Better Homes and Gardens.

Garden Doctor

Advice from the Experts™

Better Homes and Gardens® Books
Des Moines, Iowa

Garden Doctor: Advice from the Experts™
Editor: Denny Schrock
Copy Chief: Terri Fredrickson
Publishing Operations Manager: Karen Schirm
Senior Editor, Asset and Information Manager:
  Phillip Morgan
Edit and Design Production Coordinator:
  Mary Lee Gavin
Editorial Assistant: Kathleen Stevens
Book Production Managers: Pam Kvitne,
  Marjorie J. Schenkelberg, Rick von Holdt,
  Mark Weaver
Contributing Copy Editor: Barbara Feller-Roth
Contributing Design Director: Lyne Neymeyer
Contributing Designer: Beth Ann Edwards
Contributing Proofreaders: Fern Marshall Bradley,
  Fran Gardner, Missy Peterson
Contributing Technical Consultants: Deb Brown,
  Ray Rothenberger
Indexer: Ellen Sherron

Meredith® Books
Executive Director, Editorial: Gregory H. Kayko
Executive Director, Design: Matt Strelecki
Executive Editor/Group Manager:
  Benjamin W. Allen
Senior Associate Design Director: Tom Wegner
Marketing Product Manager: Isaac Petersen

Publisher and Editor in Chief: James D. Blume
Editorial Director: Linda Raglan Cunningham
Executive Director, New Business Development:
  Todd M. Davis
Executive Director, Sales: Ken Zagor
Director, Operations: George A. Susral
Director, Production: Douglas M. Johnston
Director, Marketing: Amy Nichols
Business Director: Jim Leonard

Vice President and General Manager:
Douglas J. Guendel

Thanks to: Janet Anderson

***Better Homes and Gardens*® Magazine**
Editor in Chief: Karol DeWulf Nickell
Deputy Editor, Gardens and Outdoor Living:
  Elvin McDonald

Meredith Publishing Group
President: Jack Griffin
Executive Vice President: Bob Mate

Meredith Corporation
Chairman and Chief Executive Officer:
  William T. Kerr
President and Chief Operating Officer:
  Stephen M. Lacy

In Memoriam: E.T. Meredith III (1933-2003)

All of us at Meredith® Books are dedicated to
providing you with information and ideas to
enhance your home and garden. We welcome your
comments and suggestions. Write to us at:
Meredith Books, Garden Editorial Department,
1716 Locust St., Des Moines, IA 50309-3023.

If you would like to purchase any of our gardening,
cooking, crafts, home improvement, or home
decorating and design books, check wherever
quality books are sold. Or visit us at: bhgbooks.com

Better Homes and Gardens®

Garden Doctor

Advice from the Experts™

Contents

Lawns, Grasses & Ground Covers

Lawns

LAWNS IN GENERAL

TLC for your lawn

Most lawn grasses will hold their own with little care, but they shine with weed control, regular mowing, and occasional fertilization. If you would like the grass to be a little greener on your side of the fence, check out these tips for lawn maintenance.

QUICK TIP

Growing great grass

- Height matters. An inch or two may not seem like much to you, but it does to grasses. Keeping your grass on the longer side shades the soil more, keeping the soil cooler and restricting the growth of annual weeds. The chart on the next page shows you the best height to keep your lawn mowed. Resist the temptation to mow it shorter; doing so lets more light reach the soil, giving weed seeds a chance to sprout, and makes the grass less drought-tolerant.
- A cut, not a shave. Cut your grass when it has reached a height at which you don't have to remove more than a third of the blade to get it to its optimal height. Although it may seem more efficient to mow less often and shave the grass low, this practice stresses the grass and does more harm than good.
- Mow often. If annual weeds reestablish themselves in your lawn, mow frequently to keep them in line. When they produce seed heads, dispose of the clippings where the seeds won't spread to your lawn.
- Fertilize correctly. Fertilizing your lawn at the proper times means that the nourishment goes to the lawn and not the weeds. Cool-season grasses should be fertilized in early spring and late fall. Warm-season grasses should be fed in summer.
- Water deeply. Weed seeds are usually at the surface of the soil. By watering deeply and letting the soil dry out between waterings, you encourage the grass roots to grow deeply and prevent the weed seeds from germinating.
- Control stolons. Be sure you use a lawn mower that hasn't been used on other lawns, or clean the mower well between lawns. Lawn clippings can carry weeds that reproduce by stolons and deposit them into your turf.

Rogue tree roots

I have maple and spruce trees in my yard. Their roots poke out in several places—enough that I scuff the roots with the mower blades. What should I do about them?

There's not much you can do about protruding roots. If you cut or bury the roots, you can injure or kill the trees. The best thing you can do for the trees and your mower is to eliminate grass around the roots. Cover the area with loose mulch, such as pine needles or shredded bark. Or plant a low-maintenance, shade-tolerant ground cover in the area to ramble among the roots, eliminating the need to mow. Suitable ground covers for shady areas include ajuga *(Ajuga)*, barrenwort *(Epimedium)*, lungwort *(Pulmonaria)*, sweet woodruff *(Galium odoratum)*, periwinkle *(Vinca minor)*, and wild ginger *(Asarum)*.

Grass growth chart

Maintaining the proper mowing heights for your turf is essential to the health of your lawn. Each variety has a recommended minimum and maximum height. Set your mower at the maximum height during the dry summer months and minimum height during the cooler off-season, or leave it at the higher setting all year.

A Bahiagrass, **B** Bermudagrass, **C** Buffalograss, **D** Centipedegrass, **E** Fine fescue, **F** Kentucky bluegrass, **G** Perennial ryegrass, **H** St. Augustinegrass, **I** Tall fescue, **J** Zoysiagrass

Repair or replace?

I used to have the lushest, greenest lawn in the neighborhood; now, I have brown patches. Any advice on whether I should try to repair the spots or remove the grass and start from scratch?

Don't let brown bring you down, especially if you've been successful with grass, as it seems you have. You may just need to patch, but let's take a look at your options.

Repair the patches if:

- 75 percent or more of the grass is fine-bladed, deep green, and soft to the touch.
- The grass is slightly thin overall but is generally in good shape.
- The lawn turns brown uniformly and only during the most severe droughts.
- Weeds, browning, and insect or disease damage occur in small, isolated patches.

Replace the whole lawn if:

- The yard is more than 50 percent bare, weed-infested, or diseased, or has additional problems.
- New bare spots occur because conditions have changed; for example, you use your lawn more for children's games, or trees have grown, increasing shade.
- Your lawn is a patchwork of three or more colors or textures of grass.
- Water puddles on the lawn after a rain.
- The grass wilts and takes on a grayish cast if not watered regularly.

QUICK TIP

Match care to turf type

The quality of your turf depends on several factors. Get started on the right foot by selecting a grass that matches the growing conditions of your plot with your maintenance desires.

Cool-season grasses: Kentucky bluegrass, fescue, perennial ryegrass
Planting: The best time is early fall, but planting can also be done in early spring.
Fertilizing: Fall is the best time to fertilize; you also can fertilize in spring. Apply a timed-release fertilizer for 8–12 weeks of lawn nutrition.
Weed control: Apply a preemergence herbicide in spring (or autumn if winter weeds are a problem). Apply a postemergence herbicide in early summer if needed. Postemergence broadleaf herbicides are also effective in midfall.

Warm-season grasses: St. Augustinegrass, Bermudagrass, Bahiagrass, zoysiagrass
Planting: The best time to plant is in midspring. For year-round color, overseed warm-season lawns with a cool-season grass, such as ryegrass, in fall.
Fertilizing: Fertilize once in late spring and once at the end of summer. Some warm-season grasses, such as St. Augustinegrass, do best when fertilized every 6–8 weeks.
Weed control: Apply a preemergence herbicide in early spring. Follow with a postemergence herbicide in late spring if needed.

Grass type	Sun/shade tolerance	Water needs	Mowing frequency	Texture/color	Comments
Kentucky bluegrass	Sun; moderate to high shade	Goes dormant in drought	Weekly during growing season	Medium, soft texture; dark green	Holds up well to foot traffic and use
Fine fescue	Sun; tolerant of light shade	Moderate to low	Weekly during growing season	Fine leaf blades; medium green	Often combined with bluegrass for a sun/shade mix
Tall fescue	Sun; tolerant of light shade	Moderate	Once or twice per week during growing season	Medium to coarse; medium green	Good heat tolerance
Perennial ryegrass	Sun; moderate shade	Weekly during growing season	Weekly during growing season	Medium green	Rapid germination makes it helpful for preventing erosion while establishing new lawn
Bermudagrass	Sun; poor shade tolerance;	Irrigation is often necessary in midsummer	Weekly during growing season	Medium to fine; medium green	Widely used; hybrid forms offer dense lawn; dormant in cool temperatures
Zoysiagrass	Sun; low shade tolerance	Drought-tolerant	Weekly during growing season	Stiff, upright	Long dormant period in cool climates; medium green in growing season; tolerates foot traffic; best for Zones 6, 7, and 8
St. Augustinegrass	Sun; tolerates shade	High; regular irrigation during growing season	Every few days during growing season	Coarse; medium to dark green	Popular along Gulf Coast; poor cold tolerance
Bahiagrass	Sun; tolerates shade	Low; drought-tolerant	Every few days during growing season	Coarse; medium green	Low-maintenance turf; coarse leaf blades give it an informal appearance
Buffalograss	Sun; tolerates part shade	Low; drought-tolerant, but goes dormant without water	Rarely needs mowing, but looks best if mowed regularly	Fine, blue-green	Excellent heat and cold tolerance; native to Great Plains

What grass where?

The grass seed at the garden center comes in mixtures of various kinds of grasses: one for shade, another for sun, and on and on. I walk out so confused I can't even ask an intelligent question. Do I need cool-season or warm-season grass? Why do I need a blend of grasses? Why not just buy one kind and be finished with it? Please give me a good place to start.

Something as common as grass should seemingly be simpler to understand. Here are the basics to help you buy the best grass for your yard.

- Blends and mixtures improve a lawn's appearance. A seed blend contains several varieties of the same kind of grass, such as three types of Kentucky bluegrass. A blend usually gives a lawn a more uniform look. A seed mixture combines several kinds of grasses—for example, Kentucky bluegrass, tall fescue, and perennial ryegrass. Such a combination promotes a green lawn all season.
- Cool-season grasses grow best in northern lawns. The grasses grow vigorously in spring and fall but may go dormant and turn brown in the heat of summer. Cool-season grasses commonly come in blends or mixtures.
- Warm-season grasses are adapted to growing conditions in the South. They grow well in hot weather but go dormant in cool weather.

Before buying grass seed, call your cooperative extension service. Experts there can recommend the best type of grass for your locale and situation.

Not enough light

This spring we planted a grass seed blend specifically designed for shady areas under our large oaks. At first the grass was lush and green, but now it's not growing well. My azaleas, hydrangeas, hostas, and gardenias have all done well in this shade, but my daylilies and amaryllis have been slow to bloom. Any suggestions are welcome.

Growing grass in shade is a challenge, even if the package says that the seed is good for shade. It may be that you don't really have enough sunlight for a lawn. Even shade-tolerant grasses need a fair amount of light. They're designed more for dappled light than for true shade. It also could be that your trees are so mature that they're competing with the grass for moisture, fertilizer, and light.

Because you are having good luck with other plants, I think your growing conditions are good for shade plants but maybe not for grass. Ultimately, it may be that a lawn is impractical in this location. Try planting ground covers and/or using mulches.

I want a grass that doesn't need frequent cutting. Can you help me find one?

There are a few grasses that need only infrequent cutting. One is buffalograss. It's a drought-tolerant North American native species, best adapted to the central and southern plains. A slow grower, it may need cutting only a few times a season, depending on how much you water it. (The more you water, the faster it will grow and the more often you'll need to mow it.)

Another low-maintenance grass is crested hairgrass. This is a slow-growing grass that needs mowing only every 3 weeks or so. It's not very common; check with the staff at your local nursery or garden center. They may need to special-order it.

Other options are most of the fine-leaf fescues, which are commonly sold for shady lawn areas. These grasses grow only about 6–8 inches tall. Some people let them grow all season without mowing. They create a natural look that substitutes well for a traditional lawn. You will need to mow them at least once a season, though, to get rid of the buildup of dead grass. Keep in mind that unmowed fine fescues are not lawns in the usual sense—that is, they won't have a tidy, close-cropped appearance.

I treated my yard with weed-and-feed for the first time, and half the lawn died! What did I do wrong?

There are several possible reasons for damage to your lawn from a weed-and-feed application.

Did you follow the package directions for the amount of product to use? When used at the correct dose, weed-and-feed products should cause no injury to most lawns, but too much may end up harming the lawn. (Too much fertilizer will burn the grass, especially if it is under heat or moisture stress. An overdose of weed killer can damage desirable plants as well as the targeted weeds.)

Some types of turfgrass are more sensitive to broadleaf weed killers than others. Creeping bentgrass is killed by 2,4-D herbicide, a common component in weed-and-feed products. The weed-and-feed label usually cautions against using it on bentgrass lawns.

It's also possible that an unrelated insect or disease problem occurred at the same time that you applied the weed-and-feed.

A bad patch

I have a bad patch of grass in my lawn, and I don't know what's causing it. I've tried watering and not watering, feeding and not feeding, mowing and not mowing. Any ideas about what I should try next?

Lots of things can damage a lawn. Some of them you've already identified: too much or not enough water, fertilizer, or mowing. Damage also can occur because weed killer has drifted into the area or because of weed competition or insect damage. Disease, excessive shade, or heavy wear and soil compaction can take out a section of your lawn, as well.

The first thing to do is pinpoint the cause of the problem. Often, your county extension service is the best place to find out what the problem may be. The experts there will suggest solutions that are best for your region.

Once you have identified the problem and corrected it, you have several choices for filling in the bare areas: seeding, sprigging, plugging, or sodding.

Fake grass

I heard about a product that looks like healthy green turf— something you just apply and it looks fabulous. What is out there in the way of a "virtual lawn"?

There are several artificial turf options. New products are being developed almost daily to meet the needs of homeowners who want a truly low-maintenance lawn.

Several companies make artificial turf that can be used in the home landscape. The products are essentially plastic grasses.

There also are paints that you can spray on lawns so they look green even if you let the lawn turn brown in summer. In addition, there are paints that you can spray on other surfaces, such as soil or sand, for a green appearance.

Artificial lawns require minimal maintenance, of course, but will need regular blowing or vacuuming to remove the debris that accumulates. They obviously save water, which is a big advantage in an arid climate.

Discolored sod

The lawn around my newly constructed house is about 6 months old. The sod is two different colors—some is medium green and some is an ugly lime green. Is this an acidity problem?

I think your hunch that you have a soil problem is right, but I wouldn't assume that it's an acidity issue. It's likely a fertility issue. Verify this by testing your soil. Soil test results will let you know if the soil is too acid (or too alkaline) and which nutrients, if any, might be lacking.

If your soil is too acid, apply lime at the amount recommended by the test. If it's a fertility issue, your lawn will benefit from fertilizer. Apply a turf fertilizer, and keep an eye on the grass to see whether it changes color. If so, you've found the problem, and you should begin a regular fertilizer program.

Soil on new construction sites may be a mix of topsoil and lower-fertility subsoil. Lighter green patches could be due to low fertility in those spots. Fertilizing the entire lawn will mask the differences.

Dethatching

How often should I dethatch my lawn?

Thatch is a layer that develops between the soil's surface and the grass. If the thatch layer is deep, the lawn will feel spongy. Use a spade to cut into the turf to determine the depth of the thatch. Dethatching is something I recommend doing only if the thatch is ¾ inch or more thick, not as a routine practice. Core aeration, however, can be done at least annually. Not only does it loosen soil, it helps control thatch.

If thatch is really thick and has gotten out of hand, aeration won't solve the problem. That's when you bring in a dethatcher (also called a power rake or vertical mower). But if thatch is more or less under control, it should stay that way with regular aeration.

Spring and fall are both good times to aerate cool-season grasses.

Erosion control

There was a lot of snow this winter. Now that it has melted, one part of my yard has trails where the water washed away the grass. How can I fix this?

These trails occurred where snowmelt eroded soil from you lawn. It is important to quickly fill in these waterways and reseed or resod them before more soil erodes.

If the trails are an inch or two wide, they are called rills. Fill them with quality topsoil, and sprinkle the soil with grass seed. If the trails are large, they are called gullies. Resodding is the best way to repair gullies, because water flowing through them from spring and summer rains may wash out loose topsoil and grass seed.

You may find it beneficial to mulch the seeded areas until the grass becomes established. A thin layer of weed-free straw makes a good mulch for starting grass seed. Another option is hydromulch. This product is usually made of paper fibers and is dyed blue-green. Some garden centers sell it as part of grass repair kits.

Grass in clay

What type of lawn grass will thrive in clay?

Turf-type tall fescue is a good choice for clay. This tough grass tolerates slightly wet conditions and will form a dense stand of turf. Thoroughly till the soil before seeding. While you are at it, work in compost, well-decomposed organic matter, or peat moss to improve the soil structure and promote drainage. Any amendments you can add now will help the grass thrive down the road.

Trouble with sandy soil

My lawn has been deteriorating. I've fertilized, used herbicides, and reseeded several times. The soil is sandy. Do I need to spread topsoil over the lawn and reseed again?

You are likely correct to peg your grass-growing woes on sandy soil. Sandy soil dries out quickly and doesn't hold nutrients well. Little water combined with almost no food severely stresses a lawn. The grass you seed on such a site never has a chance to get established.

To improve sandy soil, spread compost or topsoil over the existing lawn. A thin layer will help, but several inches would be better. Mix the compost or topsoil into your existing soil by rototilling it into the top 6–8 inches. Leaving a distinct layer of good topsoil on top of the poor, sandy soil will prevent grass roots from penetrating deeply into the soil. When reseeding, use a variety of grass tolerant to dry conditions. Your local seed supplier can recommend a cultivar for your area. Turf-type tall fescue may be a good choice for midlatitudes (the Transition Zone); buffalograss or crested wheatgrass for the Great Plains.

Dog damage

We have a large dog that has stamped out all of the grass in the area by his doghouse. How can I get the grass to come back? Also, there are big yellow spots from his urinating everywhere. What do I do about that?

The only way to fix the trampled grass is to loosen up that packed area by tilling and/or spading the area and adding some compost or fresh soil. Then you can reseed. Unless you keep your dog off the area, though, he'll pack it down again quickly. Perhaps you could keep an area close to the doghouse mulched with bark or pine needles instead of trying to grow a lawn there.

If you have a dog loose in your yard, yellow spots will occur. To prevent the yellow spots, flush the area with water each time the dog goes to the bathroom. The water dilutes the concentration of uric acid found in urine, preventing ammonia buildup in the soil.

Aeration test
How often should I aerate my lawn?

A simple test tells you if you need to aerate. Use a screwdriver to probe the soil a day or so after ¼ inch or more of rain has fallen. If the screwdriver penetrates the soil with little resistance, you probably don't need to core aerate. If you have a hard time getting the screwdriver into the soil, it's time to aerate.

I recommend core aerating the lawn at least every year or two to keep it healthy and prevent the soil from becoming compacted.

BERMUDAGRASS

Unwanted Bermudagrass
How can I get Bermudagrass out of my lawn without killing the lawn along with the Bermudagrass? In two sections of lawn, the Bermudagrass is very thick; I don't have any of this in the other two sections.

Unfortunately, you have little choice other than killing it all out and starting your lawn over in the affected sections. Wait until the Bermudagrass is actively growing, then spray with glyphosate (Roundup). Repeat applications may be necessary to completely kill the unwanted grass.

Hybrid Bermuda help
Help! Devilgrass is invading our hybrid Bermudagrass. Is there a way to get rid of it?

Devilgrass is another name for common Bermudagrass. This definitely would be a problem in hybrid Bermudagrass. Unfortunately, there's no option other than to spray the infested area with a nonselective herbicide such as glyphosate (Roundup), which will kill everything, then reestablish the hybrid Bermudagrass.

One way that common Bermudagrass (devilgrass) spreads is by stolons that are carried around on mowing equipment. Bits of devilgrass stem can fall from the lawn mower blades to the soil, develop new roots, and start a new colony. After you get this area under control, be sure that your lawn mower is not being used on other lawns that may have a devilgrass infestation.

The best time to aerate
Aerating is an excellent way to rejuvenate a lawn. By punching holes in the soil's surface, you allow valuable oxygen, water, and nutrients to reach the roots. Core aerate when the grass is actively growing.

- For most cool-season lawns, such as bluegrass and fescue, aerate in spring or early autumn.
- Gardeners who grow warm-season grasses, such as zoysiagrass or Bermudagrass, should core aerate in spring or early summer.
- For best results, core aerate when the soil is slightly moist.

BLUEGRASS

What can I use to dye my Kentucky bluegrass green if there's a drought this summer?

It's perfectly fine to let common Kentucky bluegrass stop growing and turn brown in midsummer. The grass copes with hot, dry weather by taking a summer siesta before greening up again as soon as rain and slightly cooler temperatures return.

If you don't like the look of a dormant lawn, turf paints that ensure the green appearance during summer's heat or winter's cold are available at sports supply stores. Mix the paint with water according to directions and apply it to your lawn with a hand mister or backpack sprayer. The average application lasts about 6 weeks.

If you choose to paint your lawn, allow it to go dormant and do not water it. Infrequent, light watering prevents the grass from resting, causing stress and inviting disease.

DISEASES

Seeing spots

My lawn has spots that start out circular and yellow, then spread outward in a ring shape, with the center completely dying out to bare ground. I tried fungicide on the rings and it seemed to help, but most keep expanding. One lawn company offered to spray for this problem, but it was expensive. Do you have any suggestions?

A number of different diseases produce that pattern in a lawn: yellow patch, necrotic ring spot, summer patch, and fusarium blight. All of these diseases are fungus-based. For immediate control, you can apply a systemic fungicide according to label directions (check with a local garden center or county extension service to see what is recommended for your area), but, as you are finding, fungicides are expensive, and you may need to use several applications.

Most healthy lawns are able to outgrow a bout with diseases; you may just have to tolerate some discoloration while the lawn recovers. Keep your lawn as healthy as possible. Fertilize regularly to encourage the lawn to fill in. Reseed seriously affected areas.

To prevent necrotic ring spot, dethatch and aerate your lawn regularly. Irrigate when necessary to avoid drought stress, and apply lawn fertilizer at regular intervals. During hot summer months, set your mower a little higher than during cool periods.

Fairy rings

How do I get rid of fairy rings in the lawn?

Fairy rings are caused by a fungus that often shows up in locations where trees once grew or in lawns with a great deal of thatch. Typical symptoms are a ring or arc of darker-colored grass with mushrooms growing in the darkened area. Sometimes a dead patch accompanies the ring. They generally appear in spring and go away quickly. They're almost impossible to eliminate, but you can mask their presence. If the circle within the ring is more yellow than the rest of the lawn, fertilize the entire area. That will help even out the coloration and make the fairy ring less noticeable. Extra irrigation also sometimes helps, because the soil-inhabiting fungi create artificial drought conditions by sucking up extra soil moisture.

Toadstools

I am having a problem with mushrooms—nasty slimy brown ones—in my lawn. I've put down a fungicide twice and it seems to help a little, but it doesn't solve the problem. I've handpicked them, raked them, and mowed them. I think one of the roots from my tree is rotten, and someone told me that it might be the source of the mushroom problem. Please help! I'll try anything.

Mushrooms usually develop in cool, wet conditions. They generally disappear once dry weather returns. Your friend is right; mushrooms derive their energy from decaying organic matter. A rotten tree root could be the source.

There's no chemical way to get rid of mushrooms. If you dislike their appearance, keep breaking them off with a rake and hope that dry conditions develop soon. The mushrooms themselves won't cause harm to your lawn, unless they grow densely enough to shade it.

Mildew on lawn

I have a shady area where the grass blades have a powdery white film on them. What is it, and how do I get rid of it?

It sounds as though your lawn has powdery mildew. This is a lawn disease that primarily affects Kentucky bluegrass, although some fescues can also get it. Severe outbreaks may occur on bluegrass growing in shaded areas at moderate temperatures and high relative humidity. The mildew usually disappears when environmental conditions change. It seldom causes injury that is severe enough to warrant spraying. If you're patient, the problem will likely take care of itself. If it comes back repeatedly, you may want to consider growing a less susceptible variety of grass in the shady area, or plant a shade-tolerant ground cover there.

Rusty lawn

My lawn has developed a faint orange tint. After some investigation, I discovered that my lawn has a disease called rust. I have since treated it with fungicide. However, I still see it in many patches in the yard. Where did the rust come from, will the fungicide eliminate it, and how can I prevent this from happening again?

Rust is a common disease. It can pop up in any lawn (newly seeded lawns frequently experience worse rust than established lawns), but it doesn't necessarily mean you have a problem that needs solving.

Because rust is not terribly harmful (it just looks bad), and because fungicides are expensive (and may require sequential applications to work well), relatively few homeowners choose this approach. If the right fungicide is used, it can cut down on the rust, but the best way to prevent rust is to keep the lawn healthy, well watered, and fertilized. In seasons when the grass grows rapidly, it will outgrow the rust, which can simply be mowed off.

Brown patch

There are a couple of brown circles in my St. Augustinegrass lawn that I think are brown patch. I treated them last summer, but the fungus still seems to be active. What do you suggest?

Although your diagnosis may be correct, remember that many turf diseases look like brown patch. Properly identify the disease by taking a sample to your county extension service. They'll need a patch that contains some healthy turf, as well as the dead brown area, to make a definite diagnosis.

If your lawn does indeed have brown patch, let the disease run its course. Like all fungal diseases, brown patch is condition-dependent—it flares up when the conditions are hot and humid and recedes when the weather turns cooler.

Control the severity of brown patch by avoiding heavy nitrogen applications in spring and autumn. Water in the morning, so the grass doesn't stay wet overnight. To prevent brown patch from spreading when it is active, remove grass clippings.

Snow mold

I live in the Chicago area. Now that the snow has melted away, it looks like grubs have eaten my lawn. What can I do?

Grubs are dormant in winter. Whatever you're seeing, it isn't grub damage (unless it was already there last fall). A fungus called snow mold can attack lawns underneath a snow cover. Did you notice any matting or webbing as the snow melted? Without seeing a sample, that's just a guess. Take a sample of the affected grass to a garden center or county extension service to see if it's snow mold or something else.

If it is snow mold, the turf may recover on its own. The fungus depends on temperatures just above freezing and high humidity for survival. So as the lawn dries out and air temperatures warm up, the problem should go away. If the infestation is not severe, the crown (growing point) of your grass may have survived and will sprout new growth once conditions improve. Help it along by vigorously raking the patch to allow more oxygen to reach the crowns. In severe cases, patches of grass may be killed. In that case, overseed or sod the dead areas.

FERTILIZING

Feed your lawn

The garden centers push the idea that I need to fertilize my lawn. My grass looks fine, so do I need to fertilize? If so, how often? And what type of fertilizer should I use?

Lawns usually need to be fed to look their best, but the diet must be strict. Overfertilizing results in grass that is weak and top-heavy, making it a perfect target for disease and insects. Plus, excess nutrients can run off lawns and into the water table. Always follow the package directions, and fertilize only during growth spurts—in spring and fall for cool-season grasses, in early summer for warm-season grasses.

Most commercial fertilizers are a combination of nitrogen, phosphorus, and potassium. Of these ingredients, the most important for grass is nitrogen, which promotes leaf growth and good color. You already have an excellent source of nitrogen: grass clippings. Leaving them on the lawn is an easy and inexpensive way to fertilize.

The fertilizer you choose depends on the type of grass you have and the nitrogen content of the fertilizer. If you are unsure about how much fertilizer to apply, do a soil test; then you can adjust the amount and type of fertilizer to correct any deficiencies.

QUICK TIP

Fertilizer quick tips
- Bags of fertilizer provide recommended application rates, which give you the details you need.
- Most lawns need regular feeding—once or twice a year—if they are to be lush and healthy. Feed cool-season grasses (the northern grasses that go dormant in fall and winter) in spring and autumn; feed warm-season grasses (grasses that generally stay green all year in the South, but turn brown with the first freezes in the North) in spring and summer.
- Apply fertilizer with a spreader for even distribution. A lawn's greatest need is for nitrogen, so the amount of fertilizer you apply will depend on its nitrogen content.

Winterizer fertilizer

When should I apply a winterizer fertilizer to my lawn?

Winter fertilizers are usually applied in late October or early November to cool-season lawns. To take full advantage of the effects of winterizer fertilizer, you should also make a fertilizer application to your lawn in early September. The early fall feeding stimulates root growth. If you plan to make only one fertilizer application in fall, the best time is late September or early October.

FESCUE

Changing to fescue

I live in Southern California and would like to get rid of my St. Augustinegrass and replace it with a fescue blend. Do you have any easy ideas for doing this project?

It depends on what you consider "easy"! You should kill the St. Augustinegrass first, or you'll never be rid of it and you'll wind up with a mix of grasses. If you don't like St. Augustinegrass alone, you'll like a mix even less. Spraying with a nonselective herbicide such as glyphosate (Roundup) is the standard way to do this. (Be sure that the grass is well watered before you spray it; glyphosate works better on actively growing plants.)

Till up the dead St. Augustinegrass and smooth the area before you establish the fescue. Fescue is most commonly started from seed, but fescue sod is available and provides faster results, though at a higher cost than seeding.

An option that avoids tilling is to kill the St. Augustinegrass, then rent a slit seeder to seed fescue right into the dead grass. The slit seeder places seeds in rows several inches apart. Although this saves the tilling step, and the fescue will grow, full coverage will take longer with the slit-seeded fescue than with broadcast fescue seed.

Fescue fizzled

I tried planting fescue in my lawn, and it worked out beautifully until the weather got hot. Now I'm told it dies in summer. Is that true, or is the grass just dormant?

Luckily, the various types of fescue don't die in summer, but if you fail to supply them with regular moisture, they will become dormant and look dead. Fescues break dormancy and regrow once wetter, cooler weather arrives in autumn. To keep your fescue from going dormant in summer, water it frequently. Doing so will keep it green from spring through fall.

Terrific tall fescue

What is the best brand of tall fescue grass seed?

Grass seed is typically sold as a mixture of several different cultivars, and often species, of grass. Read the label on a bag of seed to determine which species and cultivars it contains.

Some excellent cultivars of tall fescue include Arid 3, Dynasty, Falcon 2, Glen Eagle, Millennium, Scorpio, Shenandoah II, Southern Choice, and Watchdog. Avoid any bag of seed that includes Kentucky 31 (or K-31), Alta, or Fawn fescues—these are coarse pasture grasses and unsuitable for a lawn.

INSECTS

Grubs galore

Is there anything that gets rid of grubs? Our yard is covered with birds that are eating grubs, and they're causing damage, too. I'd like to stay away from poisonous chemicals if possible.

Chemical products such as halofenozide (sold under the name GrubEx) and imidacloprid (sold as GrubEx Season-Long Grub Control) are available at your local garden center. Both provide good grub control (when used as directed on the label) and have a low toxicity level when it comes to humans, pets, and wildlife. Some gardeners have had good success with natural products such as milky spore; others have had less luck. One reason is that milky spore disease targets Japanese beetle grubs; if other grub species infest your lawn, milky spore disease won't affect them. Other natural products that can provide some control, though not as consistently as a chemical control, are diatomaceous earth and beneficial nematodes, which are sold under the name Grub-Away.

Fix grub damage

Last year I had new sod put in my front yard. The sod was really beautiful, but now grubs have eaten my entire lawn! The grass just rolled back like a carpet. I've taken care of the grubs, but I don't know what to do now. Should I sod again or should I seed? What do you recommend?

Wait until the cooler months of late summer or early autumn before you do anything. Then try overseeding your lawn. If the grass seed doesn't fill in the spots by next May, you may have to resort to new sod. To prevent an infestation from happening again, watch your lawn for grubs. (Some products, if used in June or July, do a good job of preventing future grub infestations.) Use chemical or organic grub killers if another infestation occurs.

Smart mowing

Mowing the grass is a weekly task for many gardeners. Keep your lawn healthy and looking good with these tips.

- Keep the mower blades sharp. Regular sharpening will make cleaner cuts on the lawn, improving its appearance. The cleaner cuts also help your lawn resist disease and stress.
- Avoid mowing too low. Many people mow their lawns too short. Taller grass has more area on the leaves to gather energy from the sun. Taller grass also shades the ground better, meaning you can mow, weed, and water less.
- Leave clippings. Instead of bagging mown clippings, leave them on the lawn. They'll decompose, adding to the soil structure and the lawn's nutrient content.
- Wait for the lawn to dry. Avoid mowing when the grass is wet; wet grass can stick to the lawn mower blades and keep them from making sharp cuts. Mowing wet grass also can encourage disease.
- Vary the mowing pattern. To keep your grass from matting down in one direction, mow in a different pattern each time. For example, mow north to south one week, then east to west the next mowing.

Too many worms

When I added on to my house, the lawn was damaged by the heavy machinery. The lawn has recovered. I've added a sprinkler system to help it. But now there's an overabundance of night crawlers. They make bumps and hills all over. I want them gone so I can walk on my grass again! Any suggestions?

The night crawlers love the sprinkler system you recently added. If you cut back on watering, they will probably decline to tolerable levels. Night crawlers and other worms are welcome visitors to most gardens because they are so beneficial; they aerate the soil and disperse organic matter through the root zone. Their presence will improve the quality of your grass, so it may be worth tolerating a few bumps and hills for a healthier lawn. Although many lawn insecticides may reduce the number of night crawlers in your yard, none is labeled for that purpose. Neighborhood children might want to collect the night crawlers for bait for fishermen.

Sod webworms

Termite-looking insects are spreading their tunnels among our grass blades. What can they be and what will kill them?

The insects you describe are almost certainly *not* termites, which do not feed on lawns. One possibility is sod webworms; they make tiny burrows in lawns from which they emerge to feed, mostly at night.

Regardless of what your insects are, a general-purpose insecticide—Sevin, for example—will probably eliminate them. However, it's worth a trip to the cooperative extension service to find out for sure what the problem is. Take a sample of the damaged turf and an actual specimen of the bug, if you can find one. Experts will be able to identify it and make a recommendation.

MOWING

Mowing long grass

We accidentally let our bluegrass lawn grow very long, like field grass. It's very thick and lying down on itself. Should I mow it now or let it go dormant like this in summer? I am concerned that it might mat down and smother itself.

As you now realize, Kentucky bluegrass should not be allowed to become so tall. Mow it right away with your lawn mower at its highest setting, then rake the extra growth off the top of the turf. Lower the setting and mow again a few days later. Try not to remove any more than one-third of the grass height at once. Your lawn should come back this autumn. Keep in mind that your bluegrass may die out in spots.

What to do with clippings

Would it be better to add my grass clippings to a compost pile or use them as a mulch in the garden?

Avoid using grass clippings as mulch immediately after pesticide application and mowing. They should be composted first. Most widely used lawn-care insecticides and herbicides break down rapidly during composting or become tied to the organic matter in the compost.

A better option is to leave the grass clippings on the lawn. The clippings will gradually break down, improving soil conditions and reducing the need for fertilizer. Clippings usually do not contribute to thatch buildup, because they decompose readily. If the clippings form clumps on the surface of the lawn, you may need to rake off the excess, or mow again to evenly distribute the clippings.

QUICK TIP

Mowing safety tips

- To avoid accidents, keep children and pets away from areas being mowed.
- Always keep your feet, hands, and other body parts away from the blade when the mower is running.
- Remove sticks and other debris before mowing.
- Dress sensibly. Wear long pants to protect your legs. Use shoes that have nonskid soles and that completely cover your feet (no sandals).
- Know how your mower works. Read the operating guide before using it for the first time so you know its safety features.
- Avoid cutting the lawn at night, during lightning storms, when it's raining, or at other times when the grass is wet.
- Properly maintain your mower (such as changing the oil) to ensure that it is in working condition when you want to use it.

Mow, mow, mow your lawn

Since I purchased a home a couple years ago, I mow every Saturday morning. Is this regular schedule OK? Or can you mow too much or too little?

It's a pity to break your weekly routine, but if your grass is growing, you need to be mowing. Each grass type looks best and stays healthiest at a certain height. Letting the grass grow too long can be just as damaging as giving your lawn a too-short crew cut. Avoid cutting more than one-third of the leaf blade. If these guidelines work out to your mowing every Saturday, fine; however, weather and growth spurts may require adjusting your schedule.

Scalping the lawn is a common mistake. In the cooler spring and autumn weather, cut grasses shorter. When temperatures start topping 80°F, let the grass get taller. It won't have the same "perfect" appearance as a lawn cut shorter, but plant health will more than make up for style. Taller blades shade the ground, conserving moisture and preventing weed seeds from germinating.

Late-season mowing

It's late October and my lawn looks like it needs mowing again. If I don't mow it, will it cause any problems for the grass?

Leaving long grass blades going into winter can encourage disease development and other problems. The grass mats down under snow, creating an ideal place for fungal diseases such as snow mold to develop, and for the protected runways of voles and mice. As long as the grass is actively growing, mow it to its proper height. Growth usually slows down after a few hard freezes, when temperatures consistently remain cold.

Scalping recovery

I mowed my lawn really short and now it looks patchy with some light green and brown sections. How can I make the lawn look good again?

An extremely low mower setting causes scalping of the lawn. Ideally you should remove no more than one-third of the length of the grass blades with each mowing. Uneven ground can sometimes make this difficult to do. Areas where grass blades were cut too short will usually recover slowly, but the brown patches may be evidence that you cut into the crown (growing point) of some grass plants and killed them. If the dead patches are no more than a few inches in diameter, grass regrowth may fill in the bare spots. Larger dead patches will need to be overseeded or resodded. Avoid fertilizing the grass now. That would further stress the roots. Wait and let the grass recover on its own before feeding it. Be sure to water the lawn to prevent it from also suffering moisture stress.

Big toys for mowing

I have a suburban lot with a beautiful expanse of lawn. I say I need a riding mower to keep it uniform and healthy. My wife says a rider is overkill for the amount of grass we have. Is there such a thing as too much mower?

The answer is—there is no single correct answer. The best type of mower may not be the one you want. Your mower, more than just about any other yard and garden tool, is much like your car. It says a lot about you and how you feel about your lawn. Here are some guidelines and suggestions.

- Manual (reel) mower. The old-fashioned lawn mower has been updated for modern times. It's now made of lightweight but sturdy materials; some models feature pneumatic tires, easy-to-use blade-height settings, and adjustable handle length. The reel-mounted horizontal blades give a superior cut by slicing the grass against a lower, rigid bar. Spectacularly quiet and pollution-free, these mowers are especially useful for small lawns.
- Walk-behind power lawn mower. A gas- or electric-powered rotary mower is appropriate for lawns of more than 4,000 square feet. (Some battery-operated models have the capacity to cut up to two-thirds of an acre on one charge.) For a large expanse of lawn, self-propelled models are particularly helpful. Today almost all power lawn mowers are designed as mulching mowers, with a special blade that suspends clippings long enough to be cut several times before they fall back onto the lawn as a mulch.
- Riding mower. The newest in gas- or electric-powered convenience offers cruise control, joystick steering, zero turning radius, and even a drink holder. Most can pull a cart—useful for mulching and other gardening applications. Larger, more powerful models can handle aeration, tilling, and snow-removal attachments.
- Self-directed electric mower. This mower follows a predetermined path along cables buried in the lawn or stays within an electronic or physical border, cutting the grass while you do other things. Some models have a recharging/docking station, where the unit goes when battery power is low. At least one model is solar-powered.

Mower features

I need a new lawn mower. What features should I look for to make my mowing quicker and easier?

I don't know about quicker and easier, but I do know about safer and more enjoyable. Here are a few features to consider.

- Safety. Look for power mowers that instantly shut off the mower blade when you release the handle baffle.

- Maintenance. Ensure that the blade is accessible for ease of sharpening.
- Bagging attachments. In some instances it's handy to have a bag attachment; for example, before you overseed a lawn, mow closely and catch the clippings to avoid having to rake them up to expose the bare soil. For annual weeds, such as crabgrass, that have formed seeds, a bag attachment will catch the seed heads along with the clippings and reduce self-seeding; you can simply throw the contents into the trash.
- Mulching blades. These blades on modern power rotary mowers chop clippings into tiny pieces that fall among the grass blades and give the lawn a little extra moisture and nitrogen. The clippings don't cause thatch.

ST. AUGUSTINEGRASS

Stumped by St. Augustine

I live in east Texas. For the past two years I have planted squares of St. Augustinegrass in my small backyard, but it died both times. Both times I fed and watered it. The second time I put down new soil and bought the grass from a different company, and it still died. I would really appreciate any help you might be able to give me.

This is difficult to address because it sounds as if you're giving the grass everything it needs. It's possible that there's an unusual problem. If so, you'll need the help of a local expert, such as a county extension agent.

The amount of fertilizer and water you give your new grass plants could be a factor. Although the grass needs little fertilizer to get off to a good start, too much may cause the tender new roots to burn. Be certain to use no more than the recommended amount. Watering of new plantings can be tricky. Until new roots become established, watering will be needed more frequently than for established grass. On the other hand, excess water could cause the roots to rot. To complicate matters further, weather conditions affect the frequency of watering and amount of water needed. During dry, sunny, or windy conditions, more water will be needed than during overcast, humid, or calm weather.

If your site is sunny (no more than a few hours of shade each day), try a different grass, such as zoysiagrass or Bermudagrass. If those die as well, have a sample of your soil tested to see if there's some sort of contamination. For example, some topsoil is taken from agricultural land and may contain residues of weed killers.

The only thing you didn't mention was sunlight. Is your "small backyard" extremely shady? If so, maybe grass isn't the best choice. Check your local nursery for ideas on shade-loving perennials, ground covers, and shrubs.

Feeding St. Augustinegrass

When is the best time to fertilize my St. Augustinegrass?

St. Augustinegrass loves heat, so the hottest times of the year are when it will grow the most and need the most nutrients. Apply a nitrogen-rich turf fertilizer in late spring, then every 8 weeks or so through September. After that, St. Augustinegrass has little need for fertilizer, because it goes dormant in fall and winter.

Relieve St. Augustinegrass stress

I have a St. Augustinegrass lawn that has thinned out over the last few years. Last year the turf developed a fungal problem, which I treated. Is the thinning a result of the fungus?

Fungal problems are usually minimal in a well-maintained lawn. The thinning and the fungal problems you observed may be related to stressful growing conditions for the St. Augustinegrass. Focus on improving the soil and how you care for your lawn. There is a good chance that aeration will help—it loosens the soil, which allows water and oxygen to get to the roots. Also, St. Augustinegrass responds to nitrogen fertilizer. Apply fertilizer in spring and again every 6–8 weeks throughout the growing season. St. Augustinegrass grows aggressively and should quickly fill in if the soil and growing conditions are improved.

SEEDING AND SODDING

Seed or sod?

We have a new home in need of a lawn. We're trying to decide which method of starting a lawn to go with, seed or sod. We need to keep the price down, but we're willing to sod the front and part of the back so the kids have somewhere to play.

Your budget is the primary factor in determining whether you sod or seed. If you can afford it, sod where you most need it and seed the other areas. Sod will become established more quickly and permit use of the area faster. Eliminate foot traffic and children's play traffic on the newly sodded areas for 2 weeks, then allow only light traffic for 2 more weeks. If you sod and seed, get grass seed of a similar mix and type so your seeded and sodded areas eventually match.

Time of year can also be a consideration. Cool-season lawns, such as bluegrass and fescue, are best seeded and established at the end of summer (late August and September in most of the country). Early spring is another favorable time to seed cool-season lawns. In midsummer to late fall, sodding usually provides better results. It's difficult to keep seedlings evenly moist during the heat of summer, and if sown too late in the year they may not become well-enough established before freezing temperatures arrive to survive the rigors of winter. Warm-season grasses such as Bermudagrass, buffalograss, and zoysiagrass survive best when established in late spring or early summer.

Starting from scratch

Two areas in my yard have become overgrown with brush, weeds, and prickly bushes. I have been trimming them back every year, but I would like to get rid of all this stuff and make a nice lawn area that I can use. How do I do this?

The chore in front of you may be tough, but it can be done. Follow these steps for success.

Step 1. Clear the area. Cut, chop, or dig out all the weeds and brush. If the plants are particularly persistent, you may need to spray the area once or twice with a brush killer.

Step 2. Prepare the soil. Once you've dealt with the offending brush, prepare the area as you would any other lawn. Till the soil and add organic matter, such as well-rotted manure or peat moss. After tilling and amending the soil, smooth it with a rake.

Step 3. Select the right grass. Different grasses thrive in different areas. For example, native buffalograss resists heat and drought but not cold; Kentucky bluegrass is hardier but not as drought-resistant. Do some research to determine what kind of turf will do best in your new spot.

Step 4. Plant your turf. Spread grass seed or sod over the area. Keep the area watered well for the several weeks it takes for your lawn to become established. If you plant seed, it's helpful to lightly mulch it. Start using a weed-and-feed product after the grass becomes established to keep the weeds at bay.

Step 5. Maintain it regularly. As with any lawn, you'll need to mow frequently. Once you start regular mowing, any weeds that do sprout will be chopped up. After the grass is established, you may want to water during droughts, and you may wish to fertilize it regularly to help keep it healthy enough to prevent weeds from becoming a major problem. Take care to avoid overfertilizing, though. Too much fertilizer can actually make your lawn more susceptible to disease.

Lawn redo

How do I revitalize a lawn filled with crabgrass, clover, thatch, and bare spots? What steps should I take and in what order?

Assuming you want to preserve whatever grass is still there, the first thing to do is spray broadleaf weed killer on the lawn to get rid of the clover and other broadleaf weeds, such as dandelions and plantain. If you aren't sure what type of lawn you have, take a sample to a garden center for verification. Plan ahead. Most herbicides require a waiting period of at least several weeks before it is safe to reseed with grass. Here are the general steps to follow.

In September rent a vertical mower (or verticutter). Go over your lawn with it a couple of times. You want to get the blades down into the soil a bit and stir things up. Then rake off all the debris (thatch). Use a drop spreader (available at hardware stores, home centers, and garden centers) to overseed with whatever kind of grass you have. (The seed package will tell you how much to use.) After you sow the seed, go over your lawn one more time with the verticutter, but this time set the blades to barely nick the soil. This will mix the seeds into the soil, which helps them germinate. The lawn should become well-established during the fall and winter. Water as needed, and fertilize at least once in fall, no more than a month after you plant.

By next spring, you should be able to safely apply more broadleaf weed killer if necessary. Finally, in late spring apply a preemergence herbicide (crabgrass preventer) with fertilizer. That will keep the crabgrass from coming back next year.

Hydroseeding

What are the advantages and disadvantages of hydroseeding a lawn instead of simply sowing the seed without mulch?

For very large areas where watering to keep the seedbed moist is difficult, hydroseeding is a great boon to getting a lawn started. The thin covering of mulch sprayed on with the seed holds in moisture and helps keep the delicate seedlings from drying out too much when they're at the critical stages of germination and establishment. The primary disadvantages are that it is more expensive to hydroseed and that seeding a large area may require a professional with hydroseeding equipment. (Small patching jobs can be done without special equipment.)

The dirt on starting grass

I've decided to get rid of the weedy area in front of my house that I laughingly call my lawn. What's the most important thing to consider as I go about planting new grass?

Cultivate deep, friable (that means crumbly), fertile, well-drained soil to make the most of your lawn. If the ground lacks these qualities, fix the problems before you put in a new lawn. Build up shallow soil with a few inches of weed-free topsoil. Improve friability and fertility by working in compost or other organic matter.

Using lime

The grass seed I planted in my backyard sprouted but died. This spring I seeded again and used a high-traffic seed, because I have three kids and a dog. I have been told to use lime, but nothing works. What am I doing wrong?

People often use lime when they plant, but it's best to hold off using it unless you know that the lawn needs it. If your soil already has a high pH, the lime can be harmful, raising the pH to a level that the grass won't tolerate.

The real problem may be the heavy amount of traffic. Kids and dogs are hard on turf. A mature lawn might withstand them, but any lawn less than a year old won't stand up to extensive wear and tear. If possible, keep the dogs and kids off the lawn while it is still young. Planting your lawn in sections is one way to accomplish this.

It also matters what steps you took when you planted the lawn. Starting right is half the battle when planting seed. Before you plant, make sure that the soil is loose. Water frequently so the grass seedlings never dry out in the first 4–6 weeks. Keep traffic off the seeded section of lawn as long as possible. (Maybe you could fence off half the yard and get grass growing there, then do the other half.) If you follow these steps, you should succeed and have a healthy lawn.

Another alternative is sodding. It's more expensive, but it will give you an established lawn that tolerates foot traffic more quickly.

Patching and overseeding

My lawn doesn't look the best. Someone recommended overseeding, but the garden center said to patch. What's the difference, and how do I know which method to choose?

If your grass appears thin but you still have fairly uniform grass growth, overseeding will likely help. Patching is best where areas of the grass have completely died back.

Overseeding

- Because overseeding involves planting grass seed into your existing lawn, the secret to success is getting the seed in contact with the soil. To make sure that happens, mow the existing grass as close to the ground as possible without actually scalping it. Rake the clippings. Mow and rake a second time to help expose more bare soil. (You may not need a second mowing if your lawn is badly in need of repair.)
- After the soil is exposed, go over it with a metal garden rake to roughen the surface. A rough surface exposes more soil, making a better seedbed.
- To compensate for uneven germination in the existing grass, sow seed at the same rate as recommended for new lawns. Most people put the seed on with a drop spreader. Put half the seed on in strips across the lawn, then apply the other half from a different angle. The exact angle doesn't matter; just be sure to seed the area thoroughly on two passes to ensure consistent coverage, which makes for a thicker, greener lawn.
- You also can use something as simple as your fingers or as complicated as a slit seeder to get seed onto the soil. Slit seeders are power tools that open up slices of lawn for better seed-to-soil contact. You can find them at your local rental store.
- Go over the whole area with a weighted garden roller, or top-dress with a ¼-inch layer of good topsoil or fine compost. Water the seed in well. Mow the new grass when it is 3 inches tall at a medium-low setting so the late-sprouting seeds will get good light.
- Frequent, regular watering—about an inch per week—is essential to establishing a new stand of grass. Treat it as an established lawn in 4–6 weeks.

Patching

- To patch a lawn, begin by using a shovel or spade to dig around the edge of the area you need to patch. Strip off the grass and weeds in the patching area, making sure to remove the roots of all the weeds. Prepare the soil the same way you would if you were starting a lawn from scratch. Add amendments as necessary, digging in organic matter and a slow-release fertilizer. Rake the soil smooth and level.
- Thickly sow the area with a variety of seed that matches the surrounding lawn. Consider a seed blend or mixture to better match your patch to its surroundings. If it's impossible to duplicate the seed, use a type that grows vigorously.
- Thinly sprinkle straw over the patch to protect the seed and new grass, and water thoroughly. Keep the soil evenly moist for good germination and growth.

Hulled seed

What's the difference between hulled and unhulled grass seed? Does it matter which I use?

Hulled grass seed is seed that has its outer husk removed before it's packaged for sale. It makes little difference which type you use, except that with hulled seed you're getting more seed for your dollar because you're not paying for the weight of the hulls. Both types of seed will sprout equally well as long as you purchase good-quality seed.

Bird grass-seed buffet

Birds eat my grass seed. What should I use to keep them away?

Put an end to the bird smorgasbord on your developing lawn by spreading a light layer of straw over the seedbed. You need only about one bale of straw to cover 1,000 square feet of seedbed. Birds will have a tough time getting to the seed once it is covered, and the grass will grow right through the straw. If you apply a minimal layer of straw, it can stay on the lawn after the grass grows in.

A rocky situation

My yard has lots of rocks. How do I deal with them before I seed?

Rocks that are 2 inches or less in diameter can be covered with a 3–5-inch layer of quality topsoil. Grass seed should germinate and thrive just fine. Large rocks (those that are a few inches or more in diameter) will impede turf growth and give your lawn a rough appearance with uneven growth. Unfortunately, the only solution to dealing with these rocks is to remove them.

Sod on compacted soil

My lawn was sodded by the house builder and is about a year old. I've followed a lawn maintenance program, but my yard doesn't look much better than the yards that are not fertilized or maintained. I doubt that aeration would be necessary this soon after planting, but water runs off the top of the soil, and my grass seems to be growing runners on top of the soil instead of underneath. Do you think my soil is compacted?

You have probably already identified the problem: soil compaction.

Compaction is troublesome in new landscapes where heavy equipment has been used during construction. Aeration is definitely the cure. All the water and fertilizer in the world are little use if the grass fails to get its roots into the ground. Most grasses are pretty tough, so you can make three or four passes (not just two) with the core aerator, a minimum of once a year (twice is even better).

Preparing for sod

What preparations should I make to ensure success when planting a sod lawn? Also, I have a large mulberry tree in the middle of my yard. Must all the tree roots that extend into the lawn area be removed in order for grass to survive?

The basic process in preparing to sod is to till the soil, then rake it smooth (removing any rocks, loose roots, or other debris on the soil's surface). Then lay out your sod. Keep it well watered (daily, if the weather is warm and dry) until the sod becomes established. This generally takes a minimum of a few weeks. After 2–3 weeks, fertilize the lawn to help it become established more quickly.

You may find it helpful to wet the soil just before you lay the sod. Avoid making it muddy; just water it enough to keep the soil from being dust-dry. The moisture makes it less stressful for the sod.

Concerning the tree roots, it would be hard on the tree (and your back!) to remove the roots; instead, build up a thin layer of soil over the roots. You want to use just enough soil to create level ground for the sod. Be careful to avoid covering the tree roots with more than a couple of inches of soil, or the roots will suffocate and the tree might die. Avoid rototilling the soil within the root zone of trees.

Mulberry trees (and many other kinds) are tough on lawns. Any sod you lay right under the tree will probably fail to thrive. The shade compounds the problem. Instead of grass, consider mulching around the tree or adding a shallow-rooted ground cover.

Sod savvy

When is the best time to lay sod? What do I need to do to get the grass off to a good start?

Sod is a hefty investment, so it is critical to prepare the planting area and tend the turf with care. You can lay sod anytime during the growing season, although spring and early autumn are best, because cool temperatures combined with occasional rain help sod quickly root. If you lay sod in summer, water at least once a day for several weeks.

Begin by preparing the soil. Remove twigs, stones, and other debris littering the surface. Break up soil clods that are larger than 2 inches in diameter. Fill low areas with good quality topsoil.

If the soil is sandy or full of clay, work in organic matter. Take advantage of this opportunity to improve the soil; it's easy to add amendments when the soil is bare. Smooth the soil with a stiff garden rake. Finish preparing the area by compacting it slightly with a sod roller (often available through your local landscape equipment rental outlet).

Lay sod on a cool, overcast day to minimize plant stress. If you lay sod in the heat of summer, moisten the surface of the planting area before putting down the turf. With the help of a few friends, you can get the sod down in a hurry and have fun along the way. Stagger strips in a bricklike pattern, and be sure that all pieces fit tightly together. A utility knife or sharp spade is handy for cutting sod to fit irregular areas.

Once the sod is in place, run the sod roller over it to eliminate air pockets. Water it immediately, then water daily (depending on rainfall), moistening the soil to a depth of 4 inches, until the sod takes root (in 2–3 weeks). Avoid mowing sod until it has firmly rooted. To find out if sod has rooted, gently tug at it. If you feel resistance, roots are anchored in the underlying soil.

Plugs or sod?

I'm planning a new lawn, and in my research I've read about plugs. Are plugs different from sod? Please tell me more and whether they are a good option for my lawn.

Plugs are a good way to install Bermudagrass, zoysiagrass, St. Augustinegrass, and other creeping grass species. (Plugs don't work as well for noncreepers.) Plugs are little plants with roots, leaves, and a core of soil around the roots. After you plant them and keep them well watered, they take root and eventually fill in. The main drawback is that weeds can become a problem before the grass has a chance to fill in. Nevertheless, many people plug their lawns and do so quite successfully. Many garden centers sell plugs by the flat.

The difference with sod is that it comes in solid "sheets" or rolls, and you lay it down like carpet. It gives you a solid, weed-free turf immediately. Sod is more expensive than plugs, so your budget may determine which you use.

Sod transplant

Can I transplant sod?

Absolutely! Before moving the sod, prepare the area to be sodded by removing twigs and other debris. Fill any low spots with good quality topsoil, and break up clods that are more than 2 inches in diameter.

A sod cutter is easy to rent and will make the job of digging out the sod you'd like to transplant a lot easier. You can also use a flat spade to uproot the sod in small areas. After moving the sod, water it regularly until it is well-established.

Sod patching

There's a problem area in my yard where the grass has died. I'd like to patch it with sod. How do I do this?

Prepare the soil the same way you would for a seed patch. Dig out the area an inch or so below the soil line so the finished patch will be level with the existing grass.

Use a utility knife to cut a piece of sod the same size and shape as the area to be patched. Firm the patch into the soil, making sure the edges fit snugly into the surrounding lawn. Step on the patch to settle it, and water deeply.

Sprigs or plugs?

I've seen grass sold as sprigs and plugs. What are they? How do I plant them in my lawn?

Sprigs or plugs work best with warm-season grasses such as Bermudagrass, zoysiagrass, or St. Augustinegrass. Sprigs are 3–6-inch pieces of grass stems or runners without soil. Plugs are 2–4-inch chunks of sod—round or square—with soil around the roots. Before planting, till or dig organic matter and granular slow-release fertilizer into the soil. Smooth the soil with a rake.

Set plugs an equal distance apart in a grid pattern. The closer you set them, the sooner the patch will fill in. Weeds may try to occupy the spaces between plugs before the grass does; weed early and often.

To use sprigs, clear the patch. Then till and amend the soil. Sprinkle the sprigs relatively evenly across a moistened bed and cover them with a thin layer of topsoil. Some sprigs won't sprout, but the roots of most will take hold. Keep the area free from weeds. Mow when the sprigs or plugs reach a height of 2 inches.

WATERING

Watering during drought

I keep watering my lawn, but it continues to look sickly and spindly. We're expecting more drought conditions again next summer. What can I do to keep my grass alive?

Lawns love water, but you can spoil them by providing too much too often. New lawns require more water than established ones, but too much moisture is hazardous to any lawn's health. Overwatering keeps the top layer of soil wet and encourages grass to develop weak, shallow roots, leading to quick injury in hot, dry weather. Infrequent but deep watering stimulates deep root growth and provides the best results. Excess water also leaches nutrients from the root zone, and may lead to nitrogen deficiency.

You also may be adding to a drainage problem by leaving your sprinkler on for long periods. Improving your drainage might mean changing the grade of your yard or installing simple swales, baffles, and contours. Swales are long, narrow, shallow depressions that divert runoff. Baffles are small pieces of edging partially buried in the ground to slow runoff and let water soak in. Contours are ripples or bumps that intercept water and divert it through perforated pipes laid just under the surface.

Watering on a hot day
Is it okay to water the yard in the middle of the day when it's hot?

Peering at sweltering turf from the confines of your comfortable home might make you want to give the green carpet a drink to get it through hot weather, but resist the temptation. Rapid evaporation makes watering in the middle of the day wasteful. The best time to water grass is in the early morning. Wind and heat are usually minimal at this time, and the majority of the water will reach the lawn. Plus, the grass leaves and stems will dry by midday, lessening the chance of disease.

If you must water during the middle of the day, the grass will not be harmed. Myths abound about burning the grass from sun rays concentrated in water droplets. That is a misconception. Many top-notch golf courses spritz their greens on hot days to reduce heat stress on the grass.

Irrigation basics
I have an expanse of lawn mixed with plots of shrubs and flowers. I'll be installing a watering system that will allow me to apply different amounts of water at different intervals. How much water should I program the system to apply?

The amount of water that plants need depends on many factors, including the growth habit of the plants, soil type, nearby plants, and climate. It's nearly impossible to assign a standard amount of water to apply.

If you can, group plants with like water requirements on the same programmable zone. For example, group lawn areas so you can program a set amount of water for them. Shrubs require less water than turf and should be on a separate zone. Also consider the exposure of the planting area when setting up watering zones. Plants on the south or west sides of a building will require more water than those growing on the north. This process of mapping out the zones might seem daunting, but it is critical for an efficient system.

Once your zones are established, experiment with run times and water application until you find a proper balance. You'll soon get a feel for what run times work best at which times of the year and for which parts of the yard.

We have a large backyard with a slope toward the back. We have underground irrigation, so our yard gets plenty of water. Our lawn does well and looks nice with the exception of the slope. By early summer only weeds grow, and there are bare patches everywhere on the hill. Please help us come up with ideas to make our entire yard look great and provide an outdoor living space we can enjoy.

Almost always, the problem when lawns fail to grow on hills is lack of water penetration into the soil. The water runs downhill before it can soak in. The cure for this, if you have an in-ground sprinkler system with a timer, is to increase the frequency of irrigation and decrease the run times. In other words, instead of (for example) watering three times a week for 20 minutes each time, water six times a week for 10 minutes each time, or even more often if necessary. Keep adjusting the times until you see a difference. You'll have to poke around a little to see if the ground is getting moist several inches down.

Also, it would help to aerate your lawn with a core aerator to ensure that the soil is loose and that compaction isn't contributing to the problem.

WEEDS

Prickly thistles

We've just moved to a new home on a 1-acre lot. It seems that well over half the yard is covered in thistles that, last June, were more than 4 feet tall and full of big purple prickles. I've mowed them, but they seem to spread rapidly.

Unfortunately, thistles are tough. If you can handle some hard work, digging out the plants by hand in fall is a good way to combat them and avoid being left with prickly dead foliage in your lawn. Otherwise, in spring use a broadleaf herbicide labeled for use on thistles (check for it at your local garden center).

Another way to control individual thistle plants is to use a nonselective herbicide such as glyphosate (Roundup) in fall. Take care to spray only the thistles and not the desirable lawn grasses; it will kill grass plants it comes in contact with, as well as thistles. Spray when the air is calm, or use an old paintbrush to apply the herbicide directly to the thistle plants.

If the thistles are concentrated in certain areas of the yard, it may be simpler to spray the entire patch, grass and all, with glyphosate, and start over with new seed or sod in those areas. It will take 10 days to 2 weeks for the thistles (and grass) to die after being sprayed. After they have died, it is safe to rototill the affected areas and reseed or resod.

You may need to attack the thistles again next summer because of seeds that have not yet germinated. Prevent them from growing and blooming again, or the problem will quickly return. A couple of seasons of steady attention to weed control will eventually result in few of these difficult weeds on your lot.

Weedy beginning

Can I spray weed killer on recently seeded lawn? I don't want the weeds to take over before my new lawn gets established.

Lawns seeded in spring tend to get weedy, which is one reason why autumn is the recommended time for planting cool-season grasses (such as Kentucky bluegrass and tall fescue). Before applying an herbicide, wait until new turf grows enough that it requires mowing three times. Young grass plants are sensitive to weed killers and may be damaged if the herbicide is sprayed too soon.

Bent(grass) out of shape

I have bentgrass creeping into my Kentucky bluegrass lawn. I've been spraying the spots with Roundup, then reseeding, but there are a lot of spots. Are there any preventive measures I can take to stop bentgrass from overrunning my beautiful lawn?

Unfortunately, there is nothing that will selectively take out bentgrass while leaving the bluegrass. A nonselective herbicide (one that kills all vegetation) with the active ingredient glyphosate (Roundup) is the only long-term solution, and it's less than perfect, as you're finding out. Although it won't be cheap, your best option is to spray Roundup over the entire area where bentgrass is showing up, then reestablish bluegrass. To keep out the bentgrass from that point on, never mow it with a lawn mower that has been used elsewhere; invasive grasses (those that spread by rhizomes or stolons) spread via lawn clippings too.

Crying over oniongrass

I can't seem to find a solution to the multitude of oniongrass growing in our lawn. The regular weed killers don't affect it. Do you have any ideas?

Wild oniongrass is hard to kill with chemicals, but it can be done. Use a combination broadleaf herbicide product, such as Trimec, that contains two or three chemicals; ask for the ester formulation. You'll need to make the application in early spring, when the oniongrass is actively growing. One precaution: Ester formulations are a little more potent than other formulations of the same product. You should apply ester formulations only during cool weather (spring and fall) and never use them close to ornamentals.

Too much clover

I have clover in my yard. I think most of it came from an inexpensive bag of grass seed. I have tried several weed killers, to no avail. I was told that lime would get rid of it, but that didn't seem to work either. The only way I am able to get rid of it is to dig it up and replant grass in its place. Is there anything else I can try?

Clover can be killed with repeat applications of a combination selective broadleaf weed killer. Be sure to use a three-way herbicide such as Trimec or another brand that includes the same ingredients. Any product will do if it has two or three active ingredients from this list: 2,4-D, dichlorprop, MCPP (mecoprop), dicamba, triclopyr, or clopyralid. (Labels always list ingredients right up front, so you can easily check to see what's in a product before buying it.) Choose a spray; it's generally more effective than a granular weed-and-feed product. Carefully follow the instructions on the label.

The clover should be healthy and actively growing when you spray it so it will readily absorb the herbicide. Add a squirt of dish soap to the solution to help the spray stick to the leaves; otherwise, it may bead up and roll off. Make sure you spray when no rain is expected for the next couple of days, and avoid mowing or watering for at least 24 hours after application. Even with a thorough spraying, it's likely that you'll overlook many clover plants, and a few will manage to grow back. New ones will continue to germinate, too, so count on some follow-up applications. But it shouldn't take too long to bring the clover to a tolerable level.

Nutgrass control

We have nutgrass everywhere and it spreads like crazy. Do you have any recommendations?

There are several products on the market that selectively kill nutgrass. Is it in your lawn or your beds? If it's in your lawn, use a selective herbicide labeled as nutgrass killer, such as MSMA or Basagran. Most garden centers carry them. If nutgrass is in your flower beds, glyphosate (Roundup) should work, as long as the nutgrass is not too close to other plants. Be sure to spray when the air is calm, or use a paintbrush to selectively apply the chemical. No matter what you use, there will be some regrowth, so count on one or two follow-up applications.

Often (not always), nutgrass becomes a problem because of poor drainage. Check to see whether the nutgrass is growing in a wet area. If it is, you can probably reduce it by improving drainage and drying out the site.

Creeping Charlie crisis

Over the past two years our lawn has been taken over by what looks like purple violets with tiny pumpkin-plant leaves. It started randomly in the yard, then it spread in large patches, killing the grass where it takes over. Our water is supplied by our well, which is under our front yard, so chemical weed killer is out. We have a large yard, so pulling these by hand would take a lifetime. Are there any organic solutions that really work?

From your description I doubt you have violets. It sounds to me like creeping Charlie. This low-growing, aggressive member of the mint family has roundish leaves and purple flowers in spring. It's a tough, invasive weed, especially in shady spots. You have three primary options, all of which have drawbacks.

- Hand-pulling. For large infestations, forget it! But if you spot it early, you can probably manage to eliminate creeping Charlie by hand.
- Herbicide. Find a three-way weed killer (for example, one with Trimec in it) and use it a couple of times in spring or fall, when the soil is moist and growing conditions are good. The key is repeat applications a couple of weeks apart; one application alone will fail. Another option is glyphosate (Roundup). If applied directly to the plants' foliage, the nonselective herbicide does not go into the soil, so it should not affect your groundwater. It's designed to get inside the plant and kill it from the inside out. Glyphosate kills the grass, too, so you'll need to start new grass in treated areas.
- Borax. If you apply it in the right amount, household borax is slightly more toxic to creeping Charlie than to grass, so you can kill the weed but spare the lawn. It does have its limits: It's going to burn the grass if you apply it too heavily, and you can apply it only once a year for 2 years before you exceed the level that will harm grass. The proper mixture is 10 ounces of borax in 2½ gallons of water for 1,000 square feet of infested lawn.

Preventing crabgrass

Last spring I applied a fertilizer with a crabgrass preventer. For some reason the crabgrass was actually worse last summer. Is there something else I can do to make sure the chemical works?

There are several things that can go wrong with crabgrass preventer application. An unusually wet season can cause the chemical to wash out of the soil. Failure to water it in promptly can allow it to degrade before it ever works into the soil. An application too early in the season can wear out before the crabgrass stops germinating. (Some crabgrass preventers are effective for only 8 weeks or so, whereas crabgrass seeds may germinate until the end of summer). On the other hand, if you wait too late in the season to apply it, crabgrass seedlings may become established before the herbicide is effective. Be certain to apply the crabgrass preventer before the soil temperature reaches 55°F in spring. On south-facing slopes and near driveways or sidewalks, this may happen early in spring. One cue that many gardeners use for timing crabgrass preventer applications is when forsythia is in full bloom. Soil temperature measurements are more precise, but the bright golden forsythia blossoms serve as a good reminder.

Dollarweed dilemma

My lawn has lots of dollarweed growing in it. What can I do to kill the weed so my lawn looks good again?

Luckily, dollarweed (*Hydrocotyle umbellata*) in lawns is susceptible to most broadleaf weed killers, which you can buy at nurseries and garden centers under many brand names. Read the label carefully, though—not all weed killers work on all lawn types. If the dollarweed has crept out of your lawn and into planting beds, you won't be able to use a broadleaf weed killer, because it will also kill the nongrassy plants in the planting beds.

Dollarweed thrives in wet conditions. Keep the infested area as dry as you can without harming the lawn or ornamental plants. Drying out the planting area alone often significantly reduces dollarweed growth.

Bothersome burs

I have grass burs in my lawn. What can I do to stop them?

Grass burs (also called sandburs) are common in sandy lawns. Like most lawn weeds, grass burs are opportunists—they thrive when grass is struggling to survive. Proper mowing, fertilization, and irrigation develop a dense turf that will quickly choke out grass burs. In other words, give your lawn plenty of TLC.

Preemergence herbicides are best for getting rid of grass burs. Use a product that contains oryzalin or pendimethalin. Follow the application instructions carefully.

Oxalis options

What's the best way to get rid of oxalis in my tall fescue lawn? And when can I do so?

Control oxalis, an annual broadleaf weed, with a preemergence weed-and-feed product formulated for the pest. The main crop of oxalis seeds germinates in spring, but new plants will germinate throughout the growing season. Control these late-germinating plants (and any rogue plants the preemergence product misses) with a postemergence broadleaf herbicide in late spring and again in midsummer.

Quackgrass problems

My home sits on an acre of land that seems to be three-quarters quackgrass. I've consulted grass experts who have told me that the only thing I can do is tear up my lawn and start over. Please tell me what I can do! I long for a lush, soft lawn.

Quackgrass is one of the worst lawn weeds. Any chemical product that will kill quackgrass will also kill the grass in your lawn. That means you either have to put up with the quackgrass or kill the entire area and start over.

Here's another thought for you to keep in mind: A quackgrass infestation in your yard is mainly an aesthetic problem. Completely renovating a whole acre of lawn would be quite an undertaking. To kill all of the quackgrass in your lawn, you'll have to spray the area at least twice with an herbicide before reseeding or sodding. That's a lot of expense and backbreaking effort. Even though quackgrass is not beautiful, I find that I can live with a bit of it. My lawn, at least when it's freshly mowed, still looks pretty nice, quackgrass and all.

Cleaning up moss

Our backyard, which is partially shaded, is mostly moss. How do we kill the moss, and how long do we have to wait before we can plant grass? What kind of grass seed do you recommend for partial shade?

The concern here is that if moss is growing instead of grass, it probably means that the area is better suited to moss than grass. You can check with your local garden center for moss killers. However, to eliminate the moss and prepare the yard for grass, change the backyard's growing conditions. Moss prefers shady, moist, and acidic conditions. Change these environmental factors, and you may be able to promote the growth of grass over that of moss. Can you trim some of the trees to increase sunlight in the area? Is it possible to improve the drainage? Does the soil need lime to raise the pH? If you can't alter any of these conditions, grass may never grow well there. A shade-tolerant ground cover may be a better solution.

The need to weed

Despite my instincts to tolerate a few weeds, I still feel the need (and pressure from my neighbors) to keep my front lawn weed-free. Can I battle the weeds in my lawn without a full-blown chemical assault?

Keep your lawn well fed and healthy. Vigorously growing turf presents few opportunities for weeds to get a start. You can remove perennial weeds by hand, but if you don't get the whole plant (roots and all), you'll find yourself bending and pulling it again and again. Large areas of weed-infested lawn may demand a more drastic solution, especially if you have a chronic problem.

A preemergence control can wipe out crabgrass and other annual weeds by killing the young plants as they sprout. There are corn gluten-based preemergence products that are kinder to the environment. If you're cautious about chemicals, consider soap herbicides; they are less toxic than others. Avoid broadly applying any herbicide in summer, when your lawn is most stressed by heat.

ZOYSIAGRASS

Fed up with brown zoysia

My zoysiagrass is awful. It looks dead more often than it looks alive. Is there anything I can do about it?

Zoysiagrass is a warm-season perennial grass. It doesn't like cold—so in much of the country it is the first grass to turn brown in autumn and the last to green up in spring. Zoysiagrass is prized for its dense growth habit and low-maintenance nature, though, and is more popular in the South, where it stays green much longer.

If you want to replace the zoysiagrass, use a nonselective herbicide to kill it. Once the grass is dead, reseed your lawn. Zoysiagrass is most susceptible to herbicide soon after it greens up in early summer. Multiple applications are usually necessary for control.

Weeds in zoysia

Last year we were under drought conditions, and this year we have had too much rain. I noticed some problems with our lawn this year. We have zoysiagrass, which I thought was weed-resistant and quick spreading. We seem to be cultivating weeds this year, and the zoysiagrass seems to be dying off. Any suggestions?

Zoysiagrass is notoriously slow to green up in spring. If you have a lot of moisture in your area, weed seeds that have blown in could be taking root or at least sprouting. Zoysia thrives in hot, dry weather, so if it's been cool and wet, your turf may show some signs of stress. With luck, your weather will turn warm and dry soon. Zoysia is a tough grass, but it spreads slowly, and weeds can penetrate it.

Is it also possible that your zoysiagrass lawn is receiving more shade than it used to? Zoysiagrass has poor shade tolerance. As trees grow and produce more shade, zoysiagrass growing nearby thins and opens an opportunity for weeds to become established.

ORNAMENTAL GRASSES IN GENERAL

Grasses cut back

I left my ornamental grasses standing during the winter. When should I cut them back?

You were smart to leave the grasses standing through the winter. Not only do they add a strong architectural element to the winter garden, the seed heads also provide food for many birds. Shear grasses to about 4 inches above the ground in late winter, just before the plants begin growing.

Turfgrasses versus ornamental grasses

Everyone seems to be switching from low-growing lawn grasses to taller grasses in planters and beds. What are the benefits of these grasses in my landscape? Which ones should I plant?

Planting a variety of perennial grasses is ideal for creating an up-to-date landscape. Evergreen perennial grasses are truly sculptural and, if properly displayed, look as though they were created by an artist. To produce living sculptures, plant horsetail *(Equisetum)* in small water gardens or in simple containers as short-term houseplants. It can also be grown in a troublesome wet spot as an accent plant.

The beautifully textured heads of grasses are excellent in fresh or dried arrangements. Be sure to include a few plants for the cutting garden when choosing ornamental grasses for your landscape.

Clearing a large circular or oval area toward the center of your yard and planting it with a collection of ornamental grasses, such as eulalia grass *(Miscanthus sinensis)*, reduces your lawn-cutting chores. The high point of this island bed could be a mature Ravenna grass plant *(Saccharum ravennae)* or a maiden grass *(Miscanthus sinensis* 'Gracillimus'). Surround the planting with a ring of fountain grass *(Pennisetum)*, and finish off the edges with a line of dwarf fescue *(Festuca)*. All you'll need to maintain the grasses are sharpened shears to cut back the previous year's growth in late winter or early spring.

Invasive grasses

I've heard that I shouldn't plant Japanese blood grass because it is invasive. Is that true? Are there other ornamental grasses that I should avoid planting as well?

The green form of Japanese blood grass *(Imperata cylindrica)* can indeed spread quite readily, and some states have outlawed planting it. The cultivar 'Red Baron', a form with red-tinged foliage, is generally well-behaved in the garden. If you plant it, be sure to remove any solid green shoots that develop. They can quickly take over the entire planting.

Invasiveness of ornamental grasses often depends on location. An overachiever in one part of the country may limp along, scarcely surviving, in another. For example, pampas grass *(Cortaderia selloana)* is considered invasive in California, whereas gardeners in the Midwest have to struggle to grow it, because winters are too cold. Eulalia grass *(Miscanthus sinensis)* may self-seed in warm areas with long growing seasons, but in areas with shorter growing seasons it seldom produces viable seed. Cattails *(Typha)* may take over wetlands but will behave on drier sites. Grasses (and bamboos) with runners are almost always invasive. Ribbon grass *(Phalaris arundinacea)* and blue lyme grass *(Leymus arenarius* 'Glaucus') are examples of grasses that quickly spread in the landscape.

Ornamental grasses for shade

My backyard has partial shade. Are there some ornamental grasses I could grow there, or do they all need full sun?

Although most grasses grow best in full sun, there are several that tolerate part shade or even thrive in it. Northern sea oats *(Chasmanthium latifolium)*, bottlebrush grass *(Hystrix patula)*, variegated hakone grass *(Hakonechloa macra* 'Aureola'), and ribbon grass *(Phalaris arundinacea)* are well-adapted to shade. Blue fescue *(Festuca glauca)* and most types of *Miscanthus* will grow well as long as they get several hours of direct sunlight daily.

If you stretch the definition of grasses to grasslike plants, your options expand tremendously. Most of the sedges *(Carex)* grow well in shade. Lilyturf *(Liriope)*, mondo grass *(Ophiopogon)*, and hairy wood rush *(Luzula acuminata)* are additional grass look-alikes for shade.

When to divide grasses

When is the best time to divide ornamental grasses? How often do I need to divide them?

Some ornamental grasses can grow for many years without needing division. Their low-maintenance characteristics are one reason they're so popular. Others may need more frequent division. If a clump of ornamental grass begins to die out in the center, it's time to divide. Generally, early spring is the best time of year to divide ornamental grasses.

I would like to grow ornamental grasses in my yard, but prefer to use native plants. Are there some native ornamental grasses that would work?

Most any section of the country has native grasses that also make outstanding ornamentals. Of course, a plant that is native to one region may be an exotic in another. Check with your local cooperative extension office or garden center for suggestions of native grasses that will thrive in your area. To get you started, here are some of the more commonly available native grasses.

- Big bluestem *(Andropogon gerardii)* - Midwest and Great Plains
- Blue gramagrass *(Bouteloua gracilis)* - dry sites throughout North America
- Bottlebrush grass *(Hystrix patula)* - East Coast
- Gulf muhly *(Muhlenbergia capillaris)* - Southeast
- Indian grass *(Sorghastrum nutans)* - eastern United States
- Lindheimer muhly *(Muhlenbergia lindheimeri)* - Texas
- Little bluestem *(Schizachyrium scoparium)* - Midwest and Great Plains
- Mendocino reed grass *(Calamagrostis foliosa)* - California
- Northern sea oats *(Chasmanthium latifolium)* - south, central, and eastern North America
- Prairie dropseed *(Sporobolus heterolepis)* - Great Plains
- Purple love grass *(Eragrostis spectabilis)* - eastern United States, west to Minnesota and Arizona
- Switch grass *(Panicum virgatum)* - widespread in North America

Can you suggest some ornamental grasses that would brighten up the landscape with good fall color?

Ornamental grasses may not upstage the brilliant oranges and reds of some trees and shrubs, but a few of them can add quite a splash of color to the fall landscape. Native Indian grass *(Sorghastrum nutans)* develops excellent yellow to orange fall color. The cultivar 'Sioux Blue' adds the bonus of blue-green foliage throughout the summer. Other native species that switch from blue summer foliage to coppery fall plumage are little bluestem *(Schizachyrium scoparium)*, big bluestem *(Andropogon gerardii)*, and switch grass *(Panicum virgatum)*, especially the cultivar 'Heavy Metal'.

Flame grass *(Miscanthus* 'Purpurascens') lives up to its common name, turning vivid red-orange in fall. Red Baron Japanese blood grass *(Imperata cylindrica* 'Red Baron') has red-tinged foliage through the entire growing season.

I'd like to start some new ornamental grasses from the clumps I already have going. Can they be divided?

Most clumps of ornamental grasses increase in size enough that every few years they may be divided to start new plants. I find it easiest to dig up the entire clump in early spring before growth begins. (If you haven't already cut back last season's growth, do so before digging up the clump.) Slice through the clump with a sharp spade, shovel, or ax. Small clumps may be split in halves or quarters. Larger clumps may yield a dozen or more new divisions. Just make certain that each division has healthy roots and several growing points. Set the divisions in their new location at the same depth they were previously growing. Keep the transplants well watered until new roots are established.

BAMBOO

Other than keeping bamboo from spreading everywhere, what care do I need to provide for it?

Because bamboo grows so rapidly, it generally needs regular fertilization to keep it growing well. However, avoid fertilizing the first year after division. Keep plants watered regularly during their first year. After they become established, they will be more drought-tolerant.

Bamboo canes need periodic thinning. Remove dead or damaged canes as they appear. Otherwise, remove as many canes as you wish to keep the grove as dense or thin as you desire. A good rule is to prune out canes that are 5–7 years old.

How do I start new bamboo from my existing plants?

Division is often the easiest way to start new bamboo plants. Types with running rhizomes can usually be divided by slicing some of the outward-running rhizomes, making certain that the new divisions have healthy roots and growing points, which will emerge as new shoots. Clump formers may need to be dug and cut through with a sharp spade, saw, or heavy-duty knife. Again, make certain that each division has roots and shoots to support the new plant. Early spring is the best time to divide most bamboos.

My neighbor has bamboo growing along our fence line, and now bamboo shoots are coming up in my yard. How can I get rid of the shoots and stop more from coming up?

Growing hardy bamboo as a living fence may seem like a good idea, but bamboo has no respect for property lines. It's really a giant grass, and many hardy bamboo species spread by sending out shallow rhizomes, that pop through to the surface as shoots—the growing tips of new canes. Two or three times a year, you can use a sharp spade to slice off the new shoots that appear on your property. Once severed, they'll die back and won't need to be dug up. If you were to use an herbicide to kill the bamboo on your side of the fence line, your neighbor's mother plants could be seriously damaged.

Because it's virtually impossible to stop bamboo from spreading, the American Bamboo Society (www.bamboo.org) recommends installing a concrete or fabric barrier that works like an underground fence. In climates where bamboo spreads more slowly than it does in the South and West, a trench 18 inches deep and 12 inches wide, filled with small pebbles or pea gravel, makes a serviceable barrier. To make a pebble barrier work, each spring chop through the pebbles with a sharp spade to sever any rhizomes near the property line.

FEATHER REED GRASS

I've seen an extremely upright-growing grass that forms pencil-like tan flower stalks by early summer. Do you know what it is?

It sounds as though you're describing feather reed grass (*Calamagrostis* x*acutiflora*). This cool-season clump former grows to 4–6 feet tall and provides an attractive backdrop to flowering annuals and perennials. 'Karl Foerster' and 'Overdam' are a couple of available cultivars.

MISCANTHUS

I've seen a lot of ornamental grasses with the name *Miscanthus*, and some of them look quite different from the others. Which are the best ones for growing in the landscape?

There are indeed many species and cultivars of *Miscanthus*. All are warm-season clump formers that produce silvery seed heads late in the season. The main species is *M. sinensis*. Forms with fine-textured foliage include 'Gracillimus', 'Sarabande', 'Graziella', and 'Morning Light'. The latter has white leaf margins. 'Cabaret' has cream-colored foliage edged in green; 'Strictus' has horizontal bands of yellow on its green foliage. 'Yaku Jima' forms a broad clump less than 5 feet tall. Flame grass, *M.* 'Purpurascens', is a hybrid of *M. sinensis* and an unknown parent. It grows only 3 feet tall and develops outstanding red-orange fall color. At the other end of the size spectrum is giant miscanthus, *M.* 'Giganteus' (sometimes improperly listed as *M. floridulus*). It reaches 10–14 feet in height.

Zebra or porcupine grass?

My neighbor has a *Miscanthus* that he calls porcupine grass. It has yellowish horizontal stripes on the leaves. I've seen a similar grass that goes by the name zebra grass. Are they the same thing?

At first glance, porcupine grass and zebra grass do look alike. And the names are often confused. Both belong to the same species, and both have horizontal yellow stripes, but they are different cultivars. Porcupine grass is *Miscanthus sinensis* 'Strictus', and zebra grass is *M. s.* 'Zebrinus'. Porcupine grass is more stiffly upright (think porcupine quills); zebra grass is more open and floppy. Also, porcupine grass is reliably hardy in Zones 4–9, whereas zebra grass may need protection in Zone 4.

PAMPAS GRASS

Pamper your pampas

We planted several large (2–3 feet in diameter) pampas grass plants four years ago. They all grew to about 12 feet tall. They are planted a few feet from the house, and each spring we cut them back to about 6 inches tall. This year, new growth is appearing only on the sunny, south side of the plants. What can we do to improve their growth?

Depending on your recent winter weather, it's likely that the plants suffered some winter damage. True pampas grass (*Cortaderia selloana*), which is invasive enough to be considered a noxious weed in many areas of the country, isn't as cold-hardy as many people think. If you live in Zone 6 or colder, you may be outside the plant's comfort zone. Your grass may be a look-alike called Ravenna grass or plume grass (*Saccharum ravennae*), which is far less invasive than pampas grass but is reliably hardy only to Zone 6. Both sometimes have the problem of the older, main clump dying, with any new growth coming only from the younger edges.

These and most other ornamental grasses require full sun. If they are getting too much shade, they may need to be moved to a sunnier location.

We just bought a home (which was vacant for more than a year) that has pampas grass plants at the corners of the patio. The grasses are about 9 feet tall, appear dead, and are taking over the patio. What is the best way to trim them so they won't look so unruly?

Native to Argentina, pampas grass *(Cortaderia selloana)* is a dramatic warm-climate ornamental grass. The plants vary in their ability to produce thick, showy plumes, so observe yours for a season to see what they do.

In the meantime, in late winter or early spring before new growth appears, cut them back to about 12 inches from the ground. This is a yearly maintenance chore with large ornamental grasses. Keeping the plant intact through the winter makes it look good and enhances its ability to tolerate cold.

Use pruning shears or hedge clippers to cut back your pampas grass. To make trimming and cleanup easier, first bind the old leaves together with string, packing tape, or a bungee cord. Whatever tools you use, wear gloves and a long-sleeved shirt, because the grass blades can have sharp edges that will slice through exposed skin.

PENNISETUM

Fountain grass

I liked a grass called fountain grass that I saw at the nursery. What is it? What kind of care does it need?

The botanical name for fountain grass is *Pennisetum alopecuroides*. It's one of the most widely planted ornamental grasses and is adapted to fertile, well-drained soils in sun to part shade. It grows poorly in dry soil or on shady sites. At 2–3 feet tall and wide, it fits nicely into most perennial flower borders as a single specimen or massed in larger plantings. Its white flowers are borne on arching stems (thus the name "fountain") in summer. It remains attractive through the winter. It is virtually pest- and maintenance-free. Water new plants until they become established, mulch to keep down weeds, and cut back to the ground in late winter before new growth begins.

Purple fountain grass

What is the purple-leaved grass that I see used in so many containers? Can I grow it in the ground here in the Midwest?

It sounds as though you're describing purple fountain grass (*Pennisetum setaceum* 'Rubrum'). This colorful grass makes a striking addition to container gardens with its purple-maroon foliage and arching pink-tinged flower heads. It can also be grown in warm, sunny gardens as an accent plant or combined with flowering annuals and perennials. It is reliably hardy only in Zones 9 and 10. In colder zones, treat it as an annual.

SEDGE

Sedges for wet sites

Someone told me that sedges would be good plants for shady, poorly drained sites in my yard. Do you agree?

Most sedges (*Carex*) tolerate wet soils, though some prefer well-drained sites. Most will also grow well in partial (not dense) shade. Here are some to consider.
- Bowles Golden sedge (*C. elata* 'Bowles Golden'), Zones 5–9, has golden yellow foliage.
- Palm sedge (*C. muskingumensis*), Zones 4–9, develops whorls of green foliage on plants 2 feet tall.
- Tussock sedge (*C. stricta*), Zones 4–8, grows in standing water. It prefers sun over shade.
- Variegated silver sedge (*C. morrowii*), Zones 5–9, has silver margins on medium green leaves. 'Goldband' is a variety with gold-edged foliage.

Brown sedge

A friend bought a grassy plant that's about 2 feet tall and looks totally brown but is still alive. It didn't come with a label. I like the unique look of this plant and would like to get one for my yard. Can you tell me what it is and where to find it?

It sounds as though you're describing leatherleaf sedge (*Carex buchananii*). This New Zealand native is hardy in Zones 7–9 but could be grown as an annual in colder areas. It prefers full sun and moist but well-drained soil. If you can't find the plant at local nurseries or garden centers, check mail-order nurseries that specialize in ornamental grasses.

GROUND COVERS IN GENERAL

Ground cover defined

What do garden centers mean when they talk about a ground cover? It sounds like a blanket that you would lay on the soil, but I think they're referring to some kind of plant. What is a ground cover?

In the broadest sense of the term, ground covers could include landscape fabrics as well as plants. Landscape fabrics are spun-bonded or woven fabrics usually placed under mulch (pea gravel, decorative stones, wood chips, bark) to prevent weeds from growing in the mulch. More often, though, the term "ground cover" refers to low-growing, spreading plants used en masse in a landscape bed in place of turf. They may be herbaceous perennials, woody shrubs, or vines.

An effective ground cover rapidly fills in the space between individual plants to create a solid mass. In doing so it helps stabilize soil on slopes and chokes out most weeds. Unfortunately, there is often a fine line between "rapidly fills in space" and "grows completely out of control."

Keeping ground cover contained

I have several areas of ground cover in my yard. They're doing well—too well, in fact. They're spreading into the lawn and flower beds, and taking over. What can I do to keep them in bounds?

Some ground covers are more aggressive than others. Consider using well-behaved ground covers such as thyme *(Thymus)*, candytuft *(Iberis sempervirens)*, pinks *(Dianthus)*, or astilbe *(Astilbe)* in any new beds you start. If mowing fails to keep your errant ground covers in line, try edging around the ground cover bed. You may need to add a physical barrier between the ground cover bed and the lawn or flower bed you're trying to preserve.

Invasive ground covers

I'd like to plant some ground cover in my yard, but I have heard horror stories of ground covers getting out of hand. I don't want to create a landscape nightmare by planting the wrong thing. What ground covers should I avoid?

Some ground covers that run rampant in some areas of the country may be well-behaved in other locations. You may be able to keep aggressive ground covers in bounds by planting them in contained sites, such as a planting bed surrounded by a concrete barrier. See the Quick Tip on the next page for a list of ground covers that require containment.

Covering ground on a slope

My house sits on a steep, grassy hill. What can I plant so I won't have to mow? I'd like something inexpensive.

It sounds as though a ground cover would work for you, and there are some great choices out there. Although you won't have to mow a ground cover, it will still require some maintenance until it's well-established. Here's how to get a ground cover started.

- Remove the existing plants. Before planting, you'll have to completely kill existing grass and weeds. The easiest way to do this is to use a nonselective herbicide such as glyphosate (Roundup). Be sure to use it when the air is calm so the drift won't harm the plants you want to keep. Or smother the weeds with several layers of newspapers or a tarp held down with bricks for several weeks or months.

- Prepare the bed. Once all undesirable plants are dead, incorporate 2–3 inches of organic matter, such as composted manure, into the top 6–8 inches of soil. Rake the soil smooth and cover it with 3–4 inches of organic mulch, such as shredded leaves or bark. When you plant, spread apart the mulch, allowing 8–12 inches between plants. Give the bed a good soaking, and water as needed the first year to make sure that the plants receive 1 inch of water each week.

- Plant. Because you don't say where you live, whether the hill is sunny or shady, or what kind of soil it has, I can't recommend specific plants. Check with your local cooperative extension office for recommended ground covers, or visit a local nursery or garden center and ask what plants do well as a ground cover in your region.

- Maintain. Once plants are established, you should have to do little more than water during dry periods and pull occasional weeds. Replenishing the organic mulch every other year or so will help keep weeds from becoming established.

Ground covers for contained areas

- Ajuga *(Ajuga)*
- Creeping buttercup *(Ranunculus repens)*
- Crown vetch *(Coronilla varia)*
- English ivy *(Hedera helix)*
- Goutweed *(Aegopodium podagraria)*
- Honeysuckle *(Lonicera)*
- Knotweed *(Polygonum)*
- Lily-of-the-valley *(Convallaria majalis)*
- Mint *(Mentha)*
- Periwinkle *(Vinca minor)*
- Sweet woodruff *(Galium odoratum)*
- Wintercreeper *(Euonymus fortunei)*
- Yellow archangel *(Lamium galeobdolon)*

Planting between pavers

My patio is made up of slabs that have spaces between them. I'd like a ground cover for between the slabs. The patio doesn't get a lot of foot traffic and is in full sun. What can I plant?

Thyme is the most popular plant for growing in such spaces. It thrives in heat, so it's a good choice for hot, dry, sunny areas in Zones 5–10. Lemon thyme *(Thymus ×citriodorus)* has lemon-scented foliage year-round and develops pale lilac flowers in summer. Wild thyme *(T. serpyllum)* has dark green leaves and purple flowers in early summer. Woolly thyme *(T. pseudolanuginosus)* has fuzzy gray leaves; plants produce lilac flowers.

Several of the low-growing sedums (Zones 4–10) would also be good choices. Goldmoss sedum *(Sedum acre)* grows 2–3 inches tall and bears yellow flowers in spring. Dragon's Blood sedum *(S. spurium* 'Dragon's Blood') has red leaves and rosy flowers on plants 2–6 inches tall.

Rosette-forming hen and chicks *(Sempervivum tectorum)*, hardy in Zones 4–10, is another succulent adapted to sunny, dry sites. Cobweb hen and chicks *(S. arachnoideum)* has a finer texture and interesting hairy leaves that appear to be covered with cobwebs. It can develop red flowers in midsummer.

Ice plant *(Delosperma)* grows only 4–6 inches tall and is hardy in Zones 6–10. Plants bloom most of the summer; in warm-winter areas they bloom through the winter as well. Depending on the species, the daisylike flowers may be yellow, deep purple, or red.

Thrift *(Armeria maritima)* forms grassy clumps 3–6 inches tall in Zones 3–10. Pink flowers appear in spring in cold climates and almost year-round in warmer areas.

Lawn alternatives

Are there any ground covers that make a good alternative to a lawn? The spot I have in mind would occasionally have people walking across it.

If the site is in full sun, you have several choices of ground covers that will withstand some foot traffic. They won't hold up to weekly touch football games, and croquet would be a challenge on them, but they will withstand periodic forays through them. One supplier sells an entire line of such ground covers called Stepables. Here are a few for you to consider.

- Ajuga *(Ajuga)*
- Chamomile *(Chamaemelum nobile)*
- Creeping speedwell *(Veronica)*
- Moneywort *(Lysimachia nummularia)*
- New Zealand brass buttons *(Leptinella squalida)*
- Thyme *(Thymus)*

Shade ground covers

We just moved to a house that has a heavily shaded front garden. What do you suggest for colorful ground covers?

You'll get the most bloom for your buck by planting ground covers with long flowering cycles: plants such as ajuga *(Ajuga reptans)*, periwinkle *(Vinca minor)*, mock strawberry *(Duchesnea indica)*, bunchberry *(Cornus canadensis)*, and golden moneywort *(Lysimachia nummularia* 'Aurea').

For maximum coverage, place smaller varieties as close as 6 inches apart. An equal-sided cardboard triangle is a handy spacing guide; position the triangle on the ground and place a plant at each point. This planting technique gives your landscape a flowing look as opposed to an all-in-a-row appearance.

Ground covers under trees

The lawn under my shade trees is always thin and patchy. Is there a ground cover that would do better there?

You're in luck. Numerous ground covers thrive in shade. Because turfgrasses at best tolerate shade, these shade-loving ground covers will not only look better than your thin, patchy grass but they'll also be easier to take care of. Some excellent selections of tough, shade-loving ground covers include lily-of-the-valley *(Convallaria majalis)*, spotted dead nettle *(Lamium maculatum)*, foam flower *(Tiarella)*, bigroot geranium *(Geranium macrorrhizum)*, barrenwort *(Epimedium)*, and ajuga *(Ajuga)*. Wild ginger *(Asarum)*, hosta *(Hosta)*, cast-iron plant *(Aspidistra elatior)*, lilyturf *(Liriope)*, and mondo grass *(Ophiopogon)* are additional shade lovers to consider. Some ground covers grow so well in shade that in certain regions they may become invasive. Examples are English ivy *(Hedera helix)*, wintercreeper *(Euonymus fortunei)*, and sweet woodruff *(Galium odoratum)*. You can find ground covers at your local garden center or request them from mail-order garden companies that specialize in perennials.

Ground covers for sun

A lot of the ground covers I see for sale at the nursery grow best in the shade. What are some ground covers you'd suggest for planting on a sunny slope?

You're right that many of the common ground covers, such as ivy, periwinkle, and pachysandra, are best suited for shade. But don't despair; there are plenty of choices for a sunny site too. Several with silvery gray foliage are artemisia *(Artemisia)*, snow-in-summer *(Cerastium tomentosum)*, and woolly yarrow

(Achillea tomentosa). As a bonus, snow-in-summer bears white flowers, and woolly yarrow produces yellow blooms. Other blooming ground covers for sun include rock rose *(Helianthemum nummularium)*, moss phlox *(Phlox subulata)*, trailing lantana *(Lantana montevidensis)*, and ground cover shrub rose *(Rosa)*. The herbs lavender *(Lavandula)*, dwarf rosemary *(Rosmarinus)*, and lavender cotton *(Santolina)* are good ground covers for sun. Juniper *(Juniperus)*, sedum *(Sedum, Hylotelephium)*, and creeping manzanita *(Arctostaphylos)* are also good choices.

Up close and fragrant

One of the best things about a garden is its wonderful aromas, but I don't always have time to go off the beaten path to find fragrance. Any suggestions for bringing garden scents closer to where I spend most of my time?

The spaces between path pavers are perfect for scented creepers. Thyme *(Thymus)*, chamomile *(Chamaemelum nobile)*, and Corsican mint *(Mentha requienii)* can take some foot traffic while continuing to grow. Plus, every time you crush a bit of one, it releases delightful herbal smells.

Corsican mint thrives in damp, shady places, whereas chamomile and thyme tolerate slightly drier conditions. If you don't want to remove part of the path or patio to create herbal planting pockets, consider building a scented wall. A rocky wall with planting pockets can become home to licorice *(Glycyrrhiza glabra)*, caraway *(Carum carvi)*, and lavender *(Lavandula)*.

Ground covers for wet site

My yard has a low, poorly drained area where grass won't grow well. Could you suggest a ground cover that might grow better there than the grass?

You're wise to search for plants that are adapted to growing in the wet site rather than trying to change the site or grow something there that isn't suited for the location. You could perhaps grow a bog garden there if the spot stays consistently moist. If it dries out periodically, your idea of planting a ground cover may be the best solution. Chinese astilbe *(Astilbe chinensis)*, forget-me-not *(Myosotis scorpioides)*, hosta, and fern are moisture-loving perennials that can be grown en masse as ground covers. Lilyturf *(Liriope)*, moneywort *(Lysimachia nummularia)*, and ribbon grass *(Phalaris arundinacea)* are also good for wet sites.

Boulevard ground cover

The grass in the strip between my sidewalk and the street never looks very good. I've pretty much given up on growing grass there. I don't want to just put down gravel. What could I grow in this hell strip?

Hell strip is an appropriate name for the boulevard area between sidewalk and street. The large expanse of pavement and concrete surrounding the bed makes it excessively hot (and usually dry). In areas with winter snow and ice, the soil often has a high salt content from ice removers applied to the roads.

But don't despair, there are some plants that will rise (or, in the case of ground covers, creep) to the occasion. (See Boulevard ground covers, at right.) You can give the plants a better fighting chance by preparing the soil in advance of planting them. Add some compost or organic matter to help retain moisture. Also, leach the excess salt out of the soil by watering deeply.

Desert ground cover

I live in the desert Southwest. Most all the recommendations I see for ground covers won't grow here without a lot of extra watering. Is there something I could grow as a ground cover in my yard that won't need a lot of water?

See the list at right for several ground cover plants adapted to your region. You could check with your local cooperative extension office for a more extensive list of drought-tolerant plants that would grow well in your specific area. In addition to the low-moisture requirement, plants for the desert Southwest typically must be adapted to high-pH (alkaline) soils.

QUICK TIP

Boulevard ground covers
- Cotoneaster (*Cotoneaster*)
- Gazania (*Gazania rigens*)
- Grapeholly
  (*Mahonia repens*)
- Ice plant (*Lampranthus*)
- Juniper (*Juniperus*)
- Rosemary
  (*Rosmarinus officinalis*)
- St. Johnswort (*Hypericum*)
- Trailing lantana
  (*Lantana montevidensis*)
- Woolly yarrow
  (*Achillea tomentosa*)

Desert ground covers
- Bush morning glory
  (*Convolvulus cneorum*
  and *C. sabatius*)
- Coyote bush
  (*Baccharis pilularis*)
- Gazania (*Gazania rigens*)
- Lavender cotton (*Santolina chamaecyparissus*)
- Manzanita (*Arctostaphylos*)
- Snow-in-summer
  (*Cerastium tomentosum*)
- Trailing indigo bush
  (*Dalea greggii*)
- Trailing rosemary
  (*Rosmarinus officinalis* 'Prostratus')

Covering a rock wall

We have a slope in the front yard that we leveled out by putting in a rock retaining wall. I like having some level space in the yard, but I don't like the stark look of the retaining wall. What could we plant on the rock wall to make it less severe?

You have a couple of options for softening the effect of a rock wall. You could plant trailing vines or ground covers at the top of the wall, and allow them to drape down over the wall. English ivy *(Hedera helix)*, Virginia creeper *(Parthenocissus quinquefolia)*, Boston ivy *(Parthenocissus tricuspidata)*, and juniper *(Juniperus)* are woody creepers that will trail down over a wall. Ground-cover plants that could be tucked into small planting pockets in the wall include sedum *(Sedum),* thyme *(Thymus),* and sandwort *(Arenaria).*

CROWN VETCH

Crown vetch as ground cover

Would crown vetch be a good choice for a sunny slope in my yard? I see it used a lot along highways.

Crown vetch *(Coronilla varia)* works well as a ground cover for wide open spaces, but it can become invasive in a small landscape. A single plant can spread 6 square feet, and plants may self-seed, overtaking native plants and other landscape plantings. Another ground cover might be a better choice for your yard. Crown vetch does have many good qualities, including pink-and-white blooms from late spring to early fall, attractive foliage all season, and no serious pest problems. It's often used along highways because it is also salt-tolerant.

DEAD NETTLE

Planting lamium

A friend let me dig up some of her dead nettle. How do I plant it and get it to spread in my garden?

Spotted dead nettle *(Lamium maculatum)*, like many perennial ground covers, has the ability to send out new roots from various points along the stem. In fact, you should find roots wherever the stems come into direct contact with the soil. That said, you can dig up a section of the dead nettle and replant it in your garden. Work the soil before planting; if you're planting more than one piece, place the roots several inches apart. Keep them watered well, and fertilize in spring or early summer to help them spread faster.

Ground cover or perennial?

I've seen dead nettle recommended as a good ground cover in books, but the local nursery sells it as a perennial flower. Which is it?

The quick answer is "both." When grown in large patches, spotted dead nettle *(Lamium maculatum)* makes an effective, shade-tolerant ground cover. This mint relative forms new roots where stems touch moist soil, so it forms a solid mat. In addition, it can self-seed and spread throughout the garden. It performs best in Zones 4–10 but languishes in the heat. 'White Nancy', with silvery leaves and snow white flowers, is one of the best cultivars for warm areas. 'Beacon Silver' is a popular pink-flowered form. A cluster of several dead nettle plants brightens any shady perennial border. In this case, it's considered a flowering perennial instead of a ground cover.

IVY

Ivy as ground cover

We just purchased a house where the previous owners ignored the landscape. The front yard is quite shady, and the lawn looks terrible. I've seen English ivy used in ground cover beds, but wonder if it would work as a lawn substitute. Could I replace the lawn with English ivy?

English ivy *(Hedera helix)* can make a fine ground cover for shady areas. I've seen it used quite effectively as a lawn substitute under the arching canopy of trees. Keep in mind that although ivy requires less frequent trimming than grass, it does require regular maintenance. Occasionally trim back runners that spread across walkways, and remove shoots that climb tree trunks. In some areas, English ivy is banned because it grows so rampantly, and it's difficult to remove once established. So be certain it's what you want before planting it.

Ivy removal

How do you get rid of a bed of English ivy? It's out of control. Is there an herbicide that can be safely sprayed on the vines without killing the trees they are growing around?

English ivy is difficult to eliminate once it becomes established. If you're concerned that other nearby plants might be injured by treatment with a chemical, try repeated hand pulling, digging, and mowing instead. This will be hard work and will take persistence. If you use an herbicide, choose a brush killer. Repeat applications are often necessary. Check and follow label directions for use.

Ivy dieback

My English ivy looked great last summer and fall, but this spring it is showing a lot of dieback. Is this a sign of some kind of disease? What should I do?

The dieback you see on your ivy is likely not from a disease if the plants were healthy going into winter. Few disease problems develop during the dormant season. As a broadleaf evergreen, English ivy is susceptible to winter foliage injury. Severe leaf injury can occur in response to sudden drops in temperature or drying winter winds, which can cause the leaves to turn brown and drop from the plant. Check to see if the ivy is still alive: Scratch the woody stem with your fingernail. If the stem just below the bark is green, it's alive. The ivy should leaf out again this spring from its dormant buds and regrow to fill in your ground-cover bed. Later this summer, cut out any dead vines that have not recovered.

JUNIPER

Juniper as ground cover

Can you suggest a type of juniper that would make a good ground cover for a sunny western slope? I want something evergreen there.

Many of the junipers *(Juniperus)* make excellent ground covers in sites with full sun and well-drained soil. Creeping juniper *(J. horizontalis)* is one of the lowest growing at only 6–8 inches tall. 'Bar Harbor', 'Blue Rug', and 'Blue Chip' are cultivars with blue-green foliage. All are hardy in Zones 3–9. Shore juniper *(J. conferta)* is hardy in Zones 6–10. At 1–2 feet tall, it makes a great ground cover, especially in coastal areas or locations subject to salt spray from streets and driveways. Japanese garden juniper *(J. procumbens)*, Zones 4–9, makes a good 2-foot-tall ground cover, but it is susceptible to juniper blight, a fungal disease. Lower-growing forms of savin juniper *(J. sabina)* are also excellent ground covers. 'Arcadia' and 'Broadmoor' have bright green foliage; 'Skandia' has blue-green needles.

LILY-OF-THE-VALLEY

Removing lily-of-the-valley

Is there an easy way to get rid of a large patch of lily-of-the-valley?

Some gardeners would love to have your problem, because lily-of-the-valley *(Convallaria majalis)* is regarded as a wonderful blooming ground cover for moist, shady spots. In the upper Midwest, however, lily-of-the-valley grows so well that it is now listed as invasive. To replace your patch with something better behaved, such as hostas, begin by killing the lily-of-the-valley with a nonselective herbicide such as glyphosate (Roundup) or by digging out all you can. Herbicide-treated plants should die within a week or two. If you choose instead to dig plants, lay the plants and roots in the sun for several days before dumping them on your compost pile. After a few weeks, expect a number of new sprouts to emerge in the patch. Treat them again with herbicide or dig out the newly emerged shoots. After replanting the spot, patrol for stragglers for a year or two, because seeds may continue to sprout.

VINCA

How many vincas?

I saw vinca sold with annuals at my local garden center. It grew upright and had light pink flowers. I thought vinca was a ground cover. Are there different kinds?

There are three plants commonly known as vinca. One is botanically known as *Vinca minor*. Its other common name is periwinkle. It's a shade-loving ground cover that has purple, blue, or white flowers. It's hardy in Zones 4–9.

A close relative of this plant is large periwinkle *(Vinca major)*. Usually grown as an annual in cool-climate areas, this plant produces similar flowers and has a creeping or trailing habit. Its variegated form is grown as a trailing plant in container gardens and window boxes. It's hardy in Zones 7–11.

The type you saw at the garden center is another relative. Its botanical name is *Catharanthus roseus*; it's an upright-growing tender perennial that's grown as an annual. This vinca produces white, pink, red, or lavender flowers in summer.

Sick vinca

Why is my vinca turning brown and wilting? It's been getting plenty of moisture with all the rain we've had recently.

In rainy weather, vinca can be infected by phomopsis, a fungal disease that causes the shoot tips to wilt, turn brown, and die back to the soil's surface. Affected stems may turn black. Plants may die out in patches.

To get your problem under control, prune out and destroy infected plants so the disease will be less likely to spread to healthy plants. During dry weather this summer or fall, you may also want to thin out the healthy plants to improve air circulation and promote faster drying of the foliage. (Also consider thinning out branches of surrounding trees and shrubs to improve airflow.) These cultural steps may be enough to get the disease under control. You could also use a preventive fungicide spray to keep the disease from reoccurring.

Flowers

ANNUALS IN GENERAL

Avoid thinning annual seedlings

Every year I sow annual flowers directly in my garden, but they come up so thickly that I need to thin out many of them. It seems like such a waste. Is there some way that I can avoid having to thin out the extra seedlings?

Flower seedlings growing too closely together create competition just as weeds do. So leaving the extra seedlings in place is not a good option. You may be able to dig up the excess seedlings and transplant them to another area of the garden. That way you won't waste any of them.

You could also sow the seeds at a wider spacing using one of several options. Some garden centers and mail order catalogs carry seed tapes with seeds embedded at preset intervals. Roll out the seed tape where you want the flowers to grow, and wait for them to sprout. This option costs more than seed alone, but might be worth it to avoid the need to thin the seedlings. Precision seeders are tools that pick up one seed at a time and plant it at a spacing of your choice. An inexpensive method is to mix sand with your flower seeds before you sow them. The sand adds bulk to the mix, creating wider spacing of the seeds.

Rotating annuals

I've heard that vegetables should be planted in different areas of the garden each year. Is the same true for flowers?

Crop rotation—planting a particular plant in a different location each year—is a good gardening practice. When you grow the same type of plant year after year in the same spot diseases and insect problems often develop. To avoid problems it's wise to grow something different periodically to break the pest cycle. On the other hand, if you're having success with a certain variety of flower, you could continue to grow it until a problem occurs, then switch to something else.

Easiest annuals to grow

I plan to grow flowers from seed for the first time this year. What would be some easy ones to start with?

Large-seeded annuals such as marigold, sunflower, and zinnia are good choices for beginning gardeners, including children. Just be certain to wait until the soil warms and danger of frost has passed. These three prefer full sun and warm conditions.

Seedling setback

I hope that you can give me some advice about growing flowers from seed. My seeds never sprouted (moonflowers, four-o-clocks, forget-me-nots, money plant, painted daisies, and sweet peas). I soaked the seeds for a couple of days before planting them. The seed packets indicated that the seeds could be planted in January in my region. Is it still possible for them to sprout later on in the year? Is there any chance of them sprouting in March or April if I keep watering them?

You don't need to soak seeds so long. Soak them overnight only. Seeds are alive and require oxygen to survive. By soaking for a couple of days, you may have drowned the seeds. Some gardeners have better luck by wrapping the seeds in moist paper toweling rather than soaking them in water.

Cold soil temperature could also be the culprit. Your garden may be in a microclimate that is not conducive to seed sowing until a bit later in the season. Instead of planting seeds directly in the ground, plant them in seed starting mix in pots. Put the pots on a heat mat to keep the soil and seeds warm until they germinate. Transplant seedlings to the garden later, once they are established. Another option is to sow directly in the garden later in the season, when the soil has warmed sufficiently for rapid germination.

Seedling pot question

I tried starting seeds for the first time last week, and they're already growing! I used plastic foam cups, but now I'm thinking I should have used peat pots. Should I start over with new seeds? Will mine last long enough in the cups?

I can't tell you how long they need to grow in the cups, because the safe outdoor planting time in your region depends on what kind of seeds you are growing and where you live. I'm guessing, however, that most of the seedlings will be fine in the plastic foam cups, as long as you have drainage holes punched in the bottoms and are giving them as much light as possible. A grow-light hung just an inch or two above the seedlings is best. Growing the seedlings at cooler temperatures will slow down their growth, but avoid extreme cold, which could damage the tender plants. The best temperature depends on the type of seedling. For example, snapdragons tolerate cool temperatures, but zinnias need constant warmth to thrive.

I've tried starting flower and herb seeds indoors in our kitchen window, but it's always been a big disaster. The seedlings sprout, but they soon grow spindly and fall over. I've also noticed mold forming on the soil surface, but I'm afraid to stop watering because I don't want the seedlings to dry out. Am I overwatering?

It sounds as though the problem could be too much water and too little light. Even though seeds need lots of moisture and high humidity to sprout, once the seedlings break the soil's surface, they do better when allowed to dry slightly between waterings. Most young plants also show healthier growth in cooler temperatures (55–65°F). Cover the trays and pots with clear plastic until the seeds sprout, then remove it.

Seedlings that remain wet in a warm, humid environment will fall prey to diseases such as damping-off fungus. If your seedlings are collapsing at the base, that could be what's happening to them. Excess moisture also can cause mold on the soil's surface. Water from the bottom by adding water to the trays, and only add water when the soil surface feels dry to the touch.

Your spindly seedlings may need more consistent light. Fluorescent shop lights provide an inexpensive source of steady light. Place one an inch above the plants as they first emerge. Keep the light turned on for 16 hours each day. Gradually raise the light source as the seedlings grow taller, keeping the bulb an inch or two above the uppermost leaves.

Storing seeds successfully

Many generous people have given me seeds from their garden plants. How do I store them until I can plant them next spring?

To preserve your treasures for next year, store the fully dried seeds in airtight containers in a cool, dry place. Mason jars, plastic food storage containers, recycled film canisters, or airtight plastic bags work well. Silica gel packets added to the container will help absorb residual moisture. If the inside of a container sweats during storage, the seeds are too wet and should be dried further before storing. Remove them from the container and leave them in a warm, dry place for several days to accomplish further drying. (If seeds aren't fully dried, they may rot during storage.) Be sure to label the containers, including the name of the plant and the date. Keep them in a cool, dark place, such as an unheated basement. A refrigerator works well if space is available. Fully dried and refrigerated seeds can be viable up to 10 times longer than seeds stored at room temperature.

Timing seedling transplants

I have read all kinds of information on seedlings and am finding conflicting information. For example, one piece of literature will tell me to transplant when the seedling has two sets of true leaves, and another will say three sets of true leaves. Does it actually make a difference?

There's no hard-and-fast rule about when to transplant.; it varies from species to species. The key is to transplant the seedlings after they're sturdy enough to handle it, but before their roots become long or tangled with those of other seedlings. It's best to handle the seedlings by holding the leaves rather than the stem. The seedling can quickly recover from a torn leaf, but damage to the stem in the seedling stage will likely kill or severely stunt the plant.

Drought-friendly flowers

Can you suggest some drought-tolerant annuals for my sunny yard? My native plants are all drought-resistant; I don't want to mix varieties that have different watering needs. I grow mostly orange, yellow, and red flowers.

You're wise to site plants with similar water needs together. Many gardeners run into trouble when neighboring plants require very different care.

There are many good plants for your sunny garden. Some of the most popular annuals that resist drought and bloom in shades of red, yellow, and orange include annual salvia *(Salvia splendens* and *S. coccinea)*, marigold *(Tagetes erecta, T. patula*, and *T. tenuifolia* selections), melampodium *(Leucanthemum paludosum)*, creeping zinnia *(Sanvitalia procumbens)*, zinnia *(Zinnia elegans, Z. angustifolia*, and *Z. haageana)*, moss rose *(Portulaca grandiflora)*, annual vinca *(Catharanthus roseus)*, gazania *(Gazania)*, and cockscomb *(Celosia)*.

Annuals for midday sun

My front yard faces west. The flower bed gets direct sun from about 11 a.m. to 2 p.m. and is very hot. What kind of flowers can I plant and have success with in this type of environment? I've been fairly successful with geraniums, but I'd like to try something else.

If geraniums have been successful, you can probably plant other sun-loving annual flowers such as petunia, verbena, zinnia, marigold, salvia, and cosmos. Normally, sun-loving plants need at least 6 hours of direct sunlight a day. I'm guessing that your flower bed is shaded by the house in the morning and perhaps by trees later in the afternoon. Several hours of direct midday sun coupled with half a day or more of bright partial shade is enough to keep your plants happy.

Dried-flower color preservation

What is the best way to dry flowers to maintain their color? Are there chemicals I can use that will help?

Drying flowers is a good way to preserve the beauty of your garden long after the gardening season has ended. Although no flower will retain its full, bright garden color after it's dried, some plants hold their color better than others. To get the best color, cut flowers just before they are fully open, then tie them in bundles and hang them upside down in a dry, dark, warm location. You'll get the best color retention if you dry your plants in a dark location, because light can bleach the colors. Blue and yellow flowers retain much of their color when air-dried. Pink flowers fade. Good choices for colorful dried flowers include globe amaranth (*Gomphrena*), lavender (*Lavandula*), cockscomb (*Celosia*), statice (*Limonium*), strawflower (*Helichrysum*), annual salvia, heather (*Erica*), baby's breath (*Gypsophila*), cattail (*Typha*), and goldenrod (*Solidago*).

Unfortunately, no chemical product is available to enhance the color of dried flowers. Silica gel is used to preserve quick-drying flowers and flowers with closely packed petals such as roses and peonies.

Annuals in shade

The front of my house is very shady. I'd like to plant something pretty that blooms all summer, but because I'm renting, I don't want to buy perennials that I'll have to leave behind when I move. What can I grow?

Unfortunately, there aren't as many annuals that do well in shade as there are that do well in sun. Impatiens (*Impatiens walleriana*) is by far the most common—the plants bloom continuously through the summer in sparkling shades of nearly every color except blue and black. I'm also a big fan of browallia (*Browallia speciosa*), an underused annual that blooms in shades of blue and white. Wishbone flower (*Torenia fournieri*) is another fine choice; it produces interesting flowers in shades of pink, purple, white, and blue. Wax begonia (*Begonia semperflorens-cultorum*) bears red, pink, or white flowers on plants with waxy green or bronze foliage.

A number of tropical plants with colorful foliage do well in shade too. Among these is Persian shield (*Strobilanthes dyerianus*). It bears metallic purple leaves marked with silver. Coleus (*Solenostemon scutellarioides*) and caladium (*Caladium bicolor*) produce colorful foliage in the shade. Many houseplants, such as spotted dumb cane (*Dieffenbachia*), can also spend the summer outdoors in a shady spot.

Frost-damaged annuals

After I bought flowers for my hanging baskets, there was a frost. Now my flowers don't look good. Can they be saved?

Depending on the types of plants you had and how cold it was, your plants may recover. Some annuals, such as pansies and snapdragons, will grow back after a light frost. The best you can do is keep them watered and see if they grow again. Within a few days, the extent of dieback should be evident. Trim out the dead portions of the plants. Often new shoots will sprout from beneath the damaged areas, similar to when growing tips are removed in pinching for bushier growth.

Use this as a lesson to avoid buying plants too early in the season. If you do get plants a bit early, protect them from frost by covering them at night with a sheet, rug, or tarp. Or bring them indoors on frosty nights.

Hardy annuals?

What are hardy annuals? I thought annuals were killed by frost.

Most annual flowers won't survive over the winter in cold climates, but many tolerate some frost. Some annuals, such as pansies, violas, and flowering kale, survive heavy freezes. Some hardy annuals to try include alyssum, lobelia, phlox, cornflower, dianthus, nasturtium, poppy, pot marigold, snapdragon, stock, and sweet pea. These plants perform best in cool weather and will bloom best in spring and fall. In midsummer, when temperatures are high, most of them will stop flowering. With the return of cooler temperatures in fall, they will begin to bloom again.

When to plant annuals

When can I safely plant my annual flowers in the garden?

Find out the frost-free date for your area from your local cooperative extension office, a garden center, or an experienced gardening friend. Depending on the cold tolerance of the flowers you intend to plant, use this date as a guideline. Cool-season annuals such as pansies, snapdragons, and pot marigolds can be set out several weeks before the last frost date. Tropicals that are extremely sensitive to cold, such as impatiens and Thai basil, should wait until a couple of weeks after the frost-free date. Keep an eye on the weather; some years the weather warms up much earlier than in others. As a safeguard, be prepared to cover your flowers should an unseasonably late frosty night occur.

Remember, too, that the soil needs to warm up for annuals to grow well. If you have raised beds, which allow the soil to warm faster than soil in in-ground beds, you'll be able to plant earlier.

Hardening off annuals
Do I need to do anything to the flower seedlings that I started indoors before I plant them outside?

It's a good idea to harden off tender seedlings before planting them in the garden, whether you've started them yourself or purchased them from a greenhouse. Gradually expose plants to more sunlight, cooler temperatures, and less moisture for a transition period of about 7–10 days. Place them in a protected location such as under a deck, in the shade of a tree, or next to the house. Seedlings transplanted directly to the garden may sunburn, wilt severely, suffer moisture stress, and possibly die.

Deadheading
What does "deadheading" mean? When and why should this be done?

Deadheading means removing a plant's flowers as they fade. On some plants—especially annuals—this practice encourages more blooms. Deadhead right after the flowers fade. Deadheading not only improves the plants' appearance, it removes developing seeds. Because most annual flowers are genetically programmed to bloom, produce seed, and die, deadheading pushes the plants to develop more flowers in an attempt to produce more seeds. In other words, deadheading tricks the plants into steady bloom.

Fertilizing flowers
How often should I fertilize my flower beds? What is the best kind of fertilizer to use?

The answer to your question depends on the formulation of fertilizer you decide to use. Water-soluble fertilizers are intended for frequent application as you water. Follow the recommendations on the product label for best results. Slow-release fertilizers are designed to gradually break down and supply fertilizer over several months. For northern regions, one application per growing season will usually suffice. In southern areas with longer growing seasons, a second application may be needed. The third type of fertilizer is granules. It's a good idea to mix some granular fertilizer into the soil at planting time. To keep annuals blooming well, reapply granular fertilizer every 6 weeks through the growing season. Use one pound of 5-10-5 or 5-10-10 or similar analysis for 100 square feet of bed area.

Tropical effect in cool climates

I fell in love with the tropical plantings at Disney World. I need a planting plan and can't find one anywhere. Help please!

In temperate zones, tropical plants need to be raised in pots or grown as annuals; in the case of tender bulbs, you need to dig and store them each year. Without specifics of your yard's size and layout, and lacking more details on your wants and needs, a planting plan for your specific site is difficult to come up with. Consider consulting a local nursery or landscape professional for a plan that might include some of the following.

Popular tropicals include caladium *(Caladium bicolor)*, a tender bulb with showy foliage; bird-of-paradise *(Strelitzia reginae)*, which produces flamboyant orange flowers; calla lily *(Zantedeschia)*, a tender bulb that has elegant pink, white, red, orange, or yellow blooms; and elephant's ear *(Alocasia)*, a tender bulb with large leaves. Find these and a host of other plants at your local garden center.

Another alternative is to grow hardy plants that have a tropical look. Plume poppy *(Macleaya cordata)* bears large hand-shape foliage and is hardy in Zones 4–9. If you have a protected spot, you may be able to grow bear's breeches *(Acanthus mollis)*. Though it's commonly listed as being hardy in Zones 7–10, I've been successful with it in Zones 4 and 5. Wild senna *(Cassia marilandica)* is another hardy perennial that has a tropical look. It grows in Zones 4–7.

Fancy foliage ID

I want to add to my yard two plants I've seen. One is chartreuse and looks like a hosta. The other has plum-purple leaves with a silver cast. Can you identify these plants?

Based on your brief description, I can't be sure what plants you have seen, but I'd guess that the chartreuse plant you refer to is a variety of sweet potato *(Ipomoea batatas* 'Margarita'). The chartreuse-leaved sweet potato vine is a popular plant among gardeners. Plants start growing in a mound but eventually spread and creep along the ground. Grow it in full sun and moist, well-drained soil. Sweet potato vine isn't hardy; you'll need to treat it as an annual where you live.

The other plant could be Persian shield *(Strobilanthes dyerianus)*. Like sweet potato vine, it's frost-tender and won't survive outdoors in your area. Persian shield is a shrub that does best in shade. If you have a bright spot indoors, you may be able to keep it alive over the winter as a houseplant.

COLEUS

Colorful coleus

I bought three pretty coleus plants this spring. They have been in self-watering large pots under some tall evergreens. Is this a good spot for them? It can be very windy here.

Most coleus thrive in a shaded or partially shaded spot and in moist, well-drained soil. Some newer varieties tolerate full sun but require a steady supply of moisture to thrive there. Coleus often produces small spikes of blue flowers when it's happy. Many gardeners don't like this look, so they cut off these spikes. Depending on the age and size of your evergreens, your coleus may not get enough light. Though it thrives in shade, coleus does need some light. In deep shade, the plants will grow tall and spindly.

Coleus in sun?

I always thought coleus was a shade plant. Recently I've seen a lot of them planted in full sun and growing nicely. Are these sun-loving coleus the same species?

Coleus *(Solenostemon scutellarioides)* has not only undergone a botanical name change (it used to be *Coleus hybridus)*, but also has recently received a great deal of attention from plant breeders. Although coleus has long been noted for giving colorful splashes of reds, pinks, purples, whites, and greens to shady areas, recent introductions have incorporated sun tolerance. It's a good bet that the coleus you pick up at the garden center these days will grow in full sun as well as in shade.

FUCHSIA

Frustrating fuchsias

Why do my fuchsias die after a couple of weeks? They are my favorite flower, but they frustrate me.

Fuchsia is finicky. It likes cool days and cooler nights and is best suited to the Pacific Northwest and higher elevations that seldom receive sustained hot weather.

Fuchsia grows best in shade. Water it enough to keep the soil moist but not wet. Hot sun and dry soil will quickly kill a fuchsia.

GERANIUM

Thriving geraniums

How do you grow geraniums? Do they need acidic soil?

Annual geraniums *(Pelargonium)* are one of the easiest annuals to grow. In fact, they're considered nearly foolproof if planted in the right spot. Best of all, the plants produce numerous clusters of red, pink, lavender, orange, or white flowers all summer. Situate geraniums in well-drained soil; the plants will tolerate most soil types. Geraniums bloom best in full sun and when watered enough to keep them from wilting. To encourage a consistent parade of blooms, cut off flower heads as they fade. If you grow geraniums in containers, fertilize them with a commercial product according to the manufacturer's instructions, and water frequently.

Overwintering geraniums

I have geraniums I have "wintered over" in the house. So they wouldn't be too leggy, I recently cut them way back. Can I just plant them outside again in the ground or in my window box?

As long as they stayed healthy over the winter, geraniums will come back and do well. Give them a dose of liquid fertilizer in late winter so they can put on new, healthy growth before they move outdoors. Before you replant them, let them acclimate in their pots for a few hours a day in a sunny spot outdoors after the danger of frost is past.

Geranium mystery

I've been growing geraniums for many years, and this is the first time I've had problems with them. The backs of the leaves have brown spots on them, and the leaves eventually dry up and fall off. The plants are still blooming well. Could it be a fungus? We've had a little more rain than usual this year.

There are a number of diseases that can affect geraniums, and, yes, the extra rain may be causing the problem. Keeping the foliage as dry as possible, especially in late afternoon and nighttime hours, will help to prevent these diseases. Removing dead foliage helps too; it can prevent the disease from spreading so quickly.

If keeping the foliage drier doesn't help, you may need to resort to spraying a fungicide labeled for use on geraniums. Check for such a product at your local garden center, and use it just as the label says.

Geranium cuttings

I have a large geranium with beautiful coral flowers. I'd like to start more of these plants. Can geraniums be rooted in water? Also, what fertilizer would you recommend for geraniums?

Yes, geraniums can be rooted in water. Take cuttings about 6 inches long and remove all but the top leaves. Put the cuttings in a jar of water in a bright spot but not in direct sun. Be sure to remove all foliage from the cuttings that might fall below the water level; leaves in the water will rot. With luck, the cuttings will send out roots eventually and can be replanted. You may have greater success by rooting the cuttings in moist vermiculite or perlite. These soilless products promote excellent aeration as well as holding in moisture. Dip the lower end of the stems in rooting hormone to enhance root development. Geraniums do well with a slow-release granular fertilzer designed for annual flowers.

Mold on geraniums

My geraniums have something white and fuzzy on the flowers and some of the leaves. I cut off the flowers and leaves that have this mold, but it keeps coming back.

From your description I suspect that your geraniums have botrytis, also known as gray mold. This fungal disease affects dying flowers and older leaves. Its development is favored by high humidity and poor air circulation. Remove dead leaves and flowers (as you have been doing) to slow its spread. When conditions become warmer and drier, the problem will likely subside. In the meantime, do what you can to promote rapid drying of plant foliage. Water only early in the day; space plants farther apart, if possible; and improve airflow around the plants.

IMPATIENS

Verticillium wilt on impatiens

Can impatiens get verticillium wilt? I thought verticillium was a disease that affected woody plants.

Many plants are susceptible to verticillium wilt (including maple, strawberry, tomato, and impatiens). Avoid growing the same type of annuals in the same location year after year. Symptoms of verticillium include wilting, stunting, leaf drop, and stem death. If you notice these symptoms in impatiens and have planted them in the same location for several seasons, consider a different annual for that site for the next couple of years. Other shade-tolerant annuals that are immune to verticillium wilt include begonia, lobelia, pansy, and sweet alyssum. Some resistant perennial plants to consider include astilbe, columbine, coral bells, and ligularia.

Every year my mother and I plant impatiens, and every year they wilt and die. One day they'll be just fine, and the next day they're wilted, both in beds and pots. We thought we might have a spider mite problem, but soap spray didn't work. I water them every day, and most of my yard is in shade.

Impatiens are prone to a number of diseases, many of them carried in the soil or by insects such as thrips. Because you plant in the same places every year, your disease problems may be carried over from season to season in the soil or plant residue. You may also be overwatering, which can create a perfect habitat for fungal or bacterial organisms. Impatiens shouldn't need to be watered every day unless they are in the sun.

I suggest you amend your beds with good compost; impatiens need soil with a lot of organic matter, which holds moisture, and good drainage, which allows air to reach the roots. Impatiens planted in containers should be in sterile potting soil.

Thrips are tiny insects that feed on impatiens and can spread viral diseases. If you think the problem could be thrips, prevent an infestation from developing by using soap sprays. Be sure to get good coverage on the undersides of the leaves, and repeat the application several times. Once plants are infected with the virus, it's too late to spray.

Finally, make sure that you're buying high-quality bedding plants. If any of them show signs of disease or stress in the store, pass them by.

If you still have problems, perhaps you might take a year off from impatiens and plant coleus, begonias, or another colorful shade-loving plant to try to break the disease and pest cycle.

When starting impatiens seeds indoors under fluorescent lighting, should the container be covered until the seeds sprout? When is the right time to start these seeds?

Impatiens require about 12–16 weeks from sowing to turn into flowering-size seedlings you can plant outside. Impatiens are extremely susceptible to cold temperatures, so make certain that all danger of frost has passed before setting them out.

Sow the seeds according to package instructions. Keep the flat slightly moist and under grow-lights. Use a sterile seed-starting mix in clean plastic flats or cell-paks. Keep the container covered with a clear top until the seedlings germinate. Impatiens seeds require light to germinate, so place the seeds on the surface of the starting mix and provide them with bright light.

Can I bring my impatiens indoors over the winter and plant them outside again next year?

It's easy to start new impatiens plants from cuttings. Rather than digging up your old plants to bring indoors, you'll have better luck by taking cuttings late in the season to bring inside. Take cuttings 4–6 inches long. Remove the lower leaves, and place the cuttings in water or moist vermiculite. New roots should form in several weeks. Pot up the rooted cuttings, using a good soilless houseplant potting mix. Grow the plants in bright, indirect light. Expect much less bloom indoors than in the garden. In the spring, wait until warm weather settles in to move the plants outdoors.

MARIGOLD

Success in seeding marigolds

I planted flower seeds for the first time. My marigolds were husky, colorful, and long-lasting. It's my first crop of anything, and I'd like to save the seeds. What should I do?

Growing your own garden plants from seeds is not only fun and rewarding, it's practical. You open the door to a wide range of varieties you won't find at local nurseries. And for the price of one pack of annuals at the garden center, you can buy one packet of seeds and get 10 times the number of plants.

Marigolds are among the easiest seeds to save. The most important thing is to make sure the seeds are completely mature and dry before you store them. You can let the flowers dry in the garden, or you can dry them after cutting them off the plants. Start with a bouquet of disease-free flowers past their prime for beauty. If the flowers are cut while in full bloom, the seeds will not be completely mature. Wrap a rubber band around the stems and hang the bouquet upside down in a paper bag in a cool spot. As the seeds dry, they will fall into the bag. Store the fully dried seeds in a covered jar in a dark, cool location (a refrigerator is ideal). Next spring you can start the fun again.

Dying marigolds

Last summer we had a beautiful garden with marigolds in it until about midsummer. Then the leaves started turning brown and dying even though the flower heads were still blooming. Eventually entire plants died. Someone told us that it was aster yellows. Can we plant marigolds there again this year? Will they get the same thing?

Aster yellows is caused by a phytoplasma (similar to virus) that is spread from plant to plant by leafhoppers. Symptoms usually start as yellowing of foliage. Plants may grow numerous thin stems, and flowers become distorted. From your description, it sounds unlikely that your marigolds were affected by aster yellows, although marigolds are susceptible to the disease. To prevent aster yellows, you can spray your marigolds with an insecticide to control the leafhoppers. Also, if you see signs of the disease developing, remove affected plants to prevent its spread.

The symptoms you describe sound more like those of phytophthora root rot. This widespread soilborne fungus causes lower leaves of African marigold (*Tagetes erecta*) to wilt and die. Stems may have a dark, water-soaked appearance. Death can result within a few weeks. The problem is worse in cool, wet soil. Phytophthora remains in the soil indefinitely, so it would be wise to plant something other than marigolds in this bed this year. Dwarf French marigolds (*T. patula*) are resistant to the disease. Other resistant or tolerant annual flowers are begonia, cockscomb (*Celosia*), ageratum, and geranium (*Pelargonium*).

PANSY

Fall or spring planting?

Is it better to plant pansies in fall and let them overwinter, or plant them early in spring?

Fall planting allows pansies to establish roots in warm soil. They overwinter and come back in spring in Zone 5 or warmer. They'll have an earlier start and produce more blooms than spring-planted pansies. You'll not only have the bonus of blooms in the fall (and periodically through the winter), you'll get a more spectacular show in spring.

If you plant in fall, remove spent flowers to prevent seed set. Keep the plants fertilized until the ground freezes to promote root system establishment. After the soil freezes, mulch the plants to prevent alternate freezing and thawing cycles.

PETUNIA

For the past three years I have had hanging baskets of petunias that start out beautiful but then die branch by branch. They develop something that looks like a bud, but instead of becoming a flower, it turns hard and green. If left on the plant, it turns brown and spills out hundreds of little black specks. This kills the branch. What is this and what can I do to stop it?

It sounds as though your petunias are setting seed. As with most annual flowers, once the plant sets and matures a crop of seed, its life cycle is completed and it dies. However, you can keep your petunias blooming profusely all season by trimming off the developing seedpods before they turn brown. This will stimulate new shoots to develop from below the cut. The new stems will bear more flowers.

Most modern petunia cultivars require little deadheading. If you're growing one of the recent introductions and still have trouble with them dying out from seed set, it may be an indication that the plants are being stressed. (Plants often set seed in response to a stressful environment—in an attempt to reproduce before they die.) Container plantings are more likely to be stressed from lack of moisture and excess heat than plants growing in the ground. You might try watering and fertilizing your containers more frequently to minimize stress to the plants.

SALVIA

Salvia flowers not blooming

I have planted salvia in containers on my deck, and most are doing well. However, I have a few that have lost their flowers, so only the stems and leaves remain. What did I do wrong? Can I correct this, or do I have to start over?

You don't say what kind of salvia you are growing. Are they the common red-flowering annual plant also known as scarlet sage, or a blue-flowering annual salvia? These plants don't stay in full bloom constantly. As older flowers die out, the plant often goes green for a while until new flower stalks develop. This is especially true with new, younger plants. Also, be sure the plants have plenty of sun. Salvia requires at least 6–8 hours of direct sunlight per day.

Perennial salvias also go through cycles of bloom. Once flower stalks fade, trim off the dead blooms, and within a few weeks the plants start sending out another flush of flowers.

SNAPDRAGON

Trouble growing snaps

What is the trick to growing great snapdragons? Mine always start out nicely, but once the first flowers fade, they get leggy, fall over, and don't come back into bloom very well.

Snapdragons *(Antirrhinum majus)* prefer cool weather. In warmer parts of North America, it's best to treat them as a spring or fall annual. In Zones 6–9, they may overwinter, so a fall planting can be carried through the winter, providing nice bloom in fall and again in spring. Remove plants when hot weather hits. In cooler regions, snapdragons may grow through the summer, languish in midsummer's heat, and perk up again in fall.

It's a good idea to remove faded flower stalks to encourage side shoots to form. Also try growing one of the dwarf cultivars of snapdragon such as the Tahiti Series, which remains less than a foot tall.

Transplanting snapdragon seedlings

I planted a package of snapdragon seeds in a large container, mixing the small seeds with sand to evenly spread them as directed. They're now 2–3 inches tall and ready to be transplanted. Since the roots are so tiny and so close together, how do I separate them? Can I put the plants directly in the garden now?

If the seedlings were spaced well in the seedling tray, you should be able to separate their roots without too much difficulty. I like to pop the entire mass of plants out of the seed starting tray and tease apart the roots with a pencil. Be sure to handle the tender seedlings by their leaves rather than grabbing the delicate stems, which can easily be crushed.

Rather than transplanting these little seedlings directly into the garden, you'll have better luck potting them up into individual pots or cell-paks first. Grow the separated seedlings in the individual containers for several weeks to reestablish a healthy root system, which will more likely withstand transplanting into the garden.

SUNFLOWER

Cut sunflowers

I'm going to plant 'Velvet Queen' sunflowers. Can this variety be used as cut flowers?

Sunflowers make excellent cut flowers. When your plants start to bloom, cut the stems to any length you want (depending on the size vase you plan to use), then plunge them into water. If you'd like the sunflowers to last longer, keep the vase in a cool place and add a floral preservative to the water. (Floral preservative is available from most florists.) For the longest-lasting flowers, cut them and bring them inside when the blooms first start to unfold.

Dry sunflower leaves

Why do the leaves on my potted sunflowers turn yellow, crisp, and dry in summer? Although the plants flower, they always look scraggly with no leaves.

Annual sunflowers (*Helianthus annuus*) that grow in containers are very susceptible to drying out. Most are big plants with big root systems. When you cultivate them in containers, keep the potting mix slightly moist at all times. Remember that the plants can't send their roots deeper into the soil; they rely on you for their moisture. If they don't get enough water, their leaves may turn crisp. If your sunflowers require more water than you can supply, grow them in larger containers. The smaller the container, the more you'll need to water.

It also helps considerably to site your sunflowers where they are protected from the wind (plants lose a lot of moisture through their leaves, especially on hot, windy days) and where they get a little shade during the hottest hours of the afternoon.

SWEET PEAS

Odorless sweet peas

I planted sweet peas and they are beautiful, but they don't have a scent. Why not?

Sweet peas (*Lathyrus*) have a reputation for being fragrant, but not all varieties are packed with scent. Some selections have been bred for especially large flowers or interesting colors—these hybrids usually have little or no fragrance. Other selections are bred for their fragrance.

To determine which selections you want to grow, read the catalog or seed packet description. Both sources should mention how fragrant a particular type is.

SWEET POTATO

I've grown ornamental sweet potato vines in containers, and when I cleaned out the container, I found sweet potatoes in the soil mix! Can I eat them?

Ornamental sweet potato *(Ipomoea batatas)*, grown primarily for its purple, chartreuse, or variegated foliage, is a true sweet potato. As such, the tubers it forms are edible. However, their texture and flavor will not be as good as varieties developed specifically as a vegetable. You'd be better off with the garden types for stocking your kitchen pantry. Also, if you sprayed the ornamental type with pesticides not labeled for vegetables, the tubers should not be used as a food.

ZINNIA

Happy zinnias

I grew beautiful zinnias last year. How can I keep mildew from getting on them and ruining them?

The key to keeping zinnias healthy all season is planting them in the right spot and choosing the right variety. Plant your zinnias where there's full sun and well-drained soil. Shady conditions or wet soils encourage fungi to grow. Zinnias planted close together are more prone to fungal attacks. Avoid getting the foliage wet, especially during the evening and night; wet foliage encourages the growth of harmful fungi.

Many of the newer varieties are more disease-resistant than the older types. Choosing disease-resistant varieties is an important factor in keeping your plants healthy. The Profusion Series and Pinwheel Series of zinnias provide large-flowered, mildew-resistant zinnias in a broad array of colors. Smaller-flowered species zinnias, such as narrowleaf zinnia *(Zinnia angustifolia)* and Mexican zinnia *(Z. haageana)*, seldom are affected by powdery mildew.

BULBS IN GENERAL

Layer bulbs for color

I don't have much space, but I would like more bulbs in my garden. I've heard about layering bulbs. How can I do this?

Layering bulbs is a space-saving technique that many gardeners take advantage of. To do it, select large bulbs, such as daffodils, and also smaller bulbs, such as grape hyacinths. Some gardeners like to pair bulbs that bloom at the same time for greater impact; others choose bulbs that bloom at different times to prolong the spring show. Keep the timing in mind as you select varieties.

Once you've made your choices and are ready to plant, put the larger bulbs in the ground as usual. Then add soil and plant the smaller bulbs. Leave at least an inch between the top of the bigger bulb and the bottom of the smaller bulb, for best results. Follow recommended planting depths for each type of bulb.

Fall color from bulbs

I love all the color that bulbs provide in the spring and summer. Are there any I can plant for fall color?

Although most gardeners are familiar with bulbs that bloom in spring (such as daffodils) and summer (such as cannas), numerous wonderful bulbs for autumn are underused. Many send up leaves in spring, then go dormant by summer and bloom in autumn. Remember or mark where you planted them! Here are some good autumn-blooming choices.

• Autumn crocus, including *Crocus speciosus* and a number of other species, are great fall bloomers. *C. speciosus* has violet-blue flowers and grows about 6 inches tall. It naturalizes well and has several available cultivars. It is hardy in Zones 3–8. Another popular autumn-blooming crocus is saffron (*C. sativus*). It has lilac-purple flowers and grows about 2 inches tall. It is hardy in Zones 5–8.

• Colchicum (*Colchicum*) are sometimes called autumn crocus but isn't a crocus at all, though the two plants do share a strong resemblance. Several species and cultivars are available. 'Waterlily' is one of the more common; it has double pinkish flowers on 5-inch-tall plants. 'The Giant' has large violet-pink flowers on 8-inch-tall plants. Most colchicums are hardy in Zones 4–9.

• Lily-of-the-field (*Sternbergia lutea*) produces crocuslike yellow flowers in autumn. The plant grows about 6 inches tall and is hardy in Zones 7–9.

• Hardy cyclamen (*Cyclamen hederifolium*) has wonderful shield-shape leaves that are frequently patterned or mottled with silver or light green. It has pink blooms that are often fragrant. The plants grow 5 inches tall and are hardy in Zones 6–9 and in protected sites in Zone 5.

Timing your bulb planting

Bulb-planting dates can be confusing. Generally, planting times are based on bloom times. Spring-blooming bulbs such as tulips and daffodils require a cold period to bloom and must be planted in autumn. Summer- and many autumn-flowering bulbs tend to be injured by cold temperatures and should be planted in spring (lilies are an exception; they're hardy and can be planted in fall). Most summer-flowering bulbs are tender, so in cold climates they need to be dug up and stored indoors for the winter.

Spring- and summer-blooming bulbs to plant in autumn
- Crocus *(Crocus)*
- Crown imperial *(Fritillaria imperialis)*
- Daffodil *(Narcissus)*
- Glory-of-the-snow *(Chionodoxa)*
- Grape hyacinth *(Muscari)*
- Hyacinth *(Hyacinthus orientalis)*
- Lily *(Lilium)*
- Ornamental onion *(Allium)*
- Quamash *(Camassia)*
- Siberian squill *(Scilla siberica)*
- Snowdrop *(Galanthus)*
- Striped squill *(Puschkinia scilloides)*
- Tulip *(Tulipa)*
- Windflower *(Anemone blanda)*

Summer-blooming bulbs to plant in spring
- Caladium *(Caladium bicolor)*
- Calla *(Zantedeschia)*
- Canna *(Canna ×generalis)*
- Crocosmia *(Crocosmia)*
- Dahlia *(Dahlia)*
- Elephant's ear *(Alocasia* and *Colocasia)*
- Lily-of-the-Nile *(Agapanthus)*
- Peruvian daffodil *(Hymenocallis)*
- Tiger flower *(Tigridia pavonia)*
- Tuberose *(Polianthes tuberosa)*
- Tuberous begonia *(Begonia ×tuberhybrida)*

Bulb companions

I love spring bulbs, but I don't like the ugly fading foliage. Are there other plants I can grow to cover it up?

You can solve this problem in a couple of ways. The first is to plant spring-blooming perennials that put on a good show at the same time as the bulbs. Favorites include ajuga (*Ajuga*), pasque flower (*Pulsatilla vulgaris*), and periwinkle (*Vinca minor*). These perennials won't go dormant as bulbs do, so you'll have something in the spot all summer.

Your other choice is to plant perennial partners that come into their own after the bulbs, so you have an extended season of interest. Smaller perennials that bloom later include coral bells (*Heuchera*), bellflower (*Campanula carpatica* or *C. portenschlagiana*), or leadwort (*Ceratostigma plumbaginoides*).

Big, strong bulbs

My bulbs bloom, but they never seem to look as big or as lush as the pictures I see in the catalogs. Will fertilizing help? If so, when should I do this, and what fertilizer should I use?

Most gardeners fertilize spring-blooming bulbs in autumn at planting time. Work a fertilizer formulated for bulbs, such as bonemeal, into the soil in the area where you're planting. Follow the directions on the fertilizer packaging carefully—different products have different application rates.

If you're in the habit of amending your soil with well-rotted manure or compost each year, you probably won't need to fertilize your bulbs at all. These natural materials add sufficient amounts of nutrients to most soils.

Bulbs for shade

I have a shady corner in my yard. Are there bulbs that would bloom there all summer? I'd like something colorful that will come back each year and require little care.

That's a tall order! Most blooming bulbs flower for only several weeks. My suggestion would be to go the foliage route. Cannas are normally sun plants, but they will grow in shade too. Their foliage is spectacular, but they produce fewer blooms in shade. If you select one of the varieties with interesting foliage, you'll get the color you want all season. 'Striata', 'Phaison', and 'Cleopatra' have colorful variegated leaves. Cannas are hardy in Zones 7–11. In colder regions dig up the rhizomes and store them indoors over the winter. For more interesting foliage, try caladium (*Caladium*) and elephant's ear (*Alocasia*). Both of these bulbs come in a variety of colors and leaf sizes. Caladium and elephant's ear are tropical bulbs that will need to be lifted, stored, and replanted each year.

Moving bulbs

Last fall I planted a bulb garden, which was quite a financial and spiritual investment for me. Now, however, I have to move away. The bulbs have already started to bloom, but I don't want to leave them here. Is there any way I can take my bulbs with me?

You must be disappointed to have to leave your garden. However, trying to move spring-flowering bulbs in bloom risks killing them. It's best to make arrangements with the new owners of your home to allow you to come and dig the bulbs later in the year, after they've gone dormant. (Some bulbs will have multiplied, so you could take a share for yourself and leave enough for the new homeowners to enjoy next year.)

If you can't move the bulbs later, think of the garden you planted as a contribution to an area where you used to live, knowing you made it a more beautiful place for everyone who's still there to enjoy. Every spring, the neighborhood will appreciate your effort.

Rotten bulbs

My bulbs didn't come up, so I dug them and found that most of them were mush! What causes that?

There are several potential causes for rotten bulbs. The most likely reason is that your soil doesn't drain well. Most bulbs require well-drained soil; otherwise, they will suffocate and rot. Were the bulbs planted late in the fall? If planted too late in the season, bulbs may fail to develop roots before the soil freezes. Lack of snow cover may allow cold to penetrate deeper than usual and lead to frozen bulbs that rot.

Basal rot or other bulb diseases could have caused the rot on your bulbs. If this is the case, avoid planting bulbs in the same location for several years.

Another possibility is that you planted bulbs that aren't fully winter-hardy in your area. If they can't withstand the cold temperatures, they will die and turn to mush.

Watering wisdom

I plant spring bulbs under trees and other plants that receive quite a lot of water during the hot and often dry months of summer. Will my watering cause the bulbs to rot?

Bulbs prefer slightly dry conditions during their dormant period. If your soil drains well and you use restraint in watering, your bulbs should be OK. Soil that holds water after a rain can lead to rotten bulbs that quickly die. One advantage of planting bulbs within the root zone of trees is that the roots of the trees soak up excess moisture, leaving the bulbs dry through their summer dormant period.

When a bulb is not a bulb

Someone told me that a crocus isn't really a bulb. It looks like a bulb to me. Who's right?

Although crocus look a lot like bulbs and are treated the same way as bulbs, they're not true bulbs. True bulbs are buds surrounded by immature leaves and stem tissue. Examples of bulbs include tulips, onions, and lilies. If you cut open a true bulb, you can see the layers of tissues.

Crocus are corms, which are similar to true bulbs but aren't made up of layers of tissue. Also, individual corms are replaced by younger, stronger corms each year. Another example of plants that grow from corms is gladiolus.

Tubers, such as caladium and potato, are sometimes considered bulbs. Like corms, they're not made up of layers or rings of tissue.

Tuberous roots are different again. Although they resemble tubers, they're made up of a different kind of tissue and are more closely related to roots. Examples of plants having tuberous roots are dahlia and tuberous begonia.

Unplanted bulbs

I have about 200 spring bulbs that I wasn't able to plant in fall. Should I plant them inside now, save them until next fall, or throw them away?

I'm sorry to say that you have few options. Planting them in spring is a waste of time. Depending on the type of bulbs, you could pot them and put the pots in a cool, dark location for 12–15 weeks to force them into bloom over the winter. An extra refrigerator is an ideal spot to give the potted bulbs their artificial winter. Avoid storing the bulbs with fruits and vegetables, because most produce ethylene gas, which can disfigure or abort the developing flowers in bulbs.

Unlike seeds, bulbs are living plant parts that will dry out if left out of the soil too long. Next year, make sure you purchase or order bulbs so that they arrive in plenty of time to plant in fall. Bulbs should be planted 6–8 weeks before the ground freezes, so they have time to develop strong roots before they go into winter dormancy.

Overwintering tender bulbs

I bought some summer-flowering bulbs this spring. The package said to dig them up before winter. When and how do I do that?

Many bulbous plants hail from tropical or subtropical areas and are not able to withstand cold winter temperatures. Some gardeners simply treat them as annuals, tossing them at the end of each season. Most bulbs are relatively easy to overwinter indoors, however. Follow the steps at right for success in storing tender bulbs.

ALLIUM

Store allium?

Due to utility work, I had to dig up a section of my garden. I have many allium that were budded and close to bloom. Is there a way to save these until fall to replant?

Sorry, but it really is now or never. If your allium bulbs are that close to blooming, they need to be in the ground to grow. Success with transplanting the bulbs while they are ready to bloom will be questionable, but if you will lose the bulbs anyway, you might try growing them in containers with potting soil. Allow them to bloom out. Keep the foliage actively growing until it dies down naturally. Next fall, plant the bulbs in your new garden. Expect the bulbs to take several years to recover from this drastic treatment.

QUICK TIP

Overwintering bulbs indoors

1. Carefully dig the plants after the foliage dries up or is killed by a light frost. Avoid damaging the fleshy structure, because diseases then can readily enter and cause rotting in storage.
2. Cut back stems to 2 inches. Then shake the bulbs free of soil, leaving any remaining stems and foliage in place. Do not wash the bulbs. Lay the bulbs on paper and allow them to cure (dry) for a few days in a shady, well-ventilated spot at about 60–70°F.
3. Gently remove any remaining soil. Toss out bulbs showing signs of insects or diseases. To prevent problems in storage, dust bulbs with an insecticide-fungicide mixture labeled for the specific plant.
4. Store bulbs in dry peat moss, perlite, or vermiculite at about 50–55°F. Some bulbs require cooler temperatures; others need warmer temperatures. Check a reliable reference for details.
5. Label stored bulbs carefully to avoid losing track of what you've saved. Periodically check the bulbs during storage and remove any damaged or rotting material.

AMARYLLIS

More blooms on amaryllis

I have amaryllis in pots on my front porch receiving morning sun. I usually put them in the cellar for the winter and bring them up in March and start watering them. This year and last, they did not bloom. How can I get them to bloom again?

It sounds as though your amaryllis bulbs aren't storing up quite enough food to rebloom. I also think you are giving them a little too much time in the basement. Here are some tips that should help your plants rebloom.

First make sure the plants get enough sunlight on your porch to recharge—at least 6 hours of direct sun a day. The plants require fertilizing when they are up and growing. Use a liquid houseplant fertilizer once or twice a month at half the recommended strength. By the end of the summer, each bulb should produce 7 to 11 leaves.

Keep plants moderately moist until their leaves begin to yellow in late summer, then give them a good drink. Wait until the soil at the top of the pot is dusty and dry to water again. At the end of the summer, cut back on the water even more until the leaves die back. At that point, stop watering completely.

Bring your bulbs back inside before the first frost, and store them in a cool (but not too cold—this is a tropical bulb), dark spot. After about 2 months, pull the bulbs from the soil; remove the dead, dried leaves and roots; and discard the soil. Repot the bulbs in fresh potting soil and water thoroughly. You should see new growth fairly quickly. Once top growth begins, move the pots to a sunny window. Flowers should appear about 6 weeks after replanting.

As the flowers fade, cut them off behind the swelling at the base of each bloom so the plant does not waste energy forming seeds. Let the stems and leaves die down naturally. As long as they're green, they'll be putting energy into the bulbs for next year. Once all danger of frost is past and nights are consistently above 50°F, you can move the pots outside and start the process all over again.

Amaryllis rebloom

My amaryllis bloomed wonderfully. Can I get it to bloom again now?

Amaryllis bloom only once a season. However, most amaryllis send up at least two bloom stalks. (The older the bulb, the more blooms it can produce.) Only small bulbs put up just one stalk per season. Although the foliage isn't particularly attractive when the plants aren't in bloom, many gardeners feel that it's worth tolerating for the spectacular show when the plants are in bloom.

CALLA LILY

Planting callas

I have never planted bulbs. My husband gave me three calla bulbs but no instructions on what to do with them. How and where do I plant callas?

Callas *(Zantedeschia)* are adaptable; they thrive in the ground or in containers. I prefer containers because callas look good as container plants and are easier to store over the winter that way. (These plants are frost-tender, so they need to be put in storage in autumn.)

To plant them, fill a large pot with good-quality potting soil and set the rhizomes about 4 inches deep. Water well and place the pot in partial shade. Callas accept sun or shade but do best in a location that gets bright, filtered light. Because they are tender, do not plant them outside until all frost danger has passed.

You can also easily grow callas directly in the garden. Select the same growing conditions and plant them at the same depth as though you were growing them in containers unless your garden has heavy soil. In that case, plant them only 2–3 inches deep. In autumn, dig and store the bulbs in a frost-free place.

Calla lilies in winter

Do calla lilies need to be dug up for the winter, or can they be left in the ground? When is the best time to plant them?

Calla lilies *(Zantedeschia aethiopica)* are tropical plants that have showy flowers in shades of pink, yellow, red, orange, and white. Most varieties also have mottled or marked foliage that is attractive even when the plant is not in bloom. Callas prefer a slightly shady location but will grow in full sun if it's not too hot. Their blooms are relatively long-lasting but usually finish up by mid-July.

You can purchase calla lily rhizomes in spring at garden centers and nurseries. Plant the rhizomes in spring in pots or directly in the garden in soil amended with well-rotted compost, manure, or sphagnum peat moss. The plants are sensitive to frost, so wait to plant them until all frost danger is past. The rhizomes should be planted 4 inches deep.

Calla lilies will overwinter outdoors in Zones 9–11, but in most places they need to overwinter indoors. If you've grown the plants in pots, you can simply move the pots inside to a dark location for the winter without having to dig at all. Just repot them in fresh soil in spring. If you've planted them in the garden, dig up the rhizomes at the end of the growing season. Store them in a cool, dry location until next spring.

My calla lilies develop seedpods after blooming. Can I plant these pods to get more callas? Last year I didn't do anything with them, and this year I have calla lilies everywhere. I plan to separate them to share with friends. Will the seedpods help with the sharing?

It's generous to share garden plants with friends, though I don't think the seedpods will do you much good. Like most bulbs, calla lilies are best propagated vegetatively through their underground structure. I've never had anything develop from seedpods on my calla lilies, but that's not to say they haven't sprouted in your garden. Callas spread easily by their underground stems, and that's the best way to increase these plants. Divide rhizomes in late summer or early fall after digging them up for overwintering, or in spring before you set them in the ground.

CANNA

I live where winter temperatures routinely fall below zero. My grandmother, who lives in a more temperate climate, gave me some cannas. Can I grow these where I live?

Cannas (*Canna*) like growing conditions usually found in the tropics; they won't live through the winter in Zone 6 or colder without a little tender loving care. To make sure your plants live to bloom again, you'll need to dig them up in fall and store them properly through the winter.

Cannas grow from fleshy tubers. Carefully dig up the tubers after the first frost in your area has blackened the plants' foliage. Trim off all but a couple inches of stem, and place the tubers in a warm, airy location to dry. Once they are completely dry, place them in paper bags filled with slightly moistened peat moss or sand. Store the bagged tubers in a cool, dark place. Restart them in early spring (February or March in areas with cold winters) in flats of peat moss. Put flats in a sunny window or under grow-lights. Once the cannas sprout, transfer them to pots. Transplant them into the garden when they are at least 4 inches tall and after all danger of frost is past. You also can plant the tubers directly into the garden in fertile, well-drained soil after all possibility of frost has passed, but the plants will not bloom as quickly.

CROCOSMIA

Plant ID

I have a plant called "Lucifer", but I don't know a thing about it. The leaves look like gladiolus foliage, but the plant has red flowers. Do you know what the name is? Is it a perennial?

Your plant is a variety of crocosmia. Your noticing its resemblance to a gladiolus is right on the mark—both plants are members of the iris family. 'Lucifer' crocosmia is hardy in Zones 6–9. Plant crocosmia in full sun and well-drained soil. In northern ranges of Zone 6, cover the plant with several inches of mulch in winter, just after the soil freezes, to protect the overwintering corms.

DAFFODIL

Daffodils won't bloom

My favorite yellow-and-white daffodils haven't bloomed in 2 years. How can I get them to bloom again?

Like most perennials, daffodils *(Narcissus)* grow and spread, forming larger colonies each year. If not divided regularly, the bulbs become too crowded to bloom well. Luckily, there is an easy fix—dig your daffodils in summer or early autumn and plant the bulbs farther apart so they're no longer crowded. Pull individual daughter bulbs from the mother bulb and replant each one in its own hole. I find it helpful to mark where the bulbs are while they're in bloom, so I don't forget where they are after they go dormant.

Color change

I planted some yellow and some white daffodils a couple of years ago. This year they all came up yellow. What happened?

Some daffodil varieties are naturally more vigorous than others. When different varieties are planted together, sometimes the more vigorous type crowds out the less vigorous type. If you dig your daffodils this summer, separate the bulbs and plant them with more space between them. Then your white ones should start blooming again.

Daffodils won't open

My double yellow daffodils grow well, but the flowers won't open unless I give them a hand. Otherwise, they dry up and turn brown. What's wrong?

Most varieties of double daffodils are sensitive to a condition called bud blast. Although bud blast may sound like fun, it is no blast for gardeners. It typically occurs when temperatures warm quickly in spring. Unfortunately, there's nothing you can do to prevent it; if the weather warms up fast, you'll need to help open the buds by hand if you want to see flowers.

Bud blast is more likely when daffodils are overcrowded. Divide and replant the bulbs if this is the case.

Starting daffodils from seed

I've noticed that after my daffodils bloom, they develop pods on the stems. Are these seedpods? If so, can I collect and sow the seeds to start new plants?

Yes, those capsules you see at the daffodil stem tips are seedpods. Many experts recommend removing them so the bulbs have more energy to produce flowers the following year. You can collect this seed, but if it's from a hybrid bulb, the plant that grows from the seed may not look like the parent.

If you'd like to create your own daffodil hybrid, you'll need to take pollen from one flower while it's still blooming and place it on the reproductive organ of another flower. If pollination is successful, the pod should develop after the flower fades.

Once the pod ripens and turns brown, break the hard, dry seeds from the pod. Sow them immediately in a sheltered spot in the garden or in a cold frame. Though they'll germinate the following spring, you'll have to wait awhile to see them bloom; it takes most daffodils 5–6 years from seed to bloom.

Forcing paperwhites

I'd like to try my hand at forcing bulbs. I've heard it's not hard. What is a good bulb to start with?

Probably the easiest bulb to force is the paperwhite narcissus. In fact, these bulbs are so willing to get growing that they're likely to begin as they sit on your kitchen counter. Pot them in soil or anchor them in a container of pebbles filled with water to the base of the bulbs.

While you're at it, sprout a hyacinth in water. Just set the bulb in a glass that supports the base of the bulb and lets the water touch the roots. Bulbs that are grown in water use up all their energy, so they won't resprout if planted outside.

DAHLIA

I bought some dahlia bulbs. How do I plant them?

With their variety of colors, shapes, and sizes, dahlias bring life to your landscape from late summer into fall. Here's how to successfully plant and care for these tender plants.

1. Plant the tubers once all danger of frost has passed. Choose a location with fertile, well-drained soil that gets at least 6 hours of sun a day. The plants like sandy or loamy soil but will do fine in clay if you work in a 2–4-inch layer of well-rotted manure or compost before planting. Smaller varieties should be spaced 1–3 feet apart, larger ones 2–5 feet apart.
2. For each tuber, dig a hole about 12 inches wide and 8–10 inches deep. Mix a shovelful of compost and a handful of bonemeal into the soil you removed, or add a timed-release fertilizer according to package directions.
3. Fill each planting hole with the soil mixture until it is about 4 inches deep.
4. Taller plants may need to be staked. To avoid damage to the roots, drive a stake into the ground now, a few inches from where you plan to plant each bulb or tuber. Stakes can be made of wood or bamboo, or they can be metal fence posts.
5. Place a tuber horizontally in the bottom of each hole with the eye pointing upward and the roots down. Cover with 2 inches of soil. Shoots should emerge from the holes in about 2 weeks.
6. As the taller varieties grow, tie them to their stake with twine.

I recently purchased a beautiful dinner-plate dahlia. Unfortunately, it froze during a cold spell. What do I do now? Can it be saved?

The extent of damage to your dahlia depends on how cold it got, and for what length of time. If the plant was nipped by frost, it will probably come back; but if it was completely frozen, it may be too late to save it. If the roots didn't freeze, the dahlia should be able to grow from the roots. At this point, the best option is to wait and see if it resprouts. In the future, wait until all danger of frost has passed to set out your dahlia, or be prepared to protect it from frost on chilly nights.

Planting dahlias

When do I plant dahlia tubers? I've heard conflicting advice about the right time to plant in my area.

Plant dahlia tubers after all danger of frost has passed. When it's safe to plant tomatoes, it's safe to plant dahlias. If you'd like to get an earlier start, you can plant the tubers in a pot and start them indoors. That way you'll have a sizable plant to set out when the weather warms. In Zone 8 or warmer, you may leave dahlias in the ground over winter.

Storing dahlias

I read an article that said to store dahlia tubers in wood shavings in a box in the basement. I did this, and now they are shriveled. Is there any hope for them? How should I have stored them?

It sounds as though your dahlia tubers got too dry. Always make sure that the roots are slightly moist before putting them in storage. The wood shavings you used are a good choice, as are vermiculite, perlite, dry sand, or peat moss.

Keep the tubers cool in storage, but above freezing (40–45°F) is ideal. Check them regularly during the winter, and sprinkle a little water on them if they begin to dry out. A layer of newspaper over the top of the box will help hold in moisture. If your dahlia tubers are completely shriveled, they may be beyond salvaging. If there's any fleshiness to them, you might plant them and see what happens.

ELEPHANT'S EAR

Growing elephant's ear

I have an elephant's ear bulb and I'm not sure where to plant it. Can you help?

Luckily, elephant's ear *(Alocasia)* is easy to grow—plant yours in a shady spot that has moist soil. I've found it helpful to plant the bulb in a protected spot so the leaves don't get too tattered by wind.

Because elephant's ear doesn't tolerate freezing temperatures, it isn't a perennial in most areas. You'll have to dig and store the bulb in a frost-free place after the first frost in autumn, or consider it an annual and plant a new one each year.

GRAPE HYACINTH

Early-sprouting grape hyacinth

My grape hyacinths are starting to come up now. Will they bloom this autumn instead of spring?

In many areas, grape hyacinths *(Muscari armeniacum)* naturally send up foliage in autumn and then again in spring. It's normal and doesn't mean they'll bloom out of season. Look at them as good "marker" plants. If you plant them among your spring-flowering bulbs, their fall foliage reminds you where to dig. Don't worry about them—just enjoy the attractive blue-green foliage and the reminder of blooms to come in spring!

IRIS

Iris renovation

We recently purchased a home and are completely redoing the landscaping. I need to dig and replant the iris, but I don't know anything about them—sun, shade, how deep to plant them, etc. They are the tall purple iris you see everywhere.

You likely have bearded iris *(Iris ×germanica),* which need full sun and good drainage. The rhizome (the horizontal stem that the foliage grows from) need to be visible at the soil surface. Planting them deeper encourages rot and disease. Iris are best divided and moved in mid- to late summer, but you can move them earlier in the year if you must.

Iris takeover

I purchased several different-color iris, and they were beautiful the first year. The next year, most of them had turned to blue shades and the different colors were gone. What caused this? Will the old colors come back?

Plants rarely change color; it's more likely that the blue variety you bought was more vigorous (which is the case with many of the blue and purple cultivars). The stronger and more vigorous cultivars took over your iris bed and elbowed out the other colors. Planting your iris farther apart will help keep any one cultivar from crowding out the others.

Transplanting iris in spring

I need to move a bed of iris. Can that be done in spring?

You don't say what kind of iris you have, but I'm going to assume they are bearded iris. It's best to move them in late summer or early fall, when their bloom has ended and their growth slows down. If you must, you can move them in spring as long as you are careful to dig up a large ball of soil around them and replant them immediately. Do this when the plants are still short in early spring, long before bloom spikes begin to appear. If you wait until they are much taller, they might not bloom and could be stressed enough to do poorly all summer.

Dividing iris

I've noticed that my bearded iris are making fewer and fewer blooms each year. Do they need something to become healthier?

Bearded iris are known for their easy care, and they can fill a bed in only a few years. I suspect that yours are getting crowded. Bearded iris need to be dug and divided every 3–5 years to keep them growing well and not competing against one another for space, nutrients, and water. Divide them in late summer or early fall, following these steps.

1. Carefully dig the clumps with a garden fork or spade, taking care not to chop into the rhizomes (the creeping, horizontal stems that look like roots).
2. Divide the rhizomes by cutting them apart with a sharp knife. Slice off younger rhizomes that are growing off the largest, main rhizome. You will replant the babies and any large rhizomes that have buds or new shoots coming out of them. Large, old rhizomes that have no buds can be tossed out, because they're unlikely to rebloom.
3. Wash the soil off the rhizomes so you can inspect each one for iris borer (a fat pinkish worm) or rot. If you find a borer, destroy it. Soft, smelly, or rotting plants should also be destroyed. Some gardeners like to wash their iris rhizomes in a 10 percent bleach solution to destroy disease organisms, but that won't help plants that are already rotting.
4. Clip off the leaf blades so they're 6–8 inches long. This reduces the stress that the plant goes through as it concentrates on growing new roots instead of trying to maintain long leaves.
5. Replant the divisions, setting the rhizomes higher in the planting hole than the roots. A bit of the top surface of each rhizome should be just visible at the soil surface. Space the plants 12–18 inches apart. Water them well at planting, but do not continue to water unless the soil becomes dry. If some of the rhizomes were rotted, avoid replanting in the same area as they were growing.

Siberian no-show

I have a large clump of Siberian iris that bloomed well until I divided it. The divisions came up and the original clump seems to be healthy, but no blooms. What have I done wrong, or what can I do to encourage bloom?

If the divisions were quite small, they might be too little to bloom. In this case, you should see flowers next season or the season after.

Was your plant moved to a new location? If so, the plant may be suffering transplant shock. If this happened, it should bloom normally next year.

Also, be sure you replanted everything at the same level it was growing at originally. Replanting too deep or too shallow can prevent blooms.

Critical-condition iris

My iris are dying. The plants look terrible, and the roots close to the soil surface are soft and mushy. Should I cover the roots, transplant them, or what?

The most likely problem is iris borer, the worst pest of bearded iris. The borers are larvae of moths that lay eggs on dead iris foliage in autumn. The eggs hatch in spring, and the borers briefly feed on the leaves before heading to the roots. To get the problem under control, dig up your iris this summer, cut off all the rotted rhizomes, and put the rotted material in the garbage. Soak the good pieces in a mixture of ½ cup bleach per gallon of water, then replant them in fresh soil. In late fall, gather up the dead leaves and rake the bed as clean as you can.

Next spring, at about the time forsythias and tulips bloom, check your iris for ragged leaves or dark streaks in the foliage. If you see either condition, treat the infested plants with insecticide, or douse them with beneficial nematodes. Although adding nematodes to a garden may seem strange, studies show that beneficial nematodes are more effective for controlling iris borers than insecticides. The nematodes enter the borers' bodies and kill them, and continue to work for 4–5 weeks.

Soft, mushy rhizomes in iris may also be caused by bacterial soft rot. You can easily distinguish bacterial soft rot from iris borer because plants affected by soft rot will smell bad. Dig up and destroy affected areas of the plant. Replant healthy portions in a new area.

Going to great planting depths

I divided my iris and am ready to replant. How deep should I plant the roots?

I'll assume you are talking about the popular bearded iris, which bloom in early spring. Plant so the rhizomes (horizontal stems) are just below the soil surface. In very sandy soil, the rhizomes may be planted a little deeper, but no more than 1 inch below the surface. Improve the soil before replanting, working in a generous amount of organic matter such as rotted manure or compost. Keep the soil moist, but not wet, until the ground freezes. The best time to plant or transplant bearded iris is late summer, from about early August to mid-September.

Siberian and Japanese iris, cousins of the bearded iris, grow from fibrous roots instead of rhizomes. These iris are best divided in early spring, but they can also be divided in early fall. Plant the newly divided crowns at the same depth they were growing at originally and water well.

LILY

Planting potted lilies

I received several pots of lilies for Easter, including Oriental lilies and white Easter lilies. Can these be replanted so they will bloom next spring?

Carefully plant your lilies—Oriental and Easter—outdoors at the depth they normally grow (it varies depending on the lily type), and they should bloom when they usually would next season, which is in summer. (Most lilies are forced into spring bloom by greenhouses.) Often, Easter lilies will bloom again in the garden the same summer you plant them.

Lily leaf beetles

My lilies never have a chance because red beetles eat holes in the leaves. How can I get rid of the beetles?

It sounds as though your lilies are victims of the red lily leaf beetle, which has been spreading through Canada and New England since 1992. Handpick the larvae and adults, or spray plants with a neem-based insecticide once a week from mid-April to September. The sluglike larvae are the main leaf eaters. Most people wear latex gloves when gathering them, because the larvae are often coated with unpleasant slime. Look for adults and larvae starting the third week of April. Also look for cylindrical yellow-orange eggs on the undersides. Crush the eggs or pinch off the leaves with eggs on them.

Lily bloom season

I was told that Asiatic lilies bloom most of the summer. Mine don't seem to bloom very long. What is their normal bloom time?

Lilies *(Lilium)* are a garden staple, but they're not long-blooming. Each plant blooms once a year, and the flowers last a couple of weeks. However, with careful selection you can grow a range of Asiatic lilies that have varying bloom times. Good lily combinations (including Oriental and species types) can provide flowers through most of the summer.

TUBEROUS BEGONIA

Start with tubers

Instead of paying for a display of full-grown begonias, I'd like to start some from tubers. How should I plant them?

Plan for an indoor planting date 6–8 weeks before the tubers are to be transplanted outside, after the last frost date. Place tubers just below the surface in a flat of moist soilless potting mix. The indented, or concave, part of the tuber—where the buds, or "eyes," may be present—should face up. Tubers sprout best at temperatures at least as warm as 60°F. Keep the soil moist but not soaked. When newly sprouted leaves reach about 3 inches, shift the tubers to larger pots and continue to grow in bright light.

TULIP

No-show tulips

My tulips don't last. After the first spring, only one sickly leaf comes back. My neighbors have perfect tulips year after year. I plant in good soil in full sun, and I can grow everything else without a problem. What am I doing wrong?

Unlike the swallows to Capistrano, all tulips do not return every year. Switch to species or botanical tulips, which naturally come back each year and even grow bigger and bigger clumps. Species tulips have not been bred or hybridized and remain essentially as they are found in nature. *Tulipa turkestanica, T. tarda, T. saxatilis, T. clusiana, T. marjolettii,* and *T. humilis* are good choices for garden use.

Botanical tulips are hybrids that remain close to the original species. They include Kaufmanniana, Greigii, and Fosteriana tulips. Species and botanical tulips are generally smaller in bloom size than other tulips, but they can be just as spectacular. Most good bulb catalogs sell these.

Nonblooming tulips

My tulips have always returned in spring. However, this spring many of them did not bloom again. Any ideas why?

Did you do anything different last spring after your tulips bloomed? Bulbs that become weak or refuse to flower in subsequent years may not have been able to manufacture enough food to store up the energy they need to support flower buds. They may be growing in too much shade, or you may have removed the leaves before they turned completely brown and were done manufacturing food.

The truth is, however, that most tulips wear out quickly. Darwin hybrids and the other more flashy varieties last for only a couple of years at most. Only botanical or species tulips and their hybridized strains reliably come back year after year.

Some hybrid tulips have more of a propensity for repeat performance. Try 'Charles', 'Christmas Marvel', and 'Couleur Cardinal'. Triumph tulips, such as 'Don Quichotte', and lily-flowered 'Aladdin' and 'Ballade' should bloom reliably for more than one season. Others offering potential for a second season of color include tall Darwin hybrids such as 'Golden Parade', 'Oxford', and 'Holland's Glory'.

Cutting tulips

How and when do I cut my tulips to put them in a vase?

Tulips can be cut almost anytime you want to enjoy them. But leave the foliage. Allow it to remain attached to the bulb to build up energy for next year's blooms.

For the longest-lasting flowers, cut tulips in an advanced bud stage, when the blooms are still closed but the color of the flower is evident. Cut off at least ½ inch of the stems on an angle with a sharp knife and place them in water. Floral preservative is not necessary for tulips, but replace the water every day, making a fresh cut at the base of the stem. Tulips prefer cool room temperatures. Avoid combining tulips with paperwhite narcissus or daffodils, which exude a gummy sap that can shorten tulips' vase life. Tulip blooms last 3–7 days if given proper care.

The International Flower Bulb Centre (www.bulb.com) has identified several varieties of tulips known for their especially long vase life. If you like to bring tulips indoors as cut flowers, consider growing 'Angelique', 'Don Quichotte', 'Attila', 'Queen of Bartigons', 'Pax', 'Yokohama', 'Ile de France', 'Negrita', 'Leen van der Mark', 'Prinses Irene', or 'Rosario'.

Baby tulips

When I dug my tulips to separate them, I found many baby bulbs. How do I take care of them so I can have tulip flowers again?

Saving those baby tulips may not be worth the effort. The daughter bulbs will not likely develop into plants as beautiful as the parent. In most regions, tulips decline in vigor over time rather than increase in size. Tulips (except for species varieties) simply don't last forever—2–3 years of blooms is all you can really expect. If you want long-lived bulbs, choose species tulips when you replant.

However, if you live where tulips grow exceptionally well, and you are a bit adventurous, you could replant the daughter bulbs and see what you get. Space the bulbs as you would full-size ones. It will likely take several years for them to reach blooming size.

Tulip transplanting

I have a large garden box outside my apartment where I planted tulips last fall. The blossoms are just opening. I'm moving in a few weeks—the box is too large to move and it doesn't have a bottom. How can I transplant the tulips without damaging them?

You're probably not going to want to hear this, but you're best off leaving the tulips for the next owner to enjoy and planting new ones for yourself this autumn. It is stressful on tulips to be transplanted when they are actively growing. The best time to transplant them is in late summer or fall. If your bulbs did recover from being transplanted, they probably wouldn't bloom well anyway, because hybrid tulips bloom well for only a couple of years.

Tulips in warm regions

I garden in California. I was told that if I want tulips, I have to put the bulbs in the freezer and plant them in December. Is this right?

The information you received was not entirely correct. In your area you need to order bulbs that are already chilled. Many bulb companies sell prechilled bulbs for gardeners who live in climates such as yours. You can plant those bulbs directly into your garden for springtime blooms.

Some gardeners try to chill their own bulbs by storing them in the refrigerator, but this rarely works. Temperatures just above freezing are ideal for providing the necessary chilling. But because chilling the bulbs takes 12 weeks or more, most gardeners find it too much bother to take up valuable refrigerator space. Putting bulbs in the freezer will kill them, turning them to mush.

PERENNIALS IN GENERAL

Confusing categories

I'm new to flower gardening and get confused about the difference between perennials and annuals. I know that one comes back every year, and the other you have to plant every year. Which is which?

Gardening can be confusing to beginners—there's the challenge of figuring out what plant to grow where, along with new terms to learn.

Flower gardening basics

Perennials. These are plants that come back year after year from their root systems. Examples include bleeding heart *(Dicentra)*, purple coneflower *(Echinacea)*, and hosta. Typically more expensive than annuals at the garden center, perennials are a good investment because many are long-lived. Plus, many get bigger each year, and after a couple of years you can split them. When grown from seed, most perennials will not bloom the first year, so they do require a bit of patience. Also, many perennials bloom only for a few weeks each season.

Annuals. These plants grow, bloom, and die in one growing season. Examples include marigold *(Tagetes)*, petunia, and zinnia. Because annuals pack all of their energy into one year, many bloom all season long.

Biennials. This group of plants seems to be caught in the middle between perennials and annuals. They spend their first year of life as foliage plants. They come back a second year and bloom, then set seed and die. Examples include many foxgloves *(Digitalis)* and Canterbury bells *(Campanula medium)*.

Tender perennials. Think of tender perennials as having a secret identity: In cold climates they're annuals, but in frost-free climates they're perennials. (Gardeners in cold climates may be able to keep some tender perennials alive over winter as houseplants.) Examples include lantana, coleus *(Solenostemon)*, and geranium *(Pelargonium)*.

Short-lived perennials. Some perennials do well only for a few years, then fade. Examples include some lupines *(Lupinus)* and columbines *(Aquilegia)*. Many gardeners treat these plants as annuals, growing new ones from seed or purchasing new ones every year or two.

Self-sowers. These plants, which could be annuals, perennials, or biennials, produce seeds if the spent flowers aren't removed. The seeds drop and sprout easily in the garden—so you don't have to plant them again. Examples include gloriosa daisy *(Rudbeckia)*, spider flower *(Cleome)*, columbine *(Aquilegia)*, and foxglove *(Digitalis)*.

Zoned out

The labels on some perennials I purchased said they were hardy in Zones 5-8. What does that mean? How do I find out what zone my garden is in?

The United States Department of Agriculture (USDA) divides North America into hardiness regions, called zones, based on the average annual minimum temperature an area receives. The lower the zone number, the colder the winter. Use the zone designations as a rough guide to determine which perennials you can grow. (Because annuals don't survive from year to year, it doesn't matter how cold the winters get.) For example, if you live in Zone 5, you probably won't have good luck with a perennial that's suited to Zones 6–9, because it's too cold where you live. Likewise, if you live in Zone 9, you probably won't have luck with a plant that's suited to Zones 5–8, because it's too warm where you live. See a copy of the USDA zone map on page 603.

Transplant timing

It never fails—when a plant is prettiest and in full bloom is when I realize I should have planted it elsewhere. Then, when it's transplanting time, I can't recall what I wanted to move where. Can I move plants in bloom, or would that be deadly?

Plants in bloom are moved all the time, for reasons that range from impatience to impending construction. It's usually not deadly, just more difficult to do, and it's harder for the plant to recover. There's a good chance that stems will be broken and flower heads left in disarray, but ask around and you'll find at least one person who's beaten those odds with almost any plant you can name.

Water the plant well the day before you move it. Insert stakes close to the stems and gather them into a tight, but not stalk-breaking, cluster. Use soft, wide straps (such as lawn chair webbing, pantyhose, or carpet strips) to hold the stems together. You may have to tie neighboring plants out of the way so you have room to work.

Dig a wide hole starting at the plant's drip line, then angle in and under the roots. Take hold of the root ball, not the stems, to slide the plant out of the hole onto a tarp. Then sling it gently to its new position and fill the planting hole with soil. Water it in well. If the weather is hot and dry, shade the plant at midday for several days.

Of course, you could also resolve to improve your organizational skills and patience. When you get the inspiration to move a blooming plant, why not mark the spot in the garden where you want to move it, and wait until the time is right for transplanting it?

Dividing perennials

When is the best time to divide perennials? Is it something I will have to do often?

Most perennials benefit from division every 3–5 years and are best divided in early spring, just as new growth is emerging. A few perennials (early spring bloomers) do best when divided in fall. Some prefer to be left alone throughout their life. See the lists on the following page.

Your plant may need dividing if it becomes less floriferous or the flowers get smaller; if the plant's center dies out—leaving a hole, with all the growth around the edges; if the plant loses vigor; or if the plant outgrows its bounds.

Taking them with you

The lot I'm building on has many established perennials. I would like to move them, then replant them when the new construction is completed. Unfortunately, the ground is still frozen. Will they die if I move them now?

As long as your perennials are still dormant, they should be fine if you move them. The trick, however, will be to dig the plants when the ground is frozen. Construction is not likely to start while the ground is still frozen. Check with your builder about the construction schedule, and plan to stay a step ahead of it with your shovel and flower pots! Because the project probably will take several months to complete, you may need to keep the perennials potted for most of the growing season. Use lightweight potting mix in the containers rather than garden soil. Place the containers in a protected, partially shaded location until you're ready to plant the perennials in their permanent location. Keep them well-watered, and fertilize occasionally through the season. I have successfully moved hundreds of perennials from landscape to landscape following this method.

Blooms from seed

Is it better to plant perennials from seed or from plants to guarantee blooms and cut flowers the first year?

Hands down, the best way to see flowers from perennials the first year is by growing plants instead of seeds. There's never a guarantee that seed-started perennials will bloom the first year. Even if they do, they don't usually produce many blooms. Instead, their energy goes into establishing themselves.

Packaged perennials sprouting

I guess I was overeager when I bought some perennials (hosta, iris, ferns, and goatsbeard) at a discount store. They came packaged in soil inside a sealed plastic bag, and without instructions. They have green growth on them, so I'm going to cut the bags open and put them in the garage where it is cold but not freezing. How long will they last? And what's the best way to care for them? Should I water them or keep them dry? Give them light or darkness? I had hoped to get them in the ground at the beginning of March, but it's the end of February and we still have a foot of snow on the ground. Will they keep until March 15?

With plants, you often get what you pay for in terms of quality. The perennials you often see for sale in little boxes may cost less initially than a container-grown plant, but they take additional care to get off to a good start. Because the plants you have are already growing, keep them in a cool place that remains above freezing. The ideal thing would be to pot them up and get them started in a greenhouse or under grow-lights. At least that way they can grow, and you can move the developing plants outdoors at the right time. The best time to plant them outdoors is when the soil can be worked in spring and the danger of hard freezes has passed. If you don't have access to a greenhouse or grow-lights, you may be able to hold the plants successfully in the garage for several weeks after you pot them up.

QUICK TIP

Plants to divide in early fall
(1–2 months before a killing frost)
• Bearded iris *(Iris ×germanica)*
• Moss phlox *(Phlox subulata)*
• Oriental poppy
  (Papaver orientale)
• Siberian iris *(Iris siberica)*
• Sweet woodruff
  (Galium odoratum)

Plants to infrequently divide
• Baby's breath
  (Gypsophila paniculata)
• Balloon flower
  (Platycodon grandiflorus)
• Bugbane
  (Cimicifuga racemosa)
• Butterfly weed
  (Asclepias tuberosa)
• Carolina lupine
  (Thermopsis caroliniana)
• False indigo
  (Baptisia australis)
• Gas plant *(Dictamnus albus)*
• Goatsbeard *(Aruncus dioicus)*
• Monkshood
  (Aconitum napellus)
• Peony *(Paeonia lactiflora)*

Perennials as cut flowers

I would like to use some of my perennial flowers as cut flowers indoors. Which ones would be best?

Most perennial garden flowers can serve double duty as cut flowers. Here are a dozen to get you started: black-eyed Susan *(Rudbeckia)*, blazing star *(Liatris)*, chrysanthemum, delphinium, false sunflower *(Heliopsis)*, goldenrod *(Solidago)*, iris, obedient plant *(Physostegia)*, peony *(Paeonia)*, purple coneflower *(Echinacea)*, Shasta daisy *(Leucanthemum)*, and yarrow *(Achillea)*.

Heat treatment for cut flowers

I read that you should blanch the stem ends of freshly cut flowers in boiling water before arranging them. Why would you do that? Also, what's the best way to keep cut flowers looking fresh?

Only the stem ends of plants with milky sap (such as butterfly weed and poppies) should be seared in a candle flame or dipped in boiling water soon after harvest. Heat seals the cut and prevents the sap from leaking out, making a mess in the vase, and inhibiting water uptake. Other flowers don't need that treatment.

Soil topdressing

What is the best way to improve the soil in an established perennial bed? Is there a way to do it without digging up all the plants?

The best way to amend soil in an existing garden is by top-dressing the bed with an inch or two of compost each season. The compost will break down, improving soil structure and fertility. Plus, you'll perk up your perennials. This is particularly helpful if you live in a cold-winter climate and apply the compost as a mulch, after the soil freezes in winter. If you don't have access to compost, you could use shredded leaves or well-rotted manure. You also can use a packaged fertilizer such as 10-10-10 or fish emulsion. Here's how to successfully incorporate fertilizer around existing perennials.

- Check your timing. The best time to apply fertilizer to most plants is early to midspring, after the plants have grown a few inches above the soil but before they have so many leaves that it is difficult to work the soil around them. You can fertilize later in the season, but most perennials should not receive granular chemical fertilizer after about August 1 in the North or 6–8 weeks before frost.
- Pull away any mulch.
- Add fertilizer or compost. When using fertilizer, carefully measure the recommended amount. Avoid overdoing it. Too much can be harmful.

- Sprinkle fertilizer evenly on the ground around the plants. Avoid getting fertilizer on plant leaves or stems, because it can burn them.
- Lightly work fertilizer into the soil.
- Replace mulch.
- Soak the soil thoroughly, gently washing off any fertilizer that may have gotten on the plants.

Color all season

I am planning to make a flower bed on the sunny side of the house. We would like to go with perennials so we don't have to replant every year, but we want to have blooms in the garden throughout the growing season. Are there perennials that bloom all year long?

For constant color, I suggest you consider planting a mix of annuals and perennials. The perennials can be the backbone of the garden, and you can fill in around them (especially the first couple of years as the perennials get established) with annuals. Many perennials do have a long season of bloom or repeat cycles of bloom. Some to consider for your sunny garden are red valerian (*Centranthus ruber*), Jolly Bee geranium (*Geranium* 'Jolly Bee'), reblooming daylilies (*Hemerocallis* 'Miss Mary Mary', 'Stella de' Oro', and 'Happy Returns'), false sunflower (*Heliopsis helianthoides*), Coronation Gold yarrow (*Achillea* 'Coronation Gold'), Stokes' aster (*Stokesia laevis*), Tennessee coneflower (*Echinacea tennesseensis*), black-eyed Susan (*Rudbeckia hirta*), sedum (*Sedum* 'Matrona' or 'Brilliant'), Russian sage (*Perovskia atriplicifolia*), and catmint (*Nepeta ×faassenii*). I'd also mix in a few crocus, daffodil, and tulip bulbs for spring interest. After the bulbs fade, the perennials will take over and provide color. Also, include foliage plants that look good all year long without flowering. *Artemisia absinthium* 'Lambrook Silver' is one.

Make cut flowers last as long as possible

QUICK TIP

- Cut your flowers early in the morning, while the plants are fully hydrated; the heat of the day can make the stems soft and limp.
- Cut the stems on a slant (use a sharp knife or scissors to avoid crushing the stems) so they don't become blocked from resting flat on the bottom of the vase. All foliage below the water line should be stripped off.
- Get the blooms into warm (100°F) water quickly after cutting. Longer vase life can also be achieved by replacing the nourishment that the cut blooms are no longer receiving from the plant. Packets of floral preservative are available from most floral shops, or you can mix your own by adding 2 tablespoons of vinegar, 2 tablespoons of sugar, and ½ teaspoon of bleach to 1 quart of water.
- Bacterial growth can clog stems, so changing the water daily is a good idea. Recut the stems every day or so, too.
- When your bouquet has faded, clean the inside of the vase as thoroughly as you can, so the next bouquet will not have to battle leftover bacteria.

Late-summer color

By late summer, my perennial garden loses all its color. What can I plant to keep the blooms going?

You're not alone. Many gardeners see their perennial gardens fizzle before autumn. Luckily, lots of perennials come into their own at the end of summer and continue the show into autumn.

You can get some of your perennials that bloom in summer to bloom later than usual by pinching them back in spring. Doing so not only encourages later bloom but also produces a more compact plant that's less likely to need staking. Try this technique on the plants listed in the Quick Tip, below.

QUICK TIP

Perennials for late-summer color

- Anise hyssop *(Agastache foeniculum)* produces violet-blue spikes of fragrant flowers. It readily self-seeds, so use it with caution. It's hardy in Zones 4–9.
- Black-eyed Susan *(Rudbeckia fulgida)* produces golden-yellow flowers that have a black center. Some forms are marked with tones of burgundy and bronze. It's hardy in Zones 4–9.
- Mexican hat *(Ratibida columnifera)* produces flowers that look like golden daisies with an elongated central disk. It's hardy in Zones 3–10.
- Ornamental grasses can produce lovely plumes in late summer before the grasses turn shades of buff, gold, and purple in autumn.
- Perennial sunflowers, such as *Helianthus decapetalus,* start their show in late summer. Most have daisylike yellow flowers. Hardiness varies by species; *H. decapetalus* is hardy in Zones 5–8.
- Purple coneflower *(Echinacea purpurea)* offers lavender-mauve flowers in late summer. It's hardy in Zones 3–9.
- Russian sage *(Perovskia atriplicifolia)* bears silvery foliage and violet-blue flowers in late summer and early autumn. It's hardy in Zones 6–9 as a shrub; gardeners as far north as Zone 3 are able to grow it as a perennial.
- Turtlehead *(Chelone lyonii)* produces pink flowers that actually look like turtle heads. It does well in shade and is hardy in Zones 4–9.

Removing mulch

When should I clean out all of the mulch that I used in my beds to help protect my plants over the winter? I never know and I am always afraid of cleaning up too early or too late.

Pull back the mulch on your perennials before new growth begins to protect tender shoots during the process of removal. You don't have to entirely remove most types of mulch. They can remain in place around the perennials to hold in moisture over the summer and keep down weeds. If the mulch is no more than 2–4 inches thick, it won't hurt to leave it in place. Most perennials will push up through it anyway.

Plants sensitive to late-winter moisture may benefit from mulch removal, however. Chrysanthemums are a good example. If the soil remains too wet, their root systems may rot.

Fall wedding flowers

My fiancé and I are in the process of planning a September wedding. We would like to get married here at our house, and I would love to have beautiful fall gardens for my wedding. We have our own little greenhouse to start the seeds, but I need a list of flowers that are in bloom at the end of September. Perhaps you could suggest some flowers that would look great together.

Congratulations! I would suggest the following for surefire color at your fall wedding:
- Asters (especially valuable if you want blue and white in your wedding)
- Chrysanthemums (keep pinching them back until July to delay bloom)
- Grasses (many ornamental grasses are wonderful bouquet fillers)
- Pansies (for small bouquets and nosegays; pansies love cool weather)

There are other fall-blooming perennials as well, but for mass appeal I think I'd vote for those listed above. In all cases, you don't need to start these indoors. Just buy small plants in spring, set them in your garden or in large pots, and by fall you should have plenty of color. What's more, most garden centers carry all these plants in full bloom in fall, so if some of your homegrown plants don't do well, you can purchase replacements.

Summer foliage cutback

Is it OK to cut back the foliage of my perennials that don't look good anymore, even if it's only August? Maybe all the dry years we've had have changed my tolerance level, but I just can't stand looking at brown anymore. I don't want to do any permanent harm, though. Astilbes, ferns, and others that bother me now were beautiful a while ago, and I'm hoping they will be again next year.

Cut away. By late August, an established perennial has been photosynthesizing for long enough that the plant will be able to recover with no ill effects the following year. Because each year brings its share of extreme weather and at least a few destructive encounters—out-of-bounds soccer balls, squirrel-chasing dogs, home repair workers, errant weed whips—by late summer every garden has something that warrants cutting away before its time.

This isn't news to most horticulturists. Visit almost any botanical garden and you'll see spaces where cutbacks have occurred. However, you may miss seeing the gaps unless you're looking for them.

Don't be alarmed if a perennial grows back after being cut. This won't set it back or disrupt its next bloom, so enjoy the fresh greenery. Some plants are almost certain to grow new foliage even after a late-summer clipping—catmint *(Nepeta)*, daylily *(Hemerocallis)*, globe thistle *(Echinops)*, hardy hibiscus *(Hibiscus)*, and perennial geranium *(Geranium)* come to mind. Others are less predictable. I've seen the likes of astilbe, blue false indigo *(Baptisia australis)*, Japanese painted fern *(Athyrium nipponicum* 'Pictum')*, Joe-Pye weed *(Eupatorium purpureum)*, and queen-of-the-prairie *(Filipendula rubra)* send up some new shoots, but I've also known them to just lie back and wait for spring. Some perennials such as peony *(Paeonia)* and old-fashioned bleeding heart *(Dicentra spectabilis)* are almost sure bets to conserve their energy and hold off on foliage production until the next year.

Deadheading dilemma

I'd like to deadhead my perennials. How far back should I cut them?

Deadheading perennials is a good idea. Removing spent flowers encourages rebloom, eliminates seed production and self-seeding, and makes your garden and landscape look nicer. It does take time, but it's easy to do and it brings great satisfaction. To deadhead plants that produce single bloom stalks, such as blazing star *(Liatris)* or delphinium, cut back the flowering stem all the way to the ground, if possible. On plants that have a single flower on a stem, such as daisy, you want to get rid of only the flower that has finished blooming. Do this after the flower has become unattractive but before it sets seeds.

You can let the flower stalks fall to the ground, but for the best effect, you'll want to remove them from your garden. Deadheading shears are available that cut the stem and hold it until you release the handle. This allows you to deadhead with one hand, easily moving the spent flower stalk into a container so you can carry it to the compost pile.

Here are some pointers on where to deadhead specific types of perennials.

- Remove the entire bloom stalk of delphinium, blazing star, and other plants that flower from a single stem.
- Deadhead lilies just below the bottom flower to keep as many leaves on the plant as possible.
- On plants that produce several flower heads on one stem, such as false sunflower (*Heliopsis*), deadhead the stem at foliage level.
- Cut back plants that produce plumes, such as Russian sage (*Perovskia*), just below the bulk of the flowers.
- Shear plants such as coreopsis that produce flowers at the same level as the foliage.
- Deadhead individual flowers of plants that produce single blooms on long stems, such as Shasta daisy (*Leucanthemum*).

Deadheading dos and don'ts

Where on the stem do I cut off dead flowers? I've heard that removing spent flowers encourages more blooms.

Removing dead flowers, or deadheading, is a good gardening practice. It may make plants produce extra flowers, it makes for a neater garden, and it prevents self-sown seedlings from popping up everywhere.

To deadhead, pinch back to the next flower, bud, or leaf on a stem. On flowers such as petunias, pinch back the flower stalk to the first set of leaves below the bloom. If you simply pull off spent petunia petals, for example, you may leave behind the developing seedpod. Irises need a different method, because they produce new flowers lower on their stalks. Wait until all the flowers on a single stalk finish blooming, then cut the entire stem as close to the plant's base as possible.

QUICK TIP

Perennials to deadhead to prolong bloom
- Balloon flower (*Platycodon*)
- Bellflower (*Campanula*)
- Blanket flower (*Gaillardia*)
- Coreopsis (*Coreopsis*)
- Delphinium (*Delphinium*)
- Foxglove (*Digitalis*)
- Garden phlox (*Phlox paniculata*)
- Hollyhock (*Alcea rosea*)
- Lupine (*Lupinus*)
- Monkshood (*Aconitum*)
- Spiderwort (*Tradescantia*)
- Yarrow (*Achillea*)

Perennials that do not rebloom with deadheading
- Astilbe (*Astilbe*)
- Barrenwort (*Epimedium*)
- Bergenia (*Bergenia*)
- Bugbane (*Cimicifuga*)
- Goatsbeard (*Aruncus dioicus*)
- Lamb's-ears (*Stachys byzantina*)
- Ligularia (*Ligularia*)
- Lilyturf (*Liriope*)
- Oriental poppy (*Papaver orientale*)
- Peony (*Paeonia*)
- Siberian iris (*Iris sibirica*)

Directions for deadheading

I am new at gardening and want to know what "deadheading" means. Should this be done to all plants, and, if so, when?

Deadheading is removing a plant's flowers as they fade. This often encourages annuals, roses, and most perennials to set additional blooms. With azaleas and other spring-blooming shrubs, it won't promote more blooms, but it will make the plants look neater.

The purpose of a flower (from the plant's perspective) is to attract pollinators that will help the plant create seeds. When a flower is successfully pollinated, it wilts, sending chemical signals to the rest of the plant to slow down blooming and put more energy into developing seeds. Removing the flowers as they fade interrupts the chemical signals sent by the developing seeds, and the plant usually tries to bloom again. Most perennials benefit from deadheading as their flowers fade. Cut the whole flower stem near the base of the plant when it is finished blooming. The flower stem won't bloom again, but the plant may send up new flower stalks. Newer annual cultivars bloom longer than the old-fashioned ones, but all of them will bloom longer and look tidier if deadheaded. Pinch out or cut off the flower stems as the flowers begin to fade. It's not necessary to wait until all the blooms on the stalk are completely brown to do this.

Fall cutback

When should I clean up my perennial flower garden this fall and how should I do it?

As long as your perennials look good, leave them alone. Some die back after the first heavy freeze; others remain attractive all winter. I usually go through the garden several times each fall to cut down the plants that no longer look good. A final trip through the garden in late winter removes those that were left for winter interest. Most perennials can be cut back to within a couple of inches of the ground.

If some of your perennials were attacked by insects or diseases this past year, it would be a good idea to remove stems of those plants from the garden to reduce the likelihood that the problems will carry over in the next season. Rather than composting damaged plant material, dispose of it in the trash.

Once the perennial garden is cut back, it's a good time to apply mulch. With the stems out of the way, it's easier to maneuver around the plants. And the additional mulch will protect the roots and crowns from winter cold.

How do I stake my perennial flowers? A lot of them look great until they start blooming, but then they flop over and look ugly.

If most of your perennial flowers get tall and leggy, it may be an indication that your garden has too much shade or is receiving too much nitrogen fertilizer. Either situation can cause tall, leggy growth in perennials. Use fertilizer with lower nitrogen content, or grow more shade-tolerant perennials if your garden is shady. You could also grow dwarf versions of your favorite perennials to eliminate the need for staking.

If you must stake, get the staking in place early in the season, when new growth is just beginning. This allows plants to grow up through the supports, hiding the stakes by the time the plant is in bloom. There are several types of stakes from which to choose.

Single stakes are best for long-stemmed plants with large, heavy flowers, such as delphiniums, dahlias, and lilies. Tie the flower stalk to the stake as the stem elongates. Make sure the tie is loose enough so that the stem can move a bit. Use soft twine or garden twist ties that blend in with the foliage, and make a loose figure-eight loop around the plant stem and stake.

Twiggy branches pruned from trees or shrubs can be used as pea staking. Insert the branches into the ground around the edges of the clump. Large clumps may need a few pea stakes in the center as well. Cut the branches 6–8 inches shorter than the perennial's mature height so the staking will eventually be completely hidden.

You can also create a staking framework from bamboo stakes and twine. Place bamboo stakes in a circle along the edges of the perennial clump. Weave twine from one stake to another on the opposite side of the clump until you've connected all the stakes in a grid pattern. Place stakes before the plants begin to flop open. Keep the woven grid below the height of the mature foliage so it will be hidden from view.

Bushy perennials such as peonies can be supported with circular metal rings. Many garden centers carry peony rings and tomato cages that can be used for this purpose. The perennial foliage will grow and fill in to conceal the ring.

A no-fuss garden
I like flowers but don't want to spend a lot of time watering, fertilizing, and pruning. What would you suggest for lots of color with little work?

It's many a gardener's dream: a colorful garden that comes back year after year, requires minimal maintenance, and doesn't die if you neglect it. If that fits your vision of a perfect garden, here's one that shouldn't disappoint you.

All of these plants thrive in a sunny spot and well-drained soil. Planting them in shade or wet soil strips away their aura of invincibility. To avoid major weeding duties, use organic mulch, such as shredded bark or wood chips.

- Anise hyssop *(Agastache foeniculum)*. A heat- and drought-tolerant perennial that's native to North America, anise hyssop produces spikes of violet-blue flowers from midsummer until frost. 'Blue Fortune' is a reliable new selection. Anise hyssop grows 5 feet tall and 1 foot wide. Zones 4–9.
- Blazing star *(Liatris spicata)*. In late summer, blazing star produces exclamation points of purple that often last until early autumn. 'Kobold' is a popular dwarf selection; 'Floristan White' blooms white. Plants grow 3–5 feet tall and 2 feet wide. Zones 4–9.
- Carpathian bellflower *(Campanula carpatica)*. A first-rate ground cover, it bears blue flowers throughout the summer. 'Blue Clips' is a popular selection. For added variety, try 'White Clips', a white-flowering type. *C. carpatica* and most of its selections grow up to 1 foot tall and 2 feet wide. Zones 4–7.
- Catmint *(Nepeta ×faassenii* 'Walker's Low'). Catmint starts blooming in early summer and continues to produce spikes of lavender-blue flowers until early autumn. Taller selections are available, but they tend to flop over in the garden. 'Walker's Low' grows only 10 inches tall and 18 inches wide. Zones 4–8.
- Coreopsis *(Coreopsis verticillata* 'Zagreb'). Cheerful daisy-shape yellow flowers appear in early summer and reappear if the plant is sheared back after blooming. The popular variety 'Moonbeam' has paler flowers, as does 'Creme Brulee'. 'Zagreb' grows 1 foot tall and wide. Zones 4–9.
- Corydalis *(Corydalis lutea)*. One of the longest-blooming perennials, this golden-flower charmer starts in spring and keeps going until autumn frost. It grows 1 foot tall and wide. Zones 5–8 (however, it usually self-sows, even in colder climates).
- Daylily *(Hemerocallis* 'Stella de Oro'). A favorite of landscapers, this daylily blooms on and off from early summer to autumn, producing yellow flowers. 'Black-Eyed Stella' offers additional variety with yellow blooms that have burgundy-red centers. 'Stella de Oro' grows 1 foot tall and 2 feet wide. Zones 3–9.
- Gaura *(Gaura lindheimeri)*. Native to North America, this fine perennial produces pink or white flowers from late spring to autumn. 'Siskiyou Pink' has bright pink

flowers; 'Corrie's Gold' offers golden-edged foliage. Gaura grows 3 feet tall and wide. Zones 6–9 (though many gardeners overwinter it as far north as Zone 4).

- Geranium *(Geranium* 'Rozanne'). One of the best perennial geraniums, 'Rozanne' produces violet-blue flowers from spring to autumn. Another species, bloody cranesbill *(Geranium sanguineum),* and its cultivars offer a similar bloom season as well as scarlet autumn foliage. 'Rozanne' grows 2 feet tall and wide. Zones 5–9.

- Helen's flower *(Helenium autumnale* 'Mardi Gras'). A good plant to end the bloom season, this plant produces yellow blooms marked with orange-red in summer and continues blooming until frost. Many other selections are available that bloom in shades of yellow, orange, and red. The variety 'Mardi Gras' grows 3 feet tall and 2 feet wide. Zones 4–8.

- Pincushion flower *(Scabiosa columbaria* 'Pink Mist'). A favorite of butterflies, this perennial produces lavender-pink flowers through the summer and early autumn. Another variety, 'Butterfly Blue', offers lavender-blue flowers over the same bloom period. Both types grow 2 feet tall and 3 feet wide. Zones 3–8.

- Purple coneflower *(Echinacea purpurea).* A favorite of gardeners and butterflies, purple coneflower bears lavender-mauve flowers in late summer. Many selections are available, including 'Magnus', which has extra-large flowers on a compact plant. Purple coneflower grows 4 feet tall and 2 feet wide. Zones 3–9.

- Sedum *(Sedum* 'Matrona'). A wonderful plant to end the season, this sedum produces clusters of rose-pink flowers. The selection 'Brilliant' offers more intensely colored blooms; 'Frosty Morn' has variegated foliage. 'Matrona' grows 18 inches tall and wide. Zones 3–10.

- Shasta daisy *(Leucanthemum ×superbum).* The classic daisy, it blooms from the start of summer to the end of autumn. 'Becky' is an especially popular selection. It grows 4 feet tall and wide. Zones 5–8.

- Speedwell *(Veronica* 'Sunny Border Blue'). This award-winning perennial bears violet-blue flowers from summer to late autumn. Unfortunately, by the end of summer it tends to lose its bottom leaves even though it keeps blooming. 'Sunny Border Blue' grows 2 feet tall and 1 foot wide. Zones 4–8.

- Spiderwort *(Tradescantia virginiana* 'Purple Profusion'). The flowers of this perennial open only in the morning, but they appear from late spring until autumn. Enjoy its grassy foliage too. 'Osprey' features ice blue flowers. Spiderwort grows 2 feet tall and wide. Zones 5–9 (many gardeners overwinter it as far north as Zone 3).

- Yarrow *(Achillea millefolium* 'Cerise Queen'). This perennial resists heat and drought like a champion and produces clusters of bright pink flowers all summer. 'The Beacon' is also a choice selection; it offers scarlet red blooms. 'Cerise Queen' grows 2 feet tall and wide. Zones 3–9.

Loving that shade

We have three 'Bradford' pear trees in our front yard. What type of grass and flowers will live in the shade under them? The trees are more than 15 feet tall, and the shade area under each tree is at least 6 feet square.

You have a lot of options, and all of them will do well in your area. I wouldn't try to grow grass under the trees—it generally does less well in shade. You could grow hostas and ferns, of course, and add almost any other shade-loving perennial to that mix. Some colorful flowering choices that also have good foliage are lungwort *(Pulmonaria)*, spotted dead nettle *(Lamium)*, ajuga *(Ajuga)*, foam flower *(Tiarella)*, toad lily *(Tricyrtis)*, and astilbe. When planting, take care to avoid damage to the trees' roots as you dig, and do not add a layer of soil on top of the existing soil. Even a couple of inches of extra soil could suffocate some of the roots.

Shadeless shade garden

I have a large perennial garden shaded by three pines. The pines are diseased and I'm told they have to be removed. I can't move my entire garden, and I'm afraid I will lose most of the plants to the sun that they will be exposed to. How can I protect them?

Your best choice is moving your perennials to another shady area in your yard. Planting new trees is another option, but because your garden is large, it will likely take your new trees too long to grow enough to produce the shade your plants need. Erecting a pergola or trellis with vines to create shade over your garden is another option, but the cost may be prohibitive. You might also consider selling some of your plants and using the money to purchase plants that will like the newly sunny spot.

Southwestern shade plants

My Southern California yard is shady. I'd like to beautify it but don't know what plants to choose. Can you help?

Here are some shade-loving plants that will do well in Southern California.
- Anthurium *(Anthurium)*
- Caladium *(Caladium)*
- Elephant's ear *(Alocasia* and *Colocasia)*
- Gardenia *(Gardenia)*
- Ginger *(Alpinia, Costus,* and *Hedychium)*
- Glorybower *(Clerodendrum bungei)*
- Impatiens *(Impatiens)*

I'd like to start a cut-flower border, but my yard is quite shady. Are there any shade-loving plants that make good cut flowers?

Unfortunately, few shade-loving plants produce good cut flowers. The best types include astilbe, masterwort *(Astrantia major)*, monkshood *(Aconitum)*, coral bells *(Heuchera)*, and cardinal flower *(Lobelia cardinalis)*.

If your garden receives some direct sun, you might be able to grow more traditional cut flowers, such as gerbera daisy *(Gerbera)*, lilies *(Lilium)*, or blazing star *(Liatris)*. However, when grown in the shade, these plants won't provide as much show as they would if grown in the sun.

My parents have space to put in a small planting bed at the back of their house in an area that receives very little sun. They already have plenty of hostas and would like something different. What perennials can you suggest that have color from flowers or that have interesting variegated leaves? I can't seem to come up with anything besides hostas!

Although most people may not realize it, there are a whole host of shade-loving plants. Some of my favorites include astilbe, barrenwort *(Epimedium)*, bleeding heart *(Dicentra)*, Virginia bluebell *(Mertensia virginica)*, lungwort *(Pulmonaria)*, foam flower *(Tiarella)*, spotted dead nettle *(Lamium)*, ajuga *(Ajuga reptans)*, periwinkle *(Vinca minor)*, and toad lily *(Tricyrtis)*. All of these plants are generally available at garden centers, nurseries, and from mail-order companies that specialize in perennials.

Most of these plants are native to woodland areas; incorporate organic matter into the soil before planting to help them thrive.

I'm looking for a reliable late-season flowering perennial that can tolerate some shade. What do you suggest?

Most shade-loving perennials are spring bloomers, but there are several that come into their glory late in the year.

- Golden Fleece goldenrod *(Solidago sphacelata* 'Golden Fleece') is one of the few shade-tolerant plants with yellow blooms. It bears bright golden flowers in late summer and fall.
- Japanese anemone *(Anemone ×hybrida)* blooms into early fall, adding color to the late-season garden. Plants are 2–3 feet tall with white, pink, or rosy flowers.

- Toad lily *(Tricyrtis hirta)* is a gracefully arching plant with white and purple blooms in fall.
- Turtlehead *(Chelone lyonii)* sends up spikes of pink flowers late in the season. Blooms resemble a turtle's head poking out of its shell.

Perennial planting parameters

How do I know how far apart to plant my perennials?

You are right to take time to learn to properly space your perennials. For a modest investment up front, perennial plants will bring years of color and interest to your garden or landscape. A little time and effort spent in proper planting will pay off in the future.

Consult a good book on perennials before planting. *The Complete Perennials Book* by Ortho and the *Miracle-Gro Guide to Growing Beautiful Flowers* provide information about spacing as well as soil, sunlight, and water needs.

If you are planting nursery-grown plants, refer to the label. The preferred spacing is usually a range, such as 18–24 inches. Planting closer will give you a fuller garden more quickly, but you will probably need to divide the perennials sooner. Plants with closer spacing are more susceptible to fungal diseases caused by poor air circulation. Most perennials benefit from division after 3–5 years.

If you can't find information about a specific plant, a general rule is to space small perennials 6–12 inches apart, 2–3-foot-tall perennials 12–18 inches apart, and taller perennials 18–36 inches apart.

Perennials for hot sun

Can you suggest perennials for my hot, sunny flower garden?

The list of perennials you can grow in your garden is nearly endless. Some favorite plants for such conditions include black-eyed Susan *(Rudbeckia)*, coneflower *(Echinacea)*, aster *(Aster)*, blue false indigo *(Baptisia)*, peony *(Paeonia)*, and bearded iris *(Iris)*. Also consider the host of other plants that should be available at your local nursery or garden center, or from mail-order gardening companies that specialize in perennials.

In addition to a warm, sunny spot, all of these plants appreciate well-drained soil. Take care to avoid overwatering or fertilizing them; doing so will encourage them to produce tender growth that won't stand up to hot, windy conditions. I also advise that you mulch the soil around your perennials; this will help conserve moisture and keep soil temperatures a bit cooler.

I would like to plant flowers around a tree in my yard. The soil there is very hard and filled with roots, so I covered it with mulch. What perennials can I plant around this tree?

Planting under trees is always a tricky situation. The tree's substantial root system will absorb most of the water and nutrients from the area. Also, you can't work the soil much around the tree. Many of the tree's feeder roots are in the top 6 inches of soil; if you work this soil too much and damage these roots, you'll risk damaging or even killing your tree. Instead of working the entire area, plant in pockets among the roots so you disturb them as little as possible.

If you plan carefully, you can have a colorful shade garden from spring to fall. The key is to select the right plants, such as these.
- Corydalis *(Corydalis elata)* produces clusters of fragrant blue flowers in early spring. It may rebloom in autumn. Grows 15 inches tall. Zones 5–8.
- Dwarf goatsbeard *(Aruncus aethusifolius)* bears feathery creamy white flowers in summer. Its finely cut foliage turns yellow in autumn. Grows 18 inches tall. Zones 4–8.
- Golden hakone grass *(Hakonechloa macra* 'Aureola') has arching bright yellow-green foliage that's attractive spring to autumn. Grows 14 inches tall. Zones 5–9.
- Jack-in-the-pulpit *(Arisaema triphyllum)* bears unusual blooms similar to calla lilies in spring. Grows 2 feet tall. Zones 4–9.
- Japanese painted fern *(Athyrium nipponicum* 'Pictum') offers interest from spring to autumn because of its lovely silvery-green foliage with red highlights. The stems are also reddish. Grows 12 inches tall. Zones 5–8; but often survives in colder regions.
- Lenten rose *(Helleborus orientalis)* produces pink, white, or green flowers in late winter and spring. Grows 18 inches tall. Zones 4–9.
- Masterwort *(Astrantia major)* bears unusual spiny blooms of pink, red, or white in summer. Grows 3 feet tall. Zones 4–7.
- Navelwort *(Omphalodes cappadocica)* produces charming blue or white flowers in early spring. Grows 10 inches tall. Zones 6–8.

What perennials will grow in my backyard, which is extremely wet, especially after heavy rainfalls? A nursery I went to said that delphiniums like lots of water, so I purchased some and they died.

Delphiniums would not be my choice for your situation. Although they do appreciate moisture, they also require very good drainage (as most other perennials do). Instead of delphiniums, try perennials that don't mind wet feet. Those that can survive wet conditions include cardinal flower *(Lobelia cardinalis)*, Japanese iris *(Iris ensata)*, Siberian iris *(Iris sibirica)*, chameleon plant *(Houttuynia cordata* 'Chameleon'), common rose mallow *(Hibiscus moscheutos)*, meadowsweet *(Filipendula),* marsh marigold *(Caltha palustris)*, and quamash *(Camassia quamash)*.

To help increase the drainage, you can plant in raised beds or on berms. Soil that has been raised even a few inches above the rest of the ground will offer much better drainage.

Raised beds

I'd like to raise the soil level in my new perennial garden about 18 inches to make the garden more visible from various parts of the yard. What kind of fill can I use? Is it practical to use sod scraps to make a raised bed?

I'd avoid using anything containing live grass for fear that the grass might sprout and become a problem. (Grass has a way of growing even when sod is turned upside down.) If you can handle the wait, kill grass by putting layers of newspaper over it, topped by shredded leaves, yard waste, well-rotted manure, topsoil, peat moss, and grass clippings. After a few months, turn this temporary compost pile to create a fine raised bed. Alternatively, you can make raised beds from good, loamy topsoil, or mix compost with your existing soil to build up the raised bed.

Gulf Coast plants

I live in Zone 9, and there seem to be very few plants listed for Zones 9 and 10 in books and magazines. Perennial flowers often are rated good only to Zone 8. Where can I find information about perennials, shrubs, and small trees for my area?

In addition to your need for plants that will grow well in areas with mild winters, you also need to consider the hot summers and extensive rainfall in your area. Shop local nurseries. When you see a plant that you like growing in someone's yard, ask about it. If it is growing well for them, it should grow well for you. Also visit local botanical gardens, and consider making a trip to Baton Rouge, which has several excellent destinations for garden tourists. Also check with your local cooperative extension service for recommendations of perennials that grow well in your area.

ASTILBE

My astilbes are growing under a tree. They don't get direct sunlight but quite a bit of dappled light. I'm worried because their flowers don't open. The flowers come up but dry out before they open. What's going on, and how can I keep it from happening again?

Are your astilbe *(Astilbe)* plants growing directly beneath the tree? Any plants grown directly under trees tend to suffer because trees have extensive root systems. As a result, the tree roots absorb the majority of water and nutrients in the soil. This is particularly distressing to astilbe, which prefers moist soil. Unfortunately, there's little you can do short of moving your astilbes to a spot where they'll have moister soil and replacing them with a plant that better tolerates dry conditions.

Do you know what variety you are growing? Different astilbe varieties have varying amounts of fullness to their plumes. Many newer hybrids have larger plumes. It could be that your astilbe plumes are opening fully but are not as large and colorful as other types you've seen.

BEE BALM

I started bee balm in my garden last year. It came back beautifully, until I nipped the tops off. Now they don't look like they will flower. Did I make a mistake in nipping them? I thought this would make them fuller and lower to the ground.

Depending on how much you cut them back and how late in spring you did it, you may have prevented your bee balm *(Monarda didyma)* from flowering this year. These plants form their buds as they grow in late spring and early summer.

You were on the right track, though: You can pinch back the tips of new growth of late-summer-flowering perennials in early spring. Doing so will encourage the plants to have a fuller, more compact habit and will also make them bloom a little later in the season. If you do this, take care not to prune after early spring, and take off only the tips of the new growth.

Bee balm mildew madness

I like the hummingbirds that are attracted by my bee balm flowers, but every year the leaves turn gray and ugly. How can I keep the plants looking good?

It sounds as though your bee balm *(Monarda didyma)* suffers from powdery mildew. This fungal disease can be severe on bee balm. Plants under stress are more likely to contract the disease, so keep the soil evenly moist, and provide good air circulation to minimize the problem. However, if you're growing a susceptible cultivar, there may be little you can do to prevent your plants from turning gray by the end of summer. A better solution may be to grow one of the resistant cultivars, such as 'Colrain Red', 'Raspberry Wine', 'Violet Queen', 'Petite Delight', or 'Marshall's Delight'.

BIRD-OF-PARADISE

Slow-blooming bird

I have an orange bird-of-paradise planted on the side of my house. The flowers are trying to come out, but they are taking a long time. Is this normal? Please also give me any tips on caring for this beautiful plant.

Bird-of-paradise flowers can be slow to open, but once they do open, the blooms should last for 2 weeks or more. Native to South Africa, bird-of-paradise *(Strelitzia reginae)* doesn't need much care when grown outdoors in Zones 9 and 10. When grown in full sun or partial shade, it should reach 5 feet in height and grow into a robust clump. In future years, expect to see most of the flowers appear in early summer. Fertilize the plant in spring and again in late summer. About the only problem with this plant is that clumps are difficult to divide, so it's best to leave them undisturbed for many years.

BLEEDING HEART

Dormant bleeding hearts

The bleeding hearts at my old house used to flourish all summer. The ones at my new house are already starting to turn yellow and die. What's happening?

Are you growing the same kind of bleeding heart as you were at your old house? The old-fashioned type *(Dicentra spectabilis)* blooms in spring, then goes dormant once the weather starts to warm. It also will die down early if it gets too much sun or dries out, so don't be surprised if it's dormant by mid-summer. The fern-leaf types *(D. eximia* and *D. formosa)* bloom from spring until autumn, though they, too, usually slow down during the summer.

Bleeding heart buddies

My bleeding hearts die back and turn yellow in summer, and I'm left with a huge bare spot in my garden. How can I stop this?

Old-fashioned bleeding heart *(Dicentra spectabilis)* naturally goes dormant by midsummer. Placing the plant where it's kept cool and moist (but not wet, or it will rot) can help prolong its growing season, but it doesn't usually stay green all the way to autumn.

To prevent gaps in your garden, you can grow other plants alongside your bleeding heart. Shade lovers such as astilbe *(Astilbe)* and hosta *(Hosta)* usually come into their own about the time the bleeding heart fades away.

Dividing bleeding heart

I would like to know how to separate a bleeding heart. When is the best time to divide it?

If you'd like to divide a bleeding heart, dig it up first thing in spring when it begins to emerge from the soil. Carefully cut or pull the main clump into pieces, ensuring that each piece has a root system and a shoot system. Roots of bleeding heart can be brittle, so be gentle. Keep the transplants protected and well watered for the first growing season while they become established.

CHRISTMAS ROSE

Planting Christmas rose

I recently purchased Christmas roses from a mail-order gardening company. I would like to plant them in my backyard, but I'm concerned about how poisonous this plant may be to my dog. Would you suggest planting these perennials around the base of large trees? My soil is clay and full of roots.

All parts of the Christmas rose *(Helleborus niger)* are poisonous, but the plants are not appealing to cats or dogs. I can't promise that your pets won't be tempted to nibble, but it's highly unlikely. Other plants that contain the same kind of poison include marsh marigold *(Caltha palustris)*, buttercup *(Ranunculus)*, and baneberry *(Actaea)*.

As far as location goes, Christmas rose needs a shady location with a minimum of root competition. I suggest not planting directly under a maple or other shallow-rooted tree. Farther from the tree's trunk, but still under the canopy, would be a better spot. Improve the soil with organic matter, because the plant needs well-drained soil; it grows poorly in straight clay. You can amend small planting pockets without damaging the tree's roots.

CHRYSANTHEMUM

Overwintered mums

I planted mums this fall and don't know much about them. I was wondering if I should cut them back, since they are brown. Will they bloom again next spring and summer?

If your mums (*Chrysanthemum ×morifolium*) survive the winter, you'll see new growth developing around the base of the plant early in spring. The old, dead growth from last year can be clipped away. If nothing develops at the base of the plant, it's a sign that the plant did not survive the winter. Although garden mums are often called hardy mums, they may not survive the winter if drainage is poor or if you live in an extremely cold climate.

If numerous shoots have overwintered, divide and separate the clump. Three to five vigorous shoots are enough to make a showy clump. Once new shoots start to develop, give them a little slow-release granular flower fertilizer and leave them alone. When they are about 6 inches tall, pinch back the tops of each stem by ½ inch or so. This promotes compact, bushy growth later on. To prevent delaying the bloom, stop pinching after late June.

Normally garden chrysanthemums bloom only in fall when nights are long and days are short. (Flower bud development is a response to day length.) The mums you find blooming in spring in garden centers have been grown in a greenhouse, where they get short days to force early bloom. A few cultivars are day-neutral, flowering at any day length. So yours may develop some blooms by midsummer if not pinched. Also heat can delay bloom.

Pinching mums

My mum plants are growing now, and I would like to know when and how to trim them in order to obtain a nicely rounded flowering plant for the fall garden.

Most mum varieties hold up better in the garden if pinched a time or two. Otherwise they may flop over when in bloom. Pinch back mums when they have grown to about 6 inches tall. Pinch back just the growing tips to promote more compact growth. Repeat pinching in late June if the plant is still leggy. Avoid pinching again after the first of July, to avoid removing developing flower buds.

Alternatively, you could grow cushion or carpet mums, low-growing types that get no taller than 8–12 inches. These shorter types form a solid mound without the need for pinching.

COLUMBINE

Transplanting columbine

I have several columbines growing in a shady area of my backyard. How can I successfully transplant some of the columbines to a shaded area in my front yard?

To successfully transplant columbine, move as much of the root system with the plant as possible by keeping a large ball of soil intact around the roots. The best time to move columbine is when it is semidormant, early in spring. Plant the columbine in its new spot, making sure it's at the same depth it was growing before. Water in the transplant, and keep it watered regularly for the first growing season. (Adding a couple of inches of mulch over the soil after you water can be helpful in retaining moisture and preventing weed competition.)

Alternatively, you might collect ripe seeds after your columbine blooms, and scatter those seeds over the area where you'd like the columbine to grow. Most columbines start readily from seed (often self-seeding in the garden). If you have only one type of columbine, the plants likely will come true to type. If you have several types of columbine in your garden, the seedlings may be hybrids, developing characteristics that are a cross of the parents.

COREOPSIS

Dying coreopsis

I had several coreopsis plants for about 5 years. This spring two have completely disappeared. I am disappointed not to see them this spring and am considering replacing them with new coreopsis plants. Would this be a good idea?

It's common for coreopsis to die out after several years in the garden. It's not a particularly long-lived perennial. Five years is a good run for most coreopsis. Unless you saw evidence of disease, you can plant new ones in the same location with little danger of them dying out immediately. Large-flowered types such as 'Early Sunrise' often fade away faster than small-flowered threadleaf types *(Coreopsis verticillata)*. 'Moonbeam' and 'Zagreb' are long-lasting threadleaf types.

DAYLILY

Daylily pests

My daylilies are turning yellow at their bases. One plant is in worse shape than the others. At first I thought I fertilized too close to the plants, but now I think it may be a pest. What bugs bother daylilies? What do I use to spray?

In general, daylilies *(Hemerocallis)* have few insect problems, but an aphid attack can cause leaves to curl, yellow, and be distorted. You should be able to see a sticky, shiny substance on the leaves if aphids are present. The yellow, brown, or green insects are visible to the naked eye and are usually found in clusters in the fold near the leaf base. Control aphids by spraying them with an insecticidal soap. Spray only if you are sure you actually have them; soap sprays kill the good bugs too.

Daylily foliage can also turn yellow from leaf spot, or leaf streak. This disease starts out as spots on the leaves that gradually turn the entire leaf yellow. It's most severe in warm, humid weather. It can also be a problem if you are overwatering the plants.

To combat leaf spot or leaf streak, you'll need to spray the plants with a fungicide containing basic copper or copper sulfate. Do this every week during periods of warm, humid weather.

Another relatively recent serious problem that has hit daylilies is daylily rust. This fungal disease produces yellow-orange pustules on the foliage and can cause rapid plant decline. Rust is difficult to control. If you have a susceptible variety, it may be better to replace it with a rust-resistant one. Look for one of the All-American daylily winners such as 'Red Volunteer', a 7-inch midseason bloomer, or 'Miss Mary Mary', a double yellow repeat bloomer. Both have good to excellent rust resistance.

Master Gardeners at your local cooperative extension office, or garden store professionals, may also be able to help diagnose your daylilies' ills and provide you with recommended cultivars for your area.

Daylily propagation

Do hybrid daylilies multiply by seeds, runners, or both? I saved some seeds. Would planting them be a waste of time?

Thousands of hybrid daylilies are available; unfortunately, none can be successfully propagated true to type from seed. Seed collected from hybrid plants rarely yields true. Usually, the seeds collected from hybrid plants produce weaker or inferior plants (or plants that have traits of both parents, if two different plants were crossed to produce the seed). Because daylilies are so easy to propagate by division of their fibrous roots, I'd recommend using that method as described at right.

Daylily rotting

Last fall, around the beginning of September, I planted several daylilies that I bought from a local nursery. I covered them with leaves and spruce boughs at the end of November. When I removed the mulch this spring, I discovered that several of my daylilies had crown rot, and I lost the plants. What happened, and what should I do this year to keep this from reoccurring?

Daylilies are hardy through Zone 3. Unless you live in a colder zone, it's not necessary to cover them with winter mulch to the extent that you did. Heavy winter mulch traps moisture and encourages rot. You could put bark mulch around the plants, but avoid covering them with anything that will prevent good air circulation.

The great daylily divide

I need to transplant a large mass of daylilies. When's the best time to divide daylilies and other perennials?

Hardy daylilies are wonderful additions to any garden, but they require regular dividing to do their best. Without division every 3 years or so, plants become dense masses of foliage with few blooms. Divide daylilies in early spring, late summer, or early fall. Most experts recommend late summer, right after they finish their main flowering spurt. This gives you a full season of bloom and still gives the plants time to establish a strong new root system before winter.

Clues that it's time to divide include a dead center in the crown area, fewer and smaller blooms, and growth that appears crowded. As a rule, divide a perennial when it's not blooming. Those that bloom in midsummer should be divided in early spring when plants are 2–3 inches tall. Autumn divisions are done in late August or early September when the plants are semidormant and the temperatures are dropping. Use a spade to dig the entire clump, then use a sharp knife or shovel to cut off divisions. If you don't want to divide an entire clump, cut divisions from the edge of a clump using a spade and trowel.

A few perennials are real homebodies and don't like to be disturbed. Examples include monkshood (*Aconitum*), blue false indigo (*Baptisia*), gas plant (*Dictamnus*), sea holly and rattlesnake master (*Eryngium*), Lenten rose and Christmas rose (*Helleborus*), and Oriental poppy (*Papaver*).

Stella de Oro not reblooming

Should I deadhead daylilies? Last year my 'Stella de Oro' daylily bloomed only once. I thought it was to bloom all summer.

'Stella de Oro' is a reblooming daylily. Rather than bloom constantly, it normally has several bloom cycles each year. The longer the growing season, the more numerous the bloom cycles. You don't need to deadhead 'Stella de Oro' to get it to rebloom, but deadheading keeps the plants looking more attractive and prevents seedpods from forming. Developing seedpods can use up energy that would otherwise be put into forming more blooms.

Daylilies will grow in partial shade but bloom less. If your 'Stella de Oro' daylilies bloomed only once last year, it's likely that your plants are not getting enough sunlight or someone sold you a variety that's not really 'Stella de Oro.' 'Stella de Oro' is such a well-known variety that many imitations have shown up. Your plant may have been mislabeled.

DELPHINIUM

Dazzling delphiniums

On a recent trip to England I was amazed at the delphiniums in gardens everywhere. How can I grow them successfully here?

Plant delphiniums in moist, well-drained soil that's rich in organic matter. Add compost, peat moss, or well-rotted manure before planting, especially if you garden in clay. How much sun delphiniums need depends on where you grow them. In areas that experience cool summers—such as the Pacific Northwest or the maritime provinces of Canada—the plants thrive in full sun. In areas that experience warmer summers, the plants prefer a spot with sun in the morning and late afternoon but shade during the hottest part of the day.

Most delphiniums are hardy in Zones 3–7. They dislike hot summers and are short-lived in the Deep South, Southern California, and the desert Southwest. In these areas grow delphinium as a cool-season annual.

Delphiniums aren't drought-tolerant; they require regular watering in most areas. Spreading mulch over the soil will help keep it cool and slow evaporation.

Tall delphiniums require staking, especially when the plants are grown in an exposed area. Stake the plants by inserting a stick or pole into the ground near the plant. Tie the plant stem to the stake using a soft cloth. Use a figure-eight pattern—so the stem of the plant is in one loop and the stake is in the other loop—to prevent excess rubbing of the cloth against the stem.

Deadhead delphiniums by removing the faded flower stalks. Deadheading encourages the plants to produce a second flush of blooms.

Hundreds of delphiniums are available to gardeners. One of the best is *Delphinium grandiflorum*. This species grows less than 2 feet tall and produces clusters of true blue flowers over a mound of fine foliage. Like most delphinium species, it's rather short-lived—many gardeners treat it as an annual (or allow it to self-seed). If you prefer the taller, more stately delphiniums, Pacific Giant Hybrids typically grow 5½–6 feet tall. 'Galahad' is a variety that bears pure white flowers. 'Black Knight' produces blue blooms with black centers.

Delphinium care

My delphiniums have finished blooming for the summer. Am I supposed to split them after they bloom or do anything else?

Generally, you don't need to divide delphiniums. Delphiniums like cool summers. In warmer areas, they're short-lived and die out before they need dividing.

Many gardeners are unaware that delphiniums can produce a second flush of blooms. Right after the flowers fade, remove the flower stalk down to the top set of leaves. If your plant is situated in a spot where it's happy, it should send up another flower stalk. It probably won't be as large as the first, but you will still get two sets of blooms for the price of one!

FERNS

Fern trouble

Last year I purchased three Japanese painted ferns. Only two came back this year; both are small. Why are the ferns smaller than when I bought them?

There are many possible reasons why your ferns are failing to thrive. If the plants don't like where they are, they won't come back well. For the best luck, plant Japanese painted fern (*Athyrium nipponicum* 'Pictum') in a spot that has dappled shade and soil that's rich in organic matter. Amend the soil liberally with organic matter before planting. Even though Japanese painted fern is hardy in Zone 4, it may not come back well if you've had an especially cold winter, or a cold winter without much snow. A hot, dry summer could also weaken your plants, making them less likely to make it through the winter.

FOXGLOVE

Foxglove confusion

Do foxgloves die back to nothing after blooming? Will they come back with green leaves next spring?

It all depends on the type of foxglove *(Digitalis)* you grow. The most commonly grown foxglove *(D. purpurea)* is a biennial, meaning that it will grow only foliage its first year and bloom the next, then die after blooming.

Some types of foxglove are truly perennial, however. The most readily available perennial type is strawberry foxglove *(D. ×mertonensis)*. It looks much like the biennial type but tends to grow less tall, and the flowers are the color of crushed strawberries. The plant is hardy in Zones 3–8. Yellow foxglove *(D. grandiflora)* is another perennial type. It is also hardy in Zones 3–8. Both of these perennial foxgloves should be available at your local garden center or from mail-order nurseries.

GERBERA

Drowning gerbera daisies

I love gerbera daisies. Last year, all five that I planted just dried right up, even though they were watered and fed. This year, I planted five more in a different location; one has already dried up, and it looks like another is starting to do the same thing. The weather has been mostly cool, with only three or four days of temperatures in the upper 8os. We have had rain five out of seven days each week since spring. Can you help me?

Gerbera daisies are susceptible to a condition called foot rot, a fungus that makes the plant wilt due to damaged roots and stems. If they are too wet, they develop foot rot easily. There's no cure for this. The solution is to plant new plants in new soil, making sure the plants are not sitting in too much water. They do prefer moist soil, but it must drain well and not be soggy all the time. Rainy spring weather is probably to blame for your plants' problems. Gerbera daisies like cool temperatures, not much higher than 75°F.

Growing gerbera daisies

I grow gerbera daisies in a garden that gets lots of sun. The leaves have started to curl, turn yellow, then die. What's going on?

It sounds as though there could be a couple of things going on in your garden. First, gerbera daisy *(Gerbera jamesonii)* likes a sunny spot, but it doesn't like much heat.

Grow gerbera daisy in a bright location that's protected from sun during the hottest hours of the afternoon.

Also, gerbera daisy is sensitive to too much moisture; take care to avoid overwatering it. It's best to plant it in a sandy or well-drained soil; if your garden has clay soil, grow gerbera daisies in containers, or amend the clay liberally with organic matter before planting the flowers.

GOATSBEARD

Slow goatsbeard

I planted a goatsbeard in the spring, and it hasn't done anything. It is in a woodland, but not in deep shade. I don't think it's grown more than an inch or two. The leaves look healthy. Is this normal?

It's not at all uncommon for perennials to sit and seemingly do little the first year they're planted. The old adage "The first year it sleeps, the second year it creeps, and the third year it leaps" is true for many perennial species (despite how annoying it seems to impatient gardeners!). If your goatsbeard (*Aruncus dioicus*) looks healthy, I'd be patient and see what it does next year. You should find that it will do more. To help your goatsbeard along, top-dress the soil around the plant with organic matter and mulch. Keep the soil moist but not wet.

GOLDENROD

Allergies from goldenrod?

My neighbor planted some goldenrod in her perennial garden this spring. Doesn't goldenrod pollen cause hay fever?

Goldenrod (*Solidago*) is a late-summer bloomer with small bright yellow flowers in large clusters. Goldenrod is native throughout much of North America. Because it blooms at the peak of hay fever season, some people assume that it is responsible for seasonal allergies. However, goldenrod has gotten a bad rap. Ragweed (*Ambrosia*), which blooms at the same time and produces abundant pollen, is the real culprit. Goldenrod has become a popular cut flower, and many cultivars are available for the garden. Some of the best are the semidwarf 'Crown of Rays' and 'Golden Baby', and *S. sphacelata* 'Golden Fleece', which tolerates some shade. You can grow these goldenrods in good conscience. They won't contribute to hay fever problems unless you get close enough to sniff the flowers.

HEN AND CHICKS

How do I take care of hen and chicks? Can they be transplanted? If a chick breaks off will it still grow if placed in soil?

Hen and chicks *(Sempervivum)* is very easy to grow. It needs a sunny spot and well-drained soil. It grows well with low fertility, so there is little need to fertilize. Once established, it seldom needs watering. In fact, overwatering and poor drainage—rather than lack of moisture—are more likely to cause problems for your hen and chicks.

If a chick breaks off, you can just place it on top of the soil and it will sprout roots, provided it gets a little moisture. You can transplant these plants at any time.

HIBISCUS

Extended bloom on hibiscus

I'm six and I like to garden with my mom. We planted hibiscus last year. I love the big red flowers. It looked like it died last winter but it started growing again in spring, and I'm glad. But now my mom wants to cut it. She says cutting it will make it so it has flowers for more days. I don't want to hurt it. Are you sure it will be OK?

Hardy hibiscus *(Hibiscus moscheutos)* does make wonderfully big flowers for 3–4 weeks in late summer. As your mother says, if you make a few cuts in July, the plant will keep flowering for 2–3 extra weeks.

What can make this happen is called pinching, something gardeners do all the time to chrysanthemums so the plants don't bloom too early or get too leggy and floppy. Many other perennial flowers can be pinched too. With hibiscus, the trick is to pinch just some of the stems, so they will bloom later, but leave others alone. Some flowers open according to the normal schedule, and some open later.

Here's how to do it—and you can do it yourself. In early July, count the number of main stems on your hibiscus. If there are ten, choose about three and clip just about 2 inches off the top of those stems. Although they may not have been large enough for you to see them yet, flower buds are beginning to form on those tips. By cutting them off, you make those stems start over, so they will be a week or two later than the rest of the plant in opening their flowers.

Then, in the middle of July, cut three more stems besides the ones you cut the first time. This cut may be tough to do, because you will almost certainly be able to see flower buds on those stems. You must clip off the whole tip that has flower buds on it. Don't worry. Those stems still have plenty of time to make new flower buds that will open even later than all the rest.

Hardy hibiscus

I have a hardy hibiscus growing in sandy soil. How do I get this plant to thrive? Can I grow it where it will get only afternoon sun?

The good news is that hardy hibiscus will survive outdoors in Zones 4–9. The bad news is that for the plant to thrive and bloom well, it needs a spot where it receives full sun. A location that sees at least 6–8 hours of direct sunlight a day is best. If you situate your hardy hibiscus where it gets only half a day of sun, it may produce few blooms, if any (and the blooms will appear later in the season).

In addition to full sun, the plant prefers rich, well-drained soil. Because your garden has sandy soil, you'll want to amend the planting hole liberally with compost or well-rotted manure.

HOLLYHOCK

Rusty hollyhocks

My hollyhocks are covered in orange bumps. What could be wrong with them?

It sounds as though your plants have rust, a widespread and serious fungal disease of hollyhocks *(Alcea)*. Spores of the fungus can spread through splashing water or on air currents. The fungus also survives on cheeseweed, or mallow *(Malva)*. Remove nearby cheeseweeds; water your hollyhocks only early in the day to allow the foliage to dry overnight; and remove and destroy affected plant parts to slow the spread of the disease. Protective fungicide sprays will also help.

Hollyhocks not blooming

Last year I planted some hollyhocks that I started as seedlings. They did not bloom but had many leaves and were at least 12–14 inches tall. Do you think they will bloom this year? How can I start more of them?

The reason your plants developed leaves but no flowers the first year is because hollyhocks are biennials. They have a life span of 2 years. The plants you have now will bloom this year and die at the end of the growing season. Many gardeners think that hollyhocks are perennial because they reseed themselves freely, so there are always plants in the same location. The best thing to do to ensure more plants is to scatter ripe seedpods over the ground in fall, or start new plants from seed each year so you always have some blooming.

HOSTA

What is the secret to growing beautiful hostas? Mine are always smaller than my neighbors'. They look yellowed and moth-eaten. What am I doing wrong?

Long known for being adaptable, tough, easy-care landscape plants, hostas prefer certain sun and soil growing conditions and protection from slugs and snails to be at their best. They tolerate a wide range of conditions and are hardy in Zones 3–10. Read "Tips for growing hostas" to learn details about hosta needs.

Tips for growing hostas

- Shade. Hostas are a plant of the forest floor, and they love filtered shade. There are many cultivars in various colors, ranging from blue to green to gold to white. In general, the darker the hosta, the more shade it prefers. Green and gold hostas tolerate more light, but nearly all prefer no midday or hot afternoon sun. Many hostas tolerate a couple of hours of morning sun each day if the soil is consistently moist. Some solid green cultivars do nicely in full sun if given enough water.
- Soil. To mimic the forest-floor conditions that hostas prefer, be sure that your soil has plenty of organic matter, which retains moisture but still allows lots of air to reach the roots. Work well-rotted manure, compost, and/or sphagnum peat moss deeply into the soil for a terrific hosta bed. If you add fertilizer, the numbers on the fertilizer container should be nearly equal (for example, 10-10-10).
- Pests. Slugs and snails find a bed of hostas as appealing as many people find a buffet table. When large holes appear in your hostas, along with shiny slime trails, you can be sure it's the work of night-dining slugs or snails. Slug and snail baits have long been available, and some of the newer products pose less danger to pets and other creatures. Read the labels carefully. An easy way to collect and discard slugs is to pour beer into shallow containers (such as tuna cans or saucers), and bury the containers so the lip is near the soil line. The creatures will be attracted to the beer and fall in. Check the containers every day or so and empty and refill them as needed. You can also check for slugs and snails under garden debris during the day, and crush any that you find. Be consistent with your tactics all season, and eventually you will have few or no slugs and snails.

Horrible hostas

I moved all my big, beautiful variegated hostas from my previous home and planted them at my new one. Some are in total shade while others are in partial sun. They looked great at first, but now they are gradually turning yellow and fading away. Help!

It could be that the plants were damaged during transplanting. Or they could be turning yellow because they were given too little or too much water after transplanting. Either practice can damage the root system and lead to yellowing foliage. They also could be suffering from being planted too deeply—especially in clay soil. Lack of oxygen resulting from deep planting damages the roots. Have you fertilized them? Accidentally giving them too much fertilizer—especially right after transplanting them—could also have caused yellowing and browning of the foliage. Also, hostas often turn yellow by the end of the season. It could be that they'll come back just fine next year.

Dividing hostas

I have a large, beautiful hosta that is beginning to emerge from the soil. I have been told to divide it. I want to know when is the best time to do this and how I should go about dividing it without damaging the plant.

You can divide hostas almost anytime, but there is no need to divide them unless they are too large for their location or you want more plants to share or use in other places in your landscape. If you decide to divide them, early spring is best. Simply dig up the plant, cut it into sections with a sharp spade or knife, and replant the sections. These plants are extremely forgiving. Make certain that each section has healthy roots and buds or shoots. Water the new transplants until they are established. A layer of mulch will help maintain even soil moisture.

Let hostas flower?

Should the tall-stem flowers growing out of the hosta plants be cut or pulled out in order to let the leaves become more full?

Removing the flower stems won't affect the leaves one way or the other. The reason that some gardeners remove hosta flower stems is because they think the tall stems detract from the overall look of the plant. Other gardeners find the flowers charming and prefer to leave them on. In fact, some hostas are bred primarily for their colorful and/or fragrant flowers. Once the blooms have faded, cut the flower stalks off near the base so the foliage can disguise the cut end of the stalk.

I love hostas, but have failed to get them to grow—my plants always die within 6 months. A local gardener told me hostas don't thrive in Zone 9 and that I shouldn't waste my money. Do I have any hope?

I hate to be the bearer of bad news, but your gardening friend is right. Hostas *(Hosta)*, native to Japan and other cool areas of Asia, dislike hot weather and fail to thrive in areas warmer than Zone 8. They are temperate plants that prefer cool, mild summers and a period of cold and relative darkness during the winter. If you have a cool, moist microclimate in your yard (such as a shady site north of your house), you might get them to survive a bit longer.

Last year I acquired some hostas. The variegated one has grown quite large, but the blue-leaf variety is still small. Should I wait another year to split them? When is the best time?

You can divide hostas most anytime, but it's best to do it in early spring (when the plants are about 2 inches tall) or in late summer (about 6 weeks before the first killing frost is expected). It's best to wait until your plants are at least 3–4 years old before you cut them into sections. However, if you are in a hurry to get more plants, chances are good that they will survive dividing the first year after you plant them.

Dig around the entire clump, then lift the plant, soil and all, from the hole. Brush away enough soil so you can see the roots. Wash away the remaining soil. Use a sharp knife to cut the clump into sections. Leave as many roots as possible on each section. Replant divisions right away, and keep them moist.

Will some hostas take the sun better than others?

Although hostas prefer shade, there are some that tolerate more sun. They include 'Sunny Delight', 'Squash Casserole', 'Fragrant Bouquet', and 'Fried Bananas'. As a general rule, the yellow-leaved types can tolerate more sun. Most blue-leaved types can't handle much direct sun at all. Also as a general rule, the more organic matter in the soil, the more sun a hosta can take. Similarly, a constant moisture supply will enable hostas to tolerate a greater amount of sun.

LAVENDER

How often should lavender be trimmed? How close to the woody part can I cut? I have some 5-year-old plants that I've trimmed once, two springs ago. They're blooming well, and I keep the blooms picked, but I want to keep them in optimum condition.

Lavandula angustifolia is the lavender most often grown in North America. It is hardy to Zone 5. Trim it twice a year.

Cut lavender back hard in spring, to perhaps half its height. This pruning promotes bushiness and removes dead tips that are common after winter exposure. Lavender is not an herbaceous perennial; it is woody and evergreen. Most of the buds it sets each fall for the next year's bloom are on its youngest woody stems. So avoid cutting stems all the way back as you would a peony, which has buds belowground. Leave some portion of each leafy stem rather than stripping it of all its active growth points at one time.

Lavenders occasionally have surprised me after very hard winters during which they died right to the ground. I wrote them off as goners while clipping them back to leafless shrubs of old wood—yet vigorous shoots sprouted strongly from the lowest dormant buds at ground level.

As soon as the plant finishes it's main June–July bloom, shear it—that is, give it a haircut to remove spent flowers. Shearing may promote a second flush of bloom.

LUPINE

Lupine woes

How do I keep my lupines looking great? They seem to do well for a year or two, but then fade away. Help!

Sadly, lovely lupine *(Lupinus)* is not a particularly long-lived perennial. Most plants do well for only a few seasons; after that, they become too old to perform well. For beautiful lupines, grow new plants or seeds each year. That way, you'll always have a supply of young plants to replace the old ones. Many gardeners find that their lupines do this on their own if left to go to seed. Also be aware that lupines prefer cool climates. If summers are hot where you live, lupines will likely fail to thrive.

PEONY

Fragrant peonies

When I visited my sister-in-law a few years ago, her peonies smelled so wonderful. When I came home, I planted some of my own. I've had them for several years now, and while they're beautiful, there's no fragrance! What have I done wrong?

Peony (*Paeonia*) fragrance varies dramatically from variety to variety. Some of the older varieties often have the most fragrance. Also, double-flowered varieties tend to have much more fragrance than single-flowered ones. You'll have to do some research on peonies, and order varieties that are specifically mentioned for fragrance. Peonies are shipped in September and October, which is the best time to plant or move them.

Pining for peonies in the South

Although I now live in a small town in Texas, I loved the peonies where I grew up in the cold North. Is there a special kind of peony that can be grown in warm climates?

Most peonies require a period of cold to grow and prosper. Gardeners in some colder-microclimate areas in central or north Texas may have occasional luck with peonies, but in general they don't grow well in your area.

Precious peony plants

My wife has 50-year-old peony plants. She wants me to transplant them in our yard. They belonged to her aunt, so a successful move is important. Can you give me directions?

First, it's important that this job be completed in fall as the plants begin to go dormant, not in spring as they prepare to bloom. In September, choose a spot in full sun (at least 6 hours per day), and prepare the soil with well-rotted manure and/or compost, working it in and loosening the soil down to 18 inches.

Dig the plants carefully to minimize root injury, and remove the foliage. If the plants are large and old, they'll probably do better if they're divided. Gently wash the soil off the large roots, then use a sharp, clean knife to divide the plant's crown. Make sure each division has 3–5 pink buds or healthy stems.

Plant divisions at least 3 feet apart (peonies need good air circulation), and set each division in a hole so the soil level is no more than 2 inches above the buds on the root. If the peonies are planted too deeply, they may not bloom. As it is, peonies resent disturbance and may not bloom for several years after transplanting—especially if the plants are old.

Water them well, checking for settling to make sure they are not too deep. If rain doesn't fall, water them every week or so until the ground freezes. Use a couple of inches of mulch in winter to prevent freezing and thawing from heaving the new plants out of the ground.

If you must move them in spring or summer, dig the plants carefully, disturbing the large root ball as little as possible (dig a deep, wide hole to ensure this). Then plant the peonies as soon as you can, taking care to plant them no deeper than they were growing before.

Brown peony buds

The buds on my peonies turned brown this spring and never opened. What's wrong with them? How can I keep this from happening again?

Peony buds that turn brown and fail to open are symptomatic of a disease called botrytis. This fungal disease is worse in cool, wet conditions, so do what you can to increase air circulation around the plants to promote quick drying. Space plants far enough apart that air can flow around them. Water only at the base of the plants to avoid wetting the foliage and flower buds. Prune or remove nearby trees and shrubs to increase the amount of sunlight and wind that will reach the plants.

Fungicide sprays may also be used to prevent development of the problem. Apply the first spray when the peony shoots begin to emerge, and repeat at 10-day intervals during humid conditions or until the plants stop blooming.

Ant plants

I love cut peonies but don't like dealing with the ants. How can I rid cut flowers of ants before I bring them into the house?

Your best bet would be to gently shake or brush the ants off. Or cut the peonies as the buds just begin to open, when they are marshmallow-soft. The ants won't be as likely to be hidden in the flower petals, and the peony will bloom beautifully in a few days. You may have heard that ants play an important part in making the peonies bloom, but that is a myth.

No ants in plants

I've heard that peonies need ants to bloom. I don't see ants on my peony buds. How can I get my plants to bloom?

Don't worry; ants aren't needed to produce peony blooms. Ants often congregate on peony buds in spring because they come to harvest the sugary nectar that most peonies produce on the outside of their buds. Your peonies should flower just fine even if no ants show up.

No peony blossoms

My 10-year-old peony has never bloomed. What's wrong?

Peonies dislike root disturbance and often don't bloom the first year after transplanting. However, a 10-year-old plant certainly should have bloomed by now. Here are some common reasons why peonies don't bloom.

- Not enough sunlight. Peonies need full sun in order to grow and bloom well. If your plant receives less than 6 hours of direct sunlight a day, move it to a sunnier spot.
- Heavy soil. Peonies like well-drained soil. If your soil is slow to drain, amend it with organic matter (such as compost) to encourage better drainage.
- Deep planting. If peonies are planted too deeply, the buds in the crown of the plant won't get enough light. Buds should be planted no more than an inch or two below ground level.

Tree peony care

I recently bought a tree peony. Does it require any special care?

Tree peony *(Paeonia suffruticosa)* does best when planted in a protected spot that receives full sun (at least 6–8 hours of direct sun a day). Be sure to amend the soil with abundant organic matter (such as compost) before planting; tree peony will sulk if you grow it in clay.

   In cold-winter climates tree peony typically dies back to the ground each year. Unless it's in a really protected spot, it never grows to the 10-foot height it reaches in warmer regions.

PHLOX

Mildew-resistant phlox

Can you recommend some garden phlox cultivars that are resistant to powdery mildew? The plants I have look terrible by late summer because they are always covered with white powder.

Regional climatic differences and weather conditions can affect the amount of mildew that develops on garden phlox *(Phlox)*. But you are wise to get rid of your phlox if it is consistently infected with mildew. There are several excellent cultivars that seldom are affected by powdery mildew. Some of them are 'David', with white flowers; 'Katherine', with lavender flowers; 'Delta Snow', with white flowers; 'Eva Cullum', with pink flowers; 'Robert Poore', with purple flowers; 'Natascha', with purple flowers; and *Phlox carolina,* with lavender flowers.

RUSSIAN SAGE

Russian sage flip-flop

Why does my Russian sage flop? I've seen it in pictures in which it stands dense and upright, but mine falls over.

Russian sage *(Perovskia atriplicifolia)* has a tendency to sprawl, especially when young or grown in shade or grown in moist, fertile soil. As with all plants, this species performs best when growing conditions match its native surroundings. Russian sage is native to the seaside, where there's full sun and high atmospheric moisture, but well-drained soil that's always on the dry side. That soil also tends to be "lean," in that it doesn't provide much nitrogen.

If your plant gets fewer than 6 hours of sun per day, move it to a sunnier location. If your soil is rich and moist, understand that this condition contributes to soft, thin growth. Avoid high-nitrogen fertilizer and overwatering in the plant's vicinity. If you can't change the soil's fertility or moisture level, provide stakes to hold the plant upright.

'Little Spire' is a cultivar that's naturally shorter than the species. If you continue to have difficulty keeping your Russian sage from flopping, give it a try.

SEDUM

Transplanting sedum

When is the best time to transplant a sedum?

Sedums are tough plants that are best transplanted during the cooler temperatures of spring or fall, but you can also transplant in summer. Spring is the best time to transplant most plants because the plants have an entire growing season to recover and establish themselves before winter.

Succulent sedums also start readily from cuttings. I have often snipped off several inches of stem tips, stripped off the lower leaves, and simply stuck the cuttings in the garden where I wanted new sedum plants. Keep the planted cuttings moist, but not wet, and in a few weeks you'll have new sedum growing where you inserted the cuttings.

I have some Autumn Joy sedum. Do I need to prune them? If so, how do I do this?

You don't need to prune Autumn Joy sedum (*Hylotelephium* 'Autumn Joy') to cut out the old stems that have overwintered. Remove stems as close to ground level as possible without damaging the emerging shoots. If you've had trouble with your plants getting leggy and floppy, you can pinch off the top inch or so of growth in early- to midspring. That will encourage the plants to stay more compact and bloom a bit later than usual.

SHASTA DAISY

When is the best time to separate and transplant Shasta daisies?

Early spring is the best time to divide and separate Shasta daisy (*Leucanthemum ×superbum*), but it is an extremely tough perennial and can be moved or divided almost any time of year. Avoid dividing it during hot, dry periods of midsummer, however. Shasta daisy usually needs to be divided every few years to maintain its vigor. If the central portion of the clump begins to die out, it's a good indication that it's time to divide the plant. Dig up the entire clump, then slice through it with a sharp spade to make new plants. As long as the division has at least one healthy shoot and attached roots, it should grow in its new location.

SPEEDWELL

I am having trouble with my blue speedwell. It is in an area that gets partial shade. It is growing well but is drooping. Should I stake it? Also, would it be a good idea to pinch off the top leaves?

It sounds as though your plant (*Veronica spicata*) may not be getting enough light. Speedwell survives in part shade but does best in full sun. You can pinch back your speedwell in spring—it may grow more compact. If you pinch back in summer, though, you may remove developing flower buds, which would prevent your plant from blooming.

Your speedwell might also be getting too much fertilizer. Frequent feedings, especially if you use nitrogen-rich materials, encourage lots of quick, tender growth. Because the plants put on fast growth, the shoots aren't as strong and are more likely to flop.

YUCCA

Yucca without blooms

We have a 3-year-old yucca plant. It did not flower last year and seems not to be flowering this year. Please help me.

It sounds to me as though you are growing *Yucca filamentosa*, also called Adam's needle, which has a basal rosette of straplike evergreen leaves and is hardy to Zone 4. It thrives in the long, hot summers of the southeastern United States, where it's native. It prefers full sun and well-drained, relatively dry soil. It can take 5 years for its tall spikes of creamy white flowers to appear, so patience may be all that is required for your yucca to bloom. After blooming and fruiting, the rosette dies, sending up side shoots, known as pups, that make new plants around the former base. When your plant finishes blooming, you can trim off the flower stalk, or you can leave it and enjoy the interesting seedpods.

Planting yucca

I just purchased a yucca, and the care instructions say that it likes average to sandy, well-drained soil. What if I don't have a sandy spot for planting yucca in my flower garden?

Yucca prefers dry to average well-drained soil in full sun. If the soil doesn't drain well, the plant may suffer from rot problems. If you have clay soil, yucca isn't a good plant for your garden. Instead, try it in a container or a raised bed filled with well-drained potting mix. If you have average soil, your yucca may do all right if you avoid overwatering it. Planting it on a sunny, south-facing slope may help create the drier conditions that it enjoys.

ROSES IN GENERAL

Classifying roses

I've seen lots of different names associated with roses—old garden, hybrid tea, climber, shrub, miniature, etc. What's the difference among them?

Roses are extremely popular flowers, and hybridizers have been crossing them and selecting them for centuries. As you noted, they come in many forms. Form refers to the plant's use in the landscape. Tree roses have a long stem and a shrubby top. Miniatures grow no more than 18–24 inches tall. Ground cover roses are low growers that may spread up to 8 feet wide. Climbers have arching stems 6–20 feet long. Floribundas have clusters of medium-size blooms. Hybrid teas are the classic cut-flower rose. Grandifloras resemble hybrid teas but develop flowers in clusters. Old garden roses are types that were developed before 1867, when hybrid teas were introduced. Modern shrub roses combine old garden rose flower form and fragrance with recurrent bloom and a broader color range.

Juniper out, roses in

The one sunny spot in my yard is covered by a low-growing juniper-type plant. How do I dig out all the roots of this ground cover, and what do I need to do to prepare the soil for roses? This is my first gardening project ever, and I am really looking forward to it.

First of all, getting those roots out is going to take some work. Old junipers are hard to remove, and if they are really large you might have to resort to a backhoe. Or you might want to hire a local landscape crew to dig up these established roots. Once the roots are gone, add a layer of fresh soil, compost, peat moss, or rotted manure and till it into the existing soil. Roses require good drainage, so you need a loose, friable soil.

Because you are a beginning gardener, I suggest that you plant easy-care roses, such as shrub roses. Keep in mind that shrub roses vary in size. Plant them at least 3 feet apart; if you have the space, consider planting groups of three of the same variety and color together. Look for hardy shrub roses that are on their own roots (not grafted). Some popular and easy-to-grow roses that will bloom throughout the summer are 'Carefree Beauty', 'Bonica', and 'Graham Thomas'. Contact a reputable nursery in your area, your cooperative extension office, or the local rose society for ideas on what varieties do well in your area.

Rose requirements

I recently purchased a home that has several beautiful roses. What care do the plants need other than watering? They all have exotic names on the tags. This is my first garden, and I wouldn't want to kill the roses from my lack of plant-care knowledge.

Without knowing what types of roses you have, I can't be specific about their care, but here are some general tips you can follow.

- Prune any dead or dying branches in early spring.
- In spring, fertilize with a slow-release, granular fertilizer formulated for roses.
- Keep the plants mulched to prevent weed competition and to keep soil moisture levels consistent.
- Water with drip irrigation rather than overhead sprinklers, if possible. Roses can become diseased if their leaves stay wet.
- Remove old blooms as they fade. This encourages the plants to produce new blooms.
- Keep an eye out for insect pests, and spray only when necessary.

You are lucky that your roses still have tags that identify them. These tags will allow you to look up information on what type of roses they are and what specific care they might need. Type the name of each rose into a search engine on the Internet, and you'll probably find all sorts of helpful information.

Shade tolerance

Can you tell me about the shade tolerance of Flower Carpet and 'Zephirine Drouhin' roses? Is 4 hours of sunlight the absolute minimum for these and other shade-tolerant varieties?

Although most roses need 6 or more hours of sunshine to thrive, some bloom with only 4 hours of sunlight and withstand the fungal diseases that flourish in shade. Growing even shade-tolerant roses in partial shade, however, can decrease the number of blooms. Varieties with glossy foliage may resist black spot and mildew better because fungal spores cannot fix themselves to the slick leaf surfaces. Make sure that partially shaded roses get enough warmth for their petals to open fully. Shade-tolerant roses usually have blooms with 5 to 20 petals. Few roses with more than 40 petals will bloom well in low light.

'Zephirine Drouhin' and Flower Carpet roses offer some degree of shade tolerance, but both bloom better and are more disease-resistant in full sun. *Rosa glauca*, an old-garden rose, also tolerates shade. It's grown more for its purple-tinged grayish leaves and red stems than for its 5-petaled pink flowers and handsome red hips, which will be sparse in shady conditions.

Roses for shade
What would be the best rose to grow in a shady spot?

Most roses need full sun to grow and bloom successfully. However, some tolerate slightly less light. The minimum amount of sun needed is generally 4 hours of direct sun per day. If your garden gets less than this, consider something other than roses. Roses that are most tolerant of shade are the hybrid teas 'Blue Moon', 'Christian Dior', 'Fred Edmunds', 'Garden Party', and 'Swarthmore'. Other shade-tolerant roses include 'Alchymist' shrub rose, 'Etain' rambler, and most hybrid musk roses.

Flower Carpet quandary
My Flower Carpet roses started out with large, shiny leaves and many buds. After they bloomed, I removed the spent flowers. Now the plants have tiny yellowish leaves, no buds, and brittle black stems at the base. Three nurseries told me that samples I showed them indicated the roses were putting on new growth. What's wrong with my roses?

It's possible that the nurseries are correct. Flower Carpet roses stop blooming once in a while and may not flower for weeks. Normally, I'd suggest that instead of taking action, you wait to see what will happen to your plants. Because the leaves are turning yellow, however, you should be concerned.

Your location may affect the health of your Flower Carpet roses. If you live in a region that experiences cold winters, avoid fertilizing late in the growing season. Late feedings promote the growth of tender, new tissue that can easily be damaged by cold winter temperatures. Instead, roses need to start hardening their growth in fall. Stop fertilizing your roses about 30–45 days before the date of the first frost.

Scarce blooms
I have three rosebushes. They only bloom twice—in spring and summer—and do not have many blooms. What am I doing wrong?

Do you know what kinds of roses you're growing? Some naturally bloom all season, whereas others have only a spring and late-summer flush. This is perfectly natural behavior for many shrub roses and old-fashioned roses. In fact, a number of old-fashioned roses bloom only once a year. Are your roses growing in full sun and rich soil? If not, they won't bloom well.

148

Severe pruning

My husband trimmed our rosebushes to 7-inch stumps. I am afraid he ruined them and they won't grow anymore. What do you think?

There's still hope. Severe pruning should not kill a healthy rose, though it may affect its overall appearance and bloom production the following year. New canes will grow and replace the old ones that your husband removed. You don't say what kind of roses you have. If they are hybrid teas, you will wind up with bigger but fewer flowers. Vigorous roses such as *Rosa rugosa* and some ramblers can also come back from drastic pruning. Just make certain that new shoots arise from above the graft union (the swollen knob near the base of the plant). Shoots from below the graft union will not be the same variety as the top of the plant. If no graft union is present, the roses may be growing on their own roots, in which case any shoots that develop will be identical to the existing shoots.

Rose companions

How can I keep my roses from looking bare near the ground?

Many roses naturally lose their bottom leaves as the season progresses. Typically, there's little you can do to prevent it. That said, there is a practice of planting low plants along with roses; these companions act something like a skirt to cover up the roses' bare legs. Here are some excellent companion plants for roses.

- Annual geranium *(Pelargonium)*
- Catmint *(Nepeta)*
- Lady's mantle *(Alchemilla mollis)*
- Leadwort *(Ceratostigma plumbaginoides)*
- Perennial geranium *(Geranium)*
- Pincushion flower *(Scabiosa)*
- Pinks *(Dianthus)*
- Threadleaf coreopsis *(Coreopsis verticillata)*
- Twinspur *(Diascia)*

Waxy rose stems

I bought a rose plant this spring. Its stems came covered with wax. What is it for, and how do I get it off?

The wax is there to keep the rose from drying out while it's at the store. You don't need to do anything to remove it. It won't harm your plant, and it will wear off soon after the rose is planted in the garden.

Foundation safety

I would like to plant roses in my backyard, but I've heard that their roots are strong and may penetrate my basement if the plants are near the house. How far from the house should I plant my roses?

Fortunately, what you've heard about the rose root system isn't true. How far away from your home to plant roses depends on the size of the full-grown rose plant. If your roses mature at 5 feet wide, for example, plant them no closer than 3 feet from your home (so they don't grow against the side of your house). I advise 3 feet because the rose should grow 2½ feet—half of its total 5 feet—on all sides, and you'll want to leave a little extra room so it doesn't touch the house.

Winter protection

How do I go about protecting my roses for winter?

In areas of the country where winter temperatures dip into the single digits or colder, many types of roses need winter protection. Protect hybrid teas, grandifloras, floribundas, and climbing roses after temperatures drop into the low 20s a few times but before the soil freezes. There are several methods of protection you can use.

Tie the canes together, then mound soil 8–12 inches high around the base of the plants. Cut long canes back to 30–36 inches to prevent them from whipping in winter winds. Enclose the mounded plants with a wire cage or fence and cover the soil mound with leaves, straw, or evergreen boughs after the ground freezes.

Alternatively you can use mulch instead of soil. Mound up the mulch 15–18 inches around the plant's base. You could also use a wire-mesh cylinder or a rose cone filled with mulch.

For maximum protection, you can completely bury the rose. Dig a trench next to the plant large enough to accommodate all the canes. (Prune back excessively long canes so you won't have to dig as much.) Gently pry loose the roots on the side of the plant opposite the trench. Tie the canes together, tip the plant into the trench, and cover with soil. After the soil freezes, add mulch as additional protection.

To winterize climbing roses, remove them from their support, then lay them on the ground and cover the canes with 6–8 inches of soil. Mound the base of the climber with 8–12 inches of soil.

In all cases, in spring, gradually remove the mulch and soil as growth begins.

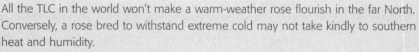
During the summer I live in Minnesota, but I spend the winters in south Texas. Are there any roses that will do well in both locations?

All the TLC in the world won't make a warm-weather rose flourish in the far North. Conversely, a rose bred to withstand extreme cold may not take kindly to southern heat and humidity.

The deep-pink-flowering climber 'William Baffin' (Zones 2–9), one of the Canadian Explorer series of roses developed specifically for northern climates, blooms repeatedly and has no trouble bouncing back when the thermometer plunges to –40°F. Equally cold-hardy are Dr. Griffith Buck's introductions, including 'Prairie Princess' (Zones 3–9), a shrub that bears semidouble coral-pink blossoms over a long period. Both will grow in the South but may not thrive as well as roses bred specifically for southern climates.

Down South, the fragrant Cherokee rose *(Rosa laevigata*, Zones 7–9) blankets hillsides in single snow white blossoms in spring. Creamy pink 'Souvenir de la Malmaison' (Zones 6–9) blooms repeatedly throughout the season. Richly scented fully double blossoms make this Bourbon rose one of the glories of the southern garden; a climbing form is also available.

Roses in containers

Can I plant roses in containers? If so, what sizes and types of containers are best?

You're in luck—virtually any rose will grow in a container. The container's size is more important than the type. Select a container that accommodates the plant's root ball and has room for the roots to grow. Smaller floribunda roses can grow in containers as small as 16 inches in diameter. Larger shrub roses will require more room, such as 24- to 36-inch containers.

Growing roses in containers is no different from growing the plants in the ground, except that roses in containers are more dependent on you for their water and nutrients, so they'll require more attention.

If you live in an area that experiences subzero temperatures, you'll need to protect your roses during that time. Two ways of doing this are to "plant" the containers somewhere in the yard during the winter, or move the potted roses to a protected place, such as an unheated garage, until severe cold has passed.

Low-maintenance roses

I like roses but have heard that they require a lot of care. Are there some you would recommend that are easier to grow than others?

These days, few gardeners have the time to inspect daily for diseases and pests. Top candidates for busy gardeners include the heirloom Gallicas, which flower before Japanese beetles attack. Fragrant *Rosa gallica* 'Versicolor', Zones 3–9, which offers deep-pink-and-white striped petals, is just one. Consider the rugosas as well. *Rosa rugosa* (Zones 2–9) bears single magenta blossoms throughout the season. Tolerant of mediocre soil, it would rather be neglected than coddled.

Lately, hybridizers have responded to the call for maintenance-free roses with some breakthrough introductions. Flower Carpet (Zones 5–9) boasts large clusters of blossoms from spring through fall on tidy shrubs that are useful as ground covers. White, pink, yellow, red, and coral selections are also available. Award-winning Knock Out (Zones 5–9) blooms continuously and asks nothing in return. With vibrant single cherry red blossoms, the shrub all but shouts, "Plant me!"

Hip, hip hooray

My roses have developed little red apples. They look pretty, but are they normal? And are they edible?

What you've observed are fruits of the rose, called rose hips. As you noted, they look similar to small apples, which are close relatives of roses. Rose hips are edible, as long as you haven't used pesticides on your plants. They are a good source of vitamin C. However, most gardeners prefer to enjoy the hips for the color they add to the fall garden.

As the gardening season winds down, it's nice to know that good things still lie ahead. For late-season interest in southern gardens, few roses can top 'Old Blush' (Zones 7–9), a beauty with semidouble lilac-pink blossoms and large orange hips (a climbing form is also available). In the North, 'Frau Dagmar Hartopp' (Zones 2–9) flaunts reddish hips the size of tiny apples, along with foliage that turns reddish purple and golden. Both roses are almost as lovely in September as they are in May.

Fragrant roses

My roses look beautiful, but they don't smell like roses. What can I do to get a stronger fragrance from them?

With hybridizers intent on producing disease resistance and ever-bigger blossoms, fragrance sometimes falls by the wayside. The roses you're growing simply may not have the potential to develop a strong aroma. Deep-coral-flowering hybrid tea

'Fragrant Cloud' (Zones 5–9) is a favorite and is on the American Rose Society's list of most fragrant roses. In general, Gallica roses are highly scented, as are hybrid musks, especially coral-pink 'Penelope' (Zones 6–9), a semidouble-flowering plant that reliably reblooms. If fragrance is on your list of must-haves, be sure the rose passes the sniff test before you splurge on it. Public rose gardens, local garden centers, and private local gardens are good places to check the fragrance of a selection.

Roses for heat

I live in Florida where summer temperatures are scorching. Are there some roses that you'd recommend for my area?

Most modern roses don't hold up well in subtropical or tropical heat. They require a winter dormancy period to thrive. Two notable exceptions are 'Iceberg' floribunda rose and Queen Elizabeth grandiflora. In general, old garden roses such as Chinas, hybrid perpetuals, and shrub roses are your best bet for growing in the heat.

Disease-resistant roses

I've always been afraid to grow roses because they have a reputation for being temperamental. Don't they get lots of disease problems you have to spray for?

Some roses are indeed susceptible to disease problems, black spot in particular. In humid climates, most roses may need protective fungicide sprays to grow well in the landscape. However, some old garden roses and many new hybrids are extremely resistant to fungal diseases.

QUICK TIP

Roses for hot climates
- Bonica ('MEIdomonac')
- Brandy ('AROcad')
- Crystalline ('ARObipy')
- French Lace ('JAClace')
- Intrigue ('JACum')
- 'Mister Lincoln'
- Moonstone ('WEKcryland')
- 'Oklahoma'
- 'Royal Highness'
- Showbiz ('TANweieke')
- Sun Flare ('JACjem')
- Sunset Celebration ('FRYxotic')
- St. Patrick ('WEKamanda')
- 'Uncle Joe'

Disease-resistant roses
- Blueberry Hill ('WEKcryplag')
- Blushing Knock Out ('RADyod')
- Carefree Sunshine ('RADsun')
- Gemini ('JACnepal')
- Gizmo ('WEKcatlart')
- Gourmet Popcorn ('WEOpop')
- Iceberg ('KORbin')
- Ingrid Bergman ('POUlman')
- Knock Out ('RADrazz')
- 'Loving Touch'
- Moonstone ('WEKcryland')
- Napa Valley ('POUlino')
- New Zealand ('MACgenev')
- Pillow Fight ('WEKpipogop')
- Pink Knock Out ('RADcon')
- 'Playboy'
- 'Sea Foam'
- Showbiz ('TANweieke')
- 'The Fairy'

CLIMBING ROSES

Nowhere to go

Our house has three climbing roses on the property. None of them has anything to climb on because of where they are planted. We would like to move them against our fence so they can climb the lattice. Can we move them now, or will this harm them?

The best time to move roses is when they are dormant or growing slowly. In most areas this is during the winter or early spring. Prepare the soil in the new bed by digging in rotted manure and compost to a depth of 12–18 inches. When you dig up the roses, take as large a root ball as you can move—the less you damage the roots, the better. Fertilize with a bit of slow-release fertilizer made for roses, if you wish. After replanting them, prune off any damaged canes, and mulch around the bases. They should do well in their new location as long as they receive full sun.

Climber lacks flowers

I have a climbing rosebush that grows well but has not bloomed for the past 2 years. Everything else I planted has done well. Does the soil lack something? Can you give me some advice?

Some climbing roses bloom only on second-year stems. A complete lack of bloom on your climbing rose makes me suspect that you are losing or removing the stems before they reach blooming age. If you live in a cold climate, you may need to remove the climber from its trellis over the winter. Lay the stems down, cover them with soil, and mulch them to permit them to survive the winter and bloom the following year. Also, avoid early-season pruning of climbing roses that normally develop just one flush of bloom, except for removal of weak or diseased canes and canes that have already bloomed. Pruning out strong, healthy first-year canes means you're removing next year's potential blooms on these varieties. Poor flowering of your climbing roses could be due to a number of causes.

- Is your rose getting at least 6 hours of sunlight each day? That much is necessary in order to set flowers on most varieties.
- Are you fertilizing your rose with too much nitrogen? Nitrogen supports leafy growth instead of flower growth.
- Are you giving your rose 1 inch of water per week through rainfall or irrigation during the growing season? Moisture-stressed roses will not bloom well.
- Is your soil pH close to 6.5? Soil that's either highly acidic or highly alkaline may keep your rose from blooming.

Quelling Queen Elizabeth®

I planted six Queen Elizabeth® climbing roses in raised spots along my fence, amending the soil with peat moss, topsoil, manure, and bonemeal. Every year the roses grow 15 feet tall, even when pruned to 22 inches. Without fertilizer, they grow as tall but don't bloom. They get windblown, acquire black spot, get termites in the mulch, dogs chew them, and they still grow 15 feet. What can I do to keep them bush size?

The climbing form of Queen Elizabeth® grows 12–15 feet tall; the bushy form is a 4½–7-foot-tall plant. Instead of trying to make your climber into something it is not, why not use its form to your advantage? Train it to grow on your fence or on lattice attached to the fence. First tie the strongest canes horizontally to the support, with equal spaces between them. Flowering shoots will emerge along this basic structure. Then, before new growth begins in spring, prune flowering shoots to two buds above the main stems, and remove any of the main canes that look dead or damaged. By managing your rose's robust growth this way, you'll get an attractive "wall" of big pink blooms and shiny leaves, which will make a fine backdrop for shorter perennials or rosebushes.

If you prefer a bush rather than a climber, grow the bush form of Queen Elizabeth® instead of the climber.

Drought-tolerant climber

Is there a climbing rose that will withstand dry climates?

Unfortunately, roses aren't the most drought-tolerant of plants. Most climbing roses have similar needs, so it's hard to single out one variety that's more drought-tolerant than others. To help your rose, add organic matter, such as compost, to the soil before planting. Organic matter helps the soil hold moisture. Mulching over the soil's surface with shredded bark also helps conserve moisture. If you use these techniques, in addition to protecting plants from scorching afternoon sun, and watering your plants occasionally, you should find that most climbing roses do well. To your advantage, a dry climate means you'll fight fewer fungal diseases than your gardening friends in more humid regions.

Pruning climbing roses

Should I cut back my climbing roses this spring as they start to turn green? Or should I have taken care of this in the winter?

Climbing roses are pruned just like their short and stout counterparts, with one exception: Climbing roses that have one beautiful flush of bloom in spring should be pruned after they flower so as not to clip off the developing flower buds. All other climbing roses can be pruned in late winter. Use a pair of sharp pruning shears to cut away dead, diseased, and weak growth. Tidy up the roses' form by cutting wayward stems back to ground level and heading back vigorous stems by 6 inches or so.

Always rake up the clippings after pruning roses. This will help control the spread of diseases such as powdery mildew, black spot, and rust.

HYBRID TEA ROSES

Transplanting hybrid teas

I have to move several hybrid tea roses. When and how would be the best time to do this?

The best time to move your hybrid tea roses is in early spring while they are still dormant. If you live in a cold climate, do this as soon as the ground thaws in late winter or early spring.

Prepare new planting holes before you dig the roses. Then dig each rose, keeping a large ball of soil around the roots if possible. Use a sharp spade to slice through the soil and roots; clean cuts will seal over more rapidly. If the plant is still dormant, you can also have success transplanting by digging the plant bare-root. Again, use a sharp spade to dig the plant, and avoid tearing the roots as you pry the plant out of the ground. If you move the plant without disturbing its roots, the plant will suffer less shock in the transplant. Mulch around the rose after you plant it, and keep the root system moist but not soggy throughout the first growing season after transplanting.

Floppy form

I recently planted some rosebushes. They are doing beautifully except for the stems, which don't seem to be strong enough to support the flowers. What can I do to keep them from drooping?

Inadequate sunlight may cause roses to produce thin canes and mediocre blooms, so make sure your roses receive at least 6 hours of sunlight each day. Droopy canes also may occur when rose plants are immature, before they have developed stems thick enough to support a full set of blooms. Perhaps your roses' stems will eventually become sturdier.

Frail canes also may be the result of improper pruning. When planting new roses, be sure to remove any weak, twiggy canes at the base. Each year when you prune your roses, continue taking off the weak canes so the plant will direct its energy to vigorous shoots. Skinny canes grow poorly and produce fewer flowers. Light pruning results in a greater number of canes per plant, but most of the canes will be smaller and weaker. Heavy pruning will encourage fewer but stronger canes from the base of the plant.

Caring for a hybrid tea rose
I purchased a hybrid tea rose and need some information about how to care for it. Can you help me?

Most hybrid teas are cared for in the same way. Here are the requirements for healthy hybrid tea rose growth.
- For lots of lush blooms, choose a site in full sun, set apart from trees and shrubs.
- Give the roses excellent drainage. If your soil is heavy clay, grow roses in a raised bed, or amend your soil with a suitable combination of compost, manure, or other organic matter.
- Mulch newly planted roses with a 2–3-inch blanket of shredded bark to help the soil stay moist, to stabilize soil temperature, and to suppress weeds.
- Water deeply each week at the base of the plant.
- Fertilize every 4–6 weeks after spring growth has begun. Cease fertilizing 6–8 weeks before the first fall frost.
- Prune annually, making sure you remove all dead, diseased wood and weak or crossing branches. Deadhead flowers as they fade to keep the roses blooming instead of spending energy producing seed. Prune out the center branches to promote good air circulation and prevent disease.

Care for cut roses
I received a dozen roses for my birthday. How can I keep them alive?

Recut the stems underwater to prevent air bubbles from reducing the water uptake, and use a floral preservative, which you can find at a florist shop, in the vase water. Floral preservative contains a type of sugar for nutrition, an acidifier to lower the pH of the water, and a compound to inhibit the growth of bacteria. Change the water every day if possible. If you recut the stems underwater every few days, your roses will live even longer. If any stem wilts, recut it. Be sure to use clean, sharp pruning shears or some other tool to avoid crushing the stem when you cut.

Pruning long-blooming roses

I have quite a few roses that flower most of the time in my Florida garden. When should I trim them, and how much should they be trimmed? Some people have told me to cut them to the lowest leaves. That scares me! Is this the best thing to do?

Your roses are probably hybrid teas or floribundas that have been grafted onto the roots of *Rosa ×fortuneana*, which is often called a Florida rootstock even though this species is native to China. Highly resistant to nematodes, this rootstock produces vigorous plants that do best when pruned lightly but continuously all year, with a more serious pruning to shape the plants in August. Each time you cut flowers to bring indoors, also remove any old blossoms as well as leaves or stems that show evidence of black spot—a fungal disease that causes black spots on leaves, with yellowing between the black patches. In August, prune out any old brown canes, then shape the plants as needed, removing up to half of the branches. When black spot or other diseases attack and get out of control, some south Florida gardeners also remove all remaining leaves at this time. However, there is no need to remove healthy leaves. Follow up this pruning with a good feeding, which will energize the plants to bloom well all winter.

MINIATURE ROSES

Keeping mini rose indoors

I received a miniature rosebush for Valentine's Day. It bloomed nicely for a few days, but now it appears to be dying. I want to plant it outside in my garden but don't think it will make it until spring. Is there anything I can do to keep it from dying?

Keep your rose in a cool location. Warm, dry conditions indoors are hard on miniature roses. Also, keep it slightly moist at all times and in the brightest spot you have—a south-facing window is ideal. On the other hand, overwatering can kill mini roses. Remove the decorative foil wrap to ensure excess water can escape.

It can be difficult to keep a miniature rose plant forced into bloom during winter in good condition until spring. (Watch for spider mites. They often attack plants stressed from dry conditions indoors.) Unless the plant dies, however, it will often rebound once planted outdoors when the weather warms. Remember to gradually harden off the rose as you move it outdoors.

Overwintering potted miniature roses

I planted several miniature roses in pots this spring. What's the best way to overwinter them?

Miniature roses are generally as hardy as hybrid tea roses. But because yours are growing in containers, you'll need to protect the root systems from low winter temperatures. Plants will be fine in the pots without any additional protection until the temperature dips into the low 20s. In fact, exposure to some frosty nights will help acclimate the plants to winter hardiness.

One option for overwintering your containers of miniature roses is to move them to an unheated garage where they will be cold but not freeze. Check the plants periodically through the winter to make certain they don't dry out too much. The soil should be moist but not wet. Another option is to sink the pots in the ground in a protected location outside. Cover the pots and plants with a mound of soil. Mulch with leaves, straw, or wood chips.

In early spring before the buds begin to grow, dig the plants and repot for the coming season.

ROSE PESTS

Infectious disease

Can you tell me why the leaves on my rosebushes have dark spots? What can I do about them?

Round black or dark brown spots and yellowing leaf tissue are symptoms of black spot, a fungal disease that also can cause premature leaf drop, poor flowering, and dark blisters on young canes. If left untreated, recurring infections can kill the plant. Black spot frequently occurs in places with high rainfall or high humidity in spring and summer. There are several ways to deal with the problem.

- Water your roses at the base of the plant, because overhead irrigation spreads the disease.
- Mulch roses to prevent soil from splashing up on the foliage.
- Prune affected stems from the plant.
- Remove diseased leaves from the stems.
- Rake diseased leaves from the ground in fall.
- Destroy infected debris rather than composting it.
- Spray with a fungicide to keep the disease in check.
- Plant resistant varieties.

Shabby rose plants

Every summer my roses produce pretty blooms, but the leaves turn brown and fall off. Do you think bad soil is the problem?

It sounds as though your roses are suffering not from bad soil but from a fungal disease such as black spot or verticillium wilt. To learn more about black spot, see "Infectious disease" on page 159.

Verticillium fungi live in the soil and enter plants through their roots, spreading through the canes by means of water-carrying vessels in the stems. The fungi block these vessels, hampering the movement of water and nutrients through the plant. The leaves will yellow at the edges, then turn brown and dry. Foliage will wilt in hot weather. Verticillium wilt has no chemical control, but fertilizing and watering your roses may promote fresh vital growth.

For a more specific diagnosis, take a plant sample to a local garden center or to your cooperative extension service.

Bothersome beetles

Beetles destroy my roses. I have tried almost everything to get rid of them and would appreciate any help you can give me.

Japanese beetles are major pests east of the Mississippi River (though the pests are gradually moving west). These metallic-green insects with coppery wing covers measure about ½ inch in length. Gangs of them attack roses from the top down, eating the tissue between the veins of tender leaves. They are active for 4–6 weeks beginning in late June to early July.

Japanese beetles do have some predators, including crows, starlings, robins, grackles, moles, and skunks. These predators consume white grubs, which are the juvenile form of the beetle, in the lawn. Unfortunately, even if you are able to control Japanese beetle grubs in your lawn, adult beetles from neighboring yards can still eat your roses.

Picking beetles by hand and drowning them in a wide-mouth container of soapy water is another approach. Do this before 7 a.m., when the beetles are less active. Japanese beetles tend to attract even more of their brethren, so fewer beetles on your plants means you're drawing fewer beetles to your property.

Avoid using pheromone traps, which often bring more beetles to your property than they capture. Chemical dusts and insecticides are more effective. Follow the directions for applying to ensure the safety of people, pets, and wildlife.

White powder on foliage

I have a white powdery substance on my climbing rosebush. Can I do something to treat this problem and make the powder disappear?

It sounds as though your rose is infected with powdery mildew, a fungal disease spread by the wind that causes curled, discolored, distorted foliage and sometimes kills infected leaves and canes. Typically, powdery mildew crops up when rainfall is low, days are dry, nights are humid, and average temperatures range from 70–80°F.

As soon as symptoms appear, spray the plant with a fungicide specifically designed for roses (available at most garden centers). Repeat applications every 7–10 days if mildew recurs.

Also, be sure your rose has adequate airflow. If not, remove any crossed canes and any congested stems in the center of the bush. Rake up and dispose of fallen rose foliage in autumn. In the future, plant rose varieties that are resistant to powdery mildew.

Something eating rose leaves

There is something attacking my roses. The leaves look like something is eating all the green coloring out of them. The leaf membranes are still there, but you can see right through the leaves.

The damage you describe sounds like that caused by European rose slugs. Rose slugs feed on the lower leaf surfaces, leaving the upper epidermis and causing a "windowpane" appearance. These insects are not true slugs but instead are sawfly larvae. They are pale green and about ½ inch in length. Slug baits are not effective on them. However, any insecticide labeled for roses will get rid of them provided you thoroughly spray the lower leaf surface where they feed.

Drooping rose flowers

What causes rosebuds to droop? I have several hybrid tea roses, and every year some of them wilt and droop without opening.

Your hybrid teas may be attacked by rose midges. The adult is a fly, but it's the feeding of the larvae that causes the flower buds to darken, shrivel, and droop. New leaves may also be affected. The larvae may still be in affected bud and leaf tissue, so prune out and destroy affected parts. Systemic insecticides may also be used to prevent rose midges from becoming a severe problem.

SHRUB ROSES

To prune or not to prune

I put in 'Nearly Wild' roses last year because I was told they are care-free. Now I'm wondering whether I should deadhead the roses when they bloom.

'Nearly Wild' roses do a good job of taking care of themselves in the landscape. They resist common rose pests and bloom well even when they are not deadheaded. Any deadheading you do will increase flower production, but it is not necessary. If you deadhead, snip off the spent flowers down to the next set of leaves.

If you keep your rose well mulched, water it from below, and scratch a slow-release fertilizer into the soil in early spring, you most likely will not need to spray.

It's a Knock Out

I've been hearing a lot about the Knock Out rose. What's so special about it? Is it a good rose to grow?

Knock Out was a 2000 winner of the All-America Rose Selection organization. It's a shrub rose that grows to about 3 feet tall and wide. It blooms from spring through fall with single cherry red flowers in clusters of 3 to 15. The glossy green foliage is tinged with shades of burgundy and has excellent disease resistance. It is considered an outstanding landscape rose. It has proven so popular that newer varieties with a broader color range have also been introduced. Blushing Knock Out is delicate pink; Pink Knock Out is fluorescent pink.

Landscaping & Outdoor Living

LANDSCAPING IN GENERAL

Value of landscape

I would like to redo the landscape in my yard and need help establishing a budget. What percentage of my home's value should be put into landscaping? What percentage of the money put into landscaping can I expect to get back if I were to sell? How much will my house appreciate due to professional landscaping?

Real estate studies suggest that you can increase the value of your home 5–15 percent by upgrading your landscape from poor to good. What constitutes a "good" landscape is somewhat arbitrary, and how much of a boost in value you'll get in a particular instance is impossible to predict, so 5–15 percent is only a rough guideline based on averages. Generally, more expensive homes have greater potential to increase in value from a well-designed and well-installed landscape. Remember that hardscape features—which can cost big bucks—such as pavers, stone walls, decks, and patios are part of the landscape investment.

Strictly going by these numbers, you might figure on spending 5–10 percent or so of the value of your home on a landscape upgrade and expect to get most of it back right away. That would buy a substantial landscape upgrade for most homes. For a $200,000 home, that would mean a $10,000 to $20,000 upgrade; for a $500,000 home, it would be $25,000 to $50,000. Consider, too, that most trees and shrubs will increase in value over time.

A few flowers and shrubs to spruce up the front yard may not add much value to your home. But if you're thinking of selling, the first impression you create with colorful flowers and tidy shrubs could make the difference between an interested buyer and a drive-by missed sale.

Expert advice

I have a big project in mind for my backyard, and I've decided it is too big for me to tackle on my own. What kind of professional do I look for to help me with the labor?

That depends on the scope of the project, how much you want to do yourself, and the amount you want to spend. Here's a summary of landscape professionals and how they can help with your project.

• Landscape architects are professionals who usually are licensed and certified. They tackle the biggest projects, such as developing a comprehensive plan for your entire outdoor space. They may charge an hourly consulting fee to walk around your property with you and make suggestions, or they may cite a flat fee for the entire project. They also may charge a fee to review your design or plan before you begin construction, which can be money well spent if it saves you grief later in the process.

- Landscape designers usually are not licensed or regulated by any agency, but they typically have some formal training in design and may belong to organizations that offer continuing education or review. If you decide to work with a landscape designer, check references carefully. Many designers, even if they aren't certified, are gifted in design and have vast plant knowledge. Designers often create planting plans rather than overall landscape designs. Also, they frequently are not the best choice for designing permanent garden structures because they lack the needed expertise.

- Landscape contractors are not overseen by a licensing agency or governed by state regulations. They often are hired to install design elements, such as a path or retaining wall formulated by a landscape architect or designer. Again, check references and ask questions about the quality and fit of materials used.

Sometimes, your local garden center is the best place to start looking for professional advice. These centers often have designers on staff or a referral relationship with a landscape architect. They frequently can supply the materials and labor needed for your dream design. You may even get a discount for a package including design, materials, and labor.

Need for approval

Do I need anyone's permission before starting my landscaping project? One neighbor says the city inspector has to approve and inspect all work; another neighbor builds pergolas and porches without asking anyone.

Projects need various levels of approval in different areas. If you're planting a perennial bed in your backyard and aren't altering any existing structures, you generally don't need governmental approval. Notice I said "generally"—the Garden Doctor wouldn't want to get you (or your neighbor) in trouble with your local officials. In some places, for example, a freestanding garden structure that doesn't connect to an existing building doesn't require building permission. But that's not the case everywhere.

The best thing to do is ask your city or county government what sorts of structures or garden changes need planning approval. Also, you may live in a development or other area that has a neighborhood association that has to approve any changes to the exterior of your home. Check local covenants.

Keep your neighbors abreast of any changes you plan so they aren't surprised when the project begins—especially if the results may somehow affect their property by altering water drainage, creating or reducing shade, or altering views.

Pick a pro

How can I make sure I'm getting the right designer or contractor for my backyard project?

Before you hire anyone, you need to ask tough questions that will make you a more informed consumer. Make a list, leaving space to write the answers as you interview prospective contractors. Here are some questions to start with.

- What professional titles do you hold?
- What professional training have you had?
- Are you certified or licensed by any group?
- What other types of projects have you done?
- How big is your typical project?
- What's the average cost of one of your projects?
- What projects have you worked on in this area?
- Can I talk to some of your clients?
- Can we visit some of the sites together?
- Do you have a specific style?
- How would you describe it?
- Can this project be done in stages?
- Can you stay within my budget?
- What happens if you don't?
- Do I pay all at once, or in stages as the work is completed?
- Can I do any of the work myself to reduce costs?
- Do you have proof of insurance?
- Are you bonded?
- What sort of guarantee do you provide on workmanship and materials?
- Can I get that in writing?
- When will the project start and when will it end?
- How soon can you provide the written contract?

Low-maintenance summer gardening

How can I prioritize my time in summer so I can spend more time enjoying my garden?

Summer—especially late summer—is best spent enjoying the garden rather than working in it. The days are hot, the insects are out, and the sun is intense. Despite these inconveniences, garden chores still need to be done. Here are some time-saving strategies to try.

- Garden in short bursts. Instead of spending an entire afternoon once every couple of weeks doing your gardening chores, spend 5 minutes in the garden each morning or evening. You'll spot weeds while they're still young and easy to pull. If you deadhead daily, you'll keep many of your perennials blooming longer and keep your garden attractive by removing faded flowers.

- Mulch. If you haven't already done so, lay a couple of inches of mulch over the soil in your garden. Mulching saves you time, because it cuts down on weeds and helps the soil conserve moisture so you can water less. Nearly any mulch material will do, but mulches made of organic matter (such as compost, peat moss, straw, or shredded bark) will enrich the soil as they decompose.
- Select the right plants. If your area's summers are especially hot or dry, stock your garden with plants that handle these conditions with ease. Species that are native to your region are especially good choices.
- Stop fertilizing. Fertilizer encourages new, lush growth in your plants when they should be winding down and getting ready for autumn. Plus, this lush growth requires more moisture and is more susceptible to disease and insect problems.

Landscape plants stuck indoors

We had to move out of our old home in June, and weren't able to move into the new one until December. The plants and trees that I had dug up in June were in containers all that time, and now they are in the basement until they can be planted this spring. The dogwood, wisteria, hostas, purple coneflower, and pear trees are starting to bloom already, and it's too early to put them in the ground. What should I do?

Because these plants are just breaking dormancy, give them as much light as possible, and keep them cool (preferably just above freezing) and moist. Move them outside as soon as the weather settles in your region. Gradually reacclimate them to the outdoor environment. Place them in a protected location out of direct sun and wind for a week or two before planting them. On a front porch, under a second-story deck, or in a shaded alcove would be a good temporary site. Be prepared to cover up the plants on frosty nights. Although all the plants you mention are hardy during midwinter dormancy, in their current state of new, tender growth they could be severely damaged by temperatures just a few degrees below freezing. Plant the trees as soon as the ground can be dug and it is not too wet. Wait until a month or so before the last expected frost date to plant the perennials.

Landscaping on a budget

We'd like to landscape our yard, but the expense seems overwhelming. Is it possible to landscape on a budget?

Yes, you just have to plan and spend wisely. Here are some hints.

- Hire a landscape designer to develop a plan, then do the work yourself. Another option is to decide on which parts of the plan you can do, then hire out the more difficult portions. You'll get the expertise in the design and save money by doing some or all of the work.
- Tackle one part of the plan at a time, and work at your own pace to spread out the cost and the work. You don't have to get the whole project done in a single day, week, or month—or even a season.
- Look for inexpensive alternatives. A retaining wall of newly quarried stone is expensive, but concrete blocks from sidewalk-replacement projects work just as well, and some contractors give them away. If there are no alternatives to an expensive part of your project, reassess its importance to the overall landscape. For example, consider what else you could have if you skip the pond.
- Plant larger trees to give your garden instant "bones" and draw attention away from unfinished portions. Shrubs, which fill in faster than trees, add structure, too, and can be purchased in smaller sizes to save money.
- Use annuals for color around new landscaping. These quick bloomers add color until your perennials have time to fill in. A couple of flats of bedding plants such as petunias, or a few seed packets of a quick-growing flower such as nasturtiums, are usually enough for full-season color.

DESIGN

Balanced plantings in sun and shade

My beds stretch the length of my property, with one side in shade and the other in full sun. Planting the sunny side is easy, but it's hard to balance the look of the garden because I can't grow colorful plants in the shady end.

It can be a challenge to get bright colors in the shade, but balance in garden design does not have to be symmetrical, with identical plantings on either side of your border. You can instead create asymmetrical or informal balance, with differing but balanced components on either end. You can use color and texture to create informal balance. For example, a dwarf gold-leaved shrub planted beside a dark green hedge can visually balance a large dark green shrub set against the same dark hedge.

As you noted, bright colors have more visual impact than do dark ones. But you may be able to counterbalance the bright red and yellow flowers of the sunny portion of the border with shade plants having variegated foliage. Creams, whites, and yellows will stand out in the shade. You can also add touches of color in the shade with annuals such as impatiens, begonias, and coleus.

Texture is another way to trick the eye into perceiving balance. Coarse-textured plants have more impact than those with a fine texture. One large-leaved hosta such as *Hosta sieboldiana* may have as much visual impact as a cluster of medium-textured chrysanthemums.

Add curb appeal

I'd like to add more curb appeal to my yard. What can I do to spruce up the front yard?

The sky's the limit when it comes to possibilities for adding pizzazz to a front yard. Your budget and personal preferences will guide your final result. Knowing where to start is often a hurdle. Here are some steps to consider.

- Know the rules. Check with your city or subdivision for ordinances regarding front-yard plantings and structures. For example, some municipalities prohibit plantings on the utility strip between the sidewalk and street. If you live in an area without sidewalks, the strip abutting the street might be public land.
- Seek professional advice. One option is to start with a professionally drawn landscape plan. Many landscapers charge a small fee for this if you do the work yourself. You won't pay separately for a plan if you're hiring a landscaper to design and install the hardscaping and plants, though.
- Build wonderful walkways. Look at the walkway from the street to your front door. Just changing a straight walk to a curving one and adding plantings can transform the whole look of a yard. Curved pathways made of stone or brick are hot items in today's market.
- Add hardscape features. Consider installing retaining walls, landscape lighting, and archways or pergolas. Keep them simple, and use materials that are reliable, require little maintenance, and compatible with the look of your home.
- Include fine touches. An easy way to add appeal is to put in window boxes or containers near doors or windows. Painting a front door or garden bench also contributes to the look of the landscape without costing much.

Getting started

I'd like a nice-looking yard, but I can't afford a professional landscaper. What can I do myself to get started?

There are lots of ways to lift a landscaping project out of the ordinary. Adapt one or more of these ideas to make your yard memorable.

- Choose plants that complement one another in height, color, and bloom time. Assign tall-growing plants to spots behind the medium-size varieties. Save the front of the border for low-growing and creeping plants.
- Put one tall plant, three medium plants, and five short plants together. Place the tall one slightly off-center; group the medium plants together; then intersperse the small, ground-hugging plants among the others.
- Dress up your yard with a flowering vine. It can transform a fence, porch pillar, arbor, or stairway railing into a bower of bloom.
- Plant vegetables and flowers in a raised bed. That way you can work the garden without walking on the bed. The plants will benefit from the enriched soil.
- Take advantage of underused locations around your house, such as side yards, alleyways, slopes, and driveway edges.
- Add an inviting path and line it with colorful plants.
- Use containers for architectural interest. Terra-cotta pots, stone urns, and window boxes offer focal points, often in places where nothing can otherwise grow, such as on decks and patios, along walkways, hanging from awnings or latticework, and on top of walls.

Setting priorities for an overgrown garden

I love my new home, but the landscape is a mess. Part of it is overgrown with shrubs, small trees, and vines. Other parts of the yard haven't been touched. What's the best way to get started on what seems to be an enormous project?

Landscaping that is done well adds a great deal to your property's value, but it should also suit your needs. Rather than start with things you can add to your landscape, begin by removing the detractors. Then you can move on to adding landscape components that bring enjoyment and value to your home. Following are some suggestions for breaking the task into workable steps.

- Trees. Mature trees are a tremendous asset, but if branches are dying, rubbing against the roof, or threatening to fall in a storm, pruning or removal is in order. For work on tall trees, call in a professional.
- Safety concerns. Does anything pose a safety hazard? For example, look for obstacles on pathways, foliage that blocks sight lines from sidewalks or driveways, crumbling retaining walls, drainage problems, or a blocked view of the front door.

- Existing beds. Examine plants to see if they are healthy and uncrowded. If you notice disease problems, determine whether they are due to an environmental condition such as compacted soil or poor air circulation.
- Lawn. Is there an apparent problem with disease or weeds? How difficult is the terrain to mow? Is there too much lawn or not enough?
- Curb appeal. Step across the street and look at your house for a few minutes. The front entry and access to it should be easy to see and look inviting. The trees, shrubs, and other plants should frame the home, make it look attractive, and not overwhelm it.
- Professional help. Even if you're on a limited budget, consider getting professional landscaping help. The more difficult and expensive the project, the more likely you are to need someone trained in this field. A good landscape architect or designer can make suggestions at differing levels of expense. The expert can help you prioritize what needs to be done first and figure out which parts you can do yourself.
- Mapping it out. Before you dig or plant, have the yard marked for utility lines, property lines, an irrigation system, or a buried pet fence. Avoid damaging the root systems of existing trees by digging too closely to them or compacting soil with heavy equipment. Check local regulations about planting near streets and sidewalks and about requirements for water gardens.
- Anchoring plants. Trees and shrubs are usually the biggest plant investments in your yard, so choose carefully. Have some idea of what you want before you go shopping. Your cooperative extension service will have good information about plants that thrive in your area.
- Hardscaping. Patios, decks, retaining walls, garden structures, and pathways can make a difference in how much you enjoy your property, and can create more outdoor living space.
- Flower beds. Adding flower beds can be a simple and inexpensive way to increase curb appeal. With any flower bed, soil preparation is key. Planting the right plants in the right soil is the first step toward that goal.

After you've made changes in your landscape, remember to take pleasure in it. Disappointed in what you see? That's all right; you can change it again. Most gardens are a work in progress. The important thing is for you and your family and friends to be out there in it, having a great time!

Focal point

All the magazines I read tell me that I need a focal point for my garden, such as a birdbath, a fancy pot, or a piece of garden art. Why is this important?

A focal point becomes part of the permanent landscape, which designers refer to as the bones of the garden. It stops the eye, creating a place to focus—hence, the term focal point. Here are some reasons you'll want to add one to your landscape.

- A focal point can transform a garden to make it yours. For example, a classical urn on a fluted pedestal adds an air of formality, whereas a copper fountain that spins and hurls water in an ever-changing pattern injects whimsy.
- An effective focal point brings with it an element of surprise. It gives visitors something they aren't expecting.
- Placing art in the garden is an ideal way to showcase the art while adding strength and character to the overall landscape.
- A focal point can be practical as well as artistic. Birdhouses, bird feeders, and birdbaths attract wildlife while adding an artistic element. The birds become an attraction too.
- A well-chosen focal point can balance a landscape design; for example, a tall piece of sculpture can offset a tree in another part of the garden. The color of the focal point can pick up hues in surrounding beds and help unify the space.

A place for art

Now that I'm finished with most of my planting, I'd like to add some art to my garden. Where do I start?

Here are four basic points to keep in mind as you're looking to place a work of garden art.

- Longevity. Make sure that you and the art are compatible over the long haul before you go to the trouble and cost of placing it in your garden. (Will you always want that massive modernist sculpture or the 101 pink flamingos?)
- Durability. Consider how long the art will last. If your heart's desire is made of wood, it will probably decay over time or require lots of maintenance. If it's made of metal, prepare to paint, or live with rust. Stone or concrete items will last longer, but they may crack from freezing and thawing or acquire a coating of moss over time.
- Stability. Create a firm base that will resist sinking under the weight of the piece or shifting at the slightest breeze. Even if the object is at the back of a flower bed, somebody may accidentally knock it over if it's unsteady.

- Use. Having in mind a specific idea, a favorite hobby, or a use for the artwork can help you narrow your choices. If you like birds, choose a birdbath that doubles as a work of art. To add the sound of water in a garden, choose a decorative fountain. Wind chimes add the element of sound and can also be eye-catching.

DRAINAGE AND SLOPES

Drainage dilemma

After we moved into our new home, we realized that there's a ditch running through our property. All drainage from neighboring homes runs into the ditch. Our whole backyard slopes from 15–25 percent. I want to add soil to change the drainage, and plant the area with shrubs and flowers rather than mow it. Do I have to call in a professional? I really can't afford to do that.

This sounds like a major project, so I suggest you contact a local expert to help you develop a plan, particularly because drainage is such an important factor. You want to make sure that your landscape design and plants are suited to the site, and also that any changes you make won't cause long-term problems for your home's foundation or for your neighbors. Avoid trying to add more soil to change the drainage yourself without thoroughly studying the situation. Making a poorly thought-out change could end up costing you much more in the long run.

Rather than changing the drainage of the site, you may be able to landscape with plants that tolerate occasional wet feet. Siberian iris *(Iris)*, redtwig dogwood *(Cornus)*, maiden grass *(Miscanthus)*, and moneywort *(Lysimachia)* are a few examples of plants that may be suited to periodic wet cycles but which also thrive during drier times.

A well-qualified professional landscape designer or architect will save you money by providing detailed plans you can follow on your own when time and money allow. Ask for references from anyone you consult, and talk to more than one professional before hiring anyone.

Rain erosion

My front yard slopes toward the house. When it rains, water runs down the hill. There is grass there, but it still makes a muddy mess! I'd like to plant a flower bed. Any suggestions?

Putting in a flower bed will only put a bandage on your problems. Your best bet is to contact a landscaper to get some on-site advice about how to drain the water away from your home. Once you get the drainage taken care of, you can work on a flower bed. You'll then have a variety of options open to you.

Moist-soil garden

I have a section of my yard that's always wet. What could I grow there?

Most plants fail to grow well where they have wet feet. If you have a spot in your sunny garden or yard that's consistently moist, try this plan. If the soil is wet enough that there's a detectable rotting odor, build the soil level up slightly and add organic matter to give your plants the best possible start. Here are some plants to try.

- Calla *(Zantedeschia aethiopica)*. Growing from a bulb that doesn't tolerate freezing temperatures, calla produces elegant, vase-shape white blooms all summer. Its arrow-shape foliage also provides interest all season. It grows 3 feet tall and 2 feet wide. Zones 9–10; elsewhere, dig bulbs and store in a frost-free location for the winter.
- Cardinal flower *(Lobelia cardinalis)*. A showstopper at the end of the season, cardinal flower produces some of the brightest red flowers you'll see. The blooms appear in late summer and autumn on clusters above the bronze-tinged foliage. This North American native grows 3 feet tall and 1 foot wide. Zones 3–9.
- Joe-Pye weed *(Eupatorium purpureum)*. A back-of-the-border plant, this North American native towers up to 7 feet tall. In summer and autumn, it produces attractive clusters of pink flowers that attract butterflies. Individual plants spread 3 feet, but form clusters that can grow much wider. Zones 3–9.
- Ligularia *(Ligularia dentata)*. This plant is grown mainly for the appeal of its large, round leaves, which are often tinged with red. It bears clusters of yellow flowers from summer to autumn and grows up to 5 feet tall and 3 feet wide. Zones 4–8.
- Moneywort *(Lysimachia nummularia)*. The variety 'Aurea' is a ground cover that provides season-long interest thanks to its brilliant golden-yellow foliage. The yellow flowers appear throughout the summer. Moneywort grows only 2 inches tall but can spread quickly when its needs are satisfied. Zones 4–8.
- Turtlehead *(Chelone lyonii)*. Native to North America, turtlehead produces bright pink flowers in late summer and autumn. The foliage is dark green and attractive throughout the growing season. Turtlehead grows 4 feet tall and 2 feet wide. Zones 3–8.

Plants for wet areas

A large area of my yard stays extremely wet—no standing water, but wet. I'd like some color there. Please give me some ideas for planting in this type of soil.

Several hardy and colorful perennials tolerate wet feet. You don't say whether your spot is sunny or shady, so I'll give you a few suggestions for both conditions. See the Quick Tip, at right, for some solutions.

Terracing a yard

Our newly purchased home sits on the high side of the street. I'd like to install steps that crisscross the slope. We have the same situation in the backyard, but the incline is not as steep. Any ideas about where I can get pictures of terraced yards?

There are a couple of places to find ideas for terracing. One of the easiest, you may already have checked: your neighborhood. Spend some time taking notes on how other people with similar conditions have handled the situation. You'll see what has been successful and what hasn't, what you like and what you don't, and which plants do best in your locale.

Second, talk to local landscapers. Dealing with a major hillside usually requires professional help. Even if you don't hire a landscape architect to do the job, it will pay off to have a professional plan in hand.

Third, check out the landscaping section at a major bookstore. Most landscaping books include information about slopes and the challenges associated with gardening on them. Although you may not find your exact situation, you'll find ideas that you can apply.

HARDSCAPES

Retaining wall

We're trying to find attractive, inexpensive material for a retaining wall about 18 inches high in the front of our home. My husband wants to use treated lumber, but I am interested in something a little better looking.

Landscape blocks are the standard material for this type of situation. I don't think you'll match the low cost of treated landscape timbers, which are about the cheapest thing out there. Nevertheless, the blocks are affordable and come in a wide range of sizes, colors, and styles, and you can get them at nearly all garden centers and home centers.

In some areas of the country, fieldstone or boulders may be readily available at nominal cost. Both are more difficult to work with than the perfectly level landscape blocks. But they provide a more natural look and will be long-lasting if installed properly. Here are several key points to remember in building your retaining wall.

- Start with a solid base. For an 18-inch-tall wall, you'll need to dig 6–12 inches deep, lay down a base of compacted sand and gravel, then lay the base course of stone, blocks, or timbers.
- Tilt each succeeding layer back into the bed. If you make the wall perfectly perpendicular, the pressure of the soil behind the wall will eventually cause the wall to push outward.
- Overlap gaps in succeeding layers. This will help tie the wall together for greater stability.

Stairs in landscape

My front yard slopes down to the street. We've decided to put in a retaining wall to create terraces. That means we'll need to have some stairs through the retaining wall. What do we need to know to do this project ourselves?

If you've had little experience in landscape construction projects, it may be well worth your time to have a professional contractor design the steps for you. (Any retaining wall over 4 feet in height should be professionally engineered to ensure structural reliability.) You could also find a good how-to book on landscape construction that will provide you detailed instructions. Here are some points to keep in mind.

- Check local codes and ordinances for regulations on stair dimensions, railing requirements, and other parameters.

- Chose a durable material that will blend well with the retaining wall and your home.
- Consider the steepness of the stairs. Treads should be a minimum of 12 inches deep. The shorter the rise (the distance stepped up between each step), the wider the tread should be. Typical combinations include a 6-inch riser with a 14-inch tread, a 5-inch riser with a 16-inch tread, and a 4-inch riser with an 18-inch tread.
- Break up long, steep slopes by curving the flight of stairs or by shortening the spans with landings.

Weeds in pavers

How do I keep weeds out of my patio pavers? When I try to pull them out, the setting sand pulls out with them.

Weeds that grow in cracks between pavers are a common nuisance. The best solution is preventive: Spread a layer of landscape fabric under the pavers when you install them. The fabric prevents weeds from rooting in deeply.

You can also kill weeds as they sprout. Various herbicides are available. Some, such as glyphosate (Roundup), kill the weeds that are present when the herbicide is sprayed but leave no residue. Others remain active in the soil after you apply them, preventing weeds from germinating for several months or more. Use caution with herbicides, and follow label directions. If you prefer to avoid chemical herbicides, carefully flame the weeds with a propane weed torch, or pour boiling water on the weeds to kill them.

LANDSCAPE LIGHTING

Lights in shrubs

I put some little white lights among my azaleas. I like the way these lights illuminate the front of my house, so I have left them up year-round. Will these lights cause any problems with the health and growth of the plants?

Using lights year-round in your shrubs should have little effect on the plants' health. You might notice that your azaleas don't bloom as well, but this will depend on the brightness of the lights and how long they are burning at night. Azaleas are sensitive to the length of the day—it's what tells them to bloom. If the plants receive too much light during the night hours, it could trick them into behaving as though the days are longer than they really are, thus keeping them from blooming at the right time.

Effect of streetlights

I've noticed that the leaves on my maple tree near a streetlight hang on through the winter, while those farther away from the light fall off at the normal time. Is the streetlight causing problems?

Bright streetlights can affect a plant's perception of day length. The plants are tricked into perceiving that days are longer than they really are by the artificial light from the street lamp. Because declining day length is one of the triggers that induces dormancy in a plant, leaf color changes and leaf drop may be delayed by proximity to a bright light. In most cases, plants will continue to grow with no ill effects. But should an extremely early cold snap hit, branch tips that have not hardened off properly may suffer dieback. Or, as in the case of your maple tree, the leaves may hang on an extra-long time. Usually as buds begin to swell next spring, the old leaves will be pushed off, and no permanent damage will be evident.

Some trees are more sensitive to the effects of security lights than others. Norway maple *(Acer platanoides)*, paper birch *(Betula papyrifera)*, sycamore *(Platanus ×acerifolia)*, American elm *(Ulmus americana),* and Japanese zelkova *(Zelkova serrata)* are some of the more sensitive. Those with low sensitivity include American holly *(Ilex opaca)*, sweet gum *(Liquidambar styraciflua)*, southern magnolia *(Magnolia grandiflora)*, Austrian pine *(Pinus nigra)*, callery pear *(Pyrus calleryana)*, and willow oak *(Quercus phellos)*.

Adding light to landscape

I'd like to add some landscape lighting next to the walkway in front of my house but wonder how safe it is and how expensive it is to keep it lit all night.

Most landscape lighting systems use low-voltage lights. The normal household voltage of 110 volts is reduced to 12 volts by a transformer. This low voltage makes the lights extremely safe; you're unlikely to get a shock even if you touch bare wires or hit a buried cable while digging in the garden. (I don't recommend trying either of these, however!)

Low-voltage systems are economical to operate. Most use less energy than a single 75-watt bulb. To save even more energy, you could put the lights on a timer that would automatically shut them off at a predetermined time each night. Or consider a solar-powered system, which harnesses sunlight during the day to power the lights at night.

PLANT SELECTION

Easy-care flowers

My mother-in-law wants me to redo her front-yard flower bed. But she is notorious for killing plants. She doesn't like to water them and keep up with their care. Can you recommend plants for me to grow for her?

You could plant annuals; they're less expensive up front and will die at the end of the season anyway. If you find that your mother-in-law can grow some annuals well, look at selecting perennials with similar growing conditions in the future.

Easy-care annuals for sun include marigold *(Tagetes),* zinnia *(Zinnia),* salvia *(Salvia),* and petunia *(Petunia ×hybrida).* If you want to try perennials, some reliable choices include purple coneflower *(Echinacea purpurea),* sedum *(Sedum; Hylotelephium),* black-eyed Susan *(Rudbeckia),* catmint *(Nepeta),* daylily *(Hemerocallis),* peony *(Paeonia),* Russian sage *(Perovskia atriplicifolia),* and coreopsis *(Coreopsis).*

Oceanside plants for Florida

I live across the street from the ocean in Florida. The gardening books I read never specify whether the plantings they feature are salt-tolerant. Can you recommend some good plants for my garden?

Although many gardeners dream of living that close to the ocean, you're discovering that such a location isn't as easy to garden in as it is to relax in. Salt tolerance is definitely an issue for gardeners who live near the sea. Luckily, there are a number of plants that will thrive in your area. They include Norfolk Island pine *(Araucaria heterophylla),* plumeria *(Plumeria),* bottlebrush *(Callistemon citrinus),* sea grape *(Coccoloba diversifolia),* yaupon *(Ilex vomitoria),* coconut *(Cocos nucifera),* Canary Island date palm *(Phoenix canariensis),* oleander *(Nerium oleander),* coontie *(Zamia integrifolia),* Japanese pittosporum *(Pittosporum tobira),* star jasmine *(Trachelospermum jasminoides),* and lilyturf *(Liriope).*

Another good way to find plants that survive salt exposure is to see what your neighbors are growing. Noting which plants grow along the beach also will provide you with good clues. Check with your local office of the cooperative extension service for plant recommendations specific to your area.

Stimulating other senses

My mother is losing her eyesight but still wants to enjoy her garden. What can I do to make her garden more appealing to her?

Brightly colored flowers aren't the only plants that give a garden appeal. Many garden designers feel that the best gardens stimulate senses other than sight.

Add plants that have textured foliage. Wonderful examples include lamb's-ears *(Stachys byzantina)*, silver sage *(Salvia argentea)*, annual dusty miller *(Senecio cineraria)*, Silver Mound artemisia *(Artemesia schmidtiana* 'Silver Mound'), and Turkish mullein *(Verbascum bombyciferum)*. All these plants have soft foliage that's pleasant to touch. To make the plants accessible, site them near pathways or seating areas.

Your mother can enjoy flowers with fragrance even if she is no longer able to see them well. Choose from the following annuals, perennials, and shrubs for olfactory delight in the garden: bearded iris *(Iris ×germanica),* butterfly bush *(Buddleia davidii)*, English lavender *(Lavandula angustifolia)*, gardenia *(Gardenia augusta)*, hyacinth *(Hyacinthus orientalis)*, lilac *(Syringa)*, Madonna lily *(Lilium candidum)*, sweet alyssum *(Lobularia maritima)*, and sweet olive *(Osmanthus fragrans).*

Select plants with fragrant foliage as well. Favorite plants that have pleasantly scented foliage include anise hyssop *(Agastache foeniculum)*, lavender *(Lavandula)*, scented geraniums *(Pelargonium)*, pineapple sage *(Salvia elegans)*, and lemon balm *(Melissa officinalis)*.

Sound is another element your mother could add to her garden. A small water garden with a waterfall or fountain makes a pleasant, soothing sound. Wind rustling through ornamental grasses, such as maiden grass *(Miscanthus sinensis* 'Gracillimus') or Indian grass *(Sorghastrum nutans),* is also a welcome addition to the garden.

Drought-resistant garden

After several years of below-normal rains, I'd like to grow plants that don't need a lot of watering. Can you suggest some?

Drought can cripple a garden. If you miss watering a time or two, your plants may develop brown foliage, malformed blooms, or no blooms. Plus, exposure to prolonged drought can make your plants more susceptible to attack by disease and insects and decrease the plants' winter hardiness.

The following plants require little watering, even during drought. Despite minimal care, they provide plenty of color throughout the summer. Use organic mulch, such as straw or shredded bark, to cover the soil's surface and reduce the number of weeds that pop up.

- Blue false indigo *(Baptisia australis)*. A North American native plant, false indigo blooms in early summer, producing clusters of dark blue flowers. The flowers turn into puffy lime green seed capsules, which turn black by the end of the season. This plant grows 4 feet tall and wide. Zones 3–9.
- Butterfly weed *(Asclepias tuberosa)*. Butterflies love to drink nectar from the orange flowers of this summer-blooming plant. It is a host plant for monarchs (meaning that the caterpillars munch on the foliage). The plant grows 3 feet tall and 1 foot wide. Zones 4–9.
- California poppy *(Eschscholzia californica)*. This annual offers up golden, orange, red, pink, or creamy white flowers throughout the summer, despite heat and drought. Its finely cut foliage is appealing too. California poppy grows 12 inches tall and 6 inches wide.
- Gazania *(Gazania rigens)*. Grown as an annual throughout much of North America, gazania resists heat and drought, producing colorful red, orange, yellow, pink, or white flowers all summer. The foliage of many selections has a silvery sheen. Gazania grows 8 inches tall and wide. Perennial in Zones 8–10.
- Globe thistle *(Echinops ritro)*. This tough perennial has prickly foliage reminiscent of thistles. It produces interesting balls of steel blue flowers in late summer and early autumn. The flowers dry well and are good for use in crafts. Globe thistle grows 4 feet tall and 2 feet wide. Zones 3–9.
- Lavender *(Lavandula angustifolia)*. Lavender is loved for its summertime purple flowers and the delightful fragrance held in its flowers and foliage. Lavender grows 3 feet tall and 4 feet wide. Zones 5–8.
- Russian sage *(Perovskia atriplicifolia)*. A shrubby perennial, Russian sage has soft silvery foliage and clusters of violet-blue flowers in summer and autumn. Both add a cooling effect to the look of the garden. Russian sage grows 5 feet tall and 4 feet wide. Zones 4–9.

Plants for privacy

I like my neighbors, but I don't like feeling exposed to the neighborhood when I'm working in my front-yard garden. A privacy fence is out for my corner lot. Any suggestions for good plants that will give me some privacy and perhaps lessen the noise of traffic?

You can grow your own living privacy fence. Tall, slender trees and shrubs such as Blue Angel holly *(Ilex ×meserveae* 'Blue Angel'), Emerald arborvitae *(Thuja occidentalis* 'Emerald'), columnar Norway maple *(Acer platanoides* 'Columnare'), and Skyrocket juniper *(Juniperus scopulorum* 'Skyrocket') are ideal for corner lots such as yours, where space and privacy are at a premium. They also are perfect for exposed front entries.

Screening electrical box

I hope you have some ideas for how to hide an awful big green electrical box in the front corner of my yard. It faces south and gets full sun. I'm looking for plant recommendations that are low maintenance but with color too.

Before planting anything around the electrical box, check with the utility company about required clearances around the box. Remember that workers will occasionally have to access the box. Anything you choose to plant there should tolerate occasional abuse and trampling. Ornamental grasses are often a good choice to screen utility boxes. Miscanthus cultivars and fountain grass *(Pennisetum alopecuroides)* grow tall enough to disguise the boxes. As a bonus, they will screen the box in winter too. For a period in spring, right after you cut down the grass, you'll be able to see the utility box. But the grass will quickly grow up and hide it again. For color, combine the grasses with low-maintenance perennials, such as purple coneflower *(Echinacea purpurea)* and black-eyed Susan *(Rudbeckia hirta)*, or annuals that will hold up in the sun, such as salvia *(Salvia)* or narrowleaf zinnia *(Zinnia angustifolia)*.

New home, new landscape

We're building a new house, and would like a nice landscape. What should a good landscape design include?

Many people think about design as simply placing plants in the landscape. Instead, think about creating outdoor "rooms". Use plants, fences, ponds, patios, or other elements to create rooms where activities take place. Functional rooms enable you to enjoy outdoor spaces.

Think about the purpose of the landscape and its function in your family's daily life. A good design meets and satisfies the needs of your family, fits the physical conditions of the site, and is attractive.

Think about your property in three main areas: the front yard, the side yards, and the backyard. Now think about the rooms to develop in these areas. They might include an entry, an outdoor living/entertaining area, places for cooking and dining, or a play area. Also include garden, work, and storage space. Link indoor living spaces to outdoor rooms with similar functions. For example, the entry, which features the front door, is an extension of the indoor foyer. Pair the garage with outdoor storage and work spaces. Patios and decks extend indoor entertaining and dining outside.

Walnut worries

I removed a black walnut tree from my yard last fall and filled the area with topsoil. I know the tree prevents some plants from growing. What plants would grow well where the tree was? Will the roots cause a problem?

Juglone, a substance produced in the roots and leaves of black walnut trees, is toxic to some plants. If there are any remnants of roots left, you may see signs of juglone toxicity for a few years, until these roots decompose completely. To be safe, you may want to consider growing plants that have shown resistance to juglone toxicity. Most annuals thrive where a black walnut once stood, as do the plants listed at right.

Where to start

There are a lot of things we'd like to change in our landscape. How do we begin?

Begin by making a scale drawing of your property. Include property lines, house, garage, other structures, driveway, and sidewalks. Here are key elements to mark on the base plan.

- Climate. Mark north, the direction summer and winter winds blow, and any microclimates you have noticed.
- Light exposure. Mark full-sun areas and partial/full-shade areas. Indicate how sunlight levels change during the day and in different seasons.
- Slope. Mark flat places and indicate poorly drained areas and steep slopes.
- Soil. Have a soil test done to determine soil pH and nutrient levels.
- Existing plants. Identify the plants on your property and note their condition. Make note of those that may need to be removed.
- Buildings. Think about shape, roofline, and location of doors and windows. Note construction materials, which can be repeated in walkways, patios, and decks.
- Views. Consider views from inside the house, as well as from outdoor living spaces. Note attractive views to enhance, and poor views to screen.
- Utilities. Mark the location of all utilities. Call your local utility location service to mark underground utilities.

   Once your base plan is completed, think about whether your landscape priorities need to be changed to fit the site.

QUICK TIP

Plants to replace a black walnut tree

Bulbs
- Crocus (*Crocus*)
- Daffodil (*Narcissus*)
- Tulip (*Tulipa*)

Perennials
- Astilbe (*Astilbe*)
- Bleeding heart (*Dicentra spectabilis*)
- Columbine (*Aquilegia*)
- Coral bells (*Heuchera*)
- Daylily (*Hemerocallis*)
- Perennial geranium (*Geranium*)
- Spiderwort (*Tradescantia*)
- Yarrow (*Achillea*)

Shrubs
- Japanese maple (*Acer palmatum*)
- Rose of Sharon (*Hibiscus syriacus*)
- Spirea (*Spiraea*)

TREES IN GENERAL

Tree planting options

When it comes to buying a tree, I find some are wrapped in burlap, others are already in pots, and the mail-order ones come bare-root. How do I choose what to buy?

If you plant your tree properly, it will likely be fine, whatever type you choose. Bear in mind that each kind has its planting nuances.

Trees sold with their roots in soil and wrapped in burlap tend to be larger and more mature. These balled-and-burlapped (B&B) trees grow in the ground and are dug in fall, late winter, or spring, then wrapped and shipped to garden centers. B&B trees are usually more expensive but can be a good value because they are large and can become established quickly.

Younger, smaller trees are often sold bare-root. This is a common method of selling trees by mail order, because it's less expensive to ship the plant without heavy soil. Low cost is the major advantage of bare-root plants. However, they require greater care to prevent roots from drying during transport and planting. Bare-root plants are available only early in spring while the plants are still dormant.

Container-grown specimens may be large, small, or somewhere in between. They may be planted almost anytime the ground can be dug. Because their entire root system is confined to the pot, they are likely to suffer little transplant stress.

Planting pointers

What's the proper way to plant trees? Can I kill them by planting them wrong?

Good planting starts as soon as you acquire a plant. Be sure to protect the roots, stems, and foliage when you transport it home. (Plants can suffer wind damage, for example, if they hang out the trunk of a car.)

When planting trees in large beds, prepare the entire area—not just individual holes. If the soil is compacted and poorly drained, create a good root zone by amending the beds with organic matter (compost or peat moss) and working it in well.

When planting an individual tree or shrub, dig a hole two to three times wider than the width of the root ball and about 2 inches shallower than its depth. Gently remove a container-grown plant from its container and set the plant in the hole so that the uppermost roots are level with or slightly higher than the surrounding soil. Avoid planting too deeply. Place a balled-and-burlapped plant in the hole so the top of the root ball is about an inch above the soil's surface. Remove any twine or wire holding the burlap in place, and cut off the burlap as far down as you can.

Fill the planting hole about two-thirds of the way with the soil you removed from the hole; avoid using compost or better topsoil. Water well to settle the soil and eliminate air pockets. When the water has drained, finish filling the hole with soil. Firm it to make sure there are no air pockets, then soak the soil thoroughly.

Finally, add a 2–4-inch-deep layer of organic mulch, such as shredded bark, to cover the soil in the planting area. This mulch conserves moisture, discourages weeds, and moderates soil temperatures. Water young plants as needed to keep the soil evenly moist.

Step-by-step bare-root guide

What's the best way to plant a bare-root tree? We ordered several from a mail-order nursery and want to be ready when the plants arrive.

As long as the frost is out of the ground, it will take minimal tools to work with your new trees. Here's what to do.

1. Before planting a bare-root tree, soak the roots for a few hours in a bucket of water to make them plump and fresh. (Avoid soaking too long; roots need oxygen as well as moisture.)

2. Dig a hole wide and deep enough to accommodate the roots without cramping them. Mound some soil into a cone shape in the center of the hole.

3. Prune back any broken roots to healthy tissue. Also remove dead roots and ones that seem unduly twisted.

4. Set the plant in the hole, spreading the roots evenly over the soil cone. The plant's original soil line should show just above ground level.

5. Backfill the hole with the dug soil until it is three-quarters full. Then water thoroughly, filling the hole and allowing the water to soak in.

6. Fill the hole with the soil until it is at ground level. If the plant has settled in too deeply during watering, pull it up gently to the correct level.

7. Firm the soil with your foot to eliminate any air pockets that may be left in the planting hole.

8. Shape a ridge of soil around the edge of the planting hole to create a watering saucer, and water again.

Removing burlap at planting

When I plant balled-and-burlapped trees, do I need to remove the burlap before planting?

You need to remove the burlap from the root ball of trees. Suppliers traditionally used standard burlap because it's tough, its natural fibers rot in the hole, it doesn't disturb the soil around the roots, and it makes planting easier. But today's burlap may be made from synthetic fibers, which are difficult to distinguish from traditional burlap and don't decay in the soil. Cut away as much burlap as possible from the sides of the root ball after you've positioned it in the hole. Because most roots grow outward rather than downward, this will allow them to grow without restraint. If the ball is encased in a wire cage, cut away the cage too. Then you can get at the burlap and remove it.

Live Christmas tree planting

I want to have a live Christmas tree that I can plant in the yard after the holidays. What is the best way to do that?

Success with a live Christmas tree requires some advance planning and cooperative weather. If you live in an extremely cold part of the country, your chances of success are diminished. Dig a planting hole for the tree before the ground freezes. Store the soil in a garage or shed where it won't freeze, or cover it with a thick layer of mulch or leaves to reduce the chance of freezing. You might also want to fill the hole with mulch or leaves to keep the surrounding soil from freezing.

Choose a healthy tree from a nursery or garden center. Keep the tree outside until just a few days before the holidays. Water to keep the root ball moist, and use mulch to protect the root ball from freezing. Move the tree to the garage or a covered porch a few days before bringing it indoors.

When you move the tree inside, keep it as cool as possible to prevent it from beginning growth. Leave it indoors for no more than a few days. Be sure the root ball stays moist but not waterlogged. Plant the tree as soon as possible after the holidays. Follow good planting procedures: Water it in thoroughly and mulch heavily.

Which trees to plant

What's the best way to pick out trees for our yard? I'm happy with having only one or two, but my wife says we have room for several.

I wouldn't want to get in the middle of a family argument, but you may both be right, depending on the types of trees you choose and the size of your yard. Take time to consider what you want the tree to do: just look pretty, shade the driveway, block the wind or a neighbor's view, or provide flowers or fruit. Will it be part of a formal planting area or grove, or will it be featured as a specimen? Consider its size at maturity. Will there be enough room for it?

Once you have answered those questions, you can move on to selecting the tree (or trees) that fits your needs. You may even find that a shrub is better suited for a particular location than a tree. Consider the factors in the table below.

Selecting trees for planting

Growth rate. The slower growers are hardwoods, which tend to live longer. If it's important to establish shade or have flowers relatively quickly, choose a fast-growing tree. Typically, they're smaller, have soft wood, and don't live as long. Their soft wood makes them more susceptible to wind or ice damage, so avoid planting them near your house.

Size. Scale trees to their surroundings. Use small or medium-size varieties for smaller houses and yards. On any site, position smaller trees near the house and taller ones farther out in the yard or at its edge.

Leaves. Trees are either deciduous or evergreen. Deciduous trees lose their leaves in fall and are bare all winter, though the leaves often give a final show of beautiful colors before they drop. Evergreen trees retain their foliage year-round. Some, such as southern magnolia (*Magnolia grandiflora*), feature broad leaves. Others, such as pines, have needlelike foliage. Of course, there are exceptions. The soft, fine-textured needles of larch (*Larix*) and bald cypress (*Taxodium distichum*) turn color in autumn and then fall off.

Hardiness. Some trees are more cold-hardy than others, so check their hardiness-zone rating. Avoid planting varieties that are marginally hardy in your area; choose only those fully hardy in your area or colder zones.

Soil. Many trees do best in rich, moist soil that's slightly acidic. Other trees prefer drier, alkaline soil that's lower in organic matter. Some trees, such as swamp maple (*Acer rubrum*) and bald cypress (*Taxodium distichum*), can handle standing water. If you're unsure about your soil, test it.

Liabilities. Trees with dangerous thorns are unsuitable for homes with children. Other trees, such as Norway maple (*Acer platanoides*) and empress tree (*Paulownia tomentosa*), may be weedy. Some are messy; sycamore (*Platanus occidentalis*) and relatives of the London plane tree (*P. xacerifolia*) drop fuzzy balls, bark, and twigs. The spiked balls from sweet gum (*Liquidambar styraciflua*) and the runaway roots of willow (*Salix*) present challenges as well. However, if you choose the right place for some of these less desirable varieties, you often can overlook their faults and enjoy their virtues instead.

Which tree where?

How do I decide whether I need an evergreen or a deciduous tree? Where is the best spot for each kind? Do you have any tips about where to put certain tree shapes?

Because a tree is a permanent part of the landscape, the most important thing about deciding where to put one is envisioning its mature size and shape. It's pretty hard to move a maple—or a pine or an oak or just about any tree—once it's established. Here are some issues to consider before planting trees.

- Evergreens are the best trees for the northwest side of your house, or between the house and the coldest winds you get on your property. The trees will block the wind, reducing heating bills and increasing your comfort in winter.
- Deciduous trees are the best choice for the southwest and southeast sides of your house. They provide shade in the heat of summer. In winter, their bare branches let the sun shine in to warm and brighten rooms. They also offer a variety of options in size and shape. Columnar trees, such as gray birch (*Betula populifolia*) and arborvitae (*Thuja*), take up little room on the ground but grow tall and stately. They make excellent hedges along property lines to screen views or block wind.
- Vase-shape and spreading trees, such as red oak (*Quercus rubra*), white oak (*Q. alba*), and sugar maple (*Acer saccharum*), produce lots of shade. Prune their lower branches as the trees mature to help increase air circulation.
- Weeping trees, such as willow (*Salix babylonica*), beech (*Fagus sylvatica* 'Pendula'), and Higan cherry (*Prunus subhirtella*), need room to spread because they grow nearly as wide as they do tall.
- Pyramid shapes include pin oak (*Quercus palustris*), littleleaf linden (*Tilia cordata*), sweet gum (*Liquidambar styraciflua*), and larch (*Larix*). Their formal look works well on lawns or along a street.
- Small flowering trees, such as dogwood (*Cornus*), crabapple (*Malus*), flowering cherry (*Prunus*), hawthorn (*Crataegus*), and magnolia (*Magnolia*) make excellent accent trees. They're ideal beneath power lines, where they can fill the view yet not interfere with wires.

Fall nursery bargains

I've noticed that the nurseries are starting to sell plants again for this fall, but I always thought spring was the best time to plant. Is this a good time to be adding to my garden?

Yes, fall is perfect for buying nursery stock and getting a jump on the next landscaping season. The bonus is that at this time of year, many nurseries hold fall clearance sales. They're a great place to find high-quality plants at affordable prices.

True, the pickings may be slim compared with spring offerings, but buying in the fall offers the following advantages besides saving money.

- Seeing is believing. You can see what many plants look like in full foliage.
- More for your money. Plants bought in the fall at your local nursery are likely to be larger than those bought through the mail, and will provide faster impact in your landscape.
- Flexible planting. Mail-order trees and shrubs are usually shipped bare-root and demand immediate attention. Nursery stock is typically sold in containers and can spend a few days in a shady spot if you can't plant right away.

Keep these tips in mind while browsing.

- Stay healthy. Avoid plants with wilted foliage, broken branches, or uneven growth. A cheap plant is no bargain if it's going to die or introduce diseases to the healthy plants in your garden.
- Stay in shape. Look for good branching structure with wide-angled branches spaced uniformly around the tree. Avoid trees with double leaders (competing main shoots of nearly equal size).
- Stay youthful. Buying younger trees and shrubs saves you money if you're willing to wait a few extra years for them to mature.

Small-tree recommendations

I am looking for a tree that has color all season long and won't grow higher than 20 feet. What do you recommend?

There are few small trees that have interest all season. Here are several to consider.

- Cockspur hawthorn *(Crataegus crus-galli)* bears white flowers in spring and has red fruits in late summer or autumn. Zones 4–7.
- Crabapple *(Malus)* flowers in spring in shades of red, white, or pink. Some selections offer colorful fruits, which attract birds in autumn. Zones 4–8.
- Downy serviceberry *(Amelanchier arborea)* offers white flowers in early spring, followed by edible red fruits. In autumn, the leaves turn burgundy-red. Zones 4–9.
- Eastern redbud *(Cercis canadensis)* produces pink or white flowers in spring and colorful leaves in fall. Some selections, such as 'Forest Pansy', have burgundy leaves during the growing season. Zones 5–9.
- Kousa dogwood *(Cornus kousa)* blooms in early summer, producing pink or white flowers followed by large fruits that resemble strawberries. Zones 5–8.

Native trees

Can you suggest some native trees to plant in my landscape?

Many gardeners know that selecting plants native to their region is one of the best routes to successful, low-maintenance landscapes. If you'd like native trees but aren't sure which are and which aren't, use this list as a starting point.

Native trees

East	American hornbeam (*Carpinus caroliniana*) American mountain ash (*Sorbus americana*) Black gum, tupelo, sour gum (*Nyssa sylvatica*) Eastern redbud (*Cercis canadensis*) Honeylocust (*Gleditsia triacanthos inermis*)
Southeast	Black gum, tupelo, sour gum (*Nyssa sylvatica*) Carolina silverbell (*Halesia tetraptera*) Sassafras (*Sassafras albidum*) Sourwood (*Oxydendrum arboreum*) Sweet gum (*Liquidambar styraciflua*)
Midwest	American linden, basswood (*Tilia americana*) Bur oak (*Quercus macrocarpa*) Honeylocust (*Gleditsia triacanthos*) Ironwood, American hophornbeam (*Ostrya virginiana*) Kentucky coffeetree (*Gymnocladus dioica*)
Northwest	Bigleaf maple, Oregon maple (*Acer macrophyllum*) Douglas fir (*Pseudotsuga menziesii*) Pacific dogwood (*Cornus nuttallii*) Saskatoon serviceberry, Pacific serviceberry (*Amelanchier alnifolia*) White fir (*Abies concolor*)
Southwest	Arizona cypress (*Cupressus arizonica*) Bigtooth maple (*Acer grandidentatum*) Gambel oak (*Quercus gambelii*) Pinyon pine (*Pinus edulis*) Ponderosa pine (*Pinus ponderosa*)

Fast-growing trees

Can you recommend shade trees that grow rapidly? I bought a new home and I have no trees. I can't wait to hang a hammock under two big shade trees!

Although I understand your desire (I wouldn't mind being in a hammock right now!), I typically don't recommend planting fast-growing trees. Fast-growing species generally develop problems, because they have soft wood that breaks easily. These trees are much more likely to lose limbs or fall during storms or periods of heavy winds. Many fast-growing species are more likely to catch diseases, and die sooner too. About the time they become effective as a shade tree, they may suddenly die or decline. Then you have to start over again.

I highly recommend planting varieties such as oaks *(Quercus)*, which are much longer lived and will not develop as many problems. In many cases, trees with a moderate growth rate have gotten a bad rap as slow growers. If provided with the right growing conditions, they can add 1–2 feet or more of growth per year.

Small tree for shade

I would like to plant a tree in a spot that's shady. It will be in front of my bedroom window, so I'd like something that's beautiful during all four seasons. I live in Zone 4.

I'm afraid that in your climate you don't have a lot of options, because there are few trees that grow in shade. I would recommend pagoda dogwood *(Cornus alternifolia)*. This native plant reaches about 20 feet tall and can be grown as a large shrub or small tree, depending on how you prune and train it. It produces small clusters of white flowers in late spring or early summer. These blooms turn into dark blue fruits that birds find appealing. In winter, you can enjoy the plant's interesting horizontal branching structure. It's hardy in Zones 4–8. For even more interest, look for the choice cultivar 'Argentea'; it bears foliage edged in bright white.

Another native tree that tolerates shade is American hornbeam *(Carpinus caroliniana)*. It grows about 40 feet tall and 50 feet wide and has blue-green leaves that turn yellow or red in autumn. In summer, it produces yellow-green catkins that look like hops. The tree's slightly fluted gray bark is attractive. American hornbeam is hardy in Zones 3–9.

If the shade is not too dense, downy serviceberry *(Amelanchier arborea)* would be a good choice. It grows 15–25 feet tall, has white blooms in spring, blue fruits in early summer, and excellent orange-red color in fall.

Right tree—right place

Planting a tree is an investment in the future. Be sure to research what growing conditions are needed for the trees to thrive in your landscape so you protect your gardening investment. Here are some considerations to get you started.

- Determine your needs. The best-case scenario is that you fall in love with a tree for its flowers or foliage (or both), determine what conditions it needs to thrive, then decide whether to buy it. An impulse purchase that you carry home and plant in the first available open space is likely to fail. Of course, there are happy accidents, but if you don't know that the plant is right for your garden, you may be wasting your time and money.

- Research the tree's needs. When you make your decision, consider all of the environmental conditions, such as cold hardiness, heat tolerance, soil needs, light and wind exposure, and moisture demands. Pay attention to the tree's mature height and width, its fragrance when it blooms, disease resistance, maintenance requirements, and potential messiness. Know the pros and cons of the species and the time commitment it requires.

- Welcome your new tree home. A common mistake is planting trees too close to one another. In later years this destroys the beauty of the trees and, with it, your investment. Unless you want a screen, avoid planting trees close together. They're more likely to develop disease and insect problems when crowded. Keep trees away from walls and foundations too. Allow room for the branches to fully expand without rubbing the wall, and for roots to extend without applying pressure to the foundation. Make certain that overhead power lines will not be in the way of the tree when it reaches mature height. Avoid planting poplars, willows, and other species with spreading roots too close to a building or underground plumbing. And if you live where it snows, keep your new tree out of the path of snow sliding off the roof.

Tree with spiny seedpods

There's a tree in my backyard and I don't know what kind it is. It's about 30 feet tall and produces spiked round balls. Can you help me identify it? What is the purpose of those balls?

It sounds like one of several options: sweet gum *(Liquidambar styraciflua)*, chestnut *(Castanea)*, or buckeye/horsechestnut *(Aesculus)*. All are common landscape trees and produce spiny pods around their seeds. The spines help protect the seeds from being eaten.

Sweet gum has glossy green leaves with five lobes, similar to a sugar maple. Fall color is variable but can be quite dramatic, with a combination of yellows, reds, and purples. It produces spiny brown balls of fruit that drop off the tree over an extended period. The spiny fruit may be used in craft projects or as mulch to deter rabbits. (If you've stepped on one barefoot, you know how painful it can be!)

American chestnut *(Castanea dentata)* used to be one of the most widespread native trees in North America, but a fungus blight wiped out most of them. Chinese chestnut *(C. mollissima)* or hybrids between the two species are more likely to be found nowadays. Leaves are simple and toothed along the margins. Fruits consist of 1 to 4 nuts enclosed in prickly burs that split open into 2 to 4 valves. Fall color is yellow or bronze.

Ohio buckeye *(Aesculus glabra)* is usually a small to medium-size tree (20–40 feet tall) with palmately compound leaves with 5 leaflets. Common horsechestnut *(A. hippocastanum)* is 50–75 feet tall and usually has 7 leaflets rather than 5. Both bear 1 or 2 nuts in a prickly or spiny capsule that splits open. Ohio buckeye turns orange-red to reddish brown in fall; horsechestnuts turn yellow or brown.

Urban trees

My homeowners' association wants to plant more trees. I've heard that some do better in the city than others. Could you give us a list of trees to choose from?

Certain trees are more tolerant of urban conditions than others. Atmospheric pollutants from industry and cars, as well as compacted soil, poor drainage, night lighting, and salt spray from snowplows all make city living less than ideal for trees. Also keep in mind that, typically, city trees have a much shorter life span than their suburban or country counterparts. See the Quick Tip, above right, for some suggestions of trees to plant in these conditions.

Tree removal

I have a large mesquite tree in my front yard. This tree is half rotten, and I am afraid the entire tree will topple over. I've decided that the tree has to go. When is the best time to cut it down?

The best time to cut down a potentially dangerous tree is as soon as you can get someone to do the job. If this tree (or any other) is threatening your home, cut it down immediately. It may be wise to enlist the help of a professional arborist or tree-service specialist to remove the tree for you. It takes experience and skill to fell a tree without causing damage to surrounding buildings, power lines, or vehicles. Unless you know what you're doing, it can be a dangerous operation.

Hiring an arborist

I need to have a tree removed. How can I be sure that the arborist I hire is reputable?

Although there are no guarantees, look for an arborist who is a member of a professional tree-care association such as the International Society of Arboriculture (ISA) or the Tree Care Industry Association (TCIA). Likewise, look for companies that employ certified arborists. Arborists who are members of ISA have demonstrated skills and been recognized nationally. You can find one near you by linking to www.treesaregood.com.

When to remove tree stakes

I moved into a new home. When should I remove the stakes from my newly planted trees?

Some experts recommend that you stake trees only for the first year after planting. Other experts recommend not staking at all. Most trees develop strong trunks faster if allowed to move freely with the wind. Sometimes newly planted trees are staked if they have a small root ball compared to their size, are heavily foliaged, or are planted on a windy site. In any case, remove the stakes from your trees as soon as they can stand alone, usually after the first growing season. The sooner the supports are removed, the faster the trees will become stronger.

Stumped by trees

We have had several trees die recently and had them cut down. Is there anything we can do to get rid of the stumps besides renting an expensive machine? Is there a chemical that will cause them to rot?

There are some stump-rotting products on the market, but they don't appreciably accelerate the process. The quickest way to get rid of stumps is to have them ground down with a stump grinder. You can rent the equipment yourself, but it's best to hire a reputable professional tree-care firm to remove the stumps. Their employees will have the know-how to do the job right. Make sure they grind the stumps down at least 6 inches below grade so you can successfully grow grass over the spot.

An alternative that is cheaper and will accelerate rotting somewhat is to cover the stumps with a dark tarp and a pile of mulch or soil. Keep it moist. This will be unsightly for a while but will do the job eventually. You could plant some morning glories in the mulch to hide the piles during the summer.

Replacement tree

I am soon to have a 100-plus-year-old swamp maple tree removed. I would like to replace this old friend with something that will be fast-growing and at the same time sure-rooted for strength. Can you recommend something that will offer good height and broad shade?

You might not be able to get a tree that meets every requirement on your wish list. The problem is that anything that grows fast is not going to be long-lived or safe in the long term (because quick growth means a weaker trunk, roots, and branches). I would suggest you think about long-term shade and safety and avoid fast-growing trees such as poplars, willows, or silver maples.

How about a red oak *(Quercus rubra)*? This might be the perfect tree for you. It has a moderate growth rate and transplants well. It also is a good shade tree with dense foliage.

Another swamp maple, also called red maple *(Acer rubrum),* might be the answer. A selection called 'Franksred' (Red Sunset) is a good possibility. It grows relatively fast for a maple, is drought tolerant, and also has a dense habit.

Be sure to match your selection with the environmental conditions of your yard. Check with your local cooperative extension service for suggested shade trees, or ask a nursery professional for recommendations of shade trees that grow well in your locale.

Trees for San Diego

Can I plant a red maple in San Diego? If not, can you recommend other suitable trees?

I would not recommend a red maple *(Acer rubrum)* for San Diego, because it's not suited to your climate. Although red maple is native to a broad range of climates from Canada to Florida, it does best in Zones 3–9 in more humid climates.

Many wonderful trees will do well in your climate, however. One favorite is drought-resistant, evergreen live oak *(Quercus agrifolia)*. This tree can be slow growing at the start, but once it's established it needs minimal watering during the summer. The tree often attracts California sister butterflies, as well as a variety of birds. Live oak usually grows about 50 feet tall and wide. It's hardy in Zones 9–11, meaning it's perfectly adapted to your area's mild winters. For smaller trees you might consider California buckeye *(Aesculus californica)*, Jerusalem thorn *(Parkinsonia aculeata),* or western redbud *(Cercis occidentalis)*.

Tree guard problem

I left the plastic wrap around the trunk of my mulberry when I planted it. Its few remaining leaves have turned brown. I just took the wrap off, and it appears that the tree was growing into the plastic. What can I do?

It sounds as if the tree was choking to death. If you don't remove those plastic wraps after planting a tree, the tree will grow into them and eventually die. Luckily, mulberries are pretty tough, so yours may recover. Water it during dry periods and apply balanced fertilizer if it recovers.

Next time remember to remove that plastic wrap when you buy a tree. Thin-barked species such as maple, apple, linden, and cherry may benefit from a protective wrap during the winter, but take off the wrap during the summer while the tree is actively growing. Mulch around the base of the tree so that weeds and grass won't grow near the trunk. That way you won't be tempted to use a weed whip near the trunk and cause injury to tender bark.

Mulching around trees

I planted several trees this year. Do I need to put wood chips around the base of these trees for the winter? If so, how much should I use?

Adding a year-round mulch at the base of your trees is a good idea. It will help your plants weather all sorts of conditions. A good mulch cover will be about 3 inches deep after it settles. An organic mulch, such as wood chips, shredded bark, or cocoa hulls, not only keeps an area free of weeds and helps conserve moisture but also improves the soil by adding organic matter as it deteriorates. Here are some mulching tips to keep in mind.

- Keep the mulch away from the trunk. Mulch should not touch the stems of your plants, because direct contact can encourage fungal disease and give voles and insects easy access to the young woody plants.
- Mulch a large enough space. The mulch layer should extend as far as the canopy of a tree. Root systems often spread 3 to 4 times the width of the canopy.
- Banish grass growing in the mulch. Grass roots compete with and slow the growth of young plants. Use herbicides with caution, however; they may damage young plants.
- Avoid too much mulch. Don't lay more than 3–4 inches of mulch around your plant. Too much mulch can keep water and air from reaching plant roots. Deep mulch also can provide a home for damage-causing insects and rodents.

I love all the color from flowering trees in the older parts of my city. We live in a newer subdivision, and I'd like to bring some of that color out here. What can you recommend?

Adding the right flowering trees and shrubs to your landscape will ensure an explosion of color in early spring. Here are some suggestions.

- Dogwood *(Cornus)*. Ranging in height from 25 to 70 feet and producing white, pink, or pale yellow flowers, dogwood can fit almost every tree need. If anthracnose is a problem on flowering dogwoods *(C. florida)* in your locale (check with your local garden center), consider the more disease-resistant kousa dogwood *(C. kousa)*. It blooms with showy white bracts a few weeks later than flowering dogwood.
- Magnolia *(Magnolia)*. For hardiness, pest resistance, and tolerance to air pollution, choose a magnolia. Depending on the species, flowers can range in color from white to light pink, deep pink, cream, and yellow. The saucer magnolia *(M. ×soulangiana)* and the southern magnolia *(M. grandiflora)* tie as the most strongly scented.
- Goldenchain tree *(Laburnum ×watereri)*. When in bloom, this tree is a showstopper. The 24-inch-long yellow racemes grace the branches in late spring and early summer. Grow this 20–30-foot-tall tree upright, or draped wisteria-fashion over an arbor in a site screened from strong winds.
- Flowering cherry *(Prunus)*. Flowering cherry is a favorite for year-round interest. In spring, trees are loaded with clouds of pink-and-white blossoms. Fall brings a whole new range of vivid leaf color, and the satiny bark is attractive all year. Japanese flowering cherry has a short to medium stature, with spreading branches. One outstanding cherry is 'Amanogawa' (Japanese for Milky Way), which displays bouquets of fragrant light pink blooms in spring.

I'm planting several new trees this spring and wonder if I should fertilize them. If so, how much?

A dilute fertilizer solution should be OK, but concentrated fertilizer may burn delicate new roots as they develop; avoid using it on newly planted trees until their second growing season. The exception is phosphorus. If your landscape soil is low in phosphorus, add it to the backfill soil. Phosphorus moves slowly in the soil, so it should be mixed in.

Preventing winter injury

With the extreme cold weather this past winter, we lost one of our favorite trees. Some of the other trees and shrubs look as if they were burned. Is there anything we can do to provide winter protection in the future?

Losing an established tree can be heartbreaking and also leave you with a gaping hole that's difficult to fill. It's good that you're thinking about this now, because, yes, there are things you can do to protect your trees from killing winter chills. Even in mild-winter Zones 7, 8, and 9, you can use these techniques when the forecasters predict below-freezing temperatures.

- Water your trees and shrubs before winter. Trees don't shut down completely in winter. They can lose water through their branches and leaves, and when the soil is frozen, their shallow roots can't replenish the moisture. That's when dehydration sets in. Prevent this by watering trees well in fall and early winter—until the ground freezes.

- Provide a sunblock. Winter sun and whipping winds can sap plants of their moisture. Shield young tree trunks from low-angled winter sun by wrapping the trunk with tree wrap. Wrap a tree trunk up to the first branch. Be sure to remove the wrap in spring.

- Mulch much. If winter would stay consistently cold, plants would be happier. Temperature fluctuations throughout the season cause repeated freezing and thawing, which damages roots near the soil's surface. In spring, that damage slows growth and makes plants more vulnerable to disease. Insulate the ground out to the drip line with a 2–4-inch-deep layer of shredded bark or wood chips. And when you are shoveling snow, add a little extra around your trees and shrubs; a thick layer of snow also can act as mulch.

Fall foliage color

Why do tree leaves change color in the fall?

The green color of leaves is due to a pigment called chlorophyll. Most leaves have other pigments, too, but they're masked by the presence of chlorophyll. In late summer and fall, with decreasing day length, leaves produce less chlorophyll, and the other pigments become visible. The red and yellow underlying pigments are produced most abundantly during warm, sunny days followed by cool nights. Red pigments are produced as a result of sugar accumulation as chlorophyll breaks down. Low sugar production under poor conditions reduces pigment production. If cloudy, cool weather hits during early fall, colors are not as spectacular.

Stripped bark on trunk

While doing yard work this spring, I noticed that the bark had been stripped off near the base of several of my young trees. The trees are budding out just fine. Is there anything I need to do? What caused this damage?

When more succulent food becomes scarce in winter, rodents strip off the bark of trees. Rabbits, mice, or voles may be to blame. Rabbits usually strip bark higher on the trunk than mice or voles, but plants partially buried in snow may have damage from any of these culprits even on side limbs. When these animals remove a circle of bark completely around the tree (girdling the tree), the tree can die. However, the tree may leaf out normally in spring even if completely girdled. This is because the xylem (water-conducting tissue) of the tree is confined to the woody tissue under the bark. As summer progresses, the tree eventually starves and dies because the phloem (food-conducting tissue) immediately beneath the bark has been removed. The roots depend on the leaves of the tree for food, so cutting off their pipeline means they'll soon starve.

If the damage is confined to a small portion of the trunk, the tree will probably recover with nothing more than a small scar. The guideline I use is that if less than 25 percent of the stem is girdled, the tree will likely recover nicely. When damage is 25–50 percent of the stem, most trees will live but will suffer noticeable stress and weakening. If more than 50 percent of the stem has been girdled, the damage is so great that removal may be the best option.

Check the wounds, and use a razor blade to cleanly cut off any hanging bark; avoid peeling off any more. Protect the trees from future damage by encircling the trees with wire-mesh cylinders that extend 2–3 inches into the ground. Or you could use spiral tree wrap to protect the trunk, or coat the trunk with rodent repellent before winter sets in.

Fall color too early

Some of my trees are turning color way ahead of schedule this summer. Why are they doing that?

Plant stress associated with root problems may cause early fall coloration. Stress conditions, such as drought, restrict the uptake of water and nutrients by the tree. Normal chlorophyll (green pigment) production shuts down, and the underlying red and yellow pigments become visible. Although early fall coloration is a warning sign of stress, there is usually no permanent damage to the tree as long as it grew well during most of the season.

Monitor stressed trees and provide them with good care. Fertilize in fall, prune out dead branches as they occur, water during dry spells, and mulch around the trees with 2–4 inches of shredded bark or wood chips.

Leaf scorch

Leaves on several of my trees turned brown this summer. They looked scorched. What causes this?

Leaf scorch develops when the plant uses water faster than it can absorb water from the soil. It's most likely to happen during drought, when high temperatures and hot, drying winds develop. Tender tissue along leaf margins is usually affected first, though any part of the leaf may turn brown if the unfavorable conditions continue. Maple *(Acer),* red oak *(Quercus rubra),* and flowering dogwood *(Cornus florida)* are most susceptible to leaf scorch.

Trees with limited root systems are especially susceptible to scorch. Recently transplanted trees that haven't had time to grow extensive root systems are obvious candidates. So are trees whose roots have been partially removed by digging near the tree or covered with a nonporous surface such as asphalt or concrete.

Lightning damage

A huge tree in my yard was struck by lightning in a recent storm. Is there anything I can do to help it survive?

Tall trees are common targets for lightning strikes. The extent of damage from lightning varies greatly. In some cases, internal injury to water-conducting tissues can happen without visible damage to the bark or branches. Bark may be split open the full length of the tree. Branches may explode. A section of the top may be killed. Roots can be killed.

Lightning strikes are more common on tall, solitary trees and those growing in moist soil or near bodies of water.

You may need to wait and see if the tree needs to be removed or if it will recover; the extent of internal damage can't be determined immediately. Trim back loose bark to where it is solidly attached. Fertilize the tree and keep it watered during dry periods.

Continue to monitor the tree's health. Remove dead branches that may appear. If the tree continues to decline, it may need to be removed.

Sapling care

I've just planted a new tree in my front yard. Any tips on how to give it the best care possible?

Raising a tree is not as complicated (or expensive) as raising a child, but it does require similar attention to needs.

Depending on the type of tree, you might wrap the tender, young trunk to prevent sunscald and protect it from damage in winter.

Water your newly planted tree deeply at least once a week through the first growing season. More is better if the summer turns hot and dry.

A layer of mulch around your tree saves water, decreases stress, and keeps the grass from competing with the tree for nutrients. The ring of mulch also keeps you and your lawn mower away from the trunk and reduces nicks in the bark, which allow insects and disease to get in. Keep the mulch away from the trunk to prevent rodents from hiding in it and gnawing the tree bark. New trees need little or no fertilizer until they have become established for a season or two.

Deicer effects

Do the deicers used on roads and sidewalks affect plants?

Salt used to melt winter ice and snow often causes plant injury. The injury may not show up until the following growing season. Salt can pull water out of plants, creating artificial droughtlike conditions around plant roots. Salt spray from roadways can directly burn the foliage of evergreens, turning it brown. Common table salt (sodium chloride), often used as road salt, also increases the sodium content of the soil. Excess sodium can damage soil structure. Chlorine from sodium chloride can cause a dried, scorched effect on leaf edges. Plants affected by road salt may have twig dieback, stunted yellowed foliage, and premature fall color.

To minimize salt damage to trees, use a deicer containing calcium chloride, which is not as harmful as sodium chloride. Or use sand or kitty litter instead of a deicer. Avoid piling snow treated with salt around trees or other plant beds.

Pruning-cut care

Should I paint the large cuts I make when pruning trees?

A tree generally seals itself effectively, and an untreated wound seals better than a painted one. Research shows that pruning paint can seal in moisture and promote decay. In most cases, you're better off avoiding the use of tree paint or wound dressings, but there are exceptions. Trees that are troubled by diseases or pests may benefit from wound dressing to keep out the pest. For example, an oak pruned during the dormant season seals itself effectively with no extra care. However, an oak that needs to be pruned in spring or summer (from storm damage, for instance) should be sealed with wound dressing to prevent sap beetles, which carry oak wilt fungus, from being attracted to the open wound.

Potted evergreens

I see many pictures in magazines of evergreen shrubs in large concrete planters at an entrance to a house. I'd like to know the planting instructions and maintenance for this type of planting.

The first decision to make in planting evergreens in containers is choosing which small-growing or dwarf variety you want. Dwarf Alberta spruce *(Picea glauca* 'Conica') or Montgomery spruce *(P. pungens* 'Montgomery') are conical in habit and suitable for containers. There are many other types to choose from, so visit a nursery or two and shop around.

After you select the right evergreens, choose the right container. In a photograph, it's sometimes hard to tell what material the planters are made of. There are many fiberglass and good-quality plastic containers that look like terra-cotta, concrete, or metal but are much lighter and easier to handle. Whatever container you choose, it must have drainage holes. Be sure the container is large enough to allow for root growth. As a rule, a 15-gallon pot will hold a 4–5-foot-tall tree.

Fill the container with a potting mix specifically prepared for containers. You can mix your own, but formulations are readily available at garden centers. It's best to choose one that has some sand in the mix. Sandy soils allow for good drainage and help develop the fine roots necessary to sustain trees in pots. The dense sand adds weight and stability to containers. If the mix is too light, when the pots need water they can be top-heavy and easily blown over.

After planting evergreens, keep them well watered. Mulch the trees after planting to delay water evaporation and keep the roots cool. Remember, container plants need to be watered more often than their cousins in the ground. The finger test is the best way to avoid under- or overwatering. To perform the test, stick your finger 2 inches into the soil. If it's dry, add water until it runs from the drainage holes. Thorough watering prevents salts and other minerals from building up in the container.

Fertilizer requirements vary depending on the type of evergreen you choose. Apply fertilizer sparingly but regularly during the growing season. Hold off fertilizing in fall and winter, and resume in spring. With container trees, avoid encouraging rapid growth.

Depending on your climate, the containers may need winter protection. In Zones 6 and colder, insulate the containers with mulch to keep the potting mix from freezing solid or keep the containers in an unheated garage.

Flower beds under trees

We want to build a raised bed for flowers under some mature trees. Will adding 4 to 6 inches of soil over the roots hurt the trees?

Adding soil over tree roots reduces the level of oxygen in the soil, and the roots suffer because of it. On sensitive trees, the roots may die; on others, the roots will grow up into the added layer of soil. When tree roots are damaged, the branches die back over time. Other symptoms of root injury include small, discolored leaves, premature fall color, suckers near the trunk, and dead twigs or branches. Because it may take several years for these symptoms to show up, many homeowners never realize that the added soil caused the dieback and other problems.

Trees most susceptible to injury from additional fill include sugar maple *(Acer saccharum)*, beech *(Fagus sylvatica)*, flowering dogwood *(Cornus florida)*, and many oaks *(Quercus), pines *(Pinus), and spruces *(Picea)*. Elm *(Ulmus), willow *(Salix)*, London plane tree *(Platanus ×acerifolia)*, pin oak *(Quercus palustris)*, and black locust *(Robinia pseudoacacia)* are least affected. Older trees and those weak from other stresses are more likely to be injured than younger, more vigorous trees.

Exposed roots

Several of the large shade trees in my backyard have exposed roots that cause my children to trip when they are playing. Is there a safe and inexpensive way to cover the roots without damaging the trees?

Covering the roots with soil may harm them. Some trees are more sensitive to added soil than others. Oaks are particularly sensitive to changes in soil level. If the roots die, the rest of the tree will soon follow. You might consider converting the area to a garden filled with shade-loving ground covers. That way your children will avoid the area altogether.

To plant shallow-rooted ground covers around the roots of a tree, cover the roots with no more than 1 inch of loose soil so that water and air can penetrate. Buy plugs of the types of plants you want to install (look for ones that thrive in dry shade); plugs are smaller and will disturb the surface roots less than larger container-grown plants would. Carefully dig around and between the roots, and find or make small planting pockets where you can work in some compost and peat moss. After the plugs are in, water well and keep watering so the ground constantly stays a little moist, which helps the newcomers get established. Once they are, they will start to spread and fill in the rooted areas, yet still allow the tree's roots to get air and moisture.

To top or thin

We have two trees that are starting to shade our vegetable garden. Is it possible to top the trees without hurting them?

Topping may be a popular practice, but it is absolutely the worst type of pruning for the health of a tree. Instead, it's best to evenly thin out the branches. Contact a licensed arborist; he or she will advise you and will prune for the safest, most prudent method of increasing light for your vegetables. Depending on the placement of the trees and your attachment to them, you might also remove one tree to create a "light window." Or consider moving your vegetable garden to a brighter spot.

Damaged in shipping

I received a small dogwood tree in the mail. The shipper packed it well, but the mail service bent the package in two! It is broken on one side. Is there any chance that the tree might make it?

It may be too late now; but in the future, if plants arrive in a damaged condition, report it immediately to the mail-order source. Reputable firms may replace the damaged goods or at least give you credit on a future order. Top-notch companies will want to know if the shipper they use is damaging their goods.

To make the best of your current situation, if the tree was shipped while it was in a dormant state, and if the main trunk wasn't broken, it probably will be fine.

Trim off any broken branches with sharp pruners, then plant the tree, and, if necessary, stake it for a year or two to straighten it out. If the main trunk was broken, trim the trunk below the break. Select the strongest (and straightest) shoot that develops as the new leader. Or you could turn the tree into a multistemmed clump by cutting it back to 6 inches above the roots and allowing several shoots to develop.

Removing moss from tree

How can I get rid of the moss that is growing on the trunks of trees in my yard?

Are you certain that what you're seeing is moss? Moss can grow on shaded, moist parts of trees (not just the north side, as advised by the old adage about finding your way out of the forest). Moss usually develops in patches and can easily be scraped off the trunk or stem. The greenish patches you are seeing may instead be lichens. Lichens are a combination of a fungus and a green or blue-green algae. They form a crustlike growth that is difficult to scrape off the trees, rocks, and other hard surfaces on which they develop. They, too, prefer shady, damp locations, though some grow in full sun. Lichens may be green, blue-green, orange, brown, or yellow. They don't penetrate the surface of the tree or cause harm to it. Therefore, no control is needed.

ASH

Leaf drop on ash

The leaves of my green ash tree are falling off. Some of the leaves have brown spots. What should I do?

It sounds as though your tree has become infected with a fungal disease called ash anthracnose. This disease attacks white ash *(Fraxinus americana)* and green ash *(F. pennsylvanica)* just after bud break in spring. It is more severe in cool, wet weather. Symptoms often don't show up until several weeks later. The fungus causes large, irregular brown patches on young leaflets, usually following the veins. Leaves may be deformed, and leaf drop can be severe, especially in the lower part of the tree where the foliage is slow to dry.

By the time you notice leaf drop, the fungus has usually run its course, and no treatment is needed. It is a disease of early spring; as the weather warms and becomes drier, reinfection is unlikely. Even with heavy leaf drop, overall tree health is rarely affected; trees usually send out a second flush of leaves. If a tree has been infected, do what you can to promote growth and avoid stress to the tree. Water the tree during dry periods; fertilize if it's not growing vigorously, and mulch around its base.

BIRCH

Yellowing birch leaves

The leaves on my river birch turned yellow and began dropping in early August. What's wrong with the tree?

Early fall leaf color in late summer is probably not a disease but rather an environmental problem related to hot, dry weather. River birch *(Betula nigra)* lives up to its name; it requires a great deal of water. During drought conditions, it benefits from periodic soaking. Mulching under the canopy of the tree will keep the soil cooler and cut down on evaporation. It is unlikely that your tree will leaf out again this season, because the defoliation happened late in summer. The tree should leaf out fine next season.

River birch care
What care does river birch need?

As you might guess from its common name, river birch (*Betula nigra*) is best suited to moist sites. It grows naturally along riverbanks and in wet bottomlands. It prefers fertile soil with a pH below 6.5. At a higher pH, iron chlorosis (noted by interveinal leaf yellowing) may develop. River birch is more heat-tolerant than most birches, but it is not drought-tolerant. It requires a lot of moisture to do well.

CRABAPPLE

Healthy crabapples
My recently planted weeping crabapple tree had been doing great, but I just noticed that several of the leaves are turning yellow and brown and are covered with dark spots. What's the problem, and what can I do about it?

Your crabapple (*Malus*) may simply be suffering transplant shock. It's not unusual for a recently transplanted tree to develop a few yellow leaves. Unless the problem progresses, you may not need to do anything other than keep the tree adequately watered. For the first growing season, you may need to water it several times a week until the new roots expand into the surrounding soil. Check the planting hole for moisture. If the soil feels dry an inch or so below the surface, it's time to water again.

It's also possible that your tree has apple scab. A fungal disease common on apple and crabapple trees, scab is an ugly and prevalent condition in many parts of the country. Humid, rainy, and warm spring weather promote the growth of the fungus, which begins as olive green spots on the foliage. The spots soon turn black, elongate, and develop a velvety appearance. In midsummer, the leaves turn yellow and drop, leaving an unsightly skeleton of a once-lovely tree.

If your tree is susceptible to scab, it will need preventive fungicide sprays in future years. For best results, begin spraying in early spring just before the flowers bloom and the leaves unfurl. Multiple applications are necessary to keep one step ahead of the disease. See the fungicide label for instructions. The best way to avoid scab is to plant a cultivar that is resistant to the disease.

Crabs with scab

Our crabapple looks terrible all year long. It has produced fruit only once in 15 years. It flowers sporadically. In spring, the few flowers it produces fall off, then so do the few leaves. What can we do?

There could be several problems happening here. Many older crabapple varieties are more susceptible to diseases than newer hybrids. It's possibile that your tree has apple scab, a fungus that defoliates trees by midsummer. Consult a certified tree specialist for diagnosis, or take a sample of the leaves to your local cooperative extension office to confirm the presence of the disease. If it is apple scab, control the disease by applying a fungicide as soon as bud growth begins in spring. You'll need to repeat the application every 7–10 days for at least 5 to 8 times to regain control. Rake up and destroy fallen leaves. They contain spores that will reinfect the tree. If all this sounds like too much work, it may be time to replace your tree with a disease-resistant variety. Tea crabapple *(Malus hupehensis)* has good scab resistance, as do many named cultivars, such as 'Adams', 'Camzam' (Camelot), 'Cardinal', 'Donald Wyman', 'Guinzam' (Guinevere), 'Indian Summer', 'Prairifire', 'Robinson', and 'Sutyzam' (Sugar Tyme).

CRAPE MYRTLE

Crape myrtle fungus

My crape myrtle tree has a powdery whitish substance on the leaves. What is this stuff, and how can I get rid of it?

The white substance you're seeing is probably powdery mildew, a fungus that appears as a white dusting on leaf surfaces. This is particularly prevalent on crape myrtle *(Lagerstroemia indica)* in hot, humid weather. It won't kill your tree, but it is unsightly, causes early leaf drop and leaf distortion, and won't go away without treatment. Spray a mix of 1 tablespoon of baking soda and a few drops of dish detergent in 1 gallon of water to get the problem under control. Or you could apply a commercial fungicide from a garden center. Clean up and discard fallen leaves promptly. Improve air circulation around infected plants to prevent infection from reoccurring. You could also remove your susceptible plant and replace it with a mildew-resistant one such as 'Catawba', 'Natchez', 'Yuma', 'Zuni', or 'Tonto'.

Tree or shrub?

I put in several young crape myrtles this year. The branches look long and leggy. Should I cut them back, and, if so, when?

Although crape myrtle *(Lagerstroemia indica)* can be pruned from anytime after the leaves have dropped in fall through early spring, I'd leave young plants alone for the first growing season and see how they shape up. Then, before you prune, decide whether you want to grow them as trees with distinct trunks or as multistemmed shrubs. If trees are your goal, remove the many suckering inner shoots as they appear. In either case, prune for shape and to remove crossing or damaged branches.

Pruning crape myrtle

When should I prune my crape myrtle?

Crape myrtle produces bushels of summer blooms. To modify its shape and size, prune it in late winter or early spring before it begins actively growing. Prune tree-form crape myrtle by removing crossing, dead, or diseased growth. Shape up a shrubby plant by cutting it back to 6 inches above ground level. It will send up a dense colony of new shoots in spring.

Encourage a second flush of flowers in late summer by deadheading (clipping off spent flower heads) right after the first bloom.

Color of blooms

My crape myrtles produce lots of blooms, but I've noticed that my neighbor's trees have brighter-color blooms. What can I do to make my trees bloom brighter?

Many factors influence a plant's bloom color. The amount of moisture the plant gets while blooming plays a role, as does the temperature during this time. What you plant next to the trees can make a difference to your eye (think about how a blue shirt may look more green when paired with one sweater and more blue when paired with another).

The most likely cause for the bloom color difference, though, is that you're growing a different variety from your neighbor. There are more than 300 crape myrtle varieties in cultivation, and many have slight differences in the color of their blooms. If this is the case, there's nothing you can do to get brighter flowers other than to replace the plants with a brighter-blooming selection.

Three years ago I planted a crape myrtle that was in bloom. The next two summers it didn't bloom. I have applied a high-phosphorus fertilizer sold specifically for crape myrtles. What else should I do?

Crape myrtle *(Lagerstroemia indica)* may not bloom for several reasons. Check to see whether it was planted too deeply. (It should have been planted at the same level as it was growing when you bought it.) Another problem could be that it is not getting enough sun. Crape myrtle requires full sun; slightly acidic, well-drained soil; and only minimal fertilizer. Lastly, have you pruned it? The trees should be pruned only from autumn through early spring. Crape myrtle blooms on new wood. If you prune during the early summer months, you may be cutting off that year's flowers.

DOGWOOD

Dogwood care and culture

What kind of care do dogwoods need? Which are the best ones to plant?

Members of the elegant and graceful dogwood clan offer remarkable variety in features from season to season. Many dogwoods offer showy flowers in spring or summer and gorgeous color in fall; others have variegated foliage, interesting bark, or brightly colored red or yellow stems in winter.

One of the most popular ornamental trees is flowering dogwood *(Cornus florida)*. This star of the woodlands and landscapes of America has had a hard time lately. Myriad pests and diseases threaten its existence in New England and the mid-Atlantic states. Many midwestern dogwoods lack bud hardiness because nurseries sell southern-grown plants to folks in colder zones. Ask your seller where the plants came from before you buy. Look for plants grown locally for the best chance of success.

Dogwoods like an acidic, well-drained soil that is mulched to maintain coolness and moisture. Most varieties prefer partial shade, but some can handle full sun. Dogwoods that experience poorly drained soil or drought conditions show signs of stress, then decline and die.

Kousa dogwood *(C. kousa)* and pagoda dogwood *(C. alternifolia)* are more disease-resistant than flowering dogwood. Redosier dogwood *(C. stolonifera)* sports bright red stems in winter and looks dramatic planted en masse in the winter landscape. A yellow-stemmed form *(C. stolonifera* 'Flaviramea') is also available. Cornelian cherry *(C. mas)* has yellow blooms early in spring, and later develops red fruits that resemble cherries.

Sick dogwood

Our dogwood trees are not blooming well. It looks like the bark is coming off, and there are several dead limbs. What kind of care do these trees need?

Flowering dogwood *(Cornus florida)* is hardy in Zones 5–9. If you live in the colder end of the range, your trees may lack flower-bud hardiness. Northern nurseries often sell stock that is southern-grown. With some plants, it makes no difference. In the case of flowering dogwoods, it does. Make certain your dogwoods came from a local source.

If that's not the problem, several disease and insect problems may be at work. From borers to anthracnose, stressed dogwoods are susceptible to many foes and woes. Make certain that your trees are planted in the right location and getting proper care. (See "Dogwood care and culture" on page 211).

You might consider replacing your flowering dogwood with pagoda dogwood *(C. alternifolia)*, hardy to Zone 3, or kousa dogwood *(C. kousa)*, hardy to Zone 5. They are more disease-resistant and hardier than flowering dogwood.

Potted dogwood

Last spring, I planted a flowering dogwood in a large pot and placed it where it receives morning sun on my deck. The leaves on the tree keep burning. The tree gets new leaves, but they also burn. I want to plant it in my yard but do not know where to put it.

Your flowering dogwood might be unhappy in its pot, because these plants don't like drying out. I suspect that moisture is more of a problem than excess sunlight.

Dogwoods require partial shade and naturally grow in locations with rich, well-drained, slightly moist soil. Dogwoods are natives of eastern woodlands and do best in a similar environment. They need protection from hot afternoon sun.

Your dogwood should do better when you plant it in the ground. If your soil is alkaline, amend it with peat moss or other types of organic matter before planting your tree. Water it well after planting. Be sure the soil has no chance to dry out, especially for the first few years, but avoid overwatering.

GINKGO

Fruitless ginkgo

We want to plant a ginkgo in our yard, but have heard that ginkgo fruits smell terrible. Are there some that don't produce fruit?

You're in luck. Ginkgo *(Ginkgo biloba)* has separate male and female trees, so purchasing a male cultivar is the best way to avoid the smelly and messy-fruiting female ginkgo. Avoid purchasing a seedling ginkgo; there's no way to know what sex the mature tree will become. Instead, purchase a named male cultivar that has been grafted onto a seedling rootstock or propagated from stem cuttings. Male cultivars to look for include 'Autumn Gold', 'Fairmount', 'PNI 2720' (Princeton Sentry), 'Saratoga', and 'Shangri-la'.

HAWTHORN

Washington hawthorn care

I have a Washington hawthorn but don't know anything about it. How tall does it grow? Will it grow into my power lines? What interesting characteristics will it offer my yard?

Washington hawthorn *(Crataegus phaenopyrum)* is a small tree that can grow to 30 feet. This North American native is hardy in Zones 4–8. The tree shouldn't interfere with your power lines unless they are low. Washington hawthorn grows at a slow to medium rate, so it should be a while before it reaches mature height. If possible, transplant Washington hawthorn in spring so its roots have a chance to become established before winter.

Plant Washington hawthorn in full sun and well-drained soil. After it is established, it requires little water and tolerates alkaline soils and salt spray from nearby streets. Like other members of the rose family, some Washington hawthorn varieties are susceptible to insects and disease. Nevertheless, the trees are prized because of their four-season interest. The tree produces small white flowers in spring and edible red or orange berries in autumn. The foliage has burgundy tones in autumn too. It's an ideal tree for attracting songbirds.

HOLLY

Cutting back holly

My Burford holly has outgrown its space. The plant is more than 5 feet tall and wide. Can I prune it back?

Unless you want to prune your holly regularly or it is a dwarf variety, I have bad news: You need to move your plant. Burford holly *(Ilex cornuta* 'Burfordii') typically grows 15 feet tall and wide. Dwarf varieties usually grow about half that. Because the plant naturally grows much larger than the space it is in, if you were to leave it where it is you would need to constantly keep it pruned, which would weaken it. If you decide to prune, avoid cutting the plant back severely. It's best to remove only a small portion of the foliage at a time.

When looking for a plant to replace it, choose one based on its mature height and spread, even though it may be tough to imagine it growing that large when you see it at the nursery. For a similar appearance, you might consider a blue holly *(Ilex xmeserveae)*. Most cultivars grow 5–10 feet tall. This species of holly has separate male and female plants. You'll need to plant at least one of each to get berries. 'Mesid' (Blue Maid) and 'Mesog' (China Girl) are females; 'Mesan' (Blue Stallion) and 'Mesdob' (China Boy) are males.

JACARANDA

Hardiness concerns

I saw a jacaranda tree and fell in love with it. Will it grow in my yard in Texas?

I'm afraid that jacaranda *(Jacaranda mimosifolia)* is a bit too tender for your climate. This tropical tree does best where the temperature doesn't drop below 45°F—and is better suited to areas such as Miami and San Diego. You can grow Texas mountain laurel *(Sophora secundiflora)*, a tree native to your area. It produces violet-blue flowers in spring. It has similarly divided foliage, as well. Texas mountain laurel typically grows 35 feet tall and 20 feet across, and is hardy in Zones 7–10.

LILAC

Caring for tree lilacs

When should I trim my tree lilac?

Japanese tree lilac *(Syringa reticulata)* has a natural grace. When planted in full sun and moist, well-drained soil, it rarely needs pruning. Preserve its graceful, informal habit by limiting pruning cuts to those that are necessary to maintain size and create a healthy branching structure. Remove dead and diseased wood and any crossing or rubbing branches. If you must prune the plant, do so right after it flowers in early summer. If you prefer, you can trim off the developing seedpods immediately after bloom to maintain a neater appearance.

MAGNOLIA

Magnolia construction damage

Last spring we expanded our patio to within 4 feet of an established magnolia that had always been healthy. This spring it has few flowers and few leaves. What can I do to restore it to its former glory?

Magnolias *(Magnolia)* have a shallow root system, which may have been damaged when you built the patio. The roots of most trees extend well beyond the branching structure. If you dug within 4 feet of the trunk, you may have removed almost half of the tree's root system. Now that the damage is done, prune out all dead wood. Restrict foot traffic around the tree out to the drip line (the place where the branches end). Spread a layer of compost, and top with mulch to a depth of no more than 4 inches combined, keeping the mulch a few inches away from the trunk. Make sure to water the tree adequately and consistently—but not excessively—throughout the growing season, especially during the hotter months. Avoid shallow watering; a long, slow soak over the entire root zone is preferable.

With time, it may recover. It all depends on how much damage was done and whether the patio interferes with the tree in any way, such as preventing water from reaching the roots. In the future, avoid digging within the drip line of trees.

Magnolia ID

We have three trees that look like magnolias but never flower. Could they be a type of magnolia, or something else?

They might be cucumbertree *(Magnolia acuminata)*. This magnolia flowers in late spring to early summer, but the flowers are nondescript green and not particularly showy. They are also borne high in the tree and are often masked by foliage. This species also doesn't flower until the tree grows to at least 20 feet in height. Leaves are dark green above and lighter green and slightly hairy on their undersides. They may be up to 10 inches long.

Magnolia care and culture

Is there more than one kind of magnolia? I've seen several different kinds of plants labeled magnolia.

Grown as specimens or in mixed groups, magnolias are basically trouble-free shrubs and trees. There are many species and hundreds of varieties from which to choose. From the handsome evergreen southern magnolia *(Magnolia grandiflora*, Zones 7–9) to the dramatic star magnolia *(M. stellata*, Zones 4–8), which covers itself in star-shape white flowers on bare wood in earliest spring, they are a treasured and valuable addition to the landscape.

Flower colors vary from white, cream, and pale yellow to pink and even purple. Southern magnolia 'Samuel Sommer' bears creamy white flowers that reach up to 14 inches wide. There is a type of magnolia for almost every region.

Magnolias prefer moist, acidic soil (pH 5.0–6.5) high in organic matter. They like full sun but will tolerate light shade. Mulch annually in early spring with compost, such as manure or leaf mold, especially if the soil is dry. In colder zones, buds of early-flowering types sometimes are damaged by late frosts.

Potted magnolia

Are there any dwarf magnolias that I can grow in a pot? I do most of my gardening in containers and would love to have a magnolia in my home landscape.

The answer is yes, but only if you have an extremely large container! The smallest varieties of "dwarf" forms grow 8–12 feet tall and 6–8 feet wide at full maturity. Most of the smaller types grow into a multistemmed shrub rather than a single-trunk tree, though you could train them into a tree form. The good news is that they are slow growing, and 'Little Gem', for example, a type of southern magnolia *(Magnolia grandiflora)*, will take 20 years to reach 20 feet. Others to consider include star magnolia *(M. stellata)*. 'Royal Star' is a superior selection with pink buds that open white. Magnolia × 'Ann' has late-blooming purplish-red blooms. 'Waterlily' has fragrant white flowers. Henry Hicks sweet bay magnolia *(M. virginiana* 'Henry Hicks') is the hardiest of the sweet bays (to Zone 5). It develops lemon-scented creamy white blooms in late spring to early summer.

To help container-grown magnolias survive, it's important to use a potting mix that contains lots of organic matter (see the potting mix package for a list of ingredients). Also, be sure to feed the tree monthly during the growing season with half-strength liquid fertilizer. Avoid fertilizing after late summer. Because the tree roots cannot search outside the pot for soil moisture, be sure to water regularly, and make sure your pot has sufficient drainage holes to prevent water from accumulating in the pot. Magnolias like cool roots, so keep a layer of mulch on the soil's surface. In cold-winter regions, protect the roots from severe freezing weather; keep the container in an unheated garage or cover it with a thick layer of mulch.

Pruning magnolia

My overgrown magnolia has multiple trunks and small flowers. When is the best time to prune it, and how far back can I cut it?

Prune your magnolia right after it blooms. Some magnolias bloom in early spring, others in summer. Regardless of type, prune after the main flush of bloom. Some southern magnolia *(Magnolia grandiflora)* cultivars such as 'Little Gem' bloom all summer. Prune these early in the growing season. Late-summer, autumn, or winter pruning can result in few, if any, flowers the following year.

Avoid pruning your magnolia too severely. A good rule when performing major rejuvenation pruning on plants such as this is to remove no more than one-third of the plant. Pruning stresses a plant and makes it more susceptible to pests and diseases. Maintain a healthy plant during pruning by removing small amounts of growth over a period of several years.

Magnolia scale

We have a magnolia that always gets scale and looks as though it is going to die. We usually spray with dormant oil in spring, but it seems we are losing the battle. Do you have any suggestions?

Once established, scale is a troublesome insect to get rid of, but you are on the right track. In early spring, before new growth begins, use a high-pressure sprayer to apply dormant oil to eradicate overwintering insects. It is essential to thoroughly coat all sides of twigs and branches each time you spray. In September, when the immature scales are active, spray with Ortho Systemic Insect Control.

MAPLE

Crack in maple

We planted a maple about 30 years ago. It has slowly grown into a beautiful tree. This year we discovered a crack running up the trunk. It is oozing sap and is filled with insects. We tried using tar to cover the crack, but it's still oozing. Is there anything we can do to save this tree?

Cracks such as this on maple *(Acer)* could be due to sunscald (though this problem usually shows up in younger trees with thin bark), freezing temperatures, or lightning. In any case, the tar won't help and in fact could be making matters worse for your tree. Trees build interior walls to seal off wounded areas. A layer of tar can seal in moisture and promote further rot. The insects you see are secondary; they're attracted to the sap and may not be harmful at all. It sounds as though you would benefit from the advice of a tree-care professional. Look for a licensed arborist in the phone book, or visit the home page of the International Society of Arboriculture at www.treesaregood.com to locate an arborist in your area.

Growth rate of maple

I just bought a lovely red maple to grow in my yard. The tag on the plant says that this tree could grow to be 50 feet tall and 50 feet wide. Right now it is only 2 feet tall and looks like a skinny stick. How long will it take to reach its full size?

The time it takes for a tree to reach maturity depends on many factors, not the least of which is genetics. Some trees are slow growers (20–30 years to reach full size) and some are fast (10–15 years). Red maple *(Acer rubrum)* is a moderately fast grower; given good growing conditions, it should put on 1–2 feet of growth per year once established. The better the growing conditions you've given it, the happier it will be and the faster it will grow. First choose a planting location with full sun and good drainage. Then help the tree get established with deep and consistent watering for the first 3 years. As it gets older, annual mulching and supplemental watering in drought times will boost its growth rate as well.

Sap flow from maple

I recently pruned my maple tree, and now sap is flowing out of the cut. Will this hurt the tree? Should I put anything on the wound?

The best time to prune maples and other trees with heavy late-winter sap flow is after they have fully leafed out in early summer. Unless you don't mind stained trunks, avoid pruning your maple tree in late winter when the majority of other trees are pruned. Maple, walnut *(Juglans)*, birch *(Betula)*, American hophornbeam *(Ostrya)*, and American hornbeam *(Carpinus caroliniana)* have free-flowing sap that seeps from open wounds in late winter and early spring. The sap flow doesn't harm the tree, but it can create unattractive wet streaks on the bark. There is no need to seal the cuts with wound dressing. Allow nature to take its course in sealing off the cuts naturally.

Maples and horses
I want to grow maple trees that have burgundy leaves. What kind of maples are they? Are they safe for my horses?

The maples you refer to are varieties of Norway maple *(Acer platanoides)* such as 'Crimson King', 'Crimson Sentry', or 'Royal Red'. They are not poisonous to horses, but avoid planting trees where horses can nibble on them. Not only will the horses disfigure the trees, but as they stand in the shade of the trees, they'll compact the soil and make it difficult for the trees to grow well.

Your best bet might be to install an attractive wood fence around the perimeter of your yard to create a barrier between the maples and the horses. Then the horses won't damage the young trees, and you will have a picture-postcard view.

Japanese maple makeover
When and how do you trim a Japanese maple?

Because Japanese maple *(Acer palmatum)* is grown for its attractive foliage rather than its flowers, you can prune it anytime from late winter to late summer. Most people like to prune these trees in early spring, just before they break dormancy. Not only can you see the outline of the tree better, but the plant gets a full growing season to adjust to the pruning. The downside to pruning at this time of year is that maples are heavy sap producers, so you might see "bleeding." Although this looks unsightly, it doesn't harm the tree. To avoid it, prune later in spring, after the leaves have appeared.

Use sharp pruning tools to make clean cuts just outside the collar (the raised area of bark where a branch joins the main trunk). Avoid pruning off more than one-third of the branches in any one year. There is no need to apply tree paint to the cuts.

Suckers on Japanese maple

I have a weeping Japanese maple. It has several shoots coming out of the base. Each shoot is going straight up and does not conform to the look of the tree. Can I cut these shoots at the base and propagate them into new trees?

If these shoots are coming from the base of the plant, they probably aren't the same variety as the weeping top part of your Japanese maple. Most named varieties, and especially weeping ones, are grafted. Grafted plants are two different varieties; one variety grows on the roots of the other. In the case of a weeping plant, an upright growing cultivar is used for the root system and trunk of the tree, and the weeping stems are grafted on top. Shoots sprouting from the base of the plant develop from the root variety. Your best option is to cut off these shoots at ground level and dispose of them. Although you could try rooting softwood cuttings, chances of success are slim unless you use rooting hormone and have a mist propagation system.

Japanese maple siting

I live in the Midwest and have an inset in front of my home that is about 8 feet deep and receives very little sun. I would like to plant a Japanese maple there. Will it like this spot?

Japanese maple *(Acer palmatum)* often fails to grow well for gardeners in the upper Midwest. The tree prefers warmer winters and cooler summers than your area typically sees. Plus, there are a number of fine shrubs that are well-adapted to your climate and enjoy partial shade. You might consider a different small tree better adapted to your region.

But if you have your heart set on a Japanese maple, and you have the right microclimate, you may be able to make it thrive. The tree likes bright but filtered light and a protected spot. The inset in front of your home may be just right for a Japanese maple. It sounds as though it's protected from scorching summer sun, and the inset may protect the tree from severe winter extremes too.

Japanese maple in a pot

Can I grow a Japanese maple in a pot on my deck?

If you're unable to grow a Japanese maple in the ground, you can grow it in a container. Here are some tips to keep in mind.
- Select a large container. Japanese maple can have a large root system. I've seen beautiful plants growing in 4-foot-wide containers. Consider pairing the container with a plant dolly—a tray on wheels. The large container full of potting soil will be heavy and difficult to move.

- Choose the right spot. Site the container in a protected place on your deck so the plant won't be exposed to full sun. Keeping it out of the wind is helpful too. A spot with morning sun and afternoon shade is ideal.
- Give it good care. Fill the container with a potting mix made for containers rather than using garden soil. Because the plant depends on you for water and nutrients, you'll need to keep the plant watered and fertilized throughout the year. During the summer, the tree may need watering daily.
- Protect it in winter. If your area experiences freezing temperatures, move your tree to an unheated garage or shed for the winter months.

OAK

Troublesome acorns

I've been told there's a way to stop oak trees from producing acorns. Do you know if this is true? They make mowing underneath the oak trees difficult.

Acorn production varies from year to year—sometimes you'll get a bumper crop and other times just a few. There isn't a simple way to prevent the acorns from forming. Florel growth regulator can be sprayed on the trees when they bloom to prevent acorn formation. But timing can be tricky for the average homeowner to detect. (Oak flowers aren't showy like those of crabapple or cherry.) And even if you get the timing right, the spray must cover the entire tree, or the portion of the tree missed by the spray will produce some acorns. Home spray equipment typically won't reach to the top of a mature oak tree. That means you'll have to hire a professional tree service to do the job. The spray is effective for only one year, so it would have to be reapplied annually. Over time, that adds up to a significant expense.

If mowing under your oak is a problem, you could mulch under the tree so you don't have to worry about whether the tree develops acorns. (And you'd spend less time mowing each week!)

Sick pin oak

My pin oak isn't doing very well. Its leaves are pale and sparse. What's wrong, and what can I do?

Pin oak *(Quercus palustris)* is an attractive landscape tree, but it can look bad when grown in the wrong spot. It sounds as if this is what is happening to yours. Pin oak likes well-drained, slightly acidic soil. If your landscape soil has too high a pH, your tree can't absorb the nutrients (iron in particular) that it needs from the soil, and as a result it develops pale leaves. Typical symptoms of iron chlorosis are yellowed leaves with green veins. A spray of chelated iron, available at garden centers, may green up the foliage. But a long-term fix will require more work.

Start with a soil test. If your soil is too alkaline, use elemental sulfur, iron sulfate, or another soil acidifier to lower the pH. Keep the tree watered well during times of drought, and mulch the soil around the tree with compost or bark chips. Fertilizing the tree in spring or early summer can help too.

PALM

Too-tall palm
Is there a way to stop a palm tree from growing once it has gotten to the desired height?

The short answer is "no." Palms grow only from their crowns; cutting the top kills the tree. Your best bet is to know how tall you want the plant to grow, then select a variety that reaches that height at maturity. Because palms vary so much in size and texture, you should be able to find one that fits your needs. Visit local botanical gardens to look at hardy varieties before choosing one for your yard.

PEAR

Pruning pear to prevent splitting
During a snowstorm, a huge limb broke off our Bradford pear and damaged one of our cars. Is it true that if we had pruned some of the thick branches out of the middle, this wouldn't have happened?

Bradford pear *(Pyrus calleryana* 'Bradford') tends to split with age because of the tight branch angles in the center of the tree. It is a relatively short-lived tree anyway, so if you have a choice of pruning limbs to avoid more damage or saving the shape of the tree, opt for sacrificing the limbs.

To avoid this situation, follow some basic pruning practices to establish a healthy growth habit at the time of planting, and maintain them throughout the tree's maturing years. Here are some tips to keep in mind.

- Establish one leader. If your young tree has multiple trunks when you plant it, choose one trunk for aesthetics and strength, then remove the others. This applies to most situations unless you are planting a clump birch or something similar. If you inherit a young tree with a double trunk, remove one of the trunks immediately, because eventually the tree will split.
- Keep it balanced. As the tree grows, make sure that the limbs are well-spaced vertically and radiate from all sides of the leader. Multiple limbs growing from one spot can cause weakness and are potentially hazardous. Selectively remove limbs to keep the tree in balance.

- Let the sun shine. Inspect your tree for branches to remove without ruining the shape of the tree. This practice allows strong winds to pass through the tree. It also improves the interior light distribution, which makes for a stronger tree.
- Navigate carefully. Lawn mowers and weed whips weaken trees by creating wounds that provide openings for disease and insects. Protect trunks from equipment damage by mulching around them. Apply the mulch no deeper than 2–4 inches, and keep it pulled away from the trunk.
- Remove dead weight. Dead wood, which is more visible after the tree leafs out, is an accident waiting to happen. Even a small storm can send dead wood crashing down.
- Call a professional. Whether you have one tree on your property or a grove of them, with some tree problems it's better to have an arborist's advice. A professional evaluation will help you head off storm damage to valuable property. An arborist can advise you about stabilizing splits and cracks in large trees and whether parts of the tree are dead and need to be removed. Let insured tree-care professionals handle removing large limbs and taking down big trees.

PINE

Pine needle yellowing

The center of my white pine tree is turning yellow. The tips are still green. Is it something I should worry about?

Pine needle drop happens every year. Some years it is more obvious or dramatic than others, but some needle loss occurs every year. Deciduous trees' leaves change color, and all drop pretty much at the same time. White pine *(Pinus strobus)* drops its third-year needles. The 1- and 2-year-old needles remain on the tree, making it "evergreen." If the tree put on a great deal of growth 3 years ago, and produced a lot of needles, the leaf drop will be more noticeable this year. This is a natural occurrence and not something to be alarmed about. Other evergreens also have seasonal needle drop, but it's usually most apparent on white pine.

POPLAR

Unpopular poplars

Our neighbors recently cut down five poplars and ground the stumps because little shoots would pop up in their lawn. Now every neighbor has poplar pop-ups. Is it possible they will damage underground pipes? How can we get rid of them?

Sadly, poplars *(Populus)* are invasive. As they get older, their roots can clog drains and pipes. In general, if everyone diligently mows the shoots, the roots will eventually die. You could call a professional lawn-care service or an arborist for treatment with a brush killer. You can also apply a brush killer especially formulated for persistent woody plants. There are a number of them, such as Ortho Brush-B-Gon Poison Ivy Killer. Read and follow the directions carefully.

REDWOOD

Suckers on redwoods

How can I eliminate the shoots that grow from the base of my redwood trees? Can I spray them with Roundup, or would that affect the whole tree?

Spraying the shoots at the base of the tree with Roundup could damage the entire tree. Roundup is a systemic herbicide. Even if you spray only the undesirable shoots, the herbicide will be absorbed by the needles and spread throughout the tree. In addition to dieback of the shoots, you may observe yellowing, browning, and disfiguration of other parts of the tree. A much better option is to prune off the unwanted shoots at ground level.

SPRUCE

Browning spruce

My dwarf Alberta spruce have been doing great, but I recently noticed that one has turned brown at the top and lost its needles. Is there any way to save this tree?

There are several possible causes of browning needles on your dwarf Alberta spruce *(Picea glauca* 'Conica'). One is the spruce spider mite. This tiny mite is active during cool fall and spring weather, feeding on needles of the spruce. If you look closely, you may see yellowish stippling on the needles; it results from a toxin injected into the needles from the mites' feeding. If populations are high, you may also see webbing. Often needles turn brown later in summer when temperatures rise. At that point, little can be done for the tree. You can spray with a miticide or horticultural oil when the mites are present in spring or fall to prevent the problem in the future.

Another possibility is winter damage on that spruce. Evergreens don't go completely dormant, so a dry autumn, drying wind, and dry soil can cause browning. The browned needles won't recover from winter damage, though the tree may produce new growth from buds on browned branches. The new growth may eventually mask the browned area. Water spruces well going into fall and winter to prevent desiccation. Midwinter watering may be needed if conditions remain dry and the soil is not frozen.

My four dwarf Alberta spruce are a perfect height but are getting too wide for my garden. I've been told they cannot be trimmed to make them skinnier. Is that true?

It sounds as though dwarf Alberta spruce wasn't the best choice for your garden. The trees can get rather wide (up to 8 feet), and it is difficult to keep them narrow. Trim back the new growth that appears on the side branches each year. By doing this, you may keep them from getting much wider than they are now. Avoid pruning back into old wood that has no green needles on it. Such a severe cutback often disfigures the conical shape of the tree.

If that doesn't sound as though it will work for you, transplant the spruces somewhere else in your yard where they will have room to grow as large as they need to. Select another, smaller tree for your garden—one with a mature size that fits the site.

SWEET GUM

Seedless sweet gum

We'd like to plant a sweet gum tree but don't want those spiny seed balls, which are a nuisance. Are there any that don't develop the gum balls?

American sweet gum (*Liquidambar styraciflua*) has male and female flowers on the same tree, so every tree can set fruit. There are a few cultivars that make a claim of bearing "few fruit," but they aren't common. You may have to search for them. Cherokee and columnar 'Shadow' are hardy to Zone 5. 'Rotundiloba' is hardy to Zone 6.

TREE FERN

Tree fern care

The home I just moved into has some type of ferny-branched tree at the entryway. What type of care does this plant need other than the automatic sprinklers below and the misting tubes from above?

My guess is that you have a tree fern. Tree ferns display beautiful, finely cut fronds on top of a treelike stem and are somewhat prehistoric in appearance. They do best in moist, well-drained soil and partial to full shade in frost-free zones. They do not like hot, dry, windy weather and should be sprayed with the garden hose during these times (hence the misting tubes). Periodically check your watering system to make sure it is working correctly to keep your plants from drying out.

WALNUT

Walnut toxicity

My black walnut tree is making my front yard dull and barren. I understand that the roots of the walnut will kill 99 percent of the flowers and shrubs planted anywhere near it. The yard receives sun all morning. Are there any plants that can survive these seemingly impossible conditions?

Although there is not a lot of conclusive scientific research on which plants thrive in proximity to black walnuts, there is much anecdotal information. An abundance of bulbs, herbs, perennials, shrubs, and annuals will grow under and near walnuts. Juglone is the substance secreted by black walnut (*Juglans nigra*), English walnut (*J. regia*), and butternut (*J. cinerea*) that is toxic to many vegetables and other garden plants.

Juglone-resistant plants include tulip (*Tulipa*), daffodil (*Narcissus*), Japanese maple (*Acer palmatum*), lilac (*Syringa*), foxglove (*Digitalis*), lady's mantle (*Alchemilla mollis*), purple coneflower (*Echinacea purpurea*), perennial geranium (*Geranium*), parsley (*Petroselinum crispum*), lavender (*Lavandula angustifolia*), begonia (*Begonia*), and impatiens (*Impatiens walleriana*). Many of the plants just mentioned are also shade-tolerant, so they would do well in your afternoon-shaded yard.

WILLOW

Weeping willow

I have been told not to plant weeping willows because they are hard on water. Is this true? I love weeping trees. Are there any others that are safer to plant?

Willows (*Salix babylonica*) aren't necessarily hard on water, but they do prefer a lot of moisture. Their root systems can be invasive in sewer systems. They are weak-wooded and messy, dropping branches during storms. In addition, they are subject to numerous disease and insect problems. Weeping willows have their place along the shorelines of lakes or for stabilizing riverbanks, but they are a poor choice for most home landscapes.

Many other trees have weeping forms, including birch, beech, pine, and crabapple. And these trees are much more suited to home landscapes than willows. Weeping forms aren't as common in the retail trade, so if you can't find a good selection at your local nursery, you may need to order one from an online nursery or mail-order source.

Willow root problem

I have a weeping willow in my backyard that I planted when my now 17-year-old son was born. It is beautiful, albeit messy. I had a sidewalk put in that runs alongside the tree. A large root has lifted the sidewalk to a point where it is now a hazard. Can I cut that root without harming the tree?

An established weeping willow can be problematic. Not only is it short-lived, it's messy and has an invasive root system. As a rule, tree roots larger than 2 inches in diameter should not be cut through. Willows regenerate roots readily, so they may not be as sensitive to root loss as some other types of trees. However, removal of a large root may also compromise the structural safety of the tree. Large roots act as structural support for the tree. (The smaller roots at the tip of the big one also take up water and nutrients.) Loss of a large support root could weaken the tree and make it more likely to blow over in a windstorm.

Weeping willow and septic systems

I have a weeping willow and a septic system in my yard. I was told that this tree will wreak havoc with the system. What can I do to prevent this from becoming a problem?

Weeping willows have invasive root systems that proliferate when given the right amount of water, nutrients, and oxygen. A leach field sets up the ideal conditions for root growth of these trees. It's likely that your tree will eventually send roots in the direction of your leach field and clog it. Before problems develop, it would be wise to remove the tree. Remember that tree roots can extend 3 to 4 times the expanse of the branches, so even if your willow is planted a good distance from the leach field, the roots may eventually grow into it.

SHRUBS IN GENERAL

When to prune

When is the best time to prune shrubs? I have several different kinds in my yard.

As they mature, many trees and shrubs need some pruning to encourage pleasing, healthy form. Pruning encourages flower and fruit production and allows more light and air to reach the inner branches. When pruning, always use sharp, clean tools, and prune at the correct time during the year. Here are some guidelines.

- Spring-flowering shrubs such as lilac *(Syringa)*, viburnum *(Viburnum)*, and forsythia *(Forsythia)* should be pruned right after they bloom.
- Summer-flowering shrubs such as butterfly bush *(Buddleia)*, beautyberry *(Callicarpa)*, and crape myrtle *(Lagerstroemia)* should be pruned in early spring before new growth begins.
- Remove branches to achieve a desirable shape.
- Prune evergreen shrubs after new growth begins. Prune mugo pines only in the candle stage (while the new shoots are elongating). Prune shrubby spruces, junipers, and yews just after new growth begins through midsummer. Boxwoods can be pruned in late spring and early summer, especially if you are training them into topiary shapes.

Reasons to prune

We've had our landscape planted for about 4 years. Some of the shrubs are starting to look a little ragged. Should I prune them?

One of the main reasons to prune shrubs is to guide their natural growth. Many shrubs grow rapidly and become overgrown, excessively twiggy, and weighted down with too much foliage. This bushiness eventually obscures the shrubs' structure, reduces flowering, and invites fungal disease. Periodic pruning makes shrubs healthier and more attractive.

Pruning to control size is a waste of time; shrubs just grow back. Instead, guide your shrubs so they reach full size and have strong stems and healthy foliage. If you need a smaller plant, consider replacing the shrub with a dwarf variety.

Clip branches individually; only hedges should be sheared. The idea is to groom the shrub to curb unruliness rather than change its basic form. It shouldn't be obvious at first glance that the shrub was just pruned.

Shrub revitalization

I moved into an old house this past winter. When the snow melted, I discovered an overgrown row of shrubs. My first thought was to yank them out, but that seems like a lot of work. What do you suggest?

Wait! Before you go to the cost and effort of replacing your shrubs, see whether they can be revitalized. Renovation involves using good pruning techniques to cut the oldest and thickest stems down to ground level and remove them. In your case, it sounds as though most of the stems are likely to be pruning candidates, so you'll need a little patience. The basic rule of thumb is to cut out no more than one-third of the bush at a time. This maintains the shrub's presence in the yard while stimulating its root system to send up vigorous replacement stems. If done gradually over several years, this process completely renews old shrubs. These shrubs respond well to renovation.

- Barberry *(Berberis)*
- Beautyberry *(Callicarpa americana)*
- Bottlebrush buckeye *(Aesculus parviflora)*
- Deutzia *(Deutzia gracilus)*
- Flowering almond *(Prunus triloba)*
- Flowering dogwood *(Cornus florida)*
- Flowering quince *(Chaenomeles speciosa)*
- Forsythia *(Forsythia ×intermedia)*
- Kerria *(Kerria japonica)*
- Lilac *(Syringa)*
- Mockorange *(Philadelphus coronarius)*
- Privet *(Ligustrum)*
- Rose of Sharon *(Hibiscus syriacus)*
- Spirea *(Spiraea)*
- Staghorn sumac *(Rhus typhina)*
- Weigela *(Weigela florida)*

QUICK TIP

Revitalizing shrubs

1. Thin the shrub when it's dormant by removing the oldest and thickest stems. After several years, shrub stems become crowded. Their leaves and flowers are sparser, and they look disheveled.
2. Use long-handled loppers to cut stems up to 1 inch in diameter. Cut each stem 1–2 feet above the ground and remove it, giving you room to properly cut the stub at ground level.
3. Use a pruning saw to cut stems larger than 1 inch in diameter. A narrow, pointed saw fits into tight spaces between crowded stems and makes a smooth cut.

Remove about one-third of the stems each year or two for thorough renovation. Cut back extra-long stems to normal length. If the leaves have emerged, avoid cutting off all the stems, or the shrub may not grow new shoots.

Four-season shrubs

What shrubs can I plant for year-round appeal? I'd like a shrub that looks good for more than a couple of weeks in the spring.

One of the great advantages of shrubs is that they combine the year-round presence of trees with the seasonal color of many herbaceous plants. As you plan your landscape, take a closer look at this list of handsome shrubs. Many are North American natives and are widely adaptable throughout the country for year-round appeal. One or more will surely be compatible with your soil conditions, climate, and garden design.

- Bottlebrush buckeye *(Aesculus parviflora)*. Grow bottlebrush buckeye for its tall spires of white flowers in late spring or early summer (much later than most other buckeyes), its mounded growth habit, its lush foliage throughout the summer, and its clear yellow foliage in fall. Bottlebrush slowly spreads to fill a planting area or cover part of a wooded slope. It's not fussy about soil or habitat. It grows best in shade; however, like many plants, it becomes denser and flowers more profusely in brighter locations. 10 feet tall. Zones 5–9.
- Common lilac *(Syringa vulgaris)*. Although the old favorites are good, some of the more recent lilac introductions broaden the color selection, extend the blooming season, and provide increased resistance to leaf mildew. Flower colors range from white to pink to lavender to purple. Plant in alkaline or neutral, well-drained soil. Lilacs do best in regions that have hard freezes and thaws, because chilling temperatures produce radiant blooms later. 6–22 feet tall, depending on cultivar. Zones 3–7.
- Kerria *(Kerria japonica)*. A low, arching shrub that functions equally well as a tall ground cover, Kerria spreads slowly into a dense clump. Its flowers are yellow and showy in spring, with bright twig coloration that lasts all winter. Double-flowering and variegated forms are available. Every few years, cut the plant to the ground in early spring to remove any winter damage. It tolerates sun or shade in most soils. 4–5 feet tall. Zones 5–9.
- Leatherleaf viburnum *(Viburnum ×rhytidophylloides)*. This hybrid combines white spring flower clusters and long-lasting pink and/or red fruit that ripens to black in late summer through fall with semievergreen foliage. It grows in full sun or partial shade in moist or dry neutral or acidic soil. 8 feet tall. Zones 5–8.
- Northern Lights azaleas *(Rhododendron* Northern Lights). Unlike most other rhododendrons, many of which are equally spectacular in mild climates, Northern Lights, bred in Minnesota, will survive temperatures as low as -40°F. Look for the cultivars 'White Lights', 'Rosy Lights', and 'Golden Lights', all named for their flower colors. They like partial shade and thrive in the same well-drained, organic, and acidic soils preferred by other rhododendrons. 5–6 feet tall. Zones 4–7.

- Oakleaf hydrangea *(Hydrangea quercifolia)*. Although most hydrangeas are grown for their summer blooms, oakleaf hydrangea also has rich crimson fall color, attractive fruit sprays, and peeling bark on old stems. Even though it grows well in moist, fertile soil, it's also more drought-tolerant than some of its cousins. 6–10 feet tall. Zones 5–9.
- Smooth sumac *(Rhus glabra)*. This shrub has tiny yellow flowers in summer followed by scarlet fruits that persist all winter. The signature red fall color arrives in early autumn. A rare cut-leaf cultivar, 'Laciniata', has extremely attractive red leaf stalks that become stunning in fall when the leaves turn, giving the shrub a two-tone effect. Plant in sun to light-shade areas in almost any soil. It readily spreads into a dense grouping of stems. 8–9 feet tall. Zones 3–9.
- Spicebush *(Lindera benzoin)*. Spicebush produces a haze of fragrant tiny greenish-yellow flowers in early spring, generates scarlet berries on female plants in late summer, and breaks out in yellow during the fall. It serves as a host plant to several species of butterflies, and its aromatic twigs are often used to stir herbal teas. Plant it in deep shade. Spicebush isn't picky about soil quality as long as it has adequate moisture. 12–15 feet tall. Zones 5–9.
- Vernal witch hazel *(Hamamelis vernalis)*. Clinging to upright limbs, vernal witch hazel's spidery yellow or reddish flowers are a sure sign that winter is winding down. (Flowers vary in size and color; choose your plant at the nursery when it is in bloom.) It has thick leaves that remain attractive all summer and, in autumn, turn a pleasing yellow that repeats the flower color. Vernal witch hazel tolerates a range of soil conditions in sun or shade. 10–12 feet tall. Zones 4–8.

How to shape shrubs

I've found information on when to prune my shrubs, but I'm still not clear on exactly how to go about it. Can you help?

When shaping shrubs, your best results will come from honoring their natural growth habit. Each shrub is genetically programmed for a certain size, shape, and branching pattern. Prune in ways that support these features and preserve each plant's character. Some of the more common pruning methods are outlined below. These techniques are for specific plants, but you can use them on plants with similar habits.

Forsythia

Overgrown shrubs look unkempt and unattractive and don't bloom well. Thinning the dense foliage-covered branches of forsythia allows light and air to penetrate and improve the plant's health.

Cut back excessively long branches. Clip them off where a leaf emerges on the stem, near the main mass of foliage. Vary the lengths of the cuts to avoid a sheared look. Reach deep within the plant to clip off particularly large or twiggy branches at the point where they join a main branch. Once you have established the general shape of the plant, give the shrub a final once-over. Be sure no branches rub against walls or tangle in nearby plants.

Evergreen hedges

To shape an evergreen hedge, taper the sides so the lower branches are wider than those at the top. If the sun reaching foliage on the sides of the hedge is insufficient, the foliage will die back. To stimulate growth, trim a hedge with hedge shears or electric clippers below the desired height in spring. When you prune later in the season, remove only a portion of new growth.

Boxwood

Boxwood is commonly used as a hedge shrub because it tolerates repeated shearing. Consider boxwood for individual plantings too; it contributes attractive, fine-textured evergreen foliage to a mixed border. To prune a boxwood that's not in a hedge, use hand pruners, rather than hedge shears, to clip off individual branches that protrude from the main body of the shrub. Cut the branches at slightly different lengths to avoid creating a sheared shape.

Shrubs for shade

When I moved to my home 23 years ago, the yard was sunny. Now I have shade because the trees I planted have grown up. What shade-tolerant shrubs should replace my sun-loving shrubs?

Look to nature for suggestions of shrubs that like shade. What shrubs grow naturally in the forest understory in your region? They should thrive in your shady yard as well. Here are a few shrubs that tolerate shade and still do beautifully.

- Beautyberry *(Callicarpa americana)* offers pink flowers in spring and early summer. These flowers give way to clusters of unusual violet fruits. This native shrub prefers a spot in partial to full shade and moist but well-drained soil. 6 feet tall and 5 feet wide. Zones 5–9.
- Glorybower *(Clerodendrum bungei)* bears clusters of fragrant dark pink flowers in late summer and autumn. A fast spreader, it is considered invasive by some gardeners. Plant it in partial to full shade and moist but well-drained soil. 6 feet tall and wide. Zones 8–10.
- Mountain laurel *(Kalmia latifolia)* produces beautiful clusters of pink, red, or white flowers in late spring and summer. It prefers afternoon shade and rich, well-drained soil. A relative of rhododendrons, it also needs acidic soil. 10 feet tall and wide. Zones 5–9.
- Oregon grapeholly *(Mahonia aquifolium)* offers yellow flowers in spring and blue-black berries in summer. A native plant, it prefers part shade and well-drained soil. 3 feet tall and 5 feet wide. Zones 5–9.

- Pagoda dogwood *(Cornus alternifolia)* produces small clusters of white flowers in early summer. If pollinated, the blooms give way to clusters of blue-black berries, which are loved by birds. A native plant, it prefers afternoon shade and moist but well-drained soil. 20 feet tall and wide. Zones 4–8.
- Summersweet *(Clethra alnifolia)* produces fragrant clusters of white or pink flowers in late summer and early autumn, a time when few other shrubs bloom. This native plant prefers partial to full shade and moist, acidic, well-drained soil. 8 feet tall and wide. Zones 3–9.

More shrubs for shade

Which shrubs or small trees do best in morning sun and afternoon shade? I'd like to have a colorful display of flowers.

Morning sun and afternoon shade are ideal for many plants that prefer partial shade. If your plants will live in afternoon shade, you can choose from various azaleas and rhododendrons *(Rhododendron)*, mountain laurel *(Kalmia latifolia)*, summersweet *(Clethra alnifolia)*, fothergilla *(Fothergilla major)*, smooth hydrangea *(Hydrangea arborescens)*, most viburnums *(Viburnum)*, and dogwoods, including kousa dogwood *(Cornus kousa)*, flowering dogwood *(C. florida)*, and pagoda dogwood *(C. alternifolia)*. Even though the area sees some sun, it may not be enough for sun-loving shrubs and trees to do well.

Shrubs for acidic soil

I'm looking for an acid-loving shrub to plant in a sunny spot. What do you recommend?

Many of the most common plants that thrive in acid soil also prefer partial shade. You do have choices, however, that will grow well in full sun. Some varieties of azaleas *(Rhododendron)*, such as the Northern Lights series, appreciate full sun in Zones 4–10. Blueberries *(Vaccinum)* are a good choice to add fall color and fruiting in Zones 3–9. Manzanita *(Arctostaphylos)* adapts to sunny acidic sites in Zones 8–10. Scotch heather *(Calluna vulgaris)* and winter heath *(Erica carnea)* are shrubby perennials for Zones 5–7. Most hollies *(Ilex)*, Zones 3–9, will grow in acidic sites in full sun. And dwarf forms of spruce *(Picea)*, such as bird's nest spruce, or pines *(Pinus)* would also be good choices. Various selections of these conifers are hardy in Zones 2–10.

Shrubs for wet site
Can you recommend some shrubs that would grow in a wet area?

Many landscapes have wet spots where it is difficult for shrubs to survive. Changing the grade or improving soil drainage are options, but they're costly and may require the assistance of a professional landscape contractor. A few shrubs adapted to wet sites include bayberry *(Myrica)*, buttonbush *(Cephalanthus occidentalis)*, pussy willow *(Salix discolor)*, red-osier dogwood *(Cornus stolonifera)*, spicebush *(Lindera benzoin)*, summersweet *(Clethra alnifolia)*, and winterberry *(Ilex verticillata)*.

Pruning overgrown shrubs
I just moved into a house that is surrounded by an overgrown landscape. Is it possible to chop some of the shrubs down and hope they regrow? Are there some I need to be more careful with?

Many gardeners inherit shrubs that have been neglected for years. In that time the shrubs may develop weak stems, tall twiggy growth, and leafless "legs."

If a shrub is pruned annually for 4–6 years after it is planted, it will develop a pleasing form and refined growth habit. Pruning in subsequent years will require less effort.

Obviously your shrubs did not receive annual early-life pruning. Overgrown shrubs can be reclaimed using one of two pruning methods. The appropriate method is determined by the growth habit of the shrub. Some plants, such as barberry *(Berberis)*, can handle renewal pruning (clipping off all the branches 4–6 inches above ground level) and will spring forth with healthy new growth. Other plants, such as rhododendron *(Rhododendron)*, may die if cut back severely. But these sensitive types can be shaped with rejuvenation pruning.

Perform renewal pruning in late winter or early spring, before the shrub begins to grow. Clip off all the stems 4–6 inches above ground level. The plant will send up new shoots during the growing season. The following winter, selectively remove about a third of the stems, keeping those that create an attractive framework. After that, prune the shrub annually to maintain the desired form. See the following page for a list of plants that can be pruned in this manner.

Rejuvenation pruning is a 3-year process. In year one, cut back one-third of the old, woody stems to ground level. In year two, remove half of the remaining old stems; in year three, cut back all remaining old, woody stems. Pruning stimulates the production of new shoots. Prune the new shoots yearly, heading them back as necessary to maintain the size and shape plant you desire.

The following plants will withstand renewal pruning.

Barberry *(Berberis)*
Bluebeard *(Caryopteris ×clandonensis)*
Bush cinquefoil *(Potentilla fruticosa)*
Butterfly bush *(Buddleia davidii)*
Crape myrtle *(Lagerstroemia indica)*
Flowering quince *(Chaenomeles)*
Forsythia *(Forsythia ×intermedia)*
Glossy abelia *(Abelia ×grandiflora)*
Heavenly bamboo *(Nandina domestica)*
Mockorange *(Philadelphus coronarius)*
Ninebark *(Physocarpus opulifolius)*
Privet *(Ligustrum)*
Redtwig dogwood *(Cornus alba* 'Sibirica'*)*
Russian almond *(Prunus tenella)*
Shrub roses *(Rosa)*
Spirea *(Spiraea)*
Weigela *(Weigela)*

Forcing bloom

What does forcing a pussy willow mean? I have a pussy willow; should I be pruning it?

Forcing refers to clipping a few branches in late winter or early spring and spurring them into bloom indoors. Forcing spring-flowering trees and shrubs into bloom in late winter is a fun way to shake off the winter doldrums. Collect a handful of 20-inch-long twigs from plants such as pussy willow, forsythia, flowering quince, peach, and redbud. Soak the twigs in room-temperature water in a bathtub or large bucket, then stand the twigs in a vase of water located in a cool, bright spot. The buds will swell and the flowers will open slowly. If the cuttings are taken close to their natural flowering time, the twigs will begin blooming in a few days. If the cuttings are taken in midwinter, it might take several weeks for flowering to occur. Change the water frequently to prevent bacterial growth.

Your pussy willow *(Salix discolor)* will benefit from annual pruning after it blooms in early spring. Trim away dead and diseased growth, and head back vigorous branches to maintain size and shape.

How can I keep my hedges looking good? They die out in the middle.

Hedges often turn brown in the middle without proper care. Luckily, maintenance is relatively easy.

If you prune your hedge into a formal shape, clip the top of the hedge narrower than the bottom so light can reach the lower branches.

Instead of shearing hedges flat, stagger your cuts. Prune some branches deeper inside the plant and others closer to the edges. This allows more light to reach the middle of the plant, keeping it from dying out.

In areas with heavy snowfall, prune formal hedges to have rounded tops. This will help protect them from heavy snow accumulation, which can break branches.

What can you suggest for a hedge 4–6 feet tall?

Would you like a sheared formal hedge or a looser informal one? Will the hedge be in sun or shade? How much trimming and pruning are you willing (or wanting) to do? Do you need the hedge to provide year-round screening or simply create a barrier? All these are questions you should consider in deciding what plants to use for your hedge.

A mixed deciduous shrub border that is densely planted offers several advantages. With a variety of plants, you can have bloom at different times of the year. You can choose plants with fall color and good winter interest. And perhaps most importantly, if one of the shrubs dies, it won't destroy the look of the entire hedge. A mixed hedge is definitely informal in appearance, and because deciduous shrubs lose their leaves in winter, you won't have a complete screen year-round.

For shrubs in the 4–6-foot range, consider summersweet *(Clethra alnifolia)*, which flowers in midsummer and is fragrant. It prefers moist, acidic soil. Oakleaf hydrangea *(Hydrangea quercifolia)* adds coarse texture, late-summer bloom, and interesting exfoliating bark in winter. Large fothergilla *(Fothergilla major)* flowers in May and has nice fall color. Regent serviceberry *(Amelanchier alnifolia* 'Regent') flowers in early spring; develops tasty berries in early summer; and turns flaming red, orange, and gold in fall. Black chokeberry *(Aronia melanocarpa)* also has white flowers in spring, berries that hang on through the winter, and good red fall color.

If you decide on an evergreen hedge, think about yew *(Taxus)*. Yew is an excellent shade-tolerant evergreen that can be sheared, but it needs well-drained soil. 'Hicksii' is a cultivar often used for hedging. Boxwood *(Buxus)* is a slow-growing broadleaf evergreen often used as a hedge. Canadian hemlock *(Tsuga canadensis)* is another choice, provided that the soil is well-drained and slightly acidic. It will require shearing to keep it at the height you desire.

ARBORVITAE

I am thinking about planting arborvitaes along my fence. If I purchase 2-foot-tall plants, how long will it take for them to reach 4–6 feet in height?

The speed at which any plant grows depends on the growing conditions (soil, moisture, light, and so forth), weather, and the particular variety (some varieties grow faster than others). Often it takes a year or two for a plant to recover from transplanting; in the process, growth is limited. However, container-grown arborvitae *(Thuja)* may suffer little transplant shock. With good growing conditions, most arborvitae will add 3–12 inches of new growth per year, depending on variety. If your plants are moderate growers, it should take about 4–5 years for them to reach 4–6 feet in height.

Arborvitae for privacy

I want to plant a 100-yard-long hedge to screen my neighbors and discourage entry onto my property. I would prefer an evergreen hedge. Please recommend several species that I can plant.

One selection I'd consider above all others is Emerald ('Smaragd') arborvitae *(Thuja occidentalis* 'Smaragd'). It grows 15 feet tall and has a dense habit. One reason for its popularity is that its emerald green foliage holds its color, even in winter. It also tolerates cold and heat and is commonly available.

It's been my experience that planting smaller conifers as hedges is the way to go. At end-of-season clearance sales, I've found 2-foot plants for as little as $5. These small plants establish themselves quickly.

When you plant your hedge of Emerald arborvitae, space the shrubs about 4 feet apart, and dig a wide hole for each plant. Avoid planting conifers too deeply; dig planting holes no deeper than the height of the pot. Remove any cord or wires binding the root ball, as well as any material (such as burlap) covering the roots.

AZALEA

Galling problem

What causes galls on azaleas and other plants? Are they harmful? What should I do to get rid of them?

Many plants are susceptible to different kinds of galls. Galls are abnormal lumps that develop on a wide range of plant parts. Various types of insects—especially wasps (some are scarcely visible to the naked eye), aphids, mites, and midges—can cause galls. Insects feed on or lay their eggs in the leaves, stems, roots, or flowers of a plant, stimulating abnormal growth and causing the plant to grow around the eggs. Sometimes fungi, bacteria, or nematodes infect plants and cause galls. Azalea leaf and flower gall is caused by the fungus *Exobasidium vaccinii*. Galls generally aren't a severe problem, though a few can girdle stems and cause dieback. Once the gall has formed, protective insecticide or fungicide sprays will be ineffective. If the problem is minor, you can trim out the affected part of the plant. In most cases, no treatment is necessary.

Distressed azaleas

I take good care of my azaleas, but they continue to die. I know they should come back and grow even bigger the following year, but they don't even survive one growing season. Help!

Several things may be at the root of your azaleas' *(Rhododendron)* problem. First, azaleas prefer acidic soil. If your soil is alkaline, your plants will surely suffer. Test your garden soil's pH, and amend the soil to be more acidic if necessary.

Most azaleas prefer moist but well-drained soil, so make sure that the azaleas in your garden have adequate drainage. If the soil is poorly drained, add compost to loosen the soil, or grow the azaleas in a raised bed with better drainage. When you're adding azaleas to your garden, check the root ball. If the roots form a congested mass, make several shallow vertical slices through them with a sharp knife to promote root branching and establishment. Keep plants watered during times of drought. Azaleas' shallow roots don't tolerate dry conditions well.

Make certain that the azaleas you're growing are adapted to your locale. Contact your local cooperative extension office for a list of cultivars that thrive in your region. That way you can be sure that the varieties you buy and plant are hardy in your area. Be sure to purchase your azaleas from a reputable nursery or garden center. Ask questions, and read labels. Some stores may carry plants that are not fully hardy in your location.

Scheduling bloom

How do I get all my azaleas to bloom at once?

If you grow different varieties of azaleas, there's nothing you can do to get them to bloom at once. Each variety has its own individual timetable.

If they're all the same variety, they should bloom pretty much together if given identical growing conditions. For example, plants that receive more moisture may bloom earlier or later than plants of the same variety that receive less moisture. Thus, to synchronize their flowering cycles, give like plants the same amount of moisture, fertilizer, and exposure to sun and wind. Also, test the soil to make sure that different planting areas contain similar amounts of organic matter and have the same level of acidity (pH).

Pruning azalea

When is the best time to prune azaleas?

It's best to prune azaleas right after their flowers fade. Deadhead deciduous and evergreen azaleas by pinching off wilted blooms between your thumb and forefinger. To keep azaleas looking natural, eliminate dead wood, cutting back the oldest stems at the base.

Azalea rebloom

If I cut the wilted flowers from my azaleas, will they bloom again this year? I've heard that deadheading promotes rebloom.

I'm sorry to say that azaleas bloom only once a season. Some types of plants will reward you with a second flush of bloom if the first blossoms are cut off as they fade. Unfortunately, azaleas and most other woody shrubs lack this capability. Although taking off dead flowers won't make the plants bloom again, it will make them look better. When the flowers are spent, snap them off where they join the center of the leaf clusters.

Color change for azaleas

I have pink azaleas in front of my house. I don't like the salmon-pink color and would prefer something darker or lighter. How can I change the color of the flowers?

Many gardeners have heard that they can change the bloom color of plants by manipulating the soil's pH. Although this is true for hydrangeas, it's not the case for most other plants (including azaleas). If you want a different color of azalea, I'm afraid you'll have to remove your current plants and replace them with a different variety.

Transplanting florist azalea

I received a potted azalea. I've kept it outside, and it's doing well. I'd like to transplant it into my yard. I know it likes acidic soil, but I don't know how much sun/shade it needs.

Azaleas sold by florists and other retailers as gift plants require well-drained, acidic soil (around pH 5.5–6.0) and partial shade. Although well-drained soil is a must, they appreciate good moisture—keep them from drying out, especially in times of drought. Most florist azaleas are hardy in Zones 7–10. Gardeners who live outside that range will need to treat the plants as annuals or short-lived gift plants.

BOXWOOD

Boxwood pruning

Can boxwoods be pruned or cut back at any time?

Whether you are sculpting boxwood (*Buxus*) into a perfect orb or simply shaping it a little, prune it in late winter and again in mid- to late June. For a graceful, natural appearance, trim boxwood by hand.

Over time, boxwood often develops a leafy outer shell and a twiggy interior. Maintain a dense, leafy interior by increasing light penetration. To do this, annually thin the plant by snapping out 6–8-inch-long twigs by hand at major branches.

Planting boxwood

I want to plant a small hedge of boxwood around my herb garden. What varieties do you recommend?

Boxwood is an excellent choice for edging beds or paths and can be grown in sun or moderate shade. It will grow in soils with a pH range of 5.0–7.5. Littleleaf boxwood (*Buxus microphylla*) and common boxwood (*B. sempervirens*) are widely available. Littleleaf boxwood has small medium-green leaves, which often turn a yellowish green in winter. Common boxwood has larger darker green leaves but is reliably hardy only into Zone 6. Korean boxwood (*B. microphylla koreana*) is an extremely hardy form of littleleaf boxwood. It can be grown in protected sites in Zone 4 and throughout Zone 5. Some hybrids have been selected for hardiness and good winter color. These include Chicagoland Green, Green Gem, 'Green Ice', 'Green Mountain', 'Green Mound', and Green Velvet. All are hardy in Zones 5–9.

BUTTERFLY BUSH

Beautifying butterfly bush

I purchased a butterfly bush last year. Should I prune off last year's branches? If so, when?

I'm glad to hear you had success with your butterfly bush *(Buddleia davidii)* last year! Sometimes the plants are fussy about growing in Zones 4 and 5. In these zones, treat butterfly bush as a perennial (not a shrub), and prune it to ground level in late winter. Most winters, the plant will be killed back to the ground in these areas, but it will send up new shoots from its root system in spring. Butterfly bush waits until the soil is warm before emerging in spring, so allow plenty of time for your plant to send up new shoots.

In warmer areas, gardeners can cut back their butterfly bush or leave it standing. If the bush is not cut back, however, the shoots become scraggly. For more compact form and a tidier appearance, cut back all old stems to about 4–6 inches above the ground in late winter or early spring. Because butterfly bush blooms on new growth, no blooms will be sacrificed.

CAMELLIA

Buds, no blooms

My camellias get many buds, but only one or two open. The rest turn brown and hard. In spring and summer the shrubs get morning sun and afternoon shade. I also have difficulty keeping azaleas alive in the same bed. What's up?

Because your azaleas won't grow either, my guess is that your soil isn't acidic enough. Both species need acidic soil. Test your soil to determine its pH. Once you know the soil pH, make the necessary adjustments. (Sulfur is typically used to lower soil pH.) Also, feed your camellias in early spring with a fertilizer designed especially for acid-loving plants.

If the shrubs are next to the house, the soil may be alkaline because of minerals leaching from concrete-based construction materials. If that's the case, move the shrubs away from the house into a protected bed that gets morning sun. Amend the area with organic matter, and set the crown a bit high in the soil.

Two years ago I planted two camellias, one on each side of my front porch steps. The leaves have started curling and are pale. Why is this happening?

If the plants are near your porch and under an overhang, they may not be getting enough water. It's easy to overlook an overhang when planning the landscape—until the plants dry out. Young plants recently transplanted are particularly sensitive to drying because their roots are limited to a small root ball. Water your camellias (*Camellia*) regularly, or move them farther away from the overhang where they can get sufficient natural rainfall.

Another possibility is the steps. Are they concrete? And are the camellia roots near them? If so, the lime that naturally leaches from the concrete may be harming the camellias. In order to thrive, camellias need acidic soil. Check the soil pH around the camellia roots. Acidify the soil by adding sulfur if necessary. Working in a little peat moss may help too. And be certain to used an acid-based fertilizer (often sold as evergreen and azalea food).

Yet another potential cause for leaf curl on your camellias is herbicide injury. Have you applied a broadleaf weed killer to nearby lawn? Your camellias could have gotten a dose of the weed killer either from drift through the air or uptake through their roots. The roots of most woody plants spread several times beyond the reach of their branches, so it's likely that your camellias have some roots under a lawn that may be 15–20 feet or more away from them.

Can a camellia be moved? If so, when do I do it? I am moving and would love to take this beauty with me.

Yes, a camellia can be moved. You'll have the best success moving a young plant in late winter or early spring, before new growth begins. Because this plant is evergreen, dig as large a root ball as possible and transplant it immediately. Add a generous amount of organic matter, such as compost, leaf mold, or coarse peat, to the soil. Avoid planting too deeply; the base of the stem should be slightly higher than the surrounding soil.

If your shrub is large, chances are it will not transplant well. You may be happier purchasing a young plant to start at your new location. With proper siting and care, it will soon catch up to where the older plant would be.

CANDLESTICK PLANT

Candlestick confusion

I recently bought three candlestick plants and planted them in full sun, 2 feet apart. The person at the nursery said they would grow quite large before blooming. What do you know about this plant?

When Texans talk about candlestick plants, they mean *Senna alata*, which used to be classified as *Cassia alata* (and is still commonly sold by some nurseries under that name). This plant also is popular in Florida, where it is often called candlebrush or candle bush. It is a fast-growing legume from Malaysia that often blooms the first year from seed. The plants may become dormant in winter where temperatures drop below about 40°F. In warmer climates, candlestick plants grow as evergreens, sometimes reaching a majestic 30 feet tall.

To get the most bloom from your plants, pinch them back in mid-spring to help induce branching. You can fertilize the plants then, too, but avoid feeding them in late summer. Plants that have to fight for ample nutrition often bloom better than those that are overfed. Expect the plants to be aflame with bright yellow blossoms in autumn. The central spike that rises from the flower clusters is the candlestick.

I've grown candlestick plant in central Iowa as a dramatic tropical foliage plant. It doesn't bloom from seed the first year, but it does grow 4–5 feet tall and develop dramatically large compound leaves. It's not hardy here, so you must start new plants from seed each year or overwinter plants in containers indoors.

DOGWOOD

Prune for good color

When and how should I prune my redtwig dogwood?

Prune your plant in late winter or early spring. Remove about one-third of the oldest, thickest canes to encourage new, vigorous canes to develop. These new canes will decorate your landscape with splashes of red this fall and winter, because 1-year-old twigs have the intense fiery red color that gives redtwig dogwood (*Cornus alba* 'Sibirica') its name. If you continue to remove one-third of the oldest stems each year, your dogwood will always have brightly colored, vigorous shoots.

Overgrown redtwig dogwoods can also be cut back completely to 6 inches above ground level. They will quickly send up new shoots.

When we bought our first home, we inherited some really overgrown shrubs. I've figured out what most of the plants are, but I need your help with the redtwig dogwoods. When should I prune these shrubs, before or after they bloom?

Redtwig dogwood (*Cornus alba* 'Sibirica') and red-osier dogwood (*C. stolonifera*) bear small white flowers, but unlike their treelike cousin flowering dogwood, they are primarily prized for their colorful red stems. Prune them in late winter or early spring while they are still dormant. First remove any dead or damaged stems. In addition, remove about a third of the oldest stems annually. The new shoots that sprout from the ground will have a brighter red color in winter. You could also prune them down to the ground annually so they put on all new growth and stay more compact. Depending on their location, redtwig dogwoods can grow to be 10 feet tall and 10 feet across.

EUONYMUS

Scorched burning bushes

The leaves on my burning bushes are drying up. The plants line my home's foundation and get plenty of water. I put a weed-and-feed product on that section of the yard but kept it 3 feet away from the burning bushes.

Burning bush (*Euonymus alatus*) is prized for its brilliant red fall foliage. However, in some regions it has become an invasive plant. It can also be susceptible to leaf scorch, a problem caused by hot temperatures. It's usually more severe on younger branches. Although you say your plants are getting a lot of water, I wonder whether it's enough. Growing along a foundation exposes them to high temperatures and perhaps soil that dries out quickly. If your roof has an overhang, the soil next to the foundation may be extremely dry. I'd be sure to keep the plants well mulched and use a drip system for watering near their roots.

If the weed-and-feed product you used contains dicamba, it could be leaching into the root zone of your burning bushes and causing the drying. Dicamba is taken up through the roots of plants, so it need not come into direct contact with your shrubs to cause injury. The roots of your burning bushes likely spread 10 feet or more into the lawn.

If you do lose your plants, consider replacing them with native plants such as red chokeberry (*Aronia arbutifolia*) or Virginia sweetspire (*Itea virginica*). Once established, these shrubs are relatively care-free and should live for many years.

**Can you give me some information on 'Greenlane' euonymus?
It appears on a landscape blueprint of my yard. I assume it is a
ground cover.**

Wintercreeper, or *Euonymus fortunei* 'Greenlane', is an evergreen shrub that often grows as a ground cover. It grows well in partial shade, but tolerates full shade. Although the young plants may be small, they mature to 3–4 feet tall and spread to 6 feet. Wintercreeper is hardy in Zones 5–9.

These plants aren't for every garden though: They're considered invasive in some areas because they might escape from gardens and naturalize in the wild. Wintercreeper has been added to several invasive plant lists. Check with your county extension service to find whether it's all right to grow it in your yard.

FLOWERING MAPLE

Thrips on flowering maple

**I have a pest problem with thrips on flowering maple (*Abutilon*).
I like to use organic methods, especially on a plant that
hummingbirds like. How can I handle those pests?**

With many pests that multiply rapidly, thrips included, it's not so much what you use but how methodically you use it that determines success or failure. Thrips can be killed with a simple solution of oil-based soap and water. Try insecticidal soap or 2 tablespoons of Murphy Oil Soap in ½ gallon of water. Spray the solution only when the air is cool so the oil doesn't burn the foliage.

Thrips are tenacious. Sprays usually don't kill their eggs, and adult thrips can fly in from nearby plants. Check thrips-prone plants faithfully at three- to five-day intervals for any new damage and deal with it promptly. Some species of thrips damage flowers and leaves, leaving them silvery or bleached, wilted, and spotted with minute red-black excrement. Others damage flowers in the bud so the emerging blooms are brown-streaked or distorted.

Organic controls are no different from other pest-control strategies in that they have consequences beyond the target plant. Even soap might put off hummingbirds, because it can spoil the nectar's taste. The first tenet of organic gardening is to help the plant itself. Ensure that soil drainage is good and water plants on a regular schedule; soggy roots or drought cause water stress, which predisposes a plant to attack by thrips. Be sure that the plant has the amount of light it prefers, because it then has the energy it needs to produce its own insect-deterring chemicals. Monitor a thrips-susceptible plant regularly; if necessary, pick off infested buds and leaves.

FORSYTHIA

Nonblooming forsythia

Why didn't my forsythia bloom this spring? It bloomed fine last year.

There are a couple of common reasons for forsythias not blooming. In very cold winters, forsythia flower buds can be killed, eliminating bloom the following spring. Sometimes all flower buds above the snow line are killed, whereas buds near ground level are unaffected because those stems were insulated by the snow. Two forsythias with greater flower-bud hardiness are 'Meadowlark' and 'Northern Sun'. These cultivars will bloom even if the temperature dips to -30–35°F. Improper pruning is another common cause of lack of bloom. Forsythia flowers form on the previous season's growth, so pruning should be done immediately after the flowers fade. Pruning later in summer or fall removes the next year's flower buds.

GARDENIA

Gardenworthy gardenias

I love the fragrance of gardenias. Do you have recommendations for the best ones to grow?

Gardenia (*Gardenia*) varieties vary in size, cold hardiness, light preferences, and when and how often they bloom, so it's best to choose the variety that best suits your climate and site.

Gardenias	
Indoor gardenias	'White Gem' grows to 2 feet tall and makes a fine subject for indoor containers. Little 'Radicans', or dwarf gardenia, seldom grows more than 2 feet tall and can be grown in containers or as a ground cover.
Coastal South	The "everblooming" gardenia 'Veitchii' is popular for growing indoors in containers or outdoors in partial shade. It grows into a loose shrub that stands 4–5 feet tall. The newer variety First Love grows a little larger and has bigger blossoms.
California	The West Coast's favorite gardenia, 'Mystery', needs full or nearly full sun and grows 6–8 feet tall. The large, mostly double flowers are produced off and on all summer.
Mid-south and Northwest	Look for 'Kleim's Hardy' or 'Daisy'. Both grow to about 3 feet tall and are often hardy to 10°F. Grow these gardenias in protected nooks, such as snuggled up against the east side of your house.

Gardenia care

What do gardenias need to look their best? Mine aren't doing well.

With the rich aroma of jasmine tinged with spicy notes of nutmeg and vanilla, graceful white gardenia blooms smell as good as they look. Whether you grow them indoors in Alaska or outdoors in Miami, you can find a glorious gardenia *(Gardenia jasminoides)* to suit any setting.

Native to China, gardenias are semitropical evergreen shrubs. They'll thrive outdoors to Zone 7b, a range that includes much of the lower South, California, and the maritime Northwest. In addition to mild winters, gardenias need acidic soil. If you're missing one or both of these requirements, don't give up. Gardenias can be happy when grown in containers that are kept indoors during the winter and moved outside after the weather warms in spring. In Texas and other mild-winter climates where the soil is alkaline, grow gardenias in tubs filled with an acidic potting mix, such as potting soil amended with sphagnum peat moss, and keep them outdoors year-round.

However you grow gardenias, it's important to know about some common problems that are easier to prevent than to cure.

Yellow leaves

- Cool soil temperatures (below 70°F) during the growing season or a pH above 6.5 can cause gardenia leaves to turn yellow, because the plant can't absorb certain nutrients even when those nutrients are present.
- Gardenias grown outdoors often shed a few yellow leaves in winter, which is normal, but when you see yellowing leaves during the summer or on plants grown indoors, take corrective measures immediately.
- The best remedy for yellow leaves is to feed plants with a good azalea fertilizer, which contains the three major plant nutrients (nitrogen, phosphorus, and potassium) as well as sulfur, which helps acidify the soil. Even if you never see yellow leaves, feed gardenias monthly during the summer and at least once during the winter.
- Yellow leaves may also be a symptom of overwatering or an infestation of root-knot nematodes. If you live in central or southern Florida, grow gardenias that have been grafted onto nematode-resistant rootstocks. Unfortunately, these rootstocks are not hardy below 28°F, so they cannot help gardenia lovers in Zones 8 and 7b.

Blossom drop

- A gardenia that has lovely dark green leaves can still have problems producing flowers, particularly if the plant is grown indoors. It is heartbreaking to watch flower buds slowly form, then drop off just before they are ready to open. The causes could be too little light, over- or underwatering, high temperatures, or low humidity.

- Give your gardenia extra attention during late spring and autumn, when gardenias are most likely to bloom. Place the plant where it will get bright morning light and cool nighttime temperatures (about 55°F). A spare bedroom where the heating vents can be closed is often a good place. Check the soil every day or two and keep it lightly moist (but not wet) at all times, and keep the air humid around the plant. When the blooms open, take the plant into your favorite room, where the fragrance can be enjoyed to the fullest.
- Bloom problems on outdoor gardenias are most often due to improper pruning. Gardenias should be pruned only to control their size or to shape the plants. Plan before you plant so you don't have to constantly prune a plant to keep it in bounds. Most well-sited gardenias need little if any pruning. If you prune your plant, do so in early summer, after spring's flowers have come and gone. Buds that open in spring form in late summer or autumn.

Pests
- Prevent problems with aphids, spider mites, scale, and other small insects by spraying plants every 4–6 weeks with insecticidal soap. If you grow gardenias in pots outdoors in summer, always inspect plants and spray them with insecticidal soap before you bring them indoors in autumn to keep pests from moving in too.

HIBISCUS

Hot for hibiscus

I love the large-flowered tropical hibiscus. Is there a way I can grow this type in the North?

With some TLC, tropical hibiscus *(Hibiscus rosa-sinensis)* will reward you with blowsy red, pink, orange, or yellow flowers throughout the growing season. Hardy in Zones 9–11, this shrub blooms for months. It must live indoors during cool weather in most of the United States. Here's how to keep it healthy.
- Soil. Grow tropical hibiscus in a large pot with light, high-quality potting soil.
- Site. Set the pot in a sunny location. Tropical hibiscus needs at least 6 hours of direct sunlight a day.
- Temperature. Tropical hibiscus prefers temperatures between 60 and 90°F. Bring your plant indoors when nighttime temperatures drop to the range of 50–55°F. Exposure to temperatures of 30°F and below can kill plants outright; temperatures higher than 90°F can cause bud drop.
- Water. Water potted hibiscus as necessary during the growing season. The soil should be moist but not wet. Too much or too little water can kill the plant.
- Fertilizer. Feed your tropical hibiscus regularly. For potted plants, that means weekly feedings with a diluted liquid fertilizer or monthly feedings with a

timed-release granular product. Unlike many flowering plants that require high-phosphorus fertilizers, hibiscus needs a fertilizer high in potassium during its period of bloom. Some gardeners prefer a balanced fertilizer such as 20-20-20.

- Pest control. Use only pesticides labeled for hibiscus, because some chemicals can damage the plant. A few hours before applying the pesticide, water the plant to ensure that it is not moisture-stressed when the spray is applied.

Absence of blooms

I purchased a beautiful hibiscus plant last summer, and it bloomed all season long. In the autumn, I moved it to my indoor plant nursery. This spring, I returned it outdoors. The foliage is great, but I've had no flowers. I feed it, and still no blooms form. What am I doing wrong?

When you put your hibiscus back outdoors, did you repot it and give it fresh light-textured potting mix? That would help. Also, your garden may have had a slow warm-up this summer. Tropical hibiscus thrives in hot, humid conditions. When conditions are cool, the plant may grow attractive foliage but will be slow to bloom.

Hibiscus flower buds are especially vulnerable to environmental stresses. They may fall off when the temperature rises into the 90s. If that's the case, shade your plant during the hottest time of day. Insect problems also can cause bud drop, as can too much or too little water. A double-flowered hibiscus is more likely to drop its buds than single-flowered forms.

Pruning winter-injured hibiscus

I have a 6-foot-tall hibiscus. Due to freezing temperatures this winter, it looks dead. I heard that it should not be cut back until spring, and there is hope it will come back. Is this true, and how far back should it be cut?

The amount and timing of pruning for your hibiscus depends on what kind of hibiscus it is, and where you live.

Tropical hibiscus (*Hibiscus rosa-sinensis*) is hardy only in Zones 9–11. If winter temperatures dipped below about 20°F, and you have a tropical hibiscus, the plant is likely dead. However, you could wait until spring to see if anything sprouts. Sometimes the stems die back, but new shoots arise from the base of the plant. Wait until the weather warms in spring, then prune back to where new, healthy growth is emerging.

Hardy hibiscus (*H. moscheutos*) is root-hardy in Zones 4–9. Plants die back completely and can be cut back to within a couple of inches of the ground in late fall or early spring. New shoots will emerge from the crown of the plant in late spring after the weather has warmed up.

HONEYSUCKLE

Deformed honeysuckle

My honeysuckle is covered with weird, deformed shoots. They are twisted and bunched up. What is wrong with it? Should I prune it?

The problem you're describing sounds like damage from honeysuckle witches'-broom aphid. As aphids feed on the stem tips of Tatarian honeysuckle (*Lonicera tatarica*), they inject a toxin into the plant stems that causes the proliferation of misshapen shoots to form. If left unchecked, the problem can eventually kill the plant.

Pruning out and destroying the witches'-brooms may help. You may also be able to dislodge the aphids from the shrub with a forceful water spray or kill them with insecticidal soap. However, they are somewhat protected inside the twisted growth, so control may require a systemic insecticide.

Another option to consider is complete removal of the honeysuckle. This problem will reoccur year after year. You could replace your susceptible honeysuckle with an aphid-resistant one. Two showy bloomers that resist these aphids are the white-flowering 'Freedom' and red-blooming 'Honey rose'. There are other aphid-resistant, shrub-type honeysuckles—'Clavey's Dwarf' and 'Emerald Mound', for example—but they are grown more for foliage than for flowers.

HYDRANGEA

Hydrangea not blooming

I have a hydrangea that was planted 10 years ago. It comes back beautifully every year but has never bloomed. What can I do?

There are several reasons why hydrangeas don't bloom. Check this list for possible adjustments to make and see if your plants recover to full bloom.
- It gets too little sunlight.
- It's planted where winter temperatures kill the flower buds (plants can still look healthy).
- It's the wrong variety for the region. Some kinds of hydrangeas are less cold-hardy than others.
- It was pruned at the wrong time. If you prune in late summer, fall, or winter you're probably pruning away the flower buds. Prune bigleaf hydrangea (*Hydrangea macrophylla*) right after blooming; prune smooth (*H. arborescens*) and panicle hydrangeas (*H. paniculata*) in early spring.
- It has been given too much or too little fertilizer.

Planting florist hydrangea

A blue hydrangea that I bought at the flower shop is sitting in a pot in my kitchen window. Can I plant it in the backyard? I have the perfect location for it. Also, please give tips for wintering the plant.

If you live in Zone 6 or warmer, your blue hydrangea should survive the winter when planted outdoors. In colder zones, the plant will probably die back to the ground over the winter and not bloom in the landscape. Plant it in spring anytime after your area no longer experiences freezing temperatures. In addition to preferring a site in partial shade, this shrub thrives in moist, well-drained soil rich in organic material, such as leaf mold and compost. Grow the plant in acidic soil (pH 5–5.8) to keep the flower color blue. To acidify the soil around your hydrangea, work iron sulfate, a soil amendment, into the soil when preparing the planting hole. (If you apply the amendment directly to the soil's surface, it will take longer to work.) For pink blooms, maintain alkaline soil (pH 7–7.5).

Winter protection depends on where your hydrangea is sited. If it's relatively protected from the elements, you won't need to do anything special. If your hydrangea is exposed to the elements, mulching around the base of the plant after the soil freezes can be helpful.

Hydrangea trimming time

Should I prune twiggy branches from hydrangeas in spring? There is a little growth on the branches, but my husband insists that these shrubs will prosper more if trimmed. What's your advice?

Hydrangeas will bloom whether or not you prune them, but for bigger flower panicles and a tidier look, consider giving them an occasional trim. Pruning times depend upon the types of hydrangeas you grow.

Bigleaf hydrangea *(Hydrangea macrophylla)* should be pruned only after it blooms in summer, because next year's buds are set on the prior year's growth. Pruning in spring forfeits that summer's flowers, unless you wait until the buds enlarge and remove only material that shows no sign of life. Avoid waiting too long to prune either, because if the bushes are pruned in late autumn, new growth may have insufficient time to harden before frost. Remove the oldest shoots to let in light and air, retaining thick new stems and some old canes. Prune out weak shoots and canes with no green growth. Cut off dead twiggy stem tips with no blooms, making your cuts above the fresh growth.

Smooth hydrangea *(H. arborescens)* and panicle hydrangea *(H. paniculata)* bloom on new wood and therefore require different pruning techniques from those used on bigleaf hydrangea. Prune all stems of smooth hydrangea ('Annabelle' is a well-known variety) to 6–12 inches from the ground in early spring. Trim panicle hydrangea in early spring to control its loose growth and encourage it to produce larger flowers. Cut it back to the last two buds on each stem, removing any branches that detract from the contours of the plant. Sometimes with age and judicious pruning, peegee hydrangea *(H. paniculata* 'Grandiflora') can grow into an impressive 20-foot tree. Pruning is not crucial to its survival. If this species is not pruned, it will develop into a large, twiggy, blooming shrub.

Growing hydrangeas

How do I take care of my hydrangeas? What care do they need to bloom well?

Irresistible flowers of pink or blue make bigleaf hydrangea *(Hydrangea macrophylla),* also known as florist's or French hydrangea, a garden favorite. To keep it blooming, the Garden Doctor offers this prescription.

- Plant bigleaf hydrangea in well-drained soil high in organic matter. Wet soil may cause root rot and kill the plant.
- Give bigleaf hydrangea morning sun and afternoon shade.
- Provide water, especially during dry spells, because bigleaf hydrangea is not drought-tolerant.
- Buy plants in bloom to make sure you get what you want. Bigleaf hydrangea is available in several forms. Mophead hydrangea produces fat, ball-like, sterile blooms; lacecap hydrangea is flatter and lighter in appearance, with showy, sterile outer florets and plain, fertile inner florets.
- Consider your gardening zone. Bigleaf hydrangea is reliably hardy in Zones 6–9. In the northern end of its range, harsh winters may kill flower buds, resulting in no blooms. There's hope for northern gardeners, however, with the introduction of Endless Summer, the first bigleaf selection that blooms reliably in Zone 4. This mildew-resistant plant flowers on old and new wood. Even if Endless Summer dies back to the crown in cold weather, it can bloom on new growth. It produces 4–6-inch mophead flowers, blue in acidic soil and pink in alkaline soil.

Snowball hydrangea not blooming

I planted a snowball hydrangea last year. It survived the winter, but it didn't flower this summer. Any suggestions?

Snowball, or smooth hydrangea *(Hydrangea arborescens)* prefers rich, well-drained soil that stays consistently moist. It does best with morning sun and afternoon shade, or dappled shade all day. The more cool morning sun it gets, the better it blooms. If you have provided your plant with these growing conditions, it might still be adapting to its new location and putting more energy into root growth than flower production. You may see flowers next year.

Excessive nitrogen fertilizer or improper pruning can also cause a lack of flowers. Snowball hydrangea blooms on new wood, so pruning in late spring or early summer will remove potential flowers.

Is it possible that the plant you picked up is a different type of hydrangea? Bigleaf hydrangea *(H. macrophylla)* is less hardy than snowball hydrangea. In Zone 5 or colder, its flower buds are often killed, but it will still put out new vegetative growth.

Removing old hydrangea flowers

What do I do with the dried flowers from last year that are still on my hydrangea? Should I prune them off?

To avoid cutting off this year's flower buds, cut the stems of the dried flowers just above where you see the top set of leaf buds on the stem. Then compost the dried flowers; if they're in decent shape, use them for crafts or dried flower arrangements.

Wilting hydrangeas

How much sun do hydrangeas need? Mine, next to my house, wilt in full sun.

Most hydrangeas like full sun to part shade, but they don't care for a location where heat beats down on them, or where they dry out readily. Newly planted hydrangeas are unable to take as much sun as established plants because their root systems are not as extensive.

If your hydrangeas are under a roof overhang, the sun may be less of a problem than the dryness. An overhang will prevent the plants under it from getting much moisture. Keeping your plants well watered and mulched can help counteract the droughty conditions there.

Oakleaf hydrangea won't bloom

My oakleaf hydrangeas have never bloomed for me in 4 years. The plants are about 5 feet tall and wide. I prune them back considerably in the spring. They are located in partial shade. What's up?

This is an easy one: Stop pruning. By pruning your oakleaf hydrangea *(Hydrangea quercifolia)* in spring, you're removing the flower buds before they get a chance to bloom. Prune oakleaf hydrangea only in summer right after the flowers fade. Although oakleaf hydrangea prefers a partially shaded spot, too much shade keeps it from blooming. Make sure it gets sun for about half a day.

Hydrangea indoors
Can I keep a hydrangea as a houseplant?

Although potted bigleaf hydrangea *(Hydrangea macrophylla)* is sold in spring with houseplants, this shrub isn't suited for growing indoors (unless you have a greenhouse or conservatory). Treat it as a short-lived gift plant (much like cut flowers), or plant it outdoors after you have enjoyed its blooms indoors.

Outdoors, the plant prefers well-drained soil and a sunny spot that sees some shade during the hottest hours of the afternoon. Most hydrangeas bloom only once a season, though some newer selections, such as Endless Summer, bloom throughout the summer.

Dried hydrangea
I love the way dried hydrangeas look in arrangements. What is the best way to dry the flowers for indoor use?

Hydrangeas are easy to air-dry—they do the work for you! Cut hydrangea flowers at any stage from green to brown, depending on what color you want in your arrangements. Most people have the best luck cutting flowers that have been allowed to dry a bit on the plant. Remove all foliage from the cut stems. Hang the stems upside down individually in a warm, dry, airy spot until they are completely dry. Wrap the flower heads in tissue paper for protection before drying if you prefer.

You can get double duty from your hydrangea flowers by enjoying them as cut flowers in a vase, then allowing them to air-dry by adding no more water to the vase once the initial fill is gone.

If these techniques seem like too much bother, simply allow the flowers to dry on the plant, then pick them when you are ready to make your arrangement.

IXORA

Pruning ixora
My ixoras are getting leggy. How and when do I prune them to keep them looking full?

Ixora *(Ixora coccinea)*, also called jungle geranium, benefits from a severe cutback called rejuvenation pruning. This is a 3-year process that involves removing old, leggy branches. In early spring of year one, cut one-third of the oldest, thickest branches to ground level; in year two, remove half of the remaining large stems; in year three, remove the last of the old, woody shoots. Beginning in year one, the plant will send up dense new growth from its base that will create an attractive, rounded shrub. Keep the new growth in check by pruning back new shoots by one-third their length in early spring.

JUNIPER

Pruning overgrown junipers

I have some overgrown junipers. Will they grow back if I cut them to the ground?

Such severe pruning will likely kill the plant. If you want to reduce the size of an overgrown juniper *(Juniperus)*, cut it back gradually over a 3-year period. Junipers can be cut back to green tissue, but avoid cutting into older wood that has no green foliage. If the plants are bare at their base, you may be better off removing the overgrown shrubs and replacing them with new ones. Start pruning the new shrubs during their first few years of growth to shape them and maintain their desired size. Minimize the amount of pruning you'll need to do by choosing varieties that won't overgrow the space you have for them.

LILAC

Few flowers

I inherited a row of lilac bushes 12–15 feet tall when I bought my house. I'm happy to have them, but they rarely give me flowers. I trim them after they bloom, but the flowers are small and don't last long. Any tips would be great.

If your plants are very old, they may be types that naturally lack large or long-lasting flowers. Here are some ideas for reinvigorating your lilacs and increasing their blooms in the future.

Lilacs *(Syringa)* prefer slightly alkaline soil. If necessary, amend the soil with lime to make it neutral or slightly alkaline instead of acidic. Feed your lilacs with some 10-10-10 fertilizer if they've been growing in the same spot for a long time. Make certain your lilacs are getting plenty of sunshine. They bloom best in full sun. If surrounding plants are shading them, prune excess growth to let in more light.

If the plants are tall, old, and scraggly, prune back one-third of the oldest, thickest stems to the ground. Follow this routine for 2 more years until you have renewed the entire shrub. A more radical pruning method is to cut all stems back to about 6 inches in March to promote new growth. The next year, choose the healthiest stems to form the structure of the renewed shrubs and eliminate the rest. Prune the remaining stems to ¼ inch above a pair of buds to stimulate the formation of side shoots. This means no flowers the next season, and perhaps for several years afterward if pruning is severe, but the plant will make more blooms in future years.

Keeping cut lilacs

Is there any way to keep lilacs from wilting in a vase?

The best time to cut lilac blossoms is early in the morning when they're fully hydrated. Cut the stems with sharp, clean pruning shears, then immediately plunge the cut stems into a bucket of water. Indoors, get a vase ready for the flowers. Make sure it's clean by running it through a dishwasher cycle or washing it by hand with a solution of 10 percent bleach and 90 percent water. Add fresh water and a floral preservative, which you can find at florist shops. Remove all leaves that would be underwater in the vase. Recut the stems at a 45-degree angle, and arrange the lilacs in the prepared container. Set the vase in indirect light and enjoy. Recut the stems and add more water as needed to prevent wilting.

Potted lilacs

Can a 'Katherine Havemeyer' French lilac be grown in a container?

This double-flowered pink French hybrid *(Syringa vulgaris* 'Katherine Havemeyer') can grow in a container, but will need root protection to survive sustained winter cold. Planted in the ground, French lilac is hardy in Zones 3–7. When in pots, even the hardiest shrubs need winter protection, because their roots are above ground and are more susceptible to freeze damage and drying out. Heavily mulch the pot and keep it in a protected location, such as a garage or shed. Make sure the lilac has a moist root ball and goes completely dormant before you move it into seclusion. Check the soil moisture several times throughout the winter to make certain that the shrub doesn't dry out too much.

Snow-flattened lilacs

A late wet spring snow flattened my 2-year-old lilacs. Will they bounce back? Any tips for preventing this in the future?

If the lilac stems are not broken, they should pop back with a bit of sun and time. Cut off broken branches to the ground. If lots of them are broken, the plants may resprout from the roots, so give them some time.

In the future, as soon as it's safe during or after a snowfall, check vulnerable shrubs and gently brush the snow from bent stems. Also, avoid planting lilacs under a roofline where heavy snow might slide down and crush them.

Lilacs lack blooms

Four summers ago I planted an old-fashioned lilac, which still hasn't bloomed. Before I dig it up, can you advise me on ways to make it bloom? It is 6 feet tall and growing nicely, but it's taking up a prime location in my yard.

Here are several reasons why a common lilac *(Syringa vulgaris)* may not bloom.
- It was pruned between midsummer and winter, removing its flower buds for the next season. Prune only in late spring, right after normal bloom time.
- It's an old variety of lilac that takes 6 years or more to bloom. You may simply need to be patient!
- It needs full sun. If the plant receives less than 6 hours of direct sunlight daily, it will never bloom well.
- Your winters are too mild to allow it to set buds. Common lilac grows best in cold-winter areas (Zones 3–7). If lack of cold is the case, a Meyer lilac *(S. meyeri)* may be a better match for your garden. Meyer lilac blooms at a young age and it flowers better in the South than most other lilacs.

Yellow lilacs

A gardening friend told me about a yellow-flowering lilac. I've only seen lilac blooms in shades of purple and white. Are there yellow lilacs? Are they the same kind as the purple and white ones?

Sometimes gardening catalogs exaggerate descriptions of creamy white lilac blooms, and one of these is probably what your friend has heard about.

The closest lilac flower color to yellow is a selection called 'Primrose'. It produces relatively small clusters of cream-colored blooms on plants that grow up to 25 feet tall.

Pale blooms on lilac

My purple lilac has hardly any color this year. How can I ensure better color next year?

Flower color is influenced by a number of conditions, including the weather. For example, warmer temperatures often encourage paler blooms; cooler temperatures often encourage more intense blooms. Soil moisture plays a part too: If your plant is dry, the flowers will be paler. It's unlikely that the flower color will permanently be pale. Be patient and hope for better weather next year.

Lilac pruning

I need advice on pruning a large, overgrown lilac. I love the flowers, but the shrub looks ugly.

Lilac *(Syringa vulgaris)* has an unattractive way of growing tall and developing bare stems. You can revive these forlorn lilacs through renewal pruning. This entails cutting all the branches back to within 6 inches of the ground in early spring. The shrub will send up new shoots during the growing season. In late winter of the following year, select and retain several strong, healthy shoots to form the shrub's framework; remove all others at ground level. Lilac wood requires 3 or more years before flowering, so you will sacrifice flowers for a few years.

A second option for rescuing a gangly lilac is to do what's called rejuvenation pruning. This 3-year process involves removing about one-third of the old, woody branches each year. You will still be able to enjoy flowers with rejuvenation pruning.

Perform regular maintenance pruning on lilacs in late spring, right after they bloom. Lilacs form buds for the following year's flowers in summer, so avoid late-winter pruning, which will snip off all buds for the coming spring.

Propagating lilac

I have a lilac that I would like to propagate. How long does propagation take? About how long before it takes root and shows new growth?

Layering is a simple way to propagate your lilac. Although layering is a natural process that occurs spontaneously with some shrubs, you may have to give your lilac a little help. Just follow these steps and you can make enough shrubs to share with your friends.

1. Prepare the soil. In spring, choose a flexible outer stem and carefully bend it until the tip touches the ground. Mark a spot on the ground about 12 inches in from the tip. Work compost into the soil around that mark.

2. Get the stem ready. With a sharp blade, carefully make a diagonal slit in the stem 12 inches from the tip, where the branch will touch the ground. Dip the cut in rooting hormone and gently turn the stem to make sure that the inside of the slit is exposed to the hormone.

3. Hold down the stem. On either side of the slit, peg the branch to the ground with landscape staples or rocks. Pile some soil on the slit and pat it down. Mulch with leaf litter and keep the branch watered throughout the summer.

4. Separate the new plant. The next spring, after roots have grown from the wounded stem, sever the connection between your new lilac and its parent. Wait a few weeks befroe moving the new plant to a site where it has space to mature.

I'm having a home built in Florida and will miss my lilacs. Will they grow in Florida?

Unfortunately, lilac *(Syringa)* won't thrive in your new yard because of the balmy climate. The plant needs cold winters to produce flowers each year.

Take heart, though. Once you move, you'll no doubt discover equally wonderful flowering shrubs you can enjoy in Florida. Some favorite fragrant shrubs include natal plum *(Carissa macrocarpa)*, crepe jasmine *(Tabernaemontana divaricata)*, and Arabian jasmine *(Jasminum sambac)*. You might also try crepe myrtle *(Lagerstroemia indica)*, also called summer lilac.

MAGNOLIA

Three years ago I purchased a magnolia shrub. Although it produces leaves and a few buds in the spring, it has not grown. Is there something I should be doing?

It often takes shrubs several years before they begin to grow and bloom well. This is because the plants need time to properly adjust to their new site. If this is just the third year since planting, I wouldn't worry about slow growth unless the plant is also showing other signs of distress such as browning or yellowing foliage. An adage that applies to perennial flowers and shrubs is: The first year it sleeps, the second year it creeps, and the third year it leaps. I suspect that your magnolia will take off and grow well this year.

Make sure your plant has good growing conditions (full sun and well-drained soil) and a site that's not too exposed. If your plant gets too little sun, is in heavy clay soil, or was planted too deeply, it may take longer to become established.

MOCKORANGE

My mockorange grows well, but I get few blossoms. I want this shrub to bloom a lot as it's near my home's entrance. I've pruned it back in the past, which doesn't seem to have helped. What can I do?

Mockorange *(Philadelphus coronarius)* is a favorite blooming shrub. Who wouldn't be attracted to the lovely white flowers and their heavenly fragrance? Some gardeners can get mockorange to grow and bloom with no effort, but other gardeners coddle it endlessly with no luck.

Here are some reasons why the shrub may not bloom.

- Improper pruning. Prune mockorange right after it blooms. If you prune it after midsummer or before it blooms in spring, you could be cutting off the flower buds.
- Freezing temperatures. Mockorange produces flower buds the year before it blooms; the buds could freeze over the winter if is is a variety not suited for your climate. Likewise, late-spring frosts could nip off the buds.
- Too much shade. Although mockorange can tolerate some shade, it won't bloom well if it gets too much. Remember that a sunny spot can gradually become shady as trees grow larger.

NATAL PLUM

Fragrant shrub

I'm stationed in Hawaii and love a plant called *Carissa macrocarpa*. I'll soon be moving back to New York. Is there a variety of this shrub that is hardy? I hate to think I'll never smell the blossoms again!

Carissa macrocarpa, sometimes called natal plum, is a tropical gem. It offers much appeal—it has lovely foliage, attractive (and edible) fruits, and fragrant flowers; it tolerates some degree of salt spray; and it is a good hedge plant. Perhaps its only downfall is that it's hardy only in Zones 9–11.

Although you won't be able to grow *Carissa* as a perennial shrub outdoors in New York, you will be able to grow it as an annual (purchasing a new plant each year), or bring it indoors and treat it as a houseplant during the winter months.

OLEANDER

Oleander pruning

I have an 8-foot-tall oleander in front of my home. I would like to trim it back to 2–3 feet tall. Its limbs are long and leggy, and it didn't flower last year. What can I do?

Maintaining a 2–3-foot-tall plant is unrealistic unless your oleander *(Nerium oleander)* is a dwarf cultivar, such as 'Petite Salmon' or 'Petite Pink', which top out at 3–4 feet tall. If you trim the plant back to 2–3 feet tall, it will send out new branches just below the cut, leaving the base of the plant bare. That said, leggy stems indicate that your plant needs corrective pruning. Begin by completely removing one-third of the large, woody stems. Cut the remaining stems back by one-quarter of their height. Late next winter, remove several more of the large, woody stems if necessary, and head back branches. Oleander grows vigorously and requires annual late-winter pruning to maintain a small size and attractive shape.

I have several oleanders in my yard, and I am having trouble with the leaves turning yellow. The plants are in a sunny, well-drained area. How can I treat this problem?

Yellowing of oleander leaves is a common symptom that the plants are too dry. Get out your hose and flood the root zone of the plants with water, them wait an hour or two and do it again. If the water runs over the surface rather than soaking in, make a raised collar of soil around the base of the plants to help retain water.

In California, yellowing of oleander leaves that begins at the tip and spreads inward is a sign of a bacterial disease called oleander leaf scorch.

My oleanders aren't thriving. They're growing in part sun. I water them when they're dry. Do I need to fertilize or do something else?

Many gardeners think of oleanders as no-care plants, because the shrubs are often used in road medians and other harsh areas. They do require some care, however.

First be sure that yours are planted in the right spot; it sounds to me as though they're not. Oleanders do best in full sun; if yours are in partial sun, they may fail to thrive because they're getting too little light. Transplanting them to a sunnier spot may solve the problem.

In most average soils, oleanders do well without fertilizing. If your yard has especially poor soil (a soil test can help confirm this for you), the plants might benefit from an application of timed-release fertilizer in spring. Follow the directions on the package to avoid overfertilizing your plants. Overfertilizing can be just as harmful to the plants' health as getting too few nutrients.

POTENTILLA

Why are my potentillas dying? The leaves turn brown and die. The plants were blooming and looking great until about a month ago.

Potentilla (*Potentilla fruticosa*) is usually among the most reliable of garden plants. It grows well in many different soils and usually blooms from June to September. It prefers full sun, and usually does well in partial shade, although it produces fewer flowers. It also adapts well to most soils, although it doesn't like wet soil, especially during winter.

Sudden browning of the foliage may indicate a root problem. I suspect that poor drainage or overly wet soils may have contributed to your potentilla's problems.

Potentilla is also susceptible to spider mites in hot, dry weather. Foliage first develops a speckled yellow coloration, and webbing may be evident. If the problem continues untreated, leaves may turn brown and die. If you see early signs of spider mites, wash them off the plants with a forceful water spray, or use an insecticidal soap to kill them.

RHODODENDRON

Rhododendron not blooming

My rhododendron didn't bloom this year. Do I have a male plant instead of a female? How do I know if mine is male or female?

Rhododendron (Rhododendron), like the majority of garden plants, produces flowers that have both male and female parts in the same bloom—so two different plants are unnecessary. In fact, a plant will bloom no matter what sex it is or whether there are any others nearby.

Getting fruit is another matter. A few species of plants, such as holly, bittersweet, and ginkgo, are dioecious—meaning that their male and female flowers are on different plants. You need to know which is which only if you want to grow one for its fruit. Only a female dioecious plant can produce fruit, and only if a male plant is nearby to pollinate it.

Lack of bloom on your rhododendron is due to some other factor. Severe winter cold could have killed the flower buds but left the vegetative buds unharmed. (Flower buds are slightly less hardy than vegetative buds.) Because flower buds form on rhododendron the previous growing season, stressful weather conditions such as drought may have limited flower bud formation. Also, if you pruned your rhododendron late in summer or in fall last year, you may have removed the flower buds for this spring.

Dividing rhododendron

I recently planted a rhododendron. How often do I need to separate the plant?

Rhododendrons should never need division. This holds true for most trees and shrubs. Division is appropriate for some perennials, but woody plants have a tough time regenerating a healthy root system. Rhododendrons rarely need pruning. They have a graceful, mounding branched habit that is particularly attractive if allowed to grow with minimal interference.

If you need to shape or limit the size of a rhododendron, make pruning cuts in late spring after the plant blooms. Also, remove dead, diseased, and weak wood annually in late spring.

Wilting rhododendrons

What is causing my rhododendrons to wilt? The leaves are rolling up. I can't see anything wrong with the plant.

At what time of year is the wilt occurring? Is the entire plant affected? Rhododendrons naturally roll their leaves during severe cold in winter. There may be nothing wrong with your plant that a little warmer weather won't cure.

If the wilt is happening during warmer weather, I suspect that your plant may have rhododendron wilt. This disease is caused by a soilborne fungus *(Phytophthora)*, which is most likely to develop in poorly drained, wet soils. Disease symptoms include stunted growth, leaf yellowing, and drooping leaves that roll inward. Usually, only one or two branches on a plant are affected at first. To remedy the problem, improve soil drainage and aeration as soon as possible. If plants are young, dig up the plants and replant them on a slight elevation after adding organic matter to the soil to improve drainage. You might also consider replacing susceptible rhododendrons with phytophthora-resistant ones. Resistant cultivars include 'Caroline', 'Professor Hugo de Vries', 'Red Head', 'Martha Isaccson', 'Pink Trumpet', and 'English Roseum.'

ROSE OF SHARON

Pruning rose of Sharon

How and when do I prune my rose of Sharon shrubs so they fill out and become thicker? Mine are getting tall and skinny.

Prune rose of Sharon *(Hibiscus syriacus)* in late winter or early spring. If you want fewer but larger flowers, prune the plants back hard. For more but smaller flowers, prune lightly.

These plants naturally have an upright growth habit—typically growing about 10 feet tall and 6 feet wide. If you'd like them to be wider than is their nature, you may be fighting a losing battle.

How close together are your shrubs? If they're crowded, they may be stretching for light. If the plants are close enough to be touching, transplant some of them.

Planting rose of Sharon

I'd like to transplant a rose of Sharon to the north side of my garage and plant another rose of Sharon with it as a privacy border. How far apart should they be? When should I transplant them?

Rose of Sharon is not likely to do well on the north side of your garage. The shrub needs full sun (at least 6–8 hours of direct sun a day). Instead of rose of Sharon, consider shade-tolerant shrubs, such as summersweet *(Clethra),* or a trellis with a shade-tolerant vine. You can buy inexpensive lengths of trellis that provide privacy.

Perhaps you can find a sunnier spot in your yard for rose of Sharon. Although you can transplant it anytime the soil isn't frozen, spring and autumn are the best time to move it. Most rose of Sharon plants develop a spread of 6–10 feet. If you plant them 5–6 feet apart they should form a solid screen 8–12 feet tall.

Rejuvenating rose of Sharon

This spring, many branches died on my rose of Sharon. I cut out the dead branches, but it still needs pruning. How and when do I do this? This plant is 22 years old; I don't want to lose it.

I'm sorry to say it, but your shrub may be coming to the end of its life span. Rose of Sharon is not a long-lived shrub; having one last this long is an accomplishment. Try cutting it back severely to stimulate new growth, then fertilize in spring with a slow-release fertilizer. Your rose of Sharon may fail to bloom next summer because of the vigorous pruning.

SPRUCE

Browning Alberta spruce

I have a dwarf Alberta spruce in my yard that is turning brown and dropping needles. What could be the problem?

Your spruce may have been attacked by spruce spider mites. Unlike most spider mites, spruce spider mites are active during the cool weather of spring and fall. When the weather turns warm, they become inactive. They suck sap out of needles, leaving yellowish speckles where they feed. When feeding is heavy, the needles become yellow or bronze and eventually drop. You may also observe webbing on needles and stems. Plants react slowly to the injury. Yellowing and needle drop often don't occur until the heat of early summer hits.

Check for spruce spider mites in fall or spring when temperatures are cool. Hold a sheet of white paper under a branch, and shake the branch over the paper. If you see moving specks on the paper, they may be spider mites. Use a magnifying glass to get a better look. If numerous mites are present, consider spraying with a miticide or insecticidal soap.

SUMMERSWEET

Pruning summersweet

I planted a summersweet last year. Brown capsules appeared last fall. Should I prune off these capsules or leave them alone?

You can prune off the capsules this spring to spruce up summersweet (*Clethra alnifolia*) a bit, but there is no need to do so. The capsules will not interfere with flower production this season and eventually will drop off on their own.

If you have time, remove spent flowers and seed heads from perennials and shrubs. When allowed to remain on the plant, spent flowers produce seeds, as your summersweet did. Seed production uses up some of the plant's energy. By removing the spent flowers, you redirect energy to other important plant functions such as root, stem, and leaf growth.

Removing spent blooms in late summer may encourage a flush of new growth, which could easily be damaged by early freezes.

VIBURNUM

Snowball viburnum care

My husband bought a snowball viburnum. I know nothing about how to care for this plant. How much sun does it need? Is planting it in full sun a bad idea?

A couple of different viburnums are commonly called snowball viburnum by gardeners, but the most common is *Viburnum plicatum*. It's popular because of its clusters of attractive white blooms in late spring, reddish-purple autumn foliage, and horizontal branching pattern. Unlike most viburnums, it doesn't produce colorful fruits. This shrub generally grows about 10 feet tall and 12 feet wide and is hardy in Zones 6–8.

It likes a spot in full sun to partial shade and moist, well-drained soil. You can help get your shrub off to a good start by amending the soil with organic matter, such as compost or peat moss, before planting. Keep it watered well during its first growing season.

Another shrub commonly called snowball viburnum is *V. opulus*, also known as European snowball. It is less desirable because it is susceptible to aphid damage.

WEIGELA

Propagating weigela
I'd like to start some more weigelas. Can I divide them?

The best way to propagate your weigelas is from stem cuttings.

Both softwood and semihardwood cuttings of weigela *(Weigela florida)* root easily. Take cuttings from the tips of weigela stems just as they begin to firm up (softwood) or when they are firm and slightly woody (semihardwood).

1. Cuttings should be about 4 inches long and have at least 3 sets of leaves. Make the bottom cut just below a node for better rooting.
2. Remove all flower buds and flowers and any lower leaves that would be buried in the rooting medium.
3. Dip the cuttings in rooting hormone, then place them in a pot filled with loose potting medium and water the medium well.
4. Cover the entire pot with a plastic bag and place the pot in indirect sunlight or under artificial lights indoors. Once the cuttings form roots (in several weeks) and begin to grow, transplant them into individual containers. Grow them in the containers in a partially shaded spot until they can be planted in the yard.

VINES IN GENERAL

Vine for full sun

I need a hardy flowering vine to climb the picket fence around our air-conditioner, which is on the west side of the house. Can any vine withstand full sun in the afternoon in addition to the heat from the air-conditioner unit?

That's a challenging site, but there are some vines that will take it. One of the toughest perennial vines for a situation such as this is trumpet vine *(Campsis radicans)*. Hummingbirds go wild for its gaudy 2-inch orange flowers that appear from midsummer to early fall. If you're not fond of orange in the garden, trumpet vine also comes with red ('Crimson Trumpet') and yellow ('Flava') flowers. I need to caution you about this vine, however; it's vigorous, fast-growing, and spreads by suckers and seeds, so you don't want to plant it close to your house's foundation. Passionflower *(Passiflora)* and climbing rose *(Rosa)* are a couple more sun-loving vines that will produce an abundance of blooms.

Several annual vines can do well in these conditions too. Some of my favorites are black-eyed Susan vine *(Thunbergia alata)* and purple hyacinth bean *(Lablab purpureus)*. Both need a little extra care to get started, as do most freshly planted annuals, but once these tough vines get going they'll withstand the blazing sun and scorching heat.

Vines for shade

I have a shady spot where I'd like to grow a flowering vine. What would you suggest?

Most flowering vines bloom more prolifically in sun. However, there are some vines that bloom and grow well in shade. Here are several to consider:

- Fiveleaf akebia *(Akebia quinata)*. The dark flowers of akebia are subtle; 'Alba' and 'Shirobana', with white flowers, and 'Rosea', with lavender flowers, are more showy. Zones 5–9.
- Climbing hydrangea *(Hydrangea petiolaris)*. Creamy white flowers in late spring. Zones 5–7.
- Dutchman's pipe *(Aristolochia macrophylla)*. Purplish-brown pipe-shaped blooms on a bold-textured vine. Zones 4–7.
- False climbing hydrangea *(Schizophragma hydrangeoides)*. Showy white blooms that resemble a lacecap hydrangea. Zones 6–8.
- Hardy kiwi *(Actinidia kolomikta)*. Flowers are fragrant but not showy. However, the pink, white, and green tricolored foliage is colorful. Zones 3–8.
- Trumpet honeysuckle *(Lonicera sempervirens)*. Pink or yellow flowers all season. Avoid planting the invasive Japanese honeysuckle *(L. japonica)*. Zones 4–9.

Vines for a fence

I would like to cover a chain-link fence with a flowering vine. Which plant would you recommend for this fence?

You're in luck—there are a lot of vines that will work for you—so many, in fact, that your hardest chore might be choosing one!

Annual vines
- Black-eyed Susan vine *(Thunbergia alata)*
- Cup and saucer vine *(Cobaea scandens)*
- Cypress vine *(Ipomoea quamoclit)*
- Moonflower *(Ipomoea alba)*
- Morning glory *(Ipomoea tricolor)*

Perennial vines
- Fiveleaf akebia *(Akebia quinata)*
- Clematis *(Clematis)*
- Passionflower *(Passiflora incarnata)*
- Trumpet vine *(Campsis radicans)*

Vines on trees

I'd like to soften the look of some tree trunks in my landscape. Could I grow vines on the trunks without hurting the trees?

Vine-covered tree trunks add lushness, color, and texture to any landscape. To grow vines on trees successfully, follow these guidelines.
- For large trees, choose a shade-tolerant vine, especially one with rootlets that attach to the trunk unaided, such as wintercreeper *(Euonymus fortunei)*, English ivy *(Hedera helix)*, or climbing hydrangea *(Hydrangea petiolaris)*.
- Grow clematis where it can grow up the north side of a small tree and into the light. *Clematis viticella* and Armand clematis *(C. armandii)* can withstand light shade; sweet autumn clematis *(C. terniflora)* and Italian clematis *(C. virginiana)* tolerate even more shade.
- Start with small specimens so the planting holes will not interfere with tree roots.
- Plant vines at least 12 inches out from the tree. Then train the vine toward the tree by tying long vine stems to the trunk or leaning a stake against the tree.
- If a desirable vine you planted starts to wrap around a trunk, cut the vine below the spot where it encircles the trunk. Let new upright shoots develop from there. If a vine completely encircles a trunk, it may girdle the tree.
- Avoid planting robust twining vines such as wisteria near trees. They can strangle and kill a tree.
- Avoid growing vines on conifers. If you have a vine-covered conifer, pull the vines

down, cut them off at the roots, and spray the vine stumps with an herbicide, being careful not to spray the tree.

- Vines can kill a tree by shading it out. If you see a vine in the tree's canopy, cut the vine at its base to give the tree a fighting chance.

QUICK TIP

Vines for fragrance
- Armand clematis *(Clematis armandii)*
- Confederate jasmine *(Trachelospermum jasminoides)*
- Madagascar jasmine *(Stephanotis floribunda)*
- Moonflower *(Ipomoea alba)*
- Pink Chinese jasmine *(Jasminum polyanthum)*
- Rose *(Rosa)*
- Sweet autumn clematis *(Clematis terniflora)*
- Sweet pea *(Lathyrus odoratus)*
- Wisteria *(Wisteria)*

Vines for fragrance

Could you suggest a blooming vine that would also have nice fragrance?

You have quite a few vines from which to select for fragrance and bloom. See the list at right for some suggestions.

Year-round color

What are some of the best plants to grow on an arbor in Zone 8? I want something that stays pretty year-round.

If you want an evergreen or semievergreen vine, an excellent choice is Gold Flame honeysuckle *(Lonicera ×heckrottii* 'Gold Flame'), which produces fragrant flowers sporadically from spring to fall, and sometimes in winter too. It will not take over your yard the way Japanese honeysuckle can. Various jasmines, such as long-blooming Spanish jasmine *(Jasminum officinale affine),* or Carolina jessamine *(Gelsemium sempervirens),* would also be good choices. Among vines that often shed their leaves in winter (or go dormant if it's cold enough) is the maypop, a native hardy passionflower *(Passiflora incarnata),* which produces exotic purple blossoms followed by egg-shape fruits.

Evergreen screening vines

I'd like to use a vine as a screen from my neighbor's property. Can you suggest an evergreen vine that would provide screening all year?

An evergreen vine can make a good screen in a narrow space. Few evergreen vines are hardy in northern climates, however. Wintercreeper *(Euonymus fortunei)* is hardy in Zones 5–9 (some in Zone 4), and English ivy *(Hedera helix)* and Persian ivy *(H. colchica)* may be grown in Zones 6–10 (some in Zone 5). Other choices for warmer areas include creeping fig *(Ficus pumila)*, Zones 8–10; Carolina jessamine *(Gelsemium sempervirens)*, Zones 8–10; Armand clematis *(Clematis armandii)*, Zones 7–9 ; cross vine *(Bignonia capreolata),* Zones 7–9; and Confederate jasmine *(Trachelospermum jasminoides)*, Zones 8–10.

Two of my neighbors have admired my allamanda and mandevilla vines, which practically grow themselves. What's the best way to propagate these vines so I can share them?

Both vines are propagated the same way, by rooting cuttings taken in spring. However, when you root cuttings, a few may not take, so it's wise to root a few more than you actually need. Here are four easy steps to growing garden-ready rooted cuttings.

1. Fill several clean 6-inch flowerpots with moist seed starting mix or a half-and-half mixture of peat moss and sand. Water well, and use a pencil to poke holes where you will place the cuttings.
2. Soon after established plants show new growth in early spring, take 3-inch-long stem cuttings. Side shoots taken from near the base of the plants work best. Dip the cut ends in rooting hormone and push them into the prepared containers. You can set 4 stem cuttings in each pot. Press soil firmly around the cuttings.
3. Enclose the containers in a loose plastic bag, using long skewers or sticks to hold the plastic above the cuttings. Keep at 75°F in filtered light until roots develop. Check regularly to make sure the soil in the pots remains constantly moist. Remove the plastic as soon as new growth appears.
4. After several weeks, when the cuttings have rooted, transplant them to individual pots, discarding any that did not root. Move the pots outdoors to a partially shaded spot. After a few days, pinch off the growing tips to encourage the development of side shoots. Wait another week or two before transplanting the rooted cuttings to the garden.

BITTERSWEET

I have a serious problem with bittersweet taking over my lilac shrubs. I've pulled and cut as much as I see, but I can't seem to get rid of it. What's the best way to get rid of it once and for all?

Oriental bittersweet *(Celastrus orbiculatus)* is a formidable foe because of its vigor, and because it can reproduce so many ways. Birds eat the seeds and spread them about, and the plants spread by developing shoots that sprout from low stems and roots. Simply cutting back the plant often stimulates the growth of new stems and root suckers. To kill a mature plant, you cut back all top growth, then treat the stumps with a brush-killer herbicide. Use caution near desirable plants such as the lilac. Stray herbicide could severely damage or kill the plants you'd like to save. Repeat this procedure in late summer to eliminate new bittersweet that sprouts from the old roots.

No bittersweet berries

My bittersweet is 7 years old. Two years ago it had a wonderful crop of fruits, but last year it didn't produce. Can I do anything this year to ensure berries?

Bittersweet *(Celastrus scandens)* depends on pollination for good berry production, so you need more than one vine. Yours produced fruits, so it's a female vine. Male flowers are borne on a different bittersweet plant. If a nearby male plant died or was removed, you'll need to plant another in order for your female plant to be pollinated. If you used insecticides in your garden while the plants were in bloom, you may have killed the insects that help pollination.

Bittersweet harvest

I have bittersweet growing on my back fence. When and how do I harvest it for the berries?

Harvest bittersweet when the first yellowish capsules of the fruit split open and you see the orange-red fruit inside. Cut stems to the length you desire, tie them together into small bundles, and hang them upside down in a warm, dry location out of direct sun. As the fruits dry, more unopened capsules will split to reveal the fruits inside.

Bittersweet can self-sow and produce plants everywhere. If you have plants where you don't want them, pull them out or transplant them in spring to a more suitable location. Bittersweet produces separate male and female plants, so you'll need at least one male plant nearby to pollinate female plants for the berries. Unfortunately there's no way to determine the sex of an immature plant, so plant several vines to ensure that you have at least one male among your plants.

BOUGAINVILLEA

Pruning bougainvillea

How do I prune my bougainvillea? It is massive, and I would like to reduce its size.

Bougainvillea *(Bougainvillea)* tolerates heavy pruning. You can safely prune off about three-quarters of the plant in late fall or early spring. Avoid the need for repeated severe pruning by lightly pruning the plant every year in late fall or early spring. Use a sharp pair of pruners to cleanly remove spent blossoms, several inches of new growth, and dead or diseased twigs.

Growing bougainvillea

I've had spotty luck with bougainvilleas. This year I bought a new one, which was beautiful, but now all the blooms are gone. How do I make sure it does well?

The delicate beauty of bougainvillea can be deceiving, because this plant needs rather harsh conditions to bloom well. In addition to a site that gets at least a half day of baking sun, bougainvillea should rarely receive water beyond the month after it is transplanted. Fertilize your plants twice a year, using a high-potassium, low-nitrogen fertilizer (the first number on the fertilizer package is nitrogen; the third number is potassium). When bougainvillea fails to bloom, it is usually due to too little sun, too much water, or too much nitrogen fertilizer. The bougainvillea bloom season stretches from December to September, depending on the cultivar.

Propagating bougainvillea

How do I propagate bougainvillea? I'd like to start some new ones from my vine.

There are a couple of methods you can use, including taking stem cuttings. The easiest way, however, is to layer the plant. Here are easy steps for layering.
1. In late summer or autumn, remove the leaves along a 12-inch section of growing stem.
2. Make a diagonal cut along the underside of the shoot, creating a small flap.
3. Lightly dust the flap with rooting hormone.
4. Lay the stem along the ground and secure it with a u-shaped wire pin. Cover the stem with about 3 inches of soil.
5. Cut the new plant from its parent after the new one develops a strong root system (about a year after the process begins). Dig it up and plant it in its permanent new home.

CAROLINA JESSAMINE

Jessamine not blooming

I have 16 Carolina jessamines that I planted near a fence and pergola. I purchased them in 5-gallon pots, and after 2½ years they still have not bloomed. I've tried watering and fertilizing them more, then tried watering them less and giving them no fertilizer. Can you help me?

I understand your frustration, and am sorry to tell you that your good intentions have worked against you. First, you might have done better to start with smaller plants—Carolina jessamine *(Gelsemium sempervirens)* is best transplanted when the plants are quite young. Older plants often need more time to become established. Misinterpreting their reluctance to bloom as a need for fertilizer was probably a mistake, too, in that well-fed vines often grow lush and green yet produce few flowers. Be patient, and don't feed your plants for at least another year or two. One trait that earned this vine the title of South Carolina's state flower is its ability to thrive with little care.

Another possiblity for poor bloom on your Carolina jessamine is temperamental spring weather. Flower buds develop on the plant in late winter or early spring. An untimely freeze could kill the buds before they have a chance to bloom.

CLEMATIS

Caring for clematis

How should I take care of my clematis?

You can baby your clematis vines or let them go; most will keep blooming. In general, they don't need much more than an occasional tidying. Many established clematis plants, however, benefit from regular low-key maintenance.

Planting clematis

How do I plant clematis rootstock? Believe it or not, I can't tell the root end from the vine end. Can you help?

You're not alone in puzzling about which end is up on a bare-root plant. The root should have fine hairlike growths on it and be much more flexible than the stem part.

When planting bare-root clematis, set it deep in the hole so the crown is 3–4 inches underground. Backfill the hole with compost. Bank more compost in a circle around the newly planted clematis and water well.

QUICK TIP

Growing healthy clematis

- Shade the roots with mulch, rocks, or low-growing plants.
- Water clematis regularly, especially if the foliage fades or goes limp.
- Side-dress with rotted manure or compost in spring and perhaps some slow-release, granular fertilizer to encourage flowering. Feed the plants all summer.
- Most clematis need at least 6–8 hours of direct sunlight to develop flowers.
- Pruning is unnecessary, but it can promote bloom, contain growth, and tidy dead stems.
- Spring bloomers, which flower on old, woody stems, need no pruning other than shaping. Do this by midsummer to avoid removing next year's flower buds.
- For early-summer bloomers, remove dead stems only in early spring.
- Cut back late-summer and fall bloomers, in winter or early spring, before the plants break dormancy. Prune these to the bottom pair of buds or to where you'd like the current season's growth to begin. They bloom on current season's growth, and will suffer no decline in bloom from a severe cutback.

Pruning sweet autumn clematis

I live in Zone 5. Should I prune sweet autumn clematis? Is spring the time to do it?

The best time to prune your sweet autumn clematis *(Clematis terniflora)* is in early spring, long before it blooms. It doesn't require pruning—it's only something to do if you want to control the plant's size. To prune, cut back the stems to the lowest pair of buds or to the height where you'd like growth to start during the current season.

Clematis wilt

Sometimes, for no reason one of my clematis vines dries up and turns crispy brown. A friend told me that a wilt disease causes this and not to plant another clematis in the same spot, since it will also get sick and die. Is this true?

When clematis wilt strikes, it takes just days for the foliage to shrivel and die. Wind spreads clematis wilt, a fungal disease affecting plants in sun and shade. *Clematis ×jackmannii* and some of its big-flowered hybrid relatives are more prone to wilt than species clematis, which have better resistance. Although infected plants look dead, the disease typically affects the stems; the roots survive. New shoots may emerge from the ground. When wilt strikes, cut back the sick parts to healthy stems, even if you have to cut them below the soil. Apply a fungicide containing copper on any new growth that appears. Also, make sure you give clematis enough water to keep it from wilting from thirst.

Replacing trellis

I need to replace a broken clematis trellis. When is the best time to do this? Will I have to cut back my clematis to remove the old trellis and put the new one in place?

The amount of pruning you'll need to do depends on how entwined your clematis and trellis have become. Ideally, you can untangle the clematis while it's dormant, then replace the trellis and tie the vine onto the new support. But untangling a twining vine can be frustrating and time-consuming. If it's too much of a headache, prune your plant as severely as necessary to remove it from the support. Do so while the plant is dormant. Severe pruning may remove next year's flowers if the clematis is a spring bloomer. But it should send out new shoots from the base that will bloom nicely the following year.

If the trellis has broken during the growing season, consider propping up the trellis with supplemental stakes or supports to get through the year until the proper pruning time.

Transplanting clematis

How do I transplant clematis? I have moved some with luck and others with no luck. I try to keep them watered and not disrupt the root balls, but still they don't survive. Are some varieties tougher than others?

As you've already discovered, clematis plants don't like to be moved once established. If you must move them, the earlier in spring you can do it, the better, before they start new growth. Some clematis varieties are definitely more robust than others. Sweet autumn clematis *(Clematis terniflora)* and pink anemone clematis *(C. montana* 'Rubens') are among the sturdiest.

CLIMBING HYDRANGEA

Boosting growth

My climbing hydrangea has many runners, but they're not growing very much and none of them has bloomed. Is there a special way to train this plant so it grows faster? I want to train it to grow up a maple tree.

Don't feel bad about your plant: Climbing hydrangea *(Hydrangea petiolaris)* can be very slow to grow. But once established, it is spectacular, so don't give up on yours. The plant climbs with holdfasts that grow along its stems, so there is little you can do to help the vines climb faster.

I don't recommend planting climbing hydrangea against a tree, especially a maple. Maples are shallow-rooted and will compete with the vine for moisture in the soil. Because the maple has a much larger root system, it will easily win the competition. If the hydrangea should happen to win the battle, it can become very large (more than 50 feet long) and very heavy. It could eventually shade out your maple tree. Instead, you might train your vine to grow up brickwork, a wood fence, or some other structure.

ENGLISH IVY

Ivy on wall

My English ivy is climbing up the brick wall of my house. Will it damage the house? Should I remove it?

Ivy climbing on a brick wall can be a beautiful sight, but it is potentially harmful to the wall. English ivy clings to trees and walls (brick or otherwise) by developing aerial rootlets called holdfasts. If you look closely at the stems of your ivy, you'll see these rootlets. Holdfasts penetrate into the mortar between the bricks. In the process the mortar is slightly damaged. All brick walls eventually need to have their mortar replaced. English ivy growing on the wall accelerates the deterioration of the mortar. If you leave the ivy growing on the wall, you'll have to repoint your house sooner than if you remove the ivy. That said, keep in mind that ivy-covered brick walls are a centuries-old tradition. The brick wall of your house can support growth of ivy and be structurally sound for many years to come if you're prepared to keep up with the extra maintenance. If you prefer lower maintenance, it may be wise to remove the ivy (see below).

Ivy invasion

We just purchased a house where the previous owners ignored the yard. English ivy is growing all over the trees and the house. The ivy stems are at least 3 inches thick at the base of the trees, and the ivy grows up about 100 feet. I'm afraid it will hurt the trees. What should I do?

You can prune back English ivy *(Hedera helix)* as severely as you need to, or remove it entirely. Ivy can grow up the trunks of trees with little danger of harming them, but it shouldn't be allowed to grow into the branches, where it can wrap around and girdle the stems, or stretch to branch tips, shading out the trees' foliage. You'll probably need to have a professional remove it from the trees if it has climbed too high and grown too thick. You also could saw out a 1-inch slice from the base of the biggest vines and let them die, then remove the vines from the trees as you are able.

MANDEVILLA

Growing mandevilla

What do I need to do to take care of my mandevilla? I love this plant's pink flowers.

Several species of mandevilla *(Mandevilla,* sometimes listed as *Dipladenia)* have become popular container plants in the North and landscape plants in the South. 'Alice du Pont' is a well-known variety. Mandevilla blooms over a long season. It is native to tropical America, so it needs warm, humid conditions for best growth. Plants are not hardy but may be overwintered in a greenhouse or bright sunroom where temperatures remain above 50°F.

Outdoors, mandevilla requires full sun to part shade. Keep the soil moderately moist, and fertilize regularly through the summer. In late summer, cease fertilizing and reduce watering. Keep the humidity high during the winter rest period. If the plant is root-bound, repot it in spring. Prune it back in late winter. Take the plant back outside when all danger of frost is past.

MORNING GLORY

Growing morning glory

I would like to plant morning glories along a wood fence. Where's the best place to put them? What care do they need?

Morning glories *(Ipomoea)* need a spot in full sun. If there's too much shade, they won't bloom. Water them throughout the summer to encourage lots of flowers. Fertilize them sparingly unless your garden has very poor soil; too much fertilizer encourages leafy growth at the expense of blooms.

In areas that experience short summers, start your morning glory seeds indoors a month or two early. Most of the season can pass before morning glories grow large enough to bloom. Many a gardener has grown them and seen only a small handful of blooms before autumn frost kills the plant.

Excess morning glory

We have a ton of pretty morning glories, but they're everywhere, overrunning the roses and apple trees as well as the bird feeder. How do I get rid of them without killing other plants?

Wherever morning glory is allowed to shed seeds, it quickly becomes a persistent summer weed. Fortunately, these vining annuals are easy to pull or hoe when they're young. To kill morning glories that have entwined themselves in other plants, use scissors or sharp-tipped pruning shears to clip the main stem close to the ground. Then simply allow the vines to shrivel.

In gardens such as yours, where the soil is richly endowed with morning glory seeds from seasons past, you can limit the number of seedlings that appear by mulching all exposed soil that basks in warm sun. Incidentally, it would be unfair to judge all morning glories by the weedy strain in your garden. Many excellent large-flower varieties reseed only modestly. Still, there are only three kinds of sites for morning glory that offset its tendency to go weedy: in a container, in a bed adjacent to a sidewalk or other hard surface, or along a fence that's bordered by a regularly mowed lawn.

PASSIONFLOWER

Growing passionflower

I would like to have a passionflower, but I do not know anything about how to grow or care for one. Where should I plant it? How long will it bloom?

A hardy perennial vine that grows wild from Texas to Virginia, and sometimes beyond, passionflower *(Passiflora incarnata)* thrives anywhere it gets at least a half day of sun. It grows in ditches, and can be kept as a houseplant if you have a sunny window. The exotic purple flowers appear from early summer to autumn, and each blossom lasts only a day. If pollinated, the plants develop egg-shape fruits, which pop loudly when stamped upon—hence the common name of maypop vine. Herbalists use the fruits as a mild sedative. The state wildflower of Tennessee, passionflower is easy to grow on a trellis or as a cover for an old stump. After the vines die back in late autumn, trim away the current season's growth. New stems will sprout from root buds in spring.

TRUMPET VINE

Bloomless trumpet vine

I bought a trumpet vine 2 years ago and it hasn't bloomed. What can I do to get it to bloom?

Trumpet vine *(Campsis radicans)*, like wisteria, is notorious for taking its time to bloom. It's common for plants to wait several years to start flowering.

   Where are you growing your plant? Trumpet vine needs full sun and well-drained soil to thrive. If yours doesn't have these growing conditions, flowering could be delayed.

Trumpet vine takeover

Last year I severely pruned an overgrown and extremely old trumpet vine. In the past few weeks it has sent up new plants all across my lawn. How can I kill these new plants, and maybe the old one too?

Trumpet vine activates dormant root buds when the parent plant is threatened. You may continue to see sprouts popping up for another year or two. Repeated mowing will kill them, or you can use a sharp knife to cut them off just below the soil line. It takes persistence to kill off the shoots. Avoid letting the shoots grow for long without removing them. By constantly mowing or pruning them off, you'll eventually starve the roots of energy.

Should you decide to get rid of the parent plant, cut off as many stems as you can, then spray the stump with a brush-killing herbicide. To give the herbicide time to kill the plant's roots, wait a month or so before digging out the stump. After the parent plant is gone, a fresh crop of trumpet vine root suckers may appear, determined to replace it, as you are finding. Continue cutting back the sprouts, and they'll eventually dwindle to nothing.

WISTERIA

Growing wisteria

I'd like to get a wisteria vine for my yard. Can you tell me where would be the best place to plant it, and what care it needs?

A wisteria vine in full bloom is enchanting. But wisterias aren't necessarily easy vines to grow. However, if you know the requirements and plan accordingly, you can grow a stunning wisteria.

- The right site. Plant your wisteria *(Wisteria)* in the right spot. To do best, the plant requires full sun (at least 6 hours a day) and well-drained soil. Especially important is a sturdy support, such as a pergola, because wisterias grow large and fast. The plant will quickly outgrow small structures and eventually the vine's heavy weight will crush them.
- Proper planting. Encourage success by planting your wisteria properly. First, work the soil well around the hole where the vine will be planted. The roots will grow through this loosened soil more easily. Second, set the plant in the ground no deeper than it was growing before. Planting it too deeply may delay or prevent blooming. Once the wisteria is planted, water it well and mulch the soil with a material such as shredded wood. Keep the wisteria watered for several weeks after planting to allow it to become established.
- Pruning practices. Prune your wisteria twice a year to keep it from growing out of bounds and to keep it flowering well. The first pruning session should happen in summer, just after the spring flush of growth. Cut off the tips of all the side shoots. Cut off any new shoots as well. The second pruning session should happen in winter. Cut back the main stems by about half. The side shoots pruned in spring can be further shortened: Cut them back to only a couple of inches from where you see the flowering spurs (which look like little pegs). This encourages the production of more flowering spurs, which means more flowers next spring.

Getting wisteria to bloom

Why doesn't my wisteria bloom?

This is one of the most common questions the Garden Doctor receives. The age of the vine and the time it takes to become established are the main issues. It can take wisteria more than 7 years after it's planted to bloom.

Improper growing conditions are also a common cause. If your wisteria was planted in heavy soil, shade, or other situations it doesn't like, the vine may fail to bloom well.

Some gardeners fertilize the plants to encourage them to grow and bloom. This, unfortunately, often works against them, because too much nitrogen causes a plant to put on leafy growth at the expense of flowers. Remember, too, that if your wisteria is growing near a lawn area, the roots may be absorbing the nitrogen-rich lawn fertilizer.

Although wisteria may be root-hardy into Zone 4, most varieties won't bloom reliably there. In Zone 5, plants may not bloom after severe winters because the cold freezes out the buds. Gardeners in Zone 5 should grow varieties such as 'Clara Mack', which have increased hardiness. In Zone 4 try Kentucky wisteria (*Wisteria macrostachya*) cultivars 'Aunt Dee' or 'Blue Moon'.

Pruning the roots with a shovel sometimes helps wisteria to bloom sooner, but this technique stresses the vine. Instead, focus on growing the plant in the right spot and pruning it properly for good blooming.

Choosing wisteria

Are there different kinds of wisteria? Which are the best ones to grow in a home garden?

There are some 50 wisteria varieties available to gardeners, but not all are suited to every garden. If you have a small garden or lack a sturdy structure on which to grow wisteria, substitute a smaller vine, such as Kentucky wisteria (*Wisteria macrostachya*) or American wisteria (*W. frutescens*). The Asian species Chinese wisteria (*W. sinensis*) and Japanese wisteria (*W. floribunda*) are considered invasive in many areas, especially the East. The American forms are smaller and don't grow as quickly, making them better suited to small gardens.

Wisteria can be invasive in the garden and is difficult to get rid of once established. To help restrain the plant's spreading root system, plant it in a courtyard where the roots can't escape into other areas or in a large container that you then place in the ground.

Tree-form wisteria

I bought a 5-foot-tall Chinese wisteria. It came with instructions saying it could be made into a small tree. I love this plant but am afraid to plant it in the ground since friends tell me it's aggressive. Can I put it in a larger pot and keep it pruned to 8 feet?

Chinese wisteria *(Wisteria sinensis)* is aggressive, but you can trim it aggressively without hurting it. Prune it after flowering and again once or twice during the summer, when you should trim back fresh long shoots to the principal stems. If necessary, prune the overall form in winter, retaining a main trunk and dense branching structure. Avoid removing the spur shoots (compact, woody stems with short internodes). These spurs, which come out of the major stems, are where most blooms appear.

Wisteria from seed

I want to start a wisteria from seed. How should I germinate the seed?

Wisteria is easy to grow from seed. Collect the mature (brown) seedpods and remove the seeds. Allow the seeds to dry, then store them in the refrigerator until spring. Sow seeds in spring after soaking them in water for 24 hours. Keep in mind that wisteria grown from seed may not closely resemble the parent plant. The seedlings that develop may not have the flower color or plant form that you would like. Also, seed-grown plants may not bloom for 10–15 years. Plants grown from cuttings or layered from a flowering plant usually begin flowering much earlier than seedlings. In addition, they'll be exact duplicates of the parent plant. For those reasons, you may want to vegetatively propagate your wisteria rather than starting new plants from seed.

Water Gardening

WATER GARDENING IN GENERAL

Pond considerations
I'd like a pond, but I want to make sure it fits into my landscape. What do I need to consider before installing one?

Ponds are wonderful in a landscape, and you're in luck, because just about any size garden can accommodate one. Ponder these questions as you look around your garden for a place to add a water element.

- How will you use your pond? Depending on how natural a setting you want, decide how many plants to place around your pond. Just about any pond will invite wildlife, but one with abundant plants draws more birds and butterflies. If your pond is more for reflection and quiet, place a chair near an area of open water where you can drink in the serenity.
- Is your landscape a place to entertain? If so, placing water near your porch or patio creates a crowd magnet. People will naturally congregate near the pond's edge, so provide a bench or a couple of chairs to allow guests to linger.
- Is your home near a busy city street? A pond with a fountain or waterfall is just right for such a spot. A recirculating water system will make pleasant splashing sounds if you give the water places to trickle and fall. If you don't have room for a waterfall, any sort of fountain that lets water return to the pond will create sound to mask the street noise.
- Are you short on space? Design a pond scaled to fit the room you have available. Consider all of your options: You may decide on a water garden in a large container or pot rather than an in-ground installation.

Siting a pond
I have a couple of places in my yard that may work for a pond. One is an open spot in the middle; the other is more natural looking but it's pretty close to a tree. Which would be better?

Without knowing the specifics about your site, I can't recommend one place over another. But consider these things as you make up your mind.

- Sunlight is important for plantings in or around your pond. Most water plants, such as water lilies, need 6–8 hours of sunlight a day to perform their best.
- You'll need a level site with well-drained soil. Though aquatic plants will be in the pond, you may want other kinds of plants (called marginal plants) around the perimeter. Marginal plants can tolerate a bog, whereas most other plants grow best in soil with good drainage.
- Select a microclimate where your pond plants can grow in calm water. Strong winds can damage delicate water plants in a matter of minutes.

- Site your pond away from trees if possible. An extensive root system will make it more difficult to dig the hole for your pond, and roots may eventually cause liner problems. Also, leaves or needles from the tree will fall into the pond, clogging the pump and filter and clouding the water. The closer your pond is to a tree, the more skimming you'll be doing.
- Consider how far away your pond is from electricity. You may need to consult a professional electrician about putting in a weatherproof electrical box near the site to plug in a pump or lighting.
- You'll also want a water supply nearby so you can top off the pond from time to time as needed.

Essential pond elements

With all the elements that go into designing a pond, it's difficult to know what I need to have versus what's nice to have. Is there a list of essentials I should include?

When designing your pond, create as naturalized an environment as possible for a flora-and-fauna aquatic haven. Here are the basics you'll need.
- Liner. This forms the basis for your pond. Purchase a preformed liner or a flexible one made of rubber. Or create your own by waterproofing a favorite container or flea-market find.
- Underlayment. Cushion an in-ground liner with underlayment. Use sand, carpet strips, or a commercial underlayment specifically designed for the task.
- Edging. Covering the edge of the liner protects and camouflages it. To blend in the edging with the pond surroundings, choose a natural material such as stone.
- Plants. A mix of surface, submerged, and marginal plants balances the plant life. Each kind of plant makes a unique contribution to the pond. In deep water, use overturned flowerpots, concrete blocks, or plastic crates to elevate water lilies and marginal plants to the shallow depths they prefer.
- Pots. Use plastic planting containers when possible. Avoid pots made of redwood or treated lumber; dye or chemicals can leach from the wood into the water and harm plants or fish.
- Pumps and filters. A filter fitted with a submersible pump will help keep your pond-cleaning chores to a minimum. A clean pond better supports fish, plants, and wildlife.
- Animals. Fish, snails, and turtles are all options for your pond. If you're new to water gardening, try growing just plants to start. Once you have the feel for water gardening, add fish and other animals a few at a time.

Water garden safety

Before we built our shed we needed a building permit. Is this also the case with installing a pond? Is there anything else I need to do before I get started?

Whether you need any special permits depends on where you live. Check with your insurer and local building officials about building codes, city ordinances, or liability concerns regarding a pond. In some places, any pond more than a few inches deep must be enclosed with a fence and a locked gate. You'll always have to watch small children around a pond, no matter what other kinds of safety precautions you take.

Because digging a pond can pose a safety hazard, check with local utilities before you thrust that shovel into the ground. Find out whether any buried gas or water lines are in the area or if there are buried wires for electricity, phone, or cable television. Many communities now have one agency or organization that will arrange to have the location of buried pipes or wires marked in your yard. Using this utility locator service is often required by law, and you could find yourself liable for repairs if you don't have the area marked before you begin digging.

Water garden workload

We've been thinking about installing a water garden, but with all the other things we have to do, we're not sure we can handle the extra workload. Are we creating a lot more work for ourselves if we put in a pond?

Although I wouldn't want to lull you into thinking that a water garden is low-maintenance, it's not as much work as you might think. Once you have established a balance of plants (and animals, if you wish), your water garden responsibilities will diminish considerably.

Establishing the garden takes the most work, but it isn't difficult, even for beginners. A local garden center can help you find the materials needed to create your design. It's up to you whether you want to do the installation yourself or hire help. After that, maintenance is key. Here are a few things to consider.

- Keep it clean. A clean pond better supports fish, plants, and wildlife. To minimize maintenance, put in a good filtration system. These systems are being refined all the time, so check with a local garden center to learn about the latest developments and to see what's recommended for the kind of pond you want. Even with the best system, though, you'll still need to regularly skim off leaves and debris.
- Top it off. Ponds lose water to evaporation, especially in places with very hot, dry summers. Periodically add water to bring the pond level up to normal. Adding water helps keep the plants and fish comfortable.

- Divide and conquer. Aquatic plants, like other garden plants, need to be divided and repotted occasionally. You will probably need to do this only once every year or two.
- Find time to feed. Fish and plants both need to be fed, though fish require a more frequent feeding schedule.
- Plan for winter. If you live where temperatures remain above freezing, you can enjoy your water garden year-round. In colder climates, you'll have more maintenance at the end of the season as you prepare to overwinter the plants and pond mechanisms.

Chlorinated tap water

Our tap water has chlorine in it. Can I use that in my water garden, or will it cause problems for fish or plants?

Chlorine dissipates from the water in a few days, or you can add a dechlorinator. After filling your water garden, let it sit for 5–7 days before adding fish or plants. Of greater concern than chlorine are chloramines, which occur naturally or may be added to water supplies. Call your water supplier to ask if they are present. If they are, treat your water with a chloramine remover before adding fish.

Water-garden winter worries

Will my pond freeze in cold weather? If it does, will this kill my plants or fish? Will winter cold crack the liner of the pond or freeze the filters?

If you live in an area with freezing temperatures, make winterizing part of your pond routine. If you grow tropical water lilies or other tender plants, bring them in for the winter and store or tend them during the cold months.

   If you have fish in your pond, it's best to keep the surface from freezing over completely. An open hole in the ice allows waste gases to vent. Also, a frozen pond surface puts pressure on the pond's liner, which may lead to cracks or splits. A small bubble fountain may be enough to keep a hole open on your pond, but if you live where it gets really cold, a floating heater is a better option.

   Another way to ease the pressure on your pond liner is to float a few objects on the surface of the water. A ball or two does the trick; a rubber duck adds a bit of whimsy to the winter months.

   Most pond liners today can withstand some freezing and thawing. Just make sure that your liner is installed according to the manufacturer's instructions and is properly supported on a soft sand base.

Muddy waters

After a rain, my water garden always looks cloudy or muddy for a while. Will that cause problems?

Muddy water in itself is usually not a problem; the silt that causes the cloudiness settles within a few hours or days. The problem could be caused by soil erosion or mud splashed into the pond by heavy rain. Check around your water feature for eroding or exposed bare soil. Spread pea gravel or organic mulch, or plant a ground cover in the problem area to prevent additional erosion. Also make certain that surface water is not flowing into the water garden. You may need to create a berm or diversion channel to channel water around the pond.

Mosquito haven?

We're considering putting in a water garden but are worried that it will be a breeding ground for mosquitoes. How can we make sure that it doesn't become one?

A neglected or badly planned water garden can indeed be a haven for mosquitoes. But you can prevent mosquitoes in a couple of ways.

First, make sure the water moves. A strong fountain or splashing waterfall will accomplish this.

Alternatively, stock the water feature with fish, especially goldfish. If the water garden is too small for goldfish, use mosquito fish. Both eat mosquito larvae.

Repairing a leak

The water level in my pond keeps dropping. I am guessing that the liner has a leak. How do I repair it?

To repair a leaky pond, drain it with a pump or siphon and locate the leak. (If your pond level drops to a certain point and stops dropping farther, you'll find the leak at that water level.) Remove anything that may have punctured the liner, such as stones or sticks. Back the puncture or tear, if possible, with damp sand or pond underlayment. Then clean and dry the surface of the liner around the leak. Using pond liner adhesive and following repair kit instructions, spread adhesive on a patch at least 2 inches longer and wider than the leak, and attach the patch to the punctured liner. Let the patch dry before refilling the pond.

You may need to move fish and plants to temporary holding quarters while the repair is being made.

Leaves in pond

Every fall my pond gets covered in falling leaves from the trees nearby. I can't keep up with scooping them out. What can I do?

Fallen leaves need to be removed almost daily so they don't decay and pollute the water. If your water feature is located under a tree, consider stretching netting over the pond to catch the leaves. Anchor the netting on the side with bricks or stakes driven into the soil. Remove the netted leaves regularly so they don't shade the water garden.

If the leaves sink to the bottom, remove them by hand or with a soft plastic rake. For larger ponds, consider investing in a pool sweep, which attaches to a garden hose and uses water pressure to remove debris and silt from the pond's bottom. A spa vacuum also works. Both are available from water garden suppliers.

EQUIPMENT AND SUPPLIES

Pump burnout

My submersible pump quit after just a few months. Is there anything I can do to make certain that won't happen right away again?

With proper care, a good-quality water garden pump should last for several years. For longest life, make sure that debris or algae don't overburden the motor. Clean the prefilter in the intake filter at least once a week during the spring, and up to three times a week in summer and fall. Keep the pump from sitting directly on the pond bottom, where it will take in more silt. Set it on a brick or flat stone. If algae clog the pump, clean the pump and make an additional filter by wrapping the pump in a large piece of fiberglass window screen, then place it inside a black plastic basket. Running the pump without water will burn out the motor.

Cracked container

I have a container I'd like to plant as a water garden—but the container has a crack in it and leaks. What can I do?

A favorite container can often make a perfect water garden. You should be able to find a water garden sealant or caulk available at your local home improvement or hardware store, or at your local garden center. Paint the product over the crack and give it time to cure before adding water. If the container has a drainage hole, use a bolt with a rubber gasket or similar piece of hardware to fill the hole.

Pump size

What size pump do I need for the filter in my water garden?

The size of pump you choose depends on the kind of filter you have. Pumps are rated by the amount of water they move in a given length of time. That's usually given in gallons per hour, sometimes listed as GPH. If you're going to use a mechanical filter, you will need a pump that moves all the water through the filter once every 2 hours. If you're using a biological filter, you can get by with only one-half to one-third that flow rate. That means your water will circulate through the biological filter once every 4–6 hours.

You don't need to choose the biggest pump in the store (bigger isn't always better). The number of gallons of water pumped per hour should never be more than the number of gallons in the pond. In other words, if you have a 100-gallon pond, buy a pump that moves 100 GPH or less.

PLANTS

Pond plants

I'd like plants in my pond, but I'm not sure where to start. Are some plants better for ponds than others? Will fish eat them?

Plants are perfect for ponds if your water feature is located where it gets at least 6 hours of direct sunlight a day. Once you have met that condition, select a range of plants that complement one another in growth habit, color, height, and bloom time. Choose a variety of water plants: surface (or floating), submerged (or oxygenating), marginal (or edge), and water lilies.

- Surface plants float on or below the surface, creating shade for underwater life. Place these plants in at least 3 inches of water. They'll float around, absorbing nutrients through suspended roots. Examples of floating plants include duckweed *(Lemna minor)*, water hyacinth *(Eichhornia crassipes),* and water lettuce *(Pistia stratiotes)*.
- Submerged plants aerate the water, which is good for fish. These bottom-dwelling plants also compete with algae for carbon dioxide, helping control the algae population. Examples of submerged plants include anacharis *(Egeria densa),* Canadian pondweed *(Elodea canadensis),* and fanwort *(Cabomba caroliniana)*.
- Marginal plants add seasonal interest, color, and height. They like to have their foliage dry and their feet wet. To grow these plants, purchase a liner with shelves, or build ledges in a rubber-lined water garden. To forgo the ledge and grow marginal plants, simply elevate the pots. Either way, position the plants so that no more than an inch of stem is below the water's surface. Examples of marginal plants include canna *(Canna)*, cattail *(Typha latifolia)*, papyrus *(Cyperus papyrus),* and sweet flag *(Acorus calamus)*.

- Water lilies *(Nymphaea)* should be planted in pots that are sunk into about 6 inches of water. The plants send up floating leaves that spread out on the surface of the pond; they also produce gorgeous blooms. There are tropical and hardy varieties available; make sure you know which plants you are growing so you can protect them accordingly.

   And, yes, koi may eat some of your water garden plants. (Most other fish do not, however.)

Winter care for hardy water lilies

I've heard that I can leave my hardy water lilies in the pond all winter. Is there anything special I need to do, or can I leave them where they are?

You can leave hardy water lilies in the pond all winter, just not in their usual locations. Here's how to have healthy, happy lilies when the snow flies in winter.

- Remove all dead and dying foliage from your plant. Lower the pot or basket containing the water lily rhizome to the deepest part of the pond, where it doesn't freeze solid. This may require moving the container from the pond's edge to the center, or it may mean removing supporting blocks or bricks that kept the container at the proper height for the lily's leaves to float to the surface. Make sure there is an opening in the surface ice that lets gases escape.
- Keeping lilies in the pond over winter is more challenging if the water feature freezes solid or if you drain the pond during cold weather. Install a floating water heater, available from your local garden center, or remove the lily, pot and all. Store the entire pot in a plastic bag kept at 40–50°F and keep the plant moist. Or remove the rhizome from the container, rinse it, and store it in moist peat moss at 40–50°F. In spring, repot it as though it were a new plant.
- In spring after the pond has thawed, return the pot to the proper growing level.

Water lily types

What is the difference between hardy water lilies and tropical water lilies? Which kind should I plant in my water garden?

It's difficult to go wrong by choosing either! Both kinds of water lilies *(Nymphaea)* are considered the crown jewels of the water garden. The main difference is that tropical water lilies love hot weather and won't make it through a cold winter, and hardy water lilies, although producing smaller flowers, are more cold-tolerant. Here are some features of each.

Tropical water lilies

- Are grown from tubers.
- Are profuse bloomers and intensely fragrant, and the only water lilies that produce blue and purple flowers. In general, they're larger and showier than the hardy varieties.
- Usually hold their blooms high above the surface of the pond.
- Bloom in the heat of the day (some blossom at night). The day-blooming lilies are sweetly scented, whereas the night bloomers have a heavy fragrance.
- Need at least 6 hours of direct sunlight a day and 2 weeks of weather with temperatures above 80°F to bloom.
- Can bloom throughout the summer, with showy 10-inch blossoms.
- Can be treated as annual plants in Zones 3–8 or brought inside if there is a danger of frost. Tend them as you would a tender perennial in Zone 9; they usually can make it through the winter on their own in Zones 10 and 11.

Hardy water lilies

- Are grown from rhizomes.
- Range in size from pygmy (those with leaves that cover less than 3 square feet of a pond's surface) to large (giants with 12 square feet of leaves, suited only for the largest ponds).
- Can live in a pond all winter if the water doesn't freeze solid and if you move them to the pond's deepest spot.
- Produce flowers that float on the water.
- Bloom in pink, white, yellow, peach, salmon, and red. Some types change color as the blossoms age and fade.
- Need at least 5–6 hours of direct sunlight to bloom.
- Can flower throughout the summer, with blossoms opening in the morning and closing in the afternoon.
- Come in varieties for almost any zone.

How many water lilies?

For our first pond, I planted a few water lilies and submerged plants. Midway through the summer the water lilies died off, causing an abundance of algae. What's the correct ratio of water lilies to other types of plants?

For successful pond life, you'll need to provide a balance of submerged and floating plants. A good rule of thumb is to have 5 or 6 stems of submerged plants in a bunch per square foot of pond surface area, and enough water lilies and floating plants to cover half the water's surface.

Submerged plants supply your pond with dissolved oxygen. Plant too few and your fish won't get enough oxygen. On the other hand, too many submerged plants clog the bottom of the pond with green growth, making it tough for water lilies and surface plants to survive. Keep an eye on submerged plants to make sure they are healthy but not too prolific.

Surface plants, and those with leaves that float, shade part of the pond's surface and deny algae the light they need for explosive growth. Without enough of these plants, sunlight can shine through the water's surface and encourage algae to grow. On the other hand, if you have too many surface plants, they rob the submerged plants of light, causing them to die and begin to decompose, making the pond water black and foul. Monitor your surface plants, allowing them to cover no more than half the water's surface for a balance.

Planting a water lily

I've ordered some water lilies. Do they need any special treatment before planting? What's the best way to plant them?

Water lilies *(Nymphaea)* are typically sold as bare-root plants. The best thing you can do for your new plants is move them to their new home right away. Begin by removing the packing material and checking the plants for any damage that may have occurred during shipping. A few yellow or bent leaves are to be expected.

Wash off any soil to avoid having this floating debris in your pond. Then place the plants in a bucket of tepid water and keep them in a cool place away from direct sunlight. You're now ready to plant. Here's how:

1. Use clean garden clippers to remove any limp brown roots. (Healthy roots are white and crisp.) Trim the root system to fit your container. Keep roots moist until planted.

2. Use aquatic planting crates with mesh sides, which allow roots to breathe underwater without letting soil escape. Fill each crate with topsoil, adding water lily fertilizer tablets; avoid using peat-based potting mixes. Create a shallow well in which to place the plant.

3. Water the container thoroughly before adding the water lily. Place a tropical lily in the center of the crate, spreading out the roots around the plant. Position a hardy lily so the growing tip pokes out of the soil at a 45-degree angle.

4. Bury the water lily roots in topsoil, pressing down firmly. The growing point, or crown, should protrude above the soil line. Water the crate again, taking care not to wash away soil or expose any roots.

5. Spread a ½-inch layer of small stones on top of the soil (avoid using limestone). Take care not to bury the crown of the water lily with stones. The stones will keep the soil in place once the crate is placed underwater.

6. Water the crate one last time. Place it in your water garden so that a tropical water lily is covered with 4–6 inches of water and a hardy lily with 6–8 inches. Watch for the first new leaves to appear in 2–3 weeks, followed by flowers.

My water lily didn't bloom this year. What did I do wrong?

Failure of a water lily to bloom can be caused by several things.

Overcrowded roots in the pot can be one reason a lily doesn't bloom. Check to see if the roots are pushing out the sides or top of the container, or if they're packed in so tightly that they're distorting the container. If so, divide the plant and repot it.

Also, check light levels. Lilies are sun lovers, requiring at least 6 hours of full sun each day. Any less and blooms will be diminished.

Make sure, too, that the lily isn't getting too much competition from other water lilies, deepwater plants or floaters. Keep yellowing or dying foliage trimmed to help the plant devote as much energy as possible to blooming.

WILDLIFE

Attracting wildlife to a pond

We just finished installing a pond and would like to attract wildlife to it, but we don't want raccoons to eat the fish. How can we attract some wildlife and keep others away?

If you build it, they will come. Birds, snails, squirrels, and, depending on where you live, even raccoons or herons will find their way to your water garden.

Moving water is a magnet for birds. Many of them prefer a splashing fountain in a pond or the activity around a waterfall to the stillness of a birdbath. Provide a food source for them by planting seed-bearing plants, such as black-eyed Susan (*Rudbeckia*) and ornamental grasses.

Ponds also attract unwanted visitors—mosquitoes. Stagnant ponds can quickly become a breeding place for these insect pests. Moving water can keep mosquitoes from breeding. In still ponds, use fish—they'll eat mosquito larvae.

Once you add fish, you are right to be concerned about raccoons. Herons and neighborhood cats may also show up looking for a quick fish snack. If predators become too much of a problem, put in more plants with foliage to provide a refuge. Or provide an area of the pond deep enough (30–36 inches) for the fish to take cover. A bridge or ledge also creates shade where fish can hide. You could also include a fish tunnel in your pond to provide shelter from predators.

The quickest route to a balanced relationship for pond wildlife may be a policy of nonintervention. It takes a little time for fish to get used to their surroundings, including plants, insects, and places to hide. The balance, in turn, may take some getting used to by the bird and mammal population. When you do need to intervene, do so minimally.

How many fish?

How many fish should I put in my pond for a healthy ratio of aquatic life to plants and water?

A good rule is 2 inches of goldfish or 1 inch of koi per 10 gallons of pond water. For example, in a 100-gallon pond, you'd need four 5-inch goldfish (a total of 20 inches of goldfish) or two 5-inch koi. In a 1,000-gallon pond, you could have forty 5-inch goldfish or ten 10-inch koi. Make sure you regulate the number of fish as they grow and multiply.

Start out on the conservative side, because the figures cited are what you should strive for to have a good balance. Work up to them slowly.

Also, avoid adding koi if the surface area of your pond is less than 100 square feet. Never put more than 2 or 3 goldfish in ponds with less than 50 gallons of water, and avoid koi in such small water gardens. If you feel the need for fishlike additions to a tiny pond, add a few tadpoles for mosquito and algae control. Tadpoles are suitable for the smallest ponds and are available from water garden suppliers. They help control mosquitoes but should not be used in areas where the adult bullfrogs are considered invasive.

Overwintering fish indoors

How do I overwinter fish indoors? Can I put them in a bucket of water in the basement?

An aquarium is ideal for overwintering water-garden fish because the fish will be easy to observe. But they can be kept in just about any clean container that hasn't held detergent or chemicals. Container size depends on the size and number of fish. Figure 1 gallon of water for every inch of fish.

Supply oxygen to the container with an air pump. Keep the water cool—between 45 and 60°F. The fish can tolerate up to 80°F, but they will need a larger container. You'll need to change the water more frequently, and feed the fish more often at the warmer temperature.

Periodically change 20 percent of the water, and keep feeding to a minimum. Fish should be ravenous when you feed them.

Koi or goldfish?

I want fish in my water garden. It's big enough for koi, but I can't decide between koi and goldfish. Are there reasons to pick one over the other?

Including fish in your water garden is a good idea. They help balance a pond, as well as eat algae and mosquitoes. Here are some qualities of each of these fish.

Koi

- Part of the carp family; feed on plants.
- Friendly—can even be taught to eat out of your hand.
- Can sell for thousands of dollars if rare, but cost as little as $10–$20, depending on size, for common ones ordered from pond suppliers. A bit more exotic and only a little more expensive, butterfly koi can be ordered for $12–$29.
- Grow 1½–3 feet long.
- Suitable for ponds with more than 100 square feet of surface area or at least 50-gallon capacity.
- Winter hardy.
- Thrive in clear, filtered water.
- Live for decades.

Goldfish

- Easy to grow; feed on mosquito larvae and other small insects
- Shy except in large numbers.
- Inexpensive and available from many pet stores and through mail order. Depending on size, comets cost $4–$8, Japanese fantails $6–$11, and shubunkins $5–$10.
- Winter hardy.
- Bright golden color.
- Grow up to 12 inches long, depending on size of pond.
- Live 10–15 years.

Power failure and fish

What happens if the power goes out? Will my fish die?

If the power goes out for just a few hours, even in hot weather, your fish should be fine. However, if the power is out for several days, the fish might become stressed for lack of oxygen. If they show signs of stress—gulping at the water's surface—install a battery-powered air pump to aerate the water. If you plan to keep expensive fish, it's wise to invest in an air pump or generator for just such emergencies.

The Kitchen Garden

FRUITS IN GENERAL

When to plant

When is the best time to plant fruit trees and raspberries?

In most areas, early spring, when the plants begin to emerge from dormancy, is the ideal time to set out any deciduous plant, including fruits. The surge of energy that results in new growth is matched belowground, as new roots stretch out in every direction. If you wait until later in spring, look for plants grown in containers; they transplant more easily than bare-root plants after they have emerged from dormancy. In mild-winter regions, late fall is a good time to plant fruit trees and berries. Cooler temperatures through the winter allow the plants to become established before the stressful heat of summer sets in.

Most fruit trees begin bearing 2–5 years after planting, but you can expect a good raspberry crop a year after planting.

Fruit planting considerations

I'd like to grow some fruit trees and berries in the yard. What should I consider before I decide what to grow?

Most fruit crops require full sun and well-drained soil. If your yard is shady, it may be best to let someone else grow the fruit for you at an orchard. Generally, strawberries and raspberries are the easiest fruits to grow. Grapes (which need a lot of pruning) and blueberries (which need moist, acidic soil) are moderately difficult to grow. And tree fruits are the most difficult to grow. In terms of pesticide treatments needed for a good-quality crop, from least to greatest, they rank like this: blueberry, raspberry, strawberry, grape, and tree fruits.

Some fruits require cross-pollination for fruit set. Apples, pears, plums, and some sweet cherries fall into this category. Two trees of different varieties should be planted within about 100 feet of each other for cross-pollination.

Fruits can be attacked by many disease and insect pests. To minimize the amount of spraying you'll need to do, choose varieties that are resistant to disease problems whenever possible.

Dormant oil spray

When is the best time to use dormant oil spray to protect my peach and apple trees?

Dormant oil effectively smothers many overwintering pests on fruit trees. A timely application of dormant oil can delay or eliminate the onset of certain diseases and insects. The best time to apply dormant oil is just before the buds break in late winter or early spring. Spray when temperatures will stay above freezing for at least 48 hours but while the trees are still dormant. Thoroughly cover all plant surfaces. Avoid spraying if the trees are already leafing out.

Preventing fruit set

Is there any way to keep fruit trees from producing fruit? I like the trees, but the fruits end up being messy every year.

There is no permanent solution to this problem. Take heart, though: Commercial growers use a spray to thin fruit. These sprays reduce the crop by applying plant hormones that cause fruit drop. When they're applied during or right after bloom, the mess is negligible. A commercially available fruit preventer is Florel. The spray must be applied during bloom, and must thoroughly cover the entire tree. Ironically, when you remove the crop, the tree puts more energy into the next year's fruit buds, ensuring a big crop if you let it go.

If you really don't want the fruit, you may be better off removing the trees and planting ornamental trees that produce flowers but no fruit.

Cross-pollination

I just bought four different kinds of fruit trees. On the tags it says to cross-pollinate. What will happen if I have only one of each tree?

Depending on what kinds of trees you have, you may get no fruit at all. Some fruit trees are "self-fruitful," meaning they don't require pollination from a different tree to bear fruit, but that doesn't sound like the case in your situation. Even for trees that are self-fruitful, yields are often increased if another variety is planted nearby for cross-pollination.

If another variety of fruit tree of the same species is within 500 feet or so of yours, and you have bees and other insects in the neighborhood, they will likely take care of the pollination for you. If your neighbors have some of the same kinds of fruit trees, you may not need to plant a pollinator. However, if the trees are not planted close together, or if insect pollinators are lacking, you may not get good yields. It won't work to just plant another tree of the same variety, either. For cross-pollination to happen, the trees must be genetically different from each other (but still the same species). For example, pollen from a 'Fuji' apple won't pollinate another Fuji apple, but it would pollinate a 'Gala' apple. And it's impossible for an apple tree to pollinate a pear, cherry, peach, or plum.

Best berries

I'd like to grow some berries in my yard. What are the best varieties?

The best varieties of berries to grow depends on your location. Few varieties grow equally well everywhere in North America. The following lists will give you a few cultivars from which to choose. For a more extensive list, check with your local cooperative extension service for recommended varieties.

Best berries to grow		
June-bearing strawberries	**Cold climates**	'Blomiden', 'Delite', 'Guardian', 'Honeoye', 'Kent', and 'Redchief'
	South	'Cardinal', 'Earliglow', 'Sunrise', 'Surecrop', and 'Tioga'
	Deep South	'Sweet Charlie'
Everbearing strawberries	**Cold climates**	'Fort Laramie' and 'Ogallala'
	South and Deep South	'Chandler'
	Pacific Northwest	'Hood', 'Redcrest', and 'Totem'
Raspberries	**Cold climates**	'Autumn Bliss', 'Canby', 'Heritage', and 'Nova'
	Pacific Northwest	'Bababerry'
	South	'Bababerry'
Blueberries	**Coldest climates**	'Chippewa', 'Northblue', 'Northsky', and 'Polaris'
	Cold climates	'Duke', 'Earliblue', 'Ozarkblue', and 'Toro'
	South	'Jubilee', 'Misty', and 'Sharpblue'
	Deep South	'Powderblue', 'Sunshine blue', and 'Tifblue'

APPLE

When to pick apples

How do I know when to pick my apples? I've never grown them before.

The most certain way to know when to pick apples is to pick one and taste it! The fruit should have developed a good color for the variety. Some are deep red, others are red with a yellow background, and yet others mature to yellow or green. Get to know the characteristics of the varieties you are growing. Mature fruits will have dark brown seeds. Cut through the core to check this.

Apples will also ripen off the tree, but not if picked too green. If you plan to store the fruit for a long time, pick the fruit slightly on the green side, because it will continue to ripen a bit after harvest. However, for best flavor allow the fruit to ripen on the tree. Keep in mind that fruit on a single tree may ripen over a couple of weeks. Fruits exposed to full sun at branch tips often ripen earlier than those hidden deep in the foliage. You may need to harvest several times to catch all fruits at their prime.

Harvesting crabapples

I bought a house that has some apple trees and a crabapple tree. When my crabapples are ripe, I would love to pick them, but I have no clue what they are good for. If I don't pick the apples, will the tree continue to produce fruit?

Most crabapples are planted mainly for the ornamental appearance of their blossoms and fruit. Depending on the variety, the fruit may hang on the tree into the fall and winter, and be left to feed the birds. One drawback to letting birds snack is that some nonnative ornamental crabapples have become invasive due to the birds spreading the seeds.

In addition to their ornamental value, some crabapples serve as pollinators for regular apples. Your crabapple may be helping the apples in your yard bear fruit.

Crabapples will continue to bear without being picked, though they may produce a heavy crop one year and little or no fruit the next. This tendency varies with variety.

Tart crabapples can add body and character to apple cider. Otherwise, try making jelly or pickled crabapples out of them. Crabapples are useful in making jelly because they contain so much natural pectin that it often isn't necessary to add commercial pectin to make the jelly set.

Chemical-free apples

I want to grow apples but don't want to have to spray all the time. Are there any varieties that don't need to be sprayed?

Many apples are susceptible to diseases such as apple scab, cedar apple rust, and fire blight. Backyard orchardists should consider growing varieties that are resistant to these diseases if they wish to avoid pesticide sprays. Scab-resistant cultivars include the early-season varieties 'Redfree', 'Prima', 'Jonafree', and 'Sir Prize'. For midseason production try 'Novamac', 'Liberty', or 'Freedom'. 'Enterprise' and 'Goldrush' are resistant late-season varieties.

Depending on your region, you'll also have insect pests such as codling moth and apple maggot to contend with. Several low-toxicity options are available to manage these pests. See "Spots on apples," on page 303.

Apples from seed

I have seeds I saved from apples purchased from the grocery store. Will they come up if I plant them? How should I plant them?

Most apples are grown from grafted trees and will not come true from seed. The seeds might germinate, and they could develop into productive trees, but the fruit might not be similar to the fruit you purchased. Fruit breeders plant thousands of apple seeds every year from controlled crosses they make. Of these seedlings, no more than one or two are expected to make it into commercial production. If you want an apple tree that develops tasty fruit, you should buy a known variety from a nursery or mail-order source. You can find almost any variety of tree available, and trees you purchase will fruit in a much shorter time. A seed-started tree could take 8–10 years to fruit. Also, apple trees started from seed will have no dwarfing characteristics. Unless you have a large yard, they may be too big for your site.

If you're the adventurous type and would like to start the seeds despite my discouragement, here's how to do it: Remove the seeds from the ripe fruit. Plant them an inch deep in a pot containing potting soil or seed germinating mix. Moisten the soil. Bury the pot outdoors in the ground in fall, or place it in a plastic bag in the refrigerator, away from ripening fruits and vegetables. Periodically check the soil mix to make certain it stays moist but not wet. After 3–4 months of temperatures just above freezing, move the pot to a location at room temperature (or wait for warm temperatures to develop naturally outdoors). If properly chilled, the seeds should germinate in several weeks.

Spots on apples

I have 'Fuji' and 'Gravenstein' apple trees. Each year the apples have black spots where an insect has laid eggs. How can I prevent this from happening so I can harvest more apples?

The usual, chemical way to achieve blemish-free fruit is with a regular fruit-tree spray program. Your county extension service or a local garden center can give you a complete program for spraying your trees.

However, some good nontoxic methods have recently become popular. One of the more interesting is Surround, a product made from a special clay. The clay forms a physical barrier on the fruit and tree that keeps most insects and diseases from coming in contact with the leaf or fruit surfaces.

Or hang sticky red spheres in the trees to trap the insects when they come to lay their eggs. When used properly, the spheres offer as much or more protection as spray. Be sure to use scent lures to make the traps much more effective.

Another thought: Are you sure the black spots are insects? Some fruit rots cause similar symptoms. Calcium deficiency of apples can cause sunken, corky spots in the fruit, for example. If you're not certain, you might take a sample apple to your local garden center or a cooperative extension agent for diagnosis.

Rejuvenating old apple tree

We just moved into a house that has several badly neglected old apple trees on the property. I don't want to lose them. What do I need to do to rejuvenate them so we can harvest fruit in the fall?

Apple trees, even neglected ones, generally can be completely renovated with 5–6 years of knowledgeable pruning. It may be unrealistic to expect a good crop for several years, until you get the trees back into shape. A good place to start is by removing any dead or damaged branches in late winter while the tree is still dormant. Next take out crossing branches and those growing inward, downward, or strongly upright. Thin out branches growing directly on top of one another. However, you should remove no more than about ¼ of the branches each year. For more detailed instructions, get a book about fruit growing and follow the pruning diagrams, or check with your county extension service for bulletins on pruning fruit trees.

AVOCADO

Growing avocados

I have two avocado trees in pots that I grew from seed. I would like to transplant them into the ground but am concerned about them surviving the winter outside. If I transplant them to a larger container, would they produce fruit? And at what age do avocados start to bear?

If you occasionally get freezing temperatures where you live, your avocados won't survive in the ground outdoors. You can transplant them into larger containers and continue to overwinter them indoors. Avocados grown from seed take 5–13 years to produce fruit and may never do so in a container indoors. Another option would be to enjoy your trees as ornamentals and purchase a Don Gillogly avocado, also known as the indoor fruiting avocado tree. If it receives bright light and proper care, it reliably bears fruit twice a year and is smaller-growing than its counterparts.

BLACKBERRY

Pruning blackberries

I have two thornless blackberry bushes on trellises. They have been there for 4 years and produce the juiciest fruit. How do I prune them? Do I have to trim off all the leaves?

Blackberries bear fruit on canes that grew the previous year. Once the canes finish bearing for the season, cut them off at the base. Remove only the canes that bore fruit that year. (They will be woodier and have fruit stalks on the canes.) New canes that started growth that spring will take their place as the bearing canes the following year. In winter, when the new canes are dormant, shorten them by about one-third to encourage branching of fruiting shoots lower down on the canes in spring.

Blackberries do best with lots of organic mulch (such as compost, shredded leaves, hay, or the like) to feed them and keep the soil moisture constant.

Sweeter blackberries

What can I add to my soil to make blackberries sweeter?

Do you know what type of blackberry you're growing? Some varieties are naturally quite tart. They're usually used for jams and pies (because you can add sugar to make them more palatable) instead of eating fresh.

You can improve the general quality and flavor of the fruit by keeping the soil around the plants well covered with organic mulch (such as compost, straw, or shredded leaves). Mulch feeds the soil, which helps strengthen the plant and thus improves the fruit quality. Mulch also helps prevent rapid drying of the soil, which can stress the plant and cause irregular, shriveled, or hard berries.

In the end, you can't overcome the heritage of a naturally tart variety, but you can get it to produce its best possible fruit. If you don't like the fruit you have even after trying the above recommendation, replace it with a sweeter-tasting variety.

Removing unwanted blackberry bushes
I have blackberry bushes all over my yard. I want to keep a few around to have blackberries for pies but would like to get rid of the rest. What is the best way to kill the rest of them without ruining the ground?

Begin by choosing the plants you want to keep. Blackberries that grow in full sun and good-quality soil generally produce the largest, best-tasting berries. To limit the future spread of your blackberry patch, make sure it's in a place where you can mow around the edges. A mowing margin provides easy access for berry picking while limiting the blackberries' spread.

You can get rid of the plants you don't want by spraying them with a woody brush-killer herbicide. Be sure to cover nearby cultivated plants—including the lawn—with plastic to prevent damage by the herbicide. Some blackberry root buds may survive and send up shoots the next season, but you can eliminate them by chopping them down with a sharp hoe.

If you prefer not to use an herbicide, you could cut off the blackberry vines at ground level. Mow or chop off any shoots that resprout.

Blackberry rust
The leaves of my blackberries are covered in orange powder. What is it? Will it harm the plants?

It sounds as though your blackberries have become infected with orange rust, a serious fungal disease that attacks blackberries and some black raspberries (but not red or purple raspberries). The orange powder you see is spores of the fungus. These spores spread from plant to plant on the wind. Quickly remove and destroy infected plants. Once infected, plants remain infected for their entire life, and produce no blossoms or fruit. No fungicide sprays are effective in controlling the disease. Failure to remove the infected plants risks spreading the disease to other blackberries nearby. If wild blackberries are growing nearby, remove them too. They may have been the source of the disease on your cultivated plantings. Establish new plantings from a disease-free source or from tissue-cultured plants.

BLUEBERRY

Growing blueberries

I'd like to grow blueberries. What do I need to know to be successful?

First, be sure you have a spot with moist but well-drained acidic soil. If your soil isn't acidic enough, the plants won't do well. If you live in an area with high-pH soil, you can grow blueberries in containers filled with an acidic peat-based potting mix, or amend the soil with an acidifying agent such as sulfur or iron sulfate.

Next, find the right type of blueberries for your area. If you live in the South, a rabbiteye type, such as 'Powderblue' or 'Tifblue', is best. In order to get fruit, grow two cultivars together. Rabbiteye blueberries are native to areas of southeastern North America.

Southern gardeners also can grow southern highbush types, such as 'Sharpblue' or 'Misty'. Unlike rabbiteye types, these plants do not need an additional variety in order to produce berries. That said, a second cultivar would be helpful in producing more fruits.

If you live in the North, plant a northern highbush type, such as 'Legacy' or 'Earliblue'. Most northern highbush types don't require a second cultivar to help them produce good fruit crops. In the Far North (Zone 4 or colder), half-high types, which are crosses between wild lowbush types and cultivated highbush types, will be your best bet. "Chippewa', 'Northsky', 'Northblue', and 'St. Cloud' are half-highbush cultivars.

Rock mulch for blueberries

I purchased a house that has blueberry bushes. They're planted in a bed covered with river rock in full sun. Should I remove the rock and replace it with mulch? If I replace the rock with mulch, do I need to work anything into the soil?

The rock over your blueberries is mulch, albeit an inert one. It discourages weeds and shelters earthworms as well as holding warmth in summer. In all but the coldest climates, it may cause overheating of the soil and injury to the shallow roots of blueberry. If you want to replace it with shredded bark, pine needles, or another organic mulch, simply pick up the rocks, pull out any weeds, and spread the new mulch over the surface. Because blueberry roots are shallow and are easily damaged if you cultivate the soil's surface, avoid the temptation to dig anything into the soil. If you want to enrich the soil, spread a shallow layer of compost or composted manure over the soil, then add your new mulch.

I want to grow blueberries near a spruce. I've heard that the 'Tophat' variety tolerates part shade. Will the spruce needles that drop off the tree kill the blueberries?

If the area you plan to plant is shady enough that lawn won't grow, it's not likely to be sunny enough for blueberries, which need 6–8 hours of sunlight a day. If grown in too much shade, blueberries produce spindly new growth and poor-quality fruits. Lack of moisture is a concern when gowing blueberries near a spruce tree. The tree roots soak up most of the available water. Spruce needles will not hurt blueberries if the plants get enough sun. If sunshine in this space is limited, hardy ferns or another shade-tolerant ground cover would be a better choice than blueberries.

CITRUS

Where can I grow citrus trees? How should I prune them?

Grow citrus where they'll get plenty of sun and in acidic, well-drained soil that's enriched with organic matter. Many experts say that growing the plants in soils rich in organic matter and using balanced organic fertilizers produces better-tasting fruit. Most citrus do not tolerate temperatures below 40°F.

In areas where citrus are marginally hardy, plant them in raised beds (where the soil warms more readily) or on the south or west side of a wall or building so that extra heat radiates onto the tree.

Gardeners who live in the North need to grow citrus indoors. Site plants where they get lots of light (direct sun is fine in most areas) and away from drafts that come from windows, doors, or heat registers. The plants prefer winter temperatures of about 65°F during the day and a few degrees cooler at night.

Grow citrus in large containers that have drainage holes at the bottom. Use an acidic potting mix, such as a peat-based mix. In areas that have alkaline water, it will be necessary to periodically use an acidifier to keep the potting-mix pH from getting too high. Water citrus enough to keep the soil moist but not wet. If you water too much, the plant roots will die and rot.

Most citrus don't need to be trained as rigorously as temperate trees such as apples, pears, and cherries. With citrus, keep these things in mind.
- Maintain an open growth habit by removing overlapping or excess shoots.
- Remove older, bearing wood to continually stimulate new growth, because most old wood becomes unfruitful after a while.
- Cut off shoots or limbs at the point where they join to another limb. Cutting back the ends of shoots instead of removing old branches can cause lots of small, brushy growth that blocks sun from the interior and encourages disease.

Flowers but no fruit

My potted orange tree has been blooming, but it doesn't ever develop any fruits. How can I get it to produce oranges?

A number of factors can cause blooming citrus not to bear fruit. Indoors, a common reason is that the blooms don't get pollinated. Use a paintbrush or cotton swab to transfer pollen to the center of the flower early in the day. If all the flowers that bloom were to set and become fruits, the plant would break down from the weight of the crop. As few as 5 percent of the flowers need to set to produce a full crop. So you need not hand-pollinate every blossom to get a decent crop.

Moisture stress (too much or too little) and nutrient deficiencies can cause fruit drop too. These problems are usually associated with leaf yellowing. Keep plants uniformly moist but not wet, and use an acid-based fertilizer formulated for citrus to prevent these environmental stresses. Low humidity in the home could also cause developing fruits to abort. Make certain that your plant has adequate humidity by grouping it with other plants or using a room humidifier.

Lemon tree care

Last year my Meyer lemon tree was covered with flowers and had a dozen lemons. I moved it outside in late May. This winter it only had two flowers. I usually give it liquid fertilizer once or twice a week. How can I get it to produce more flowers? Should I just keep it inside?

It's fine to move your lemon tree *(Citrus limon)* outside for the summer and keep it inside in the place where it's happy for the winter. Stop feeding it during the winter, and water less frequently. The soil should be allowed to dry slightly between waterings during the winter. Overfeeding will reduce flower and fruit production and cause weak roots. Feed in spring and summer only once a month. Use an acid fertilizer specifically formulated for citrus. Remove the tree from the pot every few years and repot the plant with new soil.

Orange tree ID

I bought a dwarf orange tree on the Internet. It was just a little twig when I got it in the mail. The tree is growing and has thorns, but it looks nothing like the dwarf orange tree that my friend has, which already has fruits on it. Could this be a different kind of tree?

Your tree could be almost anything, because most citrus trees will grow from seeds, and many are naturally thorny. If your friend's tree is fruiting well indoors, it is probably a calamondin orange (×*Citrofortunella microcarpa*), a productive dwarf citrus tree. Under favorable conditions, a calamondin orange will produce pungent fruit almost year-round. The fruits make fine marmalade.

Citrus from seed

How do I start an orange tree from seed? We picked up oranges at the store that have wonderful flavor, and we'd like to grow our own.

Although you can easily grow seeds collected from store-bought citrus, the plants they become usually produce less than high-quality fruit. This is because most purchased fruits are hybrids, and seed from hybrids rarely produces plants that have the same qualities as the parent fruit. However, seed-grown citrus can make for attractive foliage plants indoors (be watchful of the thorns, though). If you'd like to grow citrus for fruits, purchase a grafted named variety from a reputable nursery.

To grow oranges (or other citrus) from seed, remove the seeds from the fruit and plant them immediately. Use a seed-starting mix or potting soil, placing seeds about an inch deep in the medium. Moisten the mix and move it to a warm location until germination occurs.

Citrus pests

I'm growing oranges, lemons, and grapefruit for the first time. What pests will I have to spray for?

A number of common pests attack citrus. The usual suspects include the following.
- Whiteflies are small white insects that flutter around plants.
- Scale insects, which resemble bumps on plant stems, leaves, and fruit, and are difficult to spot.
- Mealybugs look like small clusters of cotton. Mealybugs particularly like hiding out where stems meet the trunk or along the veins of a leaf.
- Sooty mold looks like a powdery black substance on the leaves. Sooty mold typically grows on the honeydew left by aphids or scale insects.

Combat pests outdoors by using horticultural oil or insecticidal soap applied directly to the foliage. Indoors, use insecticidal soap or an insecticide designed for indoor use. Note any limitations on the use of fruit after spraying with a pesticide.

GOOSEBERRY

Making gooseberry cuttings

Can I start new gooseberry bushes from cuttings?

Most gooseberries are easy to grow from cuttings. Just follow these steps.
1. When the plants have lost their leaves in autumn (or even if there are a few leaves left), take cuttings of the healthy new wood. Avoid using shoots that appear to have holes in them (which could be infested with borers) or shoots that had disease-infected leaves. Each cutting should be at least 6 inches long.

2. Choose a protected spot in a flower bed and push the cuttings into the soil so only one-third of the length is above the soil. Space the cuttings 6 inches apart. Mark the spot well.
3. In spring, the cuttings should be rooted and beginning to grow. Care for them throughout the summer; by the end of the season, they may be as large as 1–2 feet tall.
4. In early autumn, dig the shrubs and plant them in permanent locations. In areas with especially cold winters (north of Zone 5), wait until early spring to transplant the shrubs.

GRAPES

Care of grapes
I recently moved to a house that has grapevines. They are in need of care, and I have no idea where to start.

Grapes are vigorous growers that generally need some pruning every year. Winter, before they sprout new growth, is the best time to prune them. You can cut back grapes severely if need be. There are several options when it comes to pruning styles. Do you want to grow the grapes to maximize fruit production, or would you rather simply keep them in bounds? Best fruiting comes from 2-year-old wood. Are the grapes growing on a trellis or sprawling over a pergola? How vigorous are the varieties of grapes that you have? All these are questions that need to be answered for me to provide detailed pruning instructions. Check reference books or contact your local cooperative extension office for publications on grape pruning techniques.

Grapes on arbors
How do you trim or prune grapevines on an arbor?

Do you want to grow the grapes for harvesting quality fruit? If so, when your vines are dormant, prune them to canes with spurs, removing 90–95 percent of the previous year's growth. Leaving the vines unpruned can result in a tangled mess that invites disease, looks untidy, and reduces the fruit quality. For a thorough guide to pruning and grape growing, read *The Grape Grower* by Lon Rombough.

If your vine fails to cover the arbor the way you'd like with this type of pruning, prune the plants less. You'll sacrifice some fruit quality by doing so, however.

Or grow your grapevine on a smaller arbor or trellis, cutting it back hard, and grow a nonfruiting vine, such as trumpet vine, sweet autumn clematis, or wisteria, on your arbor.

Potted grapevine

I have a grapevine in a 5-gallon nursery container, and it is sprouting leaves. I'd like to transplant it into a larger pot. What soil amendments will it need?

Any quality potting soil will do—grapes grow well in most soils. If you use a potting mix that contains a slow-release fertilizer—or you add some yourself—no additional feeding will be needed. Place the plant where you can train the vine to a sturdy post or other support. Be sure to select a container that has a drainage hole at the bottom and plenty of room for the roots. A grapevine can grow 5 feet or more a year, so it makes a good shade-providing plant for a sunny patio.

Shriveled grapes

My grapes were looking good earlier this summer, but now they're shriveling up before ripening. What's wrong with them?

It sounds as though your grapes have been attacked by black rot, a fungal disease of grapes that shows up in warm, humid weather. Infection starts as leaf spots followed by small light-brown spots on half-grown grape berries. The spots enlarge, soften, and overtake the grape in just a few days. The berry shrivels, turns black, hardens, and mummifies. These mummies remain attached to the cluster.

By the time you notice the mummies, it is too late to control black rot that season. However, take steps early next season to prevent the disease from returning. Remove mummies and diseased tendrils from the vines. Make sure the plants are growing in a sunny area with good air movement. Apply a protective fungicide early in the season, beginning at bud break, all the way through bloom for good control of black rot.

KIWI

Growing hardy kiwi

Can you tell me how to grow hardy kiwi? I've got a couple of vines that are several years old, but they have never produced fruit.

Kiwis are difficult to grow in many areas of the country. Because they bloom early in the season, flower buds are susceptible to spring frosts. Even if plants grow well, a late spring frost may wipe out the entire fruit crop for the season. They grow best in moderate climates with a long growing season.

Most kiwis have separate male and female plants. If you don't have at least one male and one female, your plants may not produce fruit, because pollen from the male is needed to produce fruits on the female vine. You could plant several more vines to increase the likelihood that you'll have at least one of each. Or you could grow a variety such as 'Issai' that produces fruit on a single vine.

Kiwis are sensitive to overfertilization. Excess nitrogen promotes vigorous growth that is less likely to be fruitful.

PASSIONFRUIT

Growing passionfruit

I'd like to grow passionfruits for making jelly. Are they something I can grow? What care do they need?

Passionfruits come from passionflower vines *(Passiflora)*. The most common species grown for its fruit is *P. edulis*. It is hardy only to Zone 10. You may find it at your local garden center or from a specialty fruit nursery. Other species that produce delicious fruit include banana passionfruit *(P. mollissima)*, hardy to Zone 7, giant granadilla *(P. quadrangularis)*, and *P. ligularis* (said to have the best-tasting fruit of any passionflower).

All passionflowers prefer full sun and well-drained soil. They do well in poor soils. If the soil is too rich or you fertilize the vines too often, they'll put on lots of rampant leafy growth at the expense of blooms and fruits.

Provide them with a sturdy support, such as a pergola. Some of the larger passionflower species can grow more than 50 feet long. That makes for a heavy plant, especially when the leaves are wet after a rainstorm.

PEACH

Watering new peach tree

I planted a 2-year-old bare-root peach tree in spring. It's not growing well. I watered it every day for 3 weeks. I'm not watering it as much now, and buds are forming. The leaves still look smaller than similar trees in the nursery. Did I harm the tree by overwatering it?

If the soil is sandy and well-drained, you may not have overwatered your peach tree. But if water stayed around the roots, you may have drowned the tree. For most soils, you need to water only once or twice per week. Less frequent, deep soakings are better than daily shallow sprinkles. The tree may also have been damaged in cold storage. If it was stored with ripening fruit, which gives off ethylene gas, stunting could result. At this point, make sure the soil is well-drained, water less frequently, and wait and see if the tree leafs out. Plants are pretty tough. You may be surprised by the growth the tree will make this year.

Bad-tasting peach

I've had a peach tree for 6 years that I purchased from a local garden center. Though the tree is beautiful, the fruits taste awful! They're not sweet, and the texture isn't good. I can't remember the variety. Can you help me?

Although a moisture or nutrient imbalance might affect fruit quality, you say the tree is lovely, which suggests that it is not lacking anything. If the tree is otherwise healthy, your tree may be an accident. Most peach trees are grafted onto a rootstock, meaning that the top part of the tree is a different variety from the roots. Sometimes the graft fails and the entire tree grows from the rootstock. Rootstock types often don't have good fruit (instead, they tend to be hardier, shorter, or more disease-resistant—traits they give to the top part of the plant). Unfortunately, you won't know this until the tree bears its low-quality fruit. I suggest three options.

- Take the fruit to the nursery to show the error and ask for a replacement tree.
- If someone at the nursery knows how to graft, or knows someone who does, ask to have a good variety, or even more than one, grafted onto the tree. That way you won't have to wait for a new tree, and you could grow a tree with several varieties of peaches.
- If you are adventurous, join a group such as North American Fruit Explorers and find a member nearby who can teach you to graft. Then you can graft other varieties onto your tree.

Dying peaches

I have been trying to grow fruit trees, but with little success. I lost all of my peaches. I think the problem is fire blight. What can I do?

Fire blight often devastates pears and apples in spring, but it does not damage peaches. It is more likely that peach tree borers are killing your trees. These are the larvae of a small, clear-winged moth that lays eggs in bark crevices in spring. The trees are damaged or killed when the eggs hatch and the larvae bore holes into the wood. Young trees with a slender trunk are often killed. Check your declining trees for evidence of borers: $1/16$-inch-diameter holes that may have a gooey substance oozing out. The holes are evidence of borers. You may be able to kill the borers in the holes by inserting a wire into the hole to skewer the wormlike larva. Prevent future borers by avoiding injury to the bark; borers seek out injured trees. Purchase pheromone traps to hang in your trees in spring to early summer, when the adult borers take to the air. These may trap them before they reproduce, and they serve as an indicator of when to apply insecticide. Spray the trunk and base of the tree with an insecticide labeled for peach tree borer.

Poor drainage also shortens the life span of peaches. They develop root rots.

Peaches from pits

I want to grow peach trees from the pits of the peaches I buy at the store. Is this possible? How do I do it?

Yes, you can grow peach trees from store-bought peaches. But there's a catch. Grocery-store peaches are not only unlikely to produce quality fruit, the trees probably wouldn't be adapted to growing in your area. So although you can use pits from the store, you may not wish to.

I do have good news, though: Many areas have heirloom peaches that have been grown from seed for generations, so they will be adapted to your climate. These heirloom types come true from seed, unlike grocery-store hybrids. You're more likely to find heirloom varieties at farm stands than at grocery stores. They should be readily available in your area, so start hunting. You will get a thrill from growing your own fruit tree from seed rather than just buying one from a nursery.

Peach pits require stratification to germinate. Plant the pits in pots buried in the ground in fall, or place the pots in a refrigerator for several months to provide the cold, moist treatment the seeds need to begin growth. Temperatures should be cold but above freezing.

Peaches are one of the few fruit trees that bear fruit relatively quickly from seed. Some peach varieties may even start to bloom and bear fruit in their second year; most will produce peaches by the third or fourth year, given good care.

Too many peaches

Although our peach tree develops loads of little green fruit each year, none of the peaches ever grows large enough to harvest. The tree gets plenty of sunshine. What's wrong?

Too much fruit can spoil the harvest. Small fruits will mature and ripen, but their diminutive size makes for poor-quality fruit. What your peach tree probably needs is a thorough thinning. As soon as the green peaches reach about an inch in diameter, selectively thin by pinching some of them from the branches. Leave the largest, healthiest-looking fruits to ripen, spaced about 6 inches apart. Your reward will be bigger fruit. Also, relieved of an overload of fruit, your peach tree's limbs are less likely to break.

Puckered peach leaves

Leaves on my peach trees are puckered and turning red. Is it something I should be worried about?

It sounds as though your tree has peach leaf curl, a fungal disease that is most prevalent in a cool, wet spring following a mild winter. New leaves are distorted and puckered and have a reddish cast. Leaves turn yellow or brown and drop.

Peach leaf curl weakens peach and nectarine trees by causing early leaf drop, making the tree more susceptible to other diseases and winter injury. Fruit production the following year is usually reduced, because trees are stressed from the leaf drop.

It's easy to control peach leaf curl with a dormant spray just as buds are beginning to grow. By the time you see the puckered red foliage, it's too late to do anything for the crop. Rake up and destroy fallen leaves to help cut down on the amount of fungal spores overwintering under the tree, and apply a fungicide in late winter next year to prevent a recurrence of the disease.

Sudden peach collapse

I have a beautiful peach tree that produced lots of peaches. Last year, the tree bloomed wonderfully and had some peaches. They grew only about a half inch in diameter, though. Also, all the leaves suddenly turned yellow and fell off. By late May, the tree looked dead. In mid-August it grew just a few shoots here and there. What happened?

Your description suggests several possibilities. I'm inclined to think that something attacked the tree's main trunk or roots, but without more information there is no way to tell whether it was an animal or a disease. Examine the main trunk for injury such as girdling from gnawing rabbits, peach tree borer damage, or injury from a weed whip or lawn mower. If you live in the northern range of peach cultivation (Zone 5), the symptoms might also be due to winter injury. Is the soil well-drained where the tree is growing? Poor drainage could have damaged the root system.

Regardless, a tree so badly shocked usually doesn't recover well. It's probably best to remove it. Avoid risk of the same thing happening by replanting a new tree in a location suited to peach tree growth. If you want to plant another type of fruit tree where the peach tree was, select a species, such as an apple or a pear that isn't a close relative.

PEAR

When to harvest pears

Last year was the first time my pear tree bore fruit, but by the time the fruit ripened, it was rotten. What can I do differently so I can harvest a good crop?

Unlike virtually every other fruit, pears must be picked when they are still quite hard. They ripen from the core outward. As you found, if pears are allowed to remain on the tree until you can feel or see ripeness, the fruit becomes mushy and brown. Check for ripeness while the fruit is still green. If you can snap the fruit off the branch briskly rather than tugging, or if you cut open a pear and find that the seed coat has darkened from white to brown or black, the pear is ready to be picked. Once harvested, most varieties ripen in a week or two. Speed up the process by sealing the pears in a bag with a ripe apple or banana.

Nonbearing 'Bartlett'

I have a 'Bartlett' pear that doesn't produce. How do I get it to bear?

If it blooms each spring, your tree may not be bearing fruit because it needs a second variety nearby to pollinate it. 'Bosc' is a common choice. If you don't have room for a second tree, have a second variety grafted onto your tree so you'll have a branch of pollinating blossoms within the canopy of your 'Bartlett'.

If your tree has not bloomed yet, it may be a maturity issue. Standard-size pear trees may take 5 years or more to reach bearing size. If you recently planted your tree, you may simply have to be patient. Pear trees should have full sun for best production. If your tree gets less than 6 hours of direct sunlight per day, excess shade could be causing lack of production.

Like apples, pears bear on spurs on 2-year-old or older wood. Excessive pruning can keep the tree from bearing fruit by removing the fruiting spurs and by forcing the growth of too much young wood, which is nonproductive. Sometimes it helps to spread branches so they grow more laterally than upright. Use limb spreaders or weights on the limbs to create wide branch angles and boost fruit production. Similarly, too much nitrogen fertilizer forces excess vegetative growth and delays fruiting. If your tree is growing vigorously, cut back on the fertilizer. (Remember that the tree may be soaking up high-nitrogen fertilizer applied to the lawn nearby.)

RASPBERRY

No raspberry fruits

Why have I never gotten fruit from my 10-year-old raspberry bush?

The problem may be the variety of raspberry you're growing. For example, a spring-bearing variety planted in your climate might be suffering from frozen fruit buds. Although raspberries are hardy in Zones 4–9, they de-acclimate very quickly during warm winter weather. A cold snap later in winter can cause dieback or damage to fruit buds. My best suggestion is to build a raised bed in full sun, with lots of organic matter in the soil, and plant a new raspberry variety that's suitable for your climate. Consider growing an everbearing raspberry such as 'Heritage'. That way, even if the summer crop is frozen off, you'll get a crop in fall.

STRAWBERRY

Fertilizing strawberries

What fertilizer do you recommend for strawberries in containers? My plants are 2 years old and produce only small, weirdly shaped berries.

One-year-old strawberry plants are more productive than older ones. If yours are on their second year, it may be time to root some of the daughter plants and replace the old parent plants. Plant them in good potting soil that contains slow-release fertilizer; you won't need to feed them until autumn. In September, clip off all old leaves that have red or brown spots, and give the plants some water-soluble plant food. Allow the plants to go dormant through the winter by keeping the container outdoors in a protected spot, or in an unheated garage. First thing in spring, move the container to a sunny spot and begin feeding the plants every 2 weeks with a general-purpose product. A few weeks later, you should have a beautiful crop of big, juicy strawberries.

From your description, I also suspect that your strawberries are being attacked by tarnished plant bugs. This insect feeds on developing blossoms. The toxin they inject while feeding causes misshapen fruits, sometimes called nubbins, to develop; the tip end of the berry becomes hard and seedy. Spray with an insecticide just before the blossoms open. Avoid using insecticide during bloom to prevent injury to pollinating insects.

Strawberry jar

Can you really grow strawberries in a pot? I've always planted them in the garden, but I saw a pretty strawberry pot at the local nursery and I'm wondering if that actually works.

One of the best things about strawberries (besides eating them with ice cream and shortcake, of course) is that you can grow them in just about any sunny home garden. With a strawberry jar you can grow these delicious berries on a balcony or patio too.

Start by filling the pot with good-quality potting soil. As the soil level reaches one of the pot's pockets, put in a strawberry plant. Continue until you reach within an inch of the top of the pot. Then plant a couple of plants at the top. Place the pot in a sunny location and keep it well watered. Because these strawberries are not set in the ground, you'll have to water them more often than the ones you have in your garden. In cold climates, the jars will need extra protection from winter cold.

Strawberry variety selection

When I lived in the East, my strawberry plants were brimming with big red fruits. Now that I live on the West Coast, my plants have a few tiny berries. What should I do to increase the size and number of strawberries?

Did you plant the same strawberry variety you had in the East? Planting a variety that did well for you back East could be the problem. Many strawberry varieties do well only in certain regions. Check to see what varieties your county extension service recommends. Or buy plants from a locally owned garden center, because it is likely to carry varieties that are adapted to your area.

To encourage healthy plants, feed them well with a balanced fertilizer (meaning that it has relatively even amounts of nitrogen, phosphorus, and potassium), and keep the plants mulched with lots of organic matter, preferably in raised beds for good drainage. Grow them in full sun; strawberries grown in shade don't have the energy to produce lots of good fruit.

Thinning strawberries

I planted a few strawberries, and now they are crowded. There are runners everywhere! Can I dig them up and put them farther apart? Can I cut off the runners?

If you're overrun by runners, a simple trick is to train them into the space between the rows in your strawberry patch to create new rows of young plants. Then remove the old rows so their spaces become the new aisles. Discard the old plants, because they're less productive than the new daughter plants.

Start by making new raised rows of soil and organic matter between the rows of established plants. Once the strawberries begin to produce runners, train them onto the new raised rows. Secure them into the soil if necessary. When the runners become established, cut them away from their parents and throw the parent plants in the compost pile or till them into the soil. The best time to get rid of the parent plants is right after the patch has finished bearing in early summer. That way the daughter plants have most of the growing season to get established and set fruit buds for next year's crop.

June bearers or day neutrals

What's the difference between June-bearing and day-neutral strawberries? Which should I grow?

For a harvest that comes on all at once, choose June-bearing strawberries. As the name implies, they bear a single crop in June in Zones 5 and north, earlier in warmer zones. With good care, you can harvest a crop from these plants for 4–5 years. They're cold-hardy to Zone 3; in areas colder than Zone 5, provide winter protection for potted plants and mulch those in the ground. Look for varieties such as 'Earliglow', 'Honeoye', 'Sweet Charlie', and 'Totem'.

Day-neutral strawberries bear fruit throughout the growing season, often into October. The plants are smaller than their June-bearing cousins, because more energy goes into fruiting. They're cold-hardy to Zone 3 too. Replace them after a couple of seasons. Look for varieties such as 'Tristar' and 'Tribute'.

Winter protection

What do I need to do to protect my strawberry patch for the winter?

In cold-winter regions of the country, strawberries need winter protection. The traditional mulch is straw (hence the name strawberry), but any weed-free, lightweight mulch may be used. In some regions, shredded corn stalks or marsh hay may be more readily available. Use whatever you can easily find. Apply the mulch 2–6 inches deep after the plants have experienced several freezes in the mid-20s. It's important to wait until cold weather settles in so the plants are dormant.

Pull the mulch off the crowns of the plants in spring when growth begins. This usually happens after high temperatures hit the low 70s for several days in a row. Be on the alert to rake the mulch back over the plants if frosty nights are predicted during bloom.

Bare-root or potted strawberries

I've heard of bare-root trees, but I see that strawberries are sold that way too. Is it better to plant bare-root strawberries or wait to buy them in pots?

Choose bare-root or potted; either way, you'll reap the benefit of strawberries, a quick-to-bear fruit you can harvest the same season you plant them. Bare-root strawberries are available at garden centers or through mail-order catalogs in late winter and early spring. They're usually sold in bundles of 10 or 25 and are often less expensive than potted plants. Plant the roots as soon as the ground is workable in spring, taking care not to bury the crown, the area where the top of the plant meets the roots.

HERBS IN GENERAL

Herbs in the heat

Herbs do not do well for me, though I can grow parsley and basil. It may just be too hot for most of the year where I live. I would especially like to grow lavender, but I have tried various types with no luck. Even mint does not do well. Do you have any suggestions?

The herbs you've mentioned require a well-drained soil with a slightly alkaline pH (7.0 to 7.3 or so). If your area is hot and humid for long stretches of the season, I'm not surprised that herbs don't grow well. Lavender, in particular, does not like high humidity with heat, but you might experiment with the French *(Lavandula stoechas)* or Spanish *(L. s. pendunculata)* types, which prefer acid soil, rather than the English *(L. angustifolia)* varieties. Because parsley and basil grow well for you, try your luck with dill, cilantro, and chives. Grow mint in an area that is protected from hot afternoon sun. French tarragon may not do well for you, but a similar-tasting herb called Mexican tarragon *(Tagetes lucida)* probably would.

You might also try growing some of the tropical herbs. Cuban oregano *(Plectranthus amboinicus)* combines the flavors of oregano, thyme, and savory and is hardy to Zone 9. Ginger *(Zingiber officinale)* is native to the tropics but survives in Zone 9, as does lemongrass *(Cymbopogon citratus)*. These three tropical herbs can be grown in containers in colder areas. Curry leaf *(Murraya koenigii)* is a small tree whose leaves are used in curry dishes. It is also hardy to Zone 9.

Herbs for shade

My yard has a lot of shade. Are there some perennial herbs that I could grow there?

Most herbs need full sun for best growth. They tolerate a few hours of light afternoon shade, but their vigor and flavor are reduced. However, a few herbs can grow in partial shade. Try some of the following: sweet flag *(Acorus gramineus)*, angelica *(Angelica archangelica)*, sweet woodruff *(Galium odoratum)*, goldenseal *(Hydrastis canadensis)*, sweet cicely *(Myrrhis odorata)*, lady's mantle *(Alchemilla mollis)*, lungwort *(Pulmonaria),* mint *(Mentha),* and bee balm *(Monarda didyma)*. Most herbs need soil that drains well. This is particularly important in shady areas, which dry more slowly than sites with full sun.

Herbs in containers

I'm growing rosemary, lemon thyme, and chives together in a clay pot. How can I keep them through the winter? They're getting crowded. Should I separate them?

You can repot them individually in late summer so they have some time outdoors to get used to their new containers. Then, before frost hits, bring them indoors and place them on a sunny windowsill (a south-facing window is essential) or under grow-lights. Make sure the pots drain well, but keep the soil slightly moist; herbs grown indoors can dry out quickly and die.

You can also plant the chives and thyme directly in the garden and let them spend the winter outdoors. They should be perfectly hardy in Zones 4–9. Rosemary is frost-sensitive and is usually hardy only to Zone 8, so it needs an indoor home during the winter in colder regions.

Fragrant herbs

I want to grow herbs that smell wonderful. What are the top fragrant herbs to grow?

Fragrance is subjective, so experiment with herbs. Hot summers are ideal for annual basil *(Ocimum basilicum)*, which smells as good as it tastes. Grow several plants, and run your hand through the leaves to release their aroma. Do the same with rosemary *(Rosmarinus officinalis)*, an herb that's evergreen in Zones 7–10. In colder climates, grow it in a pot and take it indoors over the winter. Lemon verbena *(Aloysia triphylla)* is another fine candidate. Grow it in a roomy pot that you can move into a garage or other protected place during hard freezes. Try a few scented geraniums *(Pelargonium* selections) too; they come in scents from citrus to rose and make attractive houseplants. Humidity is a problem for English lavender *(Lavandula angustifolia)*, so if your climate is damp, a better choice would be Spanish lavender *(L. stoechas)*.

Fresh herbs to harvest

I've noticed that many fine restaurants use fresh herbs, but they're expensive to buy fresh in the grocery store. How difficult is it to grow them?

Besides being some of the hardiest garden plants, most herbs are easy to grow. They are seldom picky about the soil they're planted in. If you already grow vegetables, about the only thing you need to do is find some garden space, decide what you want to grow, and get some seeds or plants. Here's a briefing on some of the more common herbs. Take your pick!

Culinary herbs

Basil (*Ocimum basilicum*) is one of the easiest herbs to grow from seed. Start it indoors and transplant it outside in rich, well-drained soil once all danger of frost has passed. Plants grow about 2 feet tall; pinch them back to encourage side growth for more yield.

Chives (*Allium spp.*) are a wonderful perennial herb and an attractive addition to your flower garden too. Grow onion chives (*A. schoenoprasum*) and garlic chives (*A. tuberosum*) for a variety of flavors. Cut onion chive leaves flush with the soil to harvest. Use the leaf tips, flowers, and knobby green seed heads of garlic chives.

Dill (*Anethum graveolens*) grows easily from seed in spring and reseeds itself if the heads are allowed to set seed. Harvest leaves regularly to keep the plant from forming a flower, although you can use the seeds for flavoring as well. Plant a second crop in midsummer for a fall harvest.

French tarragon (*Artemisia dracunculus* 'Sativa') is fairly easily propagated from seed, cuttings (in fall), or divisions (early spring). It prefers rich soil in a protected spot. Thin or transplant to 2 feet apart; divide the plant every 2–3 years. Russian tarragon (*A. dracunculus*) is hardier but less flavorful.

Oregano (*Origanum vulgare hirtum*) starts easily from cuttings or divisions taken in spring, although you can grow it from seed too. If started from seed, cover the seeds with damp cheesecloth (instead of seed-starting mix or soil) until sprouts appear. When the plants are about 6 inches tall, snip them back to encourage branching and lush foliage.

Parsley (*Petroselinum crispum*) prefers full sun, but a bit of shade is acceptable. Sow seed in spring or late summer, and thin seedlings to 9 inches apart. Parsley is a biennial, so it will come back a second year. Of the two parsley types, the flat-leaf ones are more flavorful for cooking; the curly-leaf varieties make a more eye-catching garnish.

Rosemary (*Rosmarinus officinalis*) can be started from seed in spring or from cuttings in summer. This perennial can reach 5 feet tall and grows just as wide, so it makes an eye-catching shrub for the garden in Zones 7–10. Once established, it's drought-tolerant. In colder regions, grow rosemary in a container that can be moved indoors.

Sage (*Salvia officinalis*) isn't fussy about soil as long as it gets full sun. It can be grown from seed or cuttings. Harvest the leaves before the plant flowers, and cut it back after flowering. Sage is a staple in poultry stuffing; its flavor is compatible with rosemary, thyme, bay, or oregano. Also try it with cheese and in breads.

Thyme (*Thymus vulgaris*) should be divided in spring for best results. It needs well-drained soil and protection from cold winters. Its delicate flavor complements nearly every dish. One of my favorite varieties is lemon thyme (*T. xcitriodorus*).

Growing herbs

I need information on how to cultivate herbs such as lavender, thyme, oregano, basil, and parsley in my Zone 5 garden.

Harvest the perennial herbs continually over the summer. You can cook or preserve your harvest throughout the season, but the flavor of most herbs is better before they bloom. In my Zone 5 garden, I have many perennial herbs that I cut back after the first hard frost in fall. I completely harvest herbs I treat as annuals, such as basil and parsley, in summer or clean them up after frost in fall.

Specifically, here are tips for the herbs you mentioned.

- Basil *(Ocimum basilicum)*. Harvest this annual before it blooms, then toss any remaining plants after frost takes it down.
- Lavender *(Lavandula)*. Its winter hardiness depends on species and variety. For your zone, 'Hidcote' and 'Munstead' are the hardiest English lavenders (*L. angustifolia*). French and Spanish varieties will not overwinter in your area. I don't protect my lavender, but I also do not cut it back in fall. After the new spring growth begins, I cut away any dead stems and shape the plant so that new growth comes from the center of the plant. A mulch of leaves around the base of the plant helps protect it through winter cold.
- Oregano *(Origanum vulgare hirtum)*. In your zone, traditional oregano is hardy outdoors all winter. It needs to be pinched back or harvested to keep it from looking scraggly and prevent it from reseeding all over the garden.
- Parsley *(Petroselinum crispum)*. Parsley is a biennial, so even if it makes it through the winter, it will go to seed quickly the next summer. It is best to replant it each year.
- Thyme *(Thymus vulgaris)*. Winter hardiness varies according to variety and how severe the winter is. For example, common thyme is usually hardy in Zone 4, but variegated varieties often are not. Good soil drainage is important. Mulch will help. Cut away any dead stems in spring.

Winter protection

What do I need to do to protect my sage and thyme over the winter?

Sage *(Salvia officinalis)* and thyme *(Thymus vulgaris)* are perennial herbs in Zones 5–9. They overwinter well as long as they are planted in a sunny, well-drained site. Thyme remains semievergreen through the winter; sage loses its foliage. If you would like to provide a little extra protection, mulch the plants with straw or evergreen branches after the soil freezes.

Harvesting herbs

I'm growing basil, chives, cilantro, dill, parsley, and thyme. When do I harvest these herbs?

The herbs you're growing are all good ones to start with. They're easy to grow and have few problems. Here's the scoop on how to harvest them.

- Basil. Harvest this annual by pinching the stems before flower stalks develop.
- Chives. Cut a third to half of this perennial to about an inch above the ground, or harvest individual leaves as you need them.
- Cilantro. Snip off the fresh leaves from the base of the plant for use as cilantro; allow seeds of this annual to ripen for coriander.
- Dill. Cut the fernlike leaves of this annual, or wait for the plant to flower and go to seed before harvesting.
- Parsley. Harvest the leaves of this biennial. The second year, it will quickly go to seed, so start a new plant.
- Thyme. Use scissors to harvest this perennial, leaving at least half of the plant remaining in the garden.

BASIL

Beautiful basil

I'd like to try growing some basil. What do I need to know about growing it and using it?

If you grow tomatoes (or even if you don't), plant some basil too. At home in beds or containers, basil is a fast-growing annual herb. Like tomatoes, basil loves warm weather, so wait until late spring to plant it outdoors. To keep plants producing plenty of new leaves, pinch off flower spikes as soon as they appear. Enjoy basil fresh—the leaves don't retain their flavor well when dried. Sprinkle fresh chopped basil on sun-ripened tomatoes, add it to pasta salads, or puree it into pesto. As a bonus, basil's fragrance fills the garden on warm summer days, making weeding and watering chores more enjoyable.

Basil confusion

I love growing herbs, but I'm having a hard time choosing which basil to plant. There are so many to choose from. Are some better than others for cooking?

As you are finding, one of the hardest things about growing basil is selecting one. Depending on where you buy the seeds or plants, they may be named differently. Check out the categories of basil listed on page 326 to help you decide which ones suit your needs.

Basils

Greek bush basils (*Ocimum basilicum* 'Minimum'). In the garden, these basils grow shorter and more compact than others. Chop up the succulent stems and leaves for cooking. The delicate flavor of these basils makes them perfect for using raw or adding at the end of cooking. Look for 'Spicy Globe', 'Piccolo Verde', and 'Fine Green'.

Lemon basil (*O. b.* ×'Citriodorum'). This smaller-leaved variety has a distinctive lemony aroma. Look for varieties such as 'Lime' and 'Mrs. Burns'. Use this basil in fresh or cooked dishes.

Licorice basil and cinnamon basil (*O. b.* 'Licorice', *O. b.* 'Cinnamon'). These varieties grow much the same as sweet basils but with stronger, distinctive, spicy flavors. Cinnamon basil makes a good jelly. Thai, East Indian, Puerto Rican, and Cuban basils are suited for creating the flavors of their native cuisines.

Purple basils (*O. b.* 'Purpurascens'). Add color to your herb garden with these deep purple varieties, including 'Purple Ruffles' and 'Dark Opal'. The plants won't grow as fast or as full as their green counterparts, but they provide good color. Use this basil in cooking as you would the green types; just add it later in the cooking process to allow it to keep as much of its purple color as possible.

Sweet basil (*O. b.*). This is a favorite all-purpose basil. You'll find varieties such as 'Genovese', 'Sweet Genovese', and 'Genova Profumatissima'. With this basil's large, thick leaves and pleasing flavor, making pesto is a cinch. The lettuce-leaf varieties have a more subtle basil flavor. Plants are shorter than other basils, and the large, crinkled leaves are just the right size for sandwiches. Look for varieties such as 'Mammoth' and 'Napoletano'.

Freezing basil

Can you freeze fresh basil? I planted some basil this year and it has grown abundantly. We love fresh basil but can't eat it all now.

You can freeze fresh basil, but it gets rather slimy. It tastes fine, but its texture suffers. So don't expect to use it as you would fresh basil. A better solution is to make pesto out of it and freeze the pesto. Grind the basil with olive oil, pine nuts, and Parmesan cheese and freeze it in ice cube trays—basically making pesto bouillon cubes. After the cubes are frozen solid, pop them out of the tray and store them in airtight freezer bags. You can take out as many as you need for cooking. You'll appreciate having the flavor of fresh basil during the winter.

BAY

Drying bay leaves
How do I dry bay leaves for cooking?

Sweet bay *(Laurus nobilis)* can be grown as a houseplant if you provide it with medium to bright light and cool to moderate temperatures. Keep the soil moist when the plant is actively growing, but on the dry side during the winter. Harvest full-size leaves and place them on an absorbent paper towel in a well-ventilated dark area until they are dry. In about a week or so, the leaves should be dry. Gather up the dried leaves and store them in an airtight glass jar.

GINGER

Homegrown ginger
Recently I planted a piece of sprouting ginger root, which I have been keeping moist. Once it breaks the soil's surface, what is the best way to care for it?

Edible ginger root *(Zingiber officinale)* is native to the tropical jungles of Malaysia, so it grows best in a humid place where it is shaded from hot summer sun. It also needs excellent drainage, so many gardeners grow it in raised beds. Leave room for it to grow: Ginger stems will reach at least 3 feet tall by late summer. Allow the plant to dry out in autumn. When the leafy tops die back, you can harvest some of the roots and leave the others to regrow next spring.

Ginger cannot tolerate cold soil (it is hardy to Zone 9), so you may need to transfer the root to a container and keep it in a dry place through the winter.

LAVENDER

Pruning lavender
How often should lavender be trimmed? How close to the woody part can I cut?

Lavandula angustifolia is the lavender most often grown in North America. It is hardy in Zones 5–8. Trim it twice a year. Cut lavender back hard in spring, to perhaps half its height. Spring pruning promotes bushiness and removes dead tips, which are common after winter exposure.

Most of the buds that lavender sets each fall for the next year's bloom are on its youngest woody stems, so avoid cutting these all the way back to the ground. Lavender occasionally surprises me after hard winters during which it dies right to the ground. I write off the leafless stems as goners, but, more often than not, vigorous shoots sprout from the lowest dormant buds.

As soon as the plant finishes its main summer bloom, shear it—that is, give it a haircut to remove the spent flowers. Shearing may promote a second, albeit smaller, flush of bloom.

MINT

Containing mint

No one told me that mint is so invasive! I love using this versatile herb in cooking and for making tea. I'm going to have to boycott it if I can't find a way to control it. Is there anything I can do?

Mint *(Mentha)* seems to grow anywhere and quickly spreads by rhizomes (underground stems). To keep mint from growing where you don't want it, plant it in a deep container. Set the container above ground, or sink it into a garden bed. Leave an inch or two of the pot's rim above the soil line, so the stems won't creep over the edge and root in. Another option is to grow the mint in a contained bed. For example, limiting it to a small space bordered by the foundation of your house and a sidewalk would prevent the rhizomes from taking over the rest of your yard. You may be lulled into thinking that a thin edging of brick or plastic will contain mint, but the rhizomes can burrow underground and pop up a couple of feet away.

Runaway mint

I have mint that has spread into my lawn. How can I get rid of it without killing the grass?

Mint should come with a warning label. As you have learned, it can become invasive if not contained. If you want to save a bit of your mint, dig up a small clump and plant it in a container.

To get rid of the mint in your lawn, first decide how bad the problem is. If the mint covers less than half of the lawn surface, you may be able to salvage the lawn. Use a broadleaf herbicide labeled for control of clover or other tough broadleaf weeds. The herbicide may contain 2,4-D, MCPP, and dicamba. Avoid using dicamba near trees and shrubs. It may take more than one application to control the mint. The best time to spray is late summer or early fall, though you can spray in spring too.

If the lawn is completely overrun by the mint, consider total renovation. This involves killing the entire lawn area with a nonselective herbicide such as glyphosate (Roundup). Late summer is the best time to do this. After the grass and mint are dead, reseed or resod the affected area.

PARSLEY

Bitter parsley

Last year our parsley was bitter. Is there something we can add to the soil to prevent this? Or do we need to look at something else?

In general, bitterness is caused by lack of water. Other environmental factors that cause stress to the plant could be involved too. To prevent bitterness this year, provide your parsley *(Petroselinum)* with the growing conditions it prefers. It grows best in rich, moist, well-drained soil that is slightly acidic to neutral in pH. Although parsley tolerates partial shade, it prefers full sun. Water your plant if rainfall is insufficient to keep the soil uniformly moist.

Parsley can be attacked by aster yellows, a disease spread by leafhoppers. Infected plants usually develop yellowing foliage, and flavor could be affected. Protect plants from leafhoppers with a floating row cover. Remove and destroy infected plants.

Keep in mind that parsley, if it overwinters, will have more bitterness the second year. Start new plants each year to maintain mild-flavored foliage.

ROSEMARY

Winter care for rosemary

Will my rosemary plant make it through the winter outside?

Rosemary *(Rosmarinus officinalis)* is an herb that is hardy in Zones 7–10 and protected areas of Zone 6. In colder areas, grow it outside in containers to avoid having to dig it up in fall before bringing it inside for the winter. Overwintered rosemary performs best if kept in a cool room (a basement works well) at 40–50°F with good air circulation. Because it is evergreen, it needs bright light. I keep mine in front of a large window in the basement. If you don't have good light, place the plant under fluorescent lights for 12–16 hours daily. Don't expect much growth on the plant through the winter; the idea is simply to keep it alive. Keep the soil moist, but avoid overwatering. Rosemary can develop root rot if kept too wet.

How can I make new starts off my rosemary plant?

The best way to create new rosemary plants is by taking softwood cuttings. Do this in late spring, using 3–4-inch pieces from the best-growing branches. Cut the stem just below a leaf node with a sharp knife. Remove the lower two-thirds of the foliage. Dip the stripped stem into rooting hormone, shake off the excess, and insert the cutting into seed starting mix, vermiculite, or a mixture of peat moss and perlite. Water the cuttings frequently to keep the rooting medium moist but not soggy. Cuttings should root within several weeks.

Layering is another easy way to start new plants. Take a flexible branch and bend it down so the stem touches the soil. Use a wire loop to hold the branch in contact with the soil. If you prefer, scratch the side of the branch that touches the soil, and apply rooting hormone to speed root development. In several months, when strong roots have formed, cut the new plant loose from its parent and pot it up.

STEVIA

Growing stevia

I'd like to grow the herb stevia as a natural sweetener. What care does it need? How do you harvest it?

Stevia (*Stevia rebaudiana* 'Bertoni') is native to South America, where the plant's leaves have been used for centuries as a sweetener. You can grow stevia in your home garden. Plants grow best in full sun in loamy soil with good drainage. Avoid poorly drained areas.

Start with transplants from a reliable nursery or garden center. Plants grown from seed vary in their level of sweetness, so vegetatively propagated ones are best. Plant outdoors after all danger of frost has passed. After planting, cover lightly with organic mulch to hold down weeds and conserve moisture. Water during dry periods, and use fertilizer low in nitrogen on the plants.

Harvest stems for drying in fall. The cooler temperatures and shorter days of fall intensify the sweetness in the leaves. Cut stems from the plant; strip the leaves and dry them on a screen in a sunny spot with good ventilation.

Take cuttings in late summer to carry over plants for the next year. Pot up the rooted cuttings and move them indoors before fall frosts arrive. Keep plants inside in a sunny location through the winter, and plant them outside the following spring.

THYME

How to grow thyme

Is there any special trick to growing thyme? Mine is not doing well.

Thyme *(Thymus vulgaris)* likes hot, dry, sunny sites similar to its native Mediterranean climate. Water when necessary to maintain soil moisture, but avoid overwatering. Shear off the flowers when the plant finishes blooming to keep energy concentrated in leaf production rather than in setting seed. Thyme can be propagated from cuttings, layering, or division. Harvest the entire plant by cutting it back to 2 inches above the ground in midsummer. Tie the stems in a bundle and hang them upside down in a cool, dry place to dry. When the leaves are dry, crumble them off the stems and store in an airtight glass jar for up to 2 years. You can expect one more harvest before the season ends. Pest and disease problems are few. Occasionally spider mites may attack the plants. A forceful water spray will remove them. Root rot from overwatering or poorly drained soil is the most severe problem. Avoid overwatering, and grow the plant in a raised bed if drainage is poor in your garden.

VEGETABLES IN GENERAL

Frost dates

I read about the first and last frost dates in my garden books and magazines. I understand that this is a gauge for when to plant vegetables, but how do I know these dates for my locale?

Your cooperative extension service or a local nursery can tell you the frost dates for your area. They'll be able to give you two dates: The last frost date for your area is the date when you can expect it to freeze for the last time in spring; the first frost date is the approximate date of the first fall frost.

As with all things related to Mother Nature, these dates are approximate. She can pull a fast one on you and drop in a freeze a little earlier or a little later than you planned. Be prepared with lightweight blankets and row covers for the few weeks surrounding your frost dates if you have tender plants to protect.

Lights for starting seeds

I'm setting up a seed-starting room in my basement. I don't have enough natural light, so what artificial light do I need? Will regular fluorescent lights work?

Yes regular fluorescents will do the trick. Setting up your seed-starting shop requires only two 40-watt, 48-inch-long fluorescent tubes in a shop-light fixture. The bonus? It's also one of the least expensive ways to get started. You can use grow-lights, but they're not necessary for starting seedlings. You also may want to invest in these other devices: a timer, chains to hang the light, and aluminum foil. You can also buy shelf systems especially made for growing plants under lights.

Set a timer to automatically turn the lights on for 16 hours per day. That lets you stay out late without hiring a babysitter for your seedlings, and saves energy if you forget to turn off the lights at night.

Hang the light fixture from chains so you can adjust the height of the light as your seedlings grow taller. As soon as the seedlings peek above the soil's surface, set the light to 2–4 inches above the tallest leaf. Because fluorescent light is cool, you can even let the seedlings touch the fixture.

Drape sheets of aluminum foil over the sides of the light fixture, shiny side toward the plants, to reflect as much light as possible onto the plants.

Storing leftover seeds

The seed packets I buy always have more seeds than I need for the garden this year. Can I store the leftovers to plant next year?

Keep seeds cool and dry for best storage. Put them in an airtight jar or plastic container with a small packet of silica gel in the bottom to absorb excess moisture. Place the container in the refrigerator where the temperature is about 40°F. If you have no extra room in the refrigerator, a cool basement would be a second choice.

Vegetable seeds vary in the length of time they may be stored. Beet, cucumber, muskmelon, and tomato may be stored for 5 years or more. Beans, peas, cabbage-family crops (cabbage, broccoli, cauliflower, Brussels sprouts, kale, kohlrabi), carrots, lettuce, okra, peppers, radishes, spinach, turnips, and watermelon may last 3–5 years in storage. Store sweet corn, parsley, leeks, and onions no longer than 1–2 years.

Transplant timetable

How soon before the last frost should I start my vegetable seedlings for transplanting outdoors?

Starting seeds indoors is a good way to get a jump on the growing season. You can plant them as little as 3 weeks or as long as 3 months before the last frost. Use this chart to help you decide how many weeks before your region's last frost date you can start your seeds to have them ready for transplanting outdoors at the right time.

Transplant time

Vegetable	Weeks to transplant size	Vegetable	Weeks to transplant size
Artichoke	4–6	Kale	4–6
Asparagus	plant 2–3-year-old roots	Kohlrabi	4–6
Broccoli	5–7	Lettuce	3–5
Brussels sprouts	4–6	Muskmelon	3–4
Cabbage	5–7	Okra	4–6
Cauliflower	5–7	Onion seed	12
Chives	6–8	Pepper	6–8
Collards	4–6	Spinach	6–8
Cucumber	4	Squash	3–4
Eggplant	6–9	Tomatillo	6
Endive	4–6	Tomato	5–7
		Watermelon	3–4

Seed germination test

I have some vegetable seeds left over from last year. Will they still be good to plant this year?

Some vegetable seeds store well from one year to the next, and others don't. To be certain whether your saved seeds will grow in the garden or you need to buy new ones, do a germination test on them. Moisten a paper towel and line up 10 seeds along one edge; fold the edge over the seeds. Roll up the paper towel. Place the paper towel in a covered tray or plastic bag in a warm (room temperature) location and keep it moist but not soggy. In a few days, unroll the towel to see how many seeds have germinated. This will give you an idea of what to do with your saved seed. If germination is poor, it's best to discard the seed. If most of the seeds germinated, you may be able to use the rest from that packet, but sow the seed more heavily. And if nearly all the seeds germinated, sow the seed at the normal rate.

Beginner's garden

My son recently came home from school with a sunflower plant that he had proudly started from seed. He wants to grow a garden, but I've not done that before. Do you have any suggestions for other crops to get started with?

Vegetables, fruits, and herbs can be easy to grow. Start with some of the easier ones and you'll build your confidence and graduate to growing a whole variety of produce. Once you get used to fresh produce, you'll be thanking your son for getting you started vegetable gardening.

These crops offer relatively trouble-free growing, are quick to harvest, and require a minimum of tools.

- Bush beans. No staking required for these highly productive bushes.
- Cabbage. Plant transplants as soon as the frost is out of the ground in spring.
- Cucumbers. If space permits, let them run on the ground; otherwise, a large tomato cage makes a perfect trellis.
- Onion sets. Plant onion starts close together and harvest some as green onions.
- Peas. Try both shelling peas and snow peas. Plant early in the season.
- Potatoes. Mound soil around the plant as it grows.
- Radishes. Sow seeds each week to spread out the harvest.
- Summer squash. Harvest when the fruit is young.
- Tomatoes, cherry and determinate varieties. Grow these in containers too.

Veggies in shade

Part of my garden receives afternoon shade. Are there any vegetables that would grow there? The rest of the garden has full sun.

Most vegetables require 6–8 hours of direct sunlight a day. Watch the sunshine patterns on that part of your garden, and make note of how long the sun shines directly on it. With 4–5 hours of direct sun, you can get a crop of bush beans, broccoli, cauliflower, potatoes, peas, summer squash, or rhubarb. If your area receives less than 4 hours of sunlight, you should lean toward salad crops, such as lettuce, spinach, or chard; they will tolerate more shade than fruit-bearing crops. Those crops may also actually last longer in the shady garden, because they won't get too hot in summer sun and go to seed as readily.

Veggies in small space

After growing up on a farm with plenty of elbow room and fresh vegetables, I find my suburban townhouse seems small. I'd like to grow vegetables, but how can I in such a small space?

With a little creativity, you'll be surprised how much produce you can farm in the city. First, go vertical. Save precious ground by training vining crops such as peas, pole beans, melons, squash, and cucumbers on vertical supports. Good trellises can be made of lath stakes, bamboo poles, a section of fence, or grow-netting stapled between two upright poles.

Go wide with low-growing plants such as leafy crops, onions, and root crops. Wide-row gardening works on the principle that plants sown closer together in broad bands produce up to 4 times as much harvest as the same area planted single file in separate rows. Individual plants may produce less than when they're spaced according to the seed package guidelines, but, on the whole, the volume produced is greater. Wide-row gardening also reduces weeding, because vegetables grow thickly and choke out weeds. In addition, plants shade the soil, keeping it moist during hot, dry spells.

With double-cropping, you'll get twice the harvest per square foot. To prevent crowding, combine plants with different maturities; for example, sow radishes with slower-growing carrots. When the radishes are ready to harvest, the carrots can take over. Beets planted with broccoli are another good combination.

Second-cropping involves planting in succession for constant production. Early-season vegetables, such as lettuce and green onions, leave voids after they're harvested in midsummer. Reseed empty areas with fast-growing crops such as summer squash and bush beans. Later in summer, plant more cool-season crops for a fall harvest.

My husband and I would like to grow a few more vegetables than usual. I've heard that in a larger garden it's best to rotate where the vegetables are planted each year. How do I do this? Are there certain dos and don'ts with regard to rotation?

The basic rule of rotation is to avoid planting any closely related vegetables in the same spot for at least 3 years. Some common plant families include the following.

- Tomatoes. Tomatoes, peppers, potatoes, and eggplant
- Squash. Cucumbers, melons, pumpkins, winter squash, summer squash, zucchini, and gourds
- Beans. Green beans, wax beans, lima beans, soybeans, snow peas, snap peas, and garden peas
- Cabbage. Cabbage, broccoli, cauliflower, broccoflower, Brussels sprouts, kohlrabi, kale, and collards

By rotating crops, you not only help prevent disease, you ensure that your plants get proper soil nutrients. For example, verticillium wilt can survive several years in the soil and affect tomatoes and potatoes. To keep from spreading the disease season to season, plant susceptible vegetables in different garden spots from year to year so the disease will be less likely to carry over. Rather than follow your tomato crop with tomatoes or potatoes, instead plant corn, carrots, or members of the squash family. Use crop rotation for better plant nutrient management too. Corn, for instance, uses more nitrogen than peas or beans do. In fact, members of the bean family actually add nitrogen to the soil through nitrogen fixation. By planting corn where beans or peas grew last year, you can keep your soil's nutrients better balanced and reduce the amount of additional fertilizer needed.

Safe garden wood

I'm using railroad ties to construct flower beds. I heard this is fine for flowers but not for vegetable gardens. Is this true? Can the creosote that is used to treat the ties leach into the soil and harm the vegetables?

Yes, creosote does leach out of the ties and into the soil, but worn-out ties are generally not a problem, because most of their creosote has already leached away. Whether plants take up the creosote has not been settled. However, because creosote is toxic, new ties can cause growth problems for plants that are sensitive to it. You can line your beds with plastic to prevent contact between the soil and wood, if you like. If the wood is oozing black creosote or has an odor, it shouldn't be used. Gasses released from creosote are also harmful in a closed space, so railroad ties should not be used in a greenhouse or indoors.

Many other materials can be used for constructing a raised bed, so there is no reason to give up the idea.

Because chemically pressure-treated wood is expected to last up to 40 years, most folks turn to it first when building a raised bed. If you are concerned about safety, however, be sure to research your options. Although all wood preservatives have guidelines for safe use, some of them, such as ACQ, are thought to be safer than others.

To avoid preservatives completely, choose from among several woods that are naturally rot-resistant, such as heartwood-grade redwood, knotty red cedar, cypress, catalpa, juniper, or Osage orange. Construction-grade heartwood can last so long that you'll probably want to redesign your bed before it falls apart. Availability often depends on your locale.

The plastics industry has other options, including recycled plastic and plastic mixed with sawdust. They look and handle similar to wood, will last for years outdoors, and don't leach any chemicals.

Ashes in garden

My dad wants to use the ashes from our charcoal grill on the garden. Will this have any effect?

Ashes from charcoal grills should not be added to gardens because of chemicals used in processing charcoal. Wood ashes, on the other hand, are safer for garden use. They have fertilizer value—generally less than 10 percent potash, 1 percent phosphate, and trace amounts of micronutrients—but their main effect is to raise the pH, or alkalinity, of the soil, and they can do it rather quickly. A soil pH above the optimum level limits a plant's uptake of important soil nutrients. If you live in an area with alkaline soils, adding wood ashes to the garden soil could cause nutrient deficiencies.

In areas where the soil is more acidic (generally areas east of the Mississippi), the best way to take advantage of wood ashes is to add them to the compost pile. That avoids the hassle of scattering the ashes in your gardens, and you lessen the risk of applying too much of a good thing, which can actually harm your plants.

Seeding peas and lettuce

How early can I plant peas and lettuce? It takes so long to warm up where I live, but I know that peas and lettuce can tolerate cool soil. Which varieties of lettuce and peas should I use?

Peas *(Pisum sativum)* and lettuce *(Lactuca sativa)* can be planted as early as 6 weeks before the last frost, as long as the soil is moist but not muddy. It's important to get peas in as early as possible. Yields drop dramatically on later plantings because peas tolerate heat poorly. Plant lettuce at 2-week intervals through early summer so you can extend the harvest into midsummer.

Plant lettuce again in late summer for a fall crop. You can try a late-summer planting of peas for a fall crop also. They germinate poorly in warm soil and dry conditions, so try shading the seedbed to keep the soil cooler and retain moisture. This is good advice for summer-sown lettuce too.

Perennial veggies

I grew asparagus for the first time and was amazed at how nice it was to harvest a vegetable I had planted the previous year. Do you have any suggestions for other perennial vegetables?

Perennial vegetables may take more patience than those you plant and harvest in one growing season. Many don't yield a harvest the first year after planting, but the rewards of a return harvest year after year make them worth the effort. Try these vegetables you plant once and harvest for several years.

- Artichoke *(Cynara scolymus)* is perennial in Zones 9 and warmer. In Zones 7 and 8, it overwinters in the ground if mulched. In colder zones, treat artichoke as a tender perennial, digging it up and storing it like a bulb over the winter, or grow it as an annual crop.
- Asparagus *(Asparagus officinalis)* can produce for up to 30 years, so plan on a long and fruitful relationship with these plants. For more color, add a purple variety to your mix. Grow asparagus in Zones 4–8; in warmer zones, the plants never go into their required dormancy.
- Chayote *(Sechium edule)* looks like a large green pear with a cleft. Use it in cooking as you would summer squash. This perennial vine can grow up to 90 feet and is hardy in Zones 8–10. Where the ground freezes to only an inch deep, the vines die back, but you can protect the roots with 10 inches of mulch. In climates colder than Zone 8, grow chayote as an annual vine.
- Horseradish *(Armoracia rusticana)* readily grows in most garden soils in Zones 4–8. In colder zones, overwinter the roots as you would bulbs. Wear gloves when harvesting the root; it contains an oil similar to that found in hot peppers and can burn your hands. Plant with caution. It can become invasive.

- Jerusalem artichoke *(Helianthus tuberosus)* tubers are planted like potatoes. Harvest the tubers after the plant dies back in fall. In Zones 4–9, leave a few tubers in the ground to grow the following season. In colder zones, overwinter the tubers as you would bulbs. Grow the tubers in an area where you can control the plants, because they can become invasive.
- Rhubarb *(Rheum ×cultorum)* can be grown in Zones 2–9, although it does best where the winters are cold enough to freeze the ground. In warmer zones, grow it as a winter annual. Use the thick stalks in cooking; the leaves contain toxic levels of oxalic acid and should not be eaten.

Preparing raised beds

I grew vegetables in a raised bed last summer. I haven't done anything to the soil since I planted last year. What should I do to get the soil ready for this year?

There's not much you absolutely have to do to make the soil ready for planting. I like to add a fresh layer of organic matter to the bed's surface and work that into the soil. Compost, rotted manure, leaf mold, or peat moss will help. At planting time, add a timed-release vegetable fertilizer, and dig it into the soil as you till, in preparation for planting. Keep the bed weed-free between growing seasons. By removing weeds before they set seed, you'll cut down on the need to weed while crops are growing.

Wet soil in spring

Does it matter how early I plant my vegetable garden? There's a lot of rain here in the spring, and it doesn't seem like a good idea to plant while the soil is wet.

You are absolutely right. Unless your soil is mostly sand, tilling or working it when it is wet turns it into a sticky mess. In any season, wait until the soil dries enough to pass the squeeze test. Take up a handful and squeeze it. If it forms a tight ball, it's too wet. Ideally, it should be slightly more crumbly than cookie dough.

It's perfectly OK to delay planting of tomatoes, peppers, beans, and other plants that like warm weather. However, if you wait until days become long and warm to plant cool-season crops such as lettuce, spinach, or peas, their flavor suffers and they quickly go to seed. Prepare the soil in raised beds in fall and cover them with polyethylene film through the winter to make sure you get an early start on the spring planting season. The film will keep excess moisture off the soil as well as warm the bed earlier in spring.

When to water

I have a vegetable garden that includes pole beans, red and white radishes, tomatoes, baby carrots, and green onions. What is the best time to water? It gets very hot here in the afternoon.

Early morning is usually the best time to water, especially if you are using a sprinkler or other method that wets the foliage. Watering in the morning gives the leaves enough time to dry before night. And leaves that are dry overnight are less likely to suffer from fungal diseases, because most fungi need damp leaf surfaces to spread. Morning watering also makes more efficient use of the water. Wind speeds are usually lower in early morning, meaning that less water will be lost to evaporation.

Hot, dry climates are an exception, however. Many gardeners in arid climates prefer evening watering, which raises the humidity level in the vegetable garden. A little extra humidity often enhances pollination of beans, tomatoes, and other vegetables that depend on good fruit set. Ideally, do most of your routine watering in the morning whenever possible, and switch to evening watering when your beans and tomatoes are holding a heavy set of blossoms.

Veggies in containers

This year I want to grow a few plants in pots on my back porch. I'm considering zucchini, butter beans, black-eyed peas, and green beans. What's the best way to start this project?

Begin by obtaining large containers, at least 12 inches in diameter, and site them in a sunny spot. Better yet, buy a pair of half barrels, which are ideal for veggies. To save your back, place the containers where you want them before you fill them with soil, or place them on plant dollies that you can easily roll around.

In each container or half barrel, install a 4-foot-tall teepee-type trellis. Plant a pole bean such as 'Kentucky Blue' around the base of one trellis, and a vining butter bean around the base of the other. A couple of inches inside the edges of the containers, tuck in a few seeds of a compact variety of zucchini, such as 'Gold Rush'. As for the black-eyed peas, try them in a pair of large oblong planters. Black-eyed peas take a long time to mature, and you'll need at least a dozen plants, grown 5 inches apart, to get a good yield of pods.

Season extenders

We get frosts late in the spring and early in the fall in our garden. Is there anything we can do to get our vegetables started earlier outdoors?

When it comes to gardening, starting early means you're the first on the block to serve homegrown goodness at the dinner table. Try these techniques at season's end, too, and you could be the last.

- Cloche call. Cloches protect plants from the elements. Glass cloches aren't vented; move them daily to keep plants from sizzling in the midday sun. Eliminate this daily chore by employing cloches with vents, such as milk jugs or any vented hot cap that allows heated air to escape. To use a milk jug, cut off the bottom, remove the lid, and place the top of the container over your plant. Use cloches until after the last spring frost and again when frost threatens in fall.

- Under cover. Floating row covers work on much the same principle as cloches but are a better choice for whole beds of crops such as salad greens. At season's end, the insulation from a row cover can extend the harvest of larger plants such as zucchini and tomatoes. Old sheets supported by metal hoops also make good covers. Many synthetic row covers are light enough to drape directly over the crop. Synthetic-fabric row covers may also be left on all season to give insect protection to such pest magnets as eggplant and cabbage.

- Bed warmers. Soil's insulating properties make for slow gardening in spring. Plant in raised beds, where the soil warms faster because the beds are above the main soil surface, even if only by a few inches. For gardens that aren't raised, warm the soil before you plant by covering the area with sheets of clear or black plastic or dark landscape fabric.

- Peas, please. One of the easiest ways to garden early is to grow plants that do best in cool weather. Plant these annual crops as soon as the ground can be worked, 20–40 days before the last frost in spring. Use transplants for best results. A second crop of shorter-season varieties planted in late summer will thrive in the cool weather of autumn. A few vegetables, such as cabbage and leeks, taste even better after the crop has been nipped by a light frost.

ASPARAGUS

Planting asparagus

I purchased asparagus roots. What is the correct way to plant them?

Asparagus *(Asparagus)* is a tough, persistent plant. It requires well-drained soil with a near neutral pH. Many old references suggest digging a trench, then making mounds on which to plant the asparagus, but this isn't necessary. You need to dig a trench only deep enough to cover the roots with 4 inches of soil. To tell which side is up on a dormant asparagus plant, look for knobby lumps, which are most numerous on the top. Spread out the roots as you plant them, like spokes of an umbrella. Allow enough space between plants so the tips of the roots don't overlap. Mulch with clean wheat straw or another weed-free material to cut down on weeds, which are the biggest challenge in the first 2 years after a new asparagus bed is planted.

Harvesting asparagus

How much asparagus can I harvest? I've heard that if I pick too much, I could hurt my plants.

The first year after planting, pick only large spears (pencil-size diameter or greater) that emerge early in the growing season. This means gathering only a handful of spears over a period of 2 weeks in early spring. In the second year, gather all the spears you want for a month, beginning with the emergence of the first spear. In subsequent seasons, limit your picking to a 6-week period. (Some people use the end of the spring strawberry season as the sign that asparagus season is over.) If you overharvest asparagus, the plants will produce fewer spears, because they will have less time to store energy and develop the next year's crop.

Asparagus fern

Do I need to keep all asparagus shoots picked so none of them develop into fern?

During the harvest season, pick the asparagus patch clean. If you leave some shoots to develop into fern, asparagus beetles are likely to lay their eggs on the ferny growth. As the eggs hatch, the larvae feed on and distort developing shoots. Harvest frequently enough so none of the spears develops a ferny top. This may mean harvesting daily if temperatures are warm. Stop harvesting when most of the shoots are pencil size in diameter. Allow the remaining shoots to develop into fern to build up the crown for next year's harvest. Even with thorough harvest, the beetles may become a problem and require treatment with an insecticide.

Asparagus winter care

Should I leave asparagus ferns standing through the winter or cut them down this fall?

If your asparagus plants were disease- and insect-free, leave the ferns in place over the winter. The stems catch snow for additional insulation and soil moisture. Snow cover can also delay the early emergence of asparagus in spring. (Early warm air temperatures can spur asparagus spear development; then sudden drops in temperature lead to frost damage.) In early spring, mow or cut back the old ferny growth to ground level before spears emerge.

Salt on asparagus

My grandma said that I could sprinkle salt on my asparagus beds to control the weeds. Is that true?

Asparagus is more salt tolerant than a lot of plants, so it may not be damaged by an application of table salt to the soil. However, I don't recommend it. Salt destroys soil structure and may wash into other parts of the garden, injuring other crops. You have other, better options for controlling weeds in asparagus. If the patch has perennial weeds such as dandelion or quackgrass, snap off all asparagus spears below ground level, then spray the weeds with glyphosate (Roundup). Glyphosate will be inactivated once it reaches the soil, so new spears that emerge will be unaffected. Keep your asparagus bed mulched with weed-free straw or other organic mulch to prevent weeds from germinating. Hand-pull or hoe out weeds that grow through the mulch.

BEAN

Dry bean bonanza

I want to grow beans in my vegetable garden, specifically bush-type pinto and red kidney beans. When is the best time to plant and harvest them?

Wait until all danger of frost has passed to plant shell beans (*Phaseolus*). They produce best when grown in double rows (two parallel rows about 6 inches apart). Begin harvesting beans for cooking fresh as soon as the pods become leathery; this varies from about 65 days for small red beans to 80 days for larger kidney beans and pintos. To dry beans, allow them to mature until the pods turn tan, which usually takes 2 weeks longer. If a prolonged spell of rainy weather strikes while your beans are drying, harvest them and finish drying them indoors. Shell beans quickly become moldy in wet pods.

BROCCOLI

Early-bird broccoli

When can I safely plant broccoli seedlings that I bought from the garden center?

Broccoli *(Brassica)* likes cool temperatures and tolerates frost, but exposure to too much cold can make the plant develop a head prematurely. This prematurely developed head will be small, and the plant may be permanently stunted. In spring, the prime planting time is 1–3 weeks before your last expected frost date. Until then, set your plants outside on mild, sunny days so they can become accustomed to sun. Your plants can handle a light frost after you set them out: Broccoli endures cold better than heat.

If you love broccoli, plant it again in midsummer for an autumn harvest. It will taste wonderful, and the heads will be larger. In either season, watch plants for little leaf-eating caterpillars. Pick them off by hand, or spray plants with Bt *(Bacillus thuringiensis)* insecticide, such as Thuricide.

CABBAGE

Cabbage worms

There are green worms chewing holes in my cabbage. What can I do?

Three species of cabbage worms chew on leaves of cabbage-family (Brassicaceae) crops (cabbage, broccoli, cauliflower, Brussels sprouts, kohlrabi, kale). Imported cabbage worm, cabbage looper, and diamondback moth larvae chew holes through the leaves.

Keep populations of these worms lower by removing weeds in the mustard family (wild mustard, wild radish, shepherd's purse, and peppergrass) that are alternate hosts. Use floating row covers to prevent adults from laying eggs on plants. Handpick worms from the plants. The biological insecticide Bt is effective against all three species of cabbage worms.

CORN

When to harvest

How do I know when it is time to pick my sweet corn?

Corn *(Zea)* is ripe when silks are brown and dry on top but still yellow just under the husk. Watch for the silks to change color from greenish yellow to brown as the ear of corn matures.

You may also be able to determine ripeness by feel. Many gardeners check how filled-out the cobs feel before harvesting, but if you grow different varieties, those that have thin cobs may seem as though they are still filling out.

Knowing the number of days to maturity of a variety helps (find the dates on seed packets and in seed catalogs), but keep in mind that the growth rates vary in different climates.

Some gardeners peel back the husks to look at the developing kernels. Avoid peeling back any more husks than you must, because the act invites corn earworms, raccoons, and some birds to feed on your corn.

Growing sweet corn

What does it take to grow good sweet corn? The ears never fill out well when I grow it.

Sweet corn needs warm temperatures for best growth. It needs full sun and prefers a soil pH between 5.8 and 6.5. Early plantings of standard sweet corn can be made around the frost-free date when soil temperatures have warmed to 55°F. Wait until the soil warms to at least 60°F to plant supersweet types.

Plant the seed just ½ inch deep in cool soil, and 1–1½ inches deep in warm soil. Plant two or more rows of the same variety side by side to ensure good pollination. Because corn is wind-pollinated, pollen from one row must fall or blow onto the silks of an adjoining row to pollinate the kernels. Plant corn in a block of shorter rows to ensure better pollination. Space rows 30–36 inches apart.

Supersweet corn

I like the flavor of supersweet sweet corn. Does it require any special care?

High-sugar sweet corn may be either supersweet or sugary enhanced. The supersweet varieties have the "shrunken 2" gene, abbreviated "sh2." Sugary-enhanced varieties are designated "se." Look for these designations in seed catalogs or on seed packets. The reason they are sweeter than regular sweet corn is that sugars in these types of sweet corn are slower to convert to starch.

One consideration in growing supersweet sweet corn cultivars is that they are slow to germinate and have reduced seedling vigor. Wait to plant until the soil has warmed to at least 60°F, and sow seeds shallowly.

These sweeter corns should be isolated from other types of corn. Cross-pollination with regular sweet corn results in a starchy field-corn type of kernel. Plant at least 250 feet away from other types of corn. Another option is to stagger planting dates, or select cultivars that mature at different times so the tasseling periods don't overlap. Plant at least 2 weeks apart, or use varieties with at least 14 days' difference in maturity.

CUCUMBER

Crossing cucumbers

How far apart should I plant cucumbers from squash to prevent them from cross-pollinating and ruining one another?

Cucumbers (*Cucumis*) and squash (*Cucurbita*) are not related closely enough to cross-pollinate, so they may be planted next to each other with no danger of cross-pollination. If they could cross-pollinate, it would still be all right, because the fruits wouldn't be affected. This is because the fruits are part of the mother plant; cross-pollination affects only seeds. So unless you're saving the seeds to plant next year, don't worry about squash crossing with squash (or pumpkins or any other type of vegetable).

Hollow cucumbers

Every year, my cucumbers are hollow in the center. What could be causing this?

Hollow fruits are a common problem. They usually result from a combination of nutrient deficiency and irregular watering (when the soil gets very wet for a while, then very dry). Keeping the soil consistantly moist, but not wet, will help. Too much nitrogen in the soil may make the fruits grow so fast that they "open up"—the inside can't keep up with the rest of the fruit. Reducing the amount of fertilizer would help if this is the case.

Also, some cucumber varieties are more prone to the condition than others. Check the descriptions in seed catalogs or on seed packets to identify selections that better resist hollow centers.

The hollow centers have little effect on the quality of the fruit, although affected ones are sometimes bitter as a result of the moisture stress.

Straightening bent cucumbers

I am growing a 'Bush Whopper' cucumber plant. Instead of growing long and straight, the fruits grow in a C shape and are skinny at one end. What causes this?

A couple of things can cause what you describe. Misshapen cucumbers often are caused by hot, dry conditions during fruit set, soil that's not fertile enough to support the plants, or poor pollination.

The problem happens more frequently in late summer because of high temperatures. The best prevention is to keep your plants mulched to maintain more uniform soil moisture, and improve your soil with lots of organic matter to aid water-holding capacity.

If you have good soil, poor pollination is a likely culprit. Improve the chances for good pollination by planting borage (a common herb) or other flowering plants near your cucumbers. The blue borage blooms attract bees, which will also pollinate your cucumbers more thoroughly. Avoid using insecticides in your garden; these products kill bees as well as harmful insect pests.

GARLIC

Drying garlic

How do I harvest my garlic? What is the best way to store it?

Harvest garlic *(Allium)* when the tops begin to dry and discolor naturally. This usually happens in late summer or early autumn. Dig rather than pull bulbs to avoid stem injury. Place the bulbs in a well-ventilated area to dry for several weeks. After the bulbs are dry, cut off the tops and roots to within an inch of the bulbs.

Garlic will store well for 6–7 months once it is dried. It stores best at 32°F, but a 40°F refrigerator works well too. Bulbs form sprouts quickly at temperatures above 40°F.

GOURD

Curing gourds

When should I harvest gourds? How do I preserve them?

Harvest gourds when the stems turn brown and dry. If possible, harvest them before frost hits, though mature hardshell gourds *(Lagenaria)* can withstand a light frost. Cut the gourds from the vine, leaving an inch or two of stem attached. Discard rotten, bruised, or immature gourds. These are more likely to decay.

Wash the harvested gourds with soap and water. A dip in rubbing alcohol or a 10 percent bleach solution will help remove surface molds that may cause rot. Dry the surface and place the gourds in a dark, well-ventilated area for a week or so of surface drying to harden the rind and set the color. Make certain the gourds do not touch one another; use a slatted tray or screen to allow air to circulate all around. Discard any gourds that develop decay, mold, or soft spots.

Internal drying takes at least 4 additional weeks in a warm, dark, well-ventilated room. Turn the gourds periodically to promote even curing. Wipe off surface molds that may appear. Discard any gourds that decay, shrivel, or become misshapen. When the seeds rattle inside, drying is complete.

LEEK

Growing leeks

This is the first year that I've grown leeks in my garden. What's the best way to grow them? Do I need to deadhead them as I do garlic?

Leeks *(Allium)* are a tasty winter vegetable and are usually best when used in late autumn and winter after cold temperatures have sweetened them. Because they're a cool-season vegetable, leeks will withstand a considerable amount of cold, especially when covered with layers of leaves or snow during the winter.

Leeks thrive in cool weather, and they need rich soil with lots of organic matter. They also appreciate plenty of moisture. Leeks that start to produce seed heads will be tough and low quality. However, when a leek becomes mature enough to produce seed, it will also make small bulblets around the base under the soil. Separate these bulblets and plant them to produce new leeks, much as you would an onion set.

Seed heads normally form on leeks in the second year. If seed heads form in the plants' first year, your leeks are under stress. Change the growing environment to more favorable conditions to keep them healthy.

LETTUCE

Seeding lettuce

Our family enjoys the flavor of homegrown lettuce, but I have trouble starting it in the ground. The seeds either don't germinate, or they come up so thick that thinning out the seedlings becomes a tedious job. What's the trick?

Try jump-starting your plants indoors from seed. It's easier and faster to transplant seedlings exactly where you want them than to thin out the leafy crowd in the ground. And because you'll be planting seedlings instead of seeds outside, you'll also have a head start on the growing season—a plus in areas with short summers.

Here's a tip to keep lettuce *(Lactuca)* all summer long: In spring, choose lettuces with different maturity dates. Heat-tolerant, slow-bolting types (those that don't produce seed as quickly) can be transplanted into your garden last. If you're planting lettuce where your summer garden will grow, plant it between the rows where you'll be sowing hot-weather lovers such as tomatoes and peppers.

MELON

Harvesting cantaloupes

When are cantaloupes ready to harvest? Do I wait until I see some color, or do I pick them when they seem large enough, then let them ripen indoors?

Watch for the melon's skin under the outer webbing to start turning yellowish or tan. You'll also see this color develop on the underside of the fruit. As it ripens, the whole melon *(Cucumis)* will become one color. If the color under the webbing is still green, it's not ready to pick. Melons will ripen indoors if you pick them when immature (as commercial growers do), but they won't taste as good as vine-ripened fruit. Ripe cantaloupes give you another clue that they're ready to pick—the stem end separates easily from the vine. If the color looks promising for ripeness, give the fruit a little tug. If it's ripe, the stem of the fruit will release with little effort.

Wilting melons

For the second year running, my muskmelon plants are rotting. The leaves turn yellow, then brown, and the vines wilt. I water daily, fertilize as instructed on the package, and sprinkle with a granular insecticide to keep off the bugs. What is the problem?

The problem sounds like bacterial wilt, a disease spread from plant to plant by striped and spotted cucumber beetles. Both beetle types are approximately ¼–⅜ inches long, and yellow to greenish yellow. The larvae feed on the plant roots, then the adult beetles chew on the plant leaves. The disease can hit at any time.

To diagnose the disease, cut off a wilted stem near the base of the plant, then gently squeeze out the sap (the juice inside the stem). Touch a knife to the sap and withdraw it slowly. If your plant is infected with bacterial wilt, you'll see an oozing white substance that strings out in a fine thread as you withdraw the knife.

There are no good chemical controls for bacterial wilt. Remove and discard all infected plants as soon as you notice the infection. Handpick the beetles off the plant, or use floating row covers until after the blooms have begun to appear. Spray plants every 7 days with carbaryl (Sevin) or a general insect-control product to control the beetles. If you want to use a nonchemical control, horticultural-grade diatomaceous earth also will reduce the number of beetles. Apply it to all plant surfaces.

ONION

Growing onions for storage

Can I grow yellow and red onions? How do I store them?

Buy seeds or transplants from a reliable seed company or garden center after reading the descriptions to see which are good storage types. You can also grow onions *(Allium)* from sets, but the onions that develop from sets will develop seed heads and will not store as well as those grown from seeds or transplants. Plant the onions where they'll get full sun and grow in well-drained soil. Heavy soils or poorly drained soils could cause the onions to rot.

'Southport Red Globe' is an old standby red type that stores well. 'Stuttgarter' is a yellow type for storage. But be sure you have the right variety for your climate. Onions are day-length dependent for bulb formation. Types for southern climates may not bulb up in the North, just as northern types won't grow very large in southern areas.

By late summer, when the onion bulbs have developed to full size, stop watering the plants. Doing this lets the green tops dry and encourages the bulbs to go dormant. Then you can successfully store them for long periods.

When the onions are dry, store them in mesh bags and hang them in a cool, dry, dark place. They'll store longest at temperatures just above freezing. Prevent them from freezing, however, because frozen onions will turn to mush. Inspect them regularly for signs of sprouts. Use sprouting bulbs as soon as possible.

PEPPER

Puny peppers

My green peppers do not get very big. Any ideas why?

A pepper *(Capsicum)* plant covered in blooms may seem like a blessing, but it could be a curse. The problem could be that there are too many peppers on the plant. Plants have only so much energy—too many fruits can demand more energy from the plant than it can provide. Thinning the extra fruits soon after they set can help.

Small fruit also may result from poor nutrition. Compost or other forms of organic matter worked into the soil around the plants, combined with a mulch of organic material such as leaf mold, will help hold nutrients and moisture in the soil and boost plant growth.

Poor pepper set

I am having a hard time with my habanero peppers. The blossoms never form fruit. They yellow and fall off. My Thai peppers are fine and are growing and producing right next to the habaneros. Can you help?

Pepper blossom drop (often more severe in some varieties than others) is caused by temperature fluctuations during pollination. Normal pollination and fruit set fail to occur when nighttime temperatures fall below 58°F and daytime temperatures rise above 85°F. Below or above this range, the blossoms may fall off. If partial pollination occurs and fruit begins to set, the fruit often becomes misshapen or rough. Irrigating to cool the plants is one way to minimize this problem.

Another method that helps to some degree is to hang shade cloth over the plants. Shading the plants with lath panels can help too.

Spotted peppers

My bell peppers have small dark spots on them. What is this and how can I get rid of it?

It sounds as though your peppers may have bacterial spot. This disease affects leaves and fruit and develops in moist weather. On the pepper fruits, bacterial spot appears first as small, water-soaked areas. Eventually the spots become dark, raised, and scablike.

On the leaves, spots first show up as small, irregular, water-soaked areas on the lower leaf surface. They turn purplish gray with a black center. If leaf spots are numerous, they can cause the leaves to yellow and fall from the plant. Peppers on defoliated plants may develop sunscald.

This disease usually comes from infected transplants. Make certain that you purchase plants from a reputable supplier. Bacterial spot spreads through splashing water, or by the gardener working among wet plants. Avoid wetting the plants' foliage when watering, and wait until the plants dry to work in the garden. Destroy affected plants at season's end, and plant peppers in a different location next season to prevent the disease from carrying over.

POTATO

Is it true that you can grow a potato plant from a regular potato? How is this done?

It's best to grow potatoes *(Solanum)* from specially grown seed potatoes that are certified disease-free. The potatoes you purchase in the grocery store may have been treated with a sprout inhibitor to prevent them from sprouting in your pantry. However, if you have some potatoes that are beginning to sprout (the "eyes" have swollen whitish shoots beginning to develop), simply plant a piece of the sprouting potato in the ground or in a roomy pot covered with 3 inches of soil. Within 2 weeks green shoots should emerge. These will grow into bushy plants, and after 3 months or so new spuds will develop belowground. Potatoes are ready to harvest when the plants begin to turn yellow and die back.

Most potatoes sprout quickly in spring when kept at room temperature, but the type of potato makes a difference if you want to harvest good tubers. The small red potatoes often sold as "new" potatoes are fast and fun to grow. Large baking potato plants take much longer to mature and often produce poorly in areas where hot summer weather prevails.

Potato bugs

Something is eating holes in the leaves of my potato plants. I saw some large yellow-and-black beetles. Are they the culprits?

It sounds as though your potatoes have Colorado potato beetles. This beetle has a rounded light yellowish shell marked with black stripes. Colorado potato beetle is resistant to most chemical controls. It's better to prevent infestations by using appropriate cultural practices.

Start by adjusting your planting date. Plant potatoes as early as possible in spring. By the time the beetles attack, the crop will be mature enough to escape significant damage. Use an early-maturing variety and aim for a midsummer harvest. Another option is to wait to plant until early summer. By the time the potatoes emerge, most beetles will be gone. Late-planted potatoes will mature in fall.

If you have a small planting, handpicking beetles is an effective control. Inspect plants a couple of times per week and remove all larvae and adult beetles. Place floating row covers over plants to prevent adult beetles from getting to the plants.

Bacteria called Bt *(Bacillus thuringiensis san diego* or *Bt tenebrionis)* control Colorado potato beetle larvae. These products work slowly; larvae may not die until 4–5 days after treatment. Spray Bt when the larvae are just starting to develop.

Potato scab
Why do my potatoes have a scaly substance on the peel?

It sounds as though your potatoes are infected with potato scab, a fungal disease that persists in the soil over long periods. Infection occurs through wounds and through the pores in the tuber skins when the tubers are young and growing rapidly. Potato scab is most severe in warm, dry soil that's slightly alkaline.

If your soil pH is above 5.5, lower the pH with powdered sulfur (available at your local garden center). The sulfur makes weak sulfuric acid, which lowers the soil's pH level.

Here are other ways to deal with scab.
- Rotate your potato patch so each place is used for potatoes only once every 3–4 years.
- Plant resistant varieties; several have high scab resistance.

Cutting up seed potatoes
We'd like to try our hand at growing potatoes. I know I need to purchase seed potatoes, but a friend said to cut them in pieces before I plant them. How do I do this?

Take a close look at your seed potato and notice the indentations, or eyes. Each of these eyes is capable of producing a potato plant. You can plant the potatoes without dividing them, but you can have more plants and a bigger harvest if you cut them up first.

Using a kitchen knife, divide larger potatoes into small pieces. Slice each piece so it has one or more eyes. Cut smaller potatoes in half or leave them whole. Allow the cut surfaces to dry before planting them. Lay the pieces skin side up 12 inches apart in a 2–3-inch-deep furrow, and cover each piece with a 3-inch mound of soil. As the plants grow, add more soil around the bases, leaving much of the foliage showing to provide energy for the developing tubers.

Plant potatoes as early as one month before the last frost in your area. They're an easy crop to grow, and especially suitable for children. Small children can handle the seed potato pieces more easily than tiny seeds of other vegetables. They'll learn patience as they wait for the crop, and you can share their joy as they dig up the underground surprises.

PUMPKIN

Pumpkin problems

I had great success growing big orange pumpkins for Halloween my first year, but for the last two years there has been a problem. The plants start out great, then begin to slowly die. I still get a few pumpkins, but I have to harvest early. What's happening?

When pumpkins *(Cucurbita)* or summer squash *(Cucurbita)* slowly wilt to death, the culprits are usually squash vine borers—the larvae of a large moth that lays its eggs on the stems, usually near the base of the plant. The eggs hatch and the larvae bore inside and feed on the interior of the stems. By the time you see sawdustlike frass (excrement) coming out of the holes, substantial damage has been done. There are three ways to prevent serious borer damage.

- Cover plants with floating row covers until they begin to blossom. The row cover will protect the plants from borers, squash bugs, and other pests.
- Arm yourself with beneficial nematodes. Inject small amounts (less than a teaspoon) of these microscopic critters into the base of the plants' hollow stems every 4–6 inches; nematodes quickly kill the vine borers. You can buy a garden syringe for this purpose.
- Inject the stems with Bt *(Bacillus thuringiensis)*, as described in the previous paragraph.

  You may also be able to save the plant by slitting the stem lengthwise near the frass, digging out the borer, and covering up the base of the stem with moist soil.

Pollinating pumpkin

I planted pumpkin seeds and only one grew. It bloomed many times but didn't even produce one pumpkin. What did I do wrong?

Most commercial pumpkins have both male and female flowers, but a few varieties have only female flowers. When such types are sold, seed companies always include seeds of a normal type that sets both male and female flowers, so the male flowers can provide pollen for the all-female plants. Because you had only one vine, if it was one that forms only female flowers and there wasn't any other pumpkin (or zucchini-type squash) around to pollinate it, it would produce blooms but would fail to set any pumpkins.

It's possible that the plant had male and female flowers but none was pollinated. Did you notice any insects, such as bees, around the flowers? If they were absent, that may be the reason.

You can distinguish male and female flowers by looking under the flower. Male flowers have a slender stalk attaching them to the vine. Female flowers have a swollen base that looks like a miniature pumpkin. If both are present on your vine, you can compensate for lack of insect pollinators by hand-pollinating the female blossoms. Take an artist's brush to gather pollen from the male blossom early in the morning. Transfer the pollen to a freshly opened female blossom. Within a few days you should see the swollen base beginning to enlarge into a pumpkin.

PURSLANE

Prolific purslane
Purslane is taking over my garden. How do I kill it?

You can eliminate purslane *(Portulaca)* with a thick mulch, with a hoe, or by hand-pulling. Purslane grows quickly in warm weather. Mulch that's 2–3 inches deep keeps the soil below cooler and prevents the tiny purslane seeds from pushing up through it.

Whether you dig or pull it, remove it from the garden, because purslane forms new roots as it lies on the soil. Because purslane is a succulent, it can take a long time for the severed plants to dry up. In the meantime, new roots develop and the plants begin to grow again.

You might also try developing a taste for purslane. It is edible and can be added to salads. Perhaps you'll like it so much that you'll soon be asking how to grow more of it!

RHUBARB

Harvesting rhubarb
A good friend gave me a rhubarb plant. I have been growing it now for more than a year, and the plant is very leafy. Do I trim it back? How do I harvest it?

Rhubarb *(Rheum ×cultorum)* leaves are not edible, but the leaf stalks (petioles) make a good pie. Wait until the plant is at least a year old, then harvest the stalks in spring and early summer. The stalks at the outer edge of the plant can be pulled off at the soil line when the leaves are fully open and developed. Just take hold of the stalk close to the soil line, and give a slight twist as you pull. Never take more than about a third of the stalks at one time. Stop harvesting rhubarb before midsummer, and let the plant continue to grow. Trim it to the ground when it dies back naturally or is damaged by freezing weather. Rhubarb will return year after year in gardens where temperatures are not too hot.

I planted rhubarb a month ago, and it does not want to ripen. It has lots of stalks, but they are all green. When will they turn red?

To give your rhubarb plant a healthy start, avoid harvesting it the year you plant it. So you know for future harvests, there are many different rhubarb cultivars, and not all of them are red. Some selections have green, pink, or speckled petioles (stalks). Stalk color is not an indicator of ripeness but rather a characteristic of the variety. Many people believe that the red color indicates sweetness, but it's not always the case. Color may be more intense in rhubarb grown in full sun than in part shade. Green varieties can be more productive and as sweet as red ones. If your plant's stems are all green, it's unlikely they will change color.

Flowering rhubarb

Should I cut the seed stalks out of my rhubarb, or leave them there to send strength to the plant?

If you like the flowers, you aren't required to cut the stalks; flowering does not affect the flavor or edibility of the rhubarb plant. However, most gardeners cut down the stalks before the flowers bloom so more of the plant's energy remains in the roots to help produce more leaves and edible stalks.

SQUASH

Squash slow to fruit

My summer squash plants have been blooming for a couple of weeks, but they haven't produced any squash yet. What's wrong?

Most squash *(Cucurbita)* plants produce many male flowers before female flowers appear. Because only the female flowers can develop into fruits, it's common for the plant to bloom for a while without setting any squashes. You can tell the difference by closely looking at the base of the flower. Male flowers have a slender stalk, and females have a swollen base that looks like a miniature squash.

If your plants are producing female flowers, the flowers may be lacking pollination. Squash depends on honeybees and other insects for pollination. If your garden has few bees, fruit may fail to set due to lack of pollination. You could try hand pollination. Use a small brush or cotton swab to transfer pollen from the male flower to the female flower.

Not enough zucchini

I can grow other squashes and gourds with success, but I have no luck with zucchini. I get nice-looking plants and a bunch of little fruits, then they rot. I don't think it is blossom-end rot because the rot begins from the stem side. The garden is not overly wet, and I don't see any pests.

And to think that some people complain about having too much zucchini (*Cucurbita*)! I suspect that your zucchini rot might be a disease that is common among squash and other plants in the cucurbit family: gummy stem rot. Seeds and soil carry the disease; but because you say that you have no problem with other squash and gourds, I'm guessing that it's your seeds that are infected. You may also have chosen a variety that is not resistant to the disease.

Stressed plants are more likely to contract diseases. To cover all your bases, grow zucchini plants where they've not been grown before, avoid high-nitrogen fertilizers, and mulch the plants so the fruits do not sit directly on the soil's surface. Mulch also prevents dramatic fluctuations in soil moisture, which cause plant stress and blossom-end rot, another common disease of cucurbits. Excess buildup of salts in the soil can also cause blossom-end rot. To help leach the salt from the soil, water more thoroughly each time you water, but let the bed dry out a bit before you water again.

Here's hoping you have the experience of too many zucchini next season!

Bug defense for squash

My squash vines were growing beautifully, but all of a sudden they wilted and died. What would cause them to do this?

A couple of different insects may have been to blame for the collapse of your squash vines. It is disheartening to have your squash production cut short by infested vines before they produce anything edible. Here are some pest-control tips that should mean you'll be leaving excess squash on your neighbor's doorstep.

- Squash vine borer. Borers come from the eggs of adult moths. To help prevent the adult moth from laying eggs on your squash plants, grow your plants under floating row covers until after the blooms have begun to appear. Thereafter, closely inspect the base of the vines and stems for single, tiny reddish-brown eggs and wipe them off. If a borer does manage to hatch, you can tell by the appearance of a mass of frass (crumbly borer excrement) on the vine. You'll find the borer entry hole under the frass. Use a small, sharp knife to slit open the vine lengthwise at that point and remove the white larva. Mound soil up around the stem to encourage new rooting. The plant often survives if you catch the borer soon enough.

- Squash bug. Squash bugs can do a great deal of damage by sucking juices from the leaves, which then wilt, darken, and die. Watch for a cluster of shiny brown eggs on the top or undersides of leaves, groups of green or powdery gray nymphs with black legs, and ⅝-inch-long dark brown adults with a shield-shape body. Remove each of these and drown or crush them. Soap sprays and chemical controls work on nymphs but not adults. Be sure to clean up plant debris before winter. Plant varieties of squash that are resistant to squash bugs. 'Butternut' is one of the best resistant cultivars.

SUNFLOWER

Sunflower seeds
Can I save and dry sunflowers to get my own seeds?

Yes, you can. All sunflowers *(Helianthus)* have edible seeds, but for easier eating, grow a variety that has big seeds instead of the ornamental types, which have small seeds.

After the flowers have bloomed and the petals around the edge of the flower have wilted, watch for the back of the flower head to turn yellow. At that point, cut the head, leaving some stalk attached, and hang it in a warm, dry area until it is brown and dry. If you leave it on the stalk to dry outside, it may rot, or birds may eat the seeds before it's time to harvest them. When the head is dry, rub the seeds out over a bag. If you do it carefully, you can use the dry, seedless head as an interesting decoration. Then shell the seeds and roast them or eat them raw.

SWEET POTATO

Growing sweet potato
How do I grow sweet potatoes?

Sweet potato *(Ipomoea batatas)* is easy to grow if you have plenty of space in your garden. It is a tender, warm-season plant that requires a long growing season in order to produce mature large edible roots.

Grow sweet potatoes from young plants called "slips." Plant them 12–18 inches apart in rows 3–4 feet apart after the soil warms up in spring. Plant in raised beds or ridges; these soil ridges warm up earlier in spring and drain better than a level planting area. Harvest will also be easier for plants grown in ridges.

Harvest sweet potatoes just before the first fall frost. Carefully dig under the roots to lift them. To cure the roots for storage, place them in a warm (85°F), humid location for 10–14 days. Then store them at 55°F for up to 4 months.

Yam or sweet potato?

Are yams the same thing as sweet potatoes?

Technically, they are not the same thing. Yams belong to the genus *Dioscorea* and are not even in the same family as sweet potatoes *(Ipomoea)*. True yams are starchy tubers grown in tropical climates. They are not grown in the United States. However, sweet potatoes are often called yams, and the terms are commonly used interchangeably. The USDA requires that the term "yam" always be accompanied by the term "sweet potato."

TOMATO

Dying tomatoes

My tomatoes were beautiful and healthy until about midsummer. There were many tomatoes, but they were half their normal size. The leaves turned yellow, then brown, and now they are dead. I planted tomatoes in this same spot, and I had bumper crops the last two years.

Your tomatoes *(Lycopersicon)* may have been hit by early blight or septoria leaf spot, fungal diseases that are most active during humid weather. If you see disease symptoms appearing on your tomato plants, such as yellow lesions that turn brown and crispy, spray the plants with a disease-control product for vegetables. Do this once a week for 3–4 weeks. Spraying won't get rid of spots that have already begun to develop, but it will protect new growth from becoming infected.

Next year, choose a new planting spot. Avoid replanting tomatoes in the same spot year after year, because disease and fertility problems build up over time. It's important to remove and discard all spent foliage and fruit from the garden in fall to prevent diseases from overwintering in the garden. Clean tomato cages and trellises with a disinfectant such as a 10 percent chlorine bleach solution to kill lingering spores. (Rinse metal cages with water afterward to prevent corrosion.)

In addition, it helps to plant disease-resistant varieties. Look for varieties with the letters V, F, N, and/or T after them. That means the plant has shown resistance to verticillium wilt, fusarium wilt, nematodes, and tobacco mosaic diseases. There are no early-blight-resistant types, but by planting these varieties you'll narrow down the problems. Most seed catalogs and plant tags indicate whether tomato varieties are disease-resistant.

No fruits on tomato

My tomato plants are full and lush, but I don't have many blossoms or tomatoes. I planted different types, but none looks too promising. I've grown tomatoes in the past. What might be wrong?

It was a good idea to try different varieties of tomato, even if none of them has done well so far. Make certain you grow varieties adapted to your region. Check with your local cooperative extension service for suggestions.

For now, think about what problems might cause a lack of fruit set. Tomatoes will fail to set fruit under the following conditions.

- Daytime temperatures higher than 90°F and/or nighttime temperatures less than 55°F. Have you had hot daytime temperatures or cold nighttime temperatures recently?
- Too much nitrogen in the soil. Have you been fertilizing your tomatoes heavily? Is that how you got those full, lush leaves?
- Too little moisture. Has rainfall been adequate? Do you water and mulch your tomatoes to keep the soil moist?

It sounds as though your problem could be related to a combination of these factors.

Dying tomato leaves

Why does the foliage on some of my tomatoes die? Not all of the plants are like this.

Several diseases affect tomatoes, including early and late blights, septoria leaf spot, verticillium wilt, and fusarium wilt. Varieties differ in their susceptibility to these diseases. A specific diagnosis is difficult without a sample to look at, but try the following to lessen the risk of disease.

- Mulch well to prevent the spread of disease spores that live on the soil.
- Plant in a different place every year to prevent the spread of diseases that live in and on the soil.
- Provide good airflow around the tomato plants. Most foliar diseases are worse when plants remain wet for longer periods.
- Choose disease-resistant varieties. (Look for any combination of the letters V, F, N, and/or T on the plant tag.)
- Consider spraying your plants with a protective fungicide spray.
- Try growing tomatoes in fresh potting soil in a large container on a sunny deck or in a different area of your yard.

Beefsteak tomato in pots

I was thinking of growing a tomato like 'Beefsteak' rather than a smaller, patio variety. What size pot should I use?

Most tomatoes do just fine in a 14-inch pot or larger. The keys to healthy potted tomatoes are consistently moist soil and regular feedings. Consistent soil moisture helps eliminate plant stress and prevent disease. Plants in pots tend to use up all the available nutrients in the pot, and tomatoes can be heavy feeders. If you use a liquid plant food, dilute it slightly and use it at least every other time you water. As with tomatoes grown in the garden, containerized plants should have full sun (6–8 hours per day).

Tomato seedling care

How do I keep my tomato seedlings growing long enough to transplant them into the garden? I can't plant them outside for another 4 to 5 weeks, and they're getting tall and spindly. Should I cut them back to make the stalks bigger? Do I need to transplant them into bigger pots or transplant them outdoors?

For successful tomatoes, start them in conditions that mimic the perfect outdoor conditions for them to grow in. Here are their basic requirements.

Basic requirements of tomato seedlings

- Tomato seedlings grow best at temperatures between 65–72°F. Provide air circulation with a fan and illumination with grow-lights 16 hours a day. Keep the light 1–2 inches from the top of the plant. Close, bright light helps them become stocky, not spindly.

- If the plants are big enough that their root systems are filling the pots they're currently in, transplant them into larger pots. If the root systems aren't filling the pots yet, transplanting them is unnecessary.

- Use a liquid fertilizer diluted by half. (Full-strength fertilizer can be too strong for seedlings' tender root systems.) Let the soil dry out a little between waterings so that air reaches the roots. A soil that is constantly soggy will lead to disease.

- Brush your tomatoes daily. Gently brush your hand across the top of the plants. Research shows that doing so makes sturdier transplants. (Evidently the brushing simulates wind movement outdoors and creates a response in the plants to produce sturdier cells.)

- About a week before transplanting the seedlings into the ground, set them outside for a few hours at a time to gradually acclimate them to the harsher conditions outdoors. Protect them from strong wind, rain, and cold.

Transplanting tomatoes

What's the best way to transplant my tomato seedlings into the garden?

Tomatoes are sensitive to cold temperatures, so wait until all danger of frost has passed to set out your plants. (Or provide frost protection on chilly nights.) When you're ready to plant tomato seedlings into your garden, follow these steps.

1. Pinch off the bottom leaves, retaining the leaves at the top of the plant. Remove the plant from its pot, handling it by the base of the stem.
2. Dig a trench deep enough to completely cover the root ball. Sprinkle a little slow-release fertilizer or tomato food into the trench, if you like.
3. Lay the tomato on its side in the trench, gently bending up the top of the stem as you rake soil around it.
4. Firm the soil around the roots and the lower part of the stem. (Because a tomato can grow roots from its stem, bury most of it for a stronger, more stable plant.)
5. Soak with a gentle sprinkle, not a blast from a hose. Re-cover any roots exposed by watering.
6. Mulch with dried grass clippings, straw, newspapers or plastic garden film. Put a tomato cage in place, if you have one. You can add it later, but don't wait too long. Tomatoes grow quickly!

Blossom-end rot

This summer we're having tomato problems. They're rotting on the bottom, and some of the green ones are turning black. What can we do?

When a tomato turns black or brown on the bottom, it has blossom-end rot. This problem is caused by calcium deficiency in the tissue and can be brought on by any of the following conditions.

- Fluctuations in soil moisture from extremely wet to extremely dry.
- Rapid growth early in the season followed by a sudden period of dryness that slows growth.
- Excessive rains that suffocate the root hairs of the plant.
- Excess soil salts.
- Cultivation too close to the base of the plants.

The best way to prevent blossom-end rot is to plant tomatoes in well-drained soil. Mulch your plants to maintain even soil moisture, water during periods of drought, avoid cultivating near the shallow roots, and use moderate amounts of nitrogen fertilizer.

Pruning tomatoes

I had never heard of pruning tomatoes until a friend suggested that I do so. What difference will it make?

Your friend may be right—depending on where you live and the kind of tomatoes you're growing. Because determinate tomatoes produce flowers and fruit on almost every stem, you should avoid pruning off any part of the plant. Indeterminate plants are a different story, however. Because they grow and put on flowers and fruit until the end of the season, selective pinching and pruning can keep the plants in check and open up the canopy to better air circulation and sunlight. Where summers are hot, you may want to keep more leaves to shield the fruit from the strong sun. In cooler climates, pinching out some of the suckers (secondary stems that are produced out of a leaf axis on the main stem) can create better air circulation and reduce disease problems.

Black spots on tomatoes

How should I replenish my soil after planting tomatoes? The fruits have black spots that I was told were caused by a calcium deficiency. I use a small patch to grow only tomatoes.

In an average garden, it's a good idea to change the location where you plant your tomatoes each year. This helps prevent soil pests and diseases from building up in any given spot. Tomatoes like rich, well-drained soil and should be mulched to help keep soil moisture constant rather than letting the soil dry out too much between waterings. Alternate wetting and drying contributes to problems such as "catface" tomatoes (tomatoes with a distorted, gnarled bottom).

The black spots you refer to may be blossom-end rot. This physiological condition shows up as sunken black areas on the bottom (blossom end) of the fruit. The problem is indeed caused by a lack of calcium in the fruit itself. There may be plenty of calcium in the soil, but it's failing to reach the fruit during critical stages of development. To prevent this problem, keep your plant watered consistently to keep it from going from very wet to very dry. Mulch the soil around the plants to maintain consistent moisture. To prevent damage to shallow roots, avoid cultivating near the plants. Sometimes in very hot conditions, you simply can't keep blossom-end rot from happening on susceptible varieties.

If the black spots on your tomatoes are small and scattered over the surface of the fruit, it is likely a disease problem. If this is the case, you may need to move your tomatoes to a different site or spray with fungicide. If moving the tomato patch is not feasible, try building a raised bed at the site. Adding fresh compost can keep soil life active enough to reduce the likelihood of disease or pests building up. If you are strapped for space, lay a bag of compost on its side, slit it open, poke holes in the underside, and plant directly in the compost-filled bag.

Tomatoes not ripening

My tomatoes are not ripening. I have plenty of them on the plants, but they are not turning red, just staying green. The ones that have ripened have been tough and not flavorful. I water about every other day, and daily when it's very hot.

Tomatoes that are late to ripen usually are overfed and overwatered (much to the chagrin of well-intentioned gardeners). Once the vines reach the size you want, cut back on the fertilizer unless the plants show symptoms of deficiency (such as pale or stunted foliage, or misshapen fruits). Reducing water, even to the point where a little stress (slight wilting) shows before you water again, can push the plant to ripen its fruit. Watering this way also will stop more tomatoes from setting, which is desirable in areas that have short seasons, because the late ones won't have time to ripen. If your season is long, you may wish to water enough to keep more tomatoes setting on the plant, but doing so will slow the others' ripening.

Tomato types

What's the difference between "determinate" and "indeterminate" tomatoes? I think I've grown them both, but I can't recall how the types differ.

Determinate varieties of tomatoes, also called "bush" tomatoes, are bred to grow to a compact height, usually 4 feet or less. The plants stop growing when fruit sets on the terminal, or top, bud. All the crop ripens at or near the same time, usually over a 2-week period, then the plants decline.

These tomatoes may require a limited amount of caging and/or staking for support. Avoid pruning or sucker removal, because it severely reduces the crop. Determinate tomatoes perform relatively well in a container (minimum size of 5–6 gallons). Examples are 'Rutgers', 'Roma', 'Celebrity' (called semideterminate by some), and 'Marglobe'.

Indeterminate tomatoes also are sometimes called vining tomatoes. They grow and produce fruit until killed by frost and can reach heights up to 10 feet, although 6 feet is considered more average. The plants bloom, set new fruit, and ripen fruit all at the same time throughout the growing season.

These plants require substantial caging and/or staking for support. Pruning and the removal of suckers are practiced by many but are not mandatory. The need and advisability of doing so vary from region to region; experiment and see whether pruning works best for you. Because of the need for substantial support and the large size of the plants, indeterminate varieties are not usually recommended as container plants. Examples are 'Abraham Lincoln', 'Beef Master', most "cherry" types, and 'Early Girl'.

Tomatoes from seed

Over the past few years, we've tried growing several of the new varieties of tomatoes. We buy them as plants whenever possible, but some of the more unique ones I order as seed. What is the best way to get the plants started from seed?

Although some seeds grow better started directly in the garden, tomatoes do best when started indoors where you can give them additional TLC to get them off to a good, strong start. You'll need to provide the basics to get your seedlings started— namely, light, water, soil, and warmth.

- Light can come from a window that admits bright light but not direct sun. Even though light coming in a window may seem bright to us, it may not be intense enough to sustain seedling growth. If your seedlings are spindly and elongated, provide artificial light. Set a timer so the light is on for 16 hours each day.

- Water is essential for seedling growth, but overwatering can mean the end of your seedlings. Reduce this risk by irrigating the seedlings only when they need it. Touch the soil, but also be sure to poke down a half inch or so; the soil on the surface can be dry and the soil underneath moist. Here's another tip: Fill your tray with seed starting mix and feel the weight of the tray before you water. Moisten the seed starting mix and check the weight again. It will feel heavier. As your plants are growing, check the weight of the tray; when it starts to feel light, it's time to water.

- Soil is a bit of a misnomer when we talk about starting seeds. Although you can plant seeds in soil, it's best to use a sterile seed starting mix. That eliminates the risk of unwanted soil organisms growing in the environment you've created for your seedlings. You can find bags of this mix at your local nursery.

- Seedlings also need a warm growing environment for getting started. A location that's 65–80°F day and night will be just right for your tomatoes, as well as any warm-season crops you want to grow (cool-season crops like it cooler to start). Once the seeds sprout, they grow better in a slightly cooler environment, so turn the thermostat down 5 to 10 degrees.

Staking tomatoes

Some of my tomatoes need staking, while others seem to stand up on their own. What's the best way to treat tomatoes regarding support?

What you are noticing is the difference between your determinate and indeterminate plants. Check the plant tags or your seed packets, and you'll probably discover that your determinate varieties are the ones that don't need staking. Determinate tomatoes can usually stand on their own without additional support. The plants are small enough to stay upright when they start producing fruit. That said, keep an eye on your determinate plants; you may have to give the prolific producers some support. Something as simple as tying the plant to a wooden stake or poles can do the job.

Indeterminate tomatoes have a tendency to become lanky and rangy, especially the cherry types, so plan on providing support. Buy ready-made cages, or fashion your own from 6-foot lengths of 6-inch-mesh concrete-reinforcing wire. Stake the cages to keep them upright on gusty days.

Tomato leaf roll

The leaves on my tomato plant are curled and rolled up. I don't see any bugs or leaf spots. What's causing this?

Some varieties of tomato develop physiological leaf roll. 'Beefsteak', 'Big Boy', and 'Floramerica' are three susceptible varieties. The margins of leaves roll inward toward the central vein, and leaflets become leathery. Fluctuating soil moisture, excessive heat or pruning are the usual causes. The problem is mostly cosmetic. Tomato yields are unaffected. If you'd like to avoid the problem, grow a variety that is less susceptible to leaf roll. Maintain consistent soil moisture by mulching and watering as necessary. Avoid heavy pruning of your tomatoes.

Cracking tomatoes

My tomatoes are cracking and splitting open. What am I doing wrong?

Tomatoes are affected by two types of cracking. Radial cracks run from the stem end toward the blossom end; concentric cracks form circular patterns around the stem. Cracking is usually caused by changes in the growth rate of the fruit. Rapidly growing tomatoes are more susceptible. Wide fluctuations in temperature and rain promote cracking too. Maintain uniform soil moisture to help prevent cracking. (Tomatoes often split radially when watered by irrigation or rainfall after a prolonged dry spell.) Avoid excess nitrogen fertilizer, which promotes rapid growth. Some varieties are more crack-resistant than others. Try some different cultivars if you continue to experience cracking fruits.

Worms defoliating tomato

My tomato plants have huge green worms that are completely stripping the plants. What are they?

It sounds as though your plants have been attacked by tomato hornworms. They are large (up to 4 inches long) green caterpillars with white stripes on each side of the body. They get the hornworm name from the black "horn" at the rear of their body. Tomato hornworms may also feed on tomato relatives such as eggplant, pepper, and potato.

Just a few tomato hornworms can strip a plant in a short time. The worms often escape detection until much of the foliage is gone, because they blend in so well with the green leaves. If you see hornworms on a plant, simply pick them off by hand (use gloves if you're squeamish), and crush them underfoot. If the hornworm has small white cocoons attached to its body, leave the hornworm alone. The cocoons contain the larvae of a parasitic wasp that is a natural parasite of the hornworm. By the time the cocoons are present, the hornworm is no longer able to feed, so it won't cause any more damage to your tomato. The wasps that emerge from the cocoons will parasitize other hornworms and help protect your tomato plants.

Tomato cold start

I planted my tomatoes in mid-May, but they may have been slightly hurt by some cold weather. The leaves are a little yellow, and I'm wondering if there is anything I can do to save the plants, or will I have to start over?

If the tips of the plants' leaves are still green, they will probably recover when the temperatures climb again. If the leaves are completely yellow, you should pull the plants and start over.

To prevent this from happening again, wait to plant until the nights stay above 50°F, or provide some protection for your young plants. In particular, they may need some cover on chilly spring nights. You can use a milk jug with the bottom cut away as a temporary greenhouse for a week or two, until the plant is too big for the jug and the nights are warmer. You can leave the cap on the milk jug, but be sure to uncap the jug during the day when temperatures are above 50°F.

Other devices have been developed in the last few years, such as water-filled tubes to place around the plants to insulate them against cold air. Examples of these products are Wall O' Water and Kozy-Coat.

Green tomatoes

How do I ripen green tomatoes indoors? I have lots of them I picked just before frost.

You'll have the best luck with "mature green" tomatoes. These are the ones with a whitish coloration on the blossom end of the tomato. Tomatoes should be free of blemishes. Best ripening occurs when temperatures are kept at 70–75°F. To speed ripening, you can place ripe bananas or apples with the tomatoes. These fruits give off ethylene gas, which promotes ripening.

If you have lots of tomatoes, store them in a ventilated box one layer deep. To prolong storage, keep them in a cool, dark, humid room. Protect from direct sun.

Distorted tomatoes

My tomatoes are all gnarled and distorted. What would make the fruits misshapen?

Tomato fruits distorted at the blossom end are called catface tomatoes. This scarring is a physiological problem related to initial fruit development during bloom. Cool weather during fruit set or injury from 2,4-D herbicide drift can cause catfacing. Fruits that set in warmer temperatures are usually unaffected. If 2,4-D drift was involved, you will likely also see distorted foliage on the plants. In either case, by the time you see the problem, the conditions are probably in the past. Wait for the plant to outgrow the problem.

Walnut wilt

My tomatoes suddenly wilted and died this summer. My neighbor said it was because of my walnut tree in the backyard. Will walnuts kill tomato plants?

Many plants can be affected by a toxin produced by walnut trees. Tomatoes are particularly sensitive to the substance known as juglone. Because tree roots can extend 3–4 times the distance of the spread of branches, plants 50–60 feet from the tree's trunk may be affected. Tomato plants that come into contact with walnut roots can wilt about the time the fruit is setting. Juglone eventually kills the plant. To prevent this problem from happening again, plant tomatoes beyond the tree's root zone or grow them in large tubs.

Too-tall tomatoes

Please help! My tomatoes are growing very tall but have few flower buds, and I don't know what to do about it. Is there something I can do to keep them from getting so tall and to help them get more buds?

The varieties you planted might be the problem. There are two categories of tomatoes—determinate and indeterminate. Determinate tomatoes begin to set earlier than indeterminate, and stop growing when they reach a certain size. They're preferred by many gardeners.

Indeterminate varieties continue to grow and set tomatoes as long as weather permits, and they may grow for a longer time before they begin to set. Once started, they can produce prodigious amounts of tomatoes, though. The classic example is the old type of cherry tomato, which can cover the side of a house if it is given enough space, support, and time.

Overly vigorous tomatoes can also be the result of too much water or fertilizer. Instead of using a high-nitrogen fertilizer, try something light, such as fish emulsion. Also, cut back on watering when ripening starts, to encourage the vines to ripen the crop faster and to slow vine growth.

Strange pollination partners

I live in a townhouse where I can plant only in containers. This year I planted tomatoes in the same containers with zinnias, and both are growing beautifully. However, a friend is concerned that they will cross-pollinate and the tomatoes may not be safe to eat. Is that possible?

Your friend is mistaken. Most tomatoes are self-pollinating, meaning that the pollen from another plant isn't even likely to reach the flowers. Even if stray pollen were to make it to a flower, it would have no more effect than dust falling on the plant. Plants must be closely related for pollen from one to have any effect on the other; even then, the results wouldn't affect the fruit, only the next generation's seedlings.

Edible flowers as well as herbs are natural partners for tomatoes. Even sun-loving ornamental flowers, though, will add interest and color.

Gardening in Containers

Houseplants

HOUSEPLANTS IN GENERAL

Fertilizing houseplants

Should I fertilize my houseplants year round? What kind of fertilizer is best to use?

Take your cue from the growth cycles of your houseplants to determine when and how much to fertilize them. They require more nutrients while they are actively growing. This means that most need more fertilizer in spring and summer than they do during fall or winter. As light intensifies in late winter or early spring, increase the amount and frequency of fertilizer for your plants. They need very little fertilizer during the short, dark days of winter unless you also supplement the amount of light they receive to promote growth. Likewise, a plant placed in a dark corner of your living room will grow more slowly than the same type of plant growing near a sunny window.

As a general rule, apply fertilizer at half the recommended rate or frequency listed on the label. (Fertilizer manufacturers are in the business of selling more fertilizer.) These lower rates of fertilizer usually provide adequate nutrition for your plants while diminishing the chance of fertilizer burn from excess fertilizer salts. Foliage houseplants prefer a complete fertilizer (one containing nitrogen, phosphorus, and potassium) with slightly more nitrogen than phosphorus or potassium. The fertilizer labe has three numbers on it. The first of these denotes the percentage of nitrogen, the second is potassium, and the third is phosphorus. Blooming houseplants do best with less nitrogen. Look for a fertilizer that has a nitrogen content no higher than that of either phosphorus or potassium.

Houseplants leaning toward light

My houseplants all lean toward the window. Does this mean that they're not getting enough light?

It means that one side of the plants are not receiving enough light. The shaded side of a plant stem grows faster than the sunny side because sunlight breaks down plant growth hormones, called auxins. Auxin promotes cell (and stem) elongation. You may have observed this phenomenon on your plants outdoors as well. Plants growing in shade often are oriented to the sunny side of the border.

To avoid one-sided growth on your houseplants, give them a quarter turn every week or so. That way the sunlight will uniformly reach all sides of the plant over the course of a month, and plants will grow upright.

General houseplant care

Most of my houseplants just survive without looking healthy at all. Is there any magic to growing great indoor plants?

With indoor plants, success depends on matching conditions with the type of plant you're growing. English ivy *(Hedera helix)*, for example, needs a cool, moist, partially shaded location such as a north-facing window. Croton *(Codiaeum variegatum pictum)*, on the other hand, loves warmth and bright light—a southern exposure with hot temperatures helps it thrive. Ensure success by finding out what light, moisture, and temperature conditions they require. Although all houseplants differ in some respects, here are some common practices that boost performance.

Cultivating great plants indoors

- Raise the humidity. One of the biggest problems houseplants face is dry air. In the depths of winter, the air in most homes is drier than a desert. Increase humidity around your plants by purchasing a humidifier. In addition, you can group them together, and place them on humidity trays, to encircle them with moist air.

- Add nutrition. Most indoor plants benefit from a monthly dose of liquid fertilizer in spring and summer; most tropical plants grow slowly in winter, so avoid fertilizing then. Cool-season plants, such as cyclamen *(Cyclamen* persicum), pocketbook flower *(Calceolaria* hybrids), and Rieger begonia *(Begonia ×hiemalis)*, benefit from bloom-booster fertilizer during the winter, which is their flowering season.

- Turn on the light. The ideal exposure for many houseplants year-round is an eastern window. Many plants will also thrive in southern, western, or northern windows. Too little light or too much light will produce unattractive plants. Site plants in your home according to their needs.

- Wait on the water. Too much or too little water kills more houseplants than anything else. Water plants only when the soil is dry to the touch—not just on the surface but about ½–1 inch deep. Avoid letting plants sit in water for more than a few minutes.

- Set the thermostat. Learn what temperatures your plants need and place them accordingly. Avoid placing indoor plants where heat registers blow directly on the foliage. All plants benefit from protection from blasts of hot or cold air.

- Pick up after them. On most plants, pinching out growing tips increases bushiness. Trim vining plants to keep them in bounds. Remove dead or dying leaves and blooms. Cleanliness helps prevent disease and insect infestations.

Plant lights for office

I spend a lot of time in our basement where my home office is. Unfortunately, the only natural light is from one tiny window. Can I grow plants under lights in my office?

Adding plants to your office is a good idea, and it will require minimal supplies. Supplemental lights such as full-spectrum fluorescent tubes, metal halide bulbs, and high-pressure sodium bulbs make gardening possible where there is little or no natural light. Position the lights 6–8 inches above the tops of the plants, and raise the lights as the plants grow. Use a timer to keep the lights on a schedule. With the added greenery, you'll have better air quality and prettier surroundings, so you'll no doubt be much more productive!

Plants for north window

My houseplants grow wonderfully in my south window, but every time I move one to a north window, the plant rebels. Do you have any suggestions for plants that will thrive in this window?

In the filtered light of your north window, try growing low-light tolerant plants. Chinese evergreen *(Aglaonema)*, pothos *(Epipremnum)*, heartleaf philodendron *(Philodendron)*, and snake plant *(Sansevieria)* are all good easy-care choices. Some ferns also would be good for this site. Boston fern *(Nephrolepis exaltata* 'Bostoniensis') is at home in a hanging basket or on a pedestal. Maidenhair fern *(Adiantum pedatum)* appreciates high humidity and moist soil. Fertilize every 4 weeks except in winter.

Terms of light

How can I know whether I have the correct light level for growing specific houseplants? I brought home several from the garden center, and now I'm trying to figure out where to put them.

It's good to ask this question now rather than later so you can get your plants off to a good start. You can judge the kind of light your plants will receive by holding a 12-inch-square piece of white paper where the upper part of the plant will face the light source. With your other hand held 12 inches away, cast a shadow onto the paper. If you see only the slightest shadow with indistinct edges, the light is low. If the shadow is noticeable but not distinct, the light is medium. When the light is high, the shadow will have distinct edges. Consult a good houseplant book such as *Ortho's Complete Guide to Houseplants* to learn what specific light conditions are needed by the plants you purchased.

Pinching plants
What is pinching back? How do you do it for better growth on houseplants?

Pinching back is the process of removing spindly growth to encourage branching lower down on the plant. It's appropriate only for some houseplants. Houseplants with a single growing point, such as palms, or those that grow from a crown, such as African violets, can't be pinched. But long, vining species such as Swedish ivy, philodendron, English ivy, and wandering Jew do better when they are pinched back. All you need to do is pinch off or clip off the overly long foliage just above a leaf. In a few weeks, new growth will sprout from the buds in the leaf axils just below where you made the pinch or cut.

Many gardeners are too timid with the amount of foliage they remove. If you pinch the tips of the stems, new growth will develop at the tips. If you want new growth to develop at the base of the plant, cut it back severely.

Terrarium plants
I have a small glass terrarium (5×12 inches) and want to fill it with plants. What will thrive in my terrarium? I already purchased two small African violets.

You didn't mention whether your terrarium is open on top (to permit air circulation) or if it is closed. If it's closed, African violets won't do well, because they like good air circulation and they dislike having water dripping onto their hairy leaves.

Many foliage plants thrive in both open and closed terrarium environments. Suitable choices include aluminum plant *(Pilea cadieri)*, artillery plant *(Pilea microphylla)*, and creeping fig *(Ficus pumila)*. Ferns, such as bird's-nest fern *(Asplenium nidus)* or table fern *(Pteris cretica)*, also grow well in a terrarium. Nerve plant *(Fittonia)* adds colorful leaves to your planting blend. All of these plants are easy to find at garden centers. Consider using miniature versions, which won't outgrow their contained environs as quickly as their full-size cousins will.

Most terrarium plants die as a result of overwatering. If you keep your container closed, you shouldn't need to add water after the initial planting. For an open terrarium, add water only when the soil is dry to the touch half an inch below the surface.

Easy-care plants

My son is going away to college, and I thought a few plants might liven up his dreary dorm room. There's one window at the far end of the long concrete space. Do you have any recommendations?

If your son agrees to having a plant or two, there are several that are forgiving, especially around finals week.

Peace lily (*Spathiphyllum*), snake plant (*Sansevieria trifasciata*), golden pothos (*Epipremnum aureum*), and Swiss cheese plant (*Monstera deliciosa*) all grow in medium-light conditions and tolerate neglect. Allow the soil to dry to the touch between waterings. Fertilize with a water-soluble fertilizer in spring and summer (follow the directions on the package), or pot the plant using a soil that contains a slow-release fertilizer.

Browning leaf edges

My houseplant leaves are turning brown on the tips. I don't know what to do. Is there an easy fix to this problem?

The condition you describe is known as tip burn and generally develops because the humidity isn't high enough around your plants. Most indoor plants hail from sultry, tropical locales, where humidity fluctuates between 60 and 90 percent. In the average centrally heated home in winter, humidity often falls below 15 percent.

The most reliable way to battle excessively dry air in your home is by using a humidifier. Group plants together to increase the humidity near the cluster. Other techniques include misting plants daily or placing them on a bed of pebbles in a shallow tray. Add water until it's just below the surface of the pebbles. Keep plants from sitting in the water; they should rest above it, boosted by the pebbles. As water evaporates from the tray, humidity will increase around the plants. You can purchase special humidity trays, or you can use small-cell ice cube trays filled with water to get the same effect.

Fish in terrarium

I want to make a water terrarium, where you grow a plant in a container of water that also doubles as a home for a beta fish. What houseplants will grow in water?

Many plants will thrive in water, including dwarf peace lily (*Spathiphyllum*), Chinese evergreen (*Aglaonema*), and pothos (*Epipremnum*). All grow roots apart from any contact with soil in typical indoor light conditions.

Remember that you need to feed your beta fish brine shrimp, water fleas, bloodworms, or other similar creatures in order for it to survive. Contrary to urban legend, beta fish is a carnivore and will not feed on plant roots. If you observe your fish nibbling at the plant roots, it's most likely that it is eating bacteria on the roots and not the roots themselves.

White film on pots

My clay pots have a white crust on them. How do I get rid of it?

The white crust you see on the pots is an accumulation of salts. The salts may have come from fertilizers used to feed the plants, or they may be minerals such as calcium and magnesium that are naturally dissolved in your water source.

Pull the plant out of the pot while you clean the clay. An easy way to do this is to hold the pot upside down and tap the rim on the edge of a bench or table. This usually loosens the root ball so the plant will slide out intact.

Use a wire brush to scrub the pots in a dilute bleach solution (1 part bleach to 9 parts water). Then rinse thoroughly with plain water to get rid of the bleach. If the root ball of the plant held together, you can slide it right back into the pot. Or if it's time to repot, place the plant in the next size larger container.

Coffee grounds on houseplants

Since I know I can compost coffee grounds, would it be OK to put the grounds on houseplants? Also, I like to conserve water. Can I use water from cooking sweet corn or other vegetables on my houseplants?

Coffee grounds are fine additions to compost, and you can toss the entire batch—including the filter—onto the compost pile without any concerns. But indoors, be careful using coffee grounds. As the grounds decompose, they'll harbor fungi, which can attack and even kill your plants. A thick layer of grounds may also keep soil excessively moist, which can harm your plants' roots. If you use grounds indoors, do so only sparingly, and avoid watering the plants unless the soil is dry to the touch. Coffee grounds acidify soil slightly, so although that may benefit gardenias and azaleas, which prefer acidic soils, it won't help an African violet.

Cooled vegetable cooking water is fine to add to houseplants. Do so in moderation. Reuse only unsalted cooking water; salty water could burn your plants.

Mold on soil

My potted palm is getting mold on top of the soil. Should I do something to get rid of it?

Is the "mold" soft and fuzzy or hard and crusty? If it's a soft, fuzzy growth, it is likely a true mold or fungus. It's a sign that the soil is remaining too wet. Try watering less frequently and improving air circulation near the plant. The mold may not directly attack the plant, but if the soil is wet enough to promote the growth of mold, it may also be wet enough to cause root rot to develop on your plant.

If the "mold" is hard and crusty, it means you are watering too little at a time. The crusty material is likely a buildup of salts on the soil surface. Scrape off the crust, and change the way you water. Water only when the soil's surface is dry, and then water enough that it flows through the drainage holes in the pot. Dump out the excess water that collects in the saucer under the pot when the pot has finished draining. Avoid watering again until the soil feels dry. If the mineral content of your water is high, consider using collected rainwater or distilled water to help prevent mineral buildup.

Plants on vacation

We're going on vacation for a couple of weeks. Is there some way to keep my houseplants from drying out completely while we're gone?

When you go on vacation for longer than a week, your plants will need a little attention while you are gone. You can hire someone to care for your plants, or you can employ these techniques.

- Group plants to conserve humidity and moisture. Line a tray with pebbles and fill it with water to just below the top of the pebbles. Set the plants on the tray. This method also works on a day-to-day basis for plants that prefer high humidity.
- Use this method in your bathroom: Set all your houseplants in the bathtub and turn on the shower to drench them. Drape a clear sheet of plastic over the plants, but keep it from directly touching them. They'll be fine like this for up to 2 weeks. If there's no natural light, set up a fluorescent light on a timer to turn on 12 hours per day.
- Set individual plants in large, clear plastic bags, making a mini greenhouse for each. Cut a few slits in the bags, and tuck the tops of the bags under the pots.
- If it's winter, set the thermostat at 60–65°F when you leave. Your plants will fare better in a cooler atmosphere.
- If you ask a neighbor or friend to water your plants, leave a list explaining which days to water and including any special instructions for specific plants.

Living air cleaners

I've read that houseplants can play a significant role in improving air quality. If this is true, what plants should I grow?

Yes, houseplants can play a role in improving the air quality in your home. Anytime you bring new carpeting or other furnishings into your home, you also bring in the chemicals used in their manufacture. These volatile organic compounds (VOCs) contribute to air pollution inside our homes. Even when you can't smell them anymore, VOCs pollute the air enough to irritate your respiratory tract and cause headaches, sinus congestion, and fatigue. Research from NASA shows that greenery soaks up VOCs, breaks them down, and uses them for food—all this from a simple houseplant!

Two or three plants in 8- or 10-inch pots for every 100 square feet helps clean up the air in your breathing zone. Double that, and your indoor environment becomes healthier in less time. Here are some of nature's air filters.

Nature's air filters

- Areca palm *(Chrysalidocarpus lutescens)*
- Bamboo palm *(Chamaedorea erumpens)*
- Corn plant *(Dracaena fragrans* 'Massangeana')
- English ivy *(Hedera helix)*
- Florist's mum *(Chrysanthemum grandiflorum)*
- Gerbera daisy *(Gerbera jamesonii)*
- Janet Craig dracaena *(Dracaena deremensis* 'Janet Craig')
- Kimberly Queen Australian sword fern *(Nephrolepis obliterata* 'Kimberly Queen')
- Lady palm *(Rhapis excelsa)*
- Miniature date palm *(Phoenix roebelenii)*
- Rubber plant *(Ficus elastica)*
- Spider plant *(Chlorophytum comosum)*
- Warneckii dracaena *(Dracaena deremensis* 'Warneckii')
- Weeping fig *(Ficus benjamina)*

Houseplant watering

All of my indoor plants dry out pretty badly. I water them at least once a week, but they still dry out. What should I do?

The crux of your problem is likely your soil. Most commercially raised tropical houseplants arrive in a lightweight soil mix that fails to hold water very long. It works well at the greenhouse but tends to dry out in a home environment and can be difficult to rewet thoroughly. It's best to repot newly purchased plants in a commercial soil developed for houseplants. Loosen the soil around the roots, and refill your existing pots with fresh soil, and see how things progress.

You might also try increasing humidity around your houseplants. Higher humidity decreases water needs. When you water your plants, water from the top, covering the entire surface of the soil with water. Some water will run through and gather in the saucers. Avoid letting plants sit in water overnight once you start using the new soil mix. You'll be tempted to do so, but resist! Plants that sit in water for hours at a time are more prone to develop root-rot diseases.

Fluoride sensitivity

I've heard that the fluoride they put in water to prevent tooth decay is bad for plants. Should I not be watering my plants with tap water?

Some plants are indeed sensitive to the fluoride used in some municipal water systems. Variegated forms of spider plant (*Chlorophytum comosum*) are especially sensitive to fluoride. The damage shows up as marginal leaf or tip browning. Other sensitive houseplants include Easter lily (*Lilium longiflorum*), dracaena (*Dracaena*), peace lily (*Spathiphyllum*), cast iron plant (*Aspidistra elatior*), parlor palm (*Chamaedorea elegans*), and prayer plant (*Maranta leuconeura*).

Perlite (the spongy white material included in many potting mixes) and some fertilizers may also release enough fluoride to harm sensitive plants. Flush the soil occasionally with rainwater or bottled water to reduce fluoride buildup and prevent injury to these plants.

Moving houseplants indoors

My houseplants have been outside on the deck all summer. Do I need to do anything special to them when I bring them inside for winter?

Most houseplants are tropical in origin, so bring them indoors long before frost arrives. They can suffer injury at temperatures in the 40s. In addition, it's quite a shock to them to be moved from chilly outdoor nights to a toasty warm room indoors. They'll suffer less stress if you make their move more gradual. If they've been in full sun, move them to a shady spot for a week or so before taking them to the lower light levels inside your home.

Some of the leaves on your plants may turn yellow and fall off soon after the transition. This is normal. They're simply adjusting to the lower light levels indoors. As a precaution, give them a shower to wash off pests and dust accumulated outdoors. Then inspect the plants for insects before bringing them inside. Control any pests with insecticidal soap, horticultural oil, or other appropriate pesticide. For a couple weeks keep the vacationing plants isolated from those that were left indoors all summer, until you're certain they have no other unwanted hitchhikers.

Poisonous houseplants

Our household has changed a lot in the past year. Our twins are now crawling and exploring, and we have a puppy that's into everything. I figure our new arrivals will discover the houseplants any day. Are there any plants we should keep away from them?

Most houseplants are harmless to kids and pets, but there are a few that can give a bad stomachache if eaten or a nasty rash if the sap gets on skin. The Quick Tip, above, lists some plants you should keep out of the reach of kids and pets.

Rooting in soil or water?

I want to start some houseplant cuttings. Is it better to start them in soil or water? Does rooting powder really work?

The type of roots that develop in water are different from those that develop in soil or potting mix. If you plan to grow your plants continuously in water, by all means start the cuttings in water. However, if you intend to pot them up in potting soil, use a lightweight soilless mix for starting your cuttings. Some easy-to-root plants such as spider plant *(Chlorophytum comosum)*, Swedish ivy *(Plectranthus australis)*, and coleus *(Solenostemon scutellariodes)* form roots so readily that you are unlikely to notice any difference using rooting hormone on your cuttings. But most cuttings will produce more roots of higher quality if you dip the basal end of the cutting in rooting hormone. All that is needed is a light dusting. Shake off any excess powder before inserting the cutting into a pencil hole in the rooting medium.

AFRICAN VIOLET

Growing great violets

I know that African violets are supposed to be easy to grow, but I don't have much luck with them. What's the trick to growing beautiful plants?

African violets *(Saintpaulia)* beguile novice and experienced gardeners alike with their tidy foliage topped by perky sprays of nonstop blooms. Include a violet in your houseplant collection; our basics will help you cultivate a flowering virtuoso.

- Leaves. Healthy African violet leaves have a shiny tint beneath their hairy exterior and boast a flat crown of foliage. Limp or drooping leaves indicate overwatering or bone-dry soil. Upright leaves are reaching for light. Increase light levels by moving your plants closer to a window or by adding artificial light. Hard, curled leaves in the center of the crown signify cyclamen mite infestation. If you grow other African violets, forget trying to treat it; just toss the plant. It's not worth the possibility of infecting your other plants.

- Temperature. African violets' origins reach back to East Africa. They like sultry warm days (75°F or higher) and high humidity, paired with nights in the upper 60s. In climates with harsh winters, plants located near windows may show signs of cold damage (brown spots on foliage) or may stop blooming abruptly.

- Light. Bright, indirect light suits African violets best. A northern or eastern exposure brings the best results. If your light source is a western or southern exposure, hang sheer curtains to filter the strong sunlight in spring and summer.

- Food. Fertilize monthly with a liquid fertilizer at half strength applied directly to the soil (avoid bottom feeding), or use a specialized African violet fertilizer.

- Water. African violet aficionados prove as passionate about the topic of watering as they are about the plants themselves. Use room-temperature water to avoid cold-water splashes on leaves, which create splotches. Water plants from the top or bottom, whichever works best for you. Many violet growers prefer using a wick (short nylon cord) inserted through the drainage hole and dangling into a water source. Keep the soil consistently moist.

- Flowers. Newer African violets should bloom year-round. Typically they have a heavy flush of flowers several times a year; in between, plants bear fewer flowers but still bloom. Flower buds will fail to form when temperatures fall below the mid-60s or when light levels are too low or excessively high.

Watering woes

On the whole, I find growing African violets a challenge, but I love the flowers. Lately the leaves on my violets are turning brown. I water the plants twice a week, always from the bottom. Could I be watering too much?

If your violets' leaves are turning brown and mushy, it's likely that you're overwatering the plant. Typically, watering a violet once a week is plenty. To test, push your index finger just beneath the soil surface. If the soil is dry at that depth, water the plant. Over time, as you sample the soil, you'll learn other clues that signal when to water: soil color, the weight of the pot (dry soil weighs less), and leaf color or firmness (dry leaves wilt).

White violet leaves

I grow African violets under lights. The leaves on some varieties are turning almost white. The leaves are normal size; the flowers are also healthy, but the leaves go from bright green to almost white. What should I do?

There are a few factors that could be coming into play. The plants may be getting too much light, so you might want to first try moving the plants to the sides of your light table where the light is not as intense as in the center. If the light fixtures are adjustable, you can also try moving the lights farther away from the plants.

Yellow or white foliage can also be caused by overly compacted soil or by room temperatures that are too high. If it's the former, repot the plant in the same size pot, removing as much of the old soil as possible without damaging the root ball. Replace it with fresh soil. If you have a tiered light setup or a light cart, moving the plants to the bottom level often helps, because temperatures are cooler here.

The other possible problem is that the plant may be getting insufficient nitrogen. In this case, try a fertilizer rich in nitrogen (that's the first number listed in the three-digit analysis label on fertilizers). Usually, a well-balanced fertilizer for African violets is sufficient. Avoid purchasing fertilizers that contain urea, which hinders the violet's ability to absorb nutrients and water.

You may also know that cold water on African violet foliage can discolor it. Usually the affected area turns beige and corky rather than white. Water the plant from the base or use room-temperature water.

I have had an African violet for many years, and each year it produces its beautiful flowers. The plant has failed to flower this year and has produced only tiny green leaves. What could be wrong?

If, on the whole, your plant looks healthy but has simply stopped blooming, it may be getting less light than it once did. Remember, the light entering windows can change as trees grow or as structures are added to your landscape. Try moving the plant to a brighter location. Low temperatures also inhibit flowering in African violets.

If none of these situations seems to apply, repot the violet in fresh soil, using a slightly larger pot. It could also be that the plant has outgrown its container. You'll know that this is the case if the top of the plant extends far beyond the rim of the pot, or the pot has a tendency to tip over. Remember, too, that plants need food to flower. Give your plant some liquid fertilizer developed for African violets.

If the new leaves are curled or disfigured in any way, the plant may have cyclamen mites. Take a few sample leaves to a local garden center and ask for treatment suggestions.

ALOE

Making more aloes

I have an aloe. What should I do with the pieces of leaves that fall off the main plant? Can I replant them?

Shoots that break off the base of aloe plants provide a means to start new plants. Make certain that each shoot has a growing tip and a main stem; an individual leaf won't root. Make a fresh cut at the base of the stem, and insert the cut end into a mixture of equal parts sand and commercial potting soil. Keep the soil mix moist, but avoid overwatering or you'll rot the cuttings. Hasten the rooting by dipping the cut ends of the leaves into rooting hormone (available in liquid or powder form) before inserting them into the soil mixture.

Using aloe sap

How do I extract and store the aloe from my aloe plant for use in treating burns?

It's best to harvest leaves fresh for use on burns. Simply slice off a full, plump leaf and squeeze the sap out of the leaf onto the burn. I've not experimented with trying to store the aloe sap, but I suspect that it would need to be refrigerated or molds and bacteria would start growing in it. As long as you have a healthy, growing plant, though, you can get a fresh supply as you need it.

Drainage problem

I think I have killed my *Aloe vera* plant! It was doing fine, then I repotted it into a larger pot. I put a layer of rocks at the bottom because the pot didn't have a drainage hole. Now the plant looks soggy or soft in places. Have I killed it?

When an aloe plant is being overwatered, the leaves develop what are called water-soaked spots. They look like what you describe: soggy and soft. It is almost as though the entire leaf becomes saturated and gel-like, then it turns to mush. Eventually the entire plant dies. I think that your plant is experiencing a waterlogged condition because the pot you put it in lacks a drainage hole. Avoid planting in a pot without a drainage hole. The layer of pebbles in the bottom of a pot compounds the problem. As moisture moves down through the soil, it forms what is called a perched water table over the pebbles. Not until the soil above is saturated will the water move down into the pebbles. That means your aloe's roots are constantly saturated. The soil is waterlogged, and the plant's roots are dying from lack of oxygen.

You might be able to save your plant if you dig it up and let it dry out for a day or two. Remove any leaves or tissue that appear to be dead. Then dust the dry base of the plant with rooting powder and replant it in a pot with a drainage hole. Give aloe bright light, and keep it on the dry side.

If you want to use a beautiful pot that has no drainage hole, drill a hole for drainage, or use it as a cachepot. Tuck your plant into a plain plastic pot that can fit inside the eye-catching container. Elevate the inner pot on ½ inch of pea gravel.

AMARYLLIS

Growing amaryllis

How do I take care of an amaryllis? A friend gave me one for the holidays.

Amaryllis *(Hippeastrum)* likes to be pot-bound, so make certain that the pot you grow it in is no more than an inch or two larger than the diameter of the bulb. The potting soil should be well-drained, and the container should have a drainage hole. Position the bulb so its top two-thirds is above the soil level. Water only when the soil feels dry to the touch. If the soil is too wet, the bulb will rot.

Amaryllis prefer cool (60–65°F) temperatures for growth, and need a sunny location to prevent the flower stalks and foliage from stretching. Five to six weeks after planting, a flower stalk should emerge from the bulb; large bulbs may produce 2 or 3 flower stalks. Rotate the container to prevent the flower stalk from leaning toward the light.

While the plant is actively growing, give it a dose of dilute houseplant fertilizer. After the flowers fade, cut them off to prevent seeds from forming. Remove the stalk once it turns yellow Avoid removing any leaves. They're needed to produce food for rebloom the following season. Keep the plant in a sunny location and water as needed. After all danger of frost has passed, you can move the bulb outdoors for the summer. Keep it actively growing through the summer by watering and fertilizing regularly. In fall, bring the bulb back indoors before frost hits. Stop watering the plant, and let the foliage die down naturally. Keep the bulb, pot and all, in a cool, dry, dark location for several months. After this resting period, bring it back to a warm location and start watering to initiate new growth and another bloom cycle.

AZALEA

Azalea care

I love azalea plants, but for some reason I usually end up killing them. I'm not sure what I'm doing wrong. Should I plant it outside?

Azaleas *(Rhododendron)* are difficult to keep alive indoors because they are most commonly potted in a peaty soil mix that dries out in the home. The peaty mix is good for keeping down the pH; azaleas need acidic soil. However, once peat dries out, it's difficult to rewet. Keep the soil evenly moist. If the plant dries out, plunge the entire pot into a tub of water to soak the peat again. (Dry peat floats. You may have to weight down the pot with a heavy waterproof object to prevent the rootbal from popping to the surface of the water). Keep the humidity high around your azalea. Dry air will cause it to dry out faster. Fertilize with an acid fertilizer. Look for plant food formulated for azaleas, camellias, and evergreens. Provide bright indirect light indoors.

You can also plant your azalea outdoors if all frost danger has passed in your area. Most florist azaleas are hardy only to about Zone 7, so it may not overwinter outdoors in colder regions. In these colder regions, you may have limited success getting the azalea to bloom again if you leave it outdoors late into the fall. It shouldn't be allowed to freeze, but it needs several weeks of 40°F weather to induce flowers. Bring the plant back indoors over winter. Grow it in a cool, bright location with ample humidity.

BROMELIAD

Bromeliad care

I received a gift plant that the gift giver said was a bromeliad. It is beautiful, but I can't find any information on it. Can you help me?

Bromeliads make wonderful low-maintenance houseplants. Many are tropical plants that, in nature, grow on the branches of large trees; therefore, they don't require soil. Yours is probably planted in soil or bark mix. Bromeliads are much like orchids in their growth habit. If you have the type with a "cup" on top where the leaves come together, water into the cup and let it overlfow onto the soil. Bromeliads get their nutrients from water caught in their cup. If the leaves do not form a cup, you'll need to water around the base of the plant every week or so. The plants like bright, indirect light, not direct sunlight.

Dividing bromeliad

Can you split a bromeliad? I have one that has matured, and the top edges are starting to turn brown. I see three new sprouts coming from within the bottom of the leaves.

Did the central mother plant flower? It's normal for the flowering plant to die down after bloom, and for side shoots to take over. These offsets, or "pups", can be separated from the mother plant to start new plants. Slice through the main stem to remove pups. Dip the cut end in rooting hormone. Pot the offset in a lightweight soilless mix and keep it moist but not soggy. In a few weeks, new roots should form.

CACTUS

Rotting cactus

My dish of cactus was doing fine until I bumped it and one of the plants fell over. It appears to have just rotted off at the base. I don't see any insects. What can I do to preserve the rest of the plants?

The Garden Doctor will venture a guess that overwatering was the culprit. Cacti and succulents are hardy plants except when they're exposed to too much water; root rot can quickly do in even the healthiest plants.

Check the rest of your plants, and if you find any that are showing signs of rot, cut it off, allow it to dry, and reroot in fresh cactus mix. Replace the soil, perhaps with a soil mix made especially for cacti and succulents. These soils are fast-draining, allowing the plant to take a drink when you water. The excess water is quickly released from the pot. Let the soil dry out completely between waterings. In winter, this means you could be watering every other week or even less often.

CHINESE EVERGREEN

Caring for Chinese evergreen

Someone gave me a very attractive houseplant called *Aglaonema*. How should I care for it?

Aglaonema is sometimes called Chinese evergreen. It is a common gift plant and—guess what?—it's easy to grow.

Chinese evergreen dislikes direct sun or excess water. Your plant will do fine sitting across the room from a window in a corner or on an end table, and you can err on the side of caution with watering. Water it only when the soil feels dry to the touch, and use a liquid houseplant fertilizer no more frequently than monthly. Remove any lower leaves that turn yellow. If many of the lower leaves begin to turn yellow, it's likely that you're overwatering.

CHRISTMAS CACTUS

Growing holiday cactus

I have a large Christmas cactus that's been in the family a long time. I don't have much of a green thumb. How do I get it to bloom?

Holiday cactus (*Schlumbergera*) need cool temperatures and short day length to form flower buds. Thanksgiving cactus (*S. truncata*) normally blooms a bit sooner than Christmas cactus (*S. ×buckleyi*). Care requirements for both plants are essentially the same. To induce bloom, give the plants a rest period in fall. Keep them on the dry side, but water enough to prevent the flat, leafy stems from shriveling. Maintain temperatures in the 50s to set the most flower buds, though any temperature below about 65°F will work. Place them in bright, indirect light. An unheated bedroom with an east exposure may be ideal.

Once flower buds have formed (you'll see swollen knobs on the stems), increase watering to prevent the buds from dropping. Flower buds also drop if the temperature is too warm, light levels are too low, or the plant is exposed to drafts.

Display the plant where you can enjoy the blooms, but keep in mind that the flowers last longer in cool conditions. The plant moves into active growth after flowers fade. Keep it watered and fertilized from midwinter through the summer. In fall, start the cycle over again. Plants can live for several years in the same pot if the potting medium is well-drained. If the plant becomes top-heavy, transplant it to a larger pot, or remove and root some shoots to start a new plant.

CITRUS

Indoor care of citrus

I grow lemon and orange trees indoors in the winter and on the deck in the summer. How do I take care of them? They get spider mites, scale, and mealybugs.

Keeping citrus indoors during the winter can be tricky if you don't have the right conditions. Give them plenty of sunshine (a south window is ideal), maintain even soil moisture, and keep the air as humid as possible. If you can keep the atmosphere around your plants humidified, they'll be under less environmental stress.

Spider mites in particular thrive in dry conditions. If they appear, give the plant a forceful spray of water to wash them off. Insecticidal soap can also be helpful in controlling them. Scale and mealybugs are tougher to manage. Horticultural oil may help, though you may have to use rubbing alcohol swabbed directly on the pests. For severe infestations, a pesticide labeled for their control may be needed.

Pruning can be done at any time to shape the plants, but in general they don't need much pruning indoors.

Grapefruit care

My father gave me a grapefruit tree shortly before he passed away, so it's important to me to keep this tree alive. Do I move the plant outdoors over the summer? What do I feed it? Any other tips you can provide would be helpful.

It's fine to move your grapefruit tree outside once the danger of frost has passed. Your tree will thank you for a summer vacation outdoors. Just remember that taking it outside and leaving it in full sun and wind immediately could shock the plant. Move it outdoors gradually so it can get used to the new conditions. Start by leaving it in a protected spot, such as the north side of your house. Then slowly move it to full sun (or leave it in the protected spot all summer long).

Indoors, give this plant as much light as possible, and keep the humidity high near it. Citrus trees can attract insect pests such as spider mites or mealybugs during the winter when there's dry air around them. But it's a good idea to keep an eye out for insect pests on a weekly basis all year long.

Wait to fertilize until spring, but once your plant is growing outdoors, you may want to feed it with a timed-release granular fertilizer designed for citrus.

CROTON

I have a brightly colored, waxy-leaf houseplant that I believe is a croton. It sits in a sunny spot in our garden room. I only water it when the leaves start to droop. The problem is the new leaves drop as soon as they appear. The old leaves are intact. Is an insect causing this problem?

Croton (*Codiaeum variegatum pictum*) is a true tropical plant from Malaysia and India, so it thrives in sunny locations where temperatures hit the 80s during the day and stay at least in the high 60s at night. Cold drafts of air cause plants to drop leaves. Investigate the air seals in your garden room. Do you have cold air that's blowing onto plants? During the summer, even central air-conditioning could cause the problem. Low humidity can also cause leaves to fall. Boost humidity around the plant with a room humidifier.

CYCLAMEN

House or outdoor plant?

I purchased a cyclamen plant with red blooms in a 4-inch pot. I assumed it was only a houseplant. After I got home, I noted the little stake in the pot that said it's *Cyclamen persicum* and that it makes a great ground cover for shade. Can you tell me if this is a perennial in Zone 7?

Zone 7 is too cold for *Cyclamen persicum*, which is commonly called florist's cyclamen. It is used as an ornamental indoor plant, although it is perennial in nature and can be grown outdoors in Zone 9 or warmer, such as mountainsides in Hawaii or some northern Mediterranean regions (never cold, but not extremely hot either.) It needs a rich, loamy, shady location when grown outdoors. As a houseplant it prefers cool temperatures (50–65°F) and a bright location such as a sunroom, greenhouse, or conservatory. When given these conditions, it can bloom for a couple of months.

DIEFFENBACHIA

Time to cut back

When is a good time to cut back my dieffenbachia plant? It's about 8 feet tall and ready to push through the ceiling.

Congratulations on getting your dieffenbachia *(Dieffenbachia),* also known as dumb cane, to grow to such lofty heights. You must be providing it with the care it needs to thrive. If necessary you can cut back your dieffenbachia at any time, but the best time is late winter to early spring. When day length and light levels rise in spring, the new growth that results from the cutback will be sturdier.

Poisonous dieffenbachia?

My neighbor told me my dieffenbachia plant is poisonous. Do I need to worry about my dog eating it? Sometimes he chews on leaves.

Dieffenbachia is indeed poisonous. One common name for it is dumb cane, because of the effect it has on those who accidentally ingest it. The plant sap contains calcium oxylate, a chemical compound that causes swelling of the tongue and throat. Swelling can be so severe that airflow through the throat is blocked, preventing normal speech and breathing. Obviously, this can have serious consequences. Fortunately, few accidental poisonings occur. However, to be safe, keep your dieffenbachia out of the reach of small children and pets, who may not understand that the plant needs to be left alone.

DRACAENA

Lucky bamboo

I've been growing, rather successfully, a dish of lucky bamboo. As it produces more leaves, I think it's starting to look less like bamboo. Am I seeing things?

You are amazingly perceptive! Lucky bamboo is a type of dracaena *(Dracaena sanderiana),* not a true bamboo. Your dracaena cuttings are growing into their true form. These dracaena poles, with their segmented stems, make a tropical-looking grove, but the display is temporary. Dracaena roots in water and may live in it for several years if periodically fertilized. If you want to retain the appearance of stems with few leaves, you can trim back the foliage on your plants. Or you could take your rooted cuttings out of their current container and pot them up to grow as a regular houseplant. The variegated form of lucky bamboo (green leaves with white edges) is a common houseplant known as ribbon plant.

Dragontree dropping leaves

I just bought a *Dracaena marginata* plant. It is losing all its leaves. I have it under lights, keep it warm, and give it plenty of water. What am I doing wrong?

Several conditions could lead to significant leaf loss of your Madagascar dragontree (*Dracaena marginata*). Tropical foliage plants are often grown in bright greenhouses or outdoors under shade cloth. In either case, the plants are accustomed to much more light than you can provide in the brightest of spots in your home. As the plant adjusts to reduced light conditions, it often sheds some of its lower leaves.

Another possibility is that your plant might have gotten a chill on the way home from the store. Tropical plants such as dracaena react dramatically if they have experienced cold temperatures or drafts. Make certain that the store associate wraps your tropical plants well to prevent them from getting cold in transit. Preheat the car before taking the plant outside, and drive directly home. Avoid the temptation to stop off for another errand; a car cools off quickly in cold weather.

Too much water could also be causing leaf loss. The soil should be allowed to dry to the touch between waterings. If it stays constantly wet, the roots could begin rotting. Yellowed leaves and leaf drop follow.

ENGLISH IVY

Ivy plant care

Ivy plants are my favorites. I have several and just can't seem to keep them healthy. Our house is dry, and we have a water softener—two things that I know don't help. Should I mix or purchase soil? What kinds of pests will I likely be dealing with?

Ivy can be a finicky houseplant, but once you master the basics, your plant will be stunning and reward you with lots of lush, healthy growth. Pot your plants in a good-quality, light houseplant mix. Avoid watering with softened water; it's high in salts, which can damage delicate plant roots. Catch and use rainwater, or use bottled water for your plants.

Houseplant ivies all spring from the original English ivy *(Hedera helix)*—and they crave that English countryside environment: cool and damp. The deathblow to most ivies is the hot, dry environment of our homes. Place them in the coolest room you have; aim for daytime temperatures in the upper 60s and nights about 10 degrees cooler. In winter, place the plants in a bedroom where you don't run the heat. North or east light proves perfect for healthy growth. Southern sun is too sizzling for ivies' cool-loving temperament.

Increase humidity around your plants. Above all, keep your eyes peeled for spider mites. They're so tiny that most gardeners don't notice them until their webbing drapes across ivy leaves—and by then you have a major infestation. Wash off spider mites with a forceful spray of water, or use insecticidal soap or horticultural oil to reduce their numbers.

Lastly, when spring comes and temperatures stay reliably above 55°F, move your ivies outside for a summer vacation. A protected, north-facing location rejuvenates plants and prepares them for the long winter indoors. Wash them thoroughly before bringing them back indoors.

Creating an ivy topiary

I've seen a lot of artificial topiaries being sold, but I'd prefer a live one. How hard is it to create a living topiary?

Topiary is an elegant way to dress up even the most common houseplants, and you can create one in a couple of hours. If you choose one of the more easy-care houseplants, your topiary will require minimal maintenance.

For your first topiary, use ivy as your base plant. To make an ivy topiary, you'll need the following.

- Potted ivy with at least five 24-inch stems
- Wire globe topiary frame
- Sharp knife
- Heavy terra-cotta or ceramic container
- Potting soil
- Clippers or scissors

Follow these easy steps to create your own topiary.

1. Fill the ceramic pot two-thirds full with potting soil, and insert the wire prong on the topiary frame into the soil. Remove the ivy from its pot.
2. Cut the root ball by slicing down between the stems using a sharp knife. Reassemble the divided root ball around the base of the frame so the trunk of the frame is centered. If needed, add more potting soil.
3. Twine one of the long ivy stems tightly in a spiral up the trunk of the frame, then wind it through the globe at the top. Clip off all the leaves on the trunk section. Repeat the procedure with the remaining stems until you've covered all the wires of the globe.
4. As the ivy grows, pinch new growth occasionally, and clip off errant stems to keep the globe shape dense and round.

FERN

Finicky maidenhair fern

I love maidenhair ferns but have a tough time keeping them growing inside. What care do they need?

Maidenhair fern (*Adiantum*) is native to temperate woodlands, so it enjoys rich, slightly moist soil and indirect light. It is sensitive to dry air and does best indoors when it is grown in a terrarium or glass enclosure. In nature, these ferns thrive in cool, humid situations. Unless you can match these conditions, the plants have a tendency to dry up quickly.

FICUS

Ficus leaf drop

I have a ficus tree (*Ficus benjamina*) that is dropping its leaves. What can I do to get it healthy again? I am watering it more often and have applied Osmocote to the soil. Am I doing the right things?

Ficus benjamina, also known as weeping fig, drops leaves for a variety of reasons. It is extremely sensitive to changes in temperature or light conditions, and simply moving a pot from one part of a room to another can trigger leaf drop. Or a coat of fresh paint in your house near where the weeping fig resides can cause leaves to fall. Insects could also be the culprit. Are the leaves sticky to the touch? Is there webbing stretching across the tops and undersides of the leaves, and along the places where the leaves join the stems? Any of these scenarios suggests an insect pest. Take a few leaves—fresh ones that you pick off the tree and a couple that have just dropped—to a local garden center or cooperative extension office and ask them to diagnose the problem.

I'm sorry to tell you that your responses to the leaf drop—watering more and fertilizing—are not the best ones. Sometimes leaf drop on a plant results from overwatering. Roots die, then foliage begins to fall. Until you diagnose your plant's problem, avoid giving it lots of water or fertilizer. With fewer leaves to support, the plant needs less water and fertilizer.

GARDENIA

Nonblooming gardenia

I bought a gardenia last winter. Soon after I brought it home, it stopped blooming and hasn't bloomed again. How can I get more blooms from my gardenia?

Keep in mind that the gardenia (*Gardenia*) you purchased was grown in a greenhouse with ideal light, humidity, and fertilization. It's virtually impossible to duplicate those conditions at home unless you keep your gardenia in a greenhouse or conservatory. So you shouldn't expect as much bloom as when you first got it. But with proper care, you can get your gardenia to bloom again. Gardenia prefers temperatures on the cool side—about 70°F during the day and 60°F at night. Flower buds may not set if it is too warm. Gardenia also needs a bright, sunny location indoors to set flower buds. (Outdoors, partial shade is better.) Low humidity is another bane of gardenia flower buds. Keep the humidity high around your gardenia, or flower buds will abort. Group it with other plants, use a humidifier, or set it on a pebble tray with water at the base. Fertilize through the spring and summer with acid fertilizer (evergreen and azalea food).

HIBISCUS

Hibiscus not blooming

Since October my hibiscus has not had a single flower. It bloomed nicely all summer. The plant is growing well and looks good, but I miss the flowers. What can I do?

Patience may be needed. Hibiscus (*Hibiscus*) plants need a lot of sunshine; they bloom best in a bright window, preferably a southern exposure. Even with the right exposure, they may not bloom through the darker winter months when skies are gray and days are short. During this period of slower growth, cut back on watering and fertilizing. Your goal should simply be to get the plant to survive the winter months. When days lengthen in spring, you may want to trim back the plant if it is getting leggy. Increase the frequency of watering, and use a liquid houseplant fertilizer to keep the plant well fed and promote strong new growth.

Whitefly control on hibiscus

I have a beautiful potted hibiscus that I drag indoors every winter. This year, it has been attacked by tiny white bugs that live on the undersides of the leaves. When I turn the leaves over, the bugs fly off. I have tried several houseplant insecticides, but nothing has slowed them down. How can I kill off these nasty bugs without harming my family?

You're dealing with the dreaded whitefly. Hibiscus is one of their favorite hosts. Whiteflies suck sap from plant leaves, and unless you're very astute and observant, you won't notice the damage they cause to the plant (a few leaves may appear speckled). The only way you know your plants have them is seeing them fly up when the leaves are disturbed. Whiteflies are difficult to get rid of, but it is possible!

One of the best things to do is to place yellow or blue sticky cards in your plants. These cards are coated with glue that's super sticky—to bugs and people! The color attracts the whiteflies, which fly into the cards and get stuck. You can purchase sticky cards through a well-stocked garden center or by mail.

Carefully handle the sticky cards by their edges, and keep them from touching anything. If you get them on your clothing, for example, they're stuck there for life. Feel free to cut the cards in half if you think one card is too large, but do it carefully. Make one clean cut with very sharp scissors. Change the cards when they're smothered with goo-trapped bugs. Another approach is to spray your hibiscus with horticultural oil to reduce the whitefly population. It may be impossible to completely eradicate the whiteflies indoors, but with persistence you can keep their numbers low enough to tolerate. Consider getting rid of the affected plant or haevily pruning it back before the whiteflies move to your other houseplants.

INSECTS

Gnats

Tiny black gnats are flying around my houseplants. What can I do to get rid of them?

Those tiny black gnats are fungus gnats. They lay their eggs in the soil. The eggs turn into tiny wormlike larvae that munch on soil fungi and rotting plant roots. They don't chew enough roots to damage the plant unless the infestation is excessive or the plant is small, such as a seedling. The larvae pupate, then emerge from the soil as flying gnats.

Fungus gnats may be a clue that you're overwatering your plants. They can show up in soils of well-managed plants, too, but they're more common when the soil is kept constantly moist. Allow the soil to dry more between waterings.

You can also control fungus gnats using a type of bacteria, *Bacillus thuringiensis israelensis* (Bt). It comes in a liquid form that you mix with water, then pour onto the soil of your plants. It's important to follow the label directions carefully and make follow-up applications on schedule to break the gnats' life cycle. It's not enough to control the adults; you want to wipe out the juvenile forms too. You can instantly eliminate a multitude of the hovering adults by inserting yellow or blue sticky cards into a few of your houseplants. These cards are coated with glue that ensnares the insects, which find the yellow and blue hues irresistible.

One word of warning on bacterial control methods: The Bt solution, often sold under the name Knock-Out Gnats or Gnatrol, smells horrible. You'll never want to take a whiff from the bottle! You can keep any unused solution in a sealed plastic bottle until your next watering. Just avert your nose when you remove the lid.

Spider mites

A daisy tree that I brought indoors when the weather turned cold last fall has small webs on the branches, but I haven't seen any spiders. I've spotted the same condition on a Norfolk Island pine that's in another room of the house. I have sprayed the plants with a dish detergent solution, but the webs remain. What am I battling and how do I get rid of it?

Unfortunately, your plants have spider mites. The bugs are tiny—almost too small to see with the naked eye, although if you examine the webs carefully, you will see the spiderlike mites moving about within them. Most often, gardeners learn they have the pest when they spot the webs—and by then the infestation definitely has the upper hand.

Spider mites are difficult to eradicate, especially on plants inside the house. Attack these pests by using several techniques. First, wash the plants with a soapy solution of mild dish detergent or insecticidal soap. A forceful water spray in the shower will help, too. Remove all webs, wiping upper and lower leaf surfaces. If necessary, follow this treatment by applying a pesticide designed to kill spider mites. Make follow-up applications. Isolate these plants from noninfested plants in your home.

Mites multiply in hot, dry air. Increase the humidity inside your home with a humidifier. In spring, when nighttime temperatures are reliably above 55°F, take the infested plants outside. Increased air circulation will help eliminate the pest.

I have just taken over care of a large-leaf plant at our office. There is white sticky residue on top of some of the leaves. Do you have any idea what this is?

Sticky residue on plant foliage can come from the feeding of any number of insects with piercing-sucking mouthparts. Aphids, scale, and mealybugs are common culprits. If the stickiness is associated with waxy white blobs, your plant has mealybugs. These insects look like little tufts of white cotton and attach themselves to plant stems, the undersides of leaves, and the places where leaves join the main stem. They pierce the plants and suck the juices. It's undigested sugar secreted by the insects that creates the sticky residue (honeydew). The honeydew can in turn allow fungus to grow.

To get rid of mealybugs, wash off the plant with a spray of soapy water. If the plant is small enough, carry it to a large sink or an outdoor area. Use insecticidal soap or a solution of dish detergent. Soak the top and bottom of all the leaves, and physically—with the spray of water or with your fingers—remove every cottony mass that you can see. A dab of rubbing alcohol on the cottony tuft kills the mealybugs.

Or you could apply a houseplant pesticide that's labeled effective against mealybugs. Look for a product at your local garden center. Take a leaf with you that shows the critters (carry it in a sealed, clear plastic bag) to confirm this diagnosis. Follow the directions on the pesticide carefully. You'll need to make follow-up applications at 7–10-day intervals to kill young, newly hatched mealybugs. This pest is beatable, so don't give up. If the plant is heavily infested, you can always cut off some of the most affected parts.

Whiteflies

I'm seeing whiteflies all over my houseplants. I tried treating the plants with malathion, but it seems to have harmed them. I followed the label directions and application rates. Do you have any suggestions as to what I might have done wrong, and how I can beat the whiteflies?

With any pesticide, it's crucial not only to follow recommended application rates but also to use the chemical only on those plants listed on the label. It sounds as though your plants are demonstrating what's known as a phytotoxic response. In other words, the cure nearly killed the patient. This is a common problem in treating houseplants, especially when you use a powerful product such as malathion. In the future, test-treat a portion of the plant, and wait about a week to observe the results. If leaves speckle, spot, or turn brown at the edges, your chemical is the likely culprit.

The best way to defeat an established whitefly population—without killing the plants—is to combine treatments. Hang or display yellow or blue sticky cards on stakes in pots to trap flying insects. Using the sticky cards will reduce the number of adult flies on your plants, which in turn will reduce the number of eggs they lay. To whittle down the junior members of the group, try a more gentle chemical approach, such as horticultural oil. These oils typically don't burn plants or cause harm to humans.

Make sure you consistently make follow-up applications according to package directions. Many insects reproduce every 7–10 days, so you need to apply a pesticide at weekly intervals until every egg and offspring has been zapped.

NORFOLK ISLAND PINE

Limb loss

My Norfolk Island pine is losing its lower branches. I know it won't regrow them, but is there anything at all I can do to prevent more from dropping?

Increasing the humidity around your Norfolk Island pine *(Araucaria heterophylla)* can help it hold on to its lower branches—for a while. When growing in their indigenous home in the South Pacific, these plants naturally shed their lower branches as they mature. You should expect your plant to lose some branches, but setting the pot on top of a tray of pebbles and water or using a room humidifier might slow the process.

Many people decorate these trees during the holidays. If you do, avoid using lights, which can dry out the tree, or hanging ornaments, which cause the branches to droop. Also avoid allowing the soil to dry too much. Dry conditions may lead to branch drop, too.

ORCHID

Orchid know-how

I recently bought a moth orchid that is flowering. When the blossoms fade, do they drop off or do I have to cut them off? After blooming, does the plant enter a dormant period? What kind of fertilizer should I give my orchid?

Moth orchid *(Phalaenopsis)* flowers last a long time before they dry up and drop off the stalk. When the last bloom falls, cut back the stalk to the spot just below where the first flower appeared. The orchid may send up a new flower stalk, or it may remain vegetative until next year's flowering cycle begins. Keep your orchid in a bright spot away from direct sunlight. Water the plant about once a week. During times of active growth, when the plant is producing new leaves, fertilize once a month using a full-strength houseplant fertilizer solution. During the rest of the year, fertilize every 4–6 weeks using a half-strength solution.

Repotting an orchid

What do I need to do to repot my orchid? It's about 2 years old and is outgrowing its tiny pot. Do I need soil of some sort? Do I need to trim any parts when I repot? There are baby leaves growing from inside the older ones. Do I need to do anything to those?

In the wild, rather than sinking their roots into the soil, most orchids normally grow in trees, perched high above the rain forest floor. You can replicate that environment with a special orchid bark mix (a blend of ground fir-tree bark) that's sold at garden centers. It provides the quick drainage and plentiful pockets for air that orchid roots require. Mostly, though, it helps anchor plants in pots so they can grow. For best results, mix peat moss into fir bark or orchid bark mix (use 2 parts bark to 1 part peat moss), and you're ready to plant.

There are special pots on the market created just for orchids. They're full of holes to expose the roots to more air. However, a terra-cotta or plastic pot grows great orchids; no special pot is needed. Choose a pot that's 1 inch (at the most 2 inches) larger than your present pot.

The time to transplant orchids is after they bloom, when new roots have appeared but haven't grown longer than ½ inch, or when the roots start to crawl out of the pot.

Be sure to water your orchid before you repot it. Then follow this step-by-step guide to repotting and you'll have your orchid happily settled into its new quarters in no time.

1. Soak the pot containing the orchid in water for several hours, then gently pull out the orchid.
2. Carefully loosen the roots, then remove the growing medium from the root ball.
3. Replant your orchid in a pot that's only about 1 or 2 inches larger than the previous pot. Pack orchid potting mix around the roots.
4. When the orchid is firmly in place, arrange a layer of orchid mix over the top of the roots; water well.

Basic orchid multiplication

I have rooted an orchid in water. It's about 2 inches tall with four small roots. I read that I should not plant it until it grows to about 4 inches tall. How do I plant it when it reaches that height?

Rooting orchids in water is something most gardeners never think to try. They prefer a lot of oxygen aroudn their roots. You may have better luck if you aerate the water or pot it up immediately. You'll need a less coarse mix of orchid bark, which is a tree-bark mixture created just for raising orchids. You can find it at most garden centers. Use a 3- or 4-inch-wide pot. Special pots are available for growing orchids, but any plastic or terra-cotta pot will serve the purpose.

Fill the container with the special orchid mix, create a little planting hole for your orchid, then insert your plant into the bark mixture. Be careful not to break any of the roots. It's OK if some of the roots protrude from the soil; just be sure to anchor your plant so it doesn't tumble out of the pot. You didn't mention what kind of orchid you're growing, but if it's a moth orchid *(Phalaenopsis),* insert a simple metal or plastic-coated metal stake into the pot before you add the orchid itself; use the stake to keep the plant upright as it grows.

Broken flower stalk

My husband accidentally broke the flower spike on my beautiful orchid plant. The rest of the plant is OK and secure in the soil. Can I reroot and/or repot the flower stalk, or does it have to be discarded?

The best you can do is put the flower stem in water and enjoy it. Cut orchid flowers last a long time in water and will last even longer if you change the water regularly and add floral preservative each time. You can purchase packets of floral preservative at any florist. It is especially helpful in encouraging all of the buds to open. Once the last flower fades from your orchid stem, toss the whole works. A new orchid won't grow from a flower stalk.

PALM

Brown tips on leaves

What causes brown tips on plant leaves? I have a palm tree, and the ends are turning brown. Should I cut away the brown edges of the leaves or should I cut off the whole branch?

Brown leaf tips on palms may be caused by one or more of the following.
- Dryness. If the palm is not getting enough water, or if the humidity is too low, the leaf tips will turn brown. Water more frequently and on a regular basis.

- Salt. Salts from watering accumulate in the soil over time. The salts may come from fertilizer dissolved in the water or from minerals in the water itself. Excess salts are taken up by the plant and deposited in the tips of the leaves, causing burning and browning. Prevent the salt buildup by leaching (flushing) the soil with distilled water periodically.
- Chemicals. Some chemicals such as chloride and borate can accumulate in leaf tips and cause browning. If your water source has chloride or borate, use distilled or rainwater instead to water plants.

   You can trim the brown leaf tips to keep the plant more attractive. Avoid removing the entire frond before it turns completely brown. As long as the leaf has some green tissue, it's photosynthesizing and contributing to plant growth.

Webs on palm leaves

My palm trees have webs with small white dots on the leaves. The leaves are starting to turn brown. Can you help me save them?

Those webs you've been seeing are a sure sign that your palms have been infested with spider mites. These almost-invisible pests suck plant juices and can cause a plant to go into decline. Give your palms a shower to wash off the mites. In fact, regular showers may be enough to keep the mites at bay. Palms are a favorite of spider mites, so you'll have to watch for their reappearance. Insecticidal soap, horticultural oil, or chemical houseplant miticides may be necessary to control the mites.

   Palms need more moisture indoors than they do outdoors. Keep the soil slightly moist, and place the plants in a bright, draft-free location that gets lots of indirect sun. Palms dislike direct sun.

PHILODENDRON

Philodendron propagation

I have a trailing philodendron that I would like to root. Can I do this from a cutting? If so, how do I do it?

Rooting a philodendron (Philodendron) is easy. All you need is a pair of scissors and a small container of potting soil To make a cutting, use a sharp knife or shears to cut a piece of stem about 3–6 inches long. It's best to make your cut just above another leaf on the same stem. Remove all of the leaves from the cutting except the top two or three. Place the cutting in moist vermiculite or potting soil. None of the leaves should be buried in the rooting medium. If they are, perch the cutting a little higher, or remove another leaf—just be sure that two or three leaves remain.

Put your container in bright, indirect sunlight; I usually set mine along a windowsill or on a table near a window. In two or three weeks roots will sprout, followed by new leaves. Gently tug on the cutting. If you feel resistance you'll know that roots have formed. Insert the cutting in good-quality potting soil in a pot that's 3–4 inches wide.

If your mother plant is large enough, take three to five cuttings at one time and let all of them root in the same jar. Then when you plant them, you'll have a pot that's full and lush.

POINSETTIA

Holiday blooms

I purchased 10 poinsettias for Christmas and want to keep them going so I can make them rebloom next Christmas. How do I do that?

Poinsettias (Poinsettia) are easy to maintain, but it takes some effort to make them bloom a second time. To grow them after the holidays, all you need to do is treat them similar to other houseplants: Give them bright light, allow them to slightly dry between waterings, and feed them with a liquid houseplant fertilizer according to label directions. That's the easy part. The bracts (those are the leaves that look like flower petals) will eventually fade and fall off the plant. At that point, cut back the stems to just below the flowers and let them continue to grow.

Getting the plants to rebloom is the hard part. It's likely that you won't be able to bring all 10 plants into flower again, simply because of space limitations. In spring, once nighttime temperatures are consistently above 50°F, place your poinsettias outside where they'll receive bright, indirect light. They will grow but will remain completely green all summer. Prune back the plants by one-half to one-third in midsummer, and repot them in the same pot, or in one that's slightly larger if the plant has grown significantly. Use a commercial potting soil. Feed the plants with a standard houseplant fertilizer during this time of new growth. Bring the pots indoors before nighttime temperatures fall below 50°F.

From September 21 through the end of October, the plants need 14–15 hours of uninterrupted darkness daily, and nighttime temperatures around 65°F. This is the secret to triggering new flowers to form and for the bracts to change color. This means that every day at about 5 p.m. you'll need to cover the plants. Uncover them between 7 and 8 the following morning. Absolutely no light can penetrate the darkness. If you place a box over them, it must not permit light to enter. If you place plants in an extra bedroom, no light can enter the room beneath the crack of the door or through a window. Even car headlights shining through a window are enough to interrupt the required darkness. Greenhouse growers use thick black cloths to cover their poinsettia crops, blocking out all light from passing cars and nearby shopping centers. If you successfully carry out the darkness routine, by early November your plants will be developing color, and you can end the daily darkness ritual and set the plants in bright, indirect light. By the end of November, the bracts should be coloring up nicely, and you'll be able to enjoy them through the next holiday season.

Poisonous poinsettias?
Is it safe for my children and pets if I grow poinsettias? I've heard that they're poisonous.

Poinsettias are not poisonous, although it's wise to keep children or pets from eating them, because they may have been treated with pesticides. However, they do contain a milky sap that can cause an allergic skin reaction similar to the latex allergy some people experience. If you're sensitive to latex, use caution (and wear cotton or leather gloves!) when handling poinsettias.

SNAKE PLANT

Propagating snake plant
Can snake plants be started from cuttings?

Snake plant (*Sansevieria trifasciata*) can be started several ways. Perhaps the simplest method is to divide older plants. Snake plant, or mother-in-law's tongue, as it is known by some, produces underground rhizomes that increase the size of the clump of upright shoots. Division is a way to get a large new plant quickly. And it's the only way to maintain the marginal light green stripe of variegated types. Plants started from cuttings lose this variegation.

If your snake plant is not variegated, and if you're patient, you can start new plants by taking stem cuttings. Cut the snake plant leaves into 3–4-inch-long segments, cutting a notch in the upper end of each so you can tell which end is up. It's important to mark which side is up on each cutting, because the cuttings will fail to root and grow if inserted in the rooting medium upside down. Dip the lower end of the cutting in rooting hormone and insert it in a lightweight potting mix or rooting medium such as vermiculite or perlite. Keep the mix moist but not wet; snake plant rots if kept excessively wet. In several months you'll see new shoots developing from the base of the cutting.

SPIDER PLANT

Brown leaf tips

My spider plant that used to thrive seems to be thinning out and becoming unhealthy. The ends of the leaves are turning brown. Am I watering it too much or too little?

If your spider plant *(Chlorophytum comosum)* has been in the same pot for a long time, it's probably best to repot it into something a bit larger with fresh soil. Remove the root ball from the pot to look at the roots. A pot-bound spider plant will have a cluster of thick white roots at the bottom of the pot, circling around the edges, and pushing out through the drainage hole. A good time to repot is late winter or early spring. Houseplants react to the increasing hours of daylight in spring with a growth spurt. Repotting them then ties in to the plants' natural cycle.

Those brown tips could be caused by excessive drying or by mineral buildup in the soil. If the plant was pot-bound, it may have been drying out too quickly. Repotting should remedy the situation. Spider plants are also sensitive to low humidity. Leaf tips can turn brown and shrivel when the air is too dry. You can raise the humidity with a humidifier. To prevent mineral buildup, water more thoroughly. Shallow, frequent waterings can build up minerals, which the plant takes in and deposits at the leaf tips. Be sure to allow water to drain through the pot every time you water. Also, make certain your water source contains no fluoride. Spider plant is sensitive to this chemical.

Propagating spider plant

My spider plant has a lot of babies dangling from it. Can I start new plants from these?

Yes, spider plant is one of the easiest plants to propagate. If you look closely at the babies, or plantlets, you'll see some little knobs on the underside of the cluster of leaves. Those are root initials. If you place them on potting soil, the roots will start to grow, and you'll have new plants. If you like, you can leave the plantlets attached to the mother plant until they form roots. Or you can cut the plantlets off the mother plant and put them in separate pots. Just be sure to keep the soil evenly moist until the roots are fully developed. In no time you can have enough spider plants to share with friends and neighbors.

CONTAINER GARDENING IN GENERAL

Container gardens in sunny spots

I am trying to grow container gardens on my front porch, where there's lots of sun. My plantings have done poorly in the past. What plants or shrubs can I plant in a container that will look great all summer and survive the scorching sun?

When planting container gardens, the keys are the soil, the container, and the plant selection. First, make sure you have a good-quality planting mix and an appropriate-size container. Then select the best plants. For your location, it sounds as if sun-loving annuals are your best bet. Top-performing types include ornamental sweet potato *(Ipomoea batatas)*, verbena *(Verbena)*, annual geranium *(Pelargonium)*, petunia *(Petunia)*, fan flower *(Scaevola aemula)*, moss rose *(Portulaca grandiflora)*, annual salvia *(Salvia splendens, S. coccinea)*, and herbs such as rosemary *(Rosmarinus officinalis)*, lavender *(Lavandula angustifolia)*, sage *(Salvia officinalis)*, and thyme *(Thymus vulgaris)*.

Renter's garden

I rent my house, but I'm hoping to purchase one soon. I'd like to add color to my current yard, but I don't want to plant lots of things I'll have to leave behind. What can I do?

Instead of planting things in the ground, concentrate on planting in containers. You can group containers to look like flower beds—and you can move them anytime you like. Containers are also ideal for planting under trees or other areas where you can't work the soil. Here are the basics for growing plants in containers.
- The mix. Container gardens need good soil. Start with a high-quality potting mix (one that's been formulated for containers; this information should be on the package). The best mixes are rich, light, and moisture-retentive and have a slow-release fertilizer already mixed in.
- The container. A container that is too small will cause the plants to dry out too quickly. (Many plants fail to recover well if they dry out too much.) Also, be sure the container has at least one hole in the bottom so excess water can drain. Water that doesn't escape can drown your plants in a pot with no drainage.
- Maintenance. Frequent watering is a must, especially in sunny, exposed sites. Add mulch over the potting mix to conserve moisture and keep the potting mix from growing too warm on hot summer days. If you use a potting mix without a slow-release fertilizer, add one when you plant, or feed your plants regularly during the growing season.

Planting up a container

How do I plant a container garden? Should I add pebbles to the bottom of pots for drainage?

Start with a clean container; if it has been previously used, wash it with a dilute chlorine bleach solution (1 part bleach to 9 parts water) to disinfect it. Rinse it well in plain water. Soak clay pots in water for a few minutes to fill the pore spaces; otherwise, the pots will soak up water from the potting mix. Place a piece of broken pot or a coffee filter over the drainage hole to keep the potting mix contained. Avoid adding pebbles to the bottom of a container for drainage. Rather than improving drainage in the pot, this practice keeps a larger portion of the root zone saturated and often leads to root rot. If the container is extremely large, you may add packing peanuts or crushed cans to the bottom of the pot so you won't need to use as much potting mix. Place a landscape fabric liner between the lightweight fill and the potting mix to prevent the soil from washing down into the filler.

If your potting mix has a high peat content, moisten it before potting the plants. Peat is slow to soak up moisture when it is dry. Many commercial container mixes contain a wetting agent to make the initial watering much easier. Place plants in the container at the proper depth and water them thoroughly. If you like, add an inch of mulch over the surface to hold in moisture and moderate soil temperatures.

Container selection

What should I look for when I'm choosing a pot for growing plants in a container on my patio?

With the wide array of pots available, it can be daunting to choose the right one for your situation. Consider these characteristics.

- Porous or nonporous? Glazed pots and plastic, metal, and glass containers hold moisture longer than porous containers. Porous clay pots lose moisture quickly in dry weather.
- Drainage hole. Every container should have one or more drainage holes so that excess moisture can drain out. If the pot has no holes, drill a few so the roots won't become waterlogged from overwatering or heavy rains.
- Frost resistance. If you overwinter pots outdoors, consider the container's susceptibility to frost damage. Concrete, wood, and newer synthetic composite pots may be left outside over the winter with no damage. Clay pots absorb moisture and crack in freezing weather.
- Weight. Lightweight containers are easier to move around. On windy sites, they will also blow over more easily. Polyurethane pots are lightweight and easy to move. Concrete and clay are heavy. Use wheeled platforms to help move heavy containers.

Can I grow any kind of plant in a container?

Most gardeners grow annual flowers or vegetables in containers, but perennial plants such as trees, shrubs, perennial flowers, ornamental grasses, and bulbs may be grown in containers if you protect the containers and plants over the winter. Larger containers will make it easier to protect the root zone over the winter; the large mass of soil keeps it from freezing as quickly as soil in a small pot.

Consider slow-growing or space-saving dwarf varieties when they are available. This is especially true for trees and shrubs. Standard varieties can quickly outgrow the container. By selecting dwarf types you'll cut down on the need for pruning and frequent repotting. Also make certain that the plants you grow in containers are hardy for your zone or colder. Root balls surrounded by cold air are more easily damaged than those planted in the ground.

If you grow a combination of plants in the container, make certain that they all have the same light and water needs. None should be invasive, or others in the grouping will be crowded out. Ornamental grasses are well-suited to container culture and make a nice addition of height to contrast with lower-growing perennial flowers. Fountain grass *(Pennisetum),* leatherleaf sedge *(Carex buchananii),* and smaller forms of maiden grass *(Miscanthus)* are suitable for container culture.

Bulbs in containers are usually forced for early winter bloom indoors. However, some hardy lilies grow well in containers for summer bloom, and if protected from cold can be overwintered in the pot. These include gold-banded lily *(Lilium auratum),* Formosa lily *(L. formosanum),* and Easter lily *(L. longiflorum).* The cultivars 'Black Dragon', 'Cambridge', 'Dukat', and 'Stargazer' are especially good for container culture.

How should I store plant containers for the winter? Would it be OK to leave them outside?

At the end of the growing season, remove annual flowers or vegetables from their containers. Add the potting mix to the compost pile or to planting beds. Use fresh potting mix next year. Disease organisms could be in the mix, and the soil structure breaks down over the season with repeated watering.

Clean the containers before storing them. Scrub pots with a 10 percent chlorine bleach solution. Store clay containers indoors where temperatures won't fall below freezing or outdoors protected from rain and snow. Because clay is porous, it holds moisture and can crack when water in the pot freezes and expands. Plastic, wood, concrete, and nonporous pots can be safely stored outside.

Moving heavy container gardens

Is there an easy way to move big pots around on the patio? Mine are so heavy to move.

A container full of soil and plants can be surprisingly heavy and awkward to move from one spot to another. You can save yourself a lot of back-breaking labor by potting up the container in its finished location so you can avoid having to move it. If the container is already potted and you need to change its location, try one of these suggestions.

- Tilt the pot and slowly roll it, keeping it at an angle and using the bottom edge of the pot as a wheel.
- Slide the pot onto a plant trolley with casters beneath it. Roll the trolley to the new location.
- Use a plastic sled or toboggan or a tarp under the pot to drag the container.
- Rent a furniture dolly. Slide the edge of the dolly under the pot, strap it on, and move it to the new spot.
- With the help of a friend or two, lift the container onto a garden cart, and roll the plant to the new location.

Removing salt deposits

How do I get the white deposits off my clay pots? I tried a 50/50 solution of bleach and water with a stiff brush, which worked fairly well. However, I had to scrub hard and finally use full strength bleach. Do you have any other solution to this problem?

The white areas on your clay pots are a buildup of mineral salts, a common occurrence. A dilute bleach solution (1 part bleach to 9 parts water) is good for surface sterilizing pots and general cleanup, but may be little help in removing mineral deposits. I suspect that it was all that elbow grease that finally did the trick for your encrusted pots. Once the buildup has developed, there's no easy cure. The solution is to prevent the mineral buildup to begin with. Water your plants thoroughly each time you water. Allow the water to drain out the bottom of the pot. Periodically flush the soil with collected rainwater or mineral-free bottled water to keep mineral salts from building up.

FLOWERS

I recently moved into a condo and am looking for tips on how to plant flowers in containers to provide lots of color all summer long.

When space is at a premium, or an in-ground garden is impossible, turn to containers to brighten your day. By keeping a few pointers in mind, you can grow just about anything that other gardeners in your climate can grow.

- Design your space. Determine where your containers will sit and how much daily sun that area receives. Most flowers require at least 6 hours of direct sunlight per day. Less than that means you'll have to choose flowers that thrive with less sun.
- Choose your container. Get your hands on good containers with drainage holes. Choose larger containers unless you're planting extremely small plants and will be able to water them daily or even more often.
- Select your plants. A reputable garden center can help you decide what or how many plants to put in a container. Mixing plants of different species is fine, as long as they have the same requirements for water and sun. Look around the garden center for ideas of plant combinations in preplanted containers.
- Create your container. First, purchase good-quality, sterile potting soil and fertilizer. Place plants no deeper and no higher than the soil level they had in their original containers. Because you're using sterile potting soil, your plants won't have access to the kind of fertility that in-ground plants have, so you'll need to fertilize at planting and again later in the season. You can mix a slow-release fertilizer into the planting holes or use a liquid fertilizer once the soil has been pressed around the plantings. If you chose a liquid fertilizer, apply it on a regular basis during the growing season.
- Water now and later. Containers dry out more quickly than in-ground gardens do, so being able to easily water your plants daily during hot weather is a must. If plants are allowed to wilt, they may never completely recover; if they get too wet, they can end up with diseases or attract insect pests. If there is a saucer to catch excess water, empty it if any water is left standing after an hour or so.

I live in an apartment with a patio where I have many hanging baskets. What plants would you suggest for growing in baskets?

There are many beautiful annual flowers you can grow in hanging containers. Ivy geranium *(Pelargonium peltatum)*, verbena *(Verbena* hybrids), ornamental sweet potato vine *(Ipomoea batatas)*, browallia *(Browallia speciosa)*, and fan flower *(Scaevola)* are just a few of the many colorful, trailing plants you can grow. If your patio is shady, consider tuberous begonia *(Begonia ×tuberhybrida)*, wax begonia *(Begonia semperflorens-cultorum)*, bellflower *(Campanula),* impatiens *(Impatiens walleriana),* or coleus *(Solenostemon scutellarioides)*. I suggest you tour your local garden centers and home improvement stores in spring to get an idea of the variety of plants available to you. Stop by your local cooperative extension office for a list of their annual flower recommendations.

Heat-loving plants for containers

QUICK TIP

- Calibrachoa *(Calibrachoa* hybrids)
- Cosmos *(Cosmos bipinnatus, C. sulphureus)*
- Geranium *(Pelargonium ×hortorum)*
- Moss rose *(Portulaca grandiflora)*
- Petunia *(Petunia ×hybrida)*
- Salvia *(Salvia splendens, S. farinacea)*
- Vinca *(Catharanthus roseus)*
- Zinnia *(Zinnia elegans, Z. angustifolia, Z. haageana)*

Heat-tolerant flowers

I'd like to grow some plants in containers on my deck, but it gets full afternoon sun and is always very hot. What could I grow in pots for color on the deck?

Full afternoon sun reflecting off the house adds extra heat to the site you describe. Plants in containers are more sensitive to heat than those in the ground, because their root systems are more exposed to temperature fluctuations. So you'll need to choose some extremely tough plants for your deck containers. See the list of heat lovers to consider in the Quick Tip (at right).

Flowers on deck

I plan to garden in containers on my deck. What kind of flowers should I put in my containers for morning sun and evening shade? I'd like my deck to always be in bloom.

Your flower choices depend on how much sun you get during the spring and summer. Sun-loving annuals (which are usually the heaviest-flowering plants) require at least 6 hours of direct sunlight a day. These include verbena, geranium, marigold, zinnia, and salvia. If you get less than 6 hours of sun per day, you should choose shade lovers such as begonia, caladium, fuchsia, and impatiens to provide constant color.

Watering hanging baskets

Is there an easy way to water the flowers in my hanging baskets without getting water all over myself?

As you no doubt have discovered, hanging baskets need frequent watering. And it can be difficult to do without creating a mess. A watering wand on the end of a hose is perhaps the simplest solution. The wand extends your reach so the water can be directed into the center of the basket without running down your arm. Self-watering pots are another option. With these, you fill the water reservoir at the base of the pot, and the plant soaks up moisture through capillary action. You could also use a pulley system with your hanging baskets; simply lower the basket to a comfortable height for watering. Another higher-tech option is to rig up a drip irrigation system with an emitter for each hanging basket.

FOOD GARDENS

Growing edibles in containers

I'm limited to growing plants in pots on my balcony, but I'd like to grow a few fruits and vegetables this summer. What kinds would be the best for me to try?

Plants for your balcony should be beautiful as well as productive, so the best strategy is to grow mixed vegetables in large containers. In broad pots or half barrels, plant compact varieties of upright vegetables, such as tomato, pepper, or eggplant, surrounded by colorful leafy greens, such as lettuce or Swiss chard. Leaf-lettuce varieties are best, and they come in a broad range of colors and textures. Include fast-growing radishes and green onions, which you can harvest early to make room for longer-lived plants. Let cucumbers that bear small, pickle-size fruits cascade over the edges, or include trailing edible nasturtiums.

Strawberries are the easiest fruits to grow in containers. Remove the first flush of blossoms from strawberries planted this year to keep them from setting fruit. If you plant everbearing strawberries, let the second flush of blooms produce a late-season crop for you. June-bearing types won't yield until next year.

The most challenging part of growing fruits and vegetables in containers is keeping them adequately watered. Although large containers dry out more slowly than small ones, even big containers may need daily watering in hot weather.

Edible flowers

I'd like to grow some edible flowers. Are there any that I could grow in containers?

Most edible flowers can be grown in the ground or in containers. Combine them with other flowers or vegetables, or grow them alone. No matter what combination you choose, you'll be delighted with the colorful and tasty additions they make to your kitchen garden. Here are some favorites.

- Calendula (*Calendula officinalis*)
- Chives (*Allium schoenoprasum*)
- Daylily (*Hemerocallis*)

- Lavender *(Lavandula)*
- Nasturtium *(Tropaeolum majus)*
- Pansy *(Viola ×wittrockiana)*
- Rose *(Rosa)*

SOIL MIXES

Houseplant soil outdoors

Is it OK to use potting soil that's made for indoor plants for outdoor container plants?

In most cases, it's fine to use potting soil for indoor plants in containers you'll put outdoors. However, some indoor soils are a bit heavy for outdoor use and can become waterlogged during periods of heavy rain. The best potting soil for outdoor plants has a mixture of soilless products, such as peat moss, perlite, and vermiculite, to loosen the soil and ensure good drainage. And remember, indoors or out, all containers should have adequate drainage holes.

Soil recipe

I want to mix my own potting soil for outdoor container gardens. Do you have a recipe you could suggest?

There are numerous quality container mixes available for purchase. Many include desirable additions such as wetting agents that make it easier to water when the pot dries out, water-absorbing crystals that retain more moisture in the pot, and slow-release fertilizer that supplies constant nutrition. You could add all these extras to your own mix, but you may have to search a bit to find them.

These convenience factors come at a price. Commercial mixes usually are more expensive than a basic mix you concoct yourself. A fairly standard recipe for a medium-textured mix is 50 percent (by volume) peat moss, 25 percent coarse sand or perlite, and 25 percent ground pine bark. Variations on this basic mix include 2 parts peat moss, 1 part perlite, 1 part coarse sand; 1 part peat moss, 1 part sand, 1 part pine bark; and 1 part peat moss, 1 part pine bark, and 1 part perlite. Experiment with these ingredients until you come up with a mix that suits your needs.

Water-absorbing crystals

What do you call the gel-like particles that can be mixed into potting soil to help it retain water?

These gel-like particles are usually sold as dry crystals to mix with potting soil. They go by the names Watersorb, Soil Moist Terra-Sorb, and others. The actual compound is polyacrylamide, a manufactured polymer that absorbs water, then slowly releases it back into the soil as the soil becomes drier. It's pretty much the same stuff put in disposable diapers to absorb extra moisture. It takes only about a teaspoon of the dry polymer to amend the soil in a 6-inch pot. Industry sources claim that it lasts for 7–9 years in the soil before it breaks down into carbon dioxide, water, and nitrogen.

The gels are a bit controversial for use in ground beds, but most research shows that they will reduce moisture stress and frequency of watering for container-grown plants. That can be a real bonus during those hot, dry summer days when the pots dry out almost as fast as you water them.

TREES AND SHRUBS

Winter protection for pots

This year I grew some small trees and shrubs in containers. They're too big to move into the garage for winter. Do I need to do anything special to protect them over winter?

You may leave your potted trees and shrubs outdoors over the winter provided they are hardy in your climate and provided you give them extra protection for the winter. Because the roots are aboveground, they're exposed to colder temperatures than woody ornamentals growing in the ground. Keep the soil temperature in the pots above freezing. With smaller pots, you could dig a hole in the ground and place the pots in the hole, mulching over the top to insulate the area. Because your pots are too large for that, it may be best to group the pots together and cover them with a thick layer of straw, mulch, wood chips, or shredded leaves to protect the roots from freezing. If it looks like they'll freeze, move containers to an unheated garage or shed temporarily for added protection.

Topiary

I'd like to grow some clipped topiaries flanking my front door. What would you suggest?

First determine which species are hardy in your region. Also consider the exposure. Will you need a tree or shrub that withstands full sun, or is the site shady? Choose a woody plant that tolerates frequent pruning. Here are some that fit the bill.

- Arborvitae *(Thuja)*
- Azalea *(Rhododendron)*
- Boxwood *(Buxus)*
- Hemlock *(Tsuga canadensis)*
- Juniper *(Juniperus)*
- Laurel *(Laurus nobilis)*
- Privet *(Ligustrum)*
- Weeping fig *(Ficus benjamina)*

Pests

ANIMALS IN GENERAL

Animal-resistant plants

Something is eating almost everything in our yard. I'm not sure if it's deer or rabbits or something else. Is there anything we can grow that none of these wild animals will eat?

Gardeners often ask about deer- (or rabbit- or squirrel-) proof plants. When you spend precious time and energy in the garden, the last thing you want is to have pests eat your plants so you can't enjoy them. If critters such as deer or rabbits abound in your area, try these suggestions from the Garden Doctor. The plants listed in the chart at right are typically (but not always!) avoided by critters.

BIRDS

Birdseed in lawn

I have a bird feeder hanging in a tree over my lawn. The birds knock some of their food on the ground underneath the feeder, and there's a bald spot in the middle of the lawn because of them. Can I plant grass there? Is there some type of fast-growing plant that I could grow in that shady spot instead?

Before you plant anything, prepare the area by raking the spot to loosen the soil and remove any dead grass. You can plant grass in that spot after you loosen the soil, but nothing will survive very well as long as birdseed litters it. Have you thought about buying a feeder with a pan below it to catch the seed hulls? If your birdseed includes sunflower seeds, they may prevent the grass from growing. Sunflower seed hulls have an allelopathic effect on many plants—they produce a substance that inhibits the growth of other plants.

Most grasses struggle to grow in shade. Compounded with the deluge of birdseed each winter, that means your grass has a limited chance to grow in this shady spot. You could try growing a shade-tolerant ground cover, such as hosta, periwinkle, or lilyturf in the bare spot, but you might end up with the seeds from the bird feeder sprouting around your plants, requiring you to weed the area frequently.

Animal-resistant plants

Anise hyssop (*Agastache foeniculum*) Prized for its violet-blue flowers in late summer, anise hyssop bears anise-scented foliage that pests tend to steer clear of. Native to areas of North America, anise hyssop readily self seeds and offers outstanding heat and drought tolerance. It grows 5 feet tall and 1 foot wide. Zones 4–9.

Barberry (*Berberis thunbergii 'Rose Glow'*) Barberries are dependable shrubs in the garden. This variety offers reddish foliage mottled with pink and white and looks good all season long. It bears small but sharp thorns that deer, rabbits, and other critters don't like. Barberry can be invasive in some areas. This barberry grows about 3 feet tall and 4 feet wide. Zones 4–8.

Daffodil (*Narcissus*) Spring-blooming daffodils rarely fail to put a smile on gardeners' faces. And, unlike tulips and many other bulbs, pests avoid eating daffodil flowers and bulbs, so you'll be able to enjoy these plants each year in your garden. Blooms may be yellow or white and may include splashes of orange or pink. Zones 3–9.

Daylily (*Hemerocallis*) This plant is a garden workhorse—it blooms from early summer to autumn, is heat- and drought-tolerant, and is typically left alone by rabbits and other animals. Plus, you can eat the flowers. This variety of daylily grows 1 foot tall and 2 feet wide. Zones 3–9.

Flowering onion (*Allium giganteum*) When in bloom in early summer, this allium offers the garden a whimsical touch with flowers reminiscent of giant purple lollipops. Alliums are members of the onion family, whose bulbs and foliage bear an odor that deer, rabbits, and squirrels find offensive. Flowering onion grows 5 feet tall and 1 foot wide. Zones 5–9.

Lamb's-ears (*Stachys byzantina*) Wonderful for adding texture to the garden, lamb's-ears bears silvery leaves coated in fine fuzz. There's enough fuzz that pests typically don't eat the leaves; it's like having a mouth full of felt. Lamb's-ears grows 18 inches tall and can spread to several feet across. Zones 4–8.

Russian sage (*Perovskia atriplicifolia*) A staple of late-summer gardens, Russian sage offers silvery foliage and blue flowers in late summer and autumn. Although you may enjoy this plant, deer and rabbits typically don't and leave it alone. It's very heat- and drought-tolerant too. Russian sage grows 4 feet tall and 3 feet wide. Zones 4–9.

Yarrow (*Achillea 'Fire King'*) This tidy yarrow produces clusters of red flowers all summer long; the flowers are excellent for drying and use in crafts. 'Fire King' offers fine-textured foliage with an aroma that pests find annoying. It grows 2 feet tall and wide. Zones 3–9.

Geese on lawn

Our condo has a small pond in the center of the complex. Canada geese have invaded the pond and taken over our lawns. Is there a way to keep them from making a mess of everything?

Canada geese have adapted extremely well to urban and suburban habitats. Throughout most of their range, you'll find them in backyards, on lawns, on golf courses, or in any other landscape with open water nearby. Because they live in flocks, their sheer numbers can cause problems, including damage to landscaping, gardens, and water quality from their droppings.

There is no easy solution to managing geese. Because they can fly long distances, moving them to a different location is usually fruitless. They'll simply fly back to a good habitat. However, there are steps that you can take to reduce run-ins with geese. It's important to act quickly before they become too established, and to be persistent.

Keep all vegetation mowed down around ponds or in nearby open areas. Removing this vegetation eliminates nesting cover. Keep the neighbors from feeding the geese. Once geese associate your condo complex with food, they'll keep coming back for more. Scare tactics can be effective in keeping geese away. Commercially available bird-scare devices include reflective tape and balloons. You can make your own scarecrow, or tie aluminum pie pans to a string. Change the scare devices every couple of days to keep the geese from getting used to them.

Residents with dogs may help. Let the dogs run loose, chasing the geese away. Border collies are especially effective. Check with local wildlife officials for current regulations and special permits for trapping or hunting geese.

Woodpeckers on trees

Woodpeckers are attacking several trees in my yard. What can I do to protect the trees from the birds?

Woodpeckers often drill into trees that are infested with insects. In these cases, the insects are probably causing more damage than the birds. Identify the insect pest (frequently a borer of one species or another) and treat the tree accordingly.

Sometimes, though, woodpeckers attack trees for no apparent reason. Woodpeckers are federally protected birds—so you can't kill them or trap them without a permit. (Contact your state's department of natural resources for information about obtaining permits.) You can deter them, however, by hanging objects in the tree, such as strips of brightly colored plastic, Mylar, or aluminum foil; pie tins or compact discs displayed like mobiles; or inflatable rubber snakes or globes with eye designs painted on them. If your trees are small, placing bird netting around them can exclude the birds, though it won't be pretty.

Holes in tree trunk

Something is drilling holes in a gridlike pattern on the trunks of my trees. Are these borers? Will they kill my tree?

It sounds as though your trees have been found by a yellow-bellied sapsucker (yes, there really is a bird by that name!). The sapsucker is a type of woodpecker that drills holes in precise rows to drink the sap that flows from the wounds. The bird also feeds on insects that are attracted to the sap. If the injury is substantial, an individual branch or even the entire tree can be killed.

You have a couple of options to discourage the sapsucker from drilling more holes. Wrap the affected trunk or branches with burlap. When the bird can no longer access the holes, it may move on to a different tree. Or use sticky repellent such as Tanglefoot or Stik'em Special from a garden center. Apply the repellent to the trunk. When the bird lands on the sticky goo, it finds the perch unpleasant and moves on.

Pamper the affected tree a bit for the next couple of growing seasons. Make sure it suffers no moisture stress; water when weather conditions are dry. If you haven't fertilized the tree recently, it may benefit from a boost of nutrients.

CATS

Keeping cats out of flowers

I have flower beds around my home, as well as a large vegetable garden. I also have four cats that use my gardens as a litter box. I've tried commercial repellents, but none seem to work. Are there any herbs or flowers that may assist in deterring them?

Because commercial repellents haven't worked for you, consider physical barriers, such as mats of flexible plastic spikes or buried plastic forks (tines sticking up). High-tech (and high-priced) cat-deterring methods include high-frequency sound emitters, some of which are triggered by motion sensors.

Finally, if you can't beat 'em, devote an area of your garden to them. In a corner of your garden plant, catnip *(Nepeta cataria)* or catmint *(N. xfaassenii)* and install a sandbox for the kitties. The cats will find the plants irresistible, and they'll prefer to dig in the sandbox rather than the heavier soil in your garden. These distractions may occupy the cats' attention enough to keep them from exploring the rest of the garden.

Scat, cats!

Our new home is on a street that's home to outdoor pet cats. The cats use our mulch as a litter box, they leave dead rodents behind our shrubs, and their screeching awakens us nightly. I've tried cat scat mats, and they work well. Is there anything else we can do to keep cats out of our yard?

Most municipalities now have regulations about cats at large. Research this topic with your local city government or call your animal control officier for information. Chances are that you can legally catch cats at large and haul them off to the shelter. The animal control officier may help you with this.

Otherwise, you could try several cat-scaring methods. Motion-sensor-triggered contraptions that spray water at animal intruders or emit high-frequency sounds can also keep cats at bay. Repellents work well in many situations. Try a liquid formula that you apply with a hose-end sprayer. Or purchase covered repellent holders that you fill with puffed rice impregnated with repellent oil. The covering protects the repellent from the weather, so it lasts longer.

CHIPMUNKS

Bulb-eating chipmunks

How in the world do I get rid of chipmunks in my flower beds? They destroy my bulbs and leave holes behind.

A little chipmunk skipping through a garden is cute, but a chipmunk gang becomes a problem.

The first step to deterring them is to limit their food supply. Chipmunks feed on spilled birdseed beneath feeders, and they steal food from pet food bowls. Although chipmunks love tulips and many other bulbs, they avoid eating daffodils. Plant plenty of those, as well as crocus, which they also leave alone.

The second step is to add fencing. Would your garden look attractive enclosed with a small picket fence? If so, attach ½-inch hardware cloth, which resembles coarse window screening, to the back side of the fence. To keep chipmunks from burrowing into your no-chipmunk zone, bury the hardware cloth 6 inches belowground and extend it 2 feet above the ground. Hardware cloth comes in rolls—cut it with tin snips or wire cutters.

A third step is to move the location of their nests. If chipmunk holes are present in your yard, their nests are quite close, because chipmunks seldom travel more than 50 feet from their burrows. Watch for them early in the morning and late in the afternoon, and see if you can locate their homes. If you discover that they're nesting beneath a woodpile or another source of cover, you may be able to move the cover—and the chipmunks—a good distance away from your garden.

CRAYFISH

Holes in lawn

My backyard borders a creek. The lawn near the creek is developing small mounds of soil with a hole in the middle of each mound. I can't find anything in the holes. What could be causing this? How can I get rid of them?

It sounds as though your yard may have crayfish (or crawdads, as they are sometimes known). Crayfish invade lawns that are constantly wet, whether from a high water table near a body of water, as in your case, or from poor drainage or overwatering. They create holes about an inch in diameter, surrounded by a small mound of muddy soil. These mounds can make it a challenge to mow the wet site.

There's no pesticide labeled for control of crayfish, so changing the environment to discourage them is your best bet. If you suspect that overwatering might be a factor, cut back on your irrigation. Poorly drained areas may be raised to improve drainage. But in your case, you might be better off rethinking what to grow in the wet area. Rather than trying to grow a lawn next to the creek, perhaps you could install a naturalized wetland or bog. Check with your local cooperative extension office for suggestions of native plants that will grow in wet sites. Then even if the crayfish make their mounds, mowing won't be an issue.

DEER

Deer-resistant plants

Deer seem to eat whatever I plant in my yard. I'm getting very discouraged. Are there any plants that they won't eat?

If deer are hungry enough, they'll eat almost anything. However, some plants are less palatable to deer than others. You'll want to avoid tulips, hostas, and roses, which seem to be favorite snacks of deer. Try some of the plants with reported deer resistance listed at right.

Over the winter, deer ate some of our arborvitae shrubs. Should I prune now or wait to see if they come back this spring?

Wait and see how the shrubs look when the new growth emerges. Depending on how much the deer nibbled of the shrubs, they may look fine when the new tips unfold and fill out. If the deer damage is severe, I'd still recommend waiting until the new growth has filled out completely. Many times shrubs bounce back from damage over the course of 2 years. They may look rather unsightly during the first growing season, but if you can stomach the view, it's worth the wait to see how the natural growth compensates for the damage.

DOGS

Spots in lawn from dog
I sodded my yard, but my puppy is burning holes in the lawn when she urinates. I was going to give my puppy a food additive that is supposed to stop the burning effects on the lawn, but I was told the additive can cause bladder infections. I was advised to sprinkle lime on the spots. What's your opinion?

Sadly, there's not much you can do except flush the area thoroughly with water after every urination. This burning is going to happen when you have a dog that can run at will in the backyard. You could create a small, fenced-in corner of the yard where you can place the puppy every time it needs to go. That and walking the dog instead of letting it run in the backyard would help.

Adding lime to the spots would be unhelpful. A common misperception is that the spots occur because dog urine is acidic. In truth, the spots happen because the urine is full of salts—and that's why flushing with water helps; the water dilutes the salts to levels that will not harm your lawn.

Dog-tolerant landscape
I want a nice garden in my backyard, but it's also home to my two dogs. Are there trees and plants I can use that withstand dog traffic?

Let's start with the basics. It's going to be hard to have a perfect-looking landscape with two dogs using the space. How much wear and tear your dogs will impose on the garden depends on their size and activity level as well as how much time they spend outside. In general, with dogs, it's best to use shrubs instead of perennials, mulches instead of grass or ground covers, and raised beds or planters for colorful annual flowers. Those three practices can give your garden a leg up while your dogs enjoy the yard.

Dog-safe weed control
How do I clean up weeds in my yard without poisoning my pups?

How important is it to you to have a weed-free lawn? If you don't mind a few stray dandelions or a patch of clover here or there, you may not need to spray at all for weeds. If you have a typical suburban yard, you may be able to keep weeds to a tolerable level by pulling them out of the lawn and mulching planting beds to prevent weeds from growing around trees, shrubs, and perennials.

A dousing with boiling water kills most weeds. (Use caution; the boiling water kills desirable grass and flowers too.) If you have persistent weeds and would like to use an herbicide, consider spot treatment with the nonselective herbicide glyphosate (Roundup). Glyphosate also kills grass and flowers and can damage trees and shrubs, so use it with caution. Glyphosate does not persist in the soil. Just be sure to keep your dogs out of the sprayed area until the foliage dries. As long as the dogs avoid exposure to the liquid itself, they're safe.

Dogs in flower bed
My dogs use my flower beds as a place to sleep. How can I prevent them from lying on the flowers?

The surest way to protect plantings is to separate them from your pets with a physical barrier, such as a fence. Or you could try using dog-repellent chemicals to deter your dogs. Another option is to keep your dogs in a kennel or in the house when you aren't around to supervise them.

If you're serious about keeping your dogs out of a flower bed, you might mount a motion-sensor-triggered device that sprays water or emits high-frequency sounds. Another option is a buried electric fence that works with a collar that your dog wears. A beeping sound or a small electric shock can train your dogs to keep out of areas delineated by the buried wire.

FROGS

Too many frogs
I have frogs living in my garden all year long. They hide in flowerpots and often jump into the yard. What will make them go away?

Frogs are helpful in the garden because insects are their favorite food, and even tiny tree frogs eat close to 10,000 insects a year. However, their jumping can make you jump, and too many frogs can get in the way. There are a couple of things you can do to limit how many frogs share your home grounds, including eliminating sources of standing water. Because insects attract frogs, turn off outside lights at night when possible, and pull your shades and/or close your curtains at night so fewer insects are attracted to your yard. Of course, you could try to attract predators of frogs to your yard. Snakes and owls will eat frogs if they get a chance.

GOATS

Goat-resistant plants?

I'm having a hard time finding information on plants that goats won't eat. What can I plant near my fence to help camouflage it that won't be eaten by the goats?

I am a firm believer in the statement "goats will eat anything"; I have yet to find a plant that goats will not eat. Goats are browsers—they nibble on a variety of plants throughout the day and will happily chomp on almost anything in their path. Unfortunately, this means they will gladly sample whatever you plant by the fence. You could place the plants far enough away from the fence to keep the goats from reaching the plantings.

Perhaps the best solution to your unsightly fence dilemma is to beautify the enclosure with something the goats won't eat. If you have a metal fence, decorate it with found objects. For example, lend it extra character by hanging old garden implements from it. Another quick way to dress up a dreary fence is to replace the entry gate. Search farm sales and antiques stores for interesting and decorative gates. Once in place, the gate will be the focus of attention and the fence will fade into the background.

LIZARDS

Spooked by lizards

How can I keep lizards out of my flower beds? I am afraid of them and don't like to work in the beds because of them.

Many gardeners want to attract lizards to their gardens because they do a great job of capturing nasty insects, such as large brown roaches and slugs. They may help control Lyme disease, too, because infected ticks that feed on lizards have the bacteria cleared from their systems.

Lizards like your beds because they provide safe cover and plenty of food. They probably like you, too, because as you work in your beds, you disturb the critters they want to eat (lizards hunt by sight, so they need to see insects moving). To see fewer lizards in your beds, remove logs, rock piles, or other structures that provide cover. Also cap open tubes on patio furniture, where lizards love to hide.

MOLES

Mole patrol

We have moles in our garden. We were told that one way to get rid of them is to pour gasoline into their holes and seal them. Is this true? If not, what else can we do?

Serving an eviction notice to moles is not as simple as pouring gasoline into their tunnels. That would pollute the groundwater, and could be dangerous to you. Home remedies purported to control moles abound; none is terribly effective. You'll undoubtedly find someone who tried a remedy that "worked." In all likelihood, the moles simply moved on to better feeding grounds, and there was no connection between the supposed treatment and their disappearance.

Moles dine on grubs and earthworms that live in the soil. Poison baits are ineffective because the moles are not attracted to the grain-based baits. Reduction of grub populations by applying a natural pest control, such as Grub-Away nematodes, may force the moles to move elsewhere. But it may also cause them to dig with renewed energy to find grubs to feed on.

A retired friend who is an outstanding gardener catches moles in his yard by sitting in the yard early in the morning with a pitchfork in hand. When he sees the moles digging their tunnels, he stabs the ground with the fork, skewering the critters. Grisly, but effective! Assuming that you don't have as much time (or perhaps as good aim) as Bob, you can use traps to kill the burrowing creatures. It can be a tricky process, because the traps must be set in an active runway. If the mole fails to trip the trap within a couple of days of your setting it, move it to a different runway. Trapping is the most effective means of ridding your yard of moles.

A proven mole repellent is castor oil, in liquid or dry form. Multiple methods of treatment usually work best in any pest-control situation.

Moles versus voles

I've got something digging in my garden, destroying my perennials. I'm not sure if it's moles or voles. What is the difference?

Moles and voles may be out of sight, but they'll be on your mind when they begin to damage your garden. Before going into battle, learn about these burrowing landscaping menaces.

- Appearance. Moles are dark gray with blue-black or brown tones. They're built for digging, with a long, pointy snout; narrow, slitlike eyes; large padded feet with cupped claws; and a short, virtually hairless tail. Voles are about the color and size of mice but have a shorter tail. Compared with moles, voles have long front-feet claws, clearly open eyes, and a short snout.

- Habits. Moles pass their days and nights digging about underground, whereas voles speed along the earth through established runways in grass, mulch, or ground covers, as well as burrow belowground. Voles gladly take refuge in other creatures' tunnels and are content to excavate nests beneath perennials, eating out a portion of the roots to carve a cozy niche.
- Food sources. Moles are insect eaters, feasting on grubs or worms. Although they're often accused of gobbling bulbs, they aren't the guilty party—it's the voles that gorge on bulbs and perennials, eating them from belowground. Chipmunks and squirrels also eat bulbs, but they dig them up before devouring them. Voles gnaw on the bark and small twigs of shrubs and trees, and will munch on new shoots of perennials.
- Repel them. Castor oil repellents drive out moles and voles without leaving harmful residues. The liquid form, applied using a hose-end sprayer, proves most economical for treating large lawns or flower beds; apply granular timed-release pellets to a smaller area using a broadcast or rotary spreader.
- Eliminate their food source. If numerous grubs are present, consider treating your lawn with insecticide to reduce one part of the moles' food source. As a gardener, you can't eliminate the voles' food source, but you can establish an obstacle course that makes it tough for them to get a free meal. Lining planting holes stops most voles, because they don't tunnel deeply into the soil. Encircle bulbs and perennials with hardware cloth (1/4-inch or smaller mesh) at planting. Keep your lawn mowed to limit voles' aboveground traveling lanes.
- Trap them. To set a snap trap for moles, you must know which tunnel is actually being used; fresh mounds indicate activity. For voles, mouse- or rattraps baited with peanut butter make quick work of a population. Check traps daily and dispose of animals in the garbage.

Grubs and moles

I have moles in my lawn. If I control the grubs in my lawn, will the moles leave?

It's a common misconception that controlling grub populations will get rid of moles. Moles do eat grubs, but the number one food source of moles is earthworms, not white grubs. Moles will eat almost any insect larva they come across while digging through the soil. Rather than assuming that grubs are to blame because you see moles digging in the lawn, check to see how many grubs are present. Unless your lawn has more than 10 grubs per square foot (that's a lot!), chemical treatment for grubs is likely unnecessary.

Trapping is the most reliable way to eliminate moles. Harpoon or choker traps are effective.

PORCUPINES

Porcupines chewing bark

I have a problem with porcupines eating the bark off my maple tree. Can I spray to keep them from climbing the tree and eating the bark?

Nibbling porcupines, rabbits, and rodents can quickly do a number on trees and shrubs. Once they sink their teeth into the area beneath the bark, they damage the tree's pipelines for food and water movement from the roots. Do your trees a favor and take steps—at the first sign of bark damage—to prevent further gnawing.

An effective way to curb animals from assaulting your trees is to wrap the trunks with nylon or plastic tree wrap which you can find at your local garden center. Wrap the trunk tightly from ground level up to 3–4 feet high. The tree wrap's texture will often deter nibblers. Remove the wrap during the growing season to prevent girdling the stem as the trunk expands in diameter, and to remove cover for insects and diseases to enter the trunk. Replace the wrap annually.

Another potentially effective method is to spray the bark with a deer repellent, also available at your local garden center. Made of a combination of substances that taste and/or smell bad, deer repellents deter deer as well as many other animals. One lick of the awful stuff may be enough to send your porcupine packing. Reapply the product as pests return.

RABBITS

Rabbit-resistant plants

Can you suggest some plants that rabbits won't eat? They chew on everything I plant in my yard.

You're wise to start with plants that rabbits prefer not to eat. (If they're hungry enough, they'll eat almost anything.) Although you can use fencing to exclude rabbits from your garden, and you can spray plants with rabbit repellent to discourage them from munching your landscape, you can also take the easy way out and grow trees, shrubs, and flowers that they normally avoid. See the list of rabbit-resistant plants, at right.

429

Rabbit damage to shrubs

Rabbits gnawed on my shrubs this winter. Will my plants be all right?

How well your plants survive rabbit munching depends on what shrubs you're growing and how badly they were eaten. If the shrubs typically send up new shoots from the root system, I wouldn't worry, because the new stems will come up regardless of rabbit damage to existing stems. Remove the damaged stems at ground level, and let the new shoots take over. If, however, your shrubs don't send up new stems, and the rabbits girdled existing stems (ate off the bark all around them), the girdled shoots will die. Cut back the girdled stems to just below the injury. Most deciduous shrubs will send out new growth below the cut. You may want to select one or several of the new sprouts to take over as the main shoot(s) to avoid excessive branching. Evergreens are less likely to sprout from a severe cutback, so avoid pruning them severely unless you have to.

Marauding rabbits

Rabbits are eating my perennials as soon as the plants come up. How can I keep rabbits away?

The best defense against rabbits is a 3-foot-tall chicken-wire fence (1-inch mesh or smaller) with another 6 inches buried in the soil. Or you can try odor repellents such as blood meal or powdered fox urine (available at your local garden center). These usually need to be reapplied frequently. Spray-on taste repellents such as hot pepper spray are also available. It must be put directly on the plants, so rabbits get a good taste of it when they settle in for their snack. It also needs to be reapplied periodically. You can also place a row cover over your beds while the plants are small, removing it once new growth is well under way. Because rabbits prefer tender, young growth, if you keep your flowers covered for a few weeks in spring, then switch to an odor or taste repellent when the covers are removed, the rabbits may lose interest in your garden.

Mothballs to repel rabbits

Can I use mothballs to keep rabbits out of my garden?

Many gardeners seem to think that moth crystals or mothballs must be a "safe" rabbit repellent to use in the garden, because they can use the product in their home. These products are not "natural"; they are toxic pesticides labeled for use only indoors. Their specific purpose is to repel moths, not to deter rabbits or other pests in the garden. Read and follow label directions when using any pesticide. Misuse or improper dosage can lead to problems for the user or for the plants.

SQUIRRELS

Tulip-munching squirrels

Help! I have 30 or 40 tulips planted in my yard. Every time they produce buds, squirrels bite them off. How can I stop them?

To defeat squirrels, your options are repellents, scare tactics, or traps. To protect your tulip buds, use a taste repellent such as hot pepper wax spray. The wax enables it to linger up to a month, despite rainfall. You can purchase a small, handheld pump sprayer, or buy concentrate to dilute and apply it through a hose-end sprayer. You may still lose a few tulip buds, because the squirrels don't smell the hot pepper; they have to taste it for it to be effective. Look for squirrel repellents at local garden centers and pet stores or from mail-order companies.

Another option is to hang something like a shiny, light-reflecting wind sock. Of course it scares squirrels only when the wind is blowing. And they soon become accustomed to the wind sock, so it is a less than reliable control. But with the windsock coupled with the hot pepper spray, you'll have a two-pronged approach to squirrel-proofing your tulips.

Finally, in some areas you may be able to livetrap the persistent visitors and move them to a local park or greenbelt area. Check with your state conservation department about the legality of livetrapping. Your local garden center can help in determining the size trap you'll need.

Gnawing squirrels

The squirrels in my yard chew on everything, from gnawing off maple twigs to chewing up my deck and bird feeders. What can I do?

Squirrels are rodents. Rodents have fast-growing teeth designed to gnaw on hard objects. Gnawing keeps their teeth sharp and wears down their teeth so they don't become too long. When there is a shortage of acorns, other nuts, or tree bark to chew on, squirrels may revert to gnawing on other hard objects such as the siding on your house or your deck or bird feeder. Short of providing dental sharpening and grinding service for the squirrels to keep them placated, it may be difficult to keep them from gnawing on objects you want them to avoid. You may be able to keep them at bay by covering their favored chewing sites with metal flashing or hardware cloth. This may simply force them to begin gnawing elsewhere, however. Check with your local animal control office or fish and wildlife department about the possibility of livetrapping the squirrels to relocate them.

Squirrels gnawing on branch tips in spring is usually a temporary phenomenon. They feed on the expanding buds and lap up the nutrient-rich sap from the wounds they make. Once the tree is fully leafed out, they move on to a different food source.

Squirrels are eating my ginger. They attack before the plants get above ground. Spraying around the roots seems useless. What should I try next?

Because you know that squirrels like your ginger, your only hope is to keep it out of their reach. To do this, build a chicken-wire or hardware-cloth cage (with ½-inch mesh or smaller) around the plants. Squirrels won't think twice about climbing inside to dig for what they want, so cut a piece of mesh to fit over the top of the cage as well.

VOLES

Voracious voles
Last year voles burrowed under my perennials, feasted on the roots, and ate the new growth above the soil. I caught some with mousetraps placed throughout my garden, but it seemed like a futile attempt. Do you have any suggestions for getting rid of them?

Voles are one of those pests that most gardeners don't know about until they have an infestation. The best way to control voles is to use traps. You don't mention what you're using as bait, but peanut butter alone or mixed with oatmeal lures these chewing rodents effectively. Continue to set traps. You'll know when the population is under control when the traps cease snapping.

Dry or liquid castor oil treatments will repel voles. Snakes and owls prey upon voles. Depending on where you garden, you might consider hanging an owl nest box or adding a snake to your garden. Your local extension agent or department of natural resources personnel can advise you regarding owls and snakes that frequent your area. You can protect individual plants or beds by putting up a fence of ¼-inch-mesh hardware cloth buried a foot into the ground (to prevent them from tunneling underneath) and extending a foot above the ground. Keep your garden free of grassy areas and hay or leaf mulch, which provide hiding and breeding places for the voles.

Vole populations peak annually in spring and fall. They also experience population spikes roughly every 4 years. Your garden could have been the site of a local cyclical population explosion, which means that the worst could be behind you.

WOODCHUCKS

Woodchuck removal
How do I stop woodchucks from eating my flowers and plants?

Your best bet for deterring woodchucks, also known as groundhogs, is to make them find a better place to live than your yard. Many states prohibit trapping woodchucks and releasing them into the wild, so consider the following options.

You may be able to irritate them into leaving by placing colorful beach balls in your garden; woodchucks generally dislike the balls' windblown movement. Or stuff rags soaked in ammonia into the entryways of their holes. (The main entryway will have a pile of soil beside it; there should be another entrance about 50 feet away.) The smell should cause them to move on. Another possible odor repellent is fox urine (available at your local garden center). If you encircle your garden with it, woodchucks may sense a predator and seek a safer home.

If you are in search of a permanent solution, fence your garden with chicken wire, which must be buried 12 inches below the ground and extend at least 3 feet above the ground. Leave the top part of the fence unattached to posts so it will bend outward if woodchucks try to climb it. If there are many woodchucks present, add a string of electric fence mounted 4 inches above the ground.

Or grow plants that woodchucks seldom eat. These plants include columbine (*Aquilegia*), daylily (*Hemerocallis*), blanket flower (*Gaillardia ×grandiflora*), cardinal flower (*Lobelia cardinalis*), and marigold (*Tagetes*). Another solution is to get a dog that likes to chase woodchucks.

INSECTS IN GENERAL

Beneficial insects

I know that ladybugs are good for the garden, but are there some others insects that I should be encouraging to come to my yard?

Nature often provides the best pest protection by way of helpful bugs. These bugs canvass perennial beds and vegetable patches, chasing and chomping problem bugs. Here are some good guys you're likely to see in the garden.

Beneficial insects

Assassin bugs. Eating a variety of pests, assassin bugs are light brown-green, ½ to 1 inch long, and have elongated heads and long antennae.

Dragonflies. Overlooked heroes of the garden, fast-flying dragonflies munch on mosquitoes and gnats. Dragonflies appear in a variety of colors and can be up to 6 inches long.

Ground beetles. Prowling the ground for soil-dwelling pests such as slugs and snails, ground beetles are about 1 inch long and iridescent black or brown.

Lacewings. Also known as aphid lions, young lacewings prey on aphids and other insects. Adult lacewings are slender, delicate, ½-inch-long insects with large eyes. They eat pollen.

Ladybugs, or lady beetles. Perhaps the most recognizable beneficial insect, ladybugs (there are several species) devour aphids by the dozen. Learn to recognize ladybug larvae. The yellow-and-black larvae, which to me resemble a tiny alligator, chomp down aphids.

Pirate bugs. Spider mites, caterpillars, and thrips are some of the favorite entrees of the ½-inch-long black-and-silver pirate bug.

Praying mantises. These 3–4-inch-long, winged brownish insects dine at night on a buffet of moths, flies, and mosquitoes.

Soldier beetles. Perennial beds and vegetable gardens are the favorite habitat of ½-inch-long, flat-bodied soldier beetles. Cucumber beetles, aphids, and caterpillars are common prey.

Biological controls

I don't like to use pesticides of any kind in my garden. What kind of natural products could I use to keep bugs at bay?

When deciding on a biological agent to control garden pests, the choices can be confusing. Here's a list of ones you'll commonly find at garden centers and through mail-order catalogs, along with information to help you select the best pest control.

- Predators. You likely already have predators in your garden, but you can buy them too. These are insects, spiders, and mites that eat other insects and mites. You'll find ladybugs, praying mantises, and lacewings sold as garden predators. Because you are releasing live insects into your garden, you can't ensure that they will stay in your yard. Your best bet is to encourage the predator populations that you already have.
- Parasitoids. These insects are somewhat like predators, with a twist. They attack by laying eggs on or inside the pest insect. The unsuspecting pest then becomes food for the developing parasitoid. The good insect hatches out from the shell of the pest, and the cycle continues. Look for these parasitoids: *Encarsia formosa* (a type of wasp) to control whiteflies, *Muscidifurax raptor* to control house and stable flies, *Peristenus digoneutis* to control plant bugs, and *Trichogramma ostriniae* to control European corn borers.
- Pathogens. The most common pathogen you'll find on the shelves is Bt, also known by its full name, *Bacillus thuringiensis*. This is a bacteria that is carried by a nematode (a microscopic worm) into the guts of caterpillars, loopers, and grubs, killing them by melting their gut from the inside out. It is harmless to pets and humans. Bt is usually mixed with water before it is applied to plants. You'll also find pathogens that are insect-specific viruses and fungi.

Row covers for insect control

I sometimes use floating row covers for frost protection in spring and fall, but I've heard they can also be used to protect my plants from bugs. How does that work?

Row covers are an easy way to prevent imminent damage from pests that are after something yummy in your garden. Insects can't get through the covers, and plants beneath them are safe from deer, rabbits, and other animals. Floating row covers come in different weights, or thicknesses. Thin row covers make the best pest barriers, because they retain little heat. Drape the row cover over the plants you want to protect, allowing plenty of growing room, then secure the edges with pins, boards, or soil. Let the row cover float over the tops of plants, or keep it aloft with hoops. Better yet, stud the bed or row with a few upright plants, such as dwarf sunflowers or corn, that do a good job of raising a row cover up over the tops of squash, pumpkins, or young flowers that might be devoured by bugs.

ANTS

Ant invasion

I have trouble with ants on my fruit trees and in my home. Do you have any solutions for killing them all over my yard?

I'm not sure why you want to kill each and every ant in your yard. Ants rarely harm the garden; they are more of a nuisance than anything else. The petite crawlers are probably dining on honeydew left behind by problem-causing aphids on your trees. A strong spray with the hose might dislodge aphids, and thus eliminate the ants' food source.

Another solution is to wrap or coat the tree trunks with a sticky substance that will inhibit ants from scrambling up. There are a couple of products you can use—a sticky tape or a gluey substance that you spread on the bark. Both products are available at garden centers. Raised anthills are prevalent in areas with a large number of ants. Destroy hills by dousing them with several gallons of boiling water.

Ants in the house are another problem altogether. I don't mess around with an indoor ant invasion and commonly use a commercial insecticide such as Raid to eradicate them. Remember that Raid is an indoor product; it's not meant for use in the garden.

Ants in pots

The jasmines on my second-floor balcony are infested with ants. I sprayed around the pots and in the general area. A few months ago I took the plants out of their pots and repotted them. It didn't help. Is there anything else I can do?

You certainly have some persistent ants! Have you tried spraying the jasmines with carbaryl (Sevin) insecticide? It's effective on ants; but as with most sprays, you need to apply it more than once. Check with your local garden center for carbaryl or another product specifically designed to kill ants, then apply the product according to package directions. Keep in mind that the ants may have taken up residence in the soil in the pots. You may need to treat the soil with an insecticide to rid your jasmines of ants. The good news is that the ants are not harming your jasmine plants. They may be "farming" aphids on the jasmines, though. Do you see any sticky honeydew on the foliage? If so, control the aphids with insecticidal soap. Once the aphids are gone, the ants may move on to greener pastures.

Cutting-ant control

How do I get rid of leaf-cutting ants? They are eating all the leaves off my trees and plants. How do I eradicate these voracious creatures before they eradicate my entire garden?

I hear your frustration! Leaf-cutting ants are persistent and difficult landscape pests to control, because they devour many landscape plants. Their sophisticated social system makes them incredibly efficient at gathering food and creating intricate underground colonies that can easily house a million or more ants.

Control of cutting ants needs to be a neighborhood effort. Get your neighbors together and devise an action plan. Begin by identifying the location of colonies, then choose a cutting-ant insecticide. The Texas Extension Service recommends Grant's-Kills Total Ant Killer Bait, available online and through some garden centers. Follow application directions carefully, and be sure to repeat the application as suggested. It's important for your neighborhood to join you in this control effort, or the ants will simply relocate temporarily, then return to your garden as soon as the coast is clear.

Carpenter ants

I have carpenter ants invading a tree in my landscape. How can I get rid of them?

Carpenter ants normally invade only wet or decaying wood. If they're attacking one of your trees, it's likely that the tree has internal rot, which may make the tree a structural hazard.

Get a certified arborist to assess the tree's overall health. If the tree is a hazard, have it cut down. If the tree is still structurally sound, have an exterminator treat it for carpenter ants.

Fire ants

What's the best way to get rid of fire ants?

Fire ants commonly infest lawns and landscapes in the southeastern United States. Their sting can be painful, and their mounds can cause damage to lawn-care equipment. There are several options for managing fire ants. The best one for your situation depends on how many ant colonies you have in your yard, where they are located, how much work you're willing to do, how much you're willing to spend, and how concerned you are about introducing chemicals into the environment.

One method is to broadcast a bait-formulated insecticide once or twice per year. Or use an outdoor bait station formulated for fire-ant control. Several days after applying the bait, treat nuisance ant colonies in high-use areas with an individual mound treatment.

If your yard has few fire ant mounds, you can treat individual mounds. This method gets rid of the ants temporarily, but they may reappear elsewhere in the yard. This option uses the least amount of chemical but is most labor-intensive.

If you want to eliminate all ants in an area, start with broadcast bait. Several days later, apply a contact insecticide, and repeat every 4–8 weeks. This program is the most expensive and uses the greatest amount of pesticide.

To prevent fire ants from entering your home, treat outdoor colonies near the home, and apply an outside barrier of insecticide such as chlorpyrifos or a pyrethroid around the foundation. Caulk cracks and crevices. If you see fire ants indoors, use bait labeled for indoor use. Examples are bait containing abamectin (PT 370-Ascend), hydramethylnon (MaxForce Granular Insect Bait or Amdro), or bait stations containing hydramethylnon (Maxforce, Combat) or sulfluramid (Raid Double Control Ant Baits).

APHIDS

Nonchemical aphid control

My garden is infested with aphids. What is the best remedy to eliminate these pests without using chemicals?

Succulent young shoots are the favorite food of aphids and make them all the more despised by gardeners. Small but mighty, aphids measure just ⅛ inch long and are often green, yellow, or black in color. You can spot them clustered on the undersides of leaves or crawling along stems, where they pierce tissue and suck out valuable sap.

Remove aphids from sturdy plants with a strong spray of water from the garden hose. Spray every other day if necessary. Fragile plants, as well as sturdy plants that are heavily infested, may need a pest-control product such as Safer's insecticidal soap, a nonchemical, soap-based mixture that's formulated for soft-bodied insects such as aphids. Apply the product, which is available at garden centers, weekly for 2–3 weeks.

Viburnum aphids

The leaves on my snowball viburnum are all curled and twisted. What is causing this?

Your snowball viburnum (*Viburnum opulus*) has snowball viburnum aphid (*Neoceruraphis viburnicola*). This gray to dark green aphid feeds in clusters at the tips of the branches, causing leaf curl and twisted, distorted stems. Snowball viburnum is usually the only species affected; other viburnums are immune. The aphids are protected inside the curled leaves, but you may be able to dislodge them with a high-pressure spray from the garden hose. Insecticidal soap and chemical insecticides may be used too. Damage from viburnum aphids is mostly cosmetic. Although they disfigure plants, the overall health of the plant is unaffected.

BEES AND WASPS

Beauty without bees

I have just installed a patio and want to landscape it. What plants will provide fragrance and flowers near the patio but not attract bees?

You're asking a difficult question, because the blooms that most plants produce are as attractive to bees as they are to you.

You can create an equally lovely look without blooms, however. Start with ornamental grasses—many varieties are available. Some remain less than a foot tall and others grow to more than 6 feet. Some also offer attractive foliage in shades of blue and red, or have foliage variegated with bands of silver, white, or yellow.

Add in other plants grown for their foliage interest. Examples include coleus *(Solenostemon scutellarioides)*, caladium *(Caladium),* sweet potato vine *(Ipomoea batatas)*, rex begonia *(Begonia rex)*, lamb's-ears *(Stachys byzantina)*, hosta *(Hosta),* ferns, and Joseph's coat *(Alternanthera)*.

For fragrance, consider herbs that have scented foliage. Pineapple sage *(Salvia elegans)* is one of my favorites. Other excellent choices include common sage *(Salvia officinalis)*, mint *(Mentha)*, rosemary *(Rosmarinus officinalis)*, and lemon verbena *(Aloysia triphylla)*.

Yellow jackets

We have yellow jackets nesting in our lawn. How can I get rid of the unwanted insects?

Yellow jackets are a type of wasp whose populations build up in late summer. They can be a nuisance when you disturb their nest while mowing, or if you're trying to enjoy a bug-free picnic. Throughout most of the summer they are beneficial insects, feeding on caterpillars and flies. But in late summer they switch to a high-carb diet, which is why they're attracted to sugary soda pop.

If the nest is in an out-of-the-way location, your best bet may be simply to avoid the nest. All but the queen will die out over the winter, and she'll take up residence in a different spot next year. If you must destroy the nest, use carbaryl (Sevin) dust. Wait until dusk when all the yellow jackets are back in the nest. Sprinkle some carbaryl into the opening of the nest, and move slowly away. As the yellow jackets enter and exit, they'll track the dust into the nest, eventually killing the adults.

BEETLES

Pine beetle invasion

I am struggling to protect my pine trees from pine beetles, which got into my neighbor's trees. Two of mine look dead, and two more appear infested. How do I prevent the beetles from spreading?

Pine beetles normally feed on weakened or stressed trees, but when populations explode they attack healthy trees too. It takes only one female pine beetle to start an infestation, because once she begins feeding, she emits a pheromone that calls to other beetles. Within weeks, she may be joined by thousands of friends.

Pine beetles are best managed on a community-wide basis, which usually requires the prompt removal of infested trees. Avoid cleaning up trees by trimming them. The scent of pine pitch in the air sometimes attracts more pine beetles. Check with your city forester or state department of forestry about efforts they may have under way to manage pine beetles.

Flea beetles on eggplant

Help! My eggplant leaves have small holes throughout them, as if someone stuck pins through the foliage. What happened, and how do I stop it from happening again?

It sounds as though your eggplant was attacked by flea beetles. Adult flea beetles are small (about 1/10 inch) black insects that have strong back legs, allowing them to jump like fleas or crickets.

To deter the beetles, use floating row covers in spring, right after you plant. Row covers are made from a material that allows light and water to reach your plants but creates a barrier that keeps out insects. Remove the row covers after you see that most flea beetle damage on adjacent plants has stopped and before temperatures get too high in summer.

Simply planting your eggplant outdoors a little later than usual in spring can help too. If you wait to plant until most of the beetles have emerged and fed, you will have less of a problem. Luckily, feeding of flea beetles has little effect on fruiting.

Japanese beetles

I have had problems with grubs and Japanese beetles for the last few years. Most of our neighborhood has used the little bag traps, but this isn't solving the problem. Would milky spore help?

Japanese beetle traps are usually ineffective for controlling the beetles. The pheromone scent in the trap actually attracts more beetles into the area. If you can persuade neighbors a block or two away from your yard to install the traps, you might see fewer in your yard. All the beetles will fly to your neighbors!

For long-term control, milky spore will be helpful, but you may not see results until the following season, because the spores work at killing the grubs that turn into beetles rather than the beetles themselves. Japanese beetle populations can vary dramatically from year to year. It's usually best to use milky spore in combination with other treatments. If your garden has only a few Japanese beetles, kill them with soapy water. Go out early in the morning with a small bucket of soapy water. Hold the bucket under a flower or branch where Japanese beetle adults are resting. Tap the branch; the beetles will drop off into the soapy water, where they'll be killed. If you have a lot of beetles, you can spray with an insecticide such as carbaryl (Sevin) or Malathion.

Japanese beetles on roses

Last year we planted 15 rosebushes surrounding our deck. They have been plagued by beetles. The beetles eat the leaves and flowers, leaving horrible holes in my otherwise beautiful roses. What will work to kill the beetles?

It sounds as though your roses have Japanese beetles. The only quick method of getting rid of them is with a spray designed just for them. Malathion-based sprays work well. Or you could try carbaryl (Sevin).

You could also consider your roses a trap crop for the Japanese beetles. Because roses are one of their favorites, the beetles congregate there. See the response to the previous question for the technique of killing Japanese beetles in soapy water. Other favorite plants of Japanese beetle include hollyhock (*Alcea rosea*), crape myrtle (*Lagerstroemia indica*), crabapple (*Malus*), azalea (*Rhododendron*), raspberry (*Rubus*), linden (*Tilia*), and grape (*Vitis*).

Milky spore for Japanese beetle grubs

Does milky spore work to control Japanese beetles?

Milky spore is a bacterial disease (*Bacillus popilliae*) that can help in controlling Japanese beetle grubs. It is safe to use because it affects only Japanese beetle grubs. It lasts a long time in lawns once it becomes established, but it may take several years for the spores of the bacteria to cover your entire lawn. In the meantime, avoid using chemical insecticides to control the grubs. Grubs must be present for milky spore to spread. And because other types of grubs may be present in your lawn, you may be disappointed with overall grub control.

Grubs in lawn

As a new homeowner, I have a lot to learn about taking care of my lawn. Do I have to treat for grubs every year?

Grubs are the larval stage of beetles. Several types infest lawns. Japanese beetles, June beetles, and masked chafers are some of the more common ones. The grubs cause damage by feeding on the roots of grass. Injury is most apparent in late summer and early fall.

Grub populations vary from year to year. When populations are low, you don't need to apply an insecticide to your lawn. If your lawn has a history of grub problems, consider using imidacloprid (Merit) from early to midsummer, or the molt-accelerating compound halofenozide (MACH2) from early through late summer. Merit needs to be applied before grubs hatch, whereas MACH2 may be applied after they have begun to grow.

Ladybug invasion

Ladybugs are invading my house this fall. What should I do about ridding my house of them?

Multicolored Asian ladybugs invade homes in fall in search of a site for overwintering. They can congregate by the thousands. Like their American cousins, the Asian ladybugs are (generally) beneficial insects. They feed on harmful aphids and other insects. However, their sheer numbers can be a nuisance, and they can inflict a mildly painful bite.

Because these are beneficial insects, avoid destroying them, if you find them outdoors. Vacuum them up and destroy those you find inside. Caulk cracks around doors, windows, vents, and electrical outlets to keep them out of the house.

Lily leaf beetle

I have hard-shelled red bugs on a lot of my lilies. What are they, and how do I get rid of them?

It sounds as though your garden has lily leaf beetles. The beetle was first found in the United States in 1992 and has now spread throughout New England. Lily leaf beetles lay eggs and develop only on various species of lily, including Turk's cap lilies, tiger lilies, Easter lilies, and Asiatic and Oriental lilies. However, they may also feed on fritillaria, Solomon's seal, potato, and flowering tobacco.

Adult beetles are ¼–⅜ inch long. Larvae resemble slugs, with a swollen orange, brown, yellowish, or greenish body and a black head, and cause more damage than adults. Adult beetles overwinter in the soil or plant debris.

If you have only a few lilies in your garden, handpick adults, larvae, and eggs to reduce populations. The natural insecticide neem kills larvae and repels adults. Several chemical insecticides, including carbaryl (Sevin), malathion, and imidacloprid, are effective on adults and larvae.

BORERS

Emerald ash borer

I've heard that there's a new borer affecting ash trees in some parts of the country. Is it true that all the ash trees in those areas are being removed? Should I avoid planting any ash trees?

Emerald ash borer (EAB), an invasive insect native to Asia, was first identified in Michigan in 2002 and has since been observed in other Great Lakes states and Canada. All types of true ash *(Fraxinus)* are susceptible to borer damage. Mountain ash *(Sorbus)* is not. Adults are emerald green beetles; larvae are white borers that tunnel in a serpentine pattern under the bark. Damage to water-conducting tissues can be so severe that the tree dies within 2–3 years.

EAB has the potential to be devastating to ash trees in the landscape and in native forests throughout North America. For now, containment is the primary control strategy of foresters. When an infestation is discovered, all ash trees nearby are destroyed in an attempt to prevent the borers from spreading from tree to tree. Various systemic insecticides are also being tested. Many work well, but none is 100 percent effective. There is no need to apply insecticide to your ash trees if you don't live near an infection zone.

If you're thinking of planting a new shade tree and live in the Great Lakes region, consider planting something other than an ash. Containment may eradicate the emerald ash borer, but if it fails to do so you may be setting yourself up for yearly insecticide treatments to protect your ash tree.

Initial symptoms of EAB are general yellowing and thinning of the foliage. Branches begin to die back. Often you'll see woodpeckers working on the tree, extracting the larvae that live just under the bark. If you look closely, you may see D-shaped exit holes in the bark (where larvae emerged), serpentine tunneling under the bark, or adults and larvae. If you suspect EAB damage, check with your city forestry department or county cooperative extension office to confirm the diagnosis and to find out about the most current control measures.

Iris borer

I have several varieties of iris. The leaves are healthy, but the plants don't bloom, even though they're growing in full sun. I noticed that one rhizome has holes in it and is spongy. What could the problem be?

If your irises have been in the same location for several years, they may be overcrowded and in need of division. Bearded iris usually need to be divided every 3–4 years. Lift and separate plants in late summer.

The spongy rhizome may be a sign of iris borer. This serious pest of bearded iris overwinters as an egg attached to the leaves. The borers hatch in midspring and chew their way down to the rhizome. Once in the rhizome, they continue to feed, hollowing out the insides. Foliage may yellow from injury to the rhizomes. Larvae crawl out of the rhizome in late summer to pupate. Moths hatch in early autumn and lay eggs on iris foliage and nearby garden debris.

To control iris borer, clean up and destroy garden debris around irises in late fall or early spring before eggs hatch. If you find borers in rhizomes, dig up the plants, remove the borers, destroy badly damaged sections, and replant healthy ones. You can also spray affected plants in spring with an insecticide labeled for iris borer.

Squash vine borer

Squash vine borers kill my zucchini plants every year. How can I keep my zucchini plants productive?

Have you tried letting your gardening friends know that you're in need of zucchini? They might welcome another outlet for the excess squash from their gardens!

I understand your frustration. Just as the vines are gearing up to produce, the entire vine collapses and dies. The squash vine borer larva is a grublike caterpillar that gets into plant stems. It feeds inside the stem, causing wilting and death of the plant. This borer also attacks pumpkins and winter squash ('Hubbard' is a favorite of the borer; 'Butternut' is less susceptible than other squashes).

If you have only a couple of vines, you may be able to keep the borer at bay by handpicking adults and eggs. Adults look like black wasps with orange-red markings. They lay dull red eggs on the main stem near the ground, or on the undersides of leaves. You may be able to prevent egg laying by wrapping stems with aluminum foil or old nylon stockings. Or try using floating row covers to exclude the borer adults from plants. If all else fails, apply an insecticide every 7–10 days, starting when the vines begin to run.

CATERPILLARS

Caterpillars on sedum

My sedums are under attack by a creepy little green worm. When it is not curled up on the sedum leaves, it is eating them! What can I do? Is there an organic solution?

Good news—help is on the way for your stressed young plants!

If there are just a few caterpillars, picking them off plants by hand and dropping them into a bucket of soapy water is the best solution. If you don't want to touch the insects (and I understand why), combat caterpillars organically with a product called Bt *(Bacillus thuringiensis)*. This product is a naturally occurring bacterium that disturbs the digestive system of the pest until it dies. You'll need to reapply it after every rain and at least every 7–10 days.

You can get quicker results by using an insecticide such as carbaryl (Sevin). If you spray only the caterpillars, you will limit harming nearby plants. Both products should be available at your local garden center.

Bagworms

My juniper has little brown bags hanging in it. It looks like something is eating the juniper, but I don't see any bugs.

The little brown bags you're seeing in your juniper are the protective cases of bagworms. The worm (larva) inside each bag eats the buds and foliage of the juniper. While it is feeding and growing, it carries its "house" with it. Once it matures, the larva attaches its bag to a branch.

Bagworms have a single generation per year. Eggs hatch in late spring, and new larvae begin to feed immediately. At first the bag is only about ⅛ inch long. If you notice them, this is the best time to control them biologically or chemically. These controls are ineffective on mature bagworms.

If your trees and shrubs have few bagworms, handpicking is an option. Pick them off the plant and squash them. If you notice that your plant has immature bagworms, you can spray it with Bt *(Bacillus thuringiensis)* in late spring or early summer, after all the eggs have hatched. Many chemical insecticides are also labeled for control of bagworm.

White butterflies

Suddenly I'm seeing a lot of white butterflies around my lawn. Are they bad?

White butterflies are not a problem for your lawn as they innocently gather nectar from flowers. Their larvae, however, are major pests of cabbage family crops. Somewhere nearby, the larvae, known as imported cabbage worms, are probably feeding on cabbage, broccoli, cauliflower, Brussels sprouts, kale, collards, or kohlrabi. The larvae are velvety green and up to 1½ inches long. Feeding larvae chew holes in the leaves and heads of these crops, leaving behind telltale green pellets of frass.

You can keep your cabbage worm-free by covering plants with a floating row cover so the adult butterflies can't lay their eggs on the plants. If your cabbage already has some worms blissfully chomping away, use the bacterial insecticide Bt (*Bacillus thuringiensis*). Insecticidal soap or chemical insecticides may also be used to control them.

Gypsy moth

Is there any way to control gypsy moths without spraying toxic chemicals? I don't like to use pesticides, but I don't want to lose my beautiful trees either!

Gypsy moths have been steadily advancing across North America since they were brought to Massachusetts in 1868, in an attempt to introduce a new strain of silkworms. (Young larvae of the gypsy moth produce silken threads that help them get carried on the wind to new trees.) Oak trees are their favorite food, but they eat the leaves of hundreds of species of plants.

Fortunately, there are many nonchemical options to reduce the effects of gypsy moth larvae.

• Start by maintaining your trees and shrubs well. Fertilize and water as necessary to prevent them from becoming stressed. Trees under stress are attacked first by gypsy moth larvae.

• Seek out and destroy gypsy moth egg masses on your property. Female moths like to lay their eggs in protected places, such as under a flap of bark, in a woodpile, under the eaves of your house, and on boats, trailers, or RVs. Egg masses are laid in midsummer; they hatch the following spring.

• Place a sticky band around the trunks of trees to prevent young caterpillars from climbing into the canopy. Use a nonporous material coated with insect-trapping sticky material, available from garden centers and nurseries.

• Wrap a 12–18-inch-wide cloth hiding band around the tree at chest height. Fasten the cloth to the tree with twine, folding the top half of the cloth down over the bottom half. Caterpillars will gather under the cloth. Scrape them off into a bucket of soapy water to kill them.

- Spray young larvae with insecticidal soap. Older caterpillars are less affected by the spray but can be drowned in a bucket of soapy water.
- Spray with Bt *(Bacillus thuringiensis)*. This naturally occurring bacterium paralyzes the digestive system of larvae as they feed. It is quite safe for humans and pets but will affect other caterpillars of moths and butterflies.

Cures for cutworms

My neighbors and I are having problems with cutworms destroying the seedlings in our gardens. How do we get rid of them?

Cutworms are the larvae of night-flying moths. In autumn and early spring, the moths lay their eggs near the base of grasses and weeds. As soon as the soil warms in spring, the eggs hatch and the larvae begin feeding. Most cutworms are brown or grayish caterpillars and are difficult to see because they hide in soil during the day. Cutworm feeding often goes unnoticed in lawns, but it's hard to miss in a garden. Seedlings damaged by cutworms are felled like little trees. When you find the tops of young plants lying next to the stubs, cutworms are the most likely cause.

You might think that cultivating the soil well before planting vegetables would kill the eggs and larvae, but cutworm eggs survive being tossed about by spades and tillers. To prevent cutworms, keep the area free of weeds in autumn and winter. Winter weeds such as chickweed and annual bluegrass often serve as egg-laying sites for the moths. Cutworms often appear in the same sites year after year. New beds created in areas that were previously planted with grass tend to have numerous cutworms. See the Quick Tip, at right, for additional hints to control cutworms.

Protect plants from cutworms

QUICK TIP

- In fall, closely mow lawn areas near your garden to eliminate egg-laying sites. In late winter, pull up cool-season weeds that establish themselves in beds or rows.
- Cultivate the soil before directly seeding vegetables. After planting seeds, dust the soil's surface with diatomaceous earth. You'll need to reapply it after heavy rains.
- Protect transplants from cutworms with collars made from paper towel rolls or milk cartons cut into 3-inch-long pieces, or wrap the base of each seedling with aluminum foil. The collars need to extend ½ inch below the soil surface.
- Make a sticky trap from double-sided masking tape pinned to the soil on both sides of a seeded furrow. If needed, renew the stickiness of the tape by painting it with sticky molasses.
- As soon as seedlings emerge, slip a toothpick or slender wood skewer into the soil alongside each stem. When cutworms try to girdle a stem, the wood will stop them.
- Purchase beneficial nematodes, sold as Grub-Away, which kill cutworms within a few days.

Mimosa webworm or fall webworm?

My thornless honeylocust tree has brown cobwebby masses at the tips of branches. Are these spider mites?

Spider mites create fine webbing on the foliage of plants, including honeylocust *(Gleditsia)*. If the webbing is thick on the branch tips of your honeylocust, it's likely that the trees have mimosa webworm or fall webworm.

Mimosa webworm feeds on branch tips of honeylocust trees beginning in early summer. Adults are moths; larvae are caterpillars that feed on leaves inside webbing they form at branch tips. Additional generations of webworms may develop through late summer.

Fall webworm attacks many species of trees. Some of their preferred species are walnut *(Juglans)*, American elm *(Ulmus americana)*, hickory *(Carya)*, apple *(Malus)*, and maple *(Acer)*. Their nests are large and gray. Nests may appear from midsummer to fall. Try these controls for webworms.

- For either pest, you may be able to physically remove nests on small trees. Prune out affected branch tips. Avoid burning the nests in place; this can cause additional damage to the tree.
- The bacterial insecticide Bt *(Bacillus thuringiensis)* is effective if applied when the larvae are small. Unfortunately, many gardeners don't notice the nests until the caterpillars are nearly mature. By then Bt is no longer effective.
- Spray conventional insecticides when caterpillars are young. Repeat sprays may be needed for succeeding generations.

CICADAS

Protecting plants from cicadas

I just moved into a home in which old shrubs need to be replaced, but I don't want to plant new ones if cicadas are going to eat them up. Will my plants be safe?

There are two types of cicadas. Periodical cicadas have a 13- or 17-year life cycle. They're the ones that get the press because of their enormous numbers in years that they emerge. Dog-day, or annual, cicadas have a 2–5-year life cycle, but broods overlap so that some emerge every year.

For the most part, damage from cicadas is acoustical. Their piercing calls can be a nuisance. However, they can cause damage to plants above and belowground. Adults lay eggs in branch tips. In response to egg laying, twigs split and dry up. Established trees and shrubs can handle the loss of a few branch tips, but young plants can be severely disfigured. Favorite trees for egg laying include maple *(Acer)*, oak *(Quercus)*, hickory *(Carya)*, beech *(Fagus)*, ash *(Fraxinus)*, dogwood *(Cornus)*, hawthorn *(Crataegus)*, magnolia *(Magnolia)*, willow *(Salix)*, apple *(Malus)*, and cherry *(Prunus)*. Host shrubs include rose of Sharon *(Hibiscus syriacus)*, rose *(Rosa)*, raspberry *(Rubus)*, holly *(Ilex)*, spirea *(Spiraea)*, rhododendron *(Rhododendron)*, viburnum *(Viburnum)*, juniper *(Juniperus)*, and arborvitae *(Thuja occidentalis)*. Nymphs also suck sap from roots. Their prolonged feeding may reduce plant growth.

If periodical cicadas are expected to emerge in a given year, it may be best to postpone new landscape plantings until late summer or fall, after the adult cicadas have died. Recently planted trees and shrubs can be protected from egg-laying adults by covering the plants with fine-mesh nylon netting or cheesecloth. Place the netting over the crown of the plant, and tie it tightly to the trunk or main stem. If some cicadas manage to find their way under the netting, prune out damaged twigs within 3 weeks after eggs are laid to prevent nymphs from dropping to the ground and feeding on the roots. You can also spray insecticides to reduce cicada populations. But keep in mind that you may be facing a losing battle. With millions of them in the neighborhood, you may not make much of a dent in overall numbers by spraying in your yard.

EARWIGS

Eradicating earwigs

One of my potted plants has become a haven for earwigs. I sprayed it, but they are still there. I have two cats and have to be careful with insecticides, but I can't stand the bugs. What should I do?

Earwigs love dark, damp places such as flowerpots, and they can become numerous in moist, mulched beds. Earwigs normally scavenge for moss and small insects, but their nighttime dinner parties may involve plants.

Trapping earwigs is usually more effective than spraying. The least messy trap is a section of damp newspaper rolled into a tube, baited with a moistened crust of bread, and secured with a rubber band. Place a few of these around your plants overnight. Earwigs will crawl inside at night. In the morning, gather up the traps and throw them away.

GRASSHOPPERS

Every few years I lose my garden to grasshoppers. An insecticide worked for a while, but before long there were even more grasshoppers than before I sprayed. What can I do to save my garden?

Grasshoppers are one of the most unwelcome guests in my garden. They never seem to get the hint that I loathe their presence, because they return year after year. I have found several effective methods for keeping their visits at a manageable level.

Grasshoppers are easiest to control with an insecticide such as acephate (Orthene) or carbaryl (Sevin) when they are young—measuring about ½ to ¾ inch long. I apply the insecticide in early summer according to package directions. Acephate provides residual control. Consider combining chemical control with the biological control *Nosema locustae*. This is a protozoan disease of grasshoppers. It can be an effective long-term control, but it is not quick acting. You may see some reduction in grasshopper numbers a few days or weeks after application, but in general it takes about a year after applying for it to affect grasshopper populations. *N. locustae* is sold under brand names such as Nolo Bait, Semaspore, and Grasshopper Spore.

Mature grasshoppers are nearly impossible to kill with an insecticide. I rely on native birds and my flock of chickens to help control the population in late summer. A few birdbaths combined with shrubs and small trees provide water and shelter for grasshopper-chomping birds.

At the end of the growing season, rototill your garden to expose grasshopper eggs to killing temperatures during the winter.

LEAF ROLLERS

This summer I found leaf rollers in my garden. How can I organically eradicate these pests and avoid another infestation?

In small numbers, leaf rollers are a minor pest to an otherwise healthy plant. If there are just a couple of the insects in your garden, there's no need to do anything. Leaf rollers can become a threat when they band together and attack a plant in large numbers over two or more growing seasons, however.

Leaf roller damage is most visible in late spring when the young larvae devour the leaves, causing an unsightly skeleton of foliage. In early summer, larvae spin silky webs around young leaves to form a cocoon. Over several weeks the larvae develop into moths that will lay eggs and set the stage for a leaf roller infestation the following year.

Leaf rollers are most vulnerable in late spring before they form their silky cocoons. Spray your plants with Bt *(Bacillus thuringiensis)*—a biological insecticide produced from bacteria. You also can control leaf rollers with a dormant oil spray applied in early spring just before buds open. The oil, available at garden centers, will prevent the eggs from hatching.

MOSQUITOES

Mosquito management

I can't work in the yard without mosquitoes attacking me. I'm worried about West Nile virus. How can I protect myself from these pesky biters?

Bothersome mosquitoes need not take a bite out of your gardening pleasure. Follow these tips for minimizing mosquito troubles.
- Wear light-colored clothing. Light colors keep you cooler, making you less attractive to mosquitoes. Long sleeves and pants add more protection.
- Mow and trim regularly. Overgrown brush and tall weeds are the optimal mosquito habitat. Cut down weeds and brush close to your home and garden.
- Avoid dawn and dusk. Mosquitoes are most active as the sun comes up and just before it goes down.
- Use a mosquito repellent. Many experts recommend a formula that contains DEET, a chemical known to repel mosquitoes.
- Eliminate standing water. Stagnant water is a mosquito breeding ground. Turn watering cans and other vessels upside down when not in use to eliminate pooling water. Change water in birdbaths every 2–3 days.

PLANT BUGS

Four-lined plant bug

Something is attacking my black-eyed Susans, veronicas, and asters. Whatever it is makes spots all over the leaves. Can you tell what it is and how to control it?

Your flowers are being attacked by plant bugs. No, really. Although many gardeners call anything with six legs that crawls around in their garden a bug, there is a specific group of them that are officially known as plant bugs. They have long legs and antennae, and large eyes; the adults hold their wings flat over their bodies. The immature and mature bugs feed on succulent leaf tissue. They pierce the tissue and remove the cell contents, which produces small tan or bleached spots on leaves. Leaves may be distorted, and flowers often drop off plants. A wide variety of flowers may be attacked. Some of their favorites include false sunflower *(Heliopsis helianthoides)*, Shasta daisy *(Leucanthemum ×superbum)*, and chrysanthemum *(Chrysanthemum morifolium)*.

It's important to control plant bugs before they build up to an infestation. Your plants can tolerate a few damaged leaves. (Pick off spotted leaves to improve the plant's appearance). If the problem continues, spray plants with an insecticide. Make sure that your plant is listed on the product label. If migrating plant bugs reinfest the plant, repeat the spray as necessary.

Bubbly flower stems
A bug is attacking my flowers. It leaves an iridescent sappy substance on the flower stems, which at first glance looks like bubbly water droplets. What type of insect is this, and how can I get rid of it?

You described the telltale signs of spittlebug—isn't that an attractive name! These petite insects nest in a mass of protective bubbles. In spring they feed on plants by sucking fluids from leaf and stem tissue, but seldom cause intense damage. If you see only a few of them in your garden, don't worry about controlling them. If you dislike the looks of the frothy foam, blast it off the stem with a forceful spray of water.

A liberal dusting of diatomaceous earth, available at garden centers, can control a large infestation of spittlebugs. Protect perennials, trees, and shrubs with a dormant oil spray, also available at garden centers, in early spring before leaves unfurl. The spray will prevent spittlebug eggs from hatching.

Squash bug battle
How can I get rid of squash bugs? They killed my zucchini, and now I'm afraid they'll kill my pumpkins. I've dusted with an all-purpose insecticide, which doesn't seem to help.

Squash bugs gather, mate, and lay eggs as soon as the weather warms in late spring. Because you grow squash bugs' favorite foods—summer squash and pumpkins—you'll need to plant defensively.

The best thing you can do is to protect your plants with a row cover. Install the cover at planting time, and leave it on until the plants begin to bloom. Once flowers appear, remove the cover so bees and other pollinators can get to the flowers. Squash bugs will move in, but by then your plants will be robust enough that they should produce well despite the insects. Meanwhile, reduce squash bug numbers by handpicking them off your plants and dropping them into a container of soapy water for easy disposal. Examine plants for squash bug eggs (brick red clusters on leaves), and destroy them before they hatch into nymphs.

Squash bugs will feed on the fruits of your plants, so as your plants decline, gather ripe pumpkins and store them indoors. Pull up failing plants a few at a time so any remaining squash bugs are forced to congregate on the plants left behind. As the last plants are pulled, shake them over a wheelbarrow filled with hot, soapy water. This reduces the number of adults that would otherwise spend the winter in your garden, ready to attack again next spring.

SAWFLIES

Pine sawflies

Something is eating the needles off my mugo and Scotch pines this spring. I see something that looks like caterpillars on the needles. What are they?

European pine sawflies attack mugo *(Pinus mugo)*, Scotch *(P. sylvestris)*, red *(P. resinosa)*, and Austrian pine *(P. nigra)* in early spring. The adults look like flies, but the larvae resemble caterpillars. Larvae feed on needles and can strip 1-year-old needles right down to the branch. The grayish-green larvae feed in a group, and freeze into position when disturbed.

Because these are not true caterpillars, Bt *(Bacillus thuringiensis)* will not control them. However, you can handpick them off plants and drop them in soapy water to kill them. Or spray with insecticidal soap, horticultural oil, or an insecticide labeled for use on trees.

SCALES

Euonymus scales

My euonymus has white bumps on the leaves and stems. What are they, and how do I get rid of them?

It sounds as though your euonymus has euonymus scale. Several species of scales attack euonymus. Heavy infestations cause leaf drop and may kill the plant. The insects overwinter as pregnant females. They lay eggs under their waxy white coating when temperatures rise in spring. Eggs soon hatch, and crawlers spread over the plant and begin feeding.

You can spray the plants with dormant oil spray during the winter to kill the overwintering females. Thoroughly wet the stems and undersides of leaves. If the infestation is severe, cut the plants back near ground level in spring, and spray the new growth with an insecticide to kill the crawlers.

I have been battling scales, and I am losing. What can I do to save my plants from this pest?

Scale insects are a difficult problem anywhere, because the bugs are well-defended with their shieldlike backs. They suck juices from plant cells and look innocent—like small raised bumps on plant stems and leaves. Insecticides are effective only when the young larvae (crawlers) are moving about the plants. To monitor crawlers, place pieces of double-sided tape on your plants; check them weekly for the presence of tiny beige dots, or tap infested twigs over a piece of white paper and look for moving specks. When the crawlers are active, spray the plants weekly with any all-purpose insecticide.

Adult scale insects are a more serious challenge. On seriously infested plants, spray monthly with light horticultural oil. In spring and autumn, when temperatures are mild, occasionally use insecticidal soap instead of the oil. Meanwhile, douse the soil around an infested evergreen with a product that contains imidacloprid. The plants take up the chemical through their roots, and the scale insects die as they continue to feed. This chemical is much less toxic than older systemic pesticides, but it should be used only on ornamental plants.

Pine needle scales

My mugo pine has small white flecks on its needles. I can scrape them off with my fingernail. What is this?

If your mugo pine looks as though it has been spattered with white paint, it's likely it has pine needle scale. Adults are difficult to control, but the crawler stage (young, recently hatched scales) is easy to control with insecticidal soap or horticultural oil. Eggs hatch in midspring, about the time that white bridalwreath spirea blooms. Watch for the crawlers, and spray to thoroughly cover needles and stems.

SLUGS

Controlling slugs

What can I do about slugs? These creatures munch on just about everything in my garden. My biggest concern is my vegetables, because the slugs can take down an entire seedling overnight. Is there a remedy?

Slugs are the soft-bodied, slimy, snail-like creatures that feed on plants at night. During the day, they hide from the sun in damp, dark places. You can spot their presence by the trails of slime they leave in their wake and the numerous holes they make in leaves.

To control slugs, grab a flashlight and handpick the creatures from plants at night or just before dawn. Or make a slug trap from a plastic yogurt carton. Bury the carton in soil (without the lid) so its top is level with the soil's surface, and fill it with beer. Place several of these traps around your garden; empty them every few days, and restock them with fresh beer. The slugs are drawn to the beer and fall into the cartons, where they drown. Watering in the morning, rather than at night, also helps to discourage slugs.

Slugs on hostas

We have a lot of hostas, and slugs that just love them. We've tried trapping them with beer in a container, but that hasn't worked for us. Would a band of copper around our hostas help? Can you suggest anything else?

Maybe you need to switch brands of beer! Research at Colorado State University showed differences in slugs' preference for beer. Most gardeners find beer traps effective in snaring slugs. However, if beer bait doesn't work for you, spread crushed eggshells around your hostas. Slugs don't like crawling over the sharp edges of the eggshells. Iron-phosphate-based baits such as Sluggo, Escar-Go!, and Worry Free are harmless to birds and mammals but take care of slugs right away.

Copper can be an effective repellent for slugs. When the slugs crawl across the copper, the moisture in their slime trails sets off an electrical current through the copper. Because slugs don't like to get shocked any more than you or I, they avoid crossing the copper. Of course, if you set up a copper band, and some slugs are already inside it, they won't want to leave either! And a copper band can be expensive for circling an entire garden.

SPIDER MITES

Mites on houseplants

I always get spider mites on my houseplants at this time of year. Is there an effective way to keep these pests away from my houseplants?

Spider mites don't like high humidity but thrive when the air is warm and dry. To prevent them, provide a moister atmosphere for your plants. This might mean giving the plants a shower once or twice a week. To combat the pests, use insecticidal soap or a houseplant insecticide that specifically says it will kill spider mites. Spray the upper and lower surfaces of the leaves, and repeat the spray according to label directions.

Check for spider mites

How can I tell if my spruce has spider mites?

Mites are so tiny that they are difficult to detect with a quick glance. Check susceptible plants in your landscape, such as spruce *(Picea)* and potentilla, by placing a sheet of white paper beneath a branch or stem. Give the branch a sharp tap. If mites are present, you'll see tiny flecks that begin to crawl around on the paper. You may also notice fine webbing on the foliage. By the time webbing has formed, mite populations are high and should be controlled.

Keep mite populations low by dousing plants with a forceful water spray. You can also spray with insecticidal soap or horticultural oil. These products work by coating the mites, so thorough coverage is essential. Several commercial miticides are available at garden centers as well.

TERMITES

Termites or carpenter ants?

I've seen some flying insects in my house that I think might be termites. How can I be sure?

Termites are often confused with carpenter ants. Carpenter ants normally attack only wood that is already decayed, whereas termites can go after structurally sound wood. It pays to know which you're dealing with. Here are the basic differences.

QUICK TIP

Termites	Carpenter Ants
• Straight antennae	• Elbowed antennae
• Broad waist	• Pinched or narrow waist
• Wing pairs of equal size on winged forms	• Front pair of wings larger than back pair
• Workers cream colored	• Workers brownish or black
• No sawdust at nest; may be caked with mud	• Sawdust at entrance to nest

Termites and mulch

Are termites attracted to wood chip mulch? We don't want to use it if it might bring in termites.

Any wood in contact with soil can be attractive to termites. It's unusual for them to infest mulch, but it can happen. Instead, termites are more likely to attack decaying stumps or fallen limbs that contain large pieces of dead wood.

As long as you keep the wood-based mulch a foot or so away from the house's foundation, you should be able to see any mud tunnels that termites would make as they cross the barren zone. Also, bark mulch contains few wood fibers, so it is even less attractive to termites than are wood chips. You might consider using pea gravel or crushed stone next to the foundation, and wood chips in the landscape farther away from the house.

THRIPS

Shriveled glad blooms

My gladioli had a tough summer last year. They came up just fine but never really bloomed. The flowers that opened were brown and dry. I checked for pests but didn't see anything. Any ideas?

Gladiolus is commonly attacked by gladiolus thrips. The minuscule thrips are difficult to see but feed on the shoots and flowers, leaving behind silver-streaked foliage, stunted plants, and flowers that fail to open. The thrips most likely nested in your gladiolus corms and will appear again next year if you don't take action.

Winter is the best time to control gladiolus thrips. Dig the tender gladiolus corms in autumn as usual and store them in an unheated garage or shed where the temperature remains at 35–40°F; thrips will be eliminated in these near-freezing temperatures.

Control thrips during the growing season with an insecticide spray formulated specifically for thrips or with an insecticidal soap. Follow application directions carefully, and be sure to continue treatment as recommended.

WEEVILS

Black vine weevil

Something is eating half-moon notches on the edges of my rhododendron's leaves. What sort of insect would be doing this? Is this something serious?

It sounds as though your rhododendron is being munched by black vine weevils. This blackish-brown insect is about ½ inch long. It feeds on more than a hundred different kinds of garden plants, including its favorites, rhododendron, hemlock (*Tsuga*), and yew (*Taxus*) It chews half-moon notches in the edges of the leaves.

Adult weevils feed at night. They don't fly, but can crawl from plant to plant. Larvae feed on plant roots and occasionally on stems. If stems are girdled, the plant may be killed. This insect is difficult to control because adults are active at night, and larvae develop underground, protected from insecticides. No insecticides are labeled for controlling larvae, but adults may be managed by spraying plants with an insecticide in late spring. You may also be able to reduce larval populations by cutting back on irrigation to keep the soil drier.

WHITEFLIES

Whitefly woes

How do I get rid of whiteflies?

Whiteflies are notorious greenhouse pests, but they can also thrive in the garden and raise havoc. These tiny insects resemble small flies; they suck juices from plant cells. In an open garden, beneficial whitefly predators are free to fly away, so your best strategy in a war against whiteflies is to preserve populations of helpful insects. This means avoiding the use of general-purpose insecticides, because whiteflies are resistant to many pesticides.

Ladybugs and several types of tiny wasps attack whiteflies. Or you can spray horticultural oil or insecticidal soap without worrying about harming the good bugs. Alternate the sprays by applying the oil one week and the soap the following week. Meanwhile, nab some whiteflies by installing yellow or blue sticky traps near severely infested plants. (You can make traps by coating pieces of yellow or blue plastic with honey, or you can purchase traps from your local garden center.)

Whitefly-resistant plants

I am planning to develop a patio container garden at my new home. I'd like to have an emphasis on tropical plants and plants native to my region (coastal Southern California). However, I've had difficulty dealing with whiteflies in the past. Please recommend whitefly-resistant varieties of plants that would be suitable for my plan.

Whiteflies have hundreds of hosts, so naming resistant plant types is difficult. There are several kinds of whiteflies, and the host depends on the type of whitefly. Here are some tips, which in combination will help you keep the tiny pests at bay.

- Select plants that have hairy leaf surfaces, such as lamb's-ears.
- Carefully inspect all plants before bringing them home; most whitefly infestations arrive via infested plants from the nursery. Look for scalelike discs on the undersides of leaves. These are whitefly larvae.
- Remove plants that seem especially attractive to whiteflies, and replace them with something else. African marigold *(Tagetes erecta)* and French marigold *(T. patula),* calendula, nasturtium *(Tropaeolum majus),* and basil *(Ocimum)* are said to be whitefly repellers. These could be mixed into the plantings for some suppression of the population.
- Insecticidal soap can help suppress whiteflies on severely infested plants. However, it won't eliminate them, and it will be necessary to repeat the treatment all season. Yellow or blue sticky traps (the flies are attracted to them and get stuck on them) can help to keep whitefly populations under control.
- You may be able to encourage natural control of whiteflies by purchasing and releaseing the parasitc wasp *Encarsia formosa* or the predaor *Delphastus pusillus* which feeds on sweet potato whitefly and silverleaf whitefly.

Diseases

DISEASES IN GENERAL

Yellow leaves

Some of the plants in my garden are getting yellow leaves. Is this something I should be worried about?

When you see yellow leaves on a plant, you know there's a problem. Unfortunately, this is the upset stomach of gardening—yellow leaves represent any number of conditions, including the following.

- Too much water
- Not enough water
- Too much fertilizer
- Not enough fertilizer
- Exposure to cold temperatures
- Exposure to hot temperatures
- Disease
- Physical damage to the leaves
- Damage to the roots
- Old age of individual leaves

If you see yellow leaves, look at the plant's environment and see if you can detect one of the above problems. Correcting that may easily correct the yellowness. In some cases, such as temperature-related color change, the problem may have already corrected itself. In others, such as aging foliage, you need not do anything, because it's part of the plant's natural cycle of life.

Natural disease control

Do you have an all-natural solution to control a plant fungus? I don't know what fungus it is.

There is rarely a one-size-fits-all solution to plant disease problems. Many diseases are species-specific—meaning that a wilt, spot, or rot on one plant can rarely spread to plants that are not closely related. Also, be sure the problem is a fungus—fungi cause most mildews and blights, but bacteria cause some diseases. Then again, some plant problems that look like diseases are really nutritional disorders. Regardless of the cause, all plant diseases must be treated early to get good results.

As for your desire for an all-natural solution, there are products containing neem oil and neem extracts that often effectively *prevent* outbreaks of fungal diseases such as rose black spot or powdery mildew. Neem oil is derived from a tropical tree; it works as a fungicide and an insecticide. To prevent fungal diseases, spray neem oil on plants at risk every 7–10 days. Remember: It prevents fungus spores from germinating and penetrating plant tissue. It cannot cure diseases that are already established.

ANTHRACNOSE

Dogwood disease

I recently noticed red and brown spots on my young dogwood's foliage. I've been told that it is most likely infected with anthracnose. What is this disease, and how can I control it?

I don't like to be the bearer of bad news, but anthracnose is a serious disease that plagues dogwoods. Dogwoods have been particularly hard hit by the disease in the eastern United States. Symptoms of dogwood anthracnose include deformed flowers and small, circular spots on the leaves. Several other less harmful plant diseases resemble anthracnose, so contact your county extension service for information on how to properly diagnose the problem.

Anthracnose is caused by a fungus that spreads quickly in warm, wet weather. Weakened trees and those suffering from drought, nutrient deficiency, or other diseases are most susceptible. Keep a close eye on seemingly healthy plants in your landscape, watering and feeding them as necessary to prevent plant stress. Although dogwood tolerates shade, it grows best in partial shade; morning sun with afternoon shade is ideal. If yours is growing in a shady site, the foliage may remain wet for long periods after rain or dew, providing conditions favorable for development of the disease. Consider pruning out some surrounding growth to increase airflow and promote drying.

The best control measure for your infected tree is to prune out the diseased twigs. Use a pair of sharp pruners and cut infected twigs several inches below the infected area. Sterilize the pruners in alcohol or dilute bleach between cuts to prevent spreading the disease. Gather and destroy cut twigs and fallen leaves. Fungicide sprays are most effective when applied early in the season, just before buds open.

Sycamore anthracnose

Every spring my sycamore tree drops a lot of its leaves. Why does it do that, and how can I stop it from happening?

Your sycamore tree is suffering from anthracnose. This fungal disease develops during the cool, wet conditions of springtime. The fungus overwinters on branch twigs and infects emerging buds, shoots, and leaves as they expand. Infected leaves develop brown patches along their veins, and drop a couple of weeks later. Infected shoots may develop cankers and dieback. By the time you see leaf drop and twig dieback, the infection period is usually over.

Trees typically develop new leaves by early to midsummer. Reinfection is unlikely as warmer, drier weather conditions arrive. Repeat infections over the years can result in distorted growth from cankers and dieback, but fungicide sprays are seldom necessary. Cut down on the amount of fungus in the area by raking up and destroying fallen leaves. If your tree is small, you could prune out cankered twigs, but that is impractical on a large, established tree.

ASTER YELLOWS

Aster yellows on marigold

Some of my marigolds are looking strange. The flowers stay green and never fully develop into a bloom. The plants are smaller than the others and are beginning to turn yellow. What could be causing this?

It sounds as though your marigolds have become infected with aster yellows. This disease affects numerous ornamentals and vegetables, especially those in the aster family. It is caused by a phytoplasma, a microscopic organism similar to bacteria. Phytoplasmas are spread from plant to plant by leafhoppers. As leafhoppers feed on the plant, they inject phytoplasmas into the plant sap.

Once the plant is infected, there is no cure. Keep the disease under control by roguing infected plants to decrease plant-to-plant spread. Remove nearby weeds, too, because they can harbor the disease. It may help to spray the plants with an insecticide labeled to control leafhoppers.

Plants susceptible to aster yellows

- Aster (Aster)
- Blanket flower (Gaillardia ×grandiflora)
- Broccoli (Brassica oleracea)
- Carnation (Dianthus)
- Cockscomb (Celosia cristata)
- Coreopsis (Coreopsis)
- Delphinium (Delphinium)
- Gladiolus (Gladiolus)
- Lettuce (Lactuca sativa)
- Marigold (Tagetes)
- Petunia (Petunia ×hybrida)
- Phlox (Phlox)
- Purple coneflower (Echinacea purpurea)
- Snapdragon (Antirrhinum majus)
- Tomato (Lycopersicon esculentum)

BOTRYTIS

Gray mold on strawberries

A lot of my strawberries get a fluffy gray mold on them just as they turn ripe. How can I control this fungus?

Your strawberries have gray mold *(Botrytis cinerea)*, also called botrytis blight. As you noted, it is a fungus that acts quickly to rot ripe fruits. If you look closely at your plants, you'll probably see some infected blossoms too. The disease is most common during cool, humid weather. Crowded plantings and rain and splashing water enhance its spread. Blossoms and berries become infected directly when a healthy bloom or berry touches an infected one, the ground, or a dead leaf.

Pick and destroy infected fruit to get the source of new infections out of the patch. Don't leave the rotten fruit in the patch! Mulch plantings with clean straw, pine needles, or other mulch to keep fruits off the ground. Keep proper spacing between plants to promote air movement and drying. If necessary, spray with a protective fungicide that's safe for edibles.

Brown geranium flowers

Some of the flowers in each cluster of blooms on my geraniums always turn brown. The leaves also have brown spots. What should I do to prevent this problem?

It sounds as though your geraniums are infected with botrytis blight, or gray mold. This fungal disease attacks many plants, especially during cool, wet weather. The problem can be severe in an enclosed greenhouse, during cloudy conditions, or when air circulation is poor and humidity is high.

Outdoors, the problem is usually temporary. When the weather warms up and dries out, the problem goes away on its own. You can help prevent the spread of the disease by clipping off and destroying affected flowers and leaves. Give plants wider spacing so they'll have better airflow around them and dry out more quickly. Use drip irrigation, if necessary, to avoid wetting foliage and flowers when watering. If the problem persists, spray with a protective fungicide.

CANKER

Spruce canker

I've been told that my blue spruce tree has cytospora canker. The arborist said there is no cure for this disease. Isn't there something I can do to help the tree?

Your arborist is correct in saying that there is no cure for cytospora canker. This fungal disease *(Cytospora kunzei)* is most likely to attack Norway or Colorado blue spruce under stress—growing on an unfavorable site, stressed from drought, overcrowded, or otherwise in decline. Symptoms of cytospora canker include browning needles on one or more branches. A canker develops on the stem. The canker oozes amber-color pitch that dries to white.

There is no fungicide labeled for the control or prevention of cytospora. Your best bet is to keep the tree in good health. Fertilize the tree if growth is poor. Water during dry periods. Control insect pests that may infest the tree. And avoid injury to the trunk and branches. If the disease gains a foothold, prune out dead and dying branches several inches beyond the cankered area. Disinfect pruning shears between cuts with 70 percent rubbing alcohol or a 10 percent chlorine bleach solution.

CROWN GALL

Crown gall on euonymus

I just noticed several corky swellings on the stems of my euonymus bush. Is this a disease or insect? What should I do for the plant?

Your euonymus bush has crown gall, a plant disease caused by a soil-inhabiting bacterium *(Agrobacterium tumefaciens)*. Many species of plants are susceptible to the bacteria, which can remain in the soil for several years. The bacteria produce a substance that stimulates rapid cell growth in the plant, causing gall formation on the roots, crown, and sometimes branches. Galls are most often found at the soil line (crown) of the plant.

You can't eliminate crown gall from your euonymus, but the plant may survive for many years. Prune out and destroy affected stems below the galls. Disinfect pruning shears after each cut.

If you want to replace the shrub, replant with a resistant species. Among those resistant to crown gall are abelia, andromeda *(Pieris)*, barberry *(Berberis)*, deutzia, holly *(Ilex)*, leucothoe, Oregon grapeholly *(Mahonia aquifolium)*, serviceberry *(Amelanchier)*, and sumac *(Rhus)*.

DAMPING-OFF

Seedlings collapsing

I am starting seeds and have read about damping-off disease. How can I keep my seedlings safe?

You are right to be worried about damping-off disease. Once you've gone to the work of filling flats with potting mix and seeds, it's horrible to wake up one day and find your seedlings dying from this fungus, which causes them to collapse at soil level and fall over. Damping-off fungi live at the soil line, where air meets the soil surface. They tend to attack overwatered seedlings.

There's no effective treatment for damping-off once it occurs—your best bet is to prevent it. Use sterile planting containers (use new ones, or scrub recycled containers with a solution of 1 part chlorine bleach to 9 parts water.) Fill the containers with sterile potting mix, and maintain good air circulation by installing a small fan near seedlings to keep air moving. Avoid excess water. If your plants are already infected, you may be able to save some seedlings if you allow the soil to dry out between waterings.

FIRE BLIGHT

Fire blight on pear

I have a pear tree that has several branches that suddenly turned brown and died back. What would cause this?

It sounds as though your pear tree has fire blight, a bacterial disease that can infect trees during bloom or during the growing season. It's more severe during warm, wet weather. Symptoms include brown or black leaves that cling on the tree. The tips of branches often curl into a shepherd's crook. In severe cases, the entire tree may be killed. In addition to pears, other members of the rose family—apple, crabapple, pyracantha, and cotoneaster—are susceptible.

Control can be difficult. Avoid pruning susceptible trees and shrubs during the growing season. Open wounds provide an entry point for the bacteria. However, if the disease gets started, pruning out affected branches can stop its spread. Prune 8–12 inches below the blackened area. Sterilize your pruning tool between each cut by dipping the cutting mechanism in a solution of 1 part chlorine bleach to 9 parts water. To prevent metal parts from corroding, rinse tools thoroughly with water before putting them away.

Avoid fertilizing your pear tree. It may be getting excess nutrients from lawn fertilizer applied nearby. Succulent growth from high-nitrogen fertilizer is more susceptible to fire blight attack.

LEAF SPOT

Leaf spots on impatiens

My impatiens bloomed beautifully, but the leaves are spotted and turning yellow. What can I do about this?

There are several possible causes for the spotting and yellowing of leaves you have observed on your impatiens.

Tomato spotted wilt virus (TSWV) has become a serious problem on many ornamentals, including impatiens, chrysanthemum, marigold, zinnia, aster, begonia, and petunia. One of the symptoms of the disease is ring spots on the foliage. The virus spreads from plant to plant from feeding by thrips, a type of tiny insect. Once the plant is infected with TSWV, there is no cure, so the plant should be removed to prevent further spread. Remove nearby weeds. Chickweed, dock, clover, lamb's-quarters, pigweed, and bindweed are also susceptible to the virus.

Your impatiens may also be showing symptoms of fungal leaf spot. All plants, impatiens included, are susceptible to fungal diseases when they are stressed. Drought, lack of nutrients, and harsh growing conditions all stress a plant, making the plant less resistant to fungal diseases. Promote healthy impatiens by planting them in an area that receives afternoon shade and by watering and fertilizing the plants regularly. Avoid too much water or fertilizer, though, because this encourages lush, tender growth, which is much more susceptible to disease and insect pests.

Take a sample of the damaged leaves to your cooperative extension office or a garden center to diagnose the cause of the spots. If it is a fungus, you may want to spray your plants with a fungicide, following label directions for application.

Apple scab

Our crabapple gets yellow leaves with black spots, and drops them early in the summer. Is this something I should be spraying for?

The conditions you describe sound like apple scab. This fungal disease is present every year, but some years it is more severe than others. Its development is accelerated by wet weather. The primary infection period is early spring, but if wet weather continues through the summer, additional secondary infections can occur. Defoliation can be severe on susceptible varieties of crabapple.

You can spray susceptible trees with a fungicide to prevent the disease. It will take at least two or three sprays at weekly intervals beginning with bud break in spring. Rather than setting yourself up for yearly spraying, however, consider replacing your susceptible crabapple. Numerous scab-resistant varieties are available at local garden centers.

My roses have yellowed leaves with fuzzy black spots on them. Is this a disease? Do I need to spray something to get rid of it?

Black spot is a common fungal disease on roses, especially hybrid tea roses. The disease usually starts as irregular black spots on leaves. Leaves turn yellow and drop. Repeated defoliation weakens the plants, leading to poor bloom. The fungus overwinters on fallen leaves and in cankers that can develop on canes. Infection occurs throughout the growing season when conditions are warm and humid.

If you grow susceptible rose varieties in areas where black spot is a problem, you'll almost certainly have to spray fungicides to keep the problem under control. However, you can avoid the need to spray by choosing disease-resistant roses and growing them in a favorable location. Plant roses in a sunny area with good air circulation. Avoid wetting the foliage when watering, and remove spotted or yellowing leaves from the plants. In fall, clean up all diseased leaves and remove diseased canes.

Fungicide sprays for black spot are preventive, not curative. That means you need to apply them before the disease develops. Spray a systemic fungicide such as triforine (Funginex) every 7–10 days to prevent black spot from developing. Follow label directions carefully.

MISTLETOE

What is the best way to get rid of mistletoe on my trees?

Mistletoe is a parasitic plant. It develops rootlike structures that spread through the tree branch to which it is attached. If you cut off the mistletoe, it will resprout. However, there will be no mature mistletoe present to develop seeds, which is how mistletoe spreads to new branches. Removing the host branches is a better long-term solution, especially if you can cut the branches off at least 1 foot below where the mistletoe is growing.

Keep in mind that most healthy trees can handle a light load of mistletoe. Mistletoe takes nutrients and moisture from its host tree, but trees often flourish for many decades with a few clumps of mistletoe growing on their branches.

POWDERY MILDEW

Mildew on flowers

Powdery mildew is making my garden miserable. Phlox and asters continue to suffer, even though I cut back every third stalk to allow air to circulate. What can I do?

Powdery mildew is at the top of my list of ugly garden diseases. It can turn a vibrantly hued garden into a dusty white mess in a matter of days. I have found that the best strategy for dealing with this fungal disease that attacks leaves is to squelch it as much as possible, but forget worrying about the small patches that continue to thrive despite eradication efforts.

Full sun and good air circulation are key to avoiding powdery mildew. Continue to thin plants, beginning in late spring. Whenever possible, avoid getting the plants' foliage wet—especially in the afternoon, evening, and nighttime. When selecting plants that are especially susceptible to powdery mildew, such as phlox, zinnias, and roses, look for varieties that are resistant to the disease. For example, David garden phlox is reputed to have excellent resistance to powdery mildew.

You can control a thriving case of powdery mildew with a garden fungicide formulated for the disease. You will find several excellent fungicides at your local garden center. Begin treatment as soon as you see yellow spots form—just before the powdery white spots appear on the leaves.

Mildew in garden

My garden is mildew heaven. The *Pulmonaria*, bee balm, phlox, lilacs, *Eupatorium*, and black-eyed Susan all have it. There must be one plant that's really susceptible and giving it to the rest. Can you tell me which I should take out? Or what should I spray them with to keep this from happening?

Powdery mildew disfigures but rarely kills plants. Some plants, including zinnia, garden phlox, bee balm, and lilac are simply prone to mildew. They don't "give it" to one another, however. Each plant species is prey to its own fungus species. You simply see the same symptom on different plants.

Fungicides can be used as mildew preventatives, but using them is tedious and over time it will be less fruitful as resistant fungi survive and multiply. In addition, that tactic is like smearing soothing creams on a rash rather than working on the underlying cause of the irritation. When mildew is prevalent among species, watering problems and poor air circulation may be the real culprits.

Look at your watering practices and plant combinations. Zinnias and phlox are more prone to mildew if their leaves stay moist for long periods. Bee balm

(*Monarda*) and lungwort (*Pulmonaria*) are more susceptible when grown too dry. Rearrange your garden to group plants by their varying water needs, then irrigate more carefully.

Where air doesn't circulate well, mildew spores have more time to grow and take hold on a leaf. Dead-air spots in a yard may be found near solid fences and thick plant growth. Pruning to thin overgrowth can help, as can replacing solid fencing with airier structures.

You might replace some varieties that you already have with disease-resistant types—throw out Starfire phlox and plant Franz Schubert phlox instead. You can also abandon garden phlox and grow meadow rue (*Thalictrum*) or Culver's root (*Veronicastrum virginicum*) instead. Research plants in garden encyclopedias and on the Internet before you buy, to learn the disease-resistant varieties and species.

Powdery mildew on lawn

Can powdery mildew infect lawns? The shady section of my lawn has a whitish powder on it. What can I do to get rid of it?

Powdery mildew infects many species of plants, including lawn grasses. Although the powdery white substance is similar on various species, it's actually different fungal organisms that cause the disease, so you need not worry about the mildew on your grass spreading to trees, shrubs, and flowers. The fungus that causes powdery mildew on grass, *Erysiphe graminis*, is most severe on Kentucky bluegrass, although Bermudagrass and fescues can get it too. Shaded lawns are most affected.

The disease is more unsightly than damaging. It slows the growth of the grass plant, weakening it and making it more susceptible to other problems. Excessively fertilized lawns are more susceptible to powdery mildew. Fertilize and irrigate only moderately in shaded areas to help prevent the disease. Reduce shade and improve air circulation by pruning surrounding trees and shrubs. If the problem persists, consider overseeding with grasses more tolerant to mildew. An alternative is to replace the grass with a shade-tolerant ground cover.

Air circulation

My garden is behind my garage and, for the most part, has few problems. It gets lots of sun, so I am puzzled as to why the plants in one corner never do well. They turn whitish, almost frosty looking, and die off sooner than the rest of the garden. What's going on?

From what you describe, it sounds as if you have a powdery mildew problem in your garden. I suspect that poor air circulation may be the culprit. In places such as corners of yards where fences meet buildings or in spots where plants are close together, the air circulates poorly, leaving the surfaces moist. When the plants stay damp, there's more of a chance for disease organisms to stake their claim. One way you can tell if this is the problem is to stand in various parts of your garden on a breezy day. Hold a stick with a lightweight piece of material tied to it and watch how the material moves in the wind. I'll guess there's little breeze, even on a windy day, in the part of your garden you describe. If that's the case, you might try planting disease-resistant varieties in that corner.

RUST

Rusty grass

My lawn has an orange cast to it. When I mow, my shoes turn orange! Is this a kind of rust? How do I get rid of it?

It sounds as though your lawn has rust, a type of fungal disease. Rust is most common on perennial ryegrass and susceptible cultivars of Kentucky bluegrass. The disease usually shows up in mid- to late summer when these cool-season turfgrasses are growing under stressful conditions. Stressful growing conditions for turf coupled with preferential weather for rust—warm, humid conditions, followed by hot, sunny weather—lead to infection.

Symptoms on leaf blades include orange pustules full of powdery orange spores. The spores are what turn your shoes orange. Affected patches in the lawn turn yellowish orange.

You shouldn't need to spray your lawn to control rust. Instead, fertilize and water the lawn to provide better growing conditions. Late summer and fall are the best times to fertilize your lawn. Water as needed through the summer to prevent moisture stress. If the rust persists, you can overseed with rust-resistant varieties.

Daylily rust

I've heard about the new daylily rust disease. Will I need to spray my daylilies to control it?

Daylily rust (*Puccinia hemerocallidis*) was first discovered in Florida in 2000 and has rapidly spread north and west from there. Similar to other rust diseases, daylily rust produces bright yellow or orange spots with raised pustules. Eventually leaves turn yellow and dry up. The disease spreads among gardens from gardeners who share plants or from nurseries that fail to realize that their plants are infected. Spores can also spread through the air.

If you suspect that your daylily plants are infected with rust, remove all infected foliage and bury the trimmings. Sterilize tools with 70 percent rubbing alcohol or a 10 percent bleach solution to prevent spread. Wash your hands, gardening gloves, and clothes afterward to prevent spread to the rest of the garden.

There is no specific fungicide labeled for daylily rust. Some daylilies show good resistance to rust. The All-American Daylily Selection Council (www.daylilyresearch.org) tests for rust resistance on the top varieties it recommends.

Cedar-apple rust

My juniper trees have slimy orange balls on them. What are they?

It sounds as though your juniper trees have a fungal disease called cedar-apple rust (*Gymnosporangium*). The orange balls you see are the fruiting body of the fungus. The first year of infection, the fungus forms a brownish-green swelling 1–2 inches in diameter on the juniper branch. The following spring, during warm, rainy weather, the ball sends out jellylike orange projections that produce spores that spread the disease to apple trees.

Cedar-apple rust is not a serious problem on junipers (which are commonly called cedars, although they are not true cedars), although infected twigs may die. The problem is more serious on apple trees, the alternate host for the fungus. The disease can't spread from juniper to juniper or from apple to apple. The disease alternates between the two. One way to break the cycle is to make certain that apples and junipers are planted far apart. (In urban and suburban settings, this may be less practical, because you can't control what your neighbors plant.) Another control is to remove the brownish-green balls from your juniper during their first year, before they develop their orange spore horns.

On apples, the disease shows up as orange spots on leaves and fruit. Again, the tree is not permanently damaged, but the fruit can be seriously disfigured.

SOOTY MOLD

Sooty mold on camellia

My camellia has a black sooty covering on its leaves. What is this? Will it hurt the plant?

Sooty molds can develop on almost any plant. They are caused by fungi that grow in the sticky honeydew left on the foliage by feeding from sap-sucking insects, such as aphids, mealybugs, and scales. Sooty mold is relatively harmless to plants, because the mold derives its nutrition from the honeydew rather than the plant itself. However, the black coating cuts out some light to the leaf, so photosynthesis is reduced. In severe cases, the leaf may yellow from lack of light.

More serious is the insect infestation that caused the honeydew. Aphids may be easily controlled with insecticidal soap or dislodged with a forceful water spray. Mealybugs and scales can be more difficult to manage. Use an insecticide labeled for treatment of these pests to control them.

Remove sooty mold from plants by wiping leaves with a wet rag or washing it off with a forceful spray of water.

VIRUSES

Mosaic virus on tomato

The leaves of my tomato plant are deformed and mottled yellow and green. The fruits that develop are also mottled and misshapen and don't taste very good. Is this something in the soil?

The symptoms you describe are those of mosaic virus. There are two common types that affect tomato: tobacco mosaic virus and cucumber mosaic virus. Tobacco mosaic virus may be present in cigar, pipe, or cigarette tobacco, and smokers may carry the virus on their hands. These viruses are also present in many common weeds, and aphids can spread them from plant to plant.

There is no cure for mosaic viruses. Keep aphid populations under control by spraying with insecticidal soap or other insecticide. If you are a smoker, wash your hands thoroughly after smoking and before working in the garden. Remove weeds in and around the garden. If you notice infected plants, remove and destroy them to prevent spread to healthy ones.

WILT DISEASES

Dutch elm disease

I miss the elm shade trees that used to line the streets years ago. Is Dutch elm disease always going to be with us, or are there some elms that can survive the disease?

Dutch elm disease (DED) is caused by a fungus that invades and plugs the water-conducting tissues of elm trees. It enters the tree through wounds made by the elm bark beetle. The beetles carry the spores of the fungus from tree to tree. The disease can also spread from tree to tree through root grafts. When trees are planted close together, as elms lining streets were, the root systems become intertwined, and plant sap flows from one tree to another through naturally formed grafts.

As water flow to the crown of the tree is cut off, branches die. Foliage wilts, turns yellow or brown, and drops. Eventually the entire tree becomes infected and dies. Quick removal and destruction of infected limbs may prolong the life of the tree. Controlling the bark beetles that spread the disease is not practical.

Plant breeders are working on resistant elm hybrids, so that one day you may again see the graceful forms of elms arching over streets. A few resistant cultivars include Accolade, 'Dynasty', 'Frontier', 'Homestead', 'Patriot', 'Pioneer', 'Sapporo', and 'Urban'. However, it's unlikely that city foresters will again return to the practice of planting entire sections of the city with the same species. Diversity in plant types helps prevent epidemics such as DED.

Bacterial wilt of cucumber

My cucumbers start out fine early in the season, then they wilt and die suddenly. Why?

Your cucumber plants are likely infected with bacterial wilt. The bacteria that causes this disease lives in the gut of cucumber beetles. Striped cucumber beetles (yellowish green with 3 long black stripes down the back) or spotted cucumber beetles (yellowish green with 12 black spots on the back) may spread the disease. Adult beetles are about ¼ inch long. They transmit the disease to the plant through feeding wounds.

The only control for bacterial wilt is to control the beetles. A floating row cover can exclude the beetles, but you'll need to remove the cover for a few hours each day or hand-pollinate flowers to get fruit set. Plant wilt-resistant varieties if possible. You can also spray vines with an insecticide to control beetles.

Oak wilt

My beautiful red oak tree has some dying branches on it, and I'm afraid it might be oak wilt. What does oak wilt look like? If it is oak wilt, what can I do to save the tree?

You're right to be concerned about your red oak tree. Oaks in the red oak and live oak groups (generally those with pointed lobes on leaves) are much more susceptible to oak wilt than species in the white oak group (those with rounded lobes on leaves, including white oak and bur oak). You won't be able to be certain that your red oak has oak wilt, you should have the diagnosis confirmed by a laboratory test. (Check with your state cooperative extension plant diagnostic laboratory or state department of forestry or agriculture about testing services.) However, you should suspect oak wilt if your tree has wilting, bronzing leaves that fall prematurely.

Oak wilt is caused by a fungus that spreads through water-conducting tissues, causing discoloration and plugging. Sap-feeding beetles, pruning tools, or root grafts may spread the fungus from tree to tree. Red oak branches may die quickly; within a few weeks of infection, the entire tree may die. Dieback in white oaks happens at a much slower pace. Prune out dead or damaged branches, taking care to avoid injury to healthy trees. Open wounds during the growing season attract sap beetles that spread the disease. Unless you are pruning out dead or storm-damaged branches, avoid pruning oaks except during the dormant season. If you have more than one red oak, consider severing the roots between the trees to prevent the fungus from moving from one to another.

Keep trees growing vigorously by watering during periods of drought and by fertilizing periodically.

Rhododendron wilt

The leaves on my rhododendron are rolling up and wilting. What could be causing this?

Depending on the time of year, the rolling and wilting of your rhododendron leaves could be caused by cold temperatures or a disease called rhododendron wilt. During the winter, rhododendron leaves often droop and curl in response to cold temperatures. It's their way of protecting themselves from dehydration. If you see drooping and rolling of foliage during the growing season, it's likely that your rhododendron has a wilt disease caused by the soilborne fungus phytophthora. Phytophthora is most often a problem in poorly drained, wet soils (such as by a downspout). Symptoms include stunted growth, leaf yellowing, and drooping leaves. Infected roots are dark and mushy instead of light tan and firm. Plants may be killed by rhododendron wilt.

Fungicide treatment is ineffective. A better solution is to change the growing conditions. Improve soil drainage and aeration if you want to continue growing the plant in the same location. Incorporate compost or other organic matter to loosen heavy soils. Consider installing a raised bed to improve drainage, and transplant your rhododendron into the amended raised bed.

Sudden oak death

I've been hearing a lot lately about sudden oak death. What is it? Does it affect only oaks?

Sudden oak death (SOD) is a relatively new wilt disease caused by the fungus *Phytophthora ramorum*. Tanbark oak *(Lithocarpus densiflorus)*, coast live oak *(Quercus agrifolia),* and California black oak *(Q. kelloggii)* started dying in California's coastal counties in 1995. The cause was not identified until 2000. The disease may be spread through infected wood, soil, and rainwater. However, the most important way in which humans spread the disease is by moving infected plants.

In addition to the hosts mentioned above, susceptible plants include evergreen huckleberry *(Vaccinium ovatum)*, California laurel *(Umbellularia californica)*, madrone *(Arbutus menziesii)*, California buckeye *(Aesculus californica)*, manzanita *(Arctostaphylos manzanita)*, bigleaf maple *(Acer macrophyllum)*, California rhododendron *(Rhododendron macrophyllum)*, toyon *(Heteromeles arbutifolia)*, coast redwood *(Sequoia sempervirens)*, and Douglas fir *(Pseudotsuga menziesii)*. There are a number of cultivated species that are also susceptible, including camellia, viburnum, pieris, and mountain laurel *(Kalmia latifolia)*.

Some hosts develop bark cankers; others develop foliar symptoms. Those that develop bark cankers (mostly oaks) usually die. If disease symptoms develop only on leaves and twigs, death is unlikely. In susceptible oaks and tanbark oaks, the first symptom of the disease is usually a bleeding canker in which thick sap oozes to the bark's surface. Symptoms on foliar hosts include leaf spots and twig cankers. Some shoot dieback may also be seen.

For more information on SOD, visit the California Oak Mortality Task Force's website at www.suddenoakdeath.org.

Verticillium wilt on maple

I've been told my maple is dying of verticillium wilt. I thought verticillium was a problem on tomatoes. What can you tell me about this disease?

Verticillium wilt affects many ornamental trees, shrubs, and flowers as well as fruits and vegetables such as tomatoes. Maple *(Acer)* is one of the susceptible species. The disease is caused by a soilborne fungus that enters the tree roots and spreads up into the branches through the water-conducting vessels. The vessels become discolored and plugged by the fungus. This plugging cuts off the flow of water and nutrients to the branches, causing leaf discoloration and wilting.

Some maples may recover from infection, so avoid rushing to remove wilted branches. They may leaf out again next year. If the branch dies, however, cut it out. No chemical control is available for the disease, but you may be able to help your tree overcome the disease by stimulating new growth with fertilizer and adequate water during dry periods.

If your maple tree dies, avoid planting other susceptible plants in the same location. Several red maple cultivars, including Autumn Flame, October Glory, and Franksred (Red Sunset), are reportedly resistant. Other resistant trees include crabapple *(Malus)*, mountain ash *(Sorbus)*, beech *(Fagus)*, birch *(Betula)*, dogwood *(Cornus)*, sweet gum *(Liquidambar styraciflua)*, hawthorn *(Crataegus)*, holly *(Ilex)*, katsura tree *(Cercidiphyllum japonicum)*, thornless honeylocust *(Gleditsia triacanthos inermis)*, oak *(Quercus)*, pear *(Pyrus)*, and Japanese zelkova *(Zelkova serrata)*.

WEEDS IN GENERAL

Handling herbicides

What kinds of precautions do I need to follow when spraying weed killer around the plants in my garden?

Herbicides are a big help when you're battling invasive plants, but they must be kept from coming into contact with flowers, shrubs, trees, or grasses. Here's how to make an herbicide work for you.

- Protect nearby plants. Spread plastic sheeting over large shrubs, grass, or ground covers. You can use cardboard boxes to cover smaller plants. Or cut the top and bottom from a plastic milk jug, and slip the remaining portion over a problem plant before you spray it with an herbicide. Direct the spray into the milk jug to keep it contained.
- Always wait for warm, still weather with no rain forecast in the next day to spray. When mixing small batches of herbicide from concentrate, make it in a spray bottle and use the spray bottle only for herbicides.
- Spot treat in tight places. For best results, mix a small amount of herbicide or pour the prepared solution into a clean container. Add a few drops of dishwashing liquid to help the mixture adhere to the leaves. Use a small paintbrush or sponge to dab it directly onto the plants you want to kill.

Wildflowers without weeds

I am trying to create a wildflower garden at the edge of my property. The garden is only 3 years old and some areas are well-established. How do I get rid of the weeds that keep coming up without harming the wildflowers?

I have the same problem at my house—a wildflower meadow with weeds that infiltrate. Here are several tactics I use for knocking out weedy invaders. First, I never let the weeds go to seed. If I see weeds flowering, I immediately grab my pruners and cut down the plants. I mow my meadow each fall to prevent any weeds I may have missed from setting seed.

Second, I spray the worst weeds with glyphosate (Roundup) herbicide. Weeds have a tendency to grow in clumps, so I knock out entire batches of thistles, burdock, and nettles at a time. Third, I pull as many weeds as I can to keep plants from developing mature seeds. Following these steps will take some effort, but after two or three seasons you will see a dramatic population decline in weeds.

Shingle minded

Can I use tar paper and old roofing shingles to keep weeds and grass from growing?

Although both products you mention are effective in blocking out light and holding down weed growth, I advise against using these materials, because they can contain chemicals that leach into the ground and adversely affect your plants. Instead, use sheets of newspaper covered with mulch, or landscape fabric. Even black plastic (covered in mulch to make it look more attractive) is a safer alternative.

The war against weeds

I seem to be fighting a losing battle against the weeds in my garden. The season starts out pretty well, but before the summer ends, the weeds have taken over. What can I do to keep the weeds out?

Nature rushes to cover bare soil with persistent, fast-growing plants that we call weeds. Mulch covers open spaces, and discourages weeds. But even with mulch, every garden has weeds. Here are six ways to win the war against them.

Win the war against weeds

1. Weed early and often, and avoid letting weeds bear seeds. If you have trouble telling weeds from flower and veggie seedlings, work with transplants until you become familiar with which ones are the good guys and which are the pests.

2. Pull weeds when the soil is moist. When the soil is dry, use a sharp hoe to slice them off.

3. Avoid growing perennial flowers until spreading perennial weeds such as bindweed and quackgrass are under control. Plant annuals instead.

4. Keep weed seeds from sprouting with preemergence herbicides. These herbicides are most effective in spring.

5. Cover wanted plants with cardboard boxes to protect them from herbicide injury when spraying to control weeds such as poison ivy.

6. Till soil as little as possible, because working the soil pulls weed seeds to the surface. Many weed seeds need light to sprout, so cultivating the soil to get rid of one crop of weeds could encourage another crop.

A bed of weeds

Each spring I discover that my flower beds have sprouted a bed of weeds. If only my flowers were so hardy! What can I do to prevent this?

Keep your bed of flowers from becoming a bed of weeds by topping the garden with a layer of mulch and by weeding it often. Finely shredded organic matter is one of the best mulches for flower beds. Other good choices include shredded pine bark, wood chips, pine straw, and cocoa bean hulls (which smell of cocoa but could poison dogs if they eat the hulls). Spread a 1–3-inch-deep layer of mulch over the bed. Keep it a few inches away from plant stems.

Hand weeding sounds worse than it really is. Dedicate yourself to 10 minutes of weeding two or three times a week. You'll be amazed at the large area you can cover in such a short time. If you control weeds early in the season, you'll have little trouble by midsummer.

BROADLEAF WEEDS

Bindweed

When we moved here a few years ago, a vine with leaves shaped like arrowheads was growing on our chain link fence. Each year it becomes more invasive, wrapping itself around my perennials and spreading through the ground. It's in my neighbor's yard too. Could you help us stop this monster?

You are not the first gardener to be tricked into tolerating bindweed (*Convolvulus arvensis*) by its handsome arrowhead-shape leaves and trumpet-shape blooms. In the 1920s, it became one of California's most persistent weeds after gardeners grew it as an ornamental. Bindweed has been the bane of Midwest gardeners since the 1800s, when it hitched a ride into the region with some wheat seed. As you have noticed, bindweed uses spreading roots to expand its territory. Some roots can grow to 30 feet long. Many of the kinks and elbows of bindweed roots have ready-to-grow buds. Even a small piece of root left in the ground can sprout into a new plant.

To get rid of bindweed, allow the plants to grow about 6 inches high, then cut them down. Repeat through the entire growing season. This procedure forces the plants to exhaust the food reserves they hold in their roots. Late in summer, treat surviving bindweed with an herbicide. The battle will not be over, however. Bindweed also grows from seeds, which can remain viable for 50 years. Consistent weeding and the generous use of mulches are the only ways to achieve good long-term control. It will help immensely if your neighbor joins in the control effort too.

Brush removal

How do I get rid of the briars and weedy shrubs that keep popping up all over my 1-acre property? I look forward to starting a garden.

You are smart to try to overcome the weeds before starting your garden. Gardeners often become so excited to get growing that they neglect to properly prepare the planting area. The briars and rogue shrubs are sure to cause headaches in the future unless you deal with them now.

You have two excellent options for gaining the upper hand in this weedy battle. Get quick results by using an herbicide such as a bruch killer, available at local garden centers. Following application directions carefully, apply a small amount of the herbicide to the brush foliage. The herbicide will travel through the plant to the roots, killing the shrub in 3–4 weeks. Or if there are relatively few of the plants where you want to place your garden, cut off the briars and shrubs at ground level, then apply the herbicide to the stumps, particularly the open wounds.

Landscape fabric also is handy for choking out weeds, because it prevents weed seeds that are already in the ground from getting the light they need to germinate. Cut the weeds at ground level, then cover your intended garden area with the tightly woven fabric, available at garden centers. Cover the fabric with 4–5 inches of mulch to hide it and to keep the soil cool. Then you can cut holes in the fabric and begin planting.

Mischievous mint

I want to know how I can get rid of peppermint. It keeps coming back year after year and spreading over my entire garden. I fear that it's strangling some of my plants. Is there a way to control it without killing nearby plants?

Growing mint can be a double-edged sword. Because peppermint *(Mentha ×piperata)* is such a useful herb in the kitchen, first dig up a small patch and plant it in a roomy container. Like other mints, peppermint is happy to grow in confined quarters. Also like other mints, peppermint spreads rapidly by sending out shallow rhizomes, which eagerly take over space where you want to grow other plants.

To get it under control, dig out the plant material and dispose of it in the garbage. Sift through the soil with a digging fork to make sure you get out all the little pieces. Watch the area carefully for several months, and dig out any plants that pop up. Should bits of mint appear close to other plants you want to keep, clip off the tops and cover the roots with a flat stone, a board, or several layers of newspaper. Smothering peppermint plants weakens them, making them easier to pull up when the light-blocking covers are removed several weeks later. Keep up your control efforts for the rest of the season.

Should more peppermint plants appear in spring (which they probably will), you can dig them out, smother them, or treat them with a glyphosate herbicide such as Roundup. Be careful with this or any other herbicide, because it can damage or kill a huge range of plants. When using herbicides to control mint or other weedy plants that grow near more desirable species, cover nearby cultivated plants to protect them from spray drift. Or use an old paintbrush to apply the herbicide directly to the plants you want to eliminate.

Thistle solutions

I just moved to a new home, and about half an acre of my yard is covered with thistles. Last year they were more than 4 feet tall and full of prickles. I regularly mow them, but they seem to be spreading rapidly. What can I do?

I deal with thistles in my pastures every summer and have a fairly successful campaign going. Like you, I mow frequently to keep them small and to prevent them from setting seed. Stopping seed formation is very important; a single seed head can populate an entire lawn. I follow each mowing by spraying individual plants with an herbicide called Hi-Dep, available at farm supply stores. Herbicide is not required to eradicate thistles, but it will speed the process.

Some people dig up thistles. This rarely works because any small piece of the root that is left in the ground will send up a new shoot. Regular mowing is easier and more effective than the backbreaking work of digging up the tap-rooted growers. Alternatively, cut the thistle at ground level with a sharp knife. If you do this consistently (every few weeks), the thistle roots will be exhausted and cease to sprout new shoots.

Vinca out of control

A friend gave me a small piece of periwinkle vine and it has taken over the garden! How do I get rid of it? My husband mowed over it, but it is growing back.

Periwinkle, also called vinca (*Vinca minor*), is handy in some landscapes, but as you found out it can be a bear to get rid of. It's a good replacement for grass in dense shade. It also does a great job of creeping along a slope and holding soil in place.

The most effective method to rid your yard of vinca is to spray emerging sprigs with glyphosate (Roundup) herbicide, available at garden centers. Be sure to follow label directions. Also keep in mind that glyphosate will kill other plants it comes into contact with.

GRASSY WEEDS

Crabgrass

Crabgrass has invaded one of my flower beds. It looks terrible. Should I start from scratch by removing the existing plants, or can I get rid of the crabgrass with a weed killer?

The first step you should take is to confirm that the grass growing in your flower beds is crabgrass. Grasses can be tricky to identify, so consult an expert at a garden center, nursery, or cooperative extension office if you aren't certain. It's important to know whether the grass in your flower beds is a perennial or an annual.

If it is crabgrass, the plants growing now will die when freezing temperatures arrive. However, it's still a good idea to remove the plants, because they'll set seed and come back even stronger as new plants next year. To keep crabgrass from being a problem next year, treat the beds with a preemergence herbicide (ask for it at your local garden center). Preemergence herbicides work by keeping seeds from sprouting. If you use the product in spring before the crabgrass sprouts, you won't have much of a problem. Subsequently, occasional weeding should keep the beds clean. Also, mulch the beds with shredded bark, wood chips, or pine needles. Crabgrass sprouts best in bare soil. By covering the soil with mulch, you'll prevent many seeds from germinating.

Creeping grass in lawn

Our beautiful bluegrass-sodded lawn is being taken over by a trailing grass, perhaps zoysiagrass. Is there any way to eliminate it without destroying the good turf?

If you have a weedy, creeping grass in your bluegrass lawn, you have no good options. It really doesn't matter whether the weedy grass is zoysiagrass, Bermudagrass, creeping bentgrass, or some similar rogue grass. The only way to truly get rid of the zoysiagrass (or whatever it is) is to kill the entire infested patch with glyphosate (Roundup), then reseed or resod the affected area. Treat only the undesirable grass; glyphosate kills bluegrass too. But it leaves no residue in the soil, so you can replant quickly after the weedy grass dies.

Corralling fountain grass

I have two beautiful mounds of fountain grass that reseed prolifically. Every spring I have hundreds of new little fountain grass seedlings emerging in my gardens and lawn. Is the only solution destroying the plants?

Luckily, there's no need to destroy your lovely plants. But you do need to destroy the seed. Grab your favorite pair of pruners and give your fountain grass a haircut soon after the flowering plumes emerge in late summer. By removing the flowers, you are removing the seeds and eliminating the chance of seedlings next spring.

Also, dwarf fountain grass cultivars are reputed to be less invasive than full-size selections. Look for 12-inch-tall 'Little Bunny', for example.

Nutgrass

Is it possible to get rid of nutgrass growing in my lawn?

Nutgrass, also known as nutsedge, has grassy foliage but is not a true grass. The plant grows from small, nutlike tubers in the soil. If you're persistent, pulling out all new shoots that you see every couple of weeks, you may be able to get rid of a small patch of nutsedge in your lawn by hand-pulling. There are also a couple of herbicide options. One is a chemical called bentazon (Basagran). It's available from garden centers that carry lawn chemicals. Also, you can get products with the chemical MSMA in them. Look for products with "nutgrass killer" in their name.

One last note: Often (not always), nutgrass becomes a problem because of poor drainage. Check to see whether the nutgrass is growing in a wet area. If it is, you may be able to discourage it by improving the drainage and drying out the site.

Wiregrass

Is there any way to get rid of wiregrass? We seem to have an abundance of it in our flower beds, and no matter how many times I weed, it continues to come back. I've gone down almost a foot into the ground, and still find roots. I would appreciate any help you could give me.

Wiregrass is another name for Bermudagrass *(Cynodon dactylon)*. Because it is a perennial grass, it will return again next year. As you've discovered, it's persistent. It can spread rapidly as its rhizomes creep along underground. Because digging apparently is ineffective for you, you're left with chemical control. Glyphosate (Roundup) works, but because it kills whatever it comes in contact with, it may be risky to use in a bed where ornamentals are growing. Obviously, you shouldn't use it if there's any risk of spraying your desirable plants. You could apply Roundup with a paintbrush so you touch only the grass and not your flowers. Be patient; it might be several weeks before Roundup takes effect. A second or third application often is needed to kill wiregrass. Give the area where you are going to apply it a good watering a couple of days before you apply the herbicide. This will help actively growing weeds to absorb the herbicide quickly.

Another option is the herbicide fluazifop, which is sold in garden centers as "selective grass killer" or "grassy weed control." It selectively kills grasses but leaves most ornamentals alone. You'll see a long list of plants that are and aren't harmed by it on the product's label, so be sure to read it carefully and follow all directions. It's available in ready-to-use spray bottles.

INVASIVE PLANTS

Is it invasive?

I don't want to plant anything in my yard that will become invasive. How can I find out if a plant I want to grow might become invasive?

Plants that spread where they're unwanted are called invasive. Many of these are imported (also called nonnative or exotic) species that become wildly successful when given a chance to grow in the absence of the natural predators or limiting environmental conditions that were present in their homeland. This is the case with bindweed. Other nonnative species become invasive by producing huge crops of berries (Oriental bittersweet, autumn olive, and privet, to name a few), or by growing with nearly supernatural energy, as do kudzu and Japanese honeysuckle. Sometimes even native plants can become invasive when given a boost by the comforts of cultivation. This often happens with brambles, wild vines such as trumpet vine, and even some ferns.

Whenever a plant seems to like your yard a little too well, begin to control it early, before its high spirits become a headache. Better yet, check a plant's invasive reputation before adding it to your landscape. One of the best websites for this information is www.invasive.org, where you can search for invasive plants by their name or the state where they are a problem. Some plants that are well-behaved in certain regions may be problematic in others.

Crown vetch

I wonder what to do about crown vetch, which is a real problem in my yard.

Crown vetch *(Coronilla varia)* is often used as a ground cover on steep roadside banks to hold soil in place and cut down on erosion. Although it may serve a good purpose along a roadside where it can be mowed to keep it in bounds, in a backyard it can become invasive. I'd spray it with glyphosate (Roundup) if possible. It may take repeat applications to kill the extensive taproot of this legume. Otherwise, keep pulling it. I planted one plant 10 years ago and am still finding stragglers trying to survive in my garden.

Garlic mustard

I have garlic mustard everywhere on my property. How can I control it?

Garlic mustard *(Alliaria petiolata)* is an invasive weed throughout much of the Midwest and Northeast. It forms large patches that overtake native plants. Garlic mustard grows best in shady, cultivated sites, but it can become a problem in any woodland area.

Garlic mustard germinates in spring and forms a rosette of leaves that survives the winter. The plant flowers the following spring, with clusters of four-petal white flowers in midspring to early summer. Leaves on flowering stalks are heart-shape and toothed. Crushed leaves smell like garlic.

Cut off flowering stalks before they go to seed to prevent the plant from spreading seed and to break its biennial life cycle. Remove the cut stems from the site, because cut stalks sometimes mature their developing seeds. After several years of cutting, you should have your patch of garlic mustard under control. Of course, you'll need the cooperation of neighbors, too, if garlic mustard is growing on their properties.

You can also spray garlic mustard with a nonselective herbicide, such as glyphosate (Roundup). Spray in late fall or early spring when other woodland plants are dormant but garlic mustard is actively growing.

Purple loosestrife

I have a tall plant that's come up in my garden. It's now blooming with purple flowers on a branched top. I fear that it may be purple loosestrife, which I have heard can take over a garden. Please let me know what I should do about this plant.

The first step is to identify the plant. Purple loosestrife *(Lythrum salicaria)* and several related species look much alike, and all are quite invasive. Some good photographs are posted on The Nature Conservancy Invasive Species Initiative website at http://tncweeds.ucdavis.edu/esadocs/lythsali.html.

484

Introduced from Europe in the early 1800s, purple loosestrife is now the target of 21 states struggling to keep it out of natural wetlands, where it often forms dense colonies and chokes out native plants. All of the states in the upper Midwest restrict the use of purple loosestrife in gardens, because just one healthy plant can produce 2.5 million seeds.

If you identify your plant as purple loosestrife, dig it out and destroy it. In addition to a stout taproot, expect to find a network of shallow roots spreading from the primary plant. If the plant in your garden is holding seeds, place a paper or plastic bag completely over the seed-bearing spikes and clip them off before you begin digging, to prevent accidentally spreading seeds.

POISONOUS PLANTS

Poisonous landscape plants

I have small children and two dogs. I don't want any poisonous plants in my yard. Can you tell me which ones I should avoid?

Unless you grow a landscape exclusively filled with edible plants, it may be impossible to avoid every toxic plant. Many species have very low levels of toxins that help protect the plant from marauding insects and critters. That said, some are much more toxic than others. It might be worth your while to research the degree and type of toxicity possible with plants you're considering for your yard. And it would be a good idea to teach your children (and pets) not to eat plants in the yard.

See the list of common poisonous landscape plants, at right.

Poisonous landscape plants

QUICK TIP

- Azalea *(Rhododenron)*
- Bleeding heart *(Dicentra)*
- Black locust
  (Robinia pseudoacacia)
- Castor bean
  (Ricinus communis)
- Cherry *(Prunus)*
- Daphne *(Daphne)*
- Elderberry
  (Sambucus canadensis)
- Foxglove *(Digitalis purpurea)*
- Jimsonweed *(Datura)*
- Lantana *(Lantana camara)*
- Larkspur *(Delphinium)*
- Lily-of-the-valley
  (Convallaria majalis)
- Monkshood *(Aconitum)*
- Oleander *(Nerium oleander)*
- Wisteria *(Wisteria)*
- Yew *(Taxus cuspidata)*

Nasty nettle

Last year I spent a day in one of my flower beds. A couple of days later I was covered in a horrible rash. A friend said I have a stand of nettle in my backyard. Can you tell more about nettle? If that is what I got into, I want to be sure to stay away from it in the future.

Run-ins with stinging nettle (*Urtica dioica*) are often itchy, painful experiences thanks to the tiny razor-sharp hooks on the undersides of the plant's leaves. Simply brushing against the plant will cause an itchy rash. Sensitivity to this weed varies from person to person; it sounds as though you're particularly sensitive to it. Stinging nettle is a common roadside weed that grows 3–4 feet tall and has egg-shape light green leaves.

A patch of stinging nettle need not prevent you from gardening in your backyard. You can eradicate it with a few simple steps. Mow large stands. Spray remnants of the plants with an herbicide formulated for nettle and other perennial weeds. Follow application instructions on the product label.

Poison ivy control

Poison ivy is growing on my trees and in my shrub border. What's the best way to get rid of it?

Poison ivy (*Toxicodendron radicans*) can be identified by its compound leaf consisting of three leaflets. "Leaves of three; let it be." The leaflets are 2–4 inches long with pointed tips. The plant grows as a shrub or as a woody vine. In late summer, the plant may produce waxy grayish-white berries. In fall, leaves turn red or orange.

You can get rid of poison ivy by hand-pulling (wear gloves, a long-sleeve shirt, and pants to prevent skin contact) or digging out the roots. Make certain you get the entire root, or it will resprout. If you're particularly sensitive to poison ivy, avoid this method, because urushiol, the chemical that causes skin irritation, is present in all parts of the plant. Vines growing on trees can be difficult to pull out. Cut the vine at its base and carefully remove it from the tree. Apply glyphosate (Roundup) or triclopyr (Ortho's Brush-B-Gon Poison Ivy, Poison Oak, & Brush Killer) to new shoots that emerge from the base of the old plant. Repeat applications of herbicide are usually necessary for complete control. If poison ivy is growing among desirable plants, paint individual leaflets with glyphosate to avoid damage to your landscape plants.

If you come in contact with poison ivy, wash with soap and cool water immediately. Avoid burning the poison ivy vines you remove. The smoke contains urushiol. Breathing the smoke or coming in contact with tainted clothing can cause a rash. Many nonprescription poison ivy relief products are available at drugstores, but you don't want to have to use them if you can avoid it.

Garden Basics

COMPOST

I'd like to practice composting but don't know much about it. How do I get started?

Compost truly is a gardener's best friend. It adds nutrients to the soil at a slow pace, improves the texture of sandy or clay soils, and makes an ideal mulch. It's easy to see why it's often called "black gold."

Compost is a mix of high-carbon and high-nitrogen materials combined proportionately with soil, air, and moisture. Carbon-rich materials include straw, hay, leaves, sawdust, shredded newspaper, and pine needles. Nitrogen-rich materials are generally succulent green plant parts, such as grass clippings, weeds, perennial flower prunings, and vegetables. If you lack enough of the high-nitrogen materials from your garden, you may need to add animal manure, blood meal, or cottonseed meal. Kitchen scraps, such as eggshells (rinse them first), vegetables and fruits, and coffee grounds, can also be added. Avoid adding meat scraps, bones, or grease, which attract rodents and other pests.

There is a debate about adding diseased plants, or weeds with seed heads, to compost. Some experts think that the heat of a properly working compost pile will kill the diseases and seeds. Others doubt it's worth the risk. To be safe, avoid using such materials in your compost pile.

Most gardeners build or purchase some type of bin to hold compost, but you can compost by simply piling the debris. Whatever method you use, be sure the pile is sited close enough to your garden that it is easy to bring material to the pile and haul finished compost away. It's also convenient to have a water source nearby so you can add water during dry spells.

Build your compost pile as materials become available, layering them alternately with soil. Avoid adding too much nitrogen to the pile; it could start to rot and smell bad instead of properly decomposing. Add a sprinkling of topsoil or finished compost to a new compost pile to introduce the helpful microorganisms that work to make compost.

You'll need to do a little regular maintenance. Add water as needed to keep the pile moist but not soggy. Turn your compost to get air into the pile. If you don't turn your pile, you'll still get compost; it will just take longer.

Quick compost

I have had a large compost bin for two years. I have layered brown and green items and watered the pile during the summer. The pile is composting, but slowly. How can I speed up the process?

Regular maintenance helps your compost pile work quicker. Add thin layers of topsoil or finished compost to your pile to introduce microorganisms that create compost. Water enough to keep it moist but not soggy. Turn your compost regularly—once a week if possible—to keep it aerated. If that doesn't produce compost as quickly as you desire, turn the pile more often, add more nitrogen-rich (green) materials, and shred or chop the carbon-rich (brown) materials before adding them to the pile. You'll know your compost is ready for the garden when it is dark and crumbly and most of the plant parts are decomposed.

Compost in sun or shade?

I've been advised to locate my compost pile in a shady area, with a little pit in the middle. I understand the reason for the pit—to catch rainfall—but I have always assumed a compost pile should be located in a sunny area. What do you recommend?

You're right. Compost piles usually work best if they are located in sunny spots. (They warm up faster and stay warmer than shaded ones.) However, if you live in a dry climate or are unlikely to water your pile during dry periods, it's a good idea to locate your pile in at least partial shade to keep it from drying out too quickly or too much. Dry compost piles will compost slowly or not at all. You can cover the compost bin with shade cloth or landscaping fabric to prevent moisture loss. Gardeners who live in moist climates have less concern with the compost drying out.

Another thing to consider when locating your compost pile is its proximity to your garden and other parts of your landscape. The closer it is to your garden, the less distance you have to cover when hauling waste to it and finished compost away from it. Because a compost pile is a less attractive feature of a landscape, place it out of sight. You could use attractive materials such as lattice to hide your compost pile.

Adding compost to perennials

When should I add compost to my perennial garden?

The best time to add compost to a perennial garden is before you plant anything in the garden. This allows you to work the compost into the soil where it does some good. You can also add compost when you divide or transplant your perennials. Work some into each planting hole. You can spread a thin layer of compost over the entire garden in late fall.

Compost bin plans

I am interested in different styles of compost bins that are easy to construct. I want to make one and need some designs to choose from. What would you suggest?

You can make a compost bin from just about anything. One consideration, though, is how important it is for your compost bin to look attractive. If it's tucked away in the back corner of your yard, appearance may be a low priority. If it's in full view of the deck, you may want to spend a little more cash to build a state-of-the-art bin. Here are some suggestions.

- Wrap snow fence around a square of metal stakes for a good, quick compost bin.
- Stack concrete blocks in a square several feet high.
- Stand four pallets on end and wire them together.
- Make a ring of woven wire fencing.

You can also go to www.bhg.com and search for "compost bin" to see a simple bin to build.

Composting leaves

Can I speed up the decomposition of the autumn leaves from my yard so the compost will be ready in spring?

You have several factors working against you to create quick compost from the mountains of fall leaves in your yard. Fallen tree leaves are high in carbon. They need to be mixed with high-nitrogen materials to break down quickly. Grass clippings or other green debris mixed in will help, but these are usually in short supply in autumn. You can add a nitrogen fertilizer or manure if you don't have enough "greens" on hand.

Compost needs warmth to break down yard waste. As temperatures cool off in fall, the heat will have to be generated from within the compost pile. That means active management of the pile on your part. Turn the pile weekly to mix the browns and the greens, and to move the colder outer layers to the warmer interior of the pile. Keep the pile moist but not wet. With these steps you can have usable compost by spring. If it sounds like more work than you've bargained for, be patient. The leaves will compost if left alone. It just takes longer.

MULCH

Foamy mulch

The builder landscaped our new home, sodding the front lawn and planting various perennials and shrubs. The plants are surrounded by mulch. About a week ago, I saw two foamy yellow piles on the mulch. What is it and how do I get rid of it?

It sounds as though you have a slime mold growing on your wood mulch. I'm guessing that the lawn and new plants have been heavily watered (probably to help the sod), because this slime mold generally develops when moisture is plentiful. There's not much you need to do except cut back on the moisture a bit. Luckily, the fungus won't harm anything, and it will disappear on its own when the weather warms up and dries out. If it continues to appear as the weather gets drier and you have cut back on watering, it could be a sign that the area drains poorly. Keep that in mind, and water less often in those spots. In the meantime, you can break up the foamy yellow piles with a garden rake to make them less unsightly.

Newly ground or chipped wood mulch is more likely to develop slime molds. It's best to allow the wood mulch to sit for a year or so before it's spread.

Mulch selection

What type of mulch—cypress, pine, or hardwood—is best to use on our Zone 5 perennial beds? The mulch will be against our foundation, so we're concerned about termites and black ants.

Mulch is truly a gardener's friend. It helps reduce weeds, retain soil moisture, moderate soil temperatures, and replenish soil nutrients—not to mention how it dresses up the garden.

Any organic mulch will work well in your perennial beds, including shredded bark or leaves, cocoa bean hulls, and pine needles. You may want to stay away from wood chips in a perennial bed. Their coarse texture can overwhelm perennials, and the larger chips tie up nitrogen in the soil as they decompose. Also, keep the mulch a few inches from your foundation to deprive small rodents of a place to call home. Leave a gap of 6–12 inches from the foundation if you use wood-based mulch. This will prevent termites from having direct access.

Whatever mulch you use, be sure to put down a layer 2–4 inches thick. If you use less than that, weeds may still grow through it; if you use too much mulch, you may restrict the amount of oxygen getting to the plants' roots. Replenish mulch every year or two as it decomposes.

Grass as mulch

I've heard conflicting information regarding grass clippings. I used clippings as mulch around trees. Some people say it's good for the trees; some say it may give the trees a disease. Who is correct?

Good mulches for the base of a tree include wood chips, pine needles, and shredded bark. You can use grass clippings, too, but be aware of a few things. If you put down fresh grass clippings in a layer more than a couple of inches deep, the clippings can form a mat that discourages air from penetrating the soil. This mat will eventually rot and smell bad. Make certain that the grass from which the clippings were cut has not been treated with any herbicides that might be harmful to trees. Grass clippings and other organic mulches won't directly harm trees, but they can harbor rodents in winter that feed on the bark. To reduce the chances of rodent feasting, as winter approaches pull mulch away from the trunk. Wrap young trees with hardware cloth or tree wrap.

Benefits and drawbacks of mulch

One landscaper touts mulch as a panacea for garden problems. Another says that although it helps in some areas, it can be as bad as it is good. Who should I listen to?

Mulch is versatile. It discourages weeds, adds nutrients to the soil, and protects tender plants during cold winter months. All sorts of materials can be used as mulch: shredded tree bark, leaf mold, compost, rocks, lawn clippings, and shredded newspaper. To kill all grass and weeds in an area for a new bed, large pieces of cardboard or even carpet remnants smother everything they cover. Organic mulches—those made from things that were once alive, such as grass or trees—will break down into soil-enriching components, giving their all to help your garden.

Therein lies one of the problems, however: Those organic materials need nitrogen to break down into their component parts. They take what they need from your soil. So the nitrogen fertilizer you add to help your plants may get gobbled up by your mulch. Using already-composted manure or compost from your compost pile is a good way to provide a balanced meal for your plants without taking nitrogen from the garden soil.

Mulch creates a perfect haven for earthworms, which love to slither through the stuff, aerating the area and leaving behind soil-enriching castings. But the mulch also may harbor slugs and snails, which love to eat the luscious plants that grow up through the mulch. You may have to put out slug traps to contain the additional pests that can come with the use of mulch.

How do I know how much mulch to use? Is there a formula?

It can be confusing to figure out how much mulch to buy. The good news is that there is a relatively simple formula that you can use—and it's the same for all mulch types (whether organic or inorganic).

1. Measure. Measure the size of the area you'd like to cover and determine how deep you want the mulch to be. Spread most mulches 2–4 inches deep. (Avoid mulching any deeper than this around trees.)

2. Calculate. Multiply the length of your area by the width to get its square footage. Multiply the number of square feet by the depth of your mulch in feet (for example, 3 inches is three-twelfths of a foot or 0.25 feet). This gives you the volume of your area in cubic feet.

3. Convert. Bulk mulch is sold in cubic yards. To determine the number of cubic yards you'll need, divide the number of cubic feet you need by 27.

As an example, if you have a 20×25-foot garden you want to cover with mulch to 4 inches deep, multiply 20 feet by 25 feet by 0.33 feet (4 inches is one-third of a foot). This gives you 165 cubic feet; divide that by 27 to get about 6 cubic yards.

Mulch over weed barrier

I want to add a mulched cutting garden to my yard. I've read mixed reviews on the use of fabric weed barrier. I have a large birch in this area, which I do not want to lose. I am concerned that the weed barrier will limit the water to this tree.

I've had bad experiences with fabric weed barriers because weeds can grow in the mulch on top of them. These weeds are difficult to pull because their roots grow through the fabric. The product can be difficult to remove, especially once soil accumulates on top of it. Keep in mind that if you grow annuals that need replanting each year or perennial flowers that need to be divided occasionally, the fabric weed barrier will be an obstruction to digging in the bed. A more appropriate use of the weed barrier fabric is around trees and shrubs that remain in place once planted. Your birch should suffer no ill effects from the fabric. Fabric weed barriers are porous, permitting water and air to move through them. However, avoid using impermeable black plastic as a weed barrier under the mulch. Plastic blocks air and water from reaching the roots.

You may want to consider using mulch with no weed barrier under it in your cutting garden. Transplanting and dividing chores will be easier, and as the mulch decays, it will add organic matter to the soil.

Mulch left on too long

I have a garden that was covered in leaves (to protect my plants through the winter) until recently. When I cleaned the bed, I noticed that my plants had started to grow even though they weren't getting light. They have yellow-white stems and leaves. Are they going to grow right?

Although your plants may look damaged now, they're not really in serious condition—so there's little reason to worry. The elongation and yellowing of stems and leaves is called etiolation. After a few days in the sun, your perennials should be just fine. They will color up quickly and grow normally.

In the future, check for growth of perennials under the mulch a bit earlier. If left in place too long, winter mulch can smother the emerging perennials. It can also hold in excess moisture, causing them to rot.

Spring mulch removal

When should I remove the leaves, grass clippings, and mulch that I use to cover and protect my plants in winter?

Remove winter mulch in late winter or early spring when you observe new growth under the mulch. (Dig around in the mulch periodically to check for growth.) If you see mold developing on the plants, it's time to pull back the mulch. Keep in mind that winter mulch protects plants from sudden temperature changes, so acclimate your plants by pulling off the mulch gradually, over a period of days, as the plants show signs of new growth. This allows light and air to reach the new growth slowly, eliminating the chance of shock to your plants. Do keep some of the mulch handy, just in case frost is predicted and you need to protect the tender new growth.

Termites and mulch

I added a flower bed next to my home and mulched it with wood chips from trees. Is there a danger of termites getting under my house from the mulch?

Termites generally attack solid wood and leave bark mulch alone because it doesn't provide a suitable place to live or hide. However, it sounds as though the mulch you're using has wood chips in it, so it could attract termites. Be certain to keep the mulch from directly touching siding or wood walls where termites would like to dine. The mulch can act as a convenient cover for them to move through to get to a meal. Keep the mulch 6–12 inches away from any wood structures on the home. If termites cross the wood-free zone, you'll be able to see the protective soil tubes they build. That will allow you to treat them before they become established in your home.

Black spots on siding near mulch

We put down some wood chip mulch around our foundation plantings last spring. Soon afterward I started noticing tiny black specks on the house siding. They're virtually impossible to remove. Did the mulch cause the specks? How do I get rid of them?

It sounds as though your mulch has developed "artillery" or "shotgun" fungus (*Sphaerobolus stellatus*). The black specks are spore masses of the fungus. Artillery fungus has the ability to "shoot" its spores at objects such as light-colored house siding, fences, or cars. The spores stick to most surfaces and are almost impossible to remove.

This fungus develops in wood-based mulches under cool, moist conditions. Cypress, cedar, redwood, and pine bark mulch seem to be resistant to the fungus. Penn State University has looked at cleaning products to remove the artillery fungus spores from siding. Complete removal requires substantial effort and possible damage to siding, so try these cleaners in an inconspicuous spot first. Westley's Bleech-Wite tire cleaner and Castrol Super Clean were the most effective cleaners for vinyl siding; Turtle Wax Foaming Wheel Cleaner and Botanic Gold multi-use botanical soap were best on aluminum siding. You should be able to find these cleaners at automotive stores.

Selecting mulch

How do I decide how much mulch to buy? Where do I go to find the kinds of materials that make good mulch?

Take a walk through your local garden center and you'll find many types of mulch: shredded bark in bags, washed river rock in bulk, and pebbles from pea to golf ball size. Each spring, the parking lots of discount stores fill up with mountains of bagged mulch. You also can find bulk suppliers in the telephone directory under Building Materials, Landscape Equipment and Supplies, Rock, or Stone. The choices can be confusing. Here are a few guidelines to get you started.

- Wood mulches are sold in bags or in bulk. A 2-cubic-foot bag will cover 8 square feet about 3 inches deep.
- The amount of gravel needed to cover an area will vary with the size of the pebbles. Generally, a ton of rock covers 100 square feet.
- When buying in bulk, estimate that 1 cubic yard of material will cover 100 square feet about 3 inches deep.

Cocoa-hull mulch

I applied cocoa-hull mulch around the birch tree on my front lawn so I wouldn't have to weed around it. Is that the best mulch? What do I do if it gets moldy?

You're right to mulch around your birch tree. This North American native likes to have cool roots and adequate moisture, which it doesn't always get when planted in the middle of a lawn.

Cocoa bean hulls are a popular, if slightly expensive, mulch that will do just fine around your birch. They tend to mat and get moldy during hot, wet weather, but that won't harm your tree, and the mold usually washes off with rain or watering.

If you decide that the smell of chocolate is too enticing for your inner chocoholic, other good mulches for your birch include shredded bark, wood chips, and pine needles.

Rubber mulch

I've seen mulch that is made out of recycled tires. It looks like organic mulch and seems to make sense environmentally. Are there any faults to using it?

Rubber mulches are often used in playground areas at schools, athletic fields, and parks. The sponginess of the rubber adds cushioning for falls. Crumb rubber is also sometimes used to artificially create more pore space in clay soils. Drawbacks of rubber mulch include the odor and, more importantly, the fact that rubber mulch does not break down over time as organic mulches do. When organic mulches break down, they add nutrients and structure to the soil. Because the rubber does not decompose, it would be hard to remove from the garden. That could be a problem if you need to replace any plants that die or redo the plantings.

Mulch around tree

I've just planted a new tree beside the front entrance to my house. Is there any benefit to mulching around the trunk, or should I let the grass grow back?

A layer of mulch 2–4 inches deep around your newly planted tree will save water, decrease stress on the tree, and ensure that grass doesn't compete with the tree for nutrients. The ring of mulch also will keep you and your lawn mower away from the trunk and reduce nicks in the bark, which open up paths for insects and disease to get in. Keep the mulch about 3–4 inches from the trunk to keep rodents from hiding there and gnawing the tree bark. Make the ring of mulch at least as wide as the spread of branches on your newly planted tree.

Sour mulch

Can mulch go bad? We bought some bagged mulch that had an unpleasant odor, but we used it anyway. The plants are dying back where we applied it.

Yes, mulch may be unfit to use. If organic mulch such as wood chips decomposes without enough oxygen, anaerobic decomposition sets in. When this happens, the mulch produces alcohol and organic acids that can be toxic to plants. In addition, the pH of such mulch can be extremely low. Anaerobic conditions usually develop in large, wet mulch piles, or in bagged mulch with water in the bag.

It's easy to tell if the mulch you purchased is toxic. Good mulch has a pleasant, humusy smell; acid (anaerobic) mulch has a strong, sour smell. Fortunately, you don't need to throw out the sour mulch. Simply spread it out in a thin layer for a few days on a hard surface such as your driveway or patio. Once the smell subsides, the mulch should be safe to use around your plants.

Symptoms of damage from sour mulch include chlorosis (yellowing of foliage), defoliation, scorching, and even plant death from toxic fumes or from direct contact with the mulch.

SOILS

Plants for sandy soil

The soil in my area is sandy. I'd like ideas for plants in my sunny yard but would prefer not to have to add all new topsoil. Are there any plants that will thrive in this area—Zone 6 or 7?

You don't need to bring in all new soil. However, anything you plant will do better if you amend your sandy soil with organic matter in the form of well-rotted compost or manure, peat moss, or leaf mold. Apply a layer 2–3 inches thick and work it into the top 6–8 inches of your soil.

Otherwise, you are limited to plants that can tolerate your sandy soil and sunny conditions. I suggest you look for information about plants that are native to your region. Native plants, particularly prairie plants, have evolved in tough conditions and have proved their staying power. The list of native and nonnative perennials that adapt well to sandy soils includes wormwood *(Artemisia)*, yarrow *(Achillea)*, globe thistle *(Echinops)*, lavender *(Lavandula)*, salvia *(Salvia)*, Russian sage *(Perovskia atriplicifolia)*, and sedum *(Sedum; Hylotelephium)*.

Raised bed benefits

I've been told it's good to garden in raised beds. Why are they better?

Raised beds provide an excellent environment for plants, with better drainage and earlier warming in spring. Better drainage means less likelihood of root rots developing. In the case of vegetables, more plants can be grown in a smaller area than with conventional row-cropping techniques, because no space is needed between rows. Another good thing about raised beds is that no one walks on them, so the soil never becomes compacted and tilling the soil each season is easier to do. For gardeners with limited mobility, raised beds can be built to any height, so less bending and reaching are needed to work with the plants.

Making raised beds

I'd like to try gardening in a raised bed. What's the best way to make one, and what do I use to make it?

Wood is commonly used to make raised beds. It is easy to work with and attractive. If you plan to grow edible plants, use a naturally rot-resistant wood, such as red cedar, black locust, or redwood, if you're concerned about the safety of treated wood. Under most circumstances, rot-resistant woods will last 10–15 years. To build raised beds, follow these steps.

1. Determine the size of your raised bed. Four feet wide is convenient, because lumber is readily available in 4-foot lengths; with this width, the center of the bed is easily accessible from either side. If the bed will be accessible only from one side, limit the width to 3 feet. As for depth, most plants need at least a 6–12-inch root zone, but even deeper is better. To make a raised bed wheelchair-accessible, build the walls about 2 feet tall and limit the width to about 3 feet.
2. Drill holes from top to bottom all the way through each timber every 4 feet, staying 6–8 inches in from the ends of the timbers. Place the timbers where you want them, then drive a length of construction rebar through the holes and into the ground.
3. Use decay-resistant wood stakes inside the bed to add stability. Stakes should be twice the height of the raised bed. Bury half the stake in firm ground and leave half projecting above the ground as support. Attach the timbers to the stakes.
4. Fill the raised bed with topsoil, compost, and other materials in which to grow your plants, then add the plants and garden away!

Calculating lime needs

How do I figure out how many pounds of lime my garden needs?

Lime is applied to soil to increase the soil pH, which is a measure of the soil's acidity or alkalinity. A pH below 7.0 is said to be acidic; above 7.0, it is alkaline. For most garden plants, a soil pH between 6.0 and 7.0 (slightly acidic) is ideal.

To determine whether your soil needs lime and how much, you need to answer these basic questions: What is the current pH of your soil? What do you want the pH to be (based on the plants you want to grow)? What is your soil type? To get this information, you'll need to have your soil tested. Contact your county extension service or a commercial soil-testing laboratory to order a soil test kit. The results will indicate whether your soil needs lime and how much to add. Keep in mind, however, that the kind of lime you use makes a difference; refer to the package directions for general guidelines.

Stone-filled soil

I'm preparing to landscape my backyard, which has rock-filled clay soil. Is there a good way to improve the soil? Do I need to sift it, remove all the rocks, then add topsoil? Is there anything I can add to the existing clay that will enable me to grow a wider variety of plants?

Though it would be a big job, the best thing would be to dig out and replace some of the rocky clay soil with fresh topsoil.

As another option, you could build raised beds or berms to plant in and simply cover the soil's surface with a foot or so of fresh topsoil mixed with organic matter. In the time it takes the added soil to settle, you can plan what you'll plant.

If adding loads of soil isn't an option, you'll have to rake or pull the stones. Once you have removed enough of the stones to easily work the soil, amend it liberally with organic matter (such as compost) to loosen the clay.

Improving clay soil

My new garden has heavy clay soil that's difficult to dig into, and it's lumpy and clumpy. How can I improve the soil so I can plant some things to dress up my new home?

After the weather, the favorite topic of conversation among gardeners is soil. You can't change the weather, but you can change your soil. In your case, it's just going to be a bit more of a challenge.

The best and only practical way to improve clay soil is by incorporating organic matter. Compost, rotted manure, dry grass clippings (from nonchemically treated lawns), and leaf mold will eventually turn clay soil into usable soil. If you're starting a new garden, spread 2–3 inches of organic matter over the soil and work it into the top 6–8 inches. If you have existing planting beds, you may be able to dig compost into pockets around the plantings. It's a lot of work up front, but it will be worth the effort in the end.

Well-drained soil

I'd like to know what is meant by "well-drained soil."

Almost every gardening book and magazine article you read says you need well-drained soil. What is it? Well-drained soil is a soil where water infiltrates at a medium rate—somewhere between running off and draining as though someone pulled a plug.

The best soil is about half air space and half solid mineral, with 2–5 percent organic matter. Under ideal growing conditions, about half of the air space will be filled with water. If the soil is too wet, plant roots fail to get the oxygen they need. If the soil has too much air space and drains too quickly, plant roots dry out.

Here's a simple test to find out how well your soil drains. Dig a hole that is 12–18 inches across and 12–18 inches deep. Fill the hole with water. If water drains from the hole in 10 minutes or less, you have fast drainage. If the water takes an hour or more to drain, you have poorly drained soil.

Improve soil drainage by building raised beds or by adding organic matter to existing soil in the form of well-rotted manure, compost, or peat moss.

Adding sand to clay

I'd like to loosen up my clay soil by adding some sand to it. How much sand should I add?

Adding sand alone to a clay soil is not a good idea. Clay is made up of fine particles, which is why it doesn't drain well. (Water drains through the spaces between the particles; the smaller the spaces, the slower it drains.) Sand, on the other hand, drains well because it is made up of larger particles. When sand and clay are mixed, the smaller clay particles stick to the larger sand particles, eliminating the spaces and creating a dense layer of soil that's something like concrete. If you get the right combination of sand and clay, you'll end up with adobe bricks.

It's a much better idea to add organic matter—such as peat moss or compost—to a clay soil. As organic matter breaks down, it helps create larger spaces between the clay particles and enriches the soil.

Soil runoff

I'm building a small rock garden in sandy soil, so I added peat moss and topsoil into the top 8-12 inches. After a thorough watering, the water runs down the slope. What did I do wrong, and how can I fix it?

Perhaps the runoff is because of too much peat moss, which can form a crustlike surface under or over the soil. For a rock garden, I would suggest adding loam to your sand and leaving it at that, because rock-garden plants prefer soil that is on the sandier side.

Once your plants become established, their root systems will help hold the soil in place. Until then, you may need to rig up some sort of retaining system using additional rocks to keep the water and soil from washing down the slope. Mulching around the plants also will help keep the soil in place.

Improving sandy soil

The soil in my friend's yard is very sandy. What can we do to improve the soil?

I'll tell you the same thing I tell everyone with bad soil: The best way to have a good garden is to improve the soil with organic matter, compost, or well-rotted manure. The more organic matter you put into the soil, the more productivity you'll get out of it. Organic matter helps bind the sandy particles together so the soil will hold more water when it's dry, and drain more quickly when it's wet. If you can, add organic matter two or three times during the growing season. The more you add, the better.

The sand might not be the only problem your friend has to overcome. The soil also could be especially alkaline or acidic. Do a soil test to determine the pH. The organic matter you add can help moderate extreme pH levels, but you may need other amendments that specifically deal with soil pH.

Soil test results

A soil test revealed that my soil is alkaline (pH 8.0) and low in nitrogen and phosphorus. What do I need to do to balance it out?

Most plants grow best in soil with a pH of about 6.5. To lower your soil's pH, use a soil acidifier, such as soil sulfur or ammonium sulfate. Follow the directions on the package. Then amend your soil with organic matter such as compost, well-rotted manure, or peat moss.

Soil nitrogen levels change from week to week because the nutrient quickly moves through the soil. Adding organic matter to your soil will increase nitrogen levels. Another way to increase them is by adding ammonium sulfate or any granular fertilizer containing nitrogen in the form of nitrate or ammonium. Phosphorus is more stable in the soil. To increase the phosphorus level, add superphosphate, rock phosphate, or bonemeal, all of which should be available at your local garden center. Because phosphorus moves slowly through the soil, work these products into the root zone.

Drywall as soil amendment

I've heard that drywall is good for amending clay soil. How does it work? What's the best way to add it to the soil?

Drywall (sheetrock) won't necessarily help your soil. Its main ingredient is gypsum, and gypsum is used effectively to amend soils high in sodium. Gypsum needs to be ground to a fine powder to react with the soil. Unless your clay soil has a lot of salt in it, though, the gypsum will be of little use in improving the soil.

That said, the best way to deal with clay is to amend it with lots of organic matter, such as compost, peat moss, shredded leaves, straw, composted sawdust, or well-rotted manure.

Blood meal vs. bonemeal

What's the difference between blood meal and bonemeal? Can I use them together?

They both sound like something out of a horror movie, don't they? Bonemeal and blood meal are amendments that add nutrients to soil, and they can be used together. Blood meal is dried and powdered animal blood; it increases soil nitrogen levels. Bonemeal is ground animal bones; it increases soil calcium and phosphorus levels. Bonemeal also includes small amounts of magnesium, iron, zinc, and other trace elements that plants require. Blood meal and bonemeal take time to break down and make their nutrients available to plants. The plus side is that they are quite safe to apply around plants with little danger of burning from overapplication. On the downside, if your plants need a quick boost of fertilizer, they will act too slowly.

Calculating how much soil

I am going to be adding planting beds to my yard. How do I determine how much soil I will need?

At the risk of forcing flashbacks from high school math class, there is a formula you can use to determine how much soil you need. First, figure out the square footage of the beds. To do this, multiply their length in feet by their width in feet. Then determine how deep you want the soil in the beds, convert it to feet (divide by 12 because there are 12 inches in a foot), and multiply that number by the square footage. This will give you cubic feet. Divide that number by 27 to get the number of cubic yards you'll need, because soil is usually sold by the cubic yard.

As an example, if you want to add a 10×8-foot bed, multiply 10 and 8, to get 80 square feet. If you want the soil depth to be 6 inches, multiply 80 by 0.5 (because 6 inches is half a foot or $^6/_{12}$), to get 40 cubic feet. Divide that by 27 and you'll find you need about 1.5 cubic yards of soil.

Coffee grounds for soil improvement

I read that used coffee grounds are a useful soil amendment for a flower garden. Is this true?

Coffee grounds contain a small amount of nitrogen, so they contribute nutrients to the soil. They are also slightly acidic. This is good for some soils, but not for all. I recommend composting the coffee grounds instead of just dumping them on the garden. That way you avoid the risk of applying too much of a good thing. In the absence of a compost pile, work some grounds into the soil around your acid-loving plants, such as azaleas, blueberries, and hydrangeas.

For noncoffee drinkers, check with your local coffee shop. Many offer complimentary spent grounds for gardens and compost bins if you'll simply haul them away.

Working wet soil

I've always heard that I shouldn't work my garden soil when it's wet. Why not?

Avoid working or walking on garden soils when they are wet because you'll contribute to compaction. Digging in or walking on wet soil destroys the soil structure, squeezing out some of the air spaces, or pores. When the soil is dry, the air spaces provide cushioning that allows the structure to spring back into place afterward. But if you've ever stepped in mud up to your ankles, you have a feel for just how different soil is when it is saturated.

If you must walk on wet ground, distribute the force of your step over a large area by walking on a sheet of plywood or a heavily mulched area to reduce compaction. Stay on permanent pathways to keep the compaction confined to the walkway.

Double digging

What is double digging? Does it help plants grow better?

Usually when soil is tilled or dug, the top 6–12 inches of soil is turned over. With double digging, you remove the top 12 inches of soil (or the depth of a garden spade), set it aside, then loosen the next layer of soil. If you like, add and mix in several inches of organic matter as you turn over each layer. Top off the lower layer with the amended upper layer. Continue this process to the end of the planting bed.

This is hard work; it helps if you have a strong back. You will notice a dramatic difference in the growth of plants in the double-dug beds, however. When roots have 2 feet of unimpeded growth, plants thrive. You can get some of the same benefits with less digging by building raised beds.

WATERING

Lawn watering tips

We just bought our first home. Since I'm new at yard care, could you tell me what's the best way to water the lawn on a budget?

Unless your yard is somehow blessed with perfectly timed rainfall throughout the growing season, you'll need to supplement nature's water supply. Here are some tips for watering grass wisely.

Water your grass wisely

- Water heavily at infrequent intervals. On average, a lawn needs about 1 inch of water per week, from rainfall or irrigation. This will soak the soil to a depth of 4–6 inches, putting water deep into your lawn's root system. Let the lawn dry out completely between waterings. Place small cans around the yard when you water to measure how fast your sprinklers dispense water and to ensure you're covering the entire area. A thorough watering takes a while, however, so be prepared to leave the water running.

- For best results, water in the early morning when there is less wind and heat. Cool, calm conditions limit evaporation, allow greater soil penetration, and reduce runoff.

- Pause when the water puddles or runs off the yard, and let the water soak in before starting again. Most sprinklers and sprinkling systems apply water faster than the lawn can drink it up. Water soaks in at different rates in different soil types. If you have sandy soil, it could take as little as 15 minutes for a half inch of water to soak in. With clay, it could take 10 times longer.

- Keep a newly seeded lawn moist, but not soaked, while your grass seed sprouts. Too much water can inhibit germination. A light mulch over the seed will help keep the soil damp. As the new lawn grows, reduce the frequency of watering and increase the amount of water you apply each time. After 4–6 weeks, treat the new lawn as an established one.

- Completely soak a newly sodded lawn for about 2 weeks after placement, watering every day or two. This will help the root system to become firmly established.

Time of day to water

What time of day is it safe to water? I've heard that I shouldn't water during the middle of the day because the sunlight will burn holes in the leaves.

It's a myth that water droplets on plant leaves will focus the sun's rays and burn holes in the leaves. So you can water any time of day without harm to the plant from the sun. However, watering during the middle of the day is more wasteful than watering in the morning, because warm and windy conditions cause water to evaporate quickly. Water early enough in the day that the plant dries off before nightfall. If the foliage stays wet for a long time, diseases are more likely to develop.

Water from dehumidifier

Is it safe to use the water from our dehumidifier to water flowers in the garden? I'd like to conserve water if possible, but don't want to harm the plants.

The water you collect from your dehumidifier is purer than the water from your tap. I wouldn't suggest drinking it, because bacteria could be growing in it, but it should be perfectly fine to use on your plants. The reason it is so pure is that the dehumidifier condenses water vapor out of the air. This water contains no dissolved minerals, which may be present in tap water.

Lawn watering survival tips

I don't want to water my lawn all summer, but I do want it to survive during hot, dry periods. Can I water it just part of the time?

Some lawn grasses are naturally more drought-tolerant than others. Warm-season grasses such as buffalograss, Bermudagrass, and zoysiagrass need less water to thrive and survive than cool-season grasses such as fescue, Kentucky bluegrass, or ryegrass. Turf-type tall fescue and fine fescue are fairly drought-tolerant and will remain green through most summers. Kentucky bluegrass and perennial ryegrass go dormant and turn brown when conditions become hot and dry. Grass growing along sidewalks, curbs, and driveways dries out fastest and suffers the most.

If you don't care about keeping your lawn lush and green all summer, lightly irrigate with ½ inch of water every 3–4 weeks to keep the roots and crowns alive. This is not enough water to stimulate new growth, but it will keep the growing points moist enough to live. Avoid the temptation to give the lawn a soaking that could spur new growth, especially if you don't intend to continue watering. It's stressful to the grass to go in and out of dormancy. If you start watering thoroughly, continue to water thoroughly until rainfall returns to sufficient levels.

Fall watering of evergreens

Do evergreens need to be watered in the fall?

If weather conditions are dry in fall, it's a good idea to water the evergreen trees and shrubs in your landscape to prevent winter browning. They may need another boost of water in midwinter if conditions remain dry. Water when the ground is not frozen, so the water can soak into the root zone.

Evergreens lose moisture through their needles or leaves all winter, especially when temperatures are warm, humidity is low, and wind speeds are high. Broadleaf evergreens such as magnolia and rhododendron are more sensitive to drying than needled evergreens such as pine, spruce, juniper, and fir. They may not be able to absorb water from cold or frozen soil fast enough to replace moisture loss through evaporation and transpiration. When the foliage dries out, it turns brown and dies. The tree or shrub may send out healthy new growth in spring, but overall attractiveness will be marred by the older browned foliage.

Watering during drought

Because it's been so hot and dry this summer, I've been watering the trees I planted this spring every day, but they're still wilting. How can I save my trees?

For starters, stop watering so often! It's much better to give your trees a thorough soaking less often than to water daily. You don't say how much water you're giving your trees. If it's a light sprinkle, you may be wetting only the surface. (It's common for water to begin puddling on the soil's surface when only the top inch or two of soil is wet. Sometimes the water can't soak in as fast as you're applying it.) In this case, the soil in the lower part of the root ball may be completely dry, and your trees are suffering from lack of moisture.

The opposite may also be true. If you're watering enough to soak the entire root zone of the trees daily, you may be drowning your trees. The roots need oxygen just as much as they need water. If they're deprived of oxygen, the roots can't absorb water, and they die. So although there may be plenty of water in the soil, the top of the tree won't be getting any because the roots can't drink it up.

The solution to both scenarios is to water the soil deeply once every 4–7 days. If it's warm and windy, water more frequently. Plants that were grown in pots require more frequent watering than those that were field-grown and balled and burlapped. Cover the root zone with mulch to help hold in moisture.

Watering large trees

Should I be watering my established trees during the drought we're having? Or will they survive on their own?

Well-established trees and shrubs can survive long periods of dry weather without supplemental watering. But if they suffer moisture stress, they may be more susceptible to attack by diseases, insects, or other environmental stresses. Younger trees and newer plantings should be higher on your watering priority list than established ones. However, if the leaves on your established trees begin to wilt, if you notice a change in leaf color, or if the margins of the leaves turn brown, it's time to give these trees a good soaking.

Most roots grow in the top 12 inches of soil, so wet the soil uniformly to that depth. Soak the entire area under the canopy of the tree. It's best to water with drip irrigation or a soaker hose laid on the soil's surface in concentric circles around the tree. You can also water with a sprinkler, but it's more difficult to apply water uniformly with a sprinkler, and you may have to turn it off for a while to let the water soak in, then sprinkle again to soak the soil a full foot deep. It's a good idea to dig down near the drip line of the tree to determine how deep the water has soaked in.

Rainwater harvest

I'd like to catch rainwater in a rain barrel to use for watering my plants. Do I need to do anything other than direct the downspout from the roof into a barrel?

Rainwater is usually a good source of water for houseplants or plants in your landscape. You can buy ready-made rain barrels from mail-order garden suppliers, but you can also make your own from a 55-gallon drum, some PVC couplings, and a length of hose.

Place the barrel on a solid base of gravel or sand under a downspout. Direct the flow of water into the barrel. It helps to use a screen over the downspout to prevent debris from washing into and collecting in the barrel. Place a tight-fitting lid on the barrel to keep out mosquitoes. (You want to avoid creating a breeding ground for carriers of West Nile virus.) Place a spigot in the lower portion of the barrel to drain the water for use in the landscape. (Keep the spigot at least several inches above the bottom of the barrel to keep it from being clogged from sediment that may wash into the barrel.) An overflow pipe near the top of the barrel is a handy option. The overflow can be directed into a second barrel or simply aimed away from the house's foundation.

Watering new trees

How do I know how much to water the new trees I just planted?

Water newly transplanted trees well for the first year or two, until they become established. It's best to water thoroughly but less frequently. Instead of giving the trees a light sprinkle every other day, soak them deeply once or twice a week if rainfall is inadequate. Apply enough water so that it soaks into the base of the root ball.

A 2-inch-diameter tree needs about 15 gallons of water per week; a 4-inch-diameter tree, about 25 gallons. Use drip irrigation, or place a hose running at a slow trickle over the root zone. If in doubt about how much water you're applying, run the hose at a trickle into a bucket to measure the flow. If it takes 10 minutes to fill a 5-gallon bucket, you'll need to leave the hose at the root zone for 30 minutes for a 2-inch tree or 50 minutes for a 4-inch tree.

Rain garden

I've been hearing a lot about rain gardens lately. What are they? Can I make one in my suburban yard?

Rain gardens are shallow depressions in the landscape designed to catch runoff (usually from the roof, but they can catch runoff from other hard surfaces such as driveways too) after a storm. The water slowly filters into the ground rather than running into a storm drain. Compared to a conventional lawn, a rain garden allows about 30 percent more water to soak into the ground. Most rain gardens are planted with native perennials that are adapted to alternate wet and dry cycles. As more and more land is paved for driveways, sidewalks, parking areas, and buildings, these small garden patches contribute significantly to preventing pollution from runoff, decreasing flooding, increasing aquifer recharge, enhancing the beauty of your yard, and increasing habitat for wildlife.

Make your rain garden 4–8 inches deep. Deeper gardens catch more water, but it may take too long to soak in, and in the process may provide a breeding ground for mosquitoes. A rain garden in the sun is more effective than one in the shade. And keep the rain garden at least 10 feet away from the house, to keep the water from seeping into the foundation. If your soil is poorly drained, the rain garden may be less feasible.

The size of your rain garden depends on several factors—the size of the area drained, the type of soil in the yard, and the depth you'd prefer for the rain garden. Check with your local cooperative extension service, state department of natural resources, or state conservation department for assistance in determining what's best for your specific site.

Gray-water use in landscape

Can I use the rinse water from my washing machine to water plants in my landscape?

Reusing water from the laundry, bathing, or sinks seems like an efficient way to recycle water. However, there are some drawbacks. All these sources of recycled water contain bacteria that may pose health problems. For this reason, most states regulate the use of these sources of water, called gray water, in the landscape. Check with local or state health authorities for the requirements in your area. You may need to install a filtration or settling system before you can use the gray water. Never apply it to edible crops; use it only on ornamentals. Using gray water can lead to significant water savings, but make certain that you do it right and follow the rules.

Watering veggies

When is the most critical time to water vegetables? I have a big vegetable garden and have trouble keeping everything watered all the time.

Many gardeners wait until they see their vegetables wilting before dragging out the hose. That can be a mistake. Vegetables do have critical periods during development when they need water for good production. Waiting to water until they wilt pushes them past the critical stage. A few critical watering times are listed in the chart below.

Critical watering times for vegetables

Beans	During pod enlargement
Cucumbers	During fruit enlargement
Melons	During flowering and fruit development
Peppers	From planting to fruit set and enlargement
Potatoes	During tuber set and enlargement
Sweet corn	During silking, tasseling, and ear development
Tomatoes	During flowering, fruit set, and fruit enlargement

FERTILIZING

Mixing in manure

I'd like to add some well-rotted manure to my garden. Can you tell me how much I should use?

Because manure varies in nutrient content, and fertility needs vary from soil to soil, there's no "best" ratio for adding manure or other forms of organic matter to your garden. But I can give you some general recommendations. Spread a layer of manure about an inch or two deep over the garden in winter so that by spring the rains and snows have helped leach excess salts and ammonia. Avoid applying fresh manure directly on a garden where plants are growing, because it could burn the plants. The more aged the manure, the better.

One thought: Be aware of your manure source. If the animals that have produced the manure have been eating grass or weedy hay, you may end up spreading weed seeds on your garden.

Fertilizer numbers

What do the numbers on a fertilizer bag mean? Does it make a difference what numbers I use on my flowers and lawn?

All fertilizers list their nitrogen (abbreviated as N), phosphorus (P), and potassium (K) content as percentages on the label. This is called the fertilizer analysis. The nitrogen content is listed as percentage of actual nitrogen (although the source may be nitrate, ammonium, or some other form of nitrogen), the P is listed as percentage of phosphate (P_2O_5), and the K is listed as percentage of potash (K_2O). A 24-8-16 fertilizer contains 24% nitrogen, 8% phosphate, and 16% potash. The remaining 52% may be other minor fertilizer elements (such as iron or sulfur) or filler (carrier) for the nutrients. The percentages on the label are always listed in the order N-P-K.

The relationship of N-P-K figures to one another is called the fertilizer ratio. The 24-8-16 fertilizer has a 3:1:2 ratio; a 10-10-10 fertilizer has a 1:1:1 ratio. You can substitute fertilizers of similar ratios when you can't find the exact product you want. For example, the 24-8-16 fertilizer mentioned above is recommended for use on lawns. You can use any fertilizer with a similar ratio even though the analysis is different. A 25-5-10 (ratio is 5:1:2) fertilizer will work as a substitute because it is also high in nitrogen. For flowers, the 10-10-10 fertilizer would be a better choice. Flowers prefer lower levels of nitrogen. You could substitute 20-20-20 or 11-8-8 fertilizer for flowers, because these ratios are also close to 1:1:1.

Organic vs. inorganic fertilizer

Which fertilizers are considered organic? Are they safer to use than other fertilizers?

Organic fertilizers may be derived from plant materials (compost, alfalfa meal), from animal sources (manure, bonemeal), or from naturally occurring minerals (greensand, rock phosphate). Most release their nutrients slowly, so there is little danger of burning plants by applying excess organic fertilizer. However, most have a low nutrient content per pound of material, so large volumes of them must be used, and they generally cost more per pound than manufactured fertilizers. The specific nutrients in organic fertilizers are identical to the ones in manufactured fertilizers. For example, an ammonium ion from manure is no different than one produced at a fertilizer factory. However, the side benefits from the organic matter carrier are numerous. Organic matter loosens clay soil, helps retain moisture in sandy soil, and acts as a reservoir of nutrients in any soil.

Manufactured fertilizers are usually high in nutrient content per pound of fertilizer, and the cost is low compared to organic materials. Several synthetic fertilizers contain slow-release forms of fertilizer. Examples are urea-formaldehyde (UF), isobutylidene diurea (IBDU), sulfur-coated urea (SCU), and plastic-coated fertilizers, such as Osmocote. These slow-release forms are more expensive, but they reduce the potential of burning plants from overfertilization. They also cut down on the number of applications of fertilizer you'll need to make.

Fertilizer storage

Does fertilizer go bad? I usually have some left over at the end of the summer, and don't want to throw it away.

Fertilizer comes in many different forms. Liquid forms are usually a suspension or solution of fertilizer in water. The solids may settle out over time, so you may need to shake the bottle to dissolve or suspend the fertilizer if it has been sitting around for a long time. Also, be sure to keep the container from freezing.

If you have granular or water-soluble crystals of fertilizer, keep them dry. It's not enough to protect them from rain, snow, or other precipitation; you also need to keep the humidity low. In high humidity, granules or crystals cake together and may form a solid block. If you keep them dry, they can be stored indefinitely. Keep the fertilizer in its original bag or container so there's no question about what it is. If the bag or canister has been opened, wrap the remaining fertilizer tightly in plastic to exclude moisture.

Role of fertilizer elements

I know that most fertilizers contain nitrogen, phosphorus, and potassium. What do each of these do for the plant?

In simple terms, nitrogen promotes plant growth. It is associated with leafy, vegetative growth. It's part of every protein in the plant, so it's required for virtually every process, from growing new leaves to defending against pests. Nitrogen is part of the chlorophyll molecule, which gives plants their green color and is involved in creating food for the plant through photosynthesis. Lack of nitrogen shows up as general yellowing (chlorosis) of the plant. Because nitrogen can move around in the plant, older growth often yellows more than the new growth.

Phosphorus is involved in metabolic processes responsible for transferring energy from one point to another in the plant. It's also critical in root development and flowering. Because phosphorus moves slowly through the soil, it's important to work it into the soil, where it's needed by the roots.

Potassium helps regulate plant metabolism and affects water pressure regulation inside and outside of plant cells. It is important for good rood development. For these reasons, potassium is critical to plant stress tolerance.

Light & Temperature

LIGHT

Sunscald on maple

My Japanese maple tree has a dead patch of bark on the trunk. Can I save the tree?

If the dead patch of bark is on the south or southwest side of the tree, it's likely that your Japanese maple was damaged by sunscald. Sunscald may develop in winter or summer. It is due to sudden changes in temperature caused by exposure of the bark to intense sun. In summer it's most likely to happen during dry periods of extreme heat. In winter it happens when sunny winter days alternate with cold nights. Thin-barked trees such as maple, linden, apple, crabapple, cherry, and plum are most likely to be affected.

Once the bark is injured, there is little you can do. Remove any loose bark, which may harbor insects or trap moisture underneath it. To prevent the problem from developing, wrap the trunk of newly planted trees over the winter with tree wrap, or paint the trunk with white latex paint to reflect the sun's rays. Remove the wrap during the spring and summer months. Water recent transplants throughout the summer, but especially during hot spells.

Streetlights and trees

Can the light from a streetlight kill a nearby tree?

Streetlights typically have little effect on most plants. Plants sensitive to changes in day length could be affected by the light, however. For example, chrysanthemums flower in response to short days (or, more technically, long nights). Low-level light from a streetlight can be enough to cause a delay in bloom. Similarly, many woody plants such as trees develop full winter hardiness in response to shortening day length in autumn. If a streetlight is nearby, the tree may get enough light to delay the onset of winter hardiness. A sudden, severe cold snap could create some twig dieback, although it's unlikely to severely damage the entire tree; response is often limited to branches closest to the light source. I wouldn't be worried about trees near streetlights unless the trees are growing against the lights. If they are, they could pose a safety hazard.

515

Can I use ordinary fluorescent shop lights to start all of my flower and vegetable seedlings in the house?

Fluorescent lights are the best lights to use for starting seeds indoors. Use one "warm" bulb and one "cool" bulb so you'll get the full—most natural—spectrum of light. Once seedlings sprout, give them 14–16 hours of light per day. Keep the lights about 4–6 inches above the seedlings.

Avoid using incandescent bulbs to start your seedlings. These bulbs give off so much heat that your seedlings will suffer heat damage if you keep the seedlings close to the bulbs. And incandescent bulbs provide too little range of the natural spectrum of light.

Full sun vs. partial shade

I would like to know what is considered "full sun." Is it just so many hours a day, or does it mean that the plants are in the sun during the hottest part of the day?

When you read "full sun," it means that a plant needs direct, unfiltered sunlight for at least 6 hours a day. This is the minimum amount of light a sun-loving plant needs to thrive. As you have noticed, the intensity of sunlight varies depending on the time of day. A plant that gets full sun all morning but is shaded in the afternoon has a much different growing environment from one shielded from the sun in the morning but exposed to full sun in the afternoon. Many plants that are classified as growing best in "partial shade" can take full morning sun, as long as they are protected from direct afternoon sun. Latitude and elevation play a role too. Gardens in the South receive more intense sun than those in the North. And gardens at high elevations are brighter than landscapes at sea level.

Short-day mums

My friend says that chrysanthemums are short-day plants that shouldn't bloom until the day length gets short enough in fall. Mine are blooming in my garden now and it's the middle of summer. What's going on?

Most garden chrysanthemums (*Chrysanthemum morifolium*) are short-day plants, meaning that they require short day length (or, more accurately, long nights) in order to bloom. Mums and many other plants contain a light-recognition substance called phytochrome that senses the day length. Flowering is one response that can be affected by phytochrome levels within the plant. Long, uninterrupted dark cycles trigger flowering in short-day plants such as chrysanthemum and poinsettia. Other plants require short nights (long days) to bloom. These are called long-day plants. For some plants, day length makes little difference in bloom time.

As plant breeders have selected for earlier fall bloom in chrysanthemums, they inadvertently selected some that were no longer short-day plants but instead are day neutral. Your summer-blooming mum must be one of these day-neutral types.

Can plants get sunburned?

Yes, although the process isn't quite the same as the sunburn you get on your first day at the beach each summer. Leaves (and stems) of plants adapt to the light level in which they are grown. On plants grown indoors, the leaf size, leaf thickness, and chlorophyll content will be much different from on the same type of plant grown in brighter light outdoors. If the plant is suddenly moved to brighter light, leaves may become bleached or burned from excess sun. Prevent sunburn on your plants by gradually moving them to brighter light over a period of 2 weeks or so.

I have a lilac growing under an ash tree. It's starting to grow crooked, as though it's reaching for more light. How can I keep it growing straight up?

Lilacs are best adapted to growth in full sun. When grown in the shade, they won't flower well and, as you have noticed, may grow in the direction of brighter light. Short of removing the ash tree to create full sun, you may not be able to keep your lilac growing straight upright.

Plant growth bending toward light is due to phototropism. All plants produce growth substances called auxins. Auxins promote stem elongation. The auxin on the sunny side of the plant is broken down by the sunlight, creating a higher auxin concentration on the shady side of the stem. The shaded side of the stem grows faster than the sunny side, resulting in a "bend" toward the light.

You've probably seen this with houseplants. Unless you give the plant a turn now and then, all the leaves will soon be facing the window or light source. Because you can't very well give your lilac in the ground an occasional turn, the only way to keep it growing straight is to provide it with uniform light all around. If you prefer to keep the ash tree, a solution may be to replace the lilac with a shade-tolerant shrub such as hydrangea, fothergilla, or viburnum.

Light requirement for germination

Should I start my flower and vegetable seeds in the light or in the dark? Does it make any difference?

Most seeds germinate best in darkness. (They are buried in the soil, where there is no light.) However, as soon as the seedling emerges, it needs bright light or it will stretch excessively. Seeds of a few plants actually require light for best germination. These are usually small seeds that should be sown shallowly or on the soil's surface, where light can reach them. Among the plants that need light for germination are ageratum *(Ageratum houstonianum)*, California poppy *(Eschscholzia californica)*, blanket flower *(Gaillardia ×grandiflora)*, coleus *(Solenostemon scutellarioides)*, columbine *(Aquilegia)*, love-in-a-mist *(Nigella damascena)*, snapdragon *(Antirrhinum majus)*, Shasta daisy *(Leucanthemum ×superbum)*, strawflower *(Helichrysum bracteatum)*, sweet alyssum *(Lobularia maritima)*, and lettuce *(Lactuca sativa)*.

Low-E glass and plants

We're installing low-E glass windows in our new home. Will they be bad for my houseplants?

Low-E glass is short for low-emissivity glass. It is more energy-efficient than regular glass. To make low-E glass, regular glass is coated with an ultra-thin layer of metal oxide (either tin or silver). This treatment allows virtually all the visible spectrum of light to come through the window but blocks some of the ultraviolet (UV) and infrared (IR) light. UV light can cause fading damage to furniture and carpets, as well as contribute to sunburn. IR light causes heat buildup.

Because the visible spectrum of light is most important to plants, you should see little effect on the growth of your houseplants. In fact, they may grow better because the temperature may be more moderate.

Watering on a sunny day

I've heard that I shouldn't water plants in my garden when it is sunny because the drops of water can focus the sun's rays and burn the leaves. Do I need to be careful about when I water?

This is a gardening myth that refuses to die. Think about it. How often do plants get watered naturally by a passing shower, followed by exposure to bright sunshine? It happens all the time. Yet you don't see burned leaves in the garden. Watering during the sunniest part of the day will not sunburn your plants. In some cases it may even benefit the plants by cooling them off.

Overhead sprinkling during the middle of the day is not the most efficient way to water. The wind is often stronger then than it is early in the morning, so you'll lose more water to evaporation, and some of the spray may be blown away from the plants you intend to water. It's best to water early in the day so that plants will dry off before evening. Foliage and flowers that remain wet for a long time are more likely to develop disease problems.

TEMPERATURE

Hardening off

I started plants in a small greenhouse. I know that my plants should be "hardened" before I plant them outside, but I don't know what this process involves.

Hardening off means acclimating soft and tender growth—which has been protected from wind, cold, and strong sun—to outdoor conditions. Start the process of hardening off about 2 weeks before you intend to plant the seedlings outside. Water your seedlings well, then set them outdoors in a partially shaded spot. Leave the seedlings out for about an hour the first time. Repeat this process daily, gradually working up to a full day by the time they are scheduled to be transplanted into the garden.

There's no rush to set your plants out. If they're frost-tender, be sure that all danger of frost has passed. Transplant on a cloudy day, so strong sun won't wilt your seedlings.

Degree-days

What does the term "growing degree-days" have to do with gardening?

Growing degree-days are a measure of accumulated heat during the growing season. They are calculated by taking the daily maximum and minimum temperatures, determining an average, and comparing that to a base temperature. Growing degree-days directly relate to the growth and development of plants and insects. Below certain temperatures, no growth occurs (or it happens extremely slowly). At higher temperatures, development proceeds rapidly (unless it's so hot that stress sets in).

What this knowledge brings to your garden and landscape is a better predictor of when your plants will be in a certain stage of development or when insects may attack. Weather patterns can vary from year to year, so a calendar date prediction is not reliable for temperature-dependent events. For example, your forsythia shrub may bloom 2 weeks earlier this year than last if it is warmer. By the same token, the aphids that attack it likely will show up 2 weeks earlier as well.

Hardiness zones
When a plant is listed as hardy in Zones 4–9, what does that mean?

The USDA Hardiness Zone map (see page 603) was developed by examining average minimum winter temperatures for various locations over many years. Each zone covers a temperature range of 10°F, and the lower the number, the colder the average minimum winter temperature for that site. For example, plants hardy to Zone 4 should withstand the -30 to -20°F average mimimum winter low temperatures experienced there. Those in Zone 9 on average experience a minimum winter low temperature of +20 to +30°F. Some winters are milder than others, so you might be able to grow a Zone 6 plant in Zone 5 for a few years. But it's likely that a severe winter will eventually hit and kill the tender tree, shrub, or perennial. The USDA zones don't take into account the idiosyncrasies of your yard. You may have a protected spot where tender plants will thrive outside their usual zone.

Heat zones
I'm familiar with the USDA Hardiness Zones, but recently I heard about heat zones. Are they the same thing?

The American Horticulture Society (AHS) in conjunction with the USDA has expanded on the USDA Hardiness Zone designations to develop an AHS Plant Heat-Zone map. The USDA map tracks average winter cold. The AHS map measures the number of days that the high temperature reaches 86°F or higher at a given location. The reason this temperature is critical is that above 86°F, photosynthesis begins to shut down in most plants. That puts the plants under stress. Other plants operate with a different type of physiology and can take the heat better.

Similar to the USDA Hardiness Zone map, the AHS Plant Heat-Zone numbering system ranges from Zone 1 as the coolest to Zone 12 as the warmest. However, when a plant grows in a range of heat zones, the numbers are reversed. For example, a plant may be adapted to Heat Zones 9–4, meaning that it can tolerate 120–150 days (Heat Zone 9) to 14–30 days (Heat Zone 4) above 86°F annually.

Finding the right microclimate
I'd really like to grow rosemary in my Zone 6 garden, but have been told the plant is only hardy to Zone 7. Am I out of luck?

Most rosemary (*Rosmarinus officinalis*) cultivars are fully hardy only to Zone 7, but several, including 'Madalene Hill', 'Arp', and 'Athens Blue Spire' are slightly hardier than most. If you find the right microclimate for them in your yard, you may succeed with them. A microclimate is a pocket in your yard that differs from the basic growing conditions in your area. Because rosemary thrives in full sun and well-drained soil in a protected location, those conditions are what you should try to duplicate. Perhaps a raised bed on the south side of your home would provide a little extra warmth over the winter as well as permit the plant to get full sun. You could also grow rosemary in a container and move it indoors over the winter.

Frost dates

How do I find out what the frost dates are for my area?

Frost dates vary from year to year depending on weather conditions. Cold air pockets form at the base of hills, and large bodies of water modify the temperature. A protective canopy of a large tree may shield a portion of your garden from frost. The maps on page 603 illustrate the average last spring frost dates and first fall frost dates throughout the United States and Canada. Keep in mind that these are averages, and your yard may differ. For more specific dates, check with your local cooperative extension service office.

Also remember that a light frost (32°F) won't affect cool-season annuals such as cabbage, broccoli, pansies, and snapdragons, but this temperature will kill tender tomatoes, squash, impatiens, and basil. A hard frost (28°F), sometimes called a killing freeze, will damage blossoms on fruit trees and berries.

Frost heave

I planted some pansies last fall. During a midwinter thaw, I noticed that some of them were pushing up out of the ground. I'm sure I planted them deeply enough. Why are they doing this?

Your pansies are experiencing frost heave. Their root balls likely were growing in their pots in a soil mix high in organic matter. When they were placed in the ground, there was a strong difference in soil types between their root ball and the surrounding soil. As the ground freezes and thaws, the soil expands and contracts. Differing soil types lead to different rates of expansion and contraction. In the process, the pansies' roots were pushed up and out of the ground.

If the expelled root balls haven't dried out, you may be able to save the plants by poking them back into the ground. Of course, the root systems of these root balls are limited, so treat them as brand-new plantings, watering as necessary. To prevent frost heave from happening again, cover the soil with a couple of inches of organic mulch. The insulating effect of the mulch diminishes the effects of rapid temperature changes. Once the ground becomes frozen it will more likely stay frozen beneath the mulch until sustained warm temperatures arrive.

Frost crack

I have a 20-year-old shade tree that developed a split on its trunk last winter. It looks better this spring, but is there anything I should be doing to it?

It sounds as though your tree has a frost crack. Frost cracks develop from the expansion and contraction of bark and wood during wide temperature fluctuations in winter. A weakened section of the bark splits open from the stress. The sudden break is often accompanied by a loud noise like a gunshot. Cracks usually close up during the growing season, but they may remain partially open. If a large split fails to close, consult an arborist to install a rod or bolt to hold it together.

Heat affecting pollination

It's been extremely hot here lately, and my tomatoes have stopped producing fruit. Is it because it's so hot?

You've hit on the cause of your declining tomato yields. Although tomatoes are a warm-season crop, it can get too warm for them. Generally, tomatoes grow bigger, better, and faster the warmer the weather. However, when daytime highs regularly top 95°F, the plant's pollen can be killed. With no live pollen to pollinate the flower, fruits fail to develop. Varieties such as 'Heatwave II' tolerate the heat better than do others. If you're not growing a heat-tolerant variety, wait for the weather to cool down; normal fruit development should return. Other warm-season vegetables sensitive to excessive heat include pepper, eggplant, pumpkin, squash, and cucumber.

Annuals for heat

I have a sunny area in front of my house where I'd like to plant some annual flowers for color, but everything I've tried just burns up in the middle of summer. Can you suggest something that would grow in this heat trap?

Selecting the right plants for the site is a good start. Many annual flowers thrive in sun and heat if given adequate moisture. Some to try include annual blanket flower *(Gaillardia pulchella)*, globe amaranth *(Gomphrena globosa)*, lantana *(Lantana camara, L. montevidensis)*, moss rose *(Portulaca grandiflora)*, salvia *(Salvia splendens, S. farinacea)*, sunflower *(Helianthus annuus)*, vinca *(Catharanthus roseus)*, and narrowleaf zinnia *(Zinnia angustifolia)*.

Frost and fall color

My neighbor says that trees won't develop good fall color until we've had a frost. But I've noticed that some trees color up in late summer long before we've had a freeze. Do plants need to have frost for good fall color?

There is a connection between cool temperatures and fall color, but frost isn't necessary. Most plants produce a variety of pigments all summer long, but for most of the year green chlorophyll is produced in such abundance that it masks any of the other colors. As the days grow shorter and nights get cooler, chlorophyll breaks down faster than it is produced by the plant. That allows other pigments—yellow xanthophylls or carotenoids and reddish-purple anthocyanins—to take over. Brightest colors develop when sunny days are combined with cool nights. In fact, a hard frost dulls fall color by turning the leaves brown more rapidly.

Plants for Specific Sites

My yard is sunny and often dry. What plants would you suggest I grow?

You have many choices, especially if you water the plants for the first year or so while they establish. Try some of the following:

COMMON NAME	BOTANICAL NAME	ZONES
American cranberrybush viburnum	*Viburnum trilobum*	2–7
Amur maple	*Acer tataricum ginnala*	2–7
Anglo-Japanese yew	*Taxus ×media*	(4)5–7
Anthony Waterer spirea	*Spiraea japonica* 'Anthony Waterer'	3–8
Apple serviceberry	*Amelanchier ×grandiflora*	3–8
Bearded iris	*Iris* hybrids	3–9
Blanket flower	*Gaillardia ×grandiflora*	3–8
Bluebeard	*Caryopteris ×clandonensis*	(5)6–9
Bougainvillea	*Bougainvillea glabra*	10–11
Bush cinquefoil	*Potentilla fruticosa*	2–6(7)
Butterfly weed	*Asclepias tuberosa*	4–9
Canaert eastern red cedar	*Juniperus virginiana* 'Canaertii'	3–9
Chinese holly	*Ilex cornuta*	7–9
Chinese juniper	*Juniperus chinensis*	4–9
Chinese pistachio	*Pistacia chinensis*	6–9
Chinese wisteria	*Wisteria sinensis*	5–9
Colorado blue spruce	*Picea pungens* var. *glauca*	3–7
Common lilac	*Syringa vulgaris*	3–7
Cornelian cherry	*Cornus mas*	5–7
Cranberry cotoneaster	*Cotoneaster apiculatus*	4–7
Crape myrtle	*Lagerstroemia indica*	(5)6–10
Creeping juniper	*Juniperus horizontalis*	4–9
Creeping phlox	*Phlox subulata*	2–8
Daylily	*Hemerocallis* cultivars	3–10
Deodar cedar	*Cedrus deodara*	7–9
Douglas fir	*Pseudotsuga menziesii*	(3)4–6
Dwarf coyote bush	*Baccharis pilularis*	7–10
Dwarf Meyer lilac	*Syringa meyeri* 'Palibin'	3–7
Eastern redbud	*Cercis canadensis*	4–9
Eastern white pine	*Pinus strobus*	3–7(8)
Flowering crabapple	*Malus* spp.	4–8
Forsythia	*Forsythia ×intermedia*	(4)5–8(9)
Fragrant sumac	*Rhus aromatica*	3–9
Ginkgo	*Ginkgo biloba*	4–8(9)

COMMON NAME	BOTANICAL NAME	ZONES
Italian cypress	*Cupressus sempervirens*	8–10
Japanese barberry	*Berberis thunbergii*	(4)5–8
Japanese garden juniper	*Juniperus procumbens*	4–8
Kalm's St. Johnswort	*Hypericum kalmianum*	4–7
Kerria	*Kerria japonica*	5–9
Korean barberry	*Berberis koreana*	3–7
Lanceleaf coreopsis	*Coreopsis lanceolata*	4–9
Littleleaf linden	*Tilia cordata*	4–7
Mugo pine	*Pinus mugo*	3–7(8)
Ninebark	*Physocarpus opulifolius*	2–7
Northern bayberry	*Myrica pensylvanica*	(2)3–6(7)
Northern red oak	*Quercus rubra*	3–7
Norway spruce	*Picea abies*	2–6
Oriental arborvitae	*Thuja orientalis*	6–9
Oriental poppy	*Papaver orientale*	3–7
Pepper tree	*Schinus molle*	9–10
Purple beautyberry	*Callicarpa dichotoma*	5–8
Purple coneflower	*Echinacea purpurea*	3–9
Red-osier dogwood	*Cornus stolonifera*	2–7
Rugosa rose	*Rosa rugosa*	3–7
Savin juniper	*Juniperus sabina*	3–7
Scarlet firethorn	*Pyracantha coccinea*	6–9
Showy stonecrop	*Sedum spectabile*	3–10
Silver King artemisia	*Artemisia ludoviciana* 'Silver King'	4–9
Smoke tree	*Cotinus coggygria*	(4)5–8
Spike speedwell	*Veronica spicata*	4–8
Staghorn sumac	*Rhus typhina*	4–8
Star magnolia	*Magnolia stellata*	4–8
Thornless honeylocust	*Gleditsia triacanthos* var. *inermis*	4–9
Threadleaf yarrow	*Achillea filipendula*	3–9
Trailing lantana	*Lantana montevidensis*	9–10
Trident maple	*Acer buergerianum*	5–8
Turkish filbert	*Corylus colurna*	4–8
Washington hawthorn	*Crataegus phaenopyrum*	5–8
Weeping bottlebrush	*Callistemon viminalis*	8–10
Weigela	*Weigela florida*	4–8
White ash	*Fraxinus americana*	3–9
White spruce	*Picea glauca*	2–6
Winter King hawthorn	*Crataegus viridis* 'Winter King'	4–7
White fir	*Abies ×concolor*	4–7

Plants for sunny, moist conditions

What plans would you suggest for a sunny yard? It's usually moist, but never has standing water in it.

If your yard is blessed with sun and ample moisture, your choices are almost limitless. Here are a few of the many plants you could try.

COMMON NAME	BOTANICAL NAME	ZONES
Arrowwood viburnum	*Viburnum dentatum*	3–8
Bald cypress	*Taxodium distichum*	5–10
Bee balm, Oswego tea	*Monarda didyma*	3–9
Bloody cranesbill	*Geranium sanguineum*	4–8
Clematis cultivars	*Clematis cvs.*	3–8
Common boxwood	*Buxus sempervirens*	(5)6–9
Common witch hazel	*Hamamelis virginiana*	3–8
Dawn redwood	*Metasequoia glyptostroboides*	5–8
Dwarf fothergilla	*Fothergilla gardenii*	5–8(9)
Eastern arborvitae	*Thuja occidentalis*	3–7
European beech	*Fagus sylvatica*	(4)5–7
Foxglove	*Digitalis purpurea*	3–8
Fringe tree	*Chionanthus virginicus*	4–9
Garden phlox	*Phlox paniculata*	3–8
Japanese maple	*Acer palmatum*	5–8
Katsura tree	*Cercidiphyllum japonicum*	5–8
Kentucky coffee tree	*Gymnocladus dioica*	(3)4–8
Kousa dogwood	*Cornus kousa*	5–8
Limber pine	*Pinus flexilis*	4–7
Mockorange	*Philadelphus coronarius*	4–8
Panicle hydrangea	*Hydrangea paniculata*	4–8
Pincushion flower	*Scabiosa caucasica*	3–8
Red chokeberry	*Aronia arbutifolia*	(4)5–9
Red maple	*Acer rubrum*	3–9
River birch	*Betula nigra*	4–9
Shasta daisy	*Leucanthemum xsuperbum*	4–8
Southern magnolia	*Magnolia grandiflora*	(6)7–9(10)
Spike gayfeather	*Liatris spicata*	3–9
Summersweet	*Clethra alnifolia*	4–9
Swamp white oak	*Quercus bicolor*	4–8
Virginia sweetspire	*Itea virginica*	(5)6–9
Willow oak	*Quercus phellos*	5–9
Winterberry	*Ilex verticillata*	3–9

Plants for wet site

A section of my back yard is always soggy. What plants could I grow there?

If the area is constantly wet, but not inundated, bog plants will be your best bet. The following list contains plants that thrive in wet soil.

COMMON NAME	BOTANICAL NAME	ZONES
Bigleaf ligularia	*Ligularia dentata*	3–8
Calla lily	*Zantedeschia aethiopica*	9–10
Cardinal flower	*Lobelia cardinalis*	3–9
Elephant's ear	*Alocasia* cvs.	8–10
Japanese iris	*Iris ensata*	4–9
Japanese primrose	*Primula japonica*	5–7
Moneywort	*Lysimachia nummularia*	3–8
Ostrich fern	*Matteuccia struthiopteris*	3–8
Pink turtlehead	*Chelone lyonii*	3–10
Rodgersia	*Rodgersia pinnata*	4–7
Siberian iris	*Iris sibirica*	3–9
Spiderwort	*Tradescantia virginiana*	4–9

Plants for standing water

We have a pond that slopes to a shallow edge. We'd like to grow something other than cattails. What would grow well there?

Quite a few plants tolerate shallow, standing water. Check at your local nursery or water garden supply store for some of the following plants.

COMMON NAME	BOTANICAL NAME	ZONES
Bald cypress	*Taxodium distichum*	5–10
Bowles' Golden sedge	*Carex elata* 'Bowles' Golden'	5–9
Dwarf papyrus	*Cyperus profiler*	9–10
Fragrant water lily	*Nymphaea odorata*	3–8
Giant reed	*Arundo donax*	7–10
Japanese iris	*Iris ensata*	4–9
Japanese sweet flag	*Acorus gramineus*	8–9
Marsh marigold	*Caltha palustrus*	4–7
Sacred lotus	*Nelumbo nucifera*	8–10
Soft rush	*Juncus effusus*	6–9
Taro	*Colocasia esculenta*	10–11
Yellow flag	*Iris pseudacorus*	5–9

Plants for shade

Some of our yard has dense shade, and the rest high, thin shade. What are some plants we could grow?

You've hit on a question many gardeners eventually deal with. As trees get larger, they cast more shade. What once was a sunny spot becomes partially shaded, and part shade becomes full shade. The degree of shade is relative, and changes over time. The following list of shade-tolerant plants grow in light to medium shade.

COMMON NAME	BOTANICAL NAME	ZONES
Ajuga, Bugleweed	*Ajuga reptans*	3–9
Alleghany foam flower	*Tiarella cordifolia*	3–8
Anglo-Japanese yew	*Taxus ×media*	(4)5–7
Astilbe	*Astilbe ×arendsii*	3–8
Balloon flower	*Platycodon grandiflorus*	3–8
Bay laurel	*Laurus nobilis*	8–10
Bethlehem sage	*Pulmonaria saccharata*	3–8
Big leaf hydrangea	*Hydrangea macrophylla*	(5)6–9
Bottlebrush buckeye	*Aesculus parviflora*	4–9
Carolina cherry laurel	*Prunus caroliniana*	7–10
Cast-iron plant	*Aspidistra elatior*	8–11
Catawba rhododendron	*Rhododendron catawbiense*	5–8
Chinese photinia	*Photinia serrulata*	6–9
Chinese podocarpus	*Podocarpus macrophyllus* var. *maki*	8–10
Chinese witch hazel	*Hamamelis mollis*	5–8
Columbine hybrids	*Aquilegia ×hybrida*	3–9
Common bleeding heart	*Dicentra spectabilis*	3–9
Common foxglove	*Digitalis purpurea*	3–8
Common periwinkle	*Vinca minor*	4–9
Coral bells	*Heuchera sanguinea*	3–8
Creeping phlox	*Phlox stolonifera*	2–8
Downy serviceberry	*Amelanchier arborea*	4–9
Drooping leucothoe	*Leucothoe fontanesiana*	5–8
Dwarf palmetto	*Sabal minor*	9–10
Eastern redbud	*Cercis canadensis*	4–9
English ivy	*Hedera helix*	5–10
European wild ginger	*Asarum europaeum*	4–7
False Solomon's seal	*Smilacina racemosa*	4–9
Flowering dogwood	*Cornus florida*	5–9
Fringed bleeding heart	*Dicentra eximia*	3–8
Glossy abelia	*Abelia ×grandiflora*	(5)6–9

COMMON NAME	BOTANICAL NAME	ZONES
Goatsbeard	*Aruncus dioicus*	3–7
Heavenly bamboo	*Nandina domestica*	6–9(10)
Hinoki false cypress	*Chamaecyparis obtusa*	5–8
Hosta	*Hosta* species and cultivars	3–8
Italian arum	*Arum italicum*	6–9
Japanese anemone	*Anemone ×hupehensis*	5–8
Japanese aucuba	*Aucuba japonica*	(6)7–10
Japanese camellia	*Camellia japonica*	(7)8–10
Japanese fatsia	*Fatsia japonica*	8–10
Japanese maple	*Acer palmatum*	5–8
Japanese pieris	*Pieris japonica*	5–9
Japanese pittosporum	*Pittosporum tobira*	(8)9–10
Japanese spurge	*Pachysandra terminalis*	4–8
Lady's mantle	*Alchemilla mollis*	3–7
Lamium, spotted deadnettle	*Lamium maculatum*	4–8
Large fothergilla	*Fothergilla major*	5–8(9)
Leadwort, Plumbago	*Ceratostigma plumbaginoides*	5–9
Lenten rose	*Helleborus orientalis*	4–9
Lily-of-the-valley	*Convallaria majalis*	2–7
Lilyturf	*Liriope spicata*	5–10
Maidenhair fern	*Adiantum pedatum*	3–8
Meadow rue	*Thalictrum aquilegifolium*	3–9
Mondo grass	*Ophiopogon japonicus*	7–11
Moneywort	*Lysimachia nummularia*	3–8
Monkshood	*Aconitum carmichaelii*	3–7
Oakleaf hydrangea	*Hydrangea quercifolia*	5–9
Philodendron	*Philodendron* spp.	10–11
Red barrenwort	*Epimedium ×rubrum*	4–8
Small Solomon's seal	*Polygonatum biflorum*	3–9
Spicebush	*Lindera benzoin*	5–9
Star jasmine	*Trachelospermum jasminoides*	8–10
Strawberry geranium	*Saxifraga stolonifera*	6–9
Summersweet	*Clethra alnifolia*	4–9
Toad lily	*Tricyrtis hirta*	5–9
Vinca, large periwinkle	*Vinca major*	6–9
Viola	*Viola cornuta*	5–9
Virginia bluebells	*Mertensia virginica*	3–7
White fringe tree	*Chionanthus virginicus*	4–9
Yellow archangel	*Lamium galeobdolon*	4–9

The soil in our yard is nothing but heavy clay. Do we have to amend it before we can grow anything?

While amending your garden's soil with organic matter will loosen the clay and give you more options of plants to grow, many plants will grow in unamended clay. If you prefer to avoid the work of amending the soil, try some of these clay lovers.

COMMON NAME	BOTANICAL NAME	ZONES
Bur oak	*Quercus macrocarpa*	3–8
Bush cinquefoil	*Potentilla fruticosa*	2–6(7)
Butterfly weed	*Asclepias tuberosa*	4–9
Callery pear cultivars	*Pyrus calleryana* cvs.	5–8(9)
Chinese juniper	*Juniperus chinensis*	4–9
Common lilac	*Syringa vulgaris*	3–7
Eastern arborvitae	*Thuja occidentalis*	3–7
European black alder	*Alnus glutinosa*	3–7
European larch	*Larix decidua*	(3)4–6(7)
Flowering crabapple	*Malus* spp.	4–8
Forsythia	*Forsythia* ×*intermedia*	4–8(9)
Golden rain tree	*Koelreuteria paniculata*	5–9
Hackberry	*Celtis occidentalis*	3–9
Hedge maple	*Acer campestre*	5–8
Honeysuckle	*Lonicera* spp.	2–9
Littleleaf linden	*Tilia cordata*	4–7
Northern bayberry	*Myrica pensylvanica*	(2)3–6(7)
Norway maple	*Acer platanoides*	3–7
Norway spruce	*Picea abies*	2–7
Obedient plant	*Physostegia virginiana*	3–8
Ox-eye daisy	*Leucanthemum vulgare*	4–9
Peony	*Paeonia* cvs.	3–8
Pin oak	*Quercus palustris*	4–8
Red-osier dogwood	*Cornus stolonifera*	2–7
River birch	*Betula nigra*	4–9
Russian olive	*Elaeagnus angustifolia*	2–7
Siberian peashrub	*Caragana arborescens*	2–7
Thornless honeylocust	*Gleditsia triacanthos* var. *inermis*	4–9
Viburnum	*Viburnum* spp.	2–8
White willow	*Salix alba*	2–8
Winged euonymus	*Euonymus alatus*	4–8(9)

Plants for sandy soil

Our front yard has extremely sandy soil. Sandburs and cactus grow well there, but the grass always dies out. What other ornamental plants would grow well there?

Most plants grow in sandy soil if they get enough moisture. Assuming you'd rather not irrigate constantly, choose some of the following plants that do well on sandy sites.

COMMON NAME	BOTANICAL NAME	ZONES
American holly	*Ilex opaca*	5–9
Amur privet	*Ligustrum amurense*	4–7
Butterfly bush	*Buddleia davidii*	5–9
Chinese juniper	*Juniperus chinensis*	4–9
Chinese pistachio	*Pistacia chinensis*	6–9
Creeping juniper	*Juniperus horizontalis*	3–9
Flowering quince	*Chaenomeles speciosa*	5–9
Fragrant sumac	*Rhus aromatica*	3–9
Hedge maple	*Acer campestre*	5–8
Japanese barberry	*Berberis thunbergii*	4–8
Japanese black pine	*Pinus thunbergii*	5–8
Japanese pittosporum	*Pittosporum tobira*	(8)9–10
Japanese spirea	*Spiraea japonica*	4–8
Kerria	*Kerria japonica*	5–9
Lavender cotton	*Santolina chamaecyparissus*	6–9
London plane tree	*Platanus ×acerifolia*	(5)6–8
Northern bayberry	*Myrica pensylvanica*	(2)3–6(7)
Pomegranate	*Punica granatum*	(7)8–10
Russian olive	*Elaeagnus angustifolia*	2–7
Shore juniper	*Juniperus conferta*	6–9
Trailing lantana	*Lantana montevidensis*	9–11
White spruce	*Picea glauca*	2–6

I know that blueberries need acidic soil to grow well. What other plants grow well in acidic soils?

Blueberries, azaleas, rhododendrons, heaths, and heathers require acidic growing conditions. See below for a more extensive list of acid-loving plants.

COMMON NAME	BOTANICAL NAME	ZONES
Australian tea tree	*Leptospermum laevigatum*	9–10
Azalea	*Rhododendron*	4–10
Camellia	*Camellia japonica*	(7)8–10
Canadian hemlock	*Tsuga canadensis*	(3)4–7
Carolina silverbell	*Halesia carolina*	5–9
Chinese tallow tree	*Sapium sebiferum*	8–9
Douglas fir	*Pseudotsuga menziesii*	(3)4–6
Himalayan pine	*Pinus wallichiana*	5–7
Holly	*Ilex* spp.	3–9
Japanese pieris	*Pieris japonica*	5–9
Lupine cultivars	*Lupinus* cvs.	4–8
Manzanita	*Arctostaphylos* spp.	8–10
Mountain laurel	*Kalmia latifolia*	5–9
Pin oak	*Quercus palustris*	4–8
Quaking aspen	*Populus tremuloides*	1–6
Scotch broom	*Cytisus scopularius*	5–8
Scotch heather	*Calluna vulgaris*	5–7
Sourwood	*Oxydendrum arboreum*	5–9
Spruce	*Picea* spp.	2–8
Threadleaf coreopsis	*Coreopsis verticillata*	4–9
Winter heath	*Erica carnea*	5–7

Plants for alkaline soil

The pH in our landscape is quite high—nearly 8.0. Do we need to lower the pH before installing our landscape?

You could work at lowering the pH by applying elemental sulfur or iron sulfate to the soil. Alternatively, you could grow plants adapted to the alkaline conditions in your yard, and save yourself some work. The following plants grow well in alkaline soil conditions.

COMMON NAME	BOTANICAL NAME	ZONES
American hornbeam	*Carpinus caroliniana*	3–9
American sycamore	*Platanus occidentalis*	4–9
American yellowwood	*Cladrastis kentuckea*	4–8
Black locust	*Robinia pseudoacacia*	4–8(9)
Bottlebrush buckeye	*Aesculus parviflora*	4–8
Chinese jujube	*Ziziphus jujuba*	6–9
Chinese juniper	*Juniperus chinensis*	4–9
Cornelian cherry	*Cornus mas*	5–8
Deutzia	*Deutzia* spp.	(4)5–8
Forsythia	*Forsythia* ×*intermedia*	(4)5–8(9)
Fragrant sumac	*Rhus aromatica*	3–9
Golden rain tree	*Koelreuteria paniculata*	5–9
Hackberry	*Celtis occidentalis*	3–9
Lemon bottlebrush	*Callistemon citrinus*	(8)9–11
Pawpaw	*Asimina triloba*	5–8
Persian lilac	*Syringa persica*	3–7
Queen-of-the-prairie	*Filipendula rubra*	3–9
Russian olive	*Elaeagnus angustifolia*	2–7
Sassafras	*Sassafras albidum*	(4)5–9
Scarlet firethorn	*Pyracantha coccinea*	6–9
Siberian peashrub	*Caragana arborescens*	2–7
Southern catalpa	*Catalpa bignonioides*	5–9
Speckled alder	*Alnus rugosa*	3–6
Sugarberry	*Celtis laevigata*	5–9
Wintergreen barberry	*Berberis julianae*	5–8

We have a condo on the beach and would like to do some landscaping. When it's windy, the area gets a lot of salt spray from the ocean. What plants would stand up to these harsh conditions?

Many plants are sensitive to salt, either from seaside spray or from roadside ice melt. But fortunately for you, a wide array of plants is adapted to salt spray. Select some from the following list for your landscaping project.

COMMON NAME	BOTANICAL NAME	ZONES
Aleppo pine	*Pinus halepensis*	8–10
Black locust	*Robinia pseudoacacia*	4–8(9)
Bougainvillea	*Bougainvillea glabra*	9–10
Cabbage tree	*Cordyline australis*	9–10
Chinese jujube	*Ziziphus jujuba*	6–9
Fan palm	*Chamaerops humilis*	9–10
Groundsel bush	*Baccharis halimifolia*	5–9
Japanese black pine	*Pinus thunbergii*	5–8
Japanese privet	*Ligustrum japonicum*	7–10
Natal plum	*Carissa macrocarpa*	10–11
New Zealand tea tree	*Leptospermum scoparium*	9–10
Norfolk Island pine	*Araucaria heterophylla*	10–11
Oleander	*Nerium oleander*	8–10
Pampas grass	*Cortaderia selloana*	8–10
Rose of Sharon	*Hibiscus syriacus*	5–8(9)
Rosemary	*Rosmarinus officinalis*	(6)7–9
Russian olive	*Elaeagnus angustifolia*	2–7
Scarlet firethorn	*Pyracantha coccinea*	6–9
Sea thrift	*Armeria maritima*	3–9
Siberian peashrub	*Caragana arborescens*	2–7
Southern live oak	*Quercus virginiana*	(7)8–10
Strawberry tree	*Arbutus unedo*	7–9
Tamarisk	*Tamarix ramosissima*	3(4)–8
Trailing ice plant	*Lampranthus spectabilis*	9–10
Weeping bottlebrush	*Callistemon viminalis*	8–10
White poplar	*Populus alba*	3–10

Walnut toxicity

I've heard that walnuts can kill other plants. Is this true?

Yes, walnut (Juglans spp.) is toxic to many other plants. Roots and leaves produce a toxin called juglone that adversely affects the growth of some species. Avoid growing the following plants near a walnut tree.

COMMON NAME	BOTANICAL NAME	ZONES
American linden	*Tilia americana*	3–8
Apple	*Malus sylvestris* var. *domestica*	3–10
Asparagus	*Asparagus officinalis*	4–9
Autumn crocus	*Colchicum autumnale*	5–9
Blackberry	*Rubus laciniatus*	4–9
Bush cinquefoil	*Potentilla fruticosa*	2–6(7)
Cabbage	*Brassica oleracea capitata*	NA
Common lilac	*Syringa vulgaris*	3–7
Common privet	*Ligustrum vulgare*	4–7
Cotoneaster	*Cotoneaster* spp.	4–7
Eastern white pine	*Pinus strobus*	3–7(8)
European white birch	*Betula pendula*	2–6
Flowering crabapple	*Malus* spp.	4–8
Norway spruce	*Picea abies*	2–7
Peony	*Paeonia officinalis*	3–8
Pepper	*Capsicum annuum*	NA
Potato	*Solanum tuberosum*	NA
Red pine	*Pinus resinosa*	2–6
Rhododendron, Azalea	*Rhododendron* spp.	4–10
Saucer magnolia	*Magnolia* ×*soulangiana*	4–9
Scotch pine	*Pinus sylvestris*	2–8
Tomato	*Lycopersicon esculentum*	NA

I moved from the Great Lakes area to the Gulf Coast several years ago. I loved the lupines and delphiniums I used to grow in my garden, but have had no luck with them here. Is there something I could do to grow these lovely perennials in the South?

Delphinium and lupine are cool-season perennials that thrive in Detroit, but fade quickly in New Orleans. Instead of pining for these cool-season beauties, try some warmth-loving landscape plants in your southern garden. You'll find a list below for hot-weather plants that love summer heat, and another for cool-climate plants to avoid in hot-weather regions.

Cool-climate plants—decline in hot weather

COMMON NAME	BOTANICAL NAME	ZONES
Balsam fir	*Abies balsamea*	2–5
English daisy	*Bellis perennis*	(4)5–6
European beech	*Fagus sylvatica*	(4)5–7
European black alder	*Alnus glutinosa*	3–7
Globeflower	*Trollius ×cultorum*	3–6
Goldenchain tree	*Laburnum ×watereri*	6–7
Hybrid bee delphinium	*Delphinium ×elatum*	2–7
Iceland poppy	*Papaver nudicaule*	2–8
Japanese larch	*Larix kaempferi*	4–6
Japanese primrose	*Primula japonica*	5–7
Johnny-jump-up	*Viola tricolor*	NA
Lady's mantle	*Alchemilla mollis*	3–7
Leopard's bane	*Doronicum orientale*	4–7
Lily-of-the-valley	*Convallaria majalis*	2–7
Lupine	*Lupinus* hybrids	4–8
Monkshood	*Aconitum carmichaelii*	3–7
Northern bayberry	*Myrica pensylvanica*	(2)3–6(7)
Norway maple	*Acer platanoides*	3–7
Oriental poppy	*Papaver orientale*	3–7
Pansy	*Viola ×wittrockiana*	5–8
Pinks	*Dianthus plumarius*	4–9
Pot marigold	*Calendula officinalis*	NA
Quaking aspen	*Populus tremuloides*	1–6
Rockfoil	*Saxifraga ×arendsii*	5–7
Russian olive	*Elaeagnus angustifolia*	2–7
Scotch heather	*Calluna vulgaris*	4–6
Soapwort	*Saponaria ocymoides*	3–8
Sweet pea	*Lathyrus odoratus*	NA
Winter heath	*Erica carnea*	5–7

Hot-weather plants—not frost-tolerant

COMMON NAME	BOTANICAL NAME	ZONES
Amaryllis	*Hippeastrum* cvs.	10–11
Angel's trumpet	*Brugmansia suaveolens*	10–11
Anthurium, flamingo flower	*Anthurium andraeanum*	10–11
Apricot moonflower	*Brugmansia versicolor*	9–11
Australian tree fern	*Cyathea australis*	9–10
Bengal clock vine	*Thunbergia grandiflora*	10–11
Bird of paradise	*Strelitzia reginae*	9–11
Bougainvillea	*Bougainvillea glabra*	10–11
Bower vine	*Pandorea jasminoides*	10–11
Caladium	*Caladium bicolor*	8–11
Calla lily	*Zantedeschia* cvs.	9–11
Cape leadwort	*Plumbago auriculata*	9–11
Chinese hibiscus	*Hibiscus rosa-sinensis*	10–11
Copperleaf	*Acalypha wilkesiana*	10–11
Crape myrtle	*Lagerstroemia indica*	(5)6–10
Cypress vine	*Ipomoea quamoclit*	8–10
Elephant's ear	*Alocasia macrorrhiza*	8–10
Flowering maple	*Abutilon* ×*hybridum*	8–10
Frangipani	*Plumeria rubra*	10–11
Golden trumpet	*Allamanda cathartica*	10–11
Golden vine	*Stigmaphyllon ciliatum*	10–11
Jungle flame	*Ixora coccinea*	10–11
Lily-of-the-Nile	*Agapanthus africanus*	10–11
Lobster claw	*Heliconia* spp.	10–11
Lollipop plant	*Pachystachys lutea*	10–11
Mandevilla	*Mandevilla* ×*amabilis*	10–11
Moonflower vine	*Ipomoea alba*	8–10
Morning glory	*Ipomoea tricolor*	NA
Musk mallow	*Abelmoschus moschatus*	9–11
Oleander	*Nerium oleander*	8–10
Orange jessamine	*Murraya paniculata*	10–11
Ornamental banana	*Musa* spp.	10–11
Poinsettia	*Euphorbia pulcherrima*	10–11
Red Abyssinian banana	*Ensete ventricosum* 'Maurellii'	10–11
Taro	*Colocasia esculenta*	10–11
Vinca	*Catharanthus roseus*	10–11
White ginger	*Hedychium coronarium*	9–11
Wood rose	*Ipomoea tuberosa*	10–11

Deer constantly decimate the plants in my yard. I get tired of applying repellants to deter them. Are there any plants that they won't eat?

If deer are hungry enough, they'll eat almost anything. However, they do have preferences in plants. Avoid growing plants favored by deer (see below). Instead grow those in the list of plants resistant to deer.

Plants somewhat resistant to deer

COMMON NAME	BOTANICAL NAME	ZONES
American arborvitae	*Thuja occidentalis*	3–7
Astilbe	*Astilbe ×arendsii*	3–8
Bald cypress	*Taxodium distichum*	5–10
Barberry	*Berberis* spp.	3–8
Barrenwort	*Epimedium* spp.	4–8
Boxwood	*Buxus* spp.	(5)6–9
Bugleweed	*Ajuga reptans*	3–9
Butterfly bush	*Buddleia davidii*	5–9
Cardinal flower	*Lobelia cardinalis*	3–9
Catawba rhododendron	*Rhododendron catawbiense*	5–8
Dawn redwood	*Metasequoia glyptostroboides*	5–8
Delphinium	*Delphinium* spp.	2–7
Drooping leucothoe	*Leucothoe fontanesiana*	5–8
European beech	*Fagus sylvatica*	(4)5–7
Flowering dogwood	*Cornus florida*	5–9
Forsythia	*Forsythia ×intermedia*	4–8(9)
Foxglove	*Digitalis purpurea*	3–8
Gardenia	*Gardenia* spp.	(7)8–10
Ginkgo	*Ginkgo biloba*	4–8(9)
Green Ash, white ash	*Fraxinus* spp.	(2)3–9
Heavenly bamboo	*Nandina domestica*	6–9(10)
Japanese kerria	*Kerria japonica*	5–9
Japanese pieris	*Pieris japonica*	5–9
Jasmine	*Jasminum* spp.	8–10
Juniper	*Juniperus* spp.	2–9
Larch	*Larix* spp.	(3)4–6(7)
Lenten rose	*Helleborus orientalis*	4–9
Lungwort	*Pulmonaria* cvs.	3–8
Lupine	*Lupinus* hybrids	4–8
Narcissus, daffodil	*Narcissus* spp.	3–8
Oleander	*Nerium oleander*	8–10
Oregon grapeholly	*Mahonia aquifolium*	5–9

Periwinkle	*Vinca minor*	4–9
Russian olive	*Elaeagnus angustifolia*	2–7
Russian sage	*Perovskia atriplicifolia*	3–9
Sage	*Salvia ×superba*	4–9
Scotch broom	*Cytissus scoparius*	5–8
Slender deutzia	*Deutzia gracilis*	(4)5–8
Smoke tree	*Cotinus coggygria*	(4)5–8
Speedwell	*Veronica spicata*	3–8
Spotted deadnettle	*Lamium maculatum*	4–8
Summersweet	*Clethra alnifolia*	4–9
Sweet autumn clematis	*Clematis terniflora*	5–8
Trumpet honeysuckle	*Lonicera sempervirens*	4–9
Viburnum	*Viburnum* spp.	2–8
White, Norway, Colorado spruces	*Picea* spp.	2–7
Yaupon	*Ilex vomitoria*	7–10

Plants favored by deer

COMMON NAME	BOTANICAL NAME	ZONES
Anglo-Japanese yew	*Taxus ×media*	(4)5–7
Apple	*Malus sylvestris* var. *domestica*	3–10
Azalea	*Rhododendron* spp.	4–10
Blackberry, raspberry	*Rubus* spp.	4–9
Cherry, plum	*Prunus* spp.	2–9
Coral bells	*Heuchera sanguinea*	3–8
Coralberry, snowberry	*Symphorocarpos* spp.	3–7
Daylily	*Hemerocallis* hybrids	3–10
Downy serviceberry	*Amelanchier arborea*	4–9
Eastern redbud	*Cercis canadensis*	4–9
English Ivy	*Hedera helix*	4–9
Fir	*Abies* spp.	2–7
Garden phlox	*Phlox paniculata*	3–8
Hosta	*Hosta* hybrids	3–8
Hydrangea	*Hydrangea* spp.	3–9
Japanese euonymus	*Euonymus japonicus*	7–9
Lily	*Lilium* cvs.	3–8
Norway maple	*Acer platanoides*	3–7
Red-osier dogwood	*Cornus stolonifera*	2–7
Rose	*Rosa* cvs.	3–10
Showy stonecrop	*Sedum spectabile*	3–10
Spiderwort	*Tradescantia ×virginiana*	4–9
Tulip	*Tulipa* hybrids	3–8

Rabbits plague my garden. As soon as I plant something, they chew it down. Could I plant something that they won't immediately devour?

Rascally rabbits can quickly do damage in a garden. Rabbit repellants or fencing may be worth exploring. But your selection of plants may affect the amount of damage you can expect. Some plants seem to be like candy to bunnies, while they pass up others nearby. Avoid growing their favorites (see below). Grow rabbit-resistant plants instead.

Plants somewhat resistant to rabbits

COMMON NAME	BOTANICAL NAME	ZONES
American holly	*Ilex opaca*	5–9
Butterfly bush	*Buddleia davidii*	5–9
Forsythia	*Forsythia ×intermedia*	4–8(9)
Juniper	*Juniperus* spp.	3–9
Onion, chive, garlic	*Allium* spp.	3–10
Pine	*Pinus* spp.	3–8
Spotted deadnettle	*Lamium maculatum*	3–8
Spruce	*Picea* spp.	2–8
White ash	*Fraxinus americana*	4–9
White sage	*Artemisia ludoviciana albula*	4–9
Wild thyme	*Thymus serphyllum*	4–9
Wintercreeper euonymus	*Euonymus fortunei*	4–8

Plants favored by rabbits

American hornbeam	*Carpinus caroliniana*	3–9
American linden	*Tilia americana*	3–8
American yellowwood	*Cladrastis kentuckea*	4–8
Apple	*Malus sylvestris* var. *domestica*	3–10
Babylon weeping willow	*Salix babylonica*	5–8
Blackberry, red raspberry	*Rubus* spp.	4–9
Dogwood	*Cornus* spp.	2–9
European mountain ash	*Sorbus aucuparia*	3–7
Garden pea	*Pisum sativum*	NA
Green bean, string bean	*Phaseolus vulgaris*	NA
Japanese barberry	*Berberis thunbergii*	4–8
Maple	*Acer* spp.	2–9
Oak	*Quercus* spp.	3–9(10)
Rose	*Rosa* spp.	3–10
Staghorn sumac	*Rhus typhina*	4–8
Thornless honeylocust	*Gleditsia triacanthos* var. *inermis*	4–9
Tulip	*Tulipa* hybrids	3–8

Gypsy moth-resistant trees

I understand that oaks are a favorite food of gypsy moths. What else do they like to eat? Are there some trees that they won't eat?

You're right. Gypsy moths prefer oaks of all types, but other trees are on their preferred dining list too (see below). To avoid damage to your trees from gypsy moth feeding, grow some of the trees on the list of trees resistant to gypsy moth.

Trees resistant to gypsy moth

COMMON NAME	BOTANICAL NAME	ZONES
American sycamore	*Platanus occidentalis*	(4)5–9
Balsam fir	*Abies balsamea*	2–5
Black locust	*Robinia pseudoacacia*	4–8(9)
Black walnut	*Juglans nigra*	4–9
Catalpa	*Catalpa* spp.	4–8(9)
Eastern red cedar	*Juniperus virginiana*	2–9
Flowering dogwood	*Cornus florida*	5–9
Golden larch	*Pseudolarix amabilis*	(5)6–7
Gray dogwood	*Cornus racemosa*	3–8
Green ash, white ash	*Fraxinus* spp.	(2)3–9
Holly	*Ilex* spp.	3–9
London plane tree	*Platanus ×acerifolia*	5(6)–8
Tulip tree	*Liriodendron tulipifera*	(4)5–9

Plants favored by gypsy moth

American arborvitae	*Thuja occidentalis*	3–7
American elm, Siberian elm	*Ulmus* spp.	2–9
Apple, flowering crabapple	*Malus* spp.	3–8
Black gum, black tupelo	*Nyssa sylvatica*	5–9
Canadian hemlock	*Tsuga canadensis*	(3)4–7
Cottonwood, poplar	*Populus* spp.	1–9
Douglas fir	*Pseudotsuga menziesii*	(3)4–6
European black alder	*Alnus glutinosa*	3–7
Hawthorn	*Crataegus* spp.	4–8
Hickory, pecan	*Carya* spp.	4–9
Linden	*Tilia* spp.	2–8
Maple	*Acer* spp.	2–9
Oak	*Quercus* spp.	3–9(10)
Pine	*Pinus* spp.	3–8
Sassafras	*Sassafras albidum*	(4)5–9
Spruce	*Picea* spp.	2–8
Willow	*Salix* spp.	2–8

Is there anything Japanese beetles won't eat? They're crawling all over everything in my yard.

Japanese beetle adults are general feeders, and will eat many landscape plants. A few are less attractive to them than most (see resistant plants, below). Some are especially attractive to Japanese beetles. Avoid growing these plants. Once the beetles start feeding on them, they send out a signal to others that the eating is good, and beetles from hundreds of yards away come flying in to join the feast.

Plants resistant to Japanese beetle

COMMON NAME	BOTANICAL NAME	ZONES
American holly	*Ilex opaca*	5–9
Dogwood	*Cornus* spp.	2–9
Forsythia	*Forsythia* ×*intermedia*	4–8(9)
Ginkgo	*Ginkgo biloba*	4–8(9)
Lilac	*Syringa* spp.	3–7
Silver linden	*Tilia tomentosa*	4–7
Tamarisk	*Tamarix ramosissima*	(3)4–8

Plants favored by Japanese beetle adults

American sycamore	*Platanus occidentalis*	(4)5–9
Apple, flowering crabapple	*Malus* spp.	3–8
Astilbe	*Astilbe* ×*arendsii*	3–8
Azalea	*Rhododendron* cvs.	4–10
Blueberry	*Vaccinium* spp.	3–9
Crape myrtle	*Lagerstroemia indica*	(5)6–10
Elm	*Ulmus* spp.	2–9
Flowering cherry, peach	*Prunus* spp.	3–9
Flowering quince	*Chaenomeles speciosa*	5–9
Grape	*Vitis* spp.	4–10
Hollyhock	*Alcea rosea*	3–9
Horsechestnut	*Aesculus hippocastanum*	4–7
Japanese maple, Norway maple	*Acer* spp.	4–8
Linden	*Tilia* spp.	2–8
Northern bayberry	*Myrica pensylvanica*	(2)3–6(7)
Pussy willow	*Salix discolor*	4–8
Raspberry	*Rubus idaeus*	3–7
Rose	*Rosa* spp.	3–10
Rose of Sharon	*Hibiscus syriacus*	5–8(9)
Viburnum	*Viburnum* spp.	2–8
Virginia creeper	*Parthenocissus quinquefolia*	3–9

I'd like to plant some evergreen trees in my landscape. What would you suggest?

Evergreens are a great way to add color to the winter landscape. Keep in mind that numerous trees other than needled evergreens retain their foliage through winter. Grow an assortment of needled and broadleaf evergreens for variety, texture, and color in your yard all year long.

COMMON NAME	BOTANICAL NAME	ZONES
Arborvitae	*Thuja* spp.	2–8
Arizona cypress	*Cupressus arizonica*	7–9
Atlas cedar, deodar cedar	*Cedrus* spp.	5–9
Australian tea tree	*Leptospermum laevigatum*	9–10
Balsam fir, noble fir, white fir	*Abies* spp.	3–7
Camphor tree	*Cinnamomum camphora*	9–10
Canadian hemlock	*Tsuga canadensis*	(3)4–7
China fir	*Cunninghamia lanceolata*	7–9
Coast redwood	*Sequoia sempervirens*	7–9
Colorado spruce, Norway spruce	*Picea* spp.	2–9
Douglas fir	*Pseudotsuga menziesii*	(3)4–6
Eastern red cedar	*Juniperus virginiana*	2–9
False cypress	*Chamaecyparis* spp.	5–8
Giant sequoia	*Sequoiadendron giganteum*	6–8
Holly	*Ilex* spp.	5–9
Incense cedar	*Calocedrus decurrens*	5–8
Japanese cedar	*Cryptomeria japonica*	(5)6–8
Japanese plum yew	*Cephalotaxus harringtonia*	6–9
Live oak, holly oak	*Quercus* spp.	8–10
Loquat	*Eriobotrya japonica*	8–10
Magnolia	*Magnolia* spp.	(4)5–9(10)
Norfolk Island pine	*Araucaria heterophylla*	10–11
Pine	*Pinus* spp.	2–8
Umbrella pine	*Sciadopitys verticillata*	5–7

Trees by size

Our yard is rather small so a large tree would be too big for it. Could you suggest some small trees for us to consider planting?

Tree size varies from site to site depending on soil conditions and climate. Most references provide a range of heights for trees. If conditions are favorable, the tree will grow larger; if not so favorable, it will stay smaller. As a general guideline for mature tree height, consult the list below.

Small trees—to 25 feet

COMMON NAME	BOTANICAL NAME	ZONES
Amur maple	*Acer tataricum ginnala*	2–8
Crape myrtle	*Lagerstroemia indica*	(5)6–10
Eastern redbud	*Cercis canadensis*	(4)5–9
Flowering crabapple	*Malus* spp.	4–8
Flowering dogwood	*Cornus florida*	5–9
Japanese flowering cherry	*Prunus serrulata*	5–8
Japanese maple	*Acer palmatum*	5–8
Japanese snowbell	*Styrax japonicus*	5–8
Japanese stewartia	*Stewartia pseudocamellia*	5–7(8)
Kousa dogwood	*Cornus kousa*	5–8
Loquat	*Eriobotrya japonica*	8–10
Paperbark maple	*Acer griseum*	5–8
Trident maple	*Acer buergerianum*	5–8
Washington hawthorn	*Crataegus phaenopyrum*	5–8
White fringe tree	*Chionanthus virginicus*	4–9

Medium trees—25 to 50 feet

COMMON NAME	BOTANICAL NAME	ZONES
American arborvitae	*Thuja occidentalis*	3–7
American holly	*Ilex opaca*	5–9
American hornbeam	*Carpinus caroliniana*	3–9
American yellowwood	*Cladrastis kentuckea*	4–8
Amur cork tree	*Phellodendron amurense*	(4)5–7(8)
Arizona cypress	*Cupressus arizonica*	7–9
Black gum, black tupelo	*Nyssa sylvatica*	(4)5–9
Black locust	*Robinia pseudoacacia*	4–8(9)
Callery pear	*Pyrus calleryana* cvs.	5–8(9)
Chinese elm, lacebark elm	*Ulmus parvifolia*	5–9
Chinese pistachio	*Pistacia chinensis*	6–9
Colorado spruce	*Picea pungens*	3–7(8)
Eastern red cedar	*Juniperus virginiana*	2–9
English oak	*Quercus robur*	5–8

COMMON NAME	BOTANICAL NAME	ZONES
European black alder	*Alnus glutinosa*	3–7
European mountain ash	*Sorbus aucuparia*	3–7
Golden raintree	*Koelreuteria paniculata*	5–9
Higan cherry	*Prunus subhirtella*	5–8
Incense cedar	*Calocedrus decurrens*	5–8
Japanese tree lilac	*Syringa reticulata*	3–7
Ohio buckeye	*Aesculus glabra*	4–7
Red maple	*Acer rubrum*	3–9
Sweet bay magnolia	*Magnolia virginiana*	5–9
White fir	*Abies concolor*	4–7

Large trees—over 50 feet

COMMON NAME	BOTANICAL NAME	ZONES
American linden	*Tilia americana*	3–8
American sycamore	*Platanus occidentalis*	(4)5–9
Bald cypress	*Taxodium distichum*	5–10
Canadian hemlock	*Tsuga canadensis*	(3)4–7
Dawn redwood	*Metasequoia glyptostroboides*	5–8
Deodar cedar	*Cedrus deodara*	7–9
Douglas fir	*Pseudotsuga menziesii*	(3)4–6
Eastern white pine	*Pinus strobus*	3–7(8)
European beech	*Fagus sylvatica*	(4)5–7
Ginkgo	*Ginkgo biloba*	4–8(9)
Green ash	*Fraxinus pennsylvanica*	(2)3–9
Japanese zelkova	*Zelkova serrata*	5–8
Katsura tree	*Cercidiphyllum japonicum*	5–8
Kentucky coffee tree	*Gymnocladus dioica*	(3)4–8
Littleleaf linden	*Tilia cordata*	4–7
Live oak	*Quercus virginiana*	(7)8–10
London plane tree	*Platanus ×acerifolia*	(5)6–8
Northern catalpa	*Catalpa speciosa*	4–8(9)
Norway spruce	*Picea abies*	2–7
Pin oak	*Quercus palustris*	4–8
Red oak	*Quercus rubra*	3–8
River birch	*Betula nigra*	4–9
Southern magnolia	*Magnolia grandiflora*	(6)7–9(10)
Sugar maple	*Acer saccharum*	3–8
Sweetgum	*Liquidambar styraciflua*	5–9
Thornless honeylocust	*Gleditsia triacanthos inermis*	4–9
Tulip tree	*Liriodendron tulipifera*	5–9
White ash	*Fraxinus americana*	3–9
White oak	*Quercus alba*	3–9

Besides flowering dogwood, which trees have showy blossoms?

Beautiful blooms are a bonus with many trees. Choose from among the following.

COMMON NAME	BOTANICAL NAME	ZONES
American yellowwood	*Cladrastis kentuckea*	4–8
Black locust	*Robinia pseudoacacia*	4–8(9)
Bronze acacia	*Acacia pruinosa*	10–11
Buckeye, horsechestnut	*Aesculus* spp.	4–7
Callery pear	*Pyrus calleryana*	5–8(9)
Carolina silverbell	*Halesia tetraptera*	5–8(9)
Crape myrtle	*Lagerstroemia indica*	(5)6–10
Downy serviceberry	*Amelanchier arborea*	4–9
Eastern redbud	*Cercis canadensis*	(4)5–9
Flowering cherry	*Prunus* spp.	3–8
Flowering crabapple	*Malus* spp.	3–8
Flowering dogwood	*Cornus florida*	5–9
Franklin tree	*Franklinia alatamaha*	5–8(9)
Goldenchain tree	*Laburnum ×watereri*	6–7
Golden rain tree	*Koelreuteria paniculata*	5–9
Jacaranda	*Jacaranda mimosifolia*	10–11
Japanese snowbell	*Styrax japonicus*	5–8
Japanese stewartia	*Stewartia pseudocamellia*	5–7(8)
Japanese tree lilac	*Syringa reticulata*	3–7
Kousa dogwood	*Cornus kousa*	5–8
Magnolia	*Magnolia* spp.	(4)5–9(10)
Mimosa, silk tree	*Albizia julibrissin*	6–9
Northern catalpa	*Catalpa speciosa*	4–8(9)
Panicle hydrangea	*Hydrangea paniculata*	4–8
Pussy willow	*Salix caprea*	4–8
Royal paulownia	*Paulownia tomentosa*	(5)6–9
Sourwood	*Oxydendrum arboreum*	5–9
Tulip tree	*Liriodendron tulipifera*	5–9
Washington hawthorn	*Crataegus phaenopyrum*	5–8
White fringe tree	*Chionanthus virginicus*	4–9
Witch hazel	*Hamamelis virginiana*	3–8

What trees could I plant for good fall leaf color?

Fall foliage color of trees ranges from yellow to orange, red, or purple. Take your pick from these autumn beauties.

COMMON NAME	BOTANICAL NAME	ZONES
Yellow		
American yellowwood	*Cladrastus kentuckea*	4–8
Eastern redbud	*Cercis canadensis*	(4)5–9
European beech	*Fagus sylvatica*	(4)5–7
European white birch	*Betula pendula*	2–6
Ginkgo	*Ginkgo biloba*	4–8(9)
Golden rain tree	*Koelreuteria paniculata*	5–9
Norway maple, striped maple	*Acer* spp.	2–7
Quaking aspen, white poplar	*Populus* spp.	1–9
Tulip tree	*Liriodendron tulipifera*	(4)5–9
White fringe tree	*Chionanthus virginicus*	4–9
Witch hazel	*Hamamelis virginiana*	3–8
Reddish Purple		
Eastern red cedar	*Juniperus virginiana*	2–9
Japanese stewartia	*Stewartia pseudocamellia*	5–7(8)
Kousa dogwood	*Cornus kousa*	5–8
White ash	*Fraxinus americana*	3–9
White oak	*Quercus alba*	3–9
Orange to Red		
American hornbeam	*Carpinus caroliniana*	3–9
American sweetgum	*Liquidambar styraciflua*	5–9
Downy serviceberry	*Amelanchier arborea*	4–9
European mountain ash	*Sorbus aucuparia*	3–7
Katsura tree	*Cercidiphyllum japonicum*	5–8
Red maple, sugar maple	*Acer* spp.	2–9
Sassafras	*Sassafras albidum*	(4)5–9
Red		
Amur maple, Japanese maple	*Acer* spp.	2–8
Black gum, black tupelo	*Nyssa sylvatica*	(4)5–9
Black haw viburnum	*Viburnum prunifolium*	3–9
Flowering dogwood	*Cornus florida*	5–9
Pin oak	*Quercus palustris*	4–8
Red oak	*Quercus rubra*	3–8
Sourwood	*Oxydendrum arboreum*	5–9
Washington hawthorn	*Crataegus phaenopyrum*	5–8

Shrubs by size

The shrubs that were planted next to the foundation of our house are now too large. We'd like to replace them, but aren't sure how big some of the replacements we're considering will grow. Can you give us some guidance?

Overgrown shrubs are common. It's difficult to imagine that those cute little plants in gallon containers eventually will grow to ten feet tall. So many gardeners underestimate the amount of room the plant will need. See the list below for mature shrub size guidelines.

Low shrubs—up to 3 feet

COMMON NAME	BOTANICAL NAME	ZONES
Blue mist spirea, Bluebeard	*Caryopteris ×clandonensis*	(4)5–9
Bumald spirea	*Spirea japonica* 'Bumalda'	3–8
Bush cinquefoil	*Potentilla fruticosa*	2–6(7)
Cranberry cotoneaster	*Cotoneaster apiculatus*	(4)5–7
Dwarf fothergilla	*Fothergilla gardenii*	5–8(9)
Japanese flowering quince	*Chaenomeles japonica*	5–8
Juniper	*Juniperus* spp.	3–9
Littleleaf boxwood	*Buxus microphylla*	5–9
Rockspray cotoneaster	*Cotoneaster horizontalis*	5–7
Rose daphne	*Daphne cneorum*	4–7
Slender deutzia	*Deutzia gracilis*	(4)5–8
St. Johnswort	*Hypericum* spp.	4–9

Medium shrubs—3 to 6 feet

Anglo-Japanese yew	*Taxus ×media*	(4)5–7
Fragrant sumac	*Rhus aromatica*	3–9
Gardenia	*Gardenia jasminoides*	(7)8–10
Glossy abelia	*Abelia ×grandiflora*	(5)6–9
Hydrangea	*Hydrangea* spp.	3–9
Inkberry, Japanese holly	*Ilex* spp.	4–9
Japanese pieris	*Pieris japonica*	5–9
Japanese spirea	*Spiraea japonica*	4–8
Mentor barberry, Japanese barberry	*Berberis* spp.	4–8
Oregon grapeholly	*Mahonia aquifolium*	5–9
Shrubby St. Johnswort	*Hypericum prolificum*	4–8
Snowberry	*Symphoricarpos albus*	3–7
Spreading cotoneaster	*Cotoneaster divaricatus*	(4)5–7
Summersweet	*Clethra alnifolia*	4–9
Virginia sweetspire	*Itea virginica*	(5)6–9
Winter daphne	*Daphne odora*	7–9
Winter jasmine	*Jasminum nudiflorum*	6–10

Large shrubs—over 6 feet

COMMON NAME	BOTANICAL NAME	ZONES
American cranberrybush viburnum	*Viburnum trilobum*	2–7
Bottlebrush buckeye	*Aesculus parviflora*	(4)5–8
Boxwood	*Buxus sempervirens*	(5)6–9
Butterfly bush	*Buddleia davidii*	5–9
Cherry laurel	*Prunus laurocerasus*	6–8
Chinese juniper	*Juniperus chinensis*	4–8
Chinese photinia	*Photinia serratifolia*	6–9
Common lilac	*Syringa vulgaris*	3–7
Cornelian cherry dogwood	*Cornus mas*	5–8
Double file viburnum	*Viburnum plicatum tomentosum*	5–8
European cranberrybush	*Viburnum opulus*	3–8
Flowering quince	*Chaenomeles speciosa*	5–9
Forsythia	*Forsythia ×intermedia*	(4)5–8(9)
Highbush blueberry	*Vaccinium corymbosum*	4–7
Japanese camellia	*Camellia japonica*	(7)8–10
Japanese fatsia	*Fatsia japonica*	8–10
Japanese pittosporum	*Pittosporum tobira*	(8)9–10
Japanese privet	*Ligustrum japonicum*	7–10
Jasmine	*Jasminum officinale*	8–10
Large fothergilla	*Fothergilla major*	5–8(9)
Leatherleaf viburnum	*Viburnum ×rhytidophylloides*	5–8
Mockorange	*Philadelphus coronarius*	4–8
Nandina, heavenly bamboo	*Nandina domestica*	6–9(10)
New Zealand tea tree	*Leptospermum scoparium*	9–10
Northern bayberry	*Myrica pensylvanica*	(2)3–6(7)
Oleander	*Nerium oleander*	8–10
Purple-leaf sand cherry	*Prunus ×cistena*	3–8
Red-osier dogwood	*Cornus stolonifera*	2–7
Redvein enkianthus	*Enkianthus campanulatus*	5–7
Rhododendron , azalea	*Rhododendron spp.*	4–10
Rose of Sharon	*Hibiscus syriacus*	5–8(9)
Saucer magnolia	*Magnolia ×soulangiana*	(4)5–9
Scarlet firethorn	*Pyracantha coccinea*	6–9
Siberian peashrub	*Caragana arborescens*	2–7
Smoke tree	*Cotinus coggygria*	(4)5–8
Spicebush	*Lindera benzoin*	5–9
Staghorn sumac	*Rhus typhina*	4–8
Tatarian honeysuckle	*Lonicera tatarica*	3–8
Ural false spirea	*Sorbaria sorbifolia*	2–7

Evergreen shrubs

It seems as though every landscape I see uses either junipers or yews as evergreen shrubs. I'd like something different. What could I grow?

Junipers and yews are good, tough evergreens for sun and shade, respectively. But you're wise to desire a bit of variety in your plantings. Not only will your landscape reflect your individuality, it will also create ecological diversity. To expand your evergreen shrub palette, try some of these shrubs.

Low shrubs—up to 3 feet

COMMON NAME	BOTANICAL NAME	ZONES
Gold cup St. Johnswort	Hypericum ×cyanthiflorum	5–7
Japanese garden juniper	Juniperus procumbens	4–9
Littleleaf boxwood	Buxus microphylla	5–9
Rose daphne	Daphne cneorum	(4)5–7

Medium shrubs—3 to 6 feet

Anglo-Japanese yew	Taxus ×media	5–7
David viburnum	Viburnum davidii	8–9
Drooping leucothoe	Leucothoe fontanesiana	5–8
Gardenia	Gardenia jasminoides	(7)8–10
Glossy abelia	Abelia ×grandiflora	(5)6–9
Japanese holly	Ilex crenata	6–8
Japanese pieris	Pieris japonica	5–9
Oregon grapeholly	Mahonia aquifolium	5–9
Winter daphne	Daphne odora	7–10

Large Shrubs—over 6 feet

Boxwood	Buxus sempervirens	(5)6–9
Camellia	Camellia spp.	7–10
Cherry laurel	Prunus laurocerasus	6–8
Chinese juniper	Juniperus chinensis	4–9
Holly	Ilex spp.	3–9
Holly osmanthus	Osmanthus heterophyllus	(6)7–9
Japanese fatsia	Fatsia japonica	8–10
Japanese pittosporum	Pittosporum tobira	(8)9–10
Japanese privet	Ligustrum japonicum	7–10
Leatherleaf viburnum	Viburnum ×rhytidophylloides	5–8
Oleander	Nerium oleander	8–10
Rhododendron, azalea	Rhododendron spp.	4–10
Yew pine	Podocarpus macrophyllus	8–10

What would be a good choice of shrub to provide some fall color in my yard?

Any of the following shrubs will add spectacular hues to your fall garden.

COMMON NAME	BOTANICAL NAME	ZONES
Chinese photinia	*Photinia serrulata*	6–9
Drooping leucothoe	*Leucothoe fontanesiana*	5–8
Fragrant sumac	*Rhus aromatica*	3–9
Highbush blueberry	*Vaccinium corymbosum*	4–7
Japanese barberry	*Berberis thunbergii*	(4)5–8
Large fothergilla	*Fothergilla major*	5–8(9)
Nandina, heavenly bamboo	*Nandina domestica*	6–9(10)
Oakleaf hydrangea	*Hydrangea quercifolia*	5–9
Purple-leaf sand cherry	*Prunus ×cistena*	3–8
Red chokeberry	*Aronia arbutifolia*	(4)5–9
Red-osier dogwood	*Cornus stolonifera*	2–7
Rugosa rose	*Rosa rugosa*	3–10
Smoke tree	*Cotinus coggygria*	(4)5–8
Staghorn sumac	*Rhus typhina*	4–8
Virginia sweetspire	*Itea virginica*	(5)6–9
Winged euomymus	*Euonymus alatus*	4–8(9)

Flowering shrubs
Could you suggest some flowering shrubs to plant in my landscape?

Flowering shrubs often serve double duty. In addition to colorful blooms, many develop a second season of color with ornamental fruits. The following list identifies shrubs with colorful flowers and those that also develop showy fruits.

COMMON NAME	BOTANICAL NAME	ZONES
Flowers		
Beautybush	*Kolkwitzia amabilis*	5–8
Bluebeard	*Caryopteris ×clandonensis*	(4)5–9
Bush cinquefoil	*Potentilla fruticosa*	2–6(7)
Butterfly bush	*Buddleia davidii*	5–9
Camellia	*Camellia japonica*	(7)8–10
Common lilac	*Syringa vulgaris*	3–7
Forsythia	*Forsythia ×intermedia*	4–8(9)
Hydrangea	*Hydrangea* spp.	3–9
Japanese flowering quince	*Chaenomeles japonica*	(4)5–8
Kerria	*Kerria japonica*	5–9
Magnolia	*Magnolia* spp.	(4)5–9(10)
Mockorange	*Philadelphus coronarius*	4–8
Oleander	*Nerium oleander*	8–10
Rhododendron, azalea	*Rhododendron* spp.	4–10
Rose	*Rosa* spp.	3–10
Spirea	*Spiraea* spp.	3–8
Viburnum	*Viburnum* spp.	2–8
Weigela	*Weigela florida*	4–8
Fruit		
Chinese beautyberry	*Callicarpa dichotoma*	5–8
Cotoneaster	*Cotoneaster* spp.	4–7
Holly	*Ilex* spp.	3–9
Nandina, heavenly bamboo	*Nandina domestica*	6–9(10)
Northern bayberry	*Myrica pensylvanica*	(2)3–6(7)
Oregon grapeholly	*Mahonia aquifolium*	5–9
Scarlet firethorn	*Pyracantha coccinea*	6–9
Viburnum	*Viburnum* spp.	2–8

I'd like to start a rock garden. What would be some good plants to try?

Rock garden plants require excellent drainage. Make certain you provide the proper growing conditions for them. A raised bed or a berm with porous soil is a must for success. Once you've got the right conditions for rock garden plants, select from the following.

COMMON NAME	BOTANICAL NAME	ZONES
Alpine aster	*Aster alpinus*	3–9
Aubretia	*Aubrieta ×cultorum*	6–8
Basket-of-gold	*Aurinia saxatalis*	3–7
Bellflower	*Campanula* spp.	2–7
Bloodroot	*Sanguinaria canadensis*	3–7
Bloody cranesbill	*Geranium sanguineum*	4–8
Cheddar pink	*Dianthus gratianopolitanus*	3–8
Columbine	*Aquilegia* spp.	3–9
Creeping baby's breath	*Gypsophila repens*	4–7
Creeping phlox	*Phlox subulata*	2–8
Crested iris, dwarf iris	*Iris* spp.	3–9
Evergreen candytuft	*Iberis sempervirens*	3–9
Forget-me-not	*Myosotis scorpioides*	3–9
Fringed bleeding heart	*Dicentra eximia*	3–8
Heart-leaf bergenia	*Bergenia cordifolia*	3–8
Hen and chicks, house leek	*Sempervivum* spp.	4–10
Hybrid coral bells	*Heuchera ×brizoides*	4–8
Lavender, English lavender	*Lavandula angustifolia*	5–8
Leadwort	*Ceratostigma plumbaginoides*	5–9
Maiden pink	*Dianthus deltoides*	3–8
Primrose	*Primula* spp.	4–9
Prostrate speedwell	*Veronica prostrata*	4–8
Sandwort	*Minuartia verna*	3–6
Sea thrift	*Armeria maritima*	3–9
Sedum	*Sedum* spp.	3–10
Shooting star	*Dodecatheon meadia*	3–8
Snow-in-summer	*Cerastium tomentosum*	3–7
Soapwort	*Saponaria ocymoides*	3–8
Strawberry geranium	*Saxifraga stolonifera*	5–9
Sun rose	*Helianthemum nummularium*	5–9
Wall rockcress	*Arabis caucasica*	4–8
Wild ginger	*Asarum* spp.	3–8
Wild thyme	*Thymus serpyllum*	4–9
Woolly yarrow	*Achillea tomentosa*	3–8

I just moved into a new house with nothing in the landscape. I'd like to plant some annuals for quick color this year. I need some low-growing ones to line the walkway, but I'd also like some that get quite large to fill up the empty spaces. Could you provide some guidance?

Annual flowers come in all sizes and colors. You should have no difficulty finding ones to fill your landscape needs. See below for a selection of low-growing, medium-sized or tall annual flowers.

COMMON NAME	BOTANICAL NAME
Low—for edging or front border (to 1 foot)	
Ageratum	*Ageratum houstonianum*
Annual phlox	*Phlox drummondii*
Browallia	*Browallia speciosa*
California poppy	*Eschscholzia californica*
Creeping zinnia	*Sanvitalia procumbens*
Cupflower	*Nierembergia hippomanica*
Edging lobelia	*Lobelia erinus*
Fan flower	*Scaevola aemula*
Gazania	*Gazania rigens*
Kingfisher daisy	*Felicia bergeriana*
Mignonette	*Reseda odorata*
Monkey flower	*Mimulus ×hybridus*
Moss rose	*Portulaca grandiflora*
Narrowleaf zinnia	*Zinnia angustifolia*
Pansy	*Viola ×wittrockiana*
Sweet alyssum	*Lobularia maritima*
Verbena	*Verbena ×hybrida*
Wax begonia	*Begonia Semperflorens-cultorum* hyb.
Wishbone flower	*Torenia fournieri*
Medium—for middle border (to 3 or 4 feet)	
African marigold	*Tagetes erecta*
Annual baby's breath	*Gypsophila elegans*
Bells of Ireland	*Moluccella laevis*
Blanket flower	*Gaillardia pulchella*
Blue laceflower	*Trachymene coerulea*
Butterfly flower	*Schizanthus pinnatus*
Cape marigold	*Dimorphotheca sinuata*
China aster	*Callistephus chinensis*
Cockscomb	*Celosia argentea*

COMMON NAME	BOTANICAL NAME
Coleus, painted nettle	*Solenostemon scutellarioides*
Cornflower	*Centaurea cyanus*
Flowering tobacco	*Nicotiana ×sanderae*
French marigold	*Tagetes patula*
Garden balsam	*Impatiens balsamina*
Geranium, zonal geranium	*Pelargonium ¥hortorum*
Globe amaranth	*Gomphrena globosa*
Impatiens	*Impatiens walleriana*
Nasturtium	*Tropaeolum majus*
Petunia	*Petunia ×hybrida*
Pincushion flower	*Scabiosa atropurpurea*
Pot marigold	*Calendula officinalis*
Prairie gentian	*Eustoma grandiflorum*
Scarlet sage	*Salvia splendens*
Snapdragon	*Antirrhinum majus*
Strawflower	*Helichrysum bracteatum*
Vinca	*Catharanthus roseus*
Yellow cosmos	*Cosmos sulphureus*
Zinnia	*Zinnia elegans*

Tall—for back border (over 3 feet)

American star thistle	*Centaurea americana*
Black-eyed Susan vine	*Thunbergia alata*
Castor bean	*Ricinus communis*
Cosmos	*Cosmos bipinnatus*
Dahlia	*Dahlia* spp.
Horn of plenty	*Datura metel*
Jasmine tobacco	*Nicotiana alata*
Joseph's coat	*Amaranthus tricolor*
Love-lies-bleeding	*Amaranthus caudatus*
Mexican fireweed	*Kochia scoparia*
Mexican sunflower	*Tithonia rotundifolia*
Spider flower	*Cleome hassleriana*
Sunflower	*Helianthus annuus*

It never fails. When planting my perennial garden, I always end up sticking a tall plant in front of a lower growing one. Could you help me figure out how big my plants will get?

Unless your perennial border has a formal design, an occasional "oops"—a taller plant in front of a shorter one—can add drama and interest to your flower garden. Some gardeners intentionally plant tall "see-through" plants with airy flower stems, but low-growing foliage in front of shorter plants. However, in most cases, it's understandable that you wouldn't want to hide any of the beauties in your garden. Use the following list as a guide.

COMMON NAME	BOTANICAL NAME	ZONES
Low—for front border (to 1 1/2 feet)		
Bethlehem sage	*Pulmonaria saccharata*	3–8
Bloody cranesbill	*Geranium sanguineum*	4–8
Carpathian bellflower	*Campanula carpatica*	2–7
Catmint	*Nepeta ×faassenii*	3–8
Chrysanthemum	*Chrysanthemum morifolium*	4–9
Coral bells	*Heuchera sanguinea*	3–8
Cushion spurge	*Euphorbia polychroma*	4–9
Heart-leaf bergenia	*Bergenia cordifolia*	3–8
Lady's mantle	*Alchemilla mollis*	3–7
Lamb's-ears	*Stachys byzantina*	3–8
Lavender cotton	*Santolina chamaecyparissus*	6–9
Lenten rose	*Helleborus orientalis*	4–9
Ozark sundrops	*Oenothera macrocarpa*	4–8
Pinks	*Dianthus* spp.	4–8
Sea thrift	*Armeria maritima*	3–9
Threadleaf coreopsis	*Coreopsis verticillata*	4–9
Medium—for middle border (to 4 feet)		
Astilbe	*Astilbe ×arendsii*	3–8
Baby's breath	*Gypsophila paniculata*	3–8
Balloon flower	*Platycodon grandiflorus*	3–8
Bearded iris	*Iris* bearded hybrids	3-9
Beardlip penstemon	*Penstemon barbatus*	4–9
Bee balm, Oswego tea	*Monarda didyma*	3–9
Bleeding heart	*Dicentra spectabilis*	3–9
Blue false indigo	*Baptisia australis*	3–9
Butterfly weed	*Asclepias tuberosa*	4–9
Cardinal flower	*Lobelia cardinalis*	3–9
Columbine meadow rue	*Thalictrum aquilegifolium*	3–9

COMMON NAME	BOTANICAL NAME	ZONES
Daylily	*Hemerocallis*	3–10
Featherleaf rodgersia	*Rodgersia pinnata*	4–7
Fern-leaf yarrow	*Achillea filipendulina*	3–9
Frikart's aster	*Aster ×frikartii*	5–8
Garden phlox	*Phlox paniculata*	3–8
Helen's flower	*Helenium autumnale*	3–8
Hosta	*Hosta*	3–8
Obedient plant	*Physostegia virginiana*	3–8
Oriental poppy	*Papaver orientale*	3–7
Peony	*Paeonia* spp.	3–8
Purple coneflower	*Echinacea purpurea*	3–9
Salvia	*Salvia* spp.	4–9
Shasta daisy	*Leucanthemum ×superbum*	4–8
Siberian iris	*Iris sibirica*	3–9
Speedwell	*Veronica* spp.	3–8
Spiderwort	*Tradescantia virginiana*	4–9
Spike gayfeather	*Liatris spicata*	3–9
Stoke's aster	*Stokesia laevis*	5–9
Toad lily	*Tricyrtis hirta*	5–9

Tall—for back border (over 4 feet)

False sunflower	*Heliopsis helianthoides*	3–9
Goatsbeard	*Aruncus dioicus*	3–7
Hybrid delphinium	*Delphinium*	2–7
Joe-Pye weed	*Eupatorium purpureum*	4–9
Lily	*Lilium* spp.	3–8
Monkshood cultivars	*Aconitum ×cammarum*	3–7
New England aster	*Aster novae-angliae*	4–8
New York aster	*Aster novi-belgii*	3–8
Plume poppy	*Macleaya cordata*	4–9
Queen-of-the-prairie	*Filipendula rubra*	3–9
Red hot poker	*Kniphofia uvaria*	5–9
Russian sage	*Perovskia atriplicifolia*	3–9
Snakeroot	*Cimicifuga racemosa*	3–8
White boltonia	*Boltonia asteroides latisquama*	4–9

I'd like to add some wildflowers to my shady back yard. Which would be good ones to use?

Most woodland wildflowers are spring bloomers. They explode in a riot of color before trees develop a full canopy of leaves. Here are some to consider.

COMMON NAME	BOTANICAL NAME	ZONES
Allegheny foam flower	*Tiarella cordifolia*	3–8
American trout lily	*Erythronium americanum*	3–6
Bellwort	*Uvularia sessilifolia*	4–8
Bloodroot	*Sanguinaria canadensis*	4–8
Bunchberry	*Cornus canadensis*	2–5
Canadian columbine	*Aquilegia canadensis*	3–8
Celandine poppy	*Stylophorum diphyllum*	6–8
Dutchman's breeches	*Dicentra cucullaria*	4–7
Dwarf larkspur	*Delphinium tricorne*	4–7
False Solomon's seal	*Smilacina racemosa*	4–9
Fire pink	*Silene virginica*	5–8
Great blue lobelia	*Lobelia silphilitica*	4–8
Greek valerian	*Polemonium reptans*	4–7
Hepatica	*Hepatica americana*	4–8
Jack-in-the-pulpit, Indian turnip	*Arisaema triphyllum*	2–9
May apple	*Podophyllum peltatum*	4–8
Rue-anemone	*Anemonella thalictroides*	4–8
Small Solomon's seal	*Polygonatum biflorum*	3–9
Spring beauty	*Claytonia virginica*	4–8
Tall bellflower	*Campanula americana*	4–8
Toothwort	*Cardamine laciniata*	6–8
Trailing arbutus	*Epigaea repens*	2–5
Trillium	*Trillium* spp.	3–8
Violet, viola	*Viola* spp.	3–9
Virginia bluebell	*Mertensia virginica*	3–7
Wild geranium	*Geranium maculatum*	4–8
Wintergreen	*Gaultheria procumbens*	4–7
Woodland phlox	*Phlox divaricata*	4–8

I'd like to grow some wildflowers in a sunny spot in my yard. Would native prairie wildflowers work well there?

Prairie wildflowers require full sun for best growth. If the sunny spot in your yard provides at least 6 hours of sunlight per day, you can recreate a sunny meadow with native prairie plants from the following list.

COMMON NAME	BOTANICAL NAME	ZONES
Beard tongue	*Penstemon* spp.	4–9
Bee balm, bergamot	*Monarda* spp.	3–9
Black-eyed Susan	*Rudbeckia fulgida*	3–9
Blanket flower	*Gaillardia aristata*	3–9
Blue false indigo	*Baptisia australis*	3–9
Blue sage	*Salvia azurea*	4–8
Butterfly weed	*Asclepias tuberosa*	4–9
Compass plant	*Silphium lacinatum*	4–8
Cornflower	*Centaurea cyanus*	6–8
Evening primrose	*Oenothera* spp.	4–8
Gayfeather	*Liatris spicata*	3–9
Goldenrod	*Solidago* hybrids	3–9
Helen's flower	*Helenium autumnale*	3–8
Indian paintbrush	*Castilleja coccinea*	4–8
Mexican hat	*Ratibida columnifera*	4–9
Obedient plant	*Physostegia virginiana*	3–8
Ox-eye daisy	*Leucanthemum vulgare*	3–9
Perennnial flax	*Linum perenne*	4–9
Purple coneflower	*Echinacea purpurea*	3–9
Purple poppy mallow	*Callirhoe involucrata*	4–9
Rose malva	*Lavatera assurgentiflora*	9–10
Rose vervain	*Verbena canadensis*	4–9
Soapwort	*Saponaria officinalis*	3–8
Spiderwort	*Tradescantia virginiana*	4–9
Texas bluebonnet	*Lupinus texensis*	7–8
Tickseed	*Coreopsis lanceolata*	4–9
Western sunflower	*Helianthus occidentalis*	4–9
Yarrow	*Achillea millefolium*	2–9

Plants for hedge
We'd like to put in a hedge along one edge of our property. Could you suggest some plants that would make a good hedge?

Do you want a formal or informal hedge? A formal hedge requires clipping and shaping to maintain uniform height and form. See the list below for trees and shrubs that tolerate the frequent shearing required of formal hedges. If you simply want the hedge as a screen, an informal hedge may be more appropriate. The list also includes trees and shrubs suitable for screens.

COMMON NAME	BOTANICAL NAME	ZONES
Tolerant of frequent shearing		
Alpine currant	*Ribes alpinum*	2–7
Amur maple, hedge maple	*Acer* spp.	2–8
Anglo-Japanese yew	*Taxus ×media*	(4)5–7
Arborvitae	*Thuja* spp.	2–8
Arrowwood viburnum	*Viburnum dentatum*	3–8
Boxwood	*Buxus sempervirens*	(5)6–9
Canadian hemlock	*Tsuga canadensis*	(3)4–7
Chinese holly, English holly	*Ilex* spp.	7–9
Chinese juniper	*Juniperus chinensis*	4–9
Cornelian cherry	*Cornus mas*	5–8
English laurel	*Prunus laurocerasus*	6–8
European hornbeam	*Carpinus betulus*	(4)5–7
Glossy abelia	*Abelia ×grandiflora*	(5)6–9
Hedge cotoneaster	*Cotoneaster lucidus*	3–7
Holly oak	*Quercus ilex*	9–10
Holly osmanthus	*Osmanthus heterophyllus*	(6)7–9
Japanese barberry, Mentor barberry	*Berberis* spp.	4–8
Japanese euonymus	*Euonymus japonicus*	7–9
Japanese flowering quince	*Chaenomeles japonica*	5–8
Japanese pittosporum	*Pittosporum tobira*	(8)9–10
Meyer lilac	*Syringa meyeri*	3–7
Myrtle	*Myrtis communis*	9–10
Oleander	*Nerium oleander*	8–10
Privet	*Ligustrum* spp.	(4)5–10
Russian olive	*Elaeagnus angustifolia*	2–7
Sawara false cypress	*Chamaecyparis pisifera*	5–8
Scarlet firethorn	*Pyracantha coccinea*	6–9
Siberian peashrub	*Caragana arborescens*	2–7
White fir	*Abies concolor*	4–7
White spruce	*Picea glauca*	2–6

COMMON NAME	BOTANICAL NAME	ZONES
Suitable for screening—Shrubs		
American cranberrybush	*Viburnum trilobum viburnum*	2–7
Bayberry	*Myrica pensylvanica*	(4)5–6(7)
Chinese holly, Japanese holly	*Ilex* spp.	7–9
Chinese juniper	*Juniperus chinensis*	4–9
Common lilac	*Syringa vulgaris*	3–7
Cornelian cherry	*Cornus mas*	5–8
Forsythia	*Forsythia ×intermedia*	4–8(9)
Hedge maple	*Acer campestre*	5–8
Hicks Anglo-Japanese yew	*Taxus ×media 'Hicksii'*	5–7
Japanese barberry	*Berberis thunbergii*	(4)5–8
Japanese tree lilac	*Syringa reticulata*	3–7
Mockorange	*Philadelphus coronarius*	4–8
Ninebark	*Physocarpus opulifolius*	2–7
Oleander	*Nerium oleander*	8–10
Privet	*Ligustrum* spp.	4–10
Rugosa rose	*Rosa rugosa*	3–10
Sea buckthorn	*Hippophae rhamnoides*	4–7
Sheepberry	*Viburnum lentago*	2–8
Vanhoutte spirea	*Spiraea ×vanhouttei*	3–8(9)
Vernal witch hazel	*Hamamelis vernalis*	5–8
Suitable for screening—Trees		
American arborvitae	*Thuja occidentalis*	3–7
Amur maple	*Acer tataricum ginnala*	2–8
Black haw viburnum	*Viburnum prunifolium*	3–9
Canadian hemlock	*Tsuga canadensis*	(3)4–7
Colorado spruce, Norway spruce	*Picea* spp.	2–8
Eastern red cedar	*Juniperus virginiana*	2–9
Eastern white pine	*Pinus strobus*	3–7(8)
Japanese pagoda tree	*Sophora japonica*	5–7
Littleleaf linden	*Tilia cordata*	4–7
Osage orange	*Maclura pomifera*	5–9
Sassafras	*Sassafras albidum*	(4)5–9

Windbreak plants

We live in a very windy area, and would like to plant a windbreak. What trees would you suggest?

The best windbreaks include a combination of trees and shrubs. If space permits, put in six or eight rows of plants, with shrubs in the outer rows and trees in the middle. If space is at a premium, one or two rows will provide some relief from the wind. Choose from the following wind-tolerant plants.

COMMON NAME	BOTANICAL NAME	ZONES
American arborvitae	*Thuja occidentalis*	3–7
Black walnut	*Juglans nigra*	4–9
Coast redwood	*Sequoia sempervirens*	7–9
Common lilac	*Syringa vulgaris*	3–7
Douglas fir	*Pseudotsuga menziesii*	(3)4–6
Eastern cottonwood	*Populus deltoides*	3–9
Eastern red cedar	*Juniperus virginiana*	3–9
Green ash	*Fraxinus pennsylvanica*	(2)3–9
Hackberry	*Celtis occidentalis*	3–9
Hedge maple	*Acer campestre*	5–8
Incense cedar	*Calocedrus decurrens*	5–8
Leyland cypress	*×Cupressocyparis leylandii*	6–10
Manzanita	*Arctostaphylos manzanita*	8–10
Norway spruce, white spruce	*Picea* spp.	2–8
Oleander	*Nerium oleander*	8–10
Osage orange	*Maclura pomifera*	5–9
Ponderosa pine	*Pinus ponderosa*	3–6
Rocky Mountain juniper	*Juniperus scopulorum*	3–7
Russian olive	*Elaeangnus angustifolia*	2–7
Saskatoon serviceberry	*Amelanchier alnifolia*	2–5
Shingle oak, bur oak, willow oak	*Quercus* spp.	3–9
Siberian peashrub	*Caragana arborescens*	2–7
Sweet bay	*Laurus nobilis*	8–10
Tatarian honeysuckle	*Lonicera tatarica*	3–8
Thornless honeylocust	*Gleditsia triacanthos inermis*	4–9
White willow	*Salix alba*	2–8

Plants to attract birds

My husband and I enjoy feeding and watching the birds. We'd like to attract even more of them to our yard. What plants would be good for that?

Birds require nesting sites and food sources. Most trees and shrubs can serve as nesting sites. Those in the following list provide the bonus of bearing food, too.

COMMON NAME	BOTANICAL NAME	ZONES
Shadblow serviceberry	*Amelanchier canadensis*	3–8
Red chokeberry	*Aronia arbutifolia*	(4)5–9
American bittersweet	*Celastrus scandens*	3–8
Hackberry	*Celtis occidentalis*	3–9
Buttonbush	*Cephalanthus occidentalis*	5–11
Pagoda dogwood	*Cornus alternifolia*	3–7
Cornelian cherry	*Cornus mas*	4–8
Red-osier dogwood	*Cornus stolonifera*	2–8
Washington hawthorn	*Crataegus phaenopyrum*	5–8
Possumhaw	*Ilex decidua*	5–9
American holly	*Ilex opaca*	5–9
Winterberry	*Ilex verticillata*	4–9
Eastern red cedar	*Juniperus virginiana*	2–9
European larch	*Larix decidua*	(3)4–6(7)
Honeysuckle	*Lonicera* spp.	3–8
Flowering crabapple	*Malus* spp.	3–8
Red mulberry	*Morus rubra*	5–8(9)
Wax myrtle	*Myrica cerifera*	6–9
Tupelo, black gum	*Nyssa sylvatica*	(4)5–9
Boston ivy	*Parthenocissus tricuspidata*	4–8
Cherry, plum	*Prunus* spp.	3–9
Staghorn sumac	*Rhus typhina*	4–8
American elder	*Sambucus canadensis*	3–9
European mountain ash	*Sorbus aucuparia*	3–7
Coralberry	*Symphoricarpos orbiculatus*	2–7
Canadian hemlock	*Tsuga canadensis*	(3)4–7
Black haw viburnum	*Viburnum prunifolium*	3–9
American cranberrybush	*Viburnum trilobum viburnum*	2–7

Fragrant plants

My mother loves plants and gardening, but her eyesight is failing. I'm glad to help her with her garden, but I'd like her to enjoy it too. Would a fragrance garden be a good solution?

When one sense fails, others often become more heightened. Your mother likely will appreciate plants with fragrance. Remember that foliage as well as flowers can be a potent source of aroma. Ask your mother which of the following plants she likes, and add them to her garden for olfactory enjoyment.

COMMON NAME	BOTANICAL NAME	ZONES
Fragrant foliage		
Balsam fir	*Abies balsamea*	2–5
California incense cedar	*Calocedrus decurrens*	5–8
Camphor tree	*Cinnamomum camphora*	9–10
Chives	*Allium schoenoprasum*	3–10
Colorado spruce	*Picea pungens*	3–7(8)
English lavender	*Lavandula angustifolia*	5–8
Eucalyptus	*Eucalyptus* spp.	(7)8–10
Garden sage	*Salvia officinalis*	5–10
Honey bush	*Melianthus major*	10–11
Juniper	*Juniperus* spp.	3–9
Lantana	*Lantana camara*	8–10
Laurel, sweet bay	*Laurus nobilis*	8–10
Lavender cotton	*Santolina chamaecyparissus*	6–9
Mint	*Mentha* ssp.	4–10
Oregano	*Origanum vulgare*	5–11
Pine	*Pinus* spp.	3–8
Rosemary	*Rosmarinus officinalis*	(6)7–9
Scented geraniums	*Pelargonium* spp.	9–10
Wild thyme	*Thymus serpyllum*	4–9

COMMON NAME	BOTANICAL NAME	ZONES
Fragrant flowers		
Angel's trumpet	*Brugmansia versicolor*	9–10
August lily	*Hosta plantaginea*	3–9
Bearded iris	*Iris* bearded hybrids	3–9
Black locust	*Robinia pseudoacacia*	4–8(9)
Burkwood viburnum	*Viburnum ×burkwoodii*	(4)5–8
Butterfly bush	*Buddleia davidii*	5–9
Cheddar pink	*Dianthus gratianapolitanus*	3–9
Citrus	*Citrus* spp.	8–11
Clove currant	*Ribes odoratum*	4–7
Daphne	*Daphne* spp.	(4)5–9
Fragrant viburnum	*Viburnum ×carlcephalum*	5–8
Frangipani	*Plumeria rubra*	10–11
Freesia	*Freesia* cvs.	9–10
Garden phlox	*Phlox paniculata*	3–8
Gardenia	*Gardenia jasminoides*	(7)8–10
Heliotrope	*Heliotropium arborescens*	NA
Himalayan sweet box	*Sarcococca hookeriana*	(5)6–8
Holly osmanthus	*Osmanthus heterophyllus*	(6)7–9
Hyacinth	*Hyacinthus orientalis*	4–8
Japanese wisteria	*Wisteria floribunda*	5–9
Jasmine	*Jasminum officinale*	8–10
Korean spice viburnum	*Viburnum carlesii*	4–7
Lilac	*Syringa vulgaris*	3–7
Lily	*Lilium* spp.	3–8
Lily-of-the-valley	*Convallaria majalis*	2–7
Mockorange	*Philadelphus coronarius*	4–8
Orange jessamine	*Murraya paniculata*	10–11
Peony	*Paeonia*	3–8
Rose	*Rosa* spp.	3–10
Star jasmine	*Trachelospermum jasminoides*	8–9
Summersweet	*Clethra alnifolia*	4–9
Sweet acacia	*Acacia farnesiana*	9–10
Sweet autumn clematis	*Clematis ternifolia*	5–8
Sweet bay magnolia	*Magnolia virginiana*	5–9
Sweet bouvardia	*Bouvardia longiflora*	9–10
Sweet violet	*Viola odorata*	5–9
Tuberose	*Polianthes tuberosa*	9–11
White ginger	*Hedychium coronarium*	10–11

What could I grow in my garden to attract more butterflies?

Take a 2-step approach to increasing butterfly numbers in your yard. Caterpillars, the larvae of butterflies, feed on certain plants. Provide those plants in your yard, and you'll likely see more adults after the larva mature. Adult butterflies are attracted to plants with high nectar content. Plant good nectar sources to attract and keep the colorful adults in your yard.

COMMON NAME	BOTANICAL NAME	ZONES
For nectar		
Aster	*Aster* spp.	4–8
Azalea	*Rhododendron* spp.	4–10
Butterfly bush	*Buddleia davidii*	5–9
Butterfly weed	*Asclepias tuberosa*	4–9
Egyptian star flower	*Pentas lanceolata*	9–11
Fernleaf yarrow	*Achillea filipendulina*	3–9
Garden phlox	*Phlox paniculata*	3–8
Heliotrope	*Heliotropium arborescens*	10–11
Hybrid delphinium	*Delphinium* spp.	2–7
Joe-Pye weed	*Eupatorium purpureum*	3–9
Lantana	*Lantana camara*	8–10
Orange, lemon, lime	*Citrus* spp.	8–11
Purple coneflower	*Echinacea purpurea*	3–9
Showy sedum	*Hylotelephium spectabile*	4–9
Spike gayfeather	*Liatris spicata*	3–9
Summersweet	*Clethra alnifolia*	4–9
Tickseed	*Coreopsis lanceolata*	4–9
For larval food		
Black cherry	*Prunus serotina*	3–9
Elm	*Ulmus* spp.	2–9
Flowering crabapple	*Malus* spp.	4–8
Hollyhock mallow	*Malva alcea*	3–8
Orange, lemon, lime	*Citrus* spp.	9–10
Passion flower	*Passiflora* spp.	7–10
Pink turtlehead	*Chelone lyonii*	3–8
Rose	*Rosa* spp.	3–10
Spice bush	*Lindera benzoin*	5–9
Tulip tree	*Liriodendron tulipifera*	5–9
Violet	*Viola* spp.	4–9
Willow	*Salix* spp.	2–8
Yarrow	*Achillea millefolium*	3–9

I'd like to grow a colorful houseplant in my living room. Will I need to provide bright light for it?

Color from houseplants can come from blooms or foliage. Most blooming plants and those with colorful foliage grow better in bright light, although some such as peace lily (Spathiphyllum) or variegated snake plant (Sansevieria) do well in low light. Consult the following list to see whether the plants you'd like to grow require low, medium or bright light.

COMMON NAME	BOTANICAL NAME
Tolerant of low light	
Arrowhead vine	*Syngonium podophyllum*
Cast-iron plant	*Aspidistra elatior*
Chinese evergreen	*Aglaonema commutatum*
Corn plant	*Dracaena fragrans* 'Massangeana'
Golden pothos	*Epipremnum aureum*
Grape ivy	*Cissus rhombifolia*
Heart-leaf philodendron	*Philodendron scandens*
Japanese aucuba	*Aucuba japonica*
Japanese holly fern	*Cyrtomium falcatum*
Kangaroo vine	*Cissus antarctica*
Parlor palm	*Chamaedorea elegans*
Peace lily	*Spathiphyllum wallisii*
Pleomele, song of India	*Dracaena reflexa*
Snake plant	*Sansevieria trifasciata*
Spider plant	*Chlorophytum comosum*
Spotted dumb cane	*Dieffenbachia maculata*
Table fern	*Pteris cretica*
Yew pine	*Podocarpus macrophyllus*
Best in medium light	
African violet	*Saintpaulia ionantha*
Aluminum plant	*Pilea cadierei*
Angel wing begonia	*Begonia coccinea*
Asparagus fern	*Asparagus densiflorus*
Baby rubber plant	*Peperomia obtusifolia*
Baby's tears	*Soleirolia soleirollii*
Bird's nest fern	*Asplenium nidus*
Boat lily	*Tradescantia spathacea*
Boston fern, sword fern	*Nephrolepis exaltata*
Calathea	*Calathea majestica*
Christmas cactus	*Schlumbergera ×buckleyi*

COMMON NAME	BOTANICAL NAME
Best in medium light (continued)	
Coleus, painted nettle	Solenostemon scutellarioides
Coralberry	Ardisia crispa
Devil's backbone, ribbon cactus	Pedilanthus tithymaloides
Dwarf date palm	Phoenix roebelinii
Earth star	Cryptanthus bivittatus
Easter lily	Lilium longiflorum
Emerald ripple peperomia	Peperomia caperata
Episcia, flame violet	Episcia cvs.
False aralia	Schefflera elegantissima
Flaming sword	Vriesia splendens
Flamingo flower	Anthurium scherzerianum
Gloxinia	Sinningia speciosa
Hawaiian ti plant	Cordyline terminalis
Kalanchoe	Kalanchoe blossfeldiana
Kentia palm	Howea forsteriana
Lipstick plant	Aeschynanthus radicans
Maidenhair fern	Adiantum pedatum
Medicine plant	Aloe vera
Moth orchid	Phalaenopsis cvs.
Norfolk Island pine	Araucaria heterophylla
Piggyback plant	Tolmiea menziesii
Plumosa fern	Asparagus setaceus
Prayer plant	Maranta leuconeura
Rabbit's foot fern	Davallia fejeensis
Rex begonia	Begonia Rex-cultorum hybrids
Rubber tree	Ficus elastica
Sago palm	Cycas revoluta
Schefflera	Schefflera arboricola
Screw pine	Pandanus veitchii
Swedish ivy	Plectranthus australis
Thanksgiving cactus	Schlumbergera truncata
Tree philodendron	Philodendron bipinnatifidum
Umbrella tree	Schefflera actinophylla
Vase plant	Aechmea fasciata
Wandering Jew	Tradescantia zebrina
Weeping fig	Ficus benjamina

COMMON NAME	BOTANICAL NAME
Need bright light	
Amaryllis	*Hippeastrum* spp.
Balfour aralia	*Polyscias scutellaria*
Banana	*Musa acuminata*
Bird-of-paradise	*Strelitzia reginae*
Bloodleaf	*Iresine herbstii*
Bougainvillea	*Bougainvillea glabra*
Calamondin orange	*×Citrofortunella microcarpa*
Chenille plant	*Acalypha hispida*
Chrysanthemum	*Chrysanthemum morifolium*
Crossandra, firecracker flower	*Crossandra infundibuliformis*
Croton	*Codiaeum variegatum*
Crown-of-thorns	*Euphorbia milii*
Cyclamen	*Cyclamen periscum*
Flowering maple, Chinese lantern	*Abutilon ×hybridum*
Frangipani	*Plumeria rubra*
Freesia	*Freesia* hybrids
Gardenia	*Gardenia augusta*
Geranium, zonal geranium	*Pelargonium ×hortorum*
Glorybower	*Clerodendrum thomsoniae*
Gold dust dracaena	*Dracaena surculosa*
Hydrangea	*Hydrangea macrophylla*
Jade plant	*Crassula ovata*
Meyer lemon	*Citrus meyeri*
Oxalis	*Oxalis* spp.
Panda plant	*Kalanchoe tomentosa*
Poinsettia	*Euphorbia pulcherrima*
Polka-dot plant, freckle-face	*Hypoestes phyllostachya*
Ponytail palm	*Beaucarnea recurvata*
Purple passion	*Gynura aurantiaca*
Red passion flower	*Passiflora coccinea*
Rose mallow	*Hibiscus rosa-sinensis*
Rose-scented geranium	*Pelargonium graveolens*
Shrimp plant	*Justicia brandegeana*
Snowball cactus	*Mammillaria* spp.
Wax plant	*Hoya carnosa*

Index

USDA Plant Hardiness Zone Map

This map of climate zones helps you select plants for your garden that will survive a typical winter in your region. The United States Department of Agriculture (USDA) developed the map, basing the zones on the lowest average recorded temperatures across North America. Zone 1 is the coldest area and Zone 11 is the warmest.

Plants are classified by the coldest temperature and zone they can endure. For example, plants hardy to Zone 6 normally survive where winter temperatures drop to −10° F. Those hardy to Zone 8 die long before it's that cold. These plants may grow in colder regions but must be replaced or protected over winter

each year. Plants rated for a range of hardiness zones usually survive winter in the coldest region as well as tolerate the summer heat of the warmest one.

To find your hardiness zone, note the approximate location of your community on the map, then match the color band marking that area to the key.

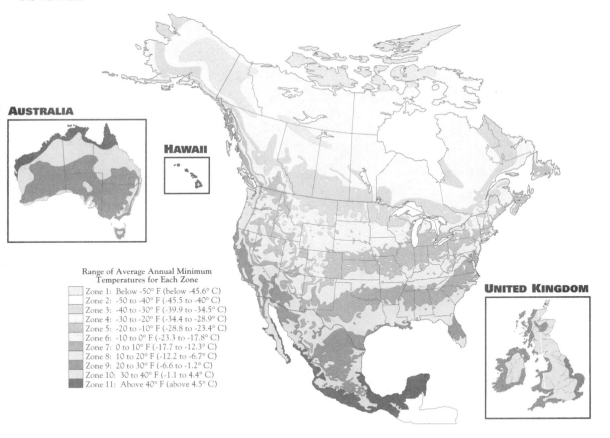

AUSTRALIA

HAWAII

Range of Average Annual Minimum Temperatures for Each Zone

Zone 1: Below -50° F (below -45.6° C)
Zone 2: -50 to -40° F (-45.5 to -40° C)
Zone 3: -40 to -30° F (-39.9 to -34.5° C)
Zone 4: -30 to -20° F (-34.4 to -28.9° C)
Zone 5: -20 to -10° F (-28.8 to -23.4° C)
Zone 6: -10 to 0° F (-23.3 to -17.8° C)
Zone 7: 0 to 10° F (-17.7 to -12.3° C)
Zone 8: 10 to 20° F (-12.2 to -6.7° C)
Zone 9: 20 to 30° F (-6.6 to -1.2° C)
Zone 10: 30 to 40° F (-1.1 to 4.4° C)
Zone 11: Above 40° F (above 4.5° C)

UNITED KINGDOM

USDA Frost Maps

**Average Dates of
First Autumn Frost**

- June 30 to July 30
- July 30 to August 30
- August 30 to September 30
- September 30 to October 30
- October 30 to November 30
- November 30 to December 30

**Average Dates of
Last Spring Frost**

- May 30 or after
- April 30 to May 30
- March 30 to April 30
- February 28 to March 30
- January 30 to February 28
- January 30 or before

Resources

Houseplants

Alannah's Greenhouses
Box 1342
Grand Forks, BC V0H 1H0, Canada
250/442-2552
www.alannahs.com

Davidson-Wilson Greenhouses
3147 E. Ladoga Rd.
Crawfordsville, IN 47933
877/723-6834

Glasshouse Works
Church St., P.O. Box 97
Stewart, OH 45778
Orders: 800/837-2142
www.glasshouseworks.com

Harborcrest Gardens
1581-H Hillside Ave., Suite 230
Victoria, BC V8T 2C1, Canada
250/642-7309
www.harborcrestgardens.com

**Kartuz Greenhouses,
Sunset Island Exotics**
1408 Sunset Dr.
Vista, CA 92085
760/941-3613
www.kartuz.com

Lauray of Salisbury
432 Undermountain Rd., Rte. 41
Salisbury, CT 06068
860/435-2263
www.lauray.com

Logee's Greenhouses
141 North St.
Danielson, CT 06239
888/330-8038
www.logees.com

Lyndon Lyon Greenhouses
P.O. Box 249
14 Mutchler St.
Dolgeville, NY 13329
315/429-8291
www.lyndonlyon.com

McKinney's Glasshouse
P.O. Box 782282
Wichita, KS 67278
316/686-9438

Northridge Gardens
9821 White Oak Ave.
Northridge, CA 91325
818/349-9798

Oak Hill Gardens
P.O. Box 25
37W 550 Binnie Rd.
Dundee, IL 60118
847/428-8500
www.oakhillgardens.com

Packer Nursery
P.O. Box 4056
Kailua-Kona, HI 96745
888/345-5566
www.alohapalms.com

P. & J. Greenhouses
20265 82nd Ave.
Langley, BC V2Y 2A9, Canada
604/888-3274

**Rainbow Gardens Nursery &
Bookshop**
1444 E. Taylor St.
Vista, CA 92084
760/758-4290
www.rainbowgardensbookshop.com

Stokes Tropicals
4806 W. Old Spanish Trail
Jeanerette, LA 70544
337/365-6998
Orders: 800/624-9706

Sunrise Nursery
13105 Canyon View
Leander, TX 78641
512/267-0023

Tiki Nursery
P.O. Box 187
Fairview, NC 28730
828/628-2212

Supplies

Eco Enterprises
1240 N.E. 175th St., Suite B
Shoreline, WA 98155
800/426-6937
www.ecogrow.com

Charley's Greenhouse & Garden
17979 State Route 536
Mount Vernon, WA 98273
800/322-4707
www.charleysgreenhouse.com

Gardener's Supply Co.
128 Intervale Rd.
Burlington, VT 05401
800/955-3370
www.gardeners.com

Hydro-Farm
755 Southpoint Blvd.
Petaluma, CA 94954
707/765-9990
www.hydrofarm.com

Indoor Gardening Supplies
P.O. Box 527
Dexter, MI 48130
800/823-5740
www.indoorgardensupplies.com

Flowers

Bluestone Perennials, Inc.
7211 Middle Ridge Road
Madison, OH 44057-3096
800/852-5243
www.bluestoneperennials.com

Cooley's Gardens
P.O. Box 126-PE
Silverton, OR 97381
800/225-5391
www.cooleysgardens.com

High Country Gardens
2902 Rufina Street
Santa Fe, NM 87507-2929
800/925-9387
www.highcountrygardens.com

Jackson & Perkins
1 Rose Lane
Medford, OR 97501
800/292-4769
www.jacksonandperkins.com

Klehm's Song Sparrow Perennial Farm
13101 E. Rye Road
Avalon, WI 53505
800/553-3715
www.songsparrow.com

Paradise Garden
474 Clotts Road
Columbus, OH 43230
614/893-0896
www.paradisegarden.com

Spring Hill Nurseries
110 West Elm Street
Tipp City, OH 45371-1699
812/537-2177
www.springhillnursery.com

Van Bourgondien
245 Route 109, P.O. Box 1000-MGA
Babylon, NY 11702-9004
800/622-9997
www.dutchbulbs.com

Wayside Gardens
1 Garden Lane
Hodges, SC 29695-0001
800/845-1124
www.waysidegardens.com

White Flower Farm
P.O. Box 50
Litchfield, CT 06759-0050
800/503-9624
www.whiteflowerfarm.com

Seeds
Ed Hume Seeds
P.O. Box 73160
Puyallup, WA 98373
Fax: 253/435-5144

McKenzie Seed Co.
30 Ninth Street
Brandon, MB R7A 6E1, Canada
204/571-7500

Park Seed
P.O. Box 31, Hwy 254
Greenwood, SC 29648
800/845-3369
www.parkseed.com

Seeds of Change
P.O. Box 15700
Santa Fe, NM 87506
888/762-7333
www.seedsofchange.com

Stokes Seeds
P.O. Box 548
Buffalo, NY 14240-0548
800/396-9238
www.stokeseeds.com

Thompson & Morgan, Inc.
P.O. Box 1308
Jackson, NJ 08527-0308
800/274-7333
www.thompson-morgan.com
Flower and vegetable seeds

Trees and Shrubs
Arborvillage
P.O. Box 227
Holt, MO 64048
816/264-3911
e-mail: arborvillage@aol.com

Bovee's Nursery
1737 SW Coronado
Portland, OR 97219
800/435-9250
www.bovees.com

Camellia Forest Nursery
9701 Carrie Rd.
Chapel Hill, NC 27516
919/968-0504
www.camforest.com

Carroll Gardens
444 E. Main St.
Westminster, MD 21157
800/638-6334
www.carrollgardens.com

Forestfarm
990 Tetherow Rd.
Williams, OR 97544
541/846-7269
www.forestfarm.com

Greer Gardens
1280 Goodpasture Island Rd.
Eugene, OR 97401
800/548-0111
www.greergardens.com

Jackson & Perkins
1 Rose Lane
Medford, OR 97501
800/854-6200
www.jacksonandperkins.com

Mellinger's
2310 W. South Range Rd.
North Lima, OH 44452-9731
800/321-7444
www.mellingers.com

Plants of the Southwest
3905 Agua Fria Rd.
Santa Fe, NM 87507
505/438-8888
Catalog: $3.50
www.plantsofthesouthwest.com

Richard Owen Nursery
2300 E. Lincoln St.
Bloomington, IL 61701
309/663-9551
www.excitinggardens.com

Roses of Yesterday & Today
803 Brown's Valley Rd.
Watsonville, CA 95076
831/728-1901
www.rosesofyesterday.com

Roslyn Nursery
211 Burr's Lane
Dix Hills, NY 11746
631/643-9347
www.roslynnursery.com

Siskiyou Rare Plant Nursery
2825 Cummings Rd.
Medford, OR 97501
541/772-6846

Wayside Gardens
1 Garden Lane
Hodges, SC 29695
800/845-1124
www.waysidegardens.com

White Flower Farm
P.O. Box 50
Litchfield, CT 06759-0050
800/503-9624
www.whiteflowerfarm.com

Woodlanders Inc.
1128 Colleton Ave.
Aiken, SC 29801
803/648-7522
www.woodlanders.net

Yucca Do Nursery
P.O. Box 907
Hempstead, TX 77445
979/826-4580
www.yuccado.com

Vegetables And Herbs
Bountiful Gardens
18001 Shafer Ranch Rd.
Willits, CA 95490-9626
707/459-6410
www.bountifulgardens.org

Comstock, Ferre & Co.
263 Main St.
Wethersfield, CT 06109
800/733-3773
www.comstockferre.com

D. Landreth Seed Co.
P.O. Box 6398
Baltimore, MD 21230
800/654-2407
www.landrethseeds.com
Catalog: $2.00

DeGiorgi Seeds & Goods
6011 N St.
Omaha, NE 68117
800/858-2580

Earl May Seed & Nursery
Shenandoah, IA 51603
800/831-4193
www.earlmay.com

Evergreen Y.H. Enterprises
P.O. Box 17538
Anaheim, CA 92817
714/637-5769
www.evergreenseeds.com

Ferry-Morse Seed Co.
P.O. Box 1620
Fulton, KY 42041
800/283-6400
www.ferry-morse.com

Harris Seeds
P.O. Box 24966
Rochester, NY 14692-0966
800/514-4441
www.harisseeds.com

High Altitude Seeds
4150B Black Oak Dr.
Hailey, ID 83333
208/788-4363
www.seedstrust.com
Catalog: $3.00

Johnny's Selected Seeds
184 Foss Hill Rd.
Albion, ME 04910-9731
207/437-4301
www.johnnyseeds.com

J.W. Jung Seed Co.
335 S. High St.
Randolph, WI 53957-0001
800/297-3123
www.jungseed.com

Native Seeds/SEARCH
526 N. 4th Ave.
Tucson, AZ 85705-8450
520/622-5561
www.nativeseeds.org

Nichols Garden Nursery
1190 N. Pacific Hwy.
Albany, OR 97321-4598
541/928-9280
www.nicholsgardennursery.com

Otis S. Twilley Seed Co., Inc.
121 Gary Rd.
Hodges, SC 29653
800/622-7333
www.twilleyseed.com

Park Seed Co.
1 Parkton Ave.
Greenwood, SC 29649
800/213-0076
www.parkseed.com

Pinetree Garden Seeds
P.O. Box 300
New Gloucester, ME 04260
207/926-3400
www.superseeds.com

Redwood City Seed Co.
P.O. Box 361
Redwood City, CA 94064
650/325-7333
www.ecoseeds.com

R.H. Shumway's
P.O. Box 1
Graniteville, SC 29829-0001
803/663-9771
www.rhshumway.com

Seeds Blum
Idaho City Stage
Boise, ID 83706
208/343-2202
Catalog: $3.00

Seeds of Change
P.O. Box 15700
Santa Fe, NM 87506
888/762-7333
www.seedsofchange.com

Stokes Seeds Inc.
P.O. Box 548
Buffalo, NY 14240-0548
800/396-9238
www.stokeseeds.com

Territorial Seed Co.
P.O. Box 157
Cottage Grove, OR 97424
541/942-9547
www.territorial-seed.com

The Cooks' Garden
P.O. Box 5010
Hodges, SC 29653-5010
800/457-9703
www.cooksgarden.com

Tomato Growers Supply Co.
P.O. Box 2237
Ft. Myers, FL 33902
888/478-7333
www.tomatogrowers.com

Vesey's Seeds Ltd.
P.O. Box 9000
Calais, ME 04619-6102
800/363-7333
www.veseys.com

Vermont Bean Seed Co.
Garden Lane
Fair Haven, VT 05743
803/663-0217
www.vermontbean.com

W. Atlee Burpee & Co.
300 Park Ave.
Warminster, PA 18991
800/888-1447
www.burpee.com

Fruits
Adams County Nursery, Inc.
26 Nursery Rd.
P.O. Box 108
Aspers, PA 17304
717/677-8105
www.acnursery.com

Ahrens Strawberry Nursery
RR1
Huntingburg, IN 47642
812/683-3055

W. F. Allen, Co.
Box 1577
Salisbury, MD 21801

Brittingham Plant Farms
P.O. Box 2538
Salisbury, MD 21801
301/749-5153

Columbia Basin Nursery
P.O. Box 458
Quincy, WA 98848
800/333-8589
www.cbnllc.com

Edible Landscaping
P.O. Box 77
Afton, VA 22920
804/361-9134
www.eat-it.com

Garden of Delights
14560 SW 14th St.
Davie, FL 33325-4217
800/741-3103
www.gardenofdelights.com

Greenmantle Nursery
3010 Ettersburg Rd.
Garberville, CA 95542
707/986-7504

Hartmann's Plantation Inc.
P.O. Box E
Grand Junction, MI 49056
616/253-4281
www.hartmannsplantcompany.com

Indiana Berry & Plant Co.
5218 West 500
South Huntingburg, IN 47542-9724
800/295-2226
www.inberry.com

Just Fruits Nursery
30 St. Frances St.
Crawfordville, FL 32327
850/926-5644

Kelly Nurseries
P.O. Box 800
Dansville, NY 14437
800/325-4180
www.kellynurseries.com

Lawson's Nursery
2730 Yellow Creek Rd.
Ball Ground, GA 30107
770/893-2141

Miller Nurseries
5060 W. Lake Rd.
Canandaigua, NY 14424-8904
800/836-9630
www.millernurseries.com

New York State Fruit Testing Cooperative Association, Inc.
P.O. Box 462
Geneva, NY 14456
315/787-2205

Nourse Farms Inc.
41 River Rd.
South Deerfield, MA 01373
413/665-2658
www.noursefarms.com

One Green World
P.O. Box 1080
Molalla, OR 97038
503/651-3005
www.onegreenworld.com

Oregon Exotics Rare Fruit Nursery
1065 Messinger Rd.
Grants Pass, OR 97527
541/846-7678
www.exoticfruit.com

Paradise Nursery
6385 Blackwater Rd.
Virginia Beach, VA 23457-1040
757/421-0201
www.paradisenursery.com

Raintree Nursery
391 Butts Rd.
Morton, WA 98356
360/496-6400
www.raintreenursery.com

Southmeadow Fruit Gardens
P.O. Box 211
Baroda, MI 49101
269/422-2411
www.southmeadowfruitgardens.com

Spring Hill Nurseries
110 W. Elm St.
Tipp City, OH 45371
513/354-1509
www.springhillnursery.com

Stark Brothers Nurseries & Orchards
P.O. Box 10
Louisiana, MO 63353
800/325-4180
www.starkbros.com

The Banana Tree, Inc.
715 Northampton St.
Easton, PA 18042
610/253-9589
www.banana-tree.com

Van Well Nursery
2821 Grant Rd.
Wenatchee, WA 98807
800/572-1553
www.vanwell.net